HUMAN KINETICS ONLINE STUDY GUIDE

How to access the supplemental online study guide

We are pleased to provide access to an online study guide that supplements *Contemporary Sport Management, Fourth Edition*. This study guide offers a variety of experiences that reinforce key material and allow you to develop and test your understanding of the diverse field of sport management. We are certain you will enjoy this unique online learning experience.

Accessing the online study guide is easy! Follow these steps if you purchased a new book:

1. Visit **www.HumanKinetics.com/ContemporarySportManagement**.
2. Click the fourth edition link next to the corresponding fourth edition book cover.
3. Click the Sign In link on the left or top of the page. If you do not have an account with Human Kinetics, you will be prompted to create one.
4. If the online product you purchased does not appear in the Ancillary Items box on the left of the page, click the Enter Key Code option in that box. Enter the key code that is printed at the right, including all hyphens. Click the Submit button to unlock your online product.
5. After you have entered your key code the first time, you will never have to enter it again to access this product. Once unlocked, a link to your product will permanently appear in the menu on the left. For future visits, all you need to do is sign in to the textbook's website and follow the link that appears in the left menu!

➜ Click the Need Help? button on the textbook's Web site if you need assistance along the way.

How to access the online study guide if you purchased a used book:

You may purchase access to the online study guide by visiting the text's Web site, **www.HumanKinetics.com/ContemporarySportManagement**, or by calling the following:

800-747-4457 . . . . U.S. customers
800-465-7301 . . . . .Canadian customers
+44 (0) 113 255 5665 . . . . European customers
08 8372 0999 . . . . Australian customers
0800 222 062 . . . . .New Zealand customers
217-351-5076 . . . . .International customers

For technical support, send an e-mail to:
support@hkusa.com . . . . U.S. and international customers
info@hkcanada.com . . . . Canadian customers
academic@hkeurope.com . . . . European customers
keycodesupport@hkaustralia.com . . . . . Australian and New Zealand customers

HUMAN KINETICS
The Information Leader in Physical Activity & Health

S: 05-2012

Product: Contemporary Sport Management, Fourth Edition online study guide

Key code: PEDERSEN-Z9HN6Z-OSG

This unique code allows you access to the online study guide.

Access is provided if you have purchased a new book.
Once submitted, the code may not be entered for any other user.

CONTEMPORARY SPORT MANAGEMENT

FOURTH EDITION

PAUL M. PEDERSEN, PhD
Indiana University

JANET B. PARKS, DA
Bowling Green State University

JEROME QUARTERMAN, PhD
Howard University

LUCIE THIBAULT, PhD
Brock University

EDITORS

HUMAN KINETICS

Library of Congress Cataloging-in-Publication Data

Contemporary sport management / Paul M. Pedersen . . . [et al.], editors. -- 4th ed.
p. cm.
Includes bibliographical references and index.
ISBN-13: 978-0-7360-8167-2 (hard cover)
ISBN-10: 0-7360-8167-4 (hard cover)
1. Sports administration. 2. Physical education and training--Administration. I. Pedersen, Paul Mark.
GV713.C66 2011
796.06'9--dc22
2010008782

ISBN-10: 0-7360-8167-4 (print)
ISBN-13: 978-0-7360-8167-2 (print)

The Web addresses cited in this text were current as of February 26, 2010, unless otherwise noted.

Acquisitions Editor: Myles Schrag; **Developmental Editor:** Amanda S. Ewing; **Assistant Editor:** Casey A. Gentis; **Copyeditor:** Bob Replinger; **Indexer:** Nancy Ball; **Permission Manager:** Dalene Reeder; **Graphic Designer:** Bob Reuther; **Graphic Artist:** Kathleen Boudreau-Fuoss; **Cover Designer:** Keith Blomberg; **Photographer (cover):** Toshifumi Kitamura/AFP/Getty Images; **Photo Asset Manager:** Laura Fitch; **Visual Production Assistant:** Joyce Brumfield; **Photo Production Manager:** Jason Allen; **Art Manager:** Kelly Hendren; **Associate Art Manager:** Alan L. Wilborn; **Illustrators:** Mic Greenberg and Alan L. Wilborn; **Printer:** Courier

Printed in the United States of America 10 9 8 7 6 5

The paper in this book is certified under a sustainable forestry program.

Human Kinetics
Web site: www.HumanKinetics.com

United States: Human Kinetics
P.O. Box 5076, Champaign, IL 61825-5076
800-747-4457
e-mail: humank@hkusa.com

Canada: Human Kinetics
475 Devonshire Road Unit 100
Windsor, ON N8Y 2L5
800-465-7301 (in Canada only)
e-mail: info@hkcanada.com

Europe: Human Kinetics
107 Bradford Road, Stanningley
Leeds LS28 6AT, United Kingdom
+44 (0) 113 255 5665
e-mail: hk@hkeurope.com

Australia: Human Kinetics
57A Price Avenue, Lower Mitcham
South Australia 5062
08 8372 0999
e-mail: info@hkaustralia.com

New Zealand: Human Kinetics
P.O. Box 80
Torrens Park, South Australia 5062
0800 222 062
e-mail: info@hknewzealand.com

E4757

Paul, Jerome, and Lucie enthusiastically dedicate
this edition of *Contemporary Sport Management* to Janet B. Parks.
We dedicate this book to Dr. Parks because she is one
of the most influential pioneers, professors, researchers,
and leaders in our field of sport management.
Besides having a leading role in founding
the North American Society for Sport Management (NASSM)
and the *Journal of Sport Management,*
she had the foresight and dedication
to develop and publish (along with coeditor Beverly R.K. Zanger)
the original *Contemporary Sport Management* (under a different title)
two decades ago. Over the past 20 years, she has led
several revisions of *Contemporary Sport Management*
with coeditors Dr. Jerome Quarterman (1998, 2003, 2007)
and Dr. Lucie Thibault (2007).
In addition to being a pioneer, scholar, teacher,
and leader in sport management, she is our coeditor and friend!
Dr. Parks, no one is more deserving of this dedication!

CONTENTS

9 YOUTH AND COMMUNITY SPORT 186

Marlene A. Dixon, PhD • Jennifer E. Bruening, PhD

10 SPORT MANAGEMENT AND MARKETING AGENCIES 206

William A. Sutton, EdD • Nicole Fowler, MBA • Mark A. McDonald, PhD

11 SPORT TOURISM 226

Heather Gibson, PhD • Sheranne Fairley, PhD

PART III SELECTED SPORT MANAGEMENT FUNCTIONS . . . 247

12 SPORT MARKETING 250

F. Wayne Blann, EdD • Ketra L. Armstrong, PhD

13 COMMUNICATION IN THE SPORT INDUSTRY 270

G. Clayton Stoldt, EdD • Stephen W. Dittmore, PhD • Paul M. Pedersen, PhD

A LETTER TO STUDENTS AND INSTRUCTORS

Welcome to the fourth edition of *Contemporary Sport Management*. Whether you are a student or an instructor, this letter will provide you with information that explains the goals, updates, and features of this new edition. Many new updates and features make this fourth edition an exciting and valuable resource, one that we are sure will broaden your understanding of sport management.

GOALS OF THIS BOOK

As with the previous editions, the goal of this fourth edition of *Contemporary Sport Management* is to introduce students to sport management, both as an academic major and as a professional endeavor. Toward that end, the book provides a broad overview of sport management rather than detailed instructions about how to manage sport enterprises. This distinction is important because the book must meet the needs of two types of students: those who have already decided to major in sport management and those who are still thinking about their choice of a major. If you are currently majoring in sport management, you probably anticipate learning more about the field, particularly about the variety of professional opportunities that await you. Those of you who are currently considering a major in sport management probably want to gain general knowledge about the field before making a final decision. After studying the information in this book, some of you will be even more intrigued with the idea of seeking a career in sport management, and you will pursue the remainder of your curriculum with enhanced understanding, insight, and maturity of purpose. On the other hand, others of you may discover that sport management is not really what you had envisioned or a field in which you want to work, and you will choose a different major. In either case, the book will have served a valuable purpose.

Contemporary Sport Management contains 20 chapters written by the four of us in concert with 37 other contributors. We invited the contributing authors to participate in this project not only because they are experts in their fields but also because they are committed to sharing their knowledge with the next generation of sport managers. We believe that you will find these contributors exceptionally credible and that you will enjoy learning from them. Their photographs and brief biographies are included at the back of the book. We are hopeful that seeing their faces and reading about their accomplishments will personalize the material in the chapters and make the book more meaningful for you. We know that you will be impressed with each contributor's experience and depth of knowledge.

SCOPE AND ORGANIZATION OF THE BOOK

The Commission on Sport Management Accreditation (COSMA) is the accrediting body for sport management curricula. This edition of *Contemporary Sport Management* addresses each of the common professional component (CPC) topical areas that COSMA considers essential to the professional preparation of sport managers. These content areas include (a) social, psychological, and international foundations of sport; (b) management (e.g., sport management principles, sport leadership, sport operations management and event and venue management, sport governance); (c) ethics in sport management; (d) sport marketing and communication; (e) finance, accounting, and economics; (f) legal aspects of sport; and (g) integrative experience (e.g., internship). The book provides basic information in all these content areas. In addition to the coverage of the sport management topical areas in specific chapters (e.g., the content area of sport marketing and communication is covered in chapter 12, "Sport Marketing," and chapter 13, "Communication in the Sport Industry"), every chapter includes a specific section or vignette on international aspects of the field and ethics in sport management, two requirements of the COSMA standards for accreditation. As you progress through the professional preparation curriculum at your college or university, you will study each content area covered in this textbook (and required by programs to meet COSMA standards) in much greater depth.

The 20 chapters of the book are organized within the following separate parts: "Introduction to Sport Management," "Selected Sport Management Sites," "Selected Sport Management Functions," and "Current Challenges in Sport Management." Each of these parts begins with a brief description of its purpose, an explanation of the types of information that you will find in the chapters in that part, and a section titled "For More Information" that identifies additional resources related to the chapter topics. After studying all the chapters, completing the international learning activities within the chapters and the additional learning activities in the Online Study Guide, and taking advantage of the "For More Information" sections, you should be able to (1) define sport management; (2) discuss the significance of sport as an international social institution; (3) exhibit desirable professional skills and attitudes; (4) describe the nature and scope of professional opportunities in the sport industry; (5) explain a variety of functions that sport managers typically perform; (6) demonstrate an understanding of theories associated with management, leadership, and organizational behavior and how these theories are applied in sport enterprises; (7) demonstrate critical thinking skills to evaluate major challenges confronting various segments of the industry; (8) explain the relevance of legal, historical, sociological, and psychological concepts to the management of sport; (9) engage in socially responsible activities and make principled decisions through a thorough knowledge of the ethical decision-making process; (10) demonstrate an appreciation of diversity through the use of unbiased language and an inclusive approach to human relations; (11) identify research questions in sport management and demonstrate the ability to analyze and interpret published research; and (12) become a member of the profession who will have a positive influence on the way that sport is managed in the future.

UPDATES TO THE FOURTH EDITION

This is the fourth edition of *Contemporary Sport Management*. We are gratified that many students over the years have found the first three editions useful, and we hope that the new, improved version will serve your needs even better. In response to suggestions made by students, colleagues, and anonymous reviewers, we have made several changes for this edition. We believe that you will appreciate and benefit from the significant modifications and updates.

A key update to this fourth edition is the Online Study Guide (OSG). This study guide (which can be accessed under the Student Resources heading at www.HumanKinetics.com/ContemporarySportManagement) provides multiple interactive learning experiences that will help you more fully understand and apply the concepts covered in each chapter. Icons throughout each chapter point you to the various activities:

Job announcements. These fabricated, but realistic, position announcements related to employment opportunities within particular sport settings will help you understand the skills that prospective employers are seeking. You can select the traits and characteristics you think are most applicable to each position. A sport management practitioner will then identify the traits and characteristics he or she thinks are most applicable to each position.

Comprehension activities. With these learning in action activities, you will encounter a multitude of activities that challenge you to complete a specific task that helps drive home the information covered in the chapter. Activities include matching exercises, multiple choice activities, and so on.

Web searches. Web activities give you the opportunity to explore a specific Web site related to a chapter's content and complete an assignment that connects the Web site's content to the chapter content.

Portfolio. The critical thinking and ethics sections in selected chapters provide background information that you will use to answer specific questions in the OSG. After completing these chapters' critical thinking and ethics questions, you will have built a portfolio that

highlights your thoughtful considerations of myriad issues related to sport management.

 **Quiz.** Short quizzes are provided to test your understanding of each chapter's main concepts.

In addition to the OSG, *Contemporary Sport Management* provides a multitude of Web site addresses. These URLs will enable you to capitalize on the vast amount of information available online. They also enable you to pursue your interests at times and locations convenient for you.

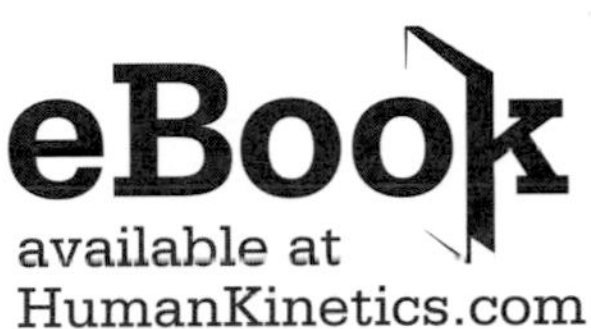

The fourth edition is an improvement of the previous editions in terms of both aesthetics and layout. For instance, this book is now in color! Even more important is that this fourth edition has been restructured to facilitate your understanding of the field. As noted earlier, the book now has four distinct parts, each of which contains at least four relevant chapters. In the first part, five unique chapters introduce you to sport management. These opening chapters provide an overview of the field, information on becoming an effective and professional sport manager, historical elements of sport management, and managerial and leadership concepts associated with this dynamic field. In the second part, six chapters detail the major settings that contain many sport management positions. These chapters examine professional and amateur sport management sites in addition to areas involving positions in sport management agencies and sport tourism. The third part of this new edition has four chapters that convey key functional areas of sport management. These areas involve sport marketing, sport communication, finance and economics in sport, and sport facility and event management. In the fourth part, five chapters examine the challenges that sport managers currently encounter and that you will face as you enter the sport industry. These challenges (and opportunities) include sport management issues related to consumer behavior, law, sociology, globalization, and research in this field. We believe the reorganization of the chapters into these four unique parts will assist you in your understanding of the field of sport management.

In addition to the restructuring, this fourth edition contains three new chapters: "Historical Aspects of the Sport Business Industry," "Interscholastic Athletics," and "Youth and Community Sport." The sport management history chapter was added because we believe that sport managers who know and appreciate the past are more likely to understand the present and more qualified to plan for the future. The other two chapters are in response to the growing need for effective leadership and sport management professionals in the areas of youth, high school, and community sport.

Complementing the three new chapters are significant revisions of and updating to the remaining chapters. Furthermore, both the running glossary and the historical moments, included in each chapter, have been expanded. We hope that the new history chapter in this edition and the expanded historical moments throughout the chapters will capture your attention as they visually communicate historical developments and connections among key events over time. Instructors can incorporate the historical information and the attendant learning activities into their lectures, assignments, and tests.

Although the chapters deal with various competencies that you should acquire as a future sport manager, two key competencies examined in select chapters are the ability to make principled ethical decisions and to think critically. First, sport managers need an understanding of ethical principles and moral psychology so they can act in a socially responsible manner and deal effectively with the numerous ethical issues they will confront. Second, because of the myriad issues that will confront you throughout your career as a sport manager, you need critical thinking skills to guide you in making sound decisions. Therefore, because of the importance of ethical decision making and critical thinking in the field of sport management, we dedicated a separate section to ethics and another to critical thinking in chapters 3 through 20 of this fourth edition. These sections permitted the authors the opportunity to analyze specific ethical and critical thinking issues related to their respective topics.

Also, because of the increased attention paid to sport as an international pursuit and the overall activities leading to the globalization of sport, current and future sport managers need an understanding and appreciation of international issues and cultures. Besides offering a specific chapter on international sport and providing steps to help you prepare for effective involvement in the global community, this edition also provides a new international vignette in each chapter. Each international sidebar is written by someone from a country other than the United States and addresses the chapter topic from an international perspective. Because we respect the linguistic customs of all countries, we have retained the voices of the sidebar authors. Consequently, some of them contain words, expressions, and spellings that might be new to you. We encourage you to take advantage of the opportunities that these new vocabularies provide for you to learn more about cultures outside the United States. We are hopeful that you will find these essays informative and that they will whet your appetite to learn more about sport and its management in other countries.

Other key features of this fourth edition of *Contemporary Sport Management* include the following:

- Each chapter reflects the inclusion of diverse populations, that is, people of different ages, genders, abilities, social classes, sexual orientations, races, ethnicities, and cultures. No separate chapter is dedicated to a topic such as "opportunities for women," or "sport for the disabled," or "the Black athlete." We believe that the inclusive nature of the text fosters a better understanding and appreciation of the variety of stakeholders that exist in the sport industry.
- The language used in the book is called gender-inclusive language. For example, athletics teams are referred to specifically as either men's teams or women's teams, a practice that acknowledges the existence of teams for both genders. The terms *fair play* and *sporting behavior* are used in place of *sportsmanship* because the inclusive terms avoid the subtle suggestion that sport is reserved for males. This use of unbiased language is a conscious attempt to reflect and embrace the diversity that is celebrated in many other ways throughout the book.
- Although each chapter of the book addresses a particular aspect of sport management, many of the chapters have important similarities. For example, most of the chapters that cover careers in sport management include lists of publications, governing bodies, and professional associations. Several chapters address ethical, legal, economic, and communication concerns. By including these topics in several chapters, we hope to reinforce important concepts that you will find useful as you progress in your professional preparation program.
- Some chapters contain real-life scenarios, case studies, profiles of sport managers, or news stories that illustrate a point. We believe that these features contribute to the user friendliness of the book.

FEATURES OF THE BOOK

This text provides many learning aids to help you understand and retain the information:

- Each of the chapters begins with learning objectives. These objectives serve as an outline for reading and studying the chapter.
- A "Historical Moments" section in each chapter presents key moments in the development of the study and practice of sport management. These key moments include dates that mark the establishment of a sport organization, the commencement of a sport journal, the arrival of a sport leader, and so on.
- A running glossary provides in-margin definitions of key terms and phrases.
- Cross-references in the book to the OSG link the text to opportunities to practice with the material presented in the text. We included a wide variety of exercises throughout the book and OSG to accommodate different learning styles and preferences.
- The review questions at the end of each chapter are linked to the objectives at the beginning of the chapter. These questions reinforce the key points of the chapter.
- Each chapter contains a reference list. Moreover, as previously noted, you will find a "For More Information" section at the beginning of each of the four parts of the book. We hope that you will use the information in these sections for further reading and exploration.

INSTRUCTOR RESOURCES

Although the preceding sections have outlined how this new edition will be useful to students, note as well that several items are useful to instructors. (And if you have not read the previous information, please be sure to do so!) This fourth edition is supported by a full array of ancillaries, including an Instructor Guide, a Test Package, a Presentation Package, and the aforementioned OSG.

- The Instructor Guide provides a sample syllabus; an explanation of what is included in the OSG, how students should use various OSG activities, and how instructors can use the OSG to prepare for and supplement their classes; an explanation of and a discussion about the importance of critical thinking in sport management; and chapter-by-chapter files that contain lecture outlines, chapter summaries, and additional activities that can be used to supplement the OSG activities.
- The Test Package includes more than 600 questions in various formats: multiple choice, true–false, fill-in-the-blank, and short answer or essay. Instructors can use these questions to build quizzes or supplement their own test questions.
- The Presentation Package includes more than 370 slides that cover the key points of each chapter. Instructors can use these slides as they are presented, but they are also encouraged to modify and add to these slides so that they more fully adhere to specific lecture outlines, class structures, and instructor preferences.
- The OSG provides students with many activity opportunities that challenge them to think about careers in sport management, demonstrate an understanding of a chapter's content, complete Web site searches and accompanying essays, thoughtfully consider critical thinking and ethical issues, and test their comprehension of a chapter's main objectives.

All of these ancillaries can be found at www.HumanKinetics.com/ContemporarySportManagement.

ACKNOWLEDGMENTS

Paul M. Pedersen, Janet B. Parks, Jerome Quarterman, and Lucie Thibault would like to express deep gratitude to numerous individuals, groups, and organizations whose collective contributions made this edition of *Contemporary Sport Management* a reality.

This project could not have been accomplished without the input and expertise of the 37 contributing authors who wrote most of the chapters in this fourth edition. These contributors are national and international leaders in their various areas of study, and the quality of this book is a direct result of their outstanding efforts. Of the 37 contributors, 12 did not contribute to the third edition, and we would especially like to acknowledge their arrival and welcome them on board. The new arrivals include Jennifer E. Bruening (University of Connecticut), Marlene A. Dixon (University of Texas at Austin), Sheranne Fairley (University of Massachusetts Amherst), Lawrence W. Fielding (Indiana University), Eric W. Forsyth (Bemidji State University), Nicole Fowler (National Basketball Association), Nicole M. LaVoi (University of Minnesota), Brenda G. Pitts (Georgia State University), Chris Reynolds (Indiana University), Sally R. Ross (University of Memphis), Luisa Velez (State University of New York at Cortland), and Warren A. Whisenant (University of Miami).

We express our sincere gratitude to the contributors of the international vignettes and learning activities integrated throughout the chapters of this new edition: John Amis, Hassan Asadi, Sungho Cho, Giorgio Gandolfi, Bill Gerrard, Morris Glimcher, Matthew Goltz, John Harris, Tassos Kaburakis, Pamm Kellett, Gi-Yong (Win) Koo, Sarah Leberman, Li Li Leung, Doris Lu-Anderson, Isaac Mwangi, Ricardo João Sonoda Nunes, Toshiyuki Ogura, John Paton, Babs Surujlal, Marijke Taks, and Xiaoyan Xing. Furthermore, we are grateful to Dr. Corinne Daprano, University of Dayton, and Dr. Andrea Eagleman, Indiana University Purdue University Indianapolis. Dr. Daprano again worked on the historical moments included in each chapter, and Dr. Eagleman revised and enhanced the Instructor Guide and Test Package. Faculty and students will benefit from the significant and useful contributions by Drs. Daprano and Eagleman.

Special notes of appreciation go to our educational institutions and publisher for their outstanding support. We are grateful to Indiana University, Bowling Green State University, Howard University, and Brock University for providing the resources that facilitated the completion of this book. We are privileged to be university professors and fortunate to work in environments that support our efforts. As always, we extend gratitude to the thousands of students whom we have had the privilege of teaching across the years. Furthermore, we sincerely appreciate Human Kinetics and the publisher's remarkable editors and professionals associated with this project. Although numerous individuals from Human Kinetics have assisted and facilitated this fourth edition, we would like to acknowledge two editors in particular. Myles Schrag, our acquisitions editor, again provided valuable advice and assistance as we conceptualized this fourth edition. The quality of the final product is due, in large measure, to Myles' expertise, imagination, energy, and enthusiasm. We are also grateful for the diligent, committed, and talented help provided by Amanda Ewing, the developmental editor for this book. Myles and Amanda made our jobs much easier by always being there with valuable information, assistance, and advice.

As with each of the previous editions, we are indebted to the anonymous reviewers and the instructors and students who have provided us with thoughtful suggestions, ideas, and critiques of the 2007 edition. Their contributions have improved, and are evident throughout, the book.

Lastly, we would like to acknowledge our various family members who have provided tremendous support of our work on *Contemporary Sport Management*. In particular, we are grateful for the patience and understanding of Brock, Carlie, Dolores, Hallie, Jennifer, and Zack.

PART I

INTRODUCTION TO SPORT MANAGEMENT

The five chapters in this section present basic information and key concepts that form the foundation of professional preparation for careers in sport management. The first three chapters take you through an overview of the field in general, examine professional considerations vital to success in the sport industry, and review key aspects of the history of the field. The last two chapters of this section involve managerial and leadership concepts applied to sport management personnel and sport organizations. Aspiring sport managers should become familiar with theories of organizational behavior, management, and leadership and be able to apply these theories in practical settings. Therefore, these last two chapters address the structure and processes of sport organizations and present desirable attributes of managers and leaders in the sport industry. The underlying theme of the two chapters is that managers have a responsibility to themselves, their employees, and their constituents to appreciate and apply theoretical concepts that will improve the effectiveness and efficiency of the workplace as well as the quality of the sport product or experience. The knowledge that you gain from these two chapters, combined with what you learn from the first three overview and historical chapters, will be useful as you study the remaining chapters in the book.

In chapter 1 Janet Parks, Jerome Quarterman, and Lucie Thibault provide an overview of the field by introducing sport management as an academic major and a career field. After defining sport and sport management, the authors delineate the types of sports in the sport industry, the settings in which sports are found, and the different ways of segmenting the sport industry. After discussing several characteristics of sport-related enterprises that distinguish them from other business pursuits, Parks, Quarterman, and Thibault then describe competencies that will be essential for success in sport management. Among the competencies examined is a strategy whereby you can develop an appreciation of critical thinking and learn to apply critical thinking skills to issues in sport management. The message of this part of the chapter is that sport managers who possess the dispositions of critical thinkers and can think critically about sport-related issues will be competent, reflective professionals who have the potential to become influential agents of change. The chapter concludes with an overview of opportunities and challenges that will face sport managers of the future. Among the challenges detailed in this part of the chapter is an extensive examination of ethics, social responsibility, and principled decision making. In the international sidebar, Marijke Taks, a native of Belgium who teaches sport management at the University of Windsor in Canada, explains the European *Sport for All* model and the effect (or lack thereof) of the economic recession on clubs and leagues in Western Europe.

Chapter 2 contains information that will help you develop a professional perspective on your studies and your career. Sally Ross, Kathryn Hoff, and JoAnn Kroll begin by providing a preview of the courses and experiences that you can expect in the professional preparation program at your college or university. Next, they discuss essential elements of a positive professional perspective—attitude, image, work transition and adjustment, and business etiquette. The authors then give special attention to career planning and management and offer sound advice related to finding a career that is compatible with your values, interests, and skills. They close the chapter by offering tips for gathering information about occupations in sport management. The international sidebar contains an essay by John Amis, a native of the United Kingdom who teaches sport management at the University of Memphis. He discusses the opportunities and advantages associated with university study abroad programs in sport management.

The purpose of chapter 3 is to provide a history of sport businesses and market structures so that you, as a future sport manager, can understand the significant historical influences on the field and develop strategies for your businesses. Lawrence Fielding, Paul M. Pedersen, and Brenda Pitts first present a historical analysis of the commercialization of sport. Within this part of the chapter the authors examine the numerous commercialization models of the developmental periods of the sport business industry. Fielding, Pedersen, and Pitts then discuss the historical aspects of the sport market. Included in this discussion are key watershed events, ranging from endorsement advertising to increased participation and spectatorship, that caused massive changes in the way that business in the sport industry was (and is) conducted. Doris Lu-Anderson, who teaches sport management at California State University at Long Beach, contributed the international sidebar for this chapter. Dr. Lu-Anderson's sidebar is a historical examination of the economic, labor, and production issues involving sporting goods manufacturing in her native Taiwan.

In chapter 4 Lucie Thibault and Jerome Quarterman define the term *organization* and describe three types of sport organizations—public, nonprofit, and commercial. This discussion is followed by explanations of organizational environment, organizational effectiveness, and organizational structure. Then the authors present various organizational designs, such as entrepreneurial, diversified, innovative, missionary, and political. The remainder of the chapter addresses organizational strategy, culture, and change. Throughout the chapter, Thibault and Quarterman present research on sport organizations and explain how the research findings apply to real-world situations in organizations. In the international sidebar, Hassan Asadi, who teaches at the University of Tehran, explains the growth, strategic planning, and organization of sport in Iran.

Chapter 5 examines the concepts of organizational behavior, human resource management, and leadership in the management of sport organizations. First, Jerome Quarterman, Ming Li, and Lucie Thibault illustrate three theoretical approaches—scientific management, human relations management, and administrative management—to managing people. After detailing the process, functions, and roles of management, the authors explain theoretical approaches to the study of leadership, ending the discussion with the integrative concept of managerial leadership. Quarterman, Li, and Thibault then present three levels of managers and explain the decision making, authority, and power aspects associated with management. They conclude the chapter by covering human resource management and organizational diversity. The international sidebar is an essay about three prominent Korean sport organizations: Korea Sports Council, Korea Foundation for the Next Generation of Sports Talent, and the Korean Society for Sport Management. Gi-Yong (Win) Koo, a native of Korea who is a teaching assistant at the University of Arkansas, contributed the sidebar.

For More Information

Professional and Scholarly Associations

- American Alliance for Health, Physical Education, Recreation and Dance (AAHPERD): www.aahperd.org/
- Asian Association for Sport Management (AASM): aasm.tw/
- European Association for Sport Management (EASM): www.easm.net/
- International Sport Management Alliance: www.nassm.com/InfoAbout/ISMA
- Japanese Association for Sport Management (JASM): e-jasm.jp/
- Korean Society for Sport Management (KSSM): www.kssm.or.kr./English
- North American Society for Sport History (NASSH): www.nassh.org/
- North American Society for Sport Management (NASSM): www.nassm.com/
- Sport Management Association of Australia and New Zealand (SMAANZ): smaanz.cadability.com.au/
- Sport Management Council of the National Association for Sport and Physical Education (NASPE): www.aahperd.org/Naspe/

Professional and Scholarly Publications

Athletic Business
Canadian Journal of Sport History
European Sport Management Quarterly
International Journal of Sport Management
International Journal of Sport Management and Marketing
International Journal of Sport Management, Recreation, & Tourism
International Journal of Sport Policy
International Journal of the History of Sport
Journal of Sport Administration & Supervision
Journal of Sport History
Journal of Sport Management
Korean Journal of Sport Management
Sport Business International
Sport History Review
Sport in History
Sport Management Education Journal
Sport Management Review
Sporting Traditions
Sports Business Daily
Street & Smith's SportsBusiness Journal

Sport Management Job Market

About.com: jobsearch.about.com/od/sportsjobs/Sports_Jobs.htm
Adventure Sports Online: www.adventuresport-sonline.com/
Athletic Business: www.athleticbusiness.com
BoardSportJobs: www.boardsportjobs.com/home.cfm
Canada.com: www.canada.com/topics/sports/index.html
Jobs in Sports: www.jobsinsports.com/
Malakye: www.malakye.com/
North American Society for Sport Management: www.nassm.com/
Online Sports: www.onlinesports.com/pages/CareerCenter.html
Quintessential Careers: www.quintcareers.com/sports_jobs.html
Sports Careers: www.sportscareers.com/
TeamWork Online: www.teamworkonline.com/
United States Olympic Committee: teamusa.org/pages/1543
Women Sports Jobs: www.womensportsjobs.com/
Women's Sports Foundation: www.womenssports-foundation.org/cgi-bin/iowa/index.html
Work in Sports: www.workinsports.com/

Additional Internet Resources

Commission on Sport Management Accreditation: www.cosmaweb.org/
Ethics in Sport: www.ausport.gov.au/information/finding_sport_information/topic/ethics
Global Sport Management News: www2.muc.edu/Academics/academic_programs/sport_business/global_sport_management_news.aspx
Institute for International Sport: www.international sport.com/
The Sport Business Education Network: www.sben.org
Sport Management Academic Programs: www.nassm.com/InfoAbout/SportMgmtPrograms
Sporting Goods Manufacturers Association (SGMA): www.sgma.com/
Sports Business News: www.sportsbusinessnews.com/
Sports Ethics Institute: www.sportsethicsinstitute.org/

HISTORICAL MOMENTS

1957	Walter O'Malley sent a letter to Dr. James Mason at Ohio University
1964	Stan Isaacs published *Careers and Opportunities in Sports*
1966	First sport administration program established at Ohio University
1970s	SMARTS, Sport Management Arts & Science Society, forerunner of NASSM, conceived by University of Massachusetts faculty
1985	North American Society for Sport Management (NASSM) established
1987	*Journal of Sport Management* (*JSM*) launched
1992	NASSM Code of Ethics adopted
1993	European Association for Sport Management (EASM) established
1994	Pitts, Fielding, and Miller's sport industry segment model introduced
1995	Sport Management Association of Australia and New Zealand (SMAANZ) established
1995	Korean Society of Sport Management (KSSM) founded
1997	Meek's economic impact model released
2001	Li, Hofacre, and Mahony's sport industry model revealed
2005	United Nations proclaimed 2005 the International Year of Sport and Physical Education
2010	More than 240 undergraduate sport management programs have been established around the world

Photo courtesy of Paul M. Pedersen.

1

MANAGING SPORT IN THE 21ST CENTURY

Janet B. Parks ■ Jerome Quarterman ■ Lucie Thibault

LEARNING OBJECTIVES

1. Discuss examples of traditional and nontraditional sporting activities.
2. Identify several different settings in which sporting activities occur.
3. Explain three different ways of organizing the sport industry.
4. Discuss four unique aspects of sport management.
5. Identify several types of positions available in sport management.
6. Explain competencies required for success in a variety of sport management jobs.
7. Apply critical thinking skills to a problem in sport management.
8. Discuss opportunities and challenges facing sport managers of the future.

Key Terms

associated spending
descriptive
discretionary funds
extreme sports
networking
organizational culture
prescriptive
principled decision making
underrepresented groups
workforce diversity

In 1957 Walter O'Malley, president and chief stockholder of the Brooklyn (now Los Angeles) Dodgers Baseball Club, anticipated the future growth of organized sport and predicted the need for professionally prepared sport administrators. O'Malley wrote a letter to Dr. James Mason, a faculty member at Ohio University, stating the following:

> I ask the question, where would one go to find a person who by virtue of education had been trained to administer a marina, race track, ski resort, auditorium, stadium, theater, convention or exhibition hall, a public camp complex, or a person to fill an executive position at a team or league level in junior athletics such as Little League baseball, football, scouting, CYO (Catholic Youth Organization), and youth activities, etc. . . . A course that would enable a graduate to read architectural and engineering plans; or having to do with specifications and contract letting, the functions of a purchasing agent in plant operations. There would be the problems of ticket selling and accounting, concessions, sale of advertising in programs, and publications, outdoor and indoor displays and related items. (Mason, Higgins, & Wilkinson, 1981, p. 44)

As a result of that inquiry, Mason and several of his colleagues created a master's-level sport administration program at Ohio University. Inaugurated in 1966, the Ohio program was the first recorded, university-sponsored attempt to provide a graduate-level curriculum specifically designed to prepare students for jobs in a variety of sport-related industries. The idea caught on, and at last count, there were 243 undergraduate sport management programs, 173 master's programs, and 41 doctoral programs in Africa, Australia, Canada, India, New Zealand, the United Kingdom, and the United States. Hundreds of college students in other countries such as Switzerland, Spain, Ireland, Netherlands, Italy, Belgium, Turkey, Iran, Japan, China, Greece, and Austria are also studying sport management (North American Society for Sport Management, 2009). (Refer to chapter 2 for more information on the content generally covered in sport management programs.)

This chapter represents the first step on your journey toward becoming a sport manager. It includes definitions of basic terms, a discussion of the nature and scope of the sport industry, and explanations of unique aspects of sport management enterprises and careers. You will also learn about desirable sport management competencies and some of the challenges and opportunities that await you as you prepare to take your place among the next generation of sport managers.

DEFINING SPORT AND SPORT MANAGEMENT

For most of us, sport implies having fun, but it can also be work (for a professional athlete), a means of employment (for a sport tourism director), or a business (for a sport marketing agency). Sport takes many forms. It may include many participants, as in team sports such as soccer and volleyball; two participants, as in dual sports such as tennis and badminton; or one person, as in individual sports such as golf and surfing. Sport includes a combination of these configurations when it involves team competitions, tournaments, or matches in dual sports (wrestling) or individual sports (in-line skating). What criteria qualify games or activities to be classified as sport? Is horse racing a sport? What about cycling, water skiing, pocket billiards, or Texas hold 'em poker and other table games? We know that football, basketball, ice and field hockey, tennis, golf, baseball, and softball are sports. Are they different from sailing, dog racing, marathoning, video gaming, and scuba diving? If so, how are they different? If not, how are they similar?

The Council of Europe (2001) defined sport as "all forms of physical activity which, through casual or organised participation, aim at expressing or improving physical

Nothing New Under the Sun

Lest we be deluded by the notion that contemporary sport management is markedly different from the ancient art of staging athletic spectacles, let us consider for a moment the following description of the games sponsored in 11 BCE by Herod the Great, king of Judea and honorary president of the Olympics:

"The games began with a magnificent dedication ceremony. Then there were athletic and musical competitions, in which large prizes were given not only to the winners but also—an unusual feature—to those who took second and third place. Bloody spectacles were also presented, with gladiators and wild beasts fighting in various combinations, and there were also horse races. Large prizes attracted contenders from all areas and this in turn drew great numbers of spectators. Cities favored by Herod sent delegations, and these he entertained and lodged at his own expense. What comes through most clearly . . . is that gigantic sums of money were spent." (Frank, 1984, p. 158)

The success of such an extravaganza relied in all likelihood on the organizational skills of the individuals charged with planning and executing the games. Certainly there was today's equivalent of a general manager, or CEO, to whom all other personnel were responsible. Additionally, assistants who were knowledgeable in economics, accounting, and finance were indispensable if the event was to become profitable. The "business managers" were responsible for obtaining financial support, purchasing equipment (and perhaps even the requisite beasts), furnishing entertainment and lodging for the VIPs, and generally being accountable for the large sums of money that were spent.

Once the financial dimension was secured, there was the challenge of attracting sufficient numbers of contestants and spectators to the games. Enter Herod's "marketing director," armed with unique and unprecedented gimmicks to assure a full complement of participants as well as a full house of onlookers. A new prize structure was devised and, in awarding prizes to musicians as well as athletes, the seeds were sown for the modern spectacle known, among other titles, as the Battle of the Bands. The marketing director must have enlisted the aid of assistants who were responsible for extending invitations, publicizing the games, and keeping records of the day's activities. In the years prior to the printing press, much less the electronic media, informing the public was no small task—to say nothing of offering enticements sufficient to persuade them to journey for days and endure what must have been extremely undesirable traveling conditions. The marketing and promotions people certainly had their hands full!

The parallel[s] could continue—there was a need for crowd control, rules decisions, award ceremonies, and so forth. After all, certain tasks must be performed regardless of the venue in which the event occurs. Now, 2000 years later, we are reminded once again of Solomon's wisdom in proclaiming in Ecclesiastes 1:9 that "there is no new thing under the sun."

fitness and mental well-being, forming social relationships or obtaining results in competition at all levels" (p. 1). Similarly, Pitts, Fielding, and Miller (1994) stated that sport is "any activity, experience, or business enterprise for which the primary focus is fitness, recreation, athletics, and leisure related" (p. 18). According to these definitions, sport does not have to be competitive, nor does it always require specialized equipment or rules; in fact, the broad concept of sport can include activities such as working out, swimming, running, boating, and dancing. For this book, we adopted these broad definitions; consequently, you should interpret the term *sport* to include an expansive variety of physical activities and associated businesses.

Many people who are employed in business endeavors associated with sport are engaged in a career field known as sport management. According to Pitts and Stotlar (2007), sport management is "the study and practice of all people, activities, businesses, or organizations involved in producing, facilitating, promoting, or organizing any sport-related business or product" (p. 4). Again, this broad definition includes an incredibly wide variety of sport-related careers.

Sport management is also the name given to many university-level academic programs designed to prepare students to assume positions in the sport industry. These programs provide two additional sources of confusion regarding vocabulary. First, you might have noticed that many professional preparation programs are titled *sport* management, whereas others are called *sports* management. In our view, people prefer one or the other based on the connotations that the words *sports* and *sport* have for them. To many academics, ourselves included, *sports* implies a collection of separate activities such as golf, soccer, hockey, volleyball, softball, and gymnastics—items in a series that we can count. On the other hand, *sport* is an all-encompassing concept. It is a collective noun that includes all sporting activities, not just those that we can place on a list. We have found that students in our classes relate well to the parallel with the different connotations of the words *religions* and *religion*. The word *religions* typically connotes several specific faiths or belief systems—different denominations or sects that we can quantify. *Religion*, on the other hand, is a broad term that we can interpret as a general reverence or faith held by any number of people. A second source of confusion is the fact that many professional preparation programs are titled sport (or sports) management, and others are called sport (or sports) administration. In both instances, we suggest that it would be counterproductive to debate which term is more appropriate. Ultimately, the quality of the curriculum is more important than the title of the program.

NATURE AND SCOPE OF THE SPORT INDUSTRY

Just as there are several definitions of sport, there are many ways to conceptualize the nature and scope of the sport industry. In the following paragraphs, we will elaborate on three concepts that, in different ways, provide overviews of sport: (1) types of sports, (2) settings in which sports are found, and (3) models of sport industry segments.

Types of Sports

One way to consider the sport industry is to examine the many types of sports that exist. An awareness of the wide diversity of sporting opportunities available to consumers is essential for anyone who anticipates becoming a decision maker in the world of sport. Sport marketers, for instance, must have a good understanding of both traditional and new sports so they can develop effective promotional strategies.

You are already familiar with traditional sports such as basketball, tennis, golf, American football, swimming, and soccer. You also know that numerous new sports and physical activities have emerged. Pitts and Stotlar (2007) identified the following activities and sports that have appeared on the scene lately: several varieties of aerobics, in-line skating, boogie boarding, snowboarding, snow kayaking, parasailing, ice surfing, mountain boarding, beach volleyball, skydive dancing, street luge, snow biking, ice climbing, the X Games, and indoor soccer.

Several of these new sports are known as extreme (action) sports, and they are becoming more popular. For example, Mawson (2002) reported that people born between 1961 and 1981 demonstrated heightened interest and engagement with action sports such as street luge, motocross biking, bungee jumping, and snow bicycling. She further noted that broadcast media had embraced **extreme sports,** as evidenced by the airing of the X Games, the Gravity Games, and the Gorge Games. Other action sporting events include the Dew Action Sports Tour, the Great Outdoor Games, and the Asian X Games (Tsuji, Bennett, & Zhang, 2007). Younger people are also learning to enjoy extreme sports. In fact, when Bennett, Henson, and Zhang (2003) asked 367 middle school and high school students about their televised sport viewing preferences, more students preferred watching the X Games than the World Series and the soccer World Cup. More students also

extreme sports (also known as action sports)—A general term for a collection of newer sports involving adrenaline-inducing action. They often feature a combination of speed, height, danger, and spectacular stunts.

preferred watching action sports to watching baseball, basketball, ice hockey, and auto racing. Both Mawson (2002) and Bennett et al. (2003) predicted that the popularity of action sports would continue to rise. Sport managers of the future, therefore, should be familiar with these sports and be prepared to make them accessible to consumers, as participatory activities, spectator events, and through the media.

The B3 Competition in South Korea is an example of how extreme sports are becoming more popular worldwide.
Photo courtesy of Paul M. Pedersen.

Settings for Sporting Activities

Another approach to the sport industry involves examining the many different settings in which sporting activities occur. This approach can provide you with ideas about where you can find sites in which sport managers might be needed. The online edition of the *Sports Market Place Directory* (Gottlieb, 2009) identified over 13,500 contacts within the following sport-related settings:

- Single sports (professional leagues, teams, organizations)
- Multi sports (athletic foundations, disabled sports organizations, high school sports, military sports, Olympic sports, professional organizations, sports commissions and convention or visitors bureaus, sports halls of fame, sports libraries and museums, state game organizations, youth sports organizations)
- College sports (college associations, college athletic conferences, college athletics departments, sport management degree programs)
- Events, meetings, and trade shows
- Media (newspapers; sports magazines and directories; sports media production; sports radio networks, local and national radio programs, satellite radio, radio stations; sports television, cable, and broadcast networks; pay-per-view television, local and national television programs, satellite television, television stations, World Wide Web)
- Sports sponsors
- Professional services (executive search services, event planning and services, event security, financial services, marketing and consulting services, technical services, sports agents, sports attorneys, sports medicine, sports travel services, statistical services, student–athlete recruiting services, ticketing services)
- Facilities (arenas and stadiums, auto race tracks, equestrian downs and parks, greyhound race tracks, facility architects and developers, facility management, facility concession services)
- Manufacturers and retailers (equipment and product manufacturers, software manufacturers, retailers)

ACTION

Go to the OSG and complete the Learning in Action activity, which helps you match several employment opportunities available in sport management with some of the categories of sport-related settings.

Sport Industry Segments

A third approach to defining the nature and scope of the sport industry is to create industry models that show the interrelationships among various segments of the sport industry. We will present three of these models, each of which represents a different approach to conceptualizing the sport industry. All three models are useful in showing you interesting and different ways to consider the world of sport.

Product Type Model

Pitts et al. (1994) developed a segmentation model of the sport industry based on the types of products sold or promoted by the businesses or organizations within them (figure 1.1). The industry segmentation approach is especially useful to sport marketers, who are typically responsible for formulating competitive strategies. Sport marketers can use their understanding of the sport product segments as they make decisions such as choosing the segments in which they wish to position their products, selecting the types of marketing strategies to use, and determining whether to create new industry segments.

The model details three product segments of the sport industry: (1) sport performance, (2) sport production, and (3) sport promotion. As shown in figure 1.1, the sport performance segment includes such varied products as school-sponsored athletics, fitness clubs, sport camps, professional sport, and municipal parks sport programs. Examples of products in the sport production segment are basketballs, fencing foils, jogging shoes, sports medicine clinics, swimming pools, and college athletic conferences. The sport promotion segment includes products such as T-shirts, giveaways, print and broadcast media, and celebrity endorsements. Sport marketers can use this product type model to plan marketing strategies, something that you will learn more about in chapter 12.

WEB

Go to the OSG and complete the Web search activity, which has you research environmental issues for sport managers.

Economic Impact Model

Meek (1997) took another approach to describing the sport industry (figure 1.2). He proposed that the industry could be defined by describing three primary sectors:

associated spending— Money spent by sport participants, spectators, and sponsors.

1. Sport entertainment and recreation such as events, teams, and individual participants; sports and related recreational activities; and **associated spending**

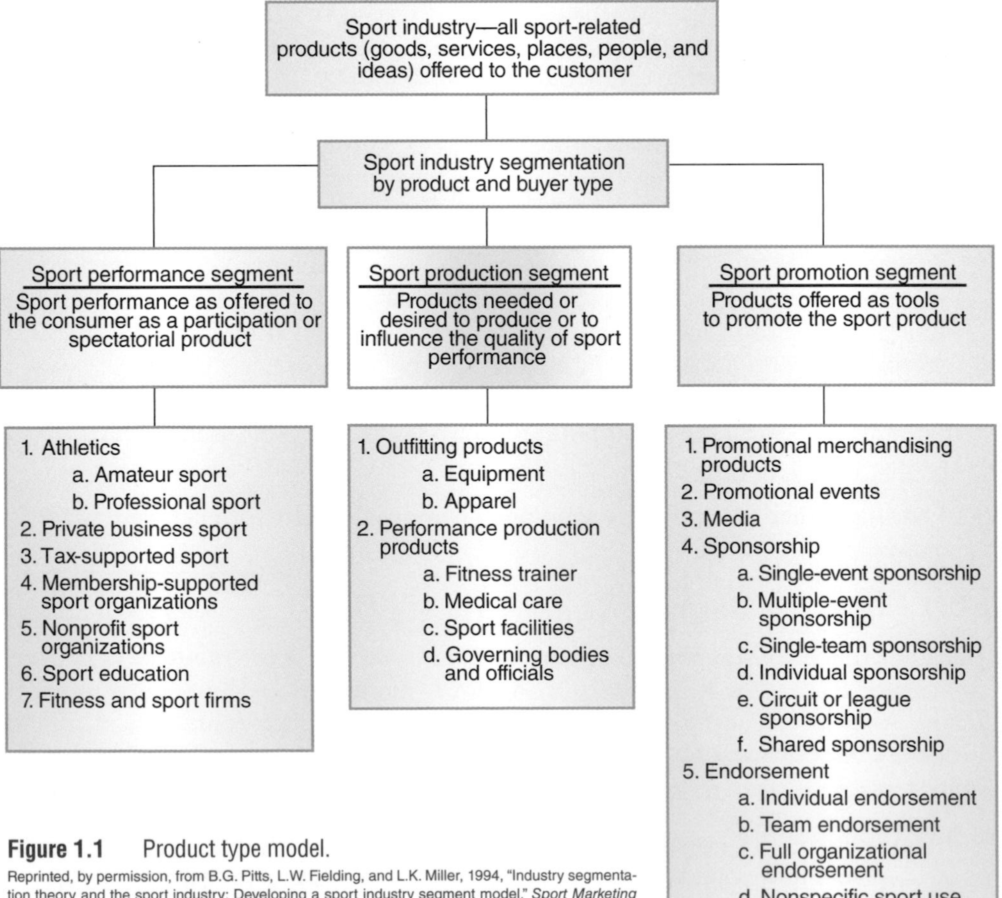

Figure 1.1 Product type model.

Reprinted, by permission, from B.G. Pitts, L.W. Fielding, and L.K. Miller, 1994, "Industry segmentation theory and the sport industry: Developing a sport industry segment model," *Sport Marketing Quarterly*, 2(1): 15–24. (Morgantown, WV: Fitness Information Technology, Inc.).

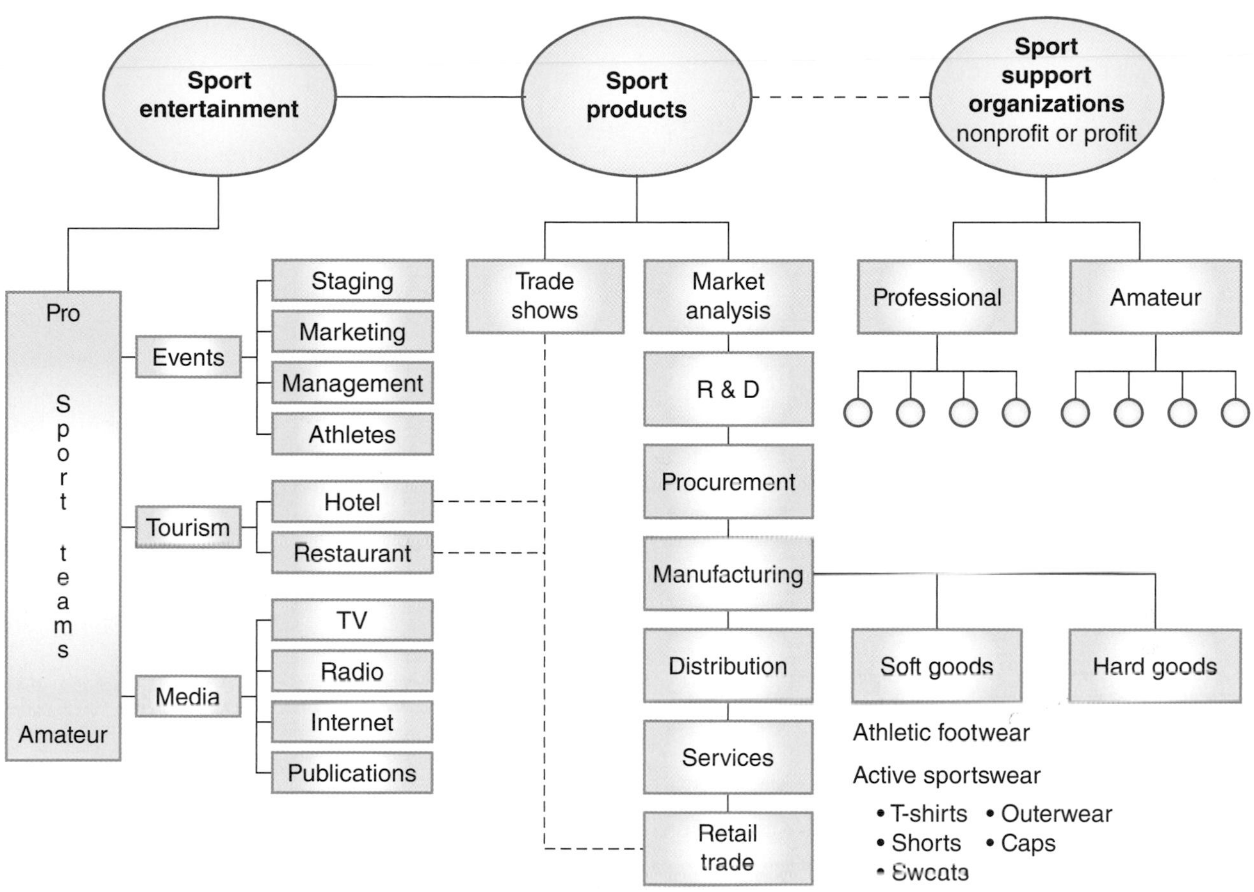

Figure 1.2 Economic impact model.

Reprinted, by permission, from A. Meek, 1997, "An estimate of the size and supported economic activity of the sports industry in the United States," *Sport Marketing Quarterly*, 6(4): 15–21. (Morgantown, WV: Fitness Information Technology, Inc.).

2. Sport products and services such as design, testing, manufacturing, and distribution of equipment, clothing, and instruments
3. Sport support organizations such as leagues, law firms, and marketing organizations (p. 16)

Meek proposed that his broad definition of sport enabled an analysis of the economic activity of the teams and businesses within each sector and the economic activity associated with sport. You will learn more about sport economics in chapter 14.

Sport Activity Model

The third model of the sport industry is based on the single characteristic that differentiates the sport industry from all other industries: sport activities, that is, games and events (Eschenfelder & Li, 2007). This model, shown in figure 1.3, defines the sport industry as the firms and organizations that

1. produce sport activities,
2. provide products and services to support the production of sport activities, and
3. sell and trade products related to sport activities.

In the sport activity model, the sport-producing sector is the core of the industry. Six supporting subsectors surround, and overlap with, the activity-producing core. Organizations in these subsectors either (1) provide products and services to the core

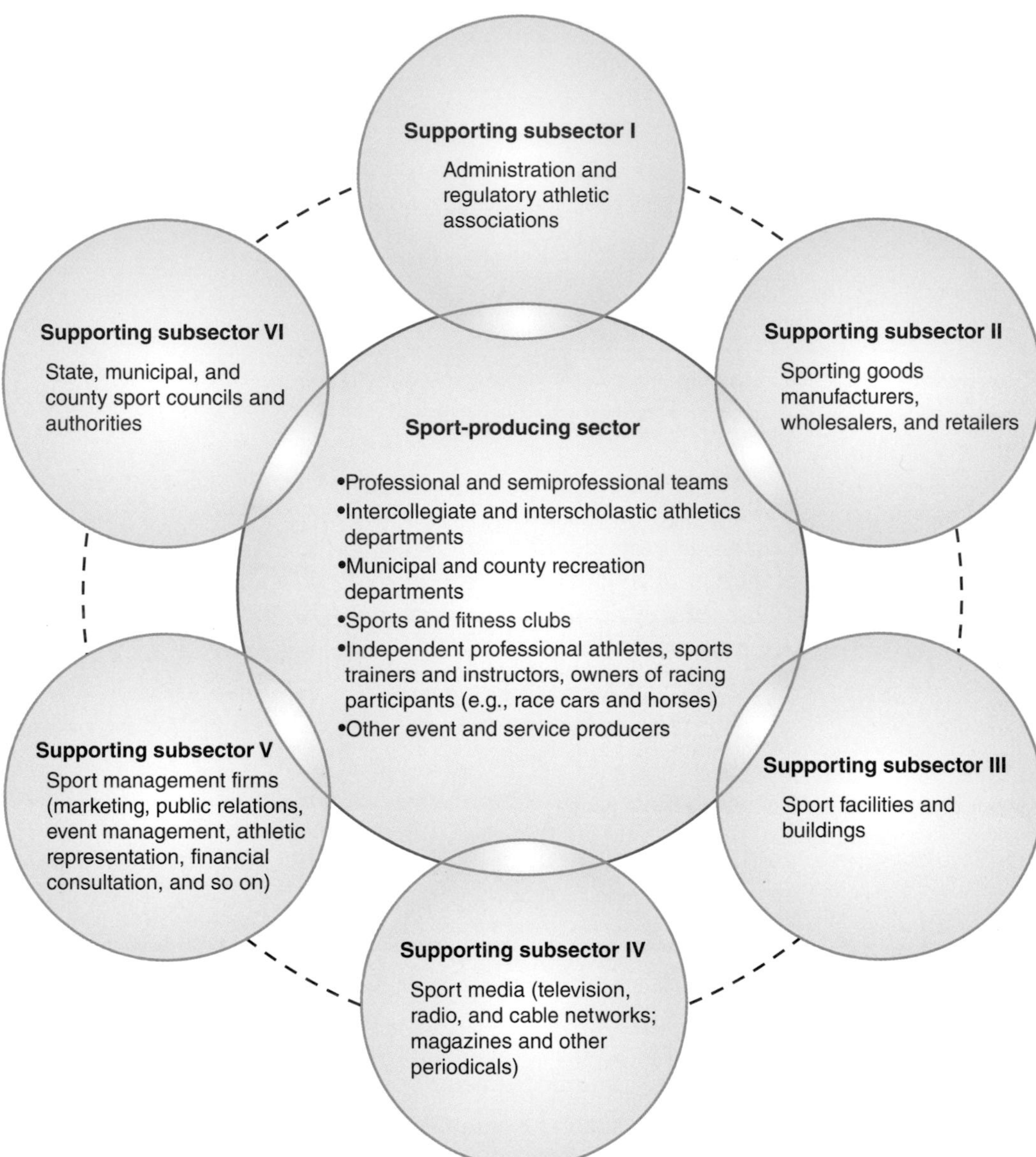

Figure 1.3 Li, Hofacre, and Mahony's sport industry model.

Reprinted, by permission, from M.J. Eschenfelder and M. Li, 2007, *Economics of sport,* 2nd ed. (Morgantown, WV: Fitness Information Technology), 6.

organizations or (2) sell or trade products related to sport. This model differs conceptually from the other two models in that it places sport at the center and illustrates the dependence of the subsectors on the production of sporting activities.

UNIQUE ASPECTS OF SPORT MANAGEMENT

Mullin (1980) provided insight into three unique aspects of sport management: sport marketing, sport enterprise financial structures, and sport industry career paths. These three aspects are just as critical today because they still make sport business different from other business enterprises and justify sport management as a distinct area of professional preparation. We add a fourth unique aspect of sport to Mullin's list: the enormous power and influence of sport as a social institution.

Sport Marketing

Sport marketing is unique because the sport product is unlike other products that consumers buy. For example, sport is consumed as quickly as it is produced. It is a perishable product that is not accompanied by any guarantees of customer satisfaction. People who provide the sport experience cannot predict the outcome because of the spontaneous nature of the activity, the inconsistency of events, and the uncertainty surrounding the results. Sport marketers, therefore, face unique challenges.

Sport Enterprise Financial Structures

Most sport businesses are financed differently from other businesses. Typically, the sale of a product or service such as clothing, food, automobiles, or home cleaning finances the business. But with the exception of sporting goods stores, sport enterprises earn a significant portion of revenue not from the sale of a service such as a game, workout, or 10K run, but from extraneous sources such as television rights, concessions, road game guarantees, parking, and merchandise. Intercollegiate athletics and municipal recreation sport programs might generate revenue from student or user fees, private donations, taxes, rentals, or licensing fees. Sport managers continually compete for the **discretionary funds** of consumers through the sale of items that might or might not be related to the apparent primary focus of the enterprise. Sport also attracts consumers who spend more money outside the sporting arena than they spend on the sport itself (e.g., travel, entertainment, souvenirs, equipment). This unique financial base requires different practices within the sport setting.

discretionary funds—Money left over after necessary expenditures (e.g., rent, food, car payment, insurance) have been made.

Sport Industry Career Paths

Traditionally, many sport management practitioners have been hired from visible groups, such as intercollegiate athletics or professional sport. An example of this phenomenon is the basketball star who becomes a basketball coach and eventually an athletics director. We can find similar career advancement patterns within municipal recreation programs, sport clubs, and professional sport teams. In some instances, then, sport is still a closed society in which obtaining employment might depend less on what the applicant knows than on whom the applicant knows (Clay, 1995).

An additional challenge is the assumption that members of **underrepresented groups** do not have the requisite skills for management positions. Arthur Triche, vice president of public relations for the Atlanta Hawks and the first African American public relations director in the National Basketball Association (NBA), credits volunteering and making contacts (i.e., **networking**) in the sport industry as important steps that he took toward overcoming this obstacle (Clay, 1995). A cautionary note about networking is in order: Mere acquaintance with influential people in the world of sport is not sufficient. Unless your acquaintances have a positive impression of your competence and work ethic, you cannot expect them to assist you in your career. You will read more about networking in chapter 2.

In spite of some advances resulting from efforts to diversify the sport management workforce, we have a long way to go before we can claim that sport is truly an equal opportunity environment (Acosta & Carpenter, 2008; Lapchick, 2009). Professional opportunities for people of color and women continue to lag behind opportunities for White males. Moreover, women and people of color in sport are occasionally subjected to public denigration, as illustrated by comments such as those uttered by media personalities Cedric "Cornbread" Maxwell and Don Imus (Brand, 2007; Kinkhabwala, 2007; McCann, 2007). As professionals, you may be in positions of authority in which your sensitivity to cultural inequities can lead to expanded **workforce diversity** and positive changes in the **organizational culture** of the sport industry (Ross & Parks, 2008).

underrepresented groups—People who traditionally have not been hired in sport management positions (e.g., women, people of color, people with disabilities).

networking—The building up or maintaining of informal relationships, especially with people who could bring advantages such as job or business opportunities (MSWord® online dictionary).

workforce diversity—People of different ages, genders, religions, physical abilities, social classes, sexual orientations, races, ethnicities, and cultures working together in an organization.

organizational culture—Workplace values, norms, and behaviors that produce patterns of behavior unique to an organization.

Sport as a Social Institution

Sport is a distinctive social activity that is frequently the basis of a person's social identity (Coakley, 2009). As such, it is a social institution of astonishing magnitude and influence. What other social pursuit is allotted several pages in the daily newspaper, has its own slot on every television and radio news program, has its own cable channels, and creates what appears to be an international withdrawal crisis when members of its workforce go on strike? The sheer power of sport mandates that people who wish to manage it acquire a sound understanding of its historical, psychological, sociological, cultural, and philosophical dimensions.

The General Assembly of the United Nations (UN) publicly recognized the power of sport when—in adopting a resolution titled "Sport as a means to promote education, health, development and peace"—it declared 2005 the International Year of Sport and Physical Education (United Nations, 2004). Further noting the major role that sport can play in promoting the UN goals of peace, dignity, and prosperity, the executive director of the United Nations Environment Programme (UNEP) stated, "The way sports events are run, the way sporting goods companies do business, and the way sports stars conduct themselves on and off the field can have profound effects far beyond the financial bottom line" (Toepfer, 2003, ¶ 9). Clearly, the immense power of sport mandates that sport managers understand the social implications of their actions. Contemporary sport enterprises need well-prepared managers who can make sound management decisions in the context of sport as an exceptionally influential social institution.

SPORT MANAGEMENT COMPETENCIES

Matt Krumrie (2009), a journalist who has been reporting on the employment industry since 1998, wrote, "The business of sports management is not about wins and losses, stats and glamour. It's about business—that's the bottom line" (¶ 11). In the same article, Becky Heidesch, CEO of Women's Sports Services LLC, a sports career-development and recruiting company, concurred. She stated, "Understanding the basics in business—sales, marketing, sponsorship, licensing—is crucial to being successful in the long run" (¶ 3).

Research suggests that sport management competencies are universal and have remained relatively stable over time (Danylchuk & Boucher, 2003; Horch & Schütte, 2003). Besides emphasizing competencies required to perform traditional tasks such as personnel management and planning, today's business world places increased importance on communication skills, communication technology, and the ability to interact in a global and multicultural society. In fact, with respect to competencies expected of sport managers, Horch and Schütte noted, "Interpersonal communication, information tasks and external representation as well as social tasks are central components of their activity" (p. 73).

Managerial Leadership Skills

Although competencies required for specific settings vary depending on particular organizations as well as specific assignments, the sport management tasks presented in figure 1.4 provide an overview of industry expectations. Most of the competencies required for these tasks are transferable, which means that you should be able to use them in a variety of vocational settings that include, but are not limited to, sport organizations.

The tasks in the core of figure 1.4 are general sport management responsibilities, those in which all sport managers must be proficient and, to varying degrees, be able to perform on the job. For example, regardless of whether you work in a sport club, the front office of a professional sport team, a sport association, or an intercollegiate

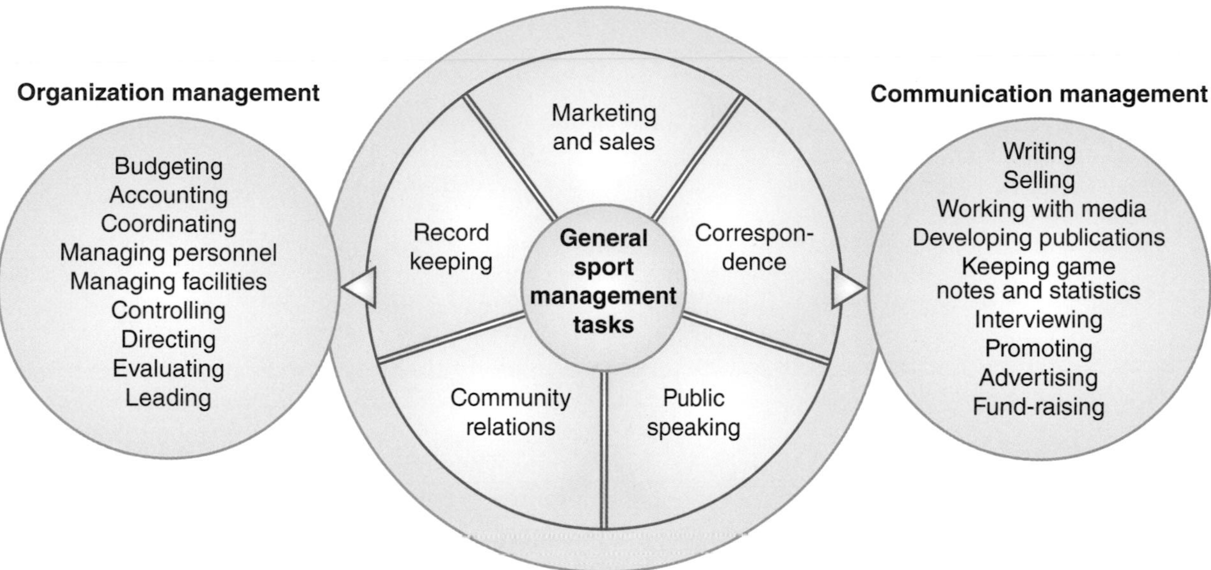

Figure 1.4 Sport management task clusters.

Adapted from J.B. Parks, P.S. Chopra, R.J. Quain, and I.E. Alguindigue, 1988, "ExSport I: An expert system for sport management career counseling." *Journal of Research on Computing in Education*, 21: 196–209.

athletics department, you need to demonstrate competence in writing, speaking, and public relations as well as in the other tasks presented in the core.

The tasks listed in the clusters branching out from the core reflect distinctions between two types of responsibilities. Leadership and management skills are necessary for performing tasks in the organization management cluster. Sport managers need good organizational skills to direct and supervise subordinates in settings such as sport clubs, municipal recreation programs, or sport associations for specific populations, such as seniors or people with differing abilities; in intercollegiate athletics and professional sport; and in the business aspect of any sport-related enterprise.

In the communication management cluster, written and oral communication skills are of paramount importance. Contemporary sport communication practitioners also must be highly skilled in computer technology related to data storage and retrieval as well as Web-based technology (Yu, 2007). Sophisticated communication management competencies are especially critical in areas such as sport marketing, media relations, and sports writing.

Note that although tasks requiring similar competencies appear within one cluster or the other, the clusters are not mutually exclusive. For example, people employed in media relations (communication management cluster) also need to be able to manage and lead personnel (organization management cluster). Conversely, employees in organization management positions need strong communication skills to be successful.

Critical Thinking Skills

An additional competency that sport management students should acquire is the ability to think critically (see the sidebar "Advice from Sport Management Academics" on p. 17). Consider, for example, the types of issues that sport managers in the second decade of the 21st century will need to address:

- Should intercollegiate athletes receive salaries?
- Should professional athletes undergo testing for drugs?
- Should the Confederate flag be flown at sporting events in the United States?
- Should male and female coaches receive equal salaries if they coach the same sport?

Job Satisfaction

Data collected from sport managers in both the United States and Europe suggest that you can expect to be satisfied with most facets of your job (Madella, 2003; Smucker & Kent, 2004). These studies have also shown, however, that you might be somewhat less satisfied with your pay and your opportunities for promotion. Of course, all jobs are different, and you might find a job that brings you immense satisfaction in all aspects, including pay and advancement. In some cases, however, the fulfillment that sport managers find in their jobs comes from their passion for sport, the camaraderie that they enjoy with their coworkers, or their love of the duties that the jobs entail. For them, salary and promotion are of lower priority.

- Should athletes in the Olympic Games receive a share of the revenues of the International Olympic Committee?
- Should young athletes be subjected to an intense, high-performance training regimen?

As managers, you will need exceptional critical thinking skills to make sound decisions about issues such as these and about additional issues that we cannot even conceptualize today. Sound decisions will not be based on expediency, the easy way out, or on what will cause the least turmoil or make the most money. You are most likely to make sound decisions if you make it a point to work toward principled justifications for your beliefs. Becoming a critical thinker is an important step toward learning to provide such justifications for your decisions.

Ideal critical thinkers possess a particular set of dispositions, or tendencies. Although many dispositions facilitate the critical thinking process (see, for example, Facione, Sánchez, Facione, & Gainen, 1995), we believe that the set of three dispositions summarized by Ennis (2000) is especially useful for the critical thinker to pursue. According to Ennis, ideal critical thinkers

- care that their beliefs are true and that their decisions are justified; that is, they care to get it right to the extent that it is possible;
- care to present a position honestly and clearly, theirs as well as others'; and
- care about the dignity and worth of every person.

Note that caring is a central aspect of the critical thinking process. The ideal critical thinker cares enough about what others have to say to make an active attempt to discover and listen to others' reasons and to be sensitive to others' feelings and levels of understanding. An important component of this caring is being truly and seriously open to points of view different from one's own, recognizing that one's own beliefs may not be sufficiently justified. Clearly, achieving this openness is more easily said than done.

What is critical thinking? You probably have encountered the term *critical thinking* many times in your daily life and in the classroom. You may also have noticed that when the term is used, its meaning is often unclear. One reason for the confusion is that the term *critical thinking* means different things to different people. Thus, you must understand the meaning of critical thinking as we are using it in this chapter and in the following chapters. Our definition, an adaptation of definitions that are widely used among scholars who systematically study critical thinking, should be helpful to you in distinguishing between critical thinking and other kinds of thinking. First, to understand what we mean by critical thinking, you need to understand what we do not mean. Critical thinking is not any of the following:

Advice from Sport Management Academics

"A true measure of whether [sport management] graduates are truly prepared is not the courses listed on their transcripts but whether they have been educated to think intelligently and make decisions about issues they will face in the dynamic world of managing a sport enterprise."

Bob Boucher, University of Windsor (1998, p. 81)

"We want our students to be strong critical thinkers who will make positive contributions to society."

Wendy Frisby, University of British Columbia (2005, p. 5)

"Students who have strong critical thinking skills, high levels of quantitative literacy, decision-making skills, and good written and oral communication skills will be able to succeed in almost any job that they choose."

Dan Mahony, Kent State University (2008, p. 8)

"Students must be encouraged not to wait until later in their education to begin the process of critical thinking and ethical decision making. Both types of thinking, in both personal and professional life, must be an ongoing activity of lived experience."

Dwight Zakus, Griffith University; David Malloy, University of Regina; Allan Edwards, Griffith University (2007, p. 148).

- Simply thinking—Critical thinking is "thinking," but it is a special form of thinking. For example, developing a good understanding of something is an important dimension of (just) thinking, but it is quite distinct from critical thinking.
- Negative thinking—To many people, critical thinking does not sound agreeable. It sounds negative. But critical thinkers are not naysayers! Critical thinkers are seeking something positive—as solid a basis for their beliefs as they can find in a world full of uncertainty. Criticisms are simply part of their search for better arguments. In this respect, critical thinking, if practiced appropriately, is positive, caring, and productive.
- Creative thinking—Certain aspects of critical thinking require our best creative efforts, which is one of its appealing components. But critical thinking stresses making evaluative judgments rather than the imaginative leaps associated with brainstorming or generating novel ideas or strategies.

Critical Thinking Questions

We have provided examples of what we do not mean, so what do we mean by critical thinking? A common feature of all critical thinking activity is the systematic evaluation of arguments (i.e., reasons and conclusions) according to explicit standards of rationality—careful thinking that helps us move forward in a continual, ongoing search to improve our opinions, decisions, or judgments. Critical thinking, as we use the term, refers to the following:

- The awareness of a set of interrelated critical questions
- The ability to ask and answer critical questions at appropriate times
- The desire to use those questions and accept their results as a guide to behavior

Central to your success in becoming a critical thinker is having a good understanding of a set of questions that you need to ask to evaluate someone's reasoning. Although there is no single correct set of critical thinking questions, we have presented eight selected questions in the sidebar on pages 18-19. The discussion of each question in

Eight Critical Thinking Questions

Question 1: What Are the Issues and the Conclusion?

You start the critical thinking process by identifying the issue and the conclusion, which will be either **prescriptive** or **descriptive.** Value preferences will have much greater influence over prescriptive conclusions than they will over descriptive conclusions. For example, values will influence the prescriptive conclusion that there should be more African American athletics directors. Conversely, the descriptive conclusion that in 2008 only 10% of NCAA Division I athletics directors were African Americans will depend on empirical evidence (Lapchick, 2009).

prescriptive—Concerns about the way the world should or ought to be.

descriptive—Concerns about the way the world is, was, or will be.

Question 2: What Are the Reasons?

Reasons are ideas that communicators use to justify their conclusions. To discover reasons, you need to ask, "What reasons do the communicators give to support their conclusion?" You should decide the merits of the conclusion based on the quality of the reasons.

Question 3: What Words or Phrases Are Ambiguous?

You cannot determine whether you agree or disagree with someone's reasoning if key terms in the reasoning could have more than one meaning and those different meanings would influence your reactions. For example, in evaluating a coach's success, if you define success as winning percentage, you may reach a different conclusion than if you define success as motivating athletes to achieve their full potential.

Question 4: What Are the Value Conflicts and Assumptions?

Assumptions are ideas that people take for granted. Values are abstract ideas that people see as worthwhile (e.g., honesty, compassion, competition, justice). In many cases, however, values are in conflict, such that embracing one value means rejecting another. The following reasoning example illustrates the influence of value conflicts and value assumptions:

- Conclusion: Sport teams should cease using American Indian symbols and traditions.
- Reason: These practices are inaccurate, disrespectful to American Indians, and offensive.
- Value assumption: The value of human dignity is more important than the value of the right of freedom of expression.

Question 5: What Are the Descriptive Assumptions?

Descriptive assumptions are unstated beliefs about how the world is, was, or will be. You discover these assumptions by asking, What ideas must be taken for granted in order for you to believe that the reason is accurate? The following scenario (Women's Sports Foundation, 2010) illustrates descriptive assumptions:

- Conclusion: Female athletes perform at higher levels when coached by men rather than by women.
- Reason: Teams with male coaches have won more championships than teams with female coaches because female coaches are not as intense and demanding as male coaches.
- Assumptions: Teams coached by women have had the same recruiting resources as teams coached by men; it is acceptable to attribute standard characteristics to all members of a given group; and intense, demanding coaches are more likely to help female athletes reach their potential.

Question 6: Does the Reasoning Contain Fallacies?

Fallacies are mistakes in reasoning that do not seem to be mistakes. The following claim illustrates a fallacy: Either we raise public moneys to finance a sport stadium or we will have to move the team to another city. This reasoning assumes that only two choices are available. If, however, it is possible to raise private moneys to build the stadium, then the reasoning contains a fallacy.

Question 7: How Good Is the Evidence?

Consider the following claims: The graduation rate of nonathletes is higher than the graduation rate of athletes; Title IX has forced several colleges to drop some men's sports; participation in sport builds good character. To evaluate such claims, ask, How good is the evidence? The greater the quality and quantity of supporting evidence, the more you can depend on it and the more you can legitimately call the claim a fact.

Question 8: What Significant Information Is Omitted?

Communicators who are trying to persuade you are likely to select and use information that supports their conclusion. Thus, you need to ask, What significant information is missing? Some examples of missing information are (a) evidence that supports different conclusions, (b) alternative value assumptions, and (c) identification of the source of the evidence presented. By looking for missing information, you can decide whether you have enough information to judge the communicator's reasoning.

Based on Browne and Keeley 2007.

the sidebar is necessarily brief. For an in-depth discussion of the eight questions, see Browne and Keeley (2007).

FUTURE CHALLENGES AND OPPORTUNITIES

Pitts and Stotlar (2007) observed that the world of sport is growing rapidly. This growth is reflected not only in the introduction of many new sports but also in the increasing number of opportunities to participate in sports and activities, an upsurge in the number and variety of sport-related magazines and sport-related Web sites on the Internet, enhanced mass media exposure of sporting activities, growth in the number and types of sport facilities and events, increased interest in sport tourism and adventure travel, and the provision of sport related goods and services for a greater variety of market segments. New professional sports have emerged, sport opportunities are being offered to a more diverse population, endorsements and sponsorships are on the rise, sport industry education is becoming more prevalent and sophisticated, marketing and promotion orientation is growing in the sport industry, sport managers are becoming more competent, and the globalization of the sport industry is progressing rapidly. Undoubtedly, these advances will create numerous job opportunities for aspiring sport managers. Madella (2003), however, cautioned that the quality of these jobs should be carefully monitored. Moreover, the status of the global economy will have major ramifications for the health of the sport industry.

The future will present sport managers with many challenges and opportunities, some that have already emerged and others that we cannot even imagine. In subsequent chapters, you will learn about a variety of such challenges within specific segments of the sport industry. Some challenges will affect all sport managers, irrespective of the segment of the industry in which they are employed. These challenges and opportunities are associated with technology, ethics and social responsibility, and the globalization of sport.

Technology

The technology explosion of the past several decades has been mind boggling, and this is only the beginning! As Danylchuk and Boucher (2003) noted, "The sport industry is already information driven. This will continue to increase and the demand for technically competent employees will continue to accelerate" (p. 293). As an example, in the sidebar "Brilliant Orange Finally Go All the Way," Westerbeek and Smith (2003) provide a hypothetical glimpse into the future with their prediction of a sport scenario in the year 2038.

Brilliant Orange Finally Go All the Way!

Amsterdam, 10 July 2038. Celebrations are under way in Amsterdam where a whole nation indulges in the "Orange Eleven's" victory in the World Cup final against Cameroon. In a capacity filled Manage-to-Manage Dome, 100,000 on-site spectators and 6 billion people worldwide celebrated a three-hour entertainment extravaganza culminating in a World Cup final that will be remembered for its brilliant soccer and mind-boggling drama.

First Time Ever Sell-Out of Virtual Stadium

Pre-match entertainment started off in spectacular fashion with hologrammatic appearances by Elvis Presley, Marilyn Monroe and Frank Sinatra, complemented by a live appearance of the Rolling Clones. Presley and Monroe performed the World Cup hymn, Sinatra treated the crowd to some classics from the last century and the Clones performed three songs from their first album, before they took the honours of kicking off the World Cup final.

The Dutch turned around what proved to be a high-scoring and equal contest throughout the four quarters of the match during extended play, when the score was still level at 4-4. Twenty minutes into extra time, after both teams were forced to take six players off the pitch (one player every three minutes) and goals were increased in height by 20 centimetres, cloned veteran striker Hans Westerbeek scored the golden goal. Westerbeek II was the first person in the world to be genetically modified with the help of "top striker" DNA. Former Dutch great Marco van Basten donated his superior genetic material through FIFA's soccer development foundation, for a modest fee of course.

Nationality gene chip measurements indicate that 88.02 per cent of all Dutch in the world witnessed this moment live, 3.02 per cent on free to air television in the continent of Africa, 1.90 per cent on pay television, 23.12 per cent on the mobile Internet, 0.1 per cent on-site (predominantly backpackers who were willing to cope with the inconvenience of actually attending the event live at no cost) and a staggering 59.52 per cent virtually live, having bought tickets in the virtual Manage-to-Manage Dome. The Quantum Entanglement technology that was trialled first at the 2006 Commonwealth Games in Melbourne, Australia, has become so popular that the virtual Manage-to-Manage Dome was sold out for the first time in the history of digital virtual stadia. The technology has become so sophisticated that it only takes a contact lens-based microchip, with a wireless link to a MoGMeD (Mobile Global Media Device) to be transported to the stadium and interact with those who also subscribed to the match. So many people (3.2 billion worldwide) wanted to log on to the server powered through the international Duff beer space station that memory capacity to interact as a live spectator in the Dome ran out. The newly introduced violence protection chip was reported to work very well, with only minor clashes reported among non-football interested cyberspace fringes. Given the effectiveness of the violence protection chip, denying access to the stadium by any spectator who is genetically predisposed to cyber violence, the virtual police had little trouble containing the culprits.

Regardless of whether the future will be exactly as Westerbeek and Smith (2003) predict, their scenario does provide food for thought. One notion to consider, however, is that technology is not an end unto itself; it is a means to an end—an innovation that facilitates progress and helps us realize other accomplishments. In the future, scientific advances in computers and communication technology will play an increasingly significant role in our society and in sport management. This progress will likely be accompanied by acknowledgment of the human need for "high-touch" activities, many of which the sport experience can provide. The challenge, therefore, is to become proficient in using technology while remaining aware of the need for human interaction in people's lives and understanding how sport can facilitate such interaction.

Ethics and Social Responsibility

Sport managers must deal with a multitude of questions that require an understanding of ethical principles and moral psychology. Consider the following questions:

- How can we best achieve gender, race, and class equity in sport?
- Do professional team owners owe primary allegiance to themselves or to the communities that support the team?
- How can we balance academic integrity with the demands of intercollegiate competition?
- Should athletes sacrifice their health for victory?
- Is winning really the bottom line of sport?
- Is intercollegiate sport an entertainment business for public consumption or an extracurricular opportunity for student development, or both, or something else?

The list is seemingly endless, and no doubt you could add your own concerns to it. DeSensi and Rosenberg (2003) noted that the number of illegal and immoral incidences in sport settings has captured the attention of the public. Many people are calling for greater accountability on the part of sport managers. In recognition of the need for a heightened focus on ethics and social responsibility in sport, DeSensi and Rosenberg advised that "being socially responsible is paramount to the execution of one's job. Developing a social consciousness and being socially responsible assists sport managers with the creation of a sound professional philosophy and subsequent ethical action" (p. 127).

In the same vein, Malloy and Zakus (1995) suggested that sport management students should understand the need to "challenge the assumptions, both overt and covert, of sport and society to enable themselves to make ethically sound decisions" (p. 54). The desire and ability to engage in **principled decision making** often distinguishes superior sport managers from their peers.

principled decision making—Basing decisions on the "Six Pillars of Character"—trustworthiness, respect, responsibility, fairness, caring, and good citizenship (responsible participation in society) (Josephson Institute of Ethics, 2002).

Now is the time to begin reflecting on ethical concerns because you surely will face them in the years to come. The sidebar "Guidelines for Making Ethical Decisions" on page 22 contains an approach to ethical decision making that was developed by scholars in the Markkula Center for Applied Ethics at Santa Clara University (*Making an Ethical Decision*, 2009). In subsequent chapters, you will be referred to this sidebar to help you examine ethical concerns in specific sport settings. The guidelines serve well as an introduction to the place of ethics in a sport manager's decision-making process.

We are hopeful that in the future, enlightened sport managers will be aware of their social responsibilities and will deliver their services in ways that reflect this understanding (see the sidebar "Code of Ethics, North American Society for Sport Management" on p. 23). For example, sport managers worldwide will be conscious of environmental concerns and will incorporate this understanding into their business practices. Environmental concerns that are important to sport managers include air and water quality, land and water use, waste management, energy management, transportation design and services, accommodation design and services, and facilities construction. Indeed, the United Nations Environment Programme (UNEP) has the following objectives for its Sport and Environment Strategy:

1. To promote the integration of environmental considerations in sports
2. To use the popularity of sports to promote environmental awareness
3. To promote the development of environmentally friendly sports facilities and the manufacture of environmentally friendly sports goods (Toepfer, 2003, ¶ 5)

Guidelines for Making Ethical Decisions

Recognize an Ethical Issue

1. Could this decision or situation be damaging to someone or to some group? Does this decision involve a choice between a good and bad alternative, or perhaps between two "goods" or between two "bads"?
2. Is this issue about more than what is legal or what is most efficient? If so, how?

Get the Facts

3. What are the relevant facts of the case? What facts are not known? Can I learn more about the situation? Do I know enough to make a decision?
4. What individuals and groups have an important stake in the outcome? Are some concerns more important than others? Why?
5. What are the options for acting? Have all the relevant persons and groups been consulted? Have I identified creative options?

Evaluate Alternative Actions

6. Evaluate the options by asking the following questions:
   - Which option will produce the most good and do the least harm (the utilitarian approach)?
   - Which option best respects the rights of all who have a stake (the rights approach)?
   - Which option treats people equally or proportionately (the justice approach)?
   - Which option best serves the community as a whole, not just some members (the common good approach)?
   - Which option leads me to act as the sort of person I want to be (the virtue approach)?

Make a Decision and Test It

7. Considering all these approaches, which option best addresses the situation?
8. If I told someone whom I respect—or told a television audience—which option I have chosen, what would they say?

Act and Reflect on the Outcome

9. How can my decision be implemented with the greatest care and attention to the concerns of all stakeholders?
10. How did my decision turn out, and what have I learned from this specific situation?

Several professional sport organizations in the United States have taken steps that reflect an understanding of environmental sustainability (Associated Press, 2007; "Pro sports go green," 2009; "To 'green' Super Bowl," 2009). Among them are the Washington Nationals, Philadelphia Eagles, National Football League (NFL), San Francisco Giants, Seattle Mariners, Indy Racing League (IRL), Minnesota Twins, New Jersey Nets, New England Patriots, Detroit Lions, St. Louis Rams, and Formula One Racing. In response to a question as to whether environmental initiatives were here to stay, Mark Andrew, founder and president of an environmental consulting and sponsorship company stated, "This is not a fad. . . . It's smart business" (Covello, 2008, ¶ 3).

Additional evidence of future sport managers' sense of social responsibility will include the routine provision of professional childcare services in sport facilities and the targeting of previously untapped and undertapped target markets, such as women

Code of Ethics, North American Society for Sport Management

The following canons or principles, arranged according to category or dimension, shall be considered by the sport manager in the performance of professional duties:

- The sport manager should hold paramount the safety, health, and welfare of the individual in the performance of professional duties.
- The sport manager should act in accordance with the highest standards of professional integrity.
- The sport manager's primary responsibility is to students/clients.
- When setting fees for service in private or commercial settings, the sport manager should ensure that they are fair, reasonable, considerate, and commensurate with the service performed and with due respect to the students'/clients' ability to pay.
- The sport manager should adhere to any and all commitments made to the employing organization. The relationship should be characterized by fairness, non-malfeasance, and truthfulness.
- The sport manager should treat colleagues with respect, courtesy, fairness, and good faith.
- The sport manager should uphold and advance the values and ethical standards, the knowledge, and the mission of the profession.
- The sport manager should promote the general welfare of society.

Reprinted, by permission, from the North American Society for Sport Management, 2010, *Ethical creed*. (Slippery Rock, PA: NASSM). Available: http://www.nassm.com/InfoAbout/NASSM/Creed

and people of differing ages, abilities, and sexual orientations. Sport managers of the future will also recognize the importance of keeping the sport experience accessible to all socioeconomic groups.

Globalization of Sport

The need to understand and appreciate other countries and cultures cannot be overstated (Danylchuk & Boucher, 2003; Thibault, 2009). In recognition of this fact, most chapters of this book contain information on the sport industry in other nations. You can take several steps to prepare yourself to interact effectively in the global community. For example, although students in many countries consider mastery of the English language a basic skill, most students in the United States do not master languages of other countries. Consequently, US students can distinguish themselves from their peers by learning a language other than English. Studying in another country for an extended period and completing courses that focus on other cultures are among the additional steps that you can take to broaden your horizons and enhance the quality of your life. Pursuing this path will also increase your value in the marketplace.

The globalization of sport brings with it many benefits. For example, more countries and athletes are participating in international events; sport is being used as a vehicle that crosses traditional lines of gender, religion, and geographical barriers; and sport is bringing people around the world together in a common interest. As you contemplate the positive aspect of the globalization of sport, however, you should understand that some advances in international sport may have come at the expense of poor people in developing countries. As with other issues that have been discussed in this chapter, critical thinking from an ethical perspective will be required to address problems such as the exploitation of third-world labor in the production of sporting goods; the recruitment and migration of athletes that results in a talent drain on their home countries; the effect of the interrelationships among transnational

SPORT CLUBS, THE *SPORT FOR ALL* MOVEMENT, AND THE RECESSION IN WESTERN EUROPE

By Marijke Taks • BELGIUM
University of Windsor, CANADA

Participant sport is delivered differently in Western Europe than it is in North America, where it is delivered primarily through the educational system. In Europe, community-based sport clubs play a dominant role in the sport delivery system. A school sport system outside the regular physical education classes does exist, but it does not receive much attention or exposure, and most people are hardly aware of its existence. The majority of participant sport takes place in sport clubs.

Community-based sport clubs have a long history and a strong tradition in European society. Sport clubs are voluntary organizations that are led by a board of directors, who are often a group of friends. Through cooperation among all the stakeholders (participants, coaches, volunteers, parents, facility operators, cafeteria owners, and so on) clubs create social networks outside the work or school environment. Camaraderie is an integral part of the sport experience!

The *Sport for All* movement, adopted in 1966 and based on the strong social values of the 1960s (i.e., democratization, participation, inclusion, and pluralism) strengthened the position of the sport clubs. Public authorities at the national, regional, and local levels started to provide direct and indirect support to voluntary sport clubs, and they still do so. The local sport authorities provide the facilities, whereas the sport clubs offer the sport

Photo courtesy of Paul M. Pedersen.

Sparta Atletik in Copenhagen, Denmark, is an example of a community-based sport club.

corporations, media, and sport organizations; and the effect of sport on the environment (Thibault, 2009).

The future will most assuredly bring change, something that can be frightening and is frequently resisted. Progressive sport managers who can anticipate and embrace change will have opportunities to be agents of change who will transform the way that sport is managed. We hope that you will be one of those managers!

Summary

In this chapter, sport is broadly defined as (1) "all forms of physical activity which, through casual or organised participation, aim at expressing or improving physical fitness and mental well-being, forming social relationships or obtaining results

programs. Nowadays, a third partner, the school, is being targeted for providing additional facilities during after-school hours.

The economic recession does not seem to have affected clubs or leagues in Western Europe. Memberships have not decreased, and large increases in participation are being noticed in popular (payable) run and bike races. In times of economic downturns, people may want to direct their attention to physical care, including sport participation and physical fitness, as a way of retaining some measure of individual control. Sport participation may play its own role in these times of economic hardship, keeping the "sport for all" philosophy alive. This situation is in contrast to professional sport and high-performance sport, in which huge dropdowns in sponsorship contracts and player salaries are taking their toll. Public sport authorities are currently refraining from investing in major sport facility projects, while waiting for better economic times.

Sport clubs in Europe offer a wide variety of sport programs and provide opportunities to children, adolescents, and adults to become involved in sport at all levels. Involvement can be as recreational participants or interclub competitors, as coaches, as administrators, as members of the board of directors, as facility providers, or even as bartenders. Each of these actors has a role to play in the sport delivery system of Europe as it strives to offer sport for all. The physical activity component and the socializing factor are two core elements of sport clubs that are particularly important during times of economic hardship and that seem to make the *Sport for All* movement and the sport club system recession proof.

INTERNATIONAL LEARNING ACTIVITY #1

Search the Internet for sport clubs in Europe. How many sports are organized on a club basis? How many of them are for men, and how many are for women? Are sport clubs available for children? Using information posted online, compare and contrast the European sport club system with the sport system in your country.

INTERNATIONAL LEARNING ACTIVITY #2

Search the Internet for information about the North American Indigenous Games (NAIG). Prepare a paper or a presentation to inform your classmates about various aspects of the Games. Moderate a class discussion about the purpose and importance of these Games.

INTERNATIONAL LEARNING ACTIVITY #3

Explore the Web site of the United Nations Environment Programme at www.unep.org/. Make a list of ways in which the environment affects sport and ways in which sport affects the environment. Then, make a list of ways in which you, as a sport manager, could advance the three major objectives of the UN Environment Programme at the local level.

in competition at all levels" (Council of Europe, 2001, p. 1) and (2) "any activity, experience, or business enterprise focused on fitness, recreation, athletics, or leisure" (Pitts et al., 1994, p. 18). The sport industry can be conceptualized based on (1) the types of sporting activities that exist, (2) the settings in which sport occurs, and (3) the industry segments into which various sport businesses and organizations can be categorized. Three models of segmentation describe the sport industry: the product type model, the economic impact model, and the sport activity model. Four unique aspects of sport management are sport marketing, the sport enterprise financial structure, career paths, and the power of sport as a social institution. Sport managers should possess general, transferable competencies as well as competencies specific to organization management and information management and the ability to think critically.

The next generation of sport managers will face challenges associated with technology, ethics and social responsibility, and globalization. Enlightened sport managers of the future will be competent in the technical aspects of their jobs and will be agents of change, both in the management of sport and in the larger society.

Review Questions

1. Name five sports that have emerged in the last few years. How has their emergence affected career opportunities in sport management?
2. List and discuss five sport business settings that might represent job opportunities for sport managers.
3. Describe three models of segmentation that have been applied to the sport industry and provide examples of sport organizations in each segment of each model.
4. Identify four unique aspects of sport management and explain how each makes the sport business different from other businesses.
5. Explain the task clusters into which sport managers' responsibilities can be classified.
6. Define critical thinking and explain the benefits of applying critical thinking skills to important issues in sport management.
7. List the dispositions that critical thinkers should possess and indicate whether you possess each of them. Explain your answers.
8. Define principled decision making and give examples of when and how sport managers need to make principled decisions.
9. Describe opportunities and challenges in technology, ethics and social responsibility, and globalization that all sport managers will face in the future.

QUIZ TIME

Did you grasp all the key points in this chapter? Go to the OSG for a short quiz to test your understanding of the material.

References

Acosta, R.V., & Carpenter, L.J. (2008). *Women in intercollegiate sport—a longitudinal, national study: Thirty-one year update 1977–2008*. Retrieved January 29, 2010, from http://webpages.charter.net/womeninsport/

Associated Press. (2007, April 22). Concerned about the earth, pro teams move to the frontier of change. *New York Times*. Retrieved April 30, 2009, from www.nytimes.com/2007/04/22/sports/baseball/22environment.html

Bennett, G., Henson, R.K., & Zhang, J. (2003). Generation Y's perceptions of the action sports industry segment. *Journal of Sport Management*, *17*, 95–115.

Boucher, R.L. (1998). Toward achieving a focal point for sport management: A binocular perspective. *Journal of Sport Management*, *12*, 76–85.

Brand, M. (2007). The women of Rutgers and social change. *NCAA News*. Retrieved May 5, 2009, from www.ncaa.org/wps/ncaa?ContentID=11333

Browne, M.N., & Keeley, S.M. (2007). *Asking the right questions: A guide to critical thinking* (8th ed.). Upper Saddle River, NJ: Prentice Hall.

Clay, B. (1995, February 1). 8 great careers in the sports industry. *Black Enterprise*, *25*(7), 158–160, 162, 164, 166.

Coakley, J. (2009). *Sports in society: Issues and controversies* (10th ed.). New York: McGraw-Hill.

Council of Europe. (2001). *The European Sports Charter* (revised). Retrieved April 15, 2009, from http://www.sportdevelopment.info/index.php?option=com_content&view=article&id=87:council-of-europe-2001-the-european-sports-charterrevised-brussels-council-of-europe-&catid=59:international-documents&Itemid=82

Covello, L. (2008, January 30). Sports teams go green: Real thing or just a fling? *FoxBusiness*. Retrieved April 14, 2009, from www.foxbusiness.com/story/personal-finance/on-topic/sports/sports-teams-green-real-thing-just-fling/

Danylchuk, K.E., & Boucher, R. (2003). The future of sport management as an academic discipline. *International Journal of Sport Management*, *4*, 281–300.

DeSensi, J.T., & Rosenberg, D. (2003). *Ethics and morality in sport management* (2nd ed.). Morgantown, WV: Fitness Information Technology.

Ennis, R.H. (2000). *Super-streamlined conception of critical thinking*. Retrieved April 18, 2009, from www.criticalthinking.net/SSConcCTApr3.html

Eschenfelder, M.J., & Li, M. (2007). *Economics of sport* (2nd ed.). Morgantown, WV: Fitness Information Technology.

Facione, P.A., Sánchez, C.A., Facione, N.C., & Gainen, J. (1995). The disposition toward critical thinking. *Journal of General Education*, *44*, 1–25.

Frank, R. (1984). Olympic myths and realities. *Arete: The Journal of Sport Literature*, *1*(2), 155–161.

Frisby, W. (2005). The good, the bad, and the ugly: Critical sport management research. *Journal of Sport Management*, *19*, 1–12.

Gottlieb, R. (2009). *Sports market place directory*. Millerton, NY: Grey House.

Horch, H., & Schütte, N. (2003). Competencies of sport managers in German sport clubs and sport federations. *Managing Leisure*, *8*, 70–84.

Isaacs, S. (1964). *Careers and opportunities in sport.* New York: Dutton.

Josephson Institute of Ethics. (2002). *Making ethical decisions.* Retrieved April 18, 2009, from www.josephsoninstitute.org/MED/MED-intro+toc.htm

Keeley, S.M., Parks, J.B., & Thibault, L. (2007). Thinking critically about sport management. In J. Parks, J. Quarterman, & L. Thibault (Eds.), *Contemporary sport management* (3rd ed., pp. 47–62). Champaign, IL: Human Kinetics.

Kinkhabwala, A. (2007, April 23). The righteous Scarlet Knights. *Sports Illustrated.* Retrieved May 5, 2009, from http://vault.sportsillustrated.cnn.com/vault/article/magazine/MAG1116097/index.htm

Krumrie, M. (2009, May 6). *Sports management.* Retrieved May 6, 2009, from http://management.monster.ca/8933_en-CA_p1.asp

Lapchick, R. (2009). *The racial and gender report card.* Retrieved April 19, 2009, from the University of Central Florida, Institute for Diversity and Ethics in Sport Web site: http://web.bus.ucf.edu/sportbusiness/?page=1445

Madella, A. (2003). Methods for analyzing sports employment in Europe. *Managing Leisure*, *8*, 56–69.

Mahony, D.F. (2008). No one can whistle a symphony: Working together for sport management's future. *Journal of Sport Management*, *22*, 1–10.

Making an ethical decision. (2009). Markkula Center for Applied Ethics, Santa Clara University. Retrieved January 29, 2010, from www.scu.edu/ethics/practicing/decision/making.pdf

Malloy, D.C., & Zakus, D.H. (1995). Ethical decision making in sport administration: A theoretical inquiry into substance and form. *Journal of Sport Management*, *9*, 36–58.

Mason, J.G., Higgins, C.R., & Wilkinson, O.J. (1981). Sports administration education 15 years later. *Athletic Purchasing and Facilities*, *5*(1), 44–45.

Mawson, L.M. (2002). The extreme sport challenge for sport managers. *International Journal of Sport Management*, *3*, 249–261.

McCann, M. (2007, February 27). *Cedric Maxwell's sexist comments about NBA referee Violet Palmer.* Retrieved May 5, 2009, from http://sports-law.blogspot.com/2007/02/cedric-maxwells-sexist-comments-about.html

Meek, A. (1997). An estimate of the size and supported economic activity of the sports industry in the United States. *Sport Marketing Quarterly*, *6*(4), 15–21.

Mullin, B.J. (1980). Sport management: The nature and utility of the concept. *Arena Review*, *4*(3), 1–11.

North American Society for Sport Management. (2009). *NASSM programs.* Retrieved April 14, 2009, from http://www.nassm.com/InfoAbout/SportMgmtPrograms

North American Society for Sport Management. (2010). *Ethical creed.* Retrieved June 14, 2010, from www.nassm.com/InfoAbout/NASSM/Creed

Parks, J.B., Chopra, P.S., Quain, R.J., & Alguindigue, I.E. (1988). ExSport: I: An expert system for sport management career counseling. *Journal of Research on Computing in Education*, *21*, 196–209.

Parks, J.B., & Olafson, G.A. (1987). Sport management and a new journal. *Journal of Sport Management*, *1*, 1–3.

Pitts, B.G., Fielding, L.W., & Miller, L.K. (1994). Industry segmentation theory and the sport industry: Developing a sport industry segmentation model. *Sport Marketing Quarterly*, *3*(1), 15–24.

Pitts, B.G., & Stotlar, D.K. (2007). *Fundamentals of sport marketing* (3rd ed.). Morgantown, WV: Fitness Information Technology.

Pro sports go green. (2009, January 31). *Environmental Leader.* Retrieved April 15, 2009, from www.environmentalleader.com/2008/01/31/pro-sports-go-green/

Ross, S.R., & Parks, J.B. (2008). Sport management students' attitudes toward women: A challenge for educators. *Sport Management Education Journal*, *2*, 1–18.

Smucker, M., & Kent, A. (2004). Satisfaction and referent comparisons in the sport industry. *International Journal of Sport Management*, *5*, 262–280.

Thibault, L. (2009). Globalization of sport: An inconvenient truth. *Journal of Sport Management*, *23*, 1–20.

Toepfer, K. (2003, December 2). *Sport and sustainable development.* Paper presented at the 5th World Conference on Sport and Environment, Turin, Italy. Retrieved April 26, 2009, from www.unep.org/Documents.Multilingual/Default.asp?DocumentID=364&ArticleID=4316&l=en

To "green" Super Bowl, NFL buys renewable energy, plants trees. (2009, January 28). *Environmental Leader.* Retrieved April 14, 2009, from www.environmentalleader.com/2009/01/28/to-green-super-bowl-nfl-buys-renewable-energy-plants-trees/

Tsuji, Y., Bennett, G., & Zhang, J. (2007). Consumer satisfaction with an action sports event. *Sport Marketing Quarterly*, *15*, 199–208.

United Nations. (2004). *Resolution adopted by the General Assembly.* Retrieved April 26, 2009, from http://daccessdds.un.org/doc/UNDOC/GEN/N04/476/80/PDF/N0447680.pdf?OpenElement

Westerbeek, H., & Smith, A. (2003). *Sport business in the global marketplace.* New York: Palgrave Macmillan.

Women's Sports Foundation. (2010). *Coaching—Do female athletes prefer male coaches? The Foundation position.* Retrieved January 29, 2010, from www.womenssportsfoundation.org/Content/Articles/Issues/Coaching/C/Coaching--Do-Female-Athletes-Prefer-Male-Coaches-The-Foundation-Position.aspx

Yu, C.C. (2007). Important computer competencies for sport management professionals. *International Journal of Applied Sports Sciences*, *19*(1), 66–85.

Zakus, D.H., Malloy, D.C., & Edwards, A. (2007). Critical and ethical thinking in sport management: Philosophical rationales and examples of methods. *Sport Management Review*, *10*, 133–158.

HISTORICAL MOMENTS

1966	National Association of Collegiate Directors of Athletics (NACDA) formed
1974	First gathering of the Stadium Managers Association held
1974	Billie Jean King founded Women's Sports Foundation
1978	North American Society for the Sociology of Sport (NASSS) formed
1986	First NASSM conference held at Kent State University
1987	Sport and Recreation Law Association (SRLA) established
1987	Association for Women in Sport Media (AWSM) formed
1987	National Association for Sport and Physical Education (NASPE) published curricular guidelines
1988	Black Coaches Association (BCA) founded (renamed Black Coaches and Administrators)
1993	NASPE–NASSM curricular standards published
1994	Sport Management Program Review Council (SMPRC) created
2002	Sport Marketing Association (SMA) established
2003	First SMA conference held
2007	College Sport Research Institute (CSRI) formed
2008	The Commission on Sport Management Accreditation (COSMA) became official accrediting body of sport management programs

Photo courtesy of Won Youl Bae.

2

DEVELOPING A PROFESSIONAL PERSPECTIVE

Sally R. Ross ■ Kathryn S. Hoff ■ JoAnn Kroll

LEARNING OBJECTIVES

1. Describe strategies to position yourself to be successful upon graduation in the competitive field of sport management.
2. Identify where entry-level opportunities exist and how to gain experience.
3. Recognize the importance of professional preparation, professional attitude, and career planning and management.
4. Explain the three components of an undergraduate sport management curriculum.
5. Describe how students can secure and optimize their involvement in field experiences.
6. Discuss ways in which your personal appearance, work transition and adjustment, and business etiquette can enhance your employability and advancement.
7. Describe the four stages involved in career planning.
8. Identify several resources that are useful in planning a career in sport management.

Key Terms

entrepreneur
etiquette
explicit norms
extracurricular activities
field experience
implicit norms
job content skills
mock interviews
values
work ethic

Achieving success in most business settings requires specific knowledge, skills, values, and understanding that students are expected to begin to acquire as undergraduates. The first step toward acquiring these essentials to success involves adopting the perspective that you are now more than simply a student. You are a professional. You cannot wait until four years from now to begin to accept the responsibilities of being a professional. Your professors expect you to conduct yourself with professionalism while on campus, and you will gain more from your degree program if you behave as a professional rather than just a student. The level of commitment that you make to sport management as an academic pursuit will influence how you approach your coursework, extracurricular activities, and relationships with fellow students and instructors. A student who develops a professional perspective early on in her or his academic career will benefit through increased knowledge and opportunities.

The field of sport management is an especially competitive one. Many schools offer a major in sport management, which translates into a large number of graduates each year. In addition, students in majors outside sport management may also be interested in working in sport. What this means is that a large pool of candidates is competing for a finite number of jobs within the sport industry. To achieve success in this competitive environment, students must be willing to put forth a great deal of effort to put themselves in the best position possible.

No matter what type of job you hope to pursue, remember that professionalism begins in the classroom. You must understand and satisfy the requirements and learning objectives of courses, and the expectations of professors. Arrive to class on time, be attentive and prepared, take notes, and show interest. You should also follow the example of professionals and use a day planner, calendar, or organizer in which you can enter assignment due dates, exam dates, work responsibilities, and meetings. Whatever apparatus you use, keep it on hand, update it when necessary, and refer to it often.

Making the decision to develop your professional perspective will allow you to take advantage of resources available to you and dedicate yourself to learning how to develop yourself into a successful professional. This chapter addresses three components of a professional perspective:

- **Professional preparation**—the courses and experiences that you can expect in your undergraduate curriculum and beyond
- **Professional attitude**—how to present a professional image, follow the fundamentals of business etiquette, develop ethical and critical thinking skills, and enter the world of work and be comfortable and productive there
- **Career planning and management**—purposeful steps that you can take and helpful resources available to you as you contemplate entering the world of work

PROFESSIONAL PREPARATION

Sport management preparation programs exist at the baccalaureate (undergraduate), master's, and doctoral levels. Baccalaureate programs prepare students for entry-level positions in the sport industry. Master's-level education prepares students for more advanced, specialized responsibilities. The doctorate usually emphasizes research. Students who seek the doctoral degree typically wish to become professors or work in some other capacity in a college or university setting.

Currently, you may be enrolled in a sport management undergraduate program, you might be a high school student, or you may be a university student in another major field who wants to learn more about opportunities in sport management. In any case, you will benefit from an explanation of what to expect in a sport management curriculum at the undergraduate level. Most undergraduate sport management programs include three components: general education courses, major courses, and field experiences.

General Education

The general education component of the undergraduate curriculum is vital because university graduates should be able to demonstrate understanding and capabilities beyond those acquired in their major courses. As a university graduate, you will be expected to express yourself well, both in writing and in speaking. You should understand and be able to discuss—at least on a topical level—areas such as art, literature, history, and social and physical sciences. With a firm foundation provided by general education courses, you should be able to deal with a changing society that reflects the cultural diversity of our world. Indeed, awareness of other cultures, as well as an understanding and appreciation of them, is essential in addressing the sport management needs of the global community (Chelladurai, 2005). Furthermore, as covered in chapter 1, as a sport manager you will also be expected to use critical thinking skills that you can acquire and develop in general education courses. As you seek to advance your career, the analytical, critical thinking, and leadership skills developed in general education courses will become even more important.

Major Courses in Sport Management

WEB Go to the OSG and complete the first Web search activity, which will help you identify ways two different organizations can help you in your sport management career.

Desire for consistency and quality in sport management curricula started in 1986 when the National Association for Sport and Physical Education (NASPE) appointed a task force to develop curricular guidelines (Brassie, 1989). Through a joint effort, NASPE and the North American Society for Sport Management (NASSM) served as the program approval agency from 1993 until 2008, when the Commission on Sport Management Accreditation (COSMA) became the accrediting body for sport management curricula.

Based on recommendations from these groups as well as published research, this textbook has been designed to introduce students to areas of study that will prepare them to pursue the rest of the sport management curriculum with enhanced insight and understanding. This book addresses topics in the content areas that have been deemed essential by the accrediting body of sport management education programs (i.e., COSMA). Reviewing the table of contents of this book will provide an overview of the scope of the sport industry and the range of employment opportunities within sport.

The courses in the sport management curriculum are designed to prepare you for a career in one of the many segments of the sport industry. But if you do not enter the sport management field, the course content prescribed in this textbook is sufficiently broad to prepare you to assume positions in a variety of other vocational fields such as advertising, promotions, sales, and communications.

Keeping up with current events in your field is essential to your academic preparation. Although numerous popular media outlets offer sport stories, students preparing to be sport managers should also read from an assortment of trade and academic journals that address sport management issues. One way to discover the most relevant reading material related to your educational and occupational goals is to pay attention to the publications that your instructors use for assignments. Several chapters of this book discuss relevant publications and professional associations specific to various careers in sport management (for examples of such associations, please refer to the sidebar "Examples of Professional Organizations" on p. 32). Membership in one or more of these associations will offer you opportunities to read publications, attend conferences, and access information exclusive to members. Some organizations have student branches, providing you with opportunities to gain experience in leadership and governance. Sharing ideas and networking with professionals at all levels will be enjoyable and helpful in your career development. Your instructors can give you advice about which professional organizations will be most helpful to you, both now and in the future.

Additional ways to learn more about your field and gain relevant work experience include becoming involved in student activities, gaining on-campus employment, and participating in community service opportunities. Participation in student organizations provides students the chance to assume leadership roles and prepare as future professionals. Student affiliate chapters of professional organizations, which are often found on campuses that have sport management programs, also provide opportunities to network with professionals, visit sport facilities, and learn about ways to gain work experience in sport settings. Students may wish to pursue community service activities such as volunteering with the Special Olympics, working with recreational sport programs, and assisting in community-sponsored events. Furthermore, numerous jobs are available on most college campuses in sport settings such as the student recreation center, the intramural sport office, and intercollegiate athletics department offices.

Extracurricular activities are an important part of professional preparation because they provide valuable skill practice and opportunities for leadership and development. Furthermore, they have been identified as especially vital to future job success. When employment recruiters were asked to examine résumés of entry-level candidates, academic performance and work experience were found to be important factors in judging potential employees, but **extracurricular activities** were most positively related to the raters' assessments of employability (Cole, Rubin, Field, & Giles, 2007).

extracurricular activities—Opportunities for involvement with clubs, organizations, and sports in which students in a school may participate but that are not part of the regular academic curriculum.

Some students may be interested in complementing their education by obtaining specialized training. Students who have completed courses in subjects such as sport marketing, management, promotions, and sales and are interested in further developing

WEB

Go to the OSG and complete the second Web search activity, which allows you to research a professional organization of your choice to see how that organization can help you on your sport management journey.

Examples of Professional Organizations

Adaptive Sports Association
American Alliance for Health, Physical Education, Recreation and Dance
American Sportscasters Association
Association for Women in Sports Media
Athletic Equipment Managers Association
Black Coaches and Administrators
College Athletic Business Management Association
College Sports Information Directors Association
European Association for Sport Management
International Association of Assembly Managers
International Ticketing Association
National Association for College Women Athletic Administrators
National Association of Collegiate Directors of Athletics
National Association of Athletic Academic Advisors
National Association of Collegiate Marketing Administrators
National Association of Concessionaires
National Association of Sports Commissions
National Recreation and Park Association
North American Society for Sport Management
Sport Marketing Association
Stadium Managers Association

and refining these skills may benefit by participating in programs offered by professional trainers. For example, Game Face offers a "Sports Career Training Camp" where students are coached by industry professionals on how to gain employment and advance in the sport industry. Another organization, the Sports Sales Combine, provides sales training and hands-on experience selling for a professional sports team. Combine attendees have the opportunity to audition for sales coaches and scouts from various professional teams and leagues, and the chance to network and interview with industry leaders.

Gaining experience through employment is an important part of professional preparation. Work experience provides students with opportunities to build networks, improve organizational skills, establish a greater sense of responsibility, expand skills, learn more about personal strengths and values, and gain self-confidence. In addition, students who gain work experience while in college are more successful in their careers, especially during the first year after graduation (Casella & Brougham, 1995). Furthermore, Skeat and Mullendore (2008) noted that students who are able to describe the skills that they have learned during their part-time work experiences may have an advantage over others when they begin to pursue full-time employment.

The National Association of Colleges and Employers (NACE) projects employment trends. The organization's *Job Outlook 2009* found that more than three-quarters of employers indicated that they prefer to hire new college graduates who have relevant work experience (National Association, 2008). Although any type of work experience may be beneficial, Marilyn Mackes, NACE executive director, believes, "College students can better position themselves with potential employers by including an internship or co-op assignment in their college plan" (National Association, 2009, ¶ 7).

Field Experiences

A **field experience** in sport management is typically referred to as an internship but may include cooperative work experiences (co-ops) or practicum experiences. A field experience allows individuals to observe and assist professionals and learn about managerial responsibilities and the scope of the sport organization in which they are employed. Field experience is a common component of the sport management curriculum, and students should expect to be supervised by an on-campus intern coordinator, as well as a professional in the agency providing the experience. Field experiences present excellent opportunities for students to apply what they have learned in the classroom to a real-life situation, thus connecting theory with practice (Cuneen & Sidwell, 1994; Young & Baker, 2004). Moreover, as Williams (2003) noted, most sport organizations do not recruit on college campuses or advertise their openings. Consequently, professional opportunities in the sport industry are "part of the 'hidden' job market" (p. 28). Given this reality, practical experience in the professional setting is an essential first step into an environment where you might be seeking employment after graduation.

field experience—A hands-on learning opportunity in which students gain professional experience in an organization while receiving class credit.

Research has shown that the best field experiences in sport management are those that require interns to expand their knowledge and learn new skills (Dixon, Cunningham, Sagas, Turner, & Kent, 2005). Many students find that their enthusiasm for the field and motivation to excel academically increase because of their internship experience. Students should give themselves sufficient time to prepare and search for a field experience. Preparing a résumé and cover letters and practicing interviewing skills (i.e., engaging in **mock interviews**) are essential. Campus career centers can be valuable sources of assistance in this preparation and may have information about available internships. Additionally, many sport organizations post internship openings on their Web sites. Your school's internship coordinator may maintain a database of available positions or a list of employers who have provided internships in the past. Your professors can also be a good source of information on planning and preparing for an internship.

mock interviews—Practice interviews in which you can rehearse your responses to questions that interviewers are likely to ask you.

Courtesy of Collegiate Licensing Company.

In Profile: Derek Eiler

Derek Eiler knows what it takes to achieve success in the competitive field of sport management. The sport marketing graduate has reached a level of achievement so impressive that he was recognized in 2009 by *Street & Smith's SportsBusiness Journal* as one of the 40 most influential sports executives under the age of 40. Eiler is senior vice president and managing director of the Collegiate Licensing Company (CLC), an IMG company that serves as the exclusive trademark-licensing representative on behalf of more than 200 colleges, universities, bowls, conferences, and the NCAA.

Eiler is enthusiastic about sharing his career experiences to help students understand how to differentiate themselves from their competition and achieve career success. He believes that aspiring sport managers must, as he states it, "be willing to sacrifice short-term rewards in order to make long-term gains." While in college, Eiler made a conscious effort to use his free time wisely, exploring different types of sport careers by doing independent research and extensive networking. After he recognized his interest in marketing, he pursued volunteer experiences that would help him land a good job after graduation.

Eiler volunteered every summer, focusing more on professional development than on financial gain. Upon graduation, he had a wide base of experience in ticketing, event management, media relations, marketing, concessions, and more. He also cultivated a network of professionals who recognized his talents, knowledge, and determination.

To learn even more about the sport industry while a student, Eiler conducted over-the-phone and in-person informational interviews with industry professionals. As he explains, "When you're a student, informational interviews are a no-pressure way to find out more about someone's job responsibilities and career path, and to build your network." He believes that students should network as much as possible while they are still in school, because it can pay "massive dividends in an internship or job search."

Through his networking, Eiler was put in touch with the president of CLC. An interview and a job offer quickly followed. In 1993, as a recent college graduate, Eiler found himself in a highly respected company in a rapidly growing industry. He has been instrumental to CLC's growth and success since then.

An executive who is now asked to give advice, Eiler shares that a good job in sport is within the reach of any student who is willing to make sacrifices to gain experience, can demonstrate a superior work ethic, and can bring quick and creative solutions to her or his sport organization.

The following shows Derek Eiler's career progression:

Collegiate Licensing Company (CLC):

Senior vice president and managing director, 2007–present
Senior vice president and chief operating officer, 2005–2006
Vice president of university services, 1997–2004
Director of university services, 1995–1996
University services representative, 1994
University services assistant, 1993

Bowling Green State University

B.S., sport marketing, 1993

Wood County Special Olympics

Intern, 1992

University of Michigan Athletic Department

Summer intern, 1991

Great Lakes State Games

Summer intern, 1991

Toledo Mud Hens

Summer intern, 1990

Advanced Education

As you look toward career advancement and additional responsibilities, you may choose, or be asked by your employer, to pursue a graduate degree. Even now, early in your academic career, you may want to begin thinking about an advanced degree. The first graduate degree after the baccalaureate is the master's. Master's degree programs typically require one or two years of additional study. Doctoral-level education builds on the background gained at the undergraduate and master's levels, is much more specialized in its focus, and is essential for anyone who aspires to be a college professor. In choosing a graduate program, students should consider the location of the program within the university, the industry focus of the program, and the experience and research interests of the faculty.

Some sport management programs are located in departments of physical education or sport management, whereas others are housed within schools of business administration, in departments of kinesiology, or in various other units. Students should make certain that their interests are in line with the offerings of the graduate program. Another important consideration when choosing a graduate program is the industry focus of the program. Some programs are geared toward preparing students for positions in athletic administration within the educational structure (e.g., intercollegiate athletics). Other programs focus on sport management in the private sector (e.g., professional sport) or public sector (e.g., community centers). Graduate programs expect candidates to have high grades, involvement in extracurricular activities, experience in the sport industry, and high scores on entrance exams such as the Graduate Records Exam (GRE) or Graduate Management Admission Test (GMAT).

PROFESSIONAL ATTITUDE

Planning your future in sport management includes paying attention to one of the most important elements of your portfolio—your professional attitude. Employers commonly share that they cannot teach people to have the mind-set for professional success. Thus, applicants who do not possess this quality are not hired or promoted. To ensure that you are a competitive candidate, one of the things that you must do is demonstrate a positive attitude in your interviews and on the job (Sukiennik, Bendat, & Raufman, 2008). An enthusiastic and professional attitude will not only enhance your opportunities for employment and advancement but also make you a more pleasant person to be around. That alone is a worthy goal. Furthermore, attitudes are demonstrated by behaviors. The following sections on ethical behavior and critical thinking are examples of how behaviors demonstrate what people consider acceptable attitudes and approaches to ethics and issues.

Ethical Decision Making

The professional codes of many sport organizations frequently articulate acceptable behaviors. Professionals in these organizations are expected to adhere to these codes, and those in sport management are no exception. For example, a quick search of the Internet using the phrase "sport code of ethics" will yield more than one million hits. The Institute of Sport Management (2010) sponsors one of those Web sites. This company, located in New South Wales, Australia, is committed to the development of the profession of sport management. The company's code of ethics as listed on its Web site notes that "the objectives of the Sport Management profession are to work to the highest standards of professionalism, to attain the highest levels of performance and generally meet the public interest requirement" (¶ 2). The Web site further notes that the objectives require "four basic needs to be met" (¶ 3): credibility, professionalism, quality of services, confidence. Take a few moments to read the Institute's entire code

STUDYING SPORT MANAGEMENT ABROAD

By John Amis • UNITED KINGDOM
University of Memphis, UNITED STATES

As the sport industry becomes increasingly globalized, students should be able to demonstrate to potential employers an appreciation of and a willingness to learn about other countries, their people, and their cultures. One avenue that can help further such understanding is a university study abroad program.

Most universities have expanded their study abroad offerings in recent years. According to the International Institute of Education, 241,791 US students participated in programs during 2006–2007, up from 99,448 in 1996–1997. Countries in Western Europe are the most favored destinations, but China's popularity is rapidly expanding, probably because of its increasing importance to US business interests.

Along with the increase in programs has come an increase in funding opportunities, ranging from traditional financial aid to dedicated study abroad scholarships. As a result, university study abroad programs are within the financial reach of most students.

University students can study abroad in three ways. First, they can participate in bilateral exchanges in which the student's home university has an agreement with a foreign university that allows students to study in each other's programs for a semester or academic year. This option offers an excellent opportunity for students to learn or improve foreign language skills, which are highly valued by many employers.

A second approach features sponsored programs, whereby a uni-

Photo courtesy of John Amis.

Students from the Sport, Commerce & Culture in the Global Marketplace study abroad program, operated jointly by the University of Maryland and the University of Memphis, pose for a photograph in the media center at Wimbledon, London.

of ethics. After you have examined the code of ethics, refer back to the ethical guidelines presented in chapter 1. In what ways does this sport organization's code of ethics intersect with the guidelines?

You have no doubt witnessed or read about many breeches of ethical behavior, often by high-profile individuals in spheres such as politics, business, and sport. People who have been caught violating social norms and formal laws can face a variety of sanctions. As discussed in chapter 1, understanding how to examine an issue thoughtfully and maintain an ethical demeanor will serve you well in any environment.

explicit norms—Formally communicated rules that govern behavior of group members.

To be successful in a classroom or a place of business, individuals must understand expectations and recognize norms that regulate group members. **Explicit norms** are

versity has agreements with third parties that provide programs in various parts of the world. These arrangements allow universities to increase the range of experiences available for their students.

Third are faculty-led programs that provide students with course credit through the home institution of faculty members who have significant experience with both the subject area and the geographic destination. In such a program, faculty members might take a group of students to another country for two weeks or so to explore ways in which issues of globalization, culture, and international management are played out in the sport industry. This approach allows students to benefit from the in-depth interest and expertise of faculty members and can lead to at least five other benefits. First, students enjoy concentrated exposure to academic and executive figures from a variety of backgrounds. Second, their worldviews are considerably enhanced as they acquire both theoretical and practical insights about ways in which sport is managed in the global marketplace. Third, they live in a foreign country and can immerse themselves in its culture. Fourth, they acquire a new frame of reference against which to compare their previous academic, professional, and personal experiences. Finally, students forge bonds with peers who are going through similar, usually brand new, experiences. When I have led such programs, I have found that the degree of understanding that students express in their culminating papers and other forms of assessment demonstrate the authenticity of their learning experiences.

Study abroad programs provide excellent opportunities for both personal and professional development. The combination of a potentially life-altering experience and the opportunity to earn academic credits makes such programs highly attractive to many students. Such experiences can also make the students highly attractive to employers.

INTERNATIONAL LEARNING ACTIVITY #1

Investigate opportunities to study abroad at your college or university. Make a list of the information necessary to inform a classmate about why these experiences are valuable and how to take advantage of the opportunities.

INTERNATIONAL LEARNING ACTIVITY #2

Go to the Cruyff Academics International Web site at www.cruyffacademics.org. Write a report about this organization. Include information about its purpose, network programs, foundation, and any other aspects of interest.

INTERNATIONAL LEARNING ACTIVITY #3

Go to the home page of the Institute for International Sport at www.internationalsport.com/. Prepare a presentation covering the Institute's mission and vision as well as other features that you think your classmates would find interesting.

formally communicated rules that govern behavior. In university communities, rules are stated in student policy manuals. In individual classrooms, explicit norms are outlined in the course syllabus and handouts. In a business environment, explicit norms are outlined in documents such as staff handbooks. To gain confidence in any situation, one should review and comprehend an organization's formal policies and procedures.

Also important is understanding informal norms, also referred to as **implicit norms,** that serve to "explain the way things happen in an organization" (Harvey & Drolet, 2004, p. 62). These informal norms can be learned, usually by observing other members of the group. As explained by Harvey and Drolet, although these expectations of

implicit norms—Unstated or informal rules understood and practiced by members of an organization.

Responsible Group Participation

While taking a college class you are randomly assigned to a three-person group that is required to research a topic and present to the class. All members of the group will work together for one overall group grade. You have a busy semester, with classes and work and family obligations, and finding a time to meet with other group members is difficult. The way that you approach this assignment may indicate how you perform in the workplace. The following are some questions that you may want to consider as you enter into this group project for the class (keep in mind that you will most likely ask yourself similar questions when engaged in group work as a professional upon entering the sport industry):

- Will you make the effort to find times to meet with group members so that you can play an equal role in the research and presentation?
- Will you avoid them, ignore their e-mails and telephone calls, and give excuses for not getting in touch with them?
- Will you allow the other members of your group to do all the work but take credit for the assignment?
- Will you actively volunteer to take on portions of the assignment, or will you remain silent, hoping that other members will do all the work and let you slide?

behavior may be informal, they are extremely important and in some cases are more powerful than formal, explicit norms.

An inability to abide by norms, combined with a skeptical view of human behavior and pressure to succeed in college, may influence students to behave unethically in their own lives. Although some students may be willing to compromise ethics and cheat to receive a better grade than they deserve, they are developing habits and behaviors that may seriously jeopardize their future success. Results based on a survey of college students suggest that "if students do not respect the climate of academic integrity while in college, they will not respect integrity in their future and personal relationships" (Nonis & Swift, 2001, p. 71).

Many students, however, have the foresight to understand that ethical behavior while in college will serve them well as they develop their professional aptitude. When preparing for a career after college, students have a responsibility to learn academic content and make good decisions on the road to future success.

As a student, you are confronted with ethical dilemmas on a weekly, if not daily, basis. What are some examples of unethical behavior that you have witnessed as a student in a sport management class? Referring to the guidelines for ethical decision making presented in chapter 1, how might you change your approach to some of the ethical issues that you face (e.g., cheating on a test, plagiarizing an article, forging a signature, explaining an absence to your professor)? How can you apply these guidelines? Why is it important to embrace ethical behavior as a student?

Critical Thinking Skills

Gaining a thorough understanding about issues is an imperative skill for students and professionals alike. As explained in chapter 1, critical thinking skills can assist a person in a quest to seek the truth. When students cultivate and practice critical thinking skills, they are less likely to act or make decisions out of habit. The development of sound critical thinking skills can allow people to thrive in academic and work environments. Mastering academic content is important, as is learning about social situations, ethics, and values. Those who challenge themselves and take the time to think, reflect, and learn give themselves a much better chance to flourish in their personal and professional lives.

Remember the eight critical thinking questions presented in chapter 1? How can you apply those questions and critical thinking to other issues that you may currently be confronting as a sport management student? (For example, should you confront a friend who uses sexist language while taunting a rival school during a tennis match? Should you join or encourage protesters outside the athletics department when school officials consider an increase in student fees to fund a new basketball arena?)

Professional Image

When first meeting you, other people rely on your physical appearance to make judgments about you. Mitchell (1998) explained that studies on the initial impression that people make "show that 7 percent of that impression is based on what a person says, 38 percent on how he or she says it, and 55 percent on what the other person *sees*" (p. 10). Although this way of judging you might seem unfair, and although initial impressions can change after someone gets to know you, you can make a first impression only once—so why not make it a good one?

The impression that you make through your physical presentation during interviews and on the job is related less to physical attractiveness than to other factors, all of which are within your control. The following items are among the many aspects of a professional image.

- *Grooming*: Attention to your grooming can pay off as you present yourself to potential employers. Aspects of grooming to consider include care of hair, nails, and teeth, as well as neatness and cleanliness.
- *Attire and accessories*: While in college, you have wide discretion in your choice of clothing and accessories, but as you move into the workplace you must understand what constitutes appropriate attire. This standard will differ depending on the organization. If you are unsure about what is acceptable attire for your organization, ask your supervisor. Web sites on professional dress and business casual dress can be especially helpful.
- *Posture*: Your sitting, standing, and walking posture (body language) conveys an impression of your attitude. People will draw different conclusions about the attitude of a person who is slouching as opposed to one who is sitting erect, with feet firmly planted on the floor, or leaning slightly forward to indicate good listening skills, interest, and enthusiasm.

Work Transition and Adjustment

Are you ready to face challenges that will present themselves in the workplace? Are you confident in your abilities and competent in your specific job skills? Are you knowledgeable about the social, political, legislative, technological, and economic trends that have influenced your field? Now is the time to begin practicing for life in the work environment. How you enter a new sport organization, approach the challenges of your new position, learn the organizational culture, develop working relationships with bosses and colleagues, participate in departmental and team meetings, communicate your ideas to others, and establish your reputation as an employee will have a major influence on your success. Valuable employees display their professional attitude in the image that they project, in the ways in which they approach work transition and adjustment, and in their business **etiquette.** The following sections offer tips on learning your job, understanding organizational culture, demonstrating your work ethic, developing written communication skills, using electronic communication, writing thank-you notes, refining teamwork skills, managing conflict, embracing diversity, being evaluated, and continuing your professional development.

etiquette—A system of rules and conventions that regulate social and professional behavior.

When starting a new job, it's important that you take the time to learn the ins and outs of the job, request feedback, and actively learn.
Photo courtesy of Paul M. Pedersen.

Learn Your Job

When you start a new job, make sure that you understand what your duties are, what you are expected to do, and how to proceed. Listen carefully to directions and ask for clarification of any instructions that you do not comprehend fully before beginning an assignment. Taking notes as you receive oral instructions is perfectly appropriate to assure understanding and thorough recall of expectations. Set up periodic meetings with your supervisor to confirm and clarify your progress on assignments to ensure that your work is accurate, thorough, and of high quality. In an entry-level or new job, you are not expected to know everything, but you are expected to show interest and actively learn.

Understand Organizational Culture

As you will learn in chapter 4, each organization has a unique culture; therefore, new employees must learn what behaviors are expected in the workplace. These expectations are sometimes stated in an organization's policy manual, but more often informal structures and unwritten ways of getting things done have evolved over time. New employees learn these unofficial procedures by observing the behaviors of others and by listening to stories told about the organization at informal gatherings. If you are unclear about expectations within your organization, it is wise to ask for clarification.

A clear understanding of expectations is essential to a fast career start, yet few new graduates take the time to do so. Astute new employees will recognize the importance of learning the organization's rules and guidelines and will distinguish themselves from others by showing their professional maturity (Holton & Naquin, 2001). Some of the key factors to pay particular attention to as a new employee include the organization's mission and guiding philosophy, values and norms, and behavioral expectations (Nardo, 1999). Often, new employee orientations and mentoring programs are offered to assist new professionals in learning about and adapting to the culture of the organization. Being mentored by a seasoned professional whom you trust and admire is an excellent approach, regardless of whether this pairing is formal or informal.

Demonstrate Your Work Ethic

work ethic—A set of values based on desirable workplace characteristics that include accountability, dependability, initiative taking, and accomplishment.

Demonstrate your commitment to the organization, supervisors, and colleagues by enthusiastically completing all job assignments within the agreed-upon deadlines, keeping your word, offering assistance, and supporting others in achieving the organization's goals. Your attitude toward work can be referred to as your **work ethic.** "Your work ethic is a set of values you work and live by," noted Curtis (1999). "The strength of your work ethic is based on the solidarity of your values" (p. 2). Identifying qualities and characteristics that you admire in others may help you determine your work values. Strive to do the right thing and gain recognition as a valuable member of the organization.

Develop Your Written Communication Skills

The ability to express thoughts and ideas in writing is one of the most important competencies of a good sport manager. Among the many types of writing that you will have to produce are business correspondence (e.g., memos, e-mail messages, responses to complaints), reports, and technical manuals. Learn to organize your thoughts logically and use grammar and punctuation correctly. Investing time and energy in learning to write well will pay huge dividends when you enter the professional world.

Use Electronic Communication Appropriately Although e-mail is often used as an informal mode of communication, adherence to the conventions of good business writing is expected in business-related e-mail messages. Good judgment regarding the content of e-mail messages is essential. Use capitalization and punctuation in your e-mails and make sure that you use the spellchecker function. Proofread your e-mails for errors and to ensure that the tone is professional and appropriate. A number of excellent Web sites address the proper uses of e-mail and the Internet and provide tips for composing electronic business correspondence (search using keywords *netiquette* or *e-mail etiquette*).

Thank Others Take the opportunity to express gratitude to anyone who provides you with information or her or his time. A good practice to follow is to send your thanks within 24 hours of a social or business contact or event. You may send a personal letter of thanks, or in many cases a well-composed e-mail will be appropriate. Making a habit of thanking people who help you will go a long way toward establishing your reputation as a professional.

Refine Your Teamwork Skills

The ability to participate as a valuable member of a team is imperative in any work setting. Tasks and assignments often utilize the talents of a work team, which is a group of people working in relationship with one another to accomplish a task or solve a problem. To be an effective team member, you need to develop skills along several dimensions including commitment to the task, communication, collaboration, confrontation, consensus building, and caring and demonstrating respect for other team members.

Learn to Manage Conflict Conflict is energy among groups of people or individuals; it is not about winning or losing. Conflict is an opportunity to acknowledge and appreciate our differences. Carney and Wells (1995) noted that workplace differences or conflicts are most likely to occur "when workers are under pressure, when their responsibilities are not clear, or when their personal expectations or needs are violated." They added that situations involving conflict "offer ideal opportunities for clarifying personal differences and for team building" (p. 179). If you disagree with a colleague, supervisor, or customer, express yourself without being unpleasant. When handled in a mature, positive way, conflict can be healthy.

Embrace Diversity Appreciate and celebrate diversity of gender, race, religion, sexual orientation, ability, age, and so on. Do not engage in racist, ageist, or sexist behaviors, and let others know, tactfully, that you do not appreciate such behaviors. Seek to understand and respect the history, values, understandings, and opinions of others. Being inclusive is the right thing to do, and it can benefit an organization's bottom line as well. A study by the National Urban League (2005) suggested "investments in the area of diversity are by no means being made at the expense of productivity. In fact, it is likely that the effective diversity practices—exemplary leadership and management practices—also result in productivity gains" (p. 15).

Performance Appraisals As a new professional, you should welcome the evaluation process, recognizing that the aim of constructive criticism is to improve your performance. Expect to be involved in setting goals that will challenge your learning process. Your progress will be measured on a recurring basis, which will help you and your supervisor identify appropriate professional development activities to help you perform to the best of your ability. Be prepared to discuss your specific needs for development and strategies to improve your job performance. The most important question to ask your supervisor is, What should I be doing to improve my job performance?

Continue Your Professional Development

As the concept of a successful career continually changes in our global sport marketplace, personal flexibility and the ability to adapt to change become even more important. Underlying the assumption that professionals can be flexible and can adapt to change is the concept of lifelong learning. Your professional education is just beginning, and it will continue throughout your life.

You should make an early commitment to lifelong learning, both formal and informal, so that you can continue to grow professionally and personally. Participation in business and professional associations (as noted earlier, some examples are listed in the sidebar "Examples of Professional Organizations" on p. 32) increases your knowledge and expands your network of associates throughout your career. A well-developed career network is vital to your professional advancement. Your network members can provide information, guidance, support, honest feedback, and access to career opportunities. Interaction with sport management colleagues is stimulating and allows you to grow professionally and contribute to your field.

ACTION

Go to the OSG and complete the Learning in Action activity, which will help you identify appropriate workplace decorum.

Business Etiquette

The academic environment is clearly a helpful setting to learn and practice manners to increase the professionalism that students bring into the sport industry. In interviews with 15 managers from five sport organizations in Northern California, Lilienthal (2004) sought to identify the professional behavior the managers expected of their new or young employees. She found that almost all the managers had recurring issues with employees' unprofessional behavior with regard to dress code and courtesy. The managers believed that classroom and workplace training in professional etiquette would be helpful. The results of a more recent survey by York College of Pennsylvania (Moltz, 2009) revealed that business leaders and human resource executives believe that many college graduates fail to exhibit appropriate levels of professionalism and workplace etiquette. As you prepare for a career in sport management, we encourage you to consider the following reminders of good manners:

- ***Telephone.*** Answering the telephone in a professional manner includes clearly identifying yourself and your organization or department; giving each caller your full attention; restating important information to check for understanding and accuracy; projecting a tone that is cheerful, natural, and attentive; ending the conversation with agreement on what is to happen next; and following up appropriately. When leaving your phone number on someone's voice mail system, speak distinctly and at a reasonable speed. Remember to leave your name, phone number, and a brief message so that the caller will be prepared when she or he returns your call.
- ***Voicemail and answering machine messages.*** Refrain from leaving inappropriate greetings for your callers, especially when you are searching for an internship or professional employment. Busy callers do not appreciate long messages, silliness, or loud music in the background.
- ***Language.*** Practice being inclusive in spoken and written language rather than using gender-biased or racially biased language. In the workplace of the 21st century, employees will interact with managers, clients, and customers who are women, people of color, or people from other cultures. Mastery of inclusive language is a good way to demonstrate your sensitivity to such concerns and to create a more pleasant workplace (Parks, Harper, & Lopez, 1994).
- ***Meeting participation.*** Expected behavior in business meetings may vary by organizational culture, but general conventions include being prepared, arriving approximately 10 minutes early, turning cell phones off or to the vibrate option, stay-

ing on task, participating openly, giving your full attention through active listening, and encouraging others to participate and offer their ideas.

- *Dining etiquette.* Many business meetings and interviews include a meal, and prospective employers, customers, and other business associates will judge your table manners. You will be more comfortable when you know what to expect. First, be prepared to engage in light conversation. Appropriate topics include current events, sports, and the arts. On the other hand, politics, religion, and sex are taboo topics. Although alcohol is never appropriate at a business lunch in the United States, know your organization's policy on alcohol at business functions or follow your host's lead.
- *International experiences.* From an international perspective, good manners can be defined in various ways. Communicating with and relating to people from other cultures requires that you learn the protocols, courtesies, customs, and behaviors of those cultures. To avoid embarrassment, investigate the customs prevalent in other countries before traveling there and before entertaining international visitors.
- *Introductions and greetings.* The host is responsible for introducing those who are meeting for the first time. When making an introduction, use the name of the most senior person first and introduce everyone else to him or her. As a general rule of respect, do not use a person's first name until invited to do so. Regardless of your gender, stand when being introduced to others. When shaking hands, both women and men should expect to use a firm grip. Grasp the person's entire hand, not just the fingers, and adjust your grip to the state of health and physical strength of the person whom you are greeting.
- *Office etiquette.* Many organizations today use dividers rather than walls, so you may find yourself working in a small space with a number of coworkers. Be conscious of their need for privacy and a quiet workplace. Be cautious in your use of music players, speakerphones, and other devices that can be distracting in a small work space.
- *Romantic relationships.* The office is not an appropriate place to engage in flirting or in more overt forms of affectionate behavior. Often, employee handbooks address issues of dating and romantic relationships in the workplace. Furthermore, be aware of your actions because others can perceive flirtatious behavior as sexual harassment (Pedersen, Osborne, Whisenant, & Lim, 2009).

A positive, professional attitude—as reflected in your professional image, work habits and behavior, and business etiquette—is essential to your future success. Do not underestimate the roles that enthusiasm and a positive self-image play in creating a successful professional attitude.

In our ever-shrinking world, it is important that you understand the customs of different cultures, including dining etiquette.

Photo courtesy of Paul M. Pedersen.

CAREER PLANNING AND MANAGEMENT

To thrive in the second decade of the 21st century, employees will need to assume responsibility for their own career planning and management. Gone are the days when a college graduate could expect to find a job after graduation and spend his or her entire career working for one organization. You will make multiple career and job choices throughout your lifespan. Estimates are that US workers will change career fields 3 to 5 times and switch jobs as many as 10 times during their working lives. Although frequent job changes will become the norm, you can achieve employment security by continuing to develop new skills through lifelong learning and by assuming personal responsibility for managing your career.

Career Decision Steps

The complex process of making career decisions involves four stages: self-awareness, occupational exploration, decision making, and career implementation. Career planning can be fascinating because you will gain new insights about yourself as well as knowledge about the variety of career options available to you. The following steps will help you in your career planning. You do not have to complete them in the order presented, and you may need to repeat a step or two as you gain new information about yourself and your career options or encounter obstacles or barriers.

- *Self-awareness* entails identifying and understanding your personal and work values, interests, abilities, aptitudes, personality traits, and desired future lifestyle.
- *Occupational exploration* entails taking a broad look at career fields and researching specific sport management occupations, work environments, and employers that may be a match with your unique career profile as identified through your self-assessment.
- *Career decision making* is the process of consciously analyzing and weighing all information that you have gathered about yourself, various sport management occupations, and career paths. At this stage you will make a tentative career decision, formulate educational and vocational goals, and develop plans to achieve them. The more you learn about yourself and the world of sport management, the better and more realistic your educational and career choices will be.
- *Career implementation* involves sharpening your job search skills. You will learn to prepare an effective résumé and cover letter, identify sources of job leads, present yourself professionally in interviews, evaluate and accept a job offer, and adjust to a new position.

Career planning is not a single, once-in-a-lifetime event. You are continually developing new interests, knowledge, and skills through your coursework, leisure activities, volunteer experiences, summer and part-time jobs, and internships. Throughout your career you may be motivated to reevaluate your options when changes in duties or work conditions of a job cause you to become less satisfied with it. Each time you face a career or job change, you will go through the career planning stages.

Your college career center offers services and programs to help you develop career goals, find the right academic and experiential programs to achieve those goals, and gain employment after graduation. Career counselors can be extremely helpful in providing guidance and direction in assessing your vocational interests, identifying skills, writing résumés and cover letters, preparing for interviews, developing a professional portfolio, and conducting the job search.

It will be helpful to you if you keep a portfolio, or collection of your work, as evidence of what you have done and, by implication, what you will be able to do as a professional. Kadlecek and Thoma (1999) suggested that the essential items in the portfolio of a sport management student are a sport marketing plan, a budget project, a sponsorship proposal, an ad media campaign, and a ticket sales campaign. Although time consuming to develop, portfolios are valuable to students in providing examples of skills. Furthermore, in the process of creating portfolios students will have an opportunity to reflect on their competencies and proficiencies.

Values

Your values are fundamental to career planning and indicate what you consider most important in your life. Zunker (2009) stated that a value can be defined as simply as "something that is important or desirable to you" (p. 16). Many factors contribute to your process of learning what you value. These include, but are not limited to, cultural background, family influences, educational opportunities, religious and spiritual experiences, friends, and peers. In an analysis of a computer-based career guidance system (SIGI[3]) that provides clarification of values, Zunker explained that eight **values** are currently being used in this system: high income, prestige, independence, helping others, security, variety, leadership, and leisure. The choices that you make about your occupational life need to be in harmony with your basic values and belief systems; otherwise, you will not find personal satisfaction in your job.

values—Indicators of what you consider most important or desirable (Zunker, 2009).

You should seek an occupation and jobs that will enhance, strengthen, and support the values that you consider important. For example, a high school coach may possess values different from those of a sport entrepreneur. The coach may be demonstrating the value that she or he places on facilitating the physical, mental, and moral development of young people, whereas the sport entrepreneur may be demonstrating the value that she or he places on providing a high level of financial security for family members.

Interests

Interests are activities in which you enthusiastically engage and find enjoyable, and subjects that arouse your curiosity or hold your attention. Interests are an integral part of your personality and are related to your values. Throughout your life, your personal experiences shape your interests. These interests often lead to competencies in the same areas. When your occupation matches your interests, you experience greater job satisfaction. If you have difficulty identifying or articulating your interests, you might want to seek the assistance of a career counselor at your university career center. Using interest inventories, career counselors can help you assess your measured interests and match those interests with appropriate occupations.

Skills

A skill is the developed aptitude, ability, or personal quality needed to perform a task competently. The three basic types of skills are job content skills, functional skills, and adaptive skills. **Job content skills** are the specialized knowledge or abilities needed to fulfill a specific job responsibility. Knowing the rules of basketball is an example of a job content skill for a basketball referee. Functional skills are general abilities that transfer to many jobs or situations. For example, the referee uses functional skills to make quick, accurate decisions and to resolve player conflicts that occur on the court. Adaptive skills are personal attributes or personality traits. In our example, the referee must remain calm and poised under stressful conditions.

job content skills—The specialized knowledge or abilities needed to fulfill specific job duties.

A survey of more than 400 US-based organizations and employers revealed that it is critical for new job entrants to possess "a combination of basic knowledge and applied skills" (Conference Board, 2006, p. 10). Professionalism and work ethic, teamwork and collaboration, and oral communication were the three highest rated

Sport Management Career Resources

Online Resources

America's Career InfoNet (www.acinet.org/acinet/)

America's Job Bank (www.jobbankinfo.org/)

Canada's Sport Information Resource Centre (www.sirc.ca/)

Career Voyages (www.careervoyages.gov/)

CareerBuilder.com (www.careerbuilder.com/)

CareerOneStop (www.careeronestop.org)

Game Face (www.gamefacesportsjobs.com)

Jobs in Sports (www.jobsinsports.com)

Monster.com (www.monster.com)

National Basketball Association (www.nba.com/careers/)

NCAA: The Market (ncaamarket.ncaa.org/search.cfm)

Nike, Inc. Web site (www.nikebiz.com/)

Occupational Outlook Handbook (www.bls.gov/OCO/)

The Official Sports Industry Job Board (www.sportsjobboard.com/)

Sports Careers (www.sportscareers.com/)

Sports Sales Combine (www.sportsalescombine.com/index.php)

Teamworkonline (www.teamworkonline.com/)

Women Sports Careers (www.womensportscareers.com/default.htm)

Book Resources

Field, S. (2004). *Career opportunities in the sports industry* (3rd ed.). New York: Checkmark.

Fischer, D. (1997). *The 50 coolest jobs in sports: What they are, who's got them, and how you can get one too!* New York: Macmillan.

Gottlieb, R. (2009). *Sports market place directory.* Millerton, NY: Grey House.

Heitzmann, W.R. (2003). *Opportunities in sports and fitness careers*. Boston: McGraw-Hill.

Robinson, M.J., Hums, M.A., Crow, R.B., & Phillips, D.R. (2001). *Profiles of sport industry professionals: The people who make the games happen.* Gaithersburg, MD: Aspen.

Wong, G.M. (2009). *The comprehensive guide to careers in sports.* Sudbury, MA: Jones & Bartlett.

applied skills needed by entrants into today's workforce. Additionally, knowledge of foreign languages was identified as the skill that will increase in importance over the coming years.

Because career success is being redefined throughout the world and our global economy is becoming more competitive, Herr, Cramer, and Niles (2004) stated that "workers must be able to function with quality and efficiency at the levels of creativity, invention, and innovation." Furthermore, the authors added that employees must be able to function "at the implementation and application levels, in customer service, in quality control, in goods production, and in services delivery" (p. 6). Knowing which skills are required to be successful in today's workplace is a good starting point for assessing your level of skill attainment. After you have identified the skills that you possess and to what degree, you can develop a plan for enhancing your level of those most pertinent to your career goals.

OCCUPATIONAL INFORMATION

Although many positions are available in existing sport management settings, you could create your own opportunity by becoming an **entrepreneur.** Making solid career decisions requires you to gather extensive information about the occupations that you wish to consider. By using a systematic approach, you will be able to compare occupations and make decisions that are compatible with your values, interests, skills, personality, and desired future lifestyle. For each occupation that you are considering, gather the following information: the nature of the work, work setting and conditions, educational and personal qualifications required, earnings, employment outlook and competition, methods of entering the occupation, opportunities for advancement, opportunities for exploring the occupation, related occupations, and sources of additional information (for a listing of online sources that may be useful in your research, refer to the sidebar "Sport Management Career Resources").

entrepreneur—A person who assumes the risks of a business or enterprise.

Another way of collecting data is through a computerized career information system. Most career centers provide an interactive, Web-based career guidance and education planning system, such as FOCUS V2 (Career Dimensions, 2010), designed to help students with important career planning tasks, including (1) understanding their interests, work values, personality, skills, and educational preferences; (2) identifying and discovering how their personal qualities relate to occupations; and (3) narrowing their options by interactively exploring and analyzing occupations.

Interviewing employees on site is an excellent way to gain additional information about jobs and work environments. Most sport managers are willing to help eager college students learn about the field. Through informational interviews you can gain an insider's view on a sport management job, obtain referrals to other professionals, and create a network of contacts.

Practice asking questions and having a conversation with a friend before you meet with the professional. Next, identify a sport manager to interview and call to arrange an appointment. When meeting with this manager, practice your professionalism. Wear business formal or business casual attire and be prepared to ask a variety of questions about how you can prepare to enter the occupation and be a successful professional. Remember to take notes. After the interview, send a thank-you letter within 24 hours.

Summary

Three elements necessary for success in sport management are professional preparation, professional attitude, and career planning and management. You can find sport management professional preparation programs at the bachelor's, master's, and doctoral levels. The typical undergraduate curriculum consists of general education courses and major courses, along with field experiences that give you opportunities to apply in sport settings what you learn in the classroom. Master's and doctoral programs will be more specific to your career goals should you wish to pursue an advanced degree.

Professional attitude is reflected in your personal appearance (e.g., hygiene, posture, self-confidence), adjustment to the workplace (e.g., academic preparation, writing skills, dependability, ethics, work habits), and business etiquette (e.g., telephone, e-mail, thank-you letters). Recruiters evaluate professional attitudes during interviews and employers evaluate them in performance appraisals.

Career planning consists of self-awareness (e.g., values, interests, skills), occupational exploration (i.e., gathering information from a variety of sources), career decision making, and career implementation. College career centers can provide valuable guidance and direction, including directing you to a multitude of resources (see the sidebar on p. 46) and helping you create an electronic portfolio.

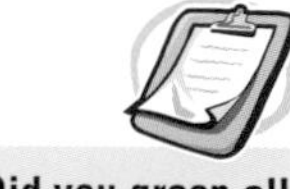

QUIZ TIME

Did you grasp all the key points in this chapter? Go to the OSG for a short quiz to test your understanding of the material.

Review Questions

1. How can professional preparation, a professional attitude, and career planning and management contribute to your success in sport management?
2. List the three components of your undergraduate sport management curriculum. Which elements within each component fulfill the content requirements of the COSMA accreditation standards?
3. Define field experiences. How do they benefit students, employers, colleges and universities, and society?
4. How would you outline an effective plan for finding an optimal field experience in sport management?
5. According to *Job Outlook 2009* (National Association, 2008), what skills and competencies will you need for a successful career in sport management? Explain how you plan to acquire these skills and competencies while in college.
6. List important elements of personal appearance, work transition and adjustment, and business etiquette. What does your conduct reveal regarding your personal perspective on each?
7. In your own words, how would you explain the four stages involved in career planning?
8. What are some print and electronic resources that you could use in seeking employment in sport management?

References

Brassie, P.S. (1989). Guidelines for programs preparing undergraduate and graduate students for careers in sport management. *Journal of Sport Management*, *3*, 158–164.

Career Dimensions. (2010). *FOCUS V2: A career & education planning system*. Retrieved June 12, 2010, from www.focus-career2.com/

Carney, C.G., & Wells, C.F. (1995). *Discover the career within you* (4th ed.). Pacific Grove, CA: Thomson Brooks/Cole.

Casella, D.A., & Brougham, C.E. (1995). Work works: Student jobs open front doors to careers. *Journal of Career Planning & Employment*, *55*(4), 24–27, 54–55.

Chelladurai, P. (2005). *Managing organizations for sport and physical activity: A systems perspective* (2nd ed.). Scottsdale, AZ: Holcomb Hathaway.

Cole, M.S., Rubin, R.S., Field, H.S., & Giles, W.F. (2007). Recruiters' perceptions and use of applicant resume information: Screening the recent college graduate. *Applied Psychology*, *56*, 319–343.

Conference Board, Partnership for 21st Century Skills, Corporate Voices for Working Families, & Society for Human Resource Management. (2006). *Are they really ready to work?* Retrieved May 8, 2009, from www.21stcenturyskills.org/documents/FINAL_REPORT_PDF09-29-06.pdf

Cuneen, J., & Sidwell, M.J. (1994). *Sport management field experiences*. Morgantown, WV: Fitness Information Technology.

Curtis & Associates. (1999). *Work culture*. Kearney, NE: Author.

Dixon, M.A., Cunningham, G.B., Sagas, M., Turner, B.A., & Kent, A. (2005). Challenge is key: An investigation of affective organizational commitment in undergraduate interns. *Journal of Education for Business*, *80*, 172–180.

Harvey, T.R., & Drolet, B. (2004). *Building teams, building people* (2nd ed.). Lanham, MD: Scarecrow Education.

Herr, E.L., Cramer, S.H., & Niles, S.G. (2004). *Career guidance and counseling through the lifespan: Systematic approaches* (6th ed.). Boston: Pearson/Allyn & Bacon.

Holton, E.F., III, & Naquin, S.S. (2001). *How to succeed in your first job: Tips for college graduates*. San Francisco: Berrett-Koehler.

Institute of Sport Management. (2010). *Code of ethics*. Retrieved January 30, 2010, from www.ismhome.com/visitor/v_ethics.htm

Kadlecek, J., & Thoma, J.E. (1999, June). *Sport management student portfolios: What practitioners want included*. Paper presented at the annual conference of the North American Society for Sport Management, Vancouver, British Columbia, Canada.

Lilienthal, S. (2004, June). *Professional etiquette of sport management students: Investigating employer perceptions*. Paper presented at the annual conference of the North American Society for Sport Management, Atlanta, GA.

Mitchell, M. (with Corr, J.). (1998). *The first five minutes: How to make a great first impression in any business situation*. New York: Wiley.

Moltz, D. (2009, October 23). Are today's grads unprofessional? *Inside Higher Ed*. Retrieved January 30, 2010, from www.insidehighered.com/news/2009/10/23/professionalism

Nardo, J. (1999). Helping new grads become successful new hires. *Journal of Career Planning and Employment*, *59*(3), 45–56.

National Association of Colleges and Employers. (2008). *Job outlook 2009: Special report*. Retrieved May 12, 2009, from www.naceweb.org/public/joboutlook_special102208.htm

National Association of Colleges and Employers. (2009, January 15). *Work experience key for new college grads seeking employment* [press release]. Retrieved May 15, 2009, from www.naceweb.org/press/display.asp?year=&prid=294

National Urban League. (2005). *Diversity practices that work: The American worker speaks*. Retrieved June 12, 2010, from www.nul.org/sites/default/files/Diversity_Practices_That_Work_2005.pdf

Nonis, S., & Swift, C.O. (2001). An examination of the relationship between academic dishonesty and workplace dishonesty:

A multi-campus investigation. *Journal of Education for Business*, *77*(2), 69–77.

Parks, J.B. (executive producer), Harper, M.C. (writer), & Lopez, P.G. (director). (1994). *One person's struggle with gender-biased language: Part 1* [Videotape]. (Available from WBGU-TV, Bowling Green State University, Bowling Green, OH 43403.)

Pedersen, P.M., Osborne, B., Whisenant, W.A., & Lim, C. (2009). An examination of the perceptions of sexual harassment by newspaper sports journalists. *Journal of Sport Management*, *23*, 335–360.

Skeat, C., & Mullendore, R.H. (2008). Student perceptions of the outcomes of on-campus employment while in college, *Michigan Journal of College Student Development*, *13*(1), 22–26.

Sukiennik, D., Bendat, W., & Raufman, L. (2008). *The career fitness program: Exercising your options* (9th ed.). Upper Saddle River, NJ: Pearson/Prentice Hall.

Williams, J. (2003). Sport management internship administration: Challenges and chances for collaboration. *NACE Journal*, *63*(2), 28–32.

Young, D.S., & Baker, R.E. (2004). Linking classroom theory to professional practice: The internship as a practical learning experience worthy of academic credit. *Journal of Physical Education, Recreation and Dance*, *75*(1), 22–24.

Zunker, V.G. (2009). *Career, work, and mental health: Integrating career & personal counseling*. Los Angeles: Sage.

HISTORICAL MOMENTS

- **1862** William H. Cammeyer began charging admission to baseball games
- **1869** Cincinnati Red Stockings become first all-professional baseball team
- **1872** Yale played Columbia in first intercollegiate football game with admission charge
- **1876** Spalding opened Baseball and Sporting Goods Emporium (Chicago)
- **1898** Golf ball patent established
- **1920** Babe Ruth sold to Yankees
- **1940** First college basketball doubleheader broadcast (NBC)—Pittsburgh v. Fordham and NYU v. Georgetown
- **1951** First live, coast-to-coast broadcast of a sporting event televised (NBC)—college football, Duke v. Pittsburgh
- **1953** Major League Baseball (MLB) Players Association formed
- **1961** Sports Broadcasting Act allowed leagues to negotiate one television contract for all their teams
- **1964** CBS bought 80% of Yankees and became first media outlet to own pro team
- **1983** National Basketball Association (NBA) salary cap instituted
- **1999** National Hockey League (NHL) Canadian teams petitioned federal government for financial aid
- **2002–03** NBA luxury tax system implemented
- **2005** Manchester United bought by American Malcolm Glazer
- **2010** United States Supreme Court rejected the NFL's request for broad antitrust law protection

Photo courtesy of Paul M. Pedersen.

HISTORICAL ASPECTS OF THE SPORT BUSINESS INDUSTRY

Lawrence W. Fielding ■ Paul M. Pedersen ■ Brenda G. Pitts

LEARNING OBJECTIVES

1. Identify the major business and market structures that allowed people to develop various sport businesses over the past 150 years.
2. Explain how the sport business industry developed through the work of several influential people and companies.
3. Discuss the influence of technology, communication, marketing, and travel on the sport business industry.
4. Identify the ways in which the sport business industry has been influenced by significant social, cultural, economic, and legal issues.
5. Detail how an understanding of the history of sport businesses and market structures can help today's sport managers develop strategies for their businesses.

Key Terms

age of organization
Battle of the Sexes
decentralized organization
distribution
diversification
emotive advertising
market share
"reason why" advertisements
vertical integration
watershed events

In 1875 the Boston Red Sox won 71 out of 79 games (.898) en route to winning the championship of the National Association of Professional Baseball Players (NAPBP). Each victory cost the baseball club US$486 (Burk, 1994). Major League Baseball's (MLB) Boston Red Sox of 2008 did not do as well. The team went 95 and 67 (.586) and failed to reach the World Series after losing to the surprising Tampa Bay Rays in the League Championship Series. With combined player salaries accounting for US$133.4 million of the team budget, each victory cost the Red Sox approximately US$1.4 million in payroll alone—which was a relative bargain in comparison to the US$2.3 million the New York Yankees had to pay out in player salaries alone (with a US$209.1 million team payroll) for each of the club's 89 victories that same year (Brown & Morrison, 2008).

A year after the Red Sox won the 1875 NAPBP championship, Albert Goodwill (A. G.) Spalding opened a retail sporting goods store in Chicago a few doors down from the Chicago White Stockings. His store, the Baseball and Sporting Goods Emporium (Spalding & Brothers), sold baseball products to professional baseball teams and department stores. Spalding, a famous pitcher and the player–coach of the White Stockings, intended to capitalize on his baseball reputation and coaching position. Ten months later his company, Spalding & Brothers, Inc., reported a profit of US$1,083 ("Once Upon a Time," 1947). Today, Spalding, one of the top four sporting goods companies in the United States, manufactures all types of sporting goods equipment, from portable basketball backboards to innovative electronic referee whistles. The firm, which pioneered the development of brand recognition in sporting goods through athlete endorsements and continues such promotional activity today with sports superstar endorsers ranging from Olympian Jennie Finch to professional basketball player Paul Pierce, is part of a sporting goods industry that sells more than US$53 billion worth of goods each year (National Sporting Goods Association, 2008).

Franchises such as the Red Sox, manufacturers such as Spalding, and athlete endorsers such as Finch are part of a sport business industry that annually produces, advertises, and sells billions of dollars in sport products and services. This chapter provides brief historical sketches in the development of the sport business industry in the United States. Because of the size and diversity of the industry, this chapter will cover only selected historical developments. Besides being able to find information in hundreds of sport history books, you can read about some historical aspects of the sport business industry not covered in the following pages by referring to some of this textbook's other chapters that include various aspects of history (e.g., chapter 8 includes a discussion of the historical aspects of interscholastic athletics; in chapter 9 you can read about the historical developments of community and youth sport participation).

HISTORICAL ASPECTS OF COMMERCIALIZATION IN SPORT

This section examines the developmental periods as well as the early commercialization models of the sport business industry. The developmental periods covered below start with the later 19th century and involve issues of urban population growth, consumer demands, modernization, and entrepreneurship. This is followed by an overview of sport business industry commercialization models, especially those associated with the sporting goods segment of the sport industry.

Developments

Numerous commercialization models have surfaced throughout the developmental periods of the sport business industry. The decade of the 1870s is a good starting point for the discussion of these commercialization models because by this time several developments were underway that made the emergence of the sport business industry possible. The urban population had grown large enough to support this new industry. At the same time, changes in response to the urban populace's demand for sport made sustainable commercialization of sport possible; the urban practice of buying sport entertainment had by this time become firmly entrenched. Various sports had become quite popular, making sport products and services viable for sustained commercial success (Rader, 2009). The process of modernizing sport, begun in harness racing, horse racing, and baseball before 1870, experienced exponential growth after 1870 (Adelman, 1986). The modernization process included the specialization of athletic skill, the development of effective organizational structures to present and control sport, the standardization and routinization of the sport product, and an educated citizenry ready to learn about and follow sport in newspapers and popular magazines. The development of the sport business industry was also aided during the last quarter of the 19th century by the growth of per capita income that left consumers with discretionary funds to spend on sport and entertainment.

Technology also influenced the beginnings of a viable sport business industry after 1870. It is difficult, for example, to imagine the development of the sport business industry without railroads to transport teams and distribute products or the telegraph to report scores and solidify business deals. By 1870 all major Eastern and Midwestern cities were interconnected by rail and telegraph. Technological developments in the newspaper press and printing industry also helped spread information about sport to an increasingly interested middle class.

Finally, by the decade of the 1870s the United States had produced a group of entrepreneurs knowledgeable about the sport business industry and eager to exploit its opportunities. During the last quarter of the 19th century, new firms organized to exploit opportunities in the leisure experience market. Sport entrepreneurs concentrated on developing techniques and processes to produce products and experiences for a growing leisure market. They also invented and experimented with methods of promoting and selling sport.

Models

Numerous commercialization models in the sport business industry developed over the last few decades of the 19th century. Several early commercialization models were associated with the sporting goods segment of the sport business industry. Between 1880 and 1890, 79 companies began to produce sporting goods products. Some of these companies had formed much earlier, such as Draper & Maynard, which organized in 1841 to manufacture men's gloves. The company converted to sporting goods and began to manufacture hunting gloves and baseball gloves during the 1880s. Other companies, such as the Weed Sewing Machine Company, changed completely. In 1878 Weed began the production of bicycles. Still others, such as B. F. Goodrich and the Narragansett Machine Company, added the manufacture of sport equipment to their other product lines. B. F. Goodrich began the production of golf balls during the 1880s, and the Narragansett Machine Company added gymnastic equipment to its product line in 1885.

Some companies began with the express objective of producing sport equipment. For example, the Nelson Johnson Manufacturing Company was established in Chicago in 1883 to produce tubular skates. The John Gloy Company was established two years later in Chicago to manufacture gymnastic equipment. Some firms were transplanted to US soil to produce sporting goods. Two companies, Slazenger and Bancroft, arrived from England in the early 1880s to produce tennis rackets. Several other firms were established to distribute and sell sporting goods. These new firms competed directly with hardware stores, which began the distribution of sporting goods during the 1870s, and department stores and mail-order houses, which began to sell sporting goods during the 1880s. Each new entrant into the sport business industry helped to popularize sport, thus developing and expanding the market.

A. G. Spalding & Brothers is an excellent example of the growth and success of the sporting goods industry during the 1880s. The Spalding firm is one of the first and certainly the most successful of the early sporting goods firms. The diversification of Spalding during the last quarter of the 19th century provides insight into the development of the industry. Spalding's experiments in marketing goods and services provide evidence of the state of the art in the late 1800s and early 1900s. Spalding & Brothers was the first modern sport business enterprise, and many other companies copied its techniques, methods, and attitudes.

vertical integration—A company's expansion by moving forward or backward within an industry; expansion along a product or service value chain. The opposite of vertical integration is horizontal integration. Horizontal integration occurs when a company adds new products and services to its organizational structure.

diversification—The act of adding new products to the company's product mix, thus diversifying the company's product offerings.

The success of Spalding & Brothers resulted from four interrelated developments within the firm: (1) vertical integration, (2) diversification, (3) the development of a modern management system, and (4) the promotional skills of A. G. Spalding himself. As noted in the chapter introduction, Spalding & Brothers began in 1876 as a retail store. By the next year, however, the firm had initiated its practice of **vertical integration** by wholesaling sporting goods from the same store. By 1884 Spalding had established wholesale centers in Chicago and New York to coordinate service for Eastern and Western markets. During the 1890s Spalding added additional wholesale centers to cover the North and South. By the beginning of the 20th century, Spalding was producing sporting goods equipment in 15 plants in the United States and 5 plants overseas. Vertical integration meant that Spalding could benefit from economies of scale and scope, thus more effectively coordinating the manufacture and distribution of sporting goods. This approach directly influenced the sale of Spalding products in local stores. Vertical integration allowed the company to control resale prices.

Diversification was another key to the company's success. Spalding began by selling baseball equipment. Its largest contract was with one of the baseball clubs in Chicago, the White Stockings. Within two years Spalding & Brothers was selling fishing equipment, ice skates, and croquet equipment. During the 1880s Spalding expanded into football, soccer, boxing, track and field, tennis, boats, canoes, and a variety of sport clothing, uniforms, and shoes. In the early 1890s Spalding produced the first basketball for James Naismith (the inventor of the game of basketball) and helped to introduce golf equipment into the US market. Spalding employees were hired out to communities interested in constructing golf courses. By the mid-1890s Spalding had become a leading contender in the burgeoning bicycle market, producing and marketing bicycles and bicycle accessories. Before the end of the 19th century Spalding manufactured nearly everything that the sport enthusiast might want or require to improve sport performance or pleasure, diversifying its offerings to meet the growing demand for sport equipment by middle-class consumer–participants.

WEB

Go to the OSG and complete the Web search activity, which will help you compare a relatively new entrant in the sport business industry with one of the first modern sport business enterprises.

Spalding & Brothers also influenced market demand for sport products in a variety of ways. The company's Library of Sports helped to expand interest and demand for sporting equipment by providing knowledge about and training in particular sports. Spalding used popular sport figures to discuss sports rules and to provide instruction in how to develop sports skills. Spalding advertisements promoted the benefits of sport for participants, helping to popularize the motives for active involvement. Spalding promotions also motivated active participation in more direct ways. The company donated trophies for tournaments, track meets, regattas, bicycle races, baseball contests, and league championships. Spalding staff members offered lessons and training for beginners as well as more advanced players and provided advice on the construction of facilities. Spalding employees taught local consumers about club organization and management of tournaments and contests. These services helped to expand local markets, brought goodwill to the company, and promoted Spalding products.

SPORTING GOODS MANUFACTURING IN TAIWAN: A HISTORICAL OVERVIEW

By Doris Lu-Anderson • TAIWAN
California State University at Long Beach, UNITED STATES

Have you ever wondered where your dad's old running shoes, your mom's tennis racket, and your high-tech BMX bicycle were manufactured? If you take a close look, you may find that many of those US brand-name products were made overseas. In some developed countries, companies that hold a trademark on a product provide manufacturing rights to manufacturers in developing countries that offer lower labor and production costs. How did this happen? Let us rewind time to the 1960s.

During the 1960s international sporting goods production orders began to shift from Japan, a major manufacturing center at the time, to Taiwan because of its lower labor costs and better quality. Taiwan began to build an export-oriented economy. During the 1970s and 1980s, Taiwanese companies attracted the business of many international brand sporting goods companies and began manufacturing products following the original order, an approach known as the original equipment manufacturer (OEM) principle. The manufacturing business grew dramatically, and companies expanded assembly lines and recruited laborers.

An example of the success of this approach is found in KENNEX, the leading racket sport manufacturer, which began producing badminton rackets in Taiwan in the early 1970s. A strong research and development (R&D) program permitted KENNEX to expand its product line to make tennis rackets for well-known brands, such as Head and Prince. KENNEX even established its own brand name, which was unusual in an OEM-oriented market. By 1987 KENNEX manufactured one of every four tennis rackets.

In the late 1970s, Taiwan-based Feng Tay Enterprise and Pou Chen Group, the dominant OEM manufacturers in the world, started producing sport shoes for Nike and adidas. When OEM profits declined, Feng Tay and Pou Chen decided to increase their profits by transforming their business from OEM to an approach known as original design manufacturer (ODM). Since then, these two manufacturers have been able to serve more clients, such as Nike, adidas, Puma, Reebok, Asics, Merrell, and Timberland. In 1992 Feng Tay and Nike joined to establish an R&D center in Taiwan, the first one outside the United States.

In the late 1980s higher labor costs in Taiwan pressured the manufacturing industry to relocate to places that could offer low labor costs. Many Taiwanese plants relocated to China and South Asia, but some companies kept their R&D centers in Taiwan.

Since the 1990s some companies with the leading brands in their categories have focused on the own branding manufacturing (OBM) principle. At the same time, they also need OEM or ODM orders to

continued ▶

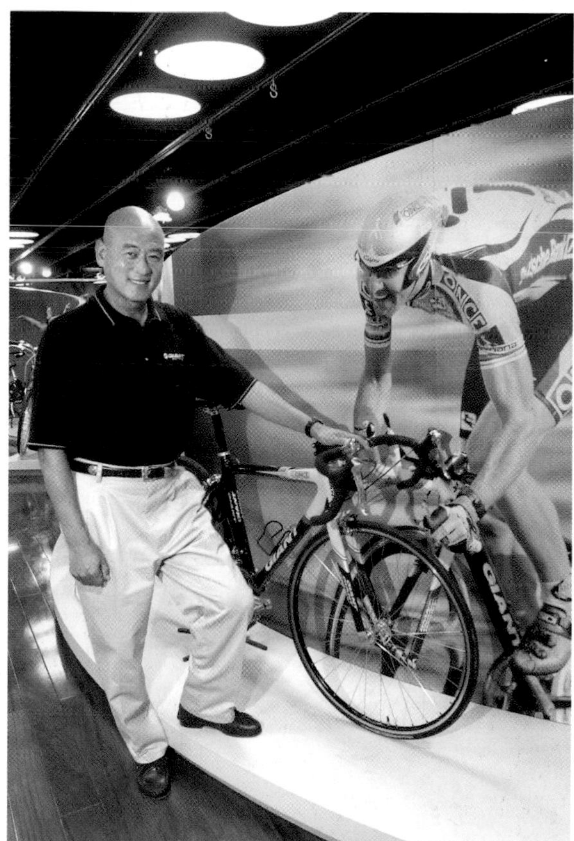

Taiwanese bicycle company Giant has made racing bicycles for some of the top teams in the Tour de France, including the Spanish club ONCE.
AP Photo/Wally Santana.

▶ continued

supplement their economic margin. For example, bicycle manufacturer Giant established its own brands but maintained its ODM product lines to produce bicycles for other brands such as Trek.

Taiwanese companies such as Giant, Johnson's Health Tech, and Cheng Shen Tire, which have been in partnership with international name brand sporting goods companies for decades, continue to operate plants in mainland China and South Asia. They have also committed to retaining competitive R&D programs in Taiwan, making the region internationally known for high-tech production and low labor costs.

INTERNATIONAL LEARNING ACTIVITY #1

Go to the "Trade" section of the Sporting Goods Manufacturers Association (SGMA) Web site (www.sgma.com/publicpolicy/trade/) and click on a link to one of the topics listed on that page. Choose one of the articles about that topic and summarize the information for a class presentation. Specifically note how the information in the article relates to international trade in sporting goods.

INTERNATIONAL LEARNING ACTIVITY #2

Using information in books, in articles, or online, write a paper describing the commercialization (commodification) of sports in countries other than the United States (e.g., rugby in England, football in Africa) or in international sport (e.g., the Olympic and Paralympic Games, the Gay Games).

The purpose of Spalding & Brothers' promotions was not just to expand the market for sport equipment but also to hawk its products. Hence, when Spalding received the contract to publish the *National League Official Rules,* the name of the rule book was changed to *Spalding's Official National League Rule Book,* and it advertised Spalding sporting goods equipment. When Spalding obtained the rights to produce the official baseball for the National League, the firm quickly announced to the baseball consumer that only Spalding could produce the real thing. Realizing the significance of being the official producer, Spalding tried to outdistance rivals by declaring its status as the official producer of footballs and soccer balls as well as golf, tennis, and track and field equipment. Spalding's pioneering use of professional and popular athletes as endorsers of the company's products resulted in the development of the unique aspect of brand recognition in sporting goods. Spalding's promotional slogans, such as "First make sure it's Spalding and then go buy," further established brand identity. Spalding helped to establish the power and popularity of "reason why" advertising during the 1880s and "negative" advertising during the 1890s.

decentralized organization—The act of developing separate divisions, subcompanies, or departments that focus on certain tasks or products of the company and can be run autonomously.

Other sporting goods entrepreneurs learned from Spalding & Brothers about **decentralized organization** and successful management techniques. Spalding was the first sporting goods firm to become a multiunit enterprise, a process that began almost immediately for the company. When A. G. Spalding purchased the Wilkins Manufacturing Company in 1878, he knew little about the manufacture of baseball bats, croquet mallets, ice skates, or baseball uniforms. To overcome this problem, Spalding retained Wilkins' staff and employees. He used the holdover employees from Wilkins to train his Spalding staff. When Wilkins sold his interest in the company three years later, Spalding had a trained administrative staff ready to take over and run the business. Spalding used the same approach when diversifying into the manufacturing of other sporting goods products. The company adopted the same approach in the development of its retail and wholesale distribution networks. Instead of searching for new employees to manage newly acquired or developed retail and wholesale outlets, Spalding hired managers away from the competition. In some instances, the acquired firm was allowed to keep its own name and to continue business as it had before the merger.

By 1894 Spalding had established two separate divisions, one in the East with headquarters in New York City and the other in the West with headquarters in Chicago. Each division was further subdivided into major activities: manufacturing, retail, and wholesale. These subdivisions were further subdivided into departments organized around sport categories (e.g., golf department, tennis department). Departments organized and administered their own functional activities such as accounting, purchasing, and advertising. To coordinate activities across divisions and departments, Spalding developed overarching functional departments. The marketing department, for example, coordinated advertising, product promotions, and markdown sales promotions nationwide. A top-level management department observed, standardized, and coordinated management techniques in each of Spalding's retail stores. This matrix organizational design proved highly effective and efficient. It gave Spalding a distinct advantage in management and proved to be an asset in the preparation of future top managers for the company. Both Julian Curtis and C. S. Lincoln, future presidents of the company, came through this system in the last decades of the 19th century.

A. G. Spalding was a pioneer in the sport business industry.

Courtesy of the Library of Congress, LC-DIG-ggbain-05154.

Just as sporting goods entrepreneurs in the 1800s learned their trade from model companies such as Spalding & Brothers, entrepreneurs in the intercollegiate athletic system benefited from observing student–athletes and student organizers. Some of the best examples of these entrepreneurs can be found in the early years of intercollegiate football.

HISTORICAL ASPECTS OF THE SPORT MARKET

Over the years in the sport business industry, **watershed events** have caused massive changes in the way that business is conducted. These events have led to new ways of doing activities (i.e., manufacturing) and new strategies and techniques for achieving business success. Although several watershed events illustrate such changes in the sport business industry, the bicycle craze of the 1890s probably provides the most instructive historical example. In 1890, 27 firms manufactured bicycles, and sales competition was relatively low. The safety bicycle, invented in England in 1887, had not had much of an effect on the US market. The pneumatic tire, invented in 1889, was just beginning to be widely used. Beginning developments in ancillary industries were under way. Dunlop, B. F. Goodrich, Goodyear, Penn Rubber Company, and a few others were beginning to manufacture bicycle tires. Miscellaneous bicycle parts such as bells, seats, and lamps were just beginning to make inroads into consumer markets. Top-grade bicycles sold for US$150. Medium-grade bicycles, introduced for the first time in 1890, sold for around US$100. Bicycles were sold primarily through hardware stores, although a few specialty shops and sporting goods stores sold bicycles. Distribution was targeted toward the larger cities in the East and Midwest. **"Reason why" advertisements** attempting to convince potential customers about the importance of the bicycle for fun, health, fitness, and self-development were placed predominantly in trade magazines. Promotions included trade shows, instructional books, and essay and poster contests.

watershed events—Events or developments in an industry that cause significant changes throughout the industry.

"reason why" advertisements—Advertising that tells consumers why they should buy a certain product.

All of this changed during the 1890s. By 1898, 312 companies were manufacturing bicycles and bicycle parts. Rapid technological improvements in the safety of the bicycle between 1890 and 1895 led firms to emphasize the need for consumers to purchase a new model each year. When technologies faltered after 1895 and the bicycle remained virtually the same from year to year, bicycle manufacturers resorted to stylistic changes so that consumers would think that it was necessary to purchase a new model each year. Bicycle sales skyrocketed after 1893, but so did competition among an ever expanding number of firms that produced bicycles. Competition spread quickly to ancillary industries as new entrants vied for **market share.** Bicycle sundries (e.g., seats, bells) also experienced a boom period between 1893 and 1898, prompting the emergence of new firms in the industry. Competition forced bicycle prices down. In 1898 top-grade bicycles could be bought for US$75, middle-grade bicycles for US$40, and low-grade bicycles for US$20. Secondhand bicycles sold for as little as US$3.

market share—Ranked position in a market determined by the percentage of a company's product sales in that market. For instance, if only three companies produce and sell basketball shoes, the company that sells the most shoes to the most consumers is considered to hold the number one market share in that product market.

The increase in competition forced bicycle firms to change the way that they did business. Beginning in 1893, firms stressed marketing and tried to meet customer needs in a variety of new ways. Firms emphasized brand equity and tried to establish entry barriers, protect against price cutting, and move bicycles through distribution channels more quickly. To accomplish these objectives, bicycle firms advertised extensively, moving into the top 10 industries in advertising volume during the 1890s. Systematic advertising became the rule as bicycle companies planned advertising campaigns across a 6- to 12-month period. Advertising agencies became the principal planners of advertising copy. Sophisticated "reason why" advertising and **emotive advertising** became commonplace. Firms developed slogans and trademarks to help establish brand-name recognition. Advertisers trotted out the established themes of fun, health, fitness, and self-improvement that were accepted parts of sport participation ideology. They also created new advertising themes to place the bicycle in the mainstream of American social movements and perceived individual needs and wants.

emotive advertising—Advertising that attempts to appeal to consumers' emotions.

During the last years of the 19th century the bicycle became at once an engine of democracy, an escape from the bonds of technology and industrialization, a tool promoting freedom for women, a moral elevator and developer for youth, and an agent for training young men. Advertisers used popular middle-class magazines and newspapers to sell bicycles. Bicycle firms began to use sales records to test advertising effectiveness. Bicycle firms employed traveling salesmen, former athletes, and former bicycle racing stars to visit local shops and hawk company products. These same traveling salesmen taught locals how to organize bicycle clubs, hold and administer bicycle races, arrange and coordinate bicycle parades and bicycle cross-country runs, and establish and direct bicycle tour routes. Traveling salesmen also helped to establish training facilities. Some of these, such as Spalding's Bicycle Training School in New York City, became famous. Most were local affairs, however, unrenowned beyond city limits. These services were designed to increase participation and improve company sales. They were part of the firm's attempt to increase or protect market share.

Bicycle firms further promoted brand equity by organizing racing teams, which were quite popular and received extensive newspaper coverage during the 1890s. Bicycle firms used them to "document" the superiority of their specific bicycle models. Firms sponsored bicycle races and bicycle tours, as well as other athletic events, in their attempts to bring their company names and products before the public eye. By the end of the decade, endorsements by prominent figures who either raced or rode bicycles became a common technique to sell bicycles.

The bicycle craze motivated many firms to enter the industry (Fielding & Miller, 1998). New entrants were successful because the demand increased each year. Demand for bicycles and bicycle accessories amounted to a product value of US$2,568,326 in 1890. Perceptive observers were well aware that demand was running well ahead of supply between 1890 and 1895. Bicycle prices remained high through 1896, and 1895 was a banner year for profits. But as the decade progressed, supply caught up to and exceeded demand. By 1898 product value had increased to US$31,915,908, but profits had dropped, and perceptive observers knew as early as 1897 that supply exceeded demand. Falling profits after 1895 were the immediate result of the intensity of competition that increased exponentially each year from 1892 through 1898. After 1898, price wars occurred frequently, replacing more solidly based marketing and promotion efforts, as firms, alarmed at shrinking profits, sold below cost to unload surplus. Despite such efforts, end-of-the-year bicycle inventories increased every year after 1897, and profits declined each year after 1895. By 1897 net earnings were less than half what they had been in 1896. Bicycle prices dropped steadily after 1895. Production costs increased slightly, while selling costs skyrocketed. In the eyes of many 1899 observers, the bicycle industry was ready for a crash. The collapse happened gradually, but was in full force by 1901. By 1909 only 94 companies remained in the bicycle industry.

The bicycle craze gave manufacturers and advertisers alike an opportunity to grow the sport business industry. This two-piece package enclosure, showing a woman wearing a bicycling costume, was created c1895 by Pope Manufacturing Co., manufacturers of Columbia Bicycles.

Courtesy of the Library of Congress, LC-USZ62-83909.

The bicycle craze and the crash that followed it served (and still serve) as examples for members of the sport business industry. It influenced thinking about business and business strategy in three key areas. First, it raised questions about how firms coped with the uncertainty created by intense competition. Overproduction and price cutting became watchwords in the sport industry. The need to curb intense competition for the good of the industry became a precept. Second, the influence of the bicycle advertising message, promoting sport in general, convinced sport firms of the necessity of promoting all kinds of sport. Third, the bicycle craze influenced marketing strategy. Successful bicycle companies employed a variety of marketing techniques in an integrated marketing strategy. Marketing strategy emphasized brand equity. Marketing techniques integrated advertising, sponsorship, and endorsements and included organizing participation through the development of local clubs and local activities, the use of traveling salesmen, and promotion through trade shows. The sport marketing mavericks from the bicycle industry had demonstrated the importance of testing for advertising success, market segmentation and market research, and the use of specialized agencies to develop and implement advertising and promotions. Perhaps far more important, the bicycle craze taught manufacturers the necessity of helping local dealers with advertising through national advertising campaigns linked to local advertising and promotional efforts.

Although the first decade of the 20th century was tough on the bicycle segment of the sport business industry, numerous sports were becoming more popular and witnessing tremendous growth (read the critical thinking section at the end of this chapter for more about the growth and popularity of sport at this time). The popularity and growth were particularly true in baseball, tennis and golf, football, basketball, fishing and target shooting, and roller skating. At this time the number of firms that manufactured sport equipment increased, as did the number of sporting goods sold. The *Sporting Goods Dealer* (*SGD*), a trade journal that provided monthly marketing reports, reported that firms selling sporting goods had tripled during the decade ("Retail Sporting Goods," 1907). The *SGD* periodically reported on what it called the "golf and tennis boom" during the decade. Equipment sales for these sports increased each year during the decade. Companies manufacturing or selling baseball equipment reported brisk business throughout the decade. Companies that made protective equipment for football, such as Rawlings Sporting Goods, reported accelerating sales each year. The roller-skating craze of 1906 through 1908, prompted by the building of outdoor skating facilities in several large cities, created a demand for roller skates. Equipment sales indicated that many people were participating in sport.

age of organization—A period of time, the 1880s and 1890s, during which companies began to organize and market sport to specific markets, such as youth.

The growth of sport participation as evidenced by the increase in sporting goods sales during the decade was influenced by the drive to organize sport participation during the **age of organization** (the decades of the 1880s and 1890s). For example, YMCAs began to organize and market sport during this period, helping to create a youth sport market by the turn of the century. The United States Lawn Tennis Association (USLTA), organized in 1881, promoted tennis for both men and women by sponsoring national tournaments during the 1890s. The United States Golf Association (USGA) offered similar opportunities for men and women golfers. As Betts (1974) explained, the National Canoe Association (1880), National Croquet Association (1882), and United States Skating Association (1884) all promoted participation and organized sport opportunities for men and women before 1900. The American Bowling Congress (ABC), organized in 1895, promoted and helped organize bowling clubs for both men and women. Men's intercollegiate athletic organizations multiplied during the 1870s, 1880s, and 1890s, codifying rules of play and organizing and administering intercollegiate contests in such diverse sports as football, soccer, track and field, cross country, baseball, and rowing (Smith, 1988). Their efforts helped to popularize sport participation and prompted participation after college. Women's colleges offered sport opportunities during the 1880s and 1890s. Women learned the joys of participation in gymnastics, basketball, golf, tennis, field hockey, and track and field. When they left college, women took with them a desire to continue to participate in sport. In addition to offering opportunities for athletic participation, just over a half century later, institutions of higher education began offering women and men opportunities to study sport management.

Segmentation

By the turn of the 20th century, perceptive observers within the sport business industry saw opportunities to make money by selling participation opportunities, charging spectators admission to watch others perform, and selling equipment for players to improve performance. The segmentation of sport marketing commenced as sport business leaders recognized that the market for sport participants, sport audiences, and sport equipment purchasers was segmented.

The sport business industry capitalized on the growing wealth of the White middle class by marketing sporting opportunities that appealed to especially men.

Courtesy of the Library of Congress, LC-USZ62-69243.

The largest of these segments was the growing number of White male middle-class sport enthusiasts in US cities. This was the key segment for financial success. Middle-class consumers far outnumbered spenders in other segments in the market, and they had the money to buy participation opportunities, tickets to games and matches, and high-priced equipment to perform. Other market segments could be ignored, but firms that overlooked the needs and wants of middle-class males did so at their peril. Astute observers of the sport scene were also aware of the second important segment—the developing youth market. Periodically, readers of the *SGD* were informed about the necessity of catering to the American boy for two important reasons. First was the fact that the participation rate for boys was up and that an increasing number of boys purchased sport equipment. Second, entrepreneurs realized that today's youth participant would become tomorrow's adult participant. Brand recognition and brand loyalty began in adolescence. White upper- and middle-class women constituted a third major segment in the sport market, particularly for specific sports. Marketers were interested in enticing women to participate and purchase golf and tennis equipment, fishing equipment, bicycles, and athletic wear.

Promoters experimented with methods of reaching the various market segments. One of the most successful experiments was store window advertising. Window displays, it was argued, attracted consumers who were not yet aware of what they needed. Window displays informed consumers about new developments in equipment technology, introduced new sport equipment, taught people about sport, and educated them about the benefits of participation. Window displays attracted attention and sold Americans on sport. Another way to attract attention and advertise a sport product was by using famous athletes as product endorsers.

Endorsement Advertising

Athlete endorsements today are commonplace, as evidenced by deals between Serena Williams and Nike, Dale Earnhardt Jr. and Pepsi, Kobe Bryant and Guitar Hero IV, and Michael Phelps and Mazda, Speedo, PowerBar, Visa, and a host of other companies and products. Such endorsements commenced years ago. For example, in 1917 J.H. Hillerich signed George Herman Ruth, otherwise known as Babe Ruth, to a contract, allowing the sporting goods company Hillerich & Bradsby (H&B) to use Ruth's autograph on its Louisville Slugger bats. Two years later the Babe Ruth–autographed Louisville Slugger was the leading seller for H&B, outdistancing the sale of any other bat sold in America. The contract with Ruth had cost H&B US$100 and a set of golf clubs—probably the most lucrative deal (for a company) in endorsement contract history.

Using an athlete's name to sell a product, particularly a sporting goods product, was not a novel idea in 1917. Hillerich had signed Honus Wagner, Hall of Fame shortstop for the Pittsburgh Pirates, to a similar deal back in 1905. Before 1910 Hillerich signed Ty Cobb and Napoleon Lajoie, both future Hall of Famers, to endorsement contracts. Wagner, Cobb, and Lajoie were chosen to endorse Louisville Slugger bats because they were expert hitters. They were excellent choices for a baseball bat company whose slogan was "the bat that gets more hits." Hillerich was using men who knew about bats, because they used them to make a living, to sell his bats. This message, endorsed by the best hitters in professional baseball, sold bats. The connection was obvious.

Indeed, the connection between experts and professionals and consumers had been made before. As mentioned earlier in this chapter, Spalding employed the idea back in the 1880s to sell baseballs. In an attempt to increase sales, bicycle manufacturers took Spalding's endorsement ideas a step further during the 1890s. Spalding chose experts from an existing professional league. Bicycle manufacturers had to create the professional league first and then sign experts to endorsement contracts. Successful professional bicycle racers endorsed bicycles and bicycle tires for companies willing to pay top dollar for their allegiance. The arms and ammo industry applied similar techniques at the turn of the century to attract buyers. Experts told less-skilled participants what products to use to improve skill, accuracy, and overall performance. Advertisers used endorsements by experts to symbolize product quality and to establish brand-name recognition. Product endorsements by experts attracted consumers who wanted to improve performance in some way. Endorsements linked participant performance to product quality.

Hillerich & Bradsby—through Ruth, Cobb, Wagner, Lajoie, and others—took the matter a step further. Ruth was more than simply an expert who informed consumers about bats. Ruth was a personality, a hero, a human interest story, a style to be copied. He was an icon, symbolizing a certain type of individuality and style. Ruth was larger than life. Indeed, vocabulary was created to describe him (e.g., people spoke of "Ruthian feats" to communicate heroic accomplishments). Consumers purchased the Ruth-autographed bat not just to improve their batting average or hit more home runs. They wanted to be like the Babe. The bat was an artifact used to accomplish Ruthian feats and, more important, to copy the Ruthian style and mode. Consumers' desire to copy the Ruthian style and mode meant that Babe Ruth endorsements could be used to sell not only baseball bats but also candy bars and other products unrelated to athletics.

Competition and Cooperation

The First World War (1914–1918) increased the attractiveness of the sporting goods industry for companies seeking long-term profitability in at least three important ways. First, military training programs that introduced and trained soldiers in sport brought a new source of revenue to the industry. Second, the war had an immediate effect on the sale of sporting goods equipment at home because the demand for all kinds of athletic equipment increased. Third, the belief that sport would nurture and develop manly traits was further solidified by the war. Throughout the war the military promoted sport as a means of training soldiers and developing better citizens. Local and state governments recognized the benefits of sport and the resultant demand for facilities. Similarly, physical education became a mandatory part of the educational curriculum, and school and college athletic programs flourished. The war functioned as a catalyst for the growth of sport during the 1920s.

Established members of the sporting goods industry were confident that demand would continue to increase after the war. This anticipation of postwar demand for sporting equipment had three important consequences. First, it led to improved manufacturing techniques. To meet the demand, manufacturers were determined to improve production facilities, increase manufacturing efficiency, and produce at full capacity. Second, several companies converted existing production capability to the manufacture of sporting goods after the war. Many of these new entrants were powerful competitors with significant capital and the ability to make large commitments to advertising and promotions to facilitate brand identity. These new entrants significantly increased the supply of sporting goods equipment. The third result was the expansion of the type of outlet in which sporting goods were distributed. The attractiveness of the sporting goods industry for investment and profit encouraged new entrants into the wholesale and retail trades. Sporting goods products began to be distributed through nontraditional outlets (e.g., drugstores, clothing stores). **Distribution** practices were further altered when many of the new jobbers and wholesalers eliminated the retailer and dealt directly with schools, industrial leagues, sport clubs, and community recreation associations. These new distributors frequently offered discounts, rebates, and gifts to generate goodwill and secure sales. Established manufacturers and traditional jobbing houses turned to direct sales to remain competitive. Improvements in manufacturing techniques meant that the supply of sporting goods products increased significantly. The proliferation

distribution—The manner in which a sport industry product or service moves from the producer or manufacturer to the consumer; distribution channels and outlets are the individuals (e.g., jobbers, dealers, salespeople, brokers) and companies (e.g., wholesalers, retailers) involved in the process of getting the product to the end user (O'Reilly & Seguin, 2009).

of sporting goods distribution outlets meant that sporting goods were more readily available to consumers. Increased supply and improved distribution resulted in both lower prices for consumers and greater competition among industry members.

Because of the new entrants into the marketplace, leaders in the sporting goods industry soon realized that the industry had become highly competitive and consequently unprofitable. The supply of sporting goods products exceeded demand as early as 1925, increasing the intensity of competition as companies vied for consumer dollars. The cost of doing business increased, and profits plummeted. To survive, manufacturers resorted to ruinous competitive practices such as price cutting. But as the industry moved into the 1930s, sporting goods leaders realized that cooperative efforts were needed to curb competition. Presidents and vice presidents of the large successful firms started the movement for cooperation, the primary vehicle for which was trade associations. Cutthroat competition decreased as industry leaders shared customer credit information, discussed solutions to common problems, talked about industry profitability, exchanged information about demand, and in general cooperated among themselves. These practices increased the individual and collective knowledge about the sporting goods industry. Competitors gained better understanding about the effects of competitive strategy on industry members and overall profitability. Cooperative efforts were used to increase market size and to gain better understanding of the industry.

The Roone Revolution in TV Sport and Entertainment

Along with the increases in sporting goods, distribution outlets, and participation opportunities in the first half of the 20th century came the arrival of televised sport, starting with a college baseball game in the late 1930s, a variety of sport broadcasts (e.g., Gillette Cavalcade of Sports) in the 1940s, and popular niche broadcasts such as roller derby and wrestling in the 1950s.

In 1960 Roone Arledge proposed to ABC executives a new plan for covering football games. The application of his plan revolutionized how sports were televised during the remainder of the 20th century. Arledge wanted to bring the TV viewer to the game, to get the audiences emotionally involved. He wanted viewers at home to experience the game as though they were at the stadium. Even if they were not football fans, reasoned Arledge, they could still enjoy the game. Bringing the consumer to the game required developing a new method for covering the game. Arledge increased the number of cameras from 3 to 9 and then to 12 or more. He introduced instant replay. To bring the action up close and personal, he used handheld and isolated cameras. Split screens and other technical devices helped the viewer experience the atmosphere of the game. To help duplicate the live atmosphere, Arledge used directional and remote microphones to capture the sounds of the game and crowd.

Arledge believed that televised sport was in the commercial entertainment business. Television programs survived only if they could draw higher ratings, support more advertising dollars, and generate greater corporate profits. The same was true for televised sport. This requirement meant that televised games had to attract a variety of viewers. Arledge realized that the casual viewer and the “sometimes” fan were far more important than the avid football consumer. The reason was simple: There were more of them. These folks required more than just sport to be entertained. Arledge believed that the participants in a sport contest were the essence of entertainment. People, he thought, watched sports to be entertained by people performing. Sport viewing was experiential. Therefore, Arledge sought to extend the entertainment value of sport beyond the game itself.

Arledge’s lessons on improving sport entertainment were copied by others. For instance, the 1970s ushered in the age of the mascot. Later in that decade, the success of the Dallas Cowboys cheerleaders prompted other teams to add cheerleaders to extend the entertainment value of the game. Additional ways that sport was tailored to appeal to more followers included exploding scoreboards, artificial grass, extended schedules and playoff systems, and rule changes to make games more action packed and exciting (Rader, 1984; Roberts & Olsen, 1989).

The abundance of sporting goods products and distribution outlets during the 1920s meant that sport equipment was widely available to a public whose interest in sport was growing steadily. As detailed by Lewis (1973), public policies begun during the First World War and expanded during the 1920s helped to influence this growing demand in several ways. During the war, army and navy officials used sport for both training and recreation, giving thousands of young men opportunities to play and watch sport. Their extensive use of sport did much to popularize sport and to legitimize sport programs as part of public policy. As part of the war effort, the War Camp Community Service began public recreation programs in hundreds of communities. After the war, local communities continued these programs, providing opportunities for participation at public expense. Between 1920 and 1930 the number of public recreation departments more than doubled. Community expenditures on public recreation increased sixfold during the 1920s. The notion that the provision of facilities and programs was public responsibility became firmly entrenched in the public mind. The war effort also encouraged the inclusion of sport instruction and the development of athletics programs in high schools and colleges throughout the nation. From the 1920s through the 1940s states passed laws requiring physical education. By 1948 only English classes had a higher enrollment in the public school system than physical education classes.

Knute Rockne and Brand Equity: Updating the Formula for Success

Between 1918 and 1930 Notre Dame football grew from an informal Saturday afternoon game to a national phenomenon. Knute Rockne, the head coach during this period, developed and applied a formula for the commercial success of big-time intercollegiate football. Because of his actions, Notre Dame football became a highly recognizable and distinguished name that consumers associated with value. Therefore, his formula produced brand equity.

The four dimensions of brand equity are brand loyalty, brand awareness, perceived quality, and brand associations or brand image (Aaker, 1991). Rockne created brand loyalty by developing a loyal following. This brand loyalty was brought about by the creation of a winning tradition, the arrival of star players who both represented and drew on the school's diverse customer base, and the establishment of an athletic culture at the university.

Rockne's formula included brand awareness, which, besides the three developments listed earlier, included such novel actions as the hiring of Archie Ward to be a student press assistant (Littlewood, 1990). Ward received tuition in return for promoting Rockne, Notre Dame football, and the team's stars.

Following Ward, Francis Wallace and then George Strickler had the same promotional assignments.

The development of perceived quality was also part of Rockne's formula. Besides the promotional work of the student press agents, Rockne understood the importance of self-promotion. His hiring of Christy Walsh, the first sport agent, helped to establish a perception of quality for Rockne and his program. For instance, Walsh got Rockne to participate in various activities (e.g., after-dinner speech circuit, radio broadcasts, movie contracts, endorsements) that helped develop the image of Rockne as an intelligent, ethical, and entrepreneurial football coach.

The development of brand associations was the final part of Rockne's formula. During the 1920s Notre Dame football developed several linkages in consumer minds. Notre Dame football players became the Fighting Irish. The Fighting Irish became synonymous with football excellence as established by a winning tradition. Notre Dame football also became synonymous with Knute Rockne, the charismatic and technically brilliant leader of the Fighting Irish. Although representing Catholics, Notre Dame football also stood for the acceptance of diversity (the new melting pot).

Overall, the creation of brand equity meant that the Fighting Irish became associated with a set of values in the minds of consumers. Those values translated into a solid nationwide fan base that prompted financial success for Notre Dame football (Oriard, 2001; Sperber, 1993; Watterson, 2000).

Increased Participation and Spectatorship

World War II severely curbed the production of sporting equipment, especially goods made from rubber, leather, wood, cotton, and petroleum. Many sporting goods companies attempted to stockpile raw materials. This action proved fruitless because government policy curbed production of sport equipment regardless of material supplies. Rationing was the rule of civilian life during this time. Many sporting and leisure activities and events were suspended, terminated, or affected in other ways. The prestigious Wimbledon championships were suspended from 1940 through 1945. Many male professional athletes were called into military duty, leaving many men's sports with less-skilled players. College and high school sport programs were cut back or eliminated altogether.

Other forms of amateur sports, however, flourished during the war. In both military life and civilian life, sport participation became a matter of policy. Inductees into the army and the navy had to be trained. Sport, including highly competitive athletic events, became part of this training as a matter of military policy. The military tried to coerce every soldier and every sailor into the sporting life. Military leaders advised civilian authorities to adopt similar policies as part of the war effort. When the war ended in 1945, hundreds of thousands of men and women returned home to the United States. The military policy to use sport as part of training and as a recreational activity had produced sport enthusiasts. Corporate business policies to organize civilian sport participants had also helped create sport enthusiasts. Postwar Americans went looking for entertainment and leisure as sport participants and as spectators. The sport industry responded to the desires of these new sport enthusiasts in other ways. Because of the growing popularity of men's football, a new professional football league began in 1946 and survived for three seasons before merging with the NFL for the 1950 season. In 1949 the men's Basketball Association of America merged with the National Basketball League to become the National Basketball Association (NBA). The end of the decade was a boom period for professional sports.

The late 1940s saw the modern color barrier broken in professional sport when Jackie Robinson signed with the Brooklyn Dodgers in 1945. Robinson was followed by Larry Doby, who signed with Cleveland in 1946. Both would play in the major leagues during the 1947 season. Professional football saw Marion Motley and Bill Willis join the Cleveland Browns in 1946 and Kenny Washington and Woody Strode play for the Los Angeles Rams that same year. Professional basketball had to wait until 1950 before Chuck Cooper joined the Celtics and Sweetwater Clifton left the Harlem Globetrotters for the New York Knicks. Several factors influenced the integration process. It was, at least in part, a response to the pressure for integration in the military during World War II. Part of it was also a question of ethics and values and of changing attitudes. Part of it was economics. African Americans constituted a large, untapped, and inexpensive talent pool. During the decades that followed, team owners became aware that African American talent often meant the difference between financial success and failure, particularly in the 1950s and 1960s as a new breed of owners took control of professional sports. Bill Veeck, an innovator who introduced new techniques to sport managers, was one of the best examples of this new breed of owners and promoters.

Go to the OSG and complete the Learning in Action activity, which will test how well you know your history of the sport business industry.

ACTION

The military policy of coercing individuals into the sporting life was directed toward all soldiers and sailors. The military developed sport programs to meet the needs of women. World War II brought substantial numbers of women into the army, navy, and coast guard. Athletic competition became part of the training program for women, which copied the men's program. Women were encouraged to participate in competitive athletics programs in volleyball, archery, basketball, bowling, tennis, table tennis, swimming, badminton, and softball. Women's military teams also took on civilian teams.

Female sport participation has grown rapidly, thanks in part to public policy and increased sporting opportunities for women. Female athletes continue to excel off the playing field as well; Indiana University field hockey defender Mutsa Mutembwa (no. 32) was named a 2010 Rhodes Scholar.
Photo courtesy of Paul M. Pedersen.

Women had been competing in industrial leagues since World War I. The 1930s had witnessed a great deal of expansion in women's industrial leagues, particularly softball leagues. World War II brought more women into more sports. Society's attitude toward the participation of women in sports began to change. An example is the women's professional baseball league. To address the sport entertainment desires of the American public, the All-American Girls Professional Baseball League (AAGPBL) was begun. Made famous by the movie *A League of Their Own*, the AAGPBL enjoyed success from 1943 to 1954. The league was the idea of Philip K. Wrigley, owner of the Wrigley chewing gum company and the Chicago Cubs, who thought that men's baseball would have to stop during the war. Although the AAGPBL is the most well-known women's baseball league, the historical record shows that women played baseball long before then—in colleges in 1866 and on professional women's teams in 1867. At its peak in 1948, 10 teams played in the AAGPBL, and over one million fans watched them play. The AAGPBL, along with other societal changes in the United States, helped bring about the beginning of a positive change in thinking toward women in sport.

Over the succeeding decades, sport participation rates for women grew dramatically. For example, between 1968 and 1980 high school girls' sport participation increased by more than 500%. Participation by women collegians increased nearly as much. The feminist movement of the late 1960s and 1970s prompted tremendous growth in the women's market for sport and sport products. The fitness boom of the 1970s and

1980s also influenced women's interest. Increased participation by women was also a matter of public policy (i.e., Title IX), and the increased opportunities translated into increased sales. Sporting goods manufacturers, distributors, and retailers strove to do their bit for public policy by selling sport shoes, sport equipment, and sport apparel and promoting participation opportunities for women athletes.

Women's sports grew exponentially, becoming more popular than ever at every level and every age. The new notion of the female athlete changed before our eyes. The 1960s and 1970s had provided an all-out assault on sexism and the traditional notions and limitations of genderized and sexualized roles. Now, with legislation and the women's rights movement making progress, women in sport charged ahead. But the rights of women in sport would be resisted by societal strongholds that clung to old traditions. Not until the 1990s would women in sport in the United States become comfortable with their muscularity and approach equality in pay to men. Along the way, it took Title IX, several lawsuits, and a series of events to reach this point. The 1973 Billie Jean King defeat of Bobby Riggs in tennis, dubbed the **Battle of the Sexes,** helped. Five years later the Women's Professional Basketball League (WBL) made history by becoming the first such professional league. The league lasted three years, folded, started again and went another three years, folded, and then repeated this sequence a few more times. Today, the Women's National Basketball Association (WNBA) and other women's professional sports leagues and intercollegiate athletics programs are so popular that they have commercial value and major corporate support. They have become mainstays in the sport business industry. Overall, the 1990s (known as the decade of the woman athlete) through the first decade of the 21st century have witnessed increased interest in women's sports and increased participation in sport by women.

Battle of the Sexes— A tennis match in 1973 between Billie Jean King and Bobby Riggs. King's much-heralded victory over Riggs represented a key triumph over sexism and provided a significant historical lesson on exceeding sexist expectations and assumptions (Nelson, 1994).

CRITICAL THINKING IN THE HISTORY OF THE SPORT BUSINESS INDUSTRY

This critical thinking section relates to the section "Historical Aspects of the Sport Market" in this chapter. Reflecting on the business of sport during the first decade of the 20th century, P. R. Robinson, president of the New York Sporting Goods Company, concluded that it had been a good decade. Robinson noted tremendous growth in the popularity of sport, particularly in baseball, tennis and golf, football, basketball, fishing and target shooting, and roller skating. Even the business panic of 1907, remarked Robinson, had not hurt the sport industry. "When general trade is down," he said, "people have more time to devote to sports." Looking to the future, Robinson saw only good times for the sport business industry. As times became better, he concluded, the demand for high-priced sporting equipment would increase because people would want to perform more effectively (Robinson, 1909).

PORTFOLIO

Complete the critical thinking portfolio activity in the OSG, consulting as needed the "Eight Critical Thinking Questions" section in chapter 1.

ETHICS IN THE HISTORY OF THE SPORT BUSINESS INDUSTRY

Beginning in 1927, Frank Bradsby, president of the Chamber of Commerce of Sporting Goods Manufacturers (later renamed the Sporting Goods Manufacturers Association, SGMA), led a concerted effort to develop a code of ethics for sporting goods manufacturers. Bradsby was prompted to lead the fight for a code of ethics by several industry-wide trade practices that hurt the image of the industry and curbed profits. Key among these unethical practices were price cutting; selling below cost; tying contracts; giving hidden rebates or discounts to secure sales; commercial bribery; piracy

PORTFOLIO

Complete the ethical issues portfolio activity in the OSG, consulting as needed the "Guidelines for Making Ethical Decisions" section in chapter 1.

of trademarks, brand names, and athletic endorsements; piracy of the term *official;* misbranding of products relative to grade, quality and guarantees; and interference with existing contracts. Through the auspices of the SGMA, Bradsby was able to enlist several sporting goods industry leaders (including Julian Curtis of Spalding Brothers; H. B. Canby of Crawford, McGregor & Canby; E. Goldsmith of Goldsmith Sons; and L. B. Icely of Wilson Sporting Goods). Between 1927 and 1930 leaders in the SGMA established a set of ethical trade practices for sporting goods manufacturers. These practices were endorsed by the entire membership of the SGMA at the industry-wide meeting in 1930 in Sulfur Spring, Virginia.

Summary

This chapter provides sketches of some of the significant developments that took place starting in the 1870s and described the foundation for the development of the sport business industry in the United States. The key events, innovations, and entrepreneurs presented here are only a few of the myriad activities and individuals who have played some crucial role in the development and history of sport management. The sketches provided in this chapter are useful because history offers many lessons relevant to your studies and career in the sport business industry.

Review Questions

1. What are some of the ways that the history of the sport business industry can be helpful to a sport management executive today?
2. How has commercialization affected the sport business industry over the years, and how is it currently influencing the industry?
3. What are some events that have significantly influenced and changed the sport business industry?
4. How have advances in manufacturing processes influenced the growth of the sport business industry?
5. What are some advances in technology that have influenced the development of the sport business industry?
6. What are the factors that have affected the growth and development of participatory, spectator, and professional sports for girls and women?
7. How have historical developments related to endorsement and sponsorship marketing affected the sport business industry?

QUIZ TIME

Did you grasp all the key points in this chapter? Go to the OSG for a short quiz to test your understanding of the material.

References

Aaker, D.A. (1991). *Managing brand equity*. New York: Free Press.

Adelman, M.L. (1986). *A sporting time: New York City and the rise of modern athletics, 1820–70*. Urbana: University of Illinois Press.

Betts, J.R. (1974). *America's sporting heritage 1850–1950*. Reading, MA: Addison-Wesley.

Brown, G., & Morrison, M. (Eds.). (2008). *ESPN sports almanac 2009*. New York: Ballantine.

Burk, R.F. (1994). *Never just a game: Players, owners, and American baseball to 1920*. Chapel Hill: University of North Carolina Press.

Fielding, L.W., & Miller, L.K. (1998). The ABC trust: A chapter in the history of capitalism in the sporting goods industry. *Sport History Review*, *29*(1), 44–58.

Lewis, G. (1973). World War I and the emergence of sport for the masses. *Maryland Historian, 4,* 109–122.

Littlewood, T.B. (1990). *Arch: A promoter, not a poet: The story of Arch Ward*. Ames: Iowa State University Press.

National Sporting Goods Association. (2008, June 3). *U.S. sporting goods sales reach $53.5 billion in 2007; NSGA expects flat 2008*. Mount Prospect, IL: Author.

Nelson, M.B. (1994). *The stronger women get, the more men love football: Sexism and the American culture of sports*. New York: Harcourt Brace.

Once upon a time: Turning back the pages of Spalding's first ledger. (1947). *Sporting Goods Dealer*, *96*, 128–130.

O'Reilly, N., & Seguin, B. (2009). *Sport marketing: A Canadian perspective*. Toronto: Nelson.

Oriard, M. (2001). *King football: Sport & spectacles in the golden age of radio & newsreels, movies & magazines, the weekly & the daily press.* Chapel Hill: University of North Carolina Press.

Rader, B.G. (1984). *In its own image: How television has transformed sports.* New York: Free Press.

Rader, B.G. (2009). *American sports: From the age of folk games to the age of televised sports* (6th ed.). Upper Saddle River, NJ: Prentice Hall.

Retail sporting goods dealers' association. (1907). *Sporting Goods Dealer, 17*, 14.

Roberts, R., & Olsen, J. (1989). *Winning is the only thing: Sports in America since 1945.* Baltimore: Johns Hopkins University Press.

Robinson, P.R. (1909, January). Trade prospects for 1909. *Sporting Goods Dealer, 20*, 31–32.

Smith, R.A. (1988). *Sports & freedom: The rise of college athletics.* New York: Oxford University Press.

Sperber, M. (1993). *Shake down the thunder: The creation of Notre Dame football.* New York: Henry Holt.

Watterson, J.S. (2000). *College football: History, spectacle, controversy.* Baltimore: Johns Hopkins University Press.

HISTORICAL MOMENTS

1910	Classical management school of thought emerged
1911	Taylor's *Principles of Scientific Management* presented productivity improvement strategies
1917	Fayol's *Administration Industrielle et Générale* proposed 14 principles still considered foundational to management theory
1920s	Follett promoted power sharing, employee participation, and negotiations in organizations
1938	Barnard's *Functions of the Executive* focused on roles of executives in organizations
1940s	Systems theory proposed cross-disciplinary problem solving (e.g., mathematics, statistics, engineering)
1950s	Total quality management movement (Japanese-style focus on quality assurances) emerged
1964	Big Ten Conference on Body-of-Knowledge Projec implemented
1975	*Administrative Theory and Practice in Physical Education and Athletics* published by Ziegler and Spaeth
1980	"Sport Management: The Nature and Utility of the Concept" by Mullin, published in *Arena Review*, discussed sport management as a unique profession
1984	*Sport Management Curricula: The Business and Education Nexus* edited by Zanger and Parks
1982	The groundbreaking book *In Search of Excellence* by Peters and Waterman published
1990	Senge's *Learning Organizations* focused on gaining competitive advantage through training organization members to think critically and creatively
1997	First edition of *Understanding Sport Organizations: The Application of Organization Theory* by Slack published
2009	Third edition of *Managing Organizations for Sport and Physical Activity* by Chelladurai published (first edition published in 2001)

Photo courtesy of Paul M. Pedersen.

4

MANAGEMENT CONCEPTS AND PRACTICE IN SPORT ORGANIZATIONS

Lucie Thibault ■ Jerome Quarterman

LEARNING OBJECTIVES

1. Identify concepts of management theory and understand how these concepts can help leaders and managers better manage their sport organizations.
2. Define organizational environment and describe its influence on sport organizations.
3. Define organizational effectiveness and explain how it is measured in sport organizations.
4. Discuss the structure and design of sport organizations.
5. Explain the importance of strategic planning, organizational culture, and organizational change.
6. Explain the importance of critical thinking in management concepts and practice in the sport industry.
7. Explain the role ethics plays in the management of sport.

Key Terms

demography
economies of scale
economies of scope
effectiveness
efficiency
environment
organization
organizational culture
organizational design
organizational structure

GET A JOB!

☑ Continue on your journey in sport management by going to the Online Study Guide (OSG) at www.HumanKinetics.com/ContemporarySportManagement. Check out the job opportunities and consider the skills and experiences that can help you succeed in sport management.

We are surrounded by organizations. Most of us were born in hospitals, we have been and continue to be educated in schools, we regularly shop for goods and services in stores, and we are protected by organizations (e.g., fire departments, police departments). Even in death, we rely on organizations. Organizations associated with sport also surround us. Most children are introduced to active participation in sport and develop sport skills through schools. Children often stay involved in sport through physical education courses, intramural activities, and interschool competitions in the education system. They may also take advantage of community sports organized by local governments and nonprofit sport clubs. For highly skilled, competitive athletes, opportunities are available in college and university sport programs, amateur sport organizations, and professional sport organizations.

Other types of organizations provide us with opportunities for passive participation in sport. For example, media organizations keep us informed about sport in various ways (e.g., the Internet, television, radio, magazines, newspapers). We may attend sport competitions at our community gathering spaces, in school facilities, and in professional sport venues. Anyone who consumes sport either actively or passively will be exposed to many different types of organizations.

In the first issue of the *Journal of Sport Management,* Earle F. Zeigler (1987) wrote that sport and physical activity over the previous 100 years had "blossomed into a large and complex enterprise that demands a multitude of good managers" (p. 10). Slack and Parent (2006) emphasized this point by noting that "increased amounts of discretionary income, a heightened awareness of the relationship between an active lifestyle and good health, and a greater number of opportunities to participate in sport have all contributed" (p. 3) to the rapid growth and increasing diversity of the sport industry.

Publications such as *Street & Smith's SportsBusiness Journal, Sports Business Daily,* and *Sport Business International* consistently report on the financial and economic state of high-profile sport around the world. Clearly, in most industrialized nations the sport sector plays an important role in the national economy as well as in the country's social and cultural fabric.

Given the importance of the sport sector in society, sport leaders and managers must understand management concepts and organizational structures and processes so that they can adopt and implement the best managerial and organizational practices. In this chapter, we will apply management concepts and practices in the realm of sport organizations. We provide illustrations, exercises, and activities to help you understand how sport organizations function. First, we define the term *organization* and describe three different types of sport organizations. Then we address major topics that are central to understanding how organizations are structured and how they operate. This chapter provides only a basic introduction to management concepts and practice applied to sport organizations. As you progress through your professional preparation program, you will have opportunities to learn much more about them.

ORGANIZATION DEFINED

organization—Social entity created to coordinate the efforts of individuals with the intent to achieve goals.

Daft (2010) defined **organizations** as "social entities that are goal-directed, are designed as deliberately structured and coordinated activity systems, and are linked to the external environment" (p. 11). Coordinated actions lead to the creation of social entities (i.e., organizations) in which people work collectively to achieve goals. In essence, people work collectively because achieving goals is often easier when working together rather than working independently. Shown in figure 4.1 is an organizational chart for a fictitious professional baseball club. Here it is conceptualized that a variety of individuals and groups work collectively. One person would almost certainly be unable to perform all the tasks and responsibilities required for the baseball organization to

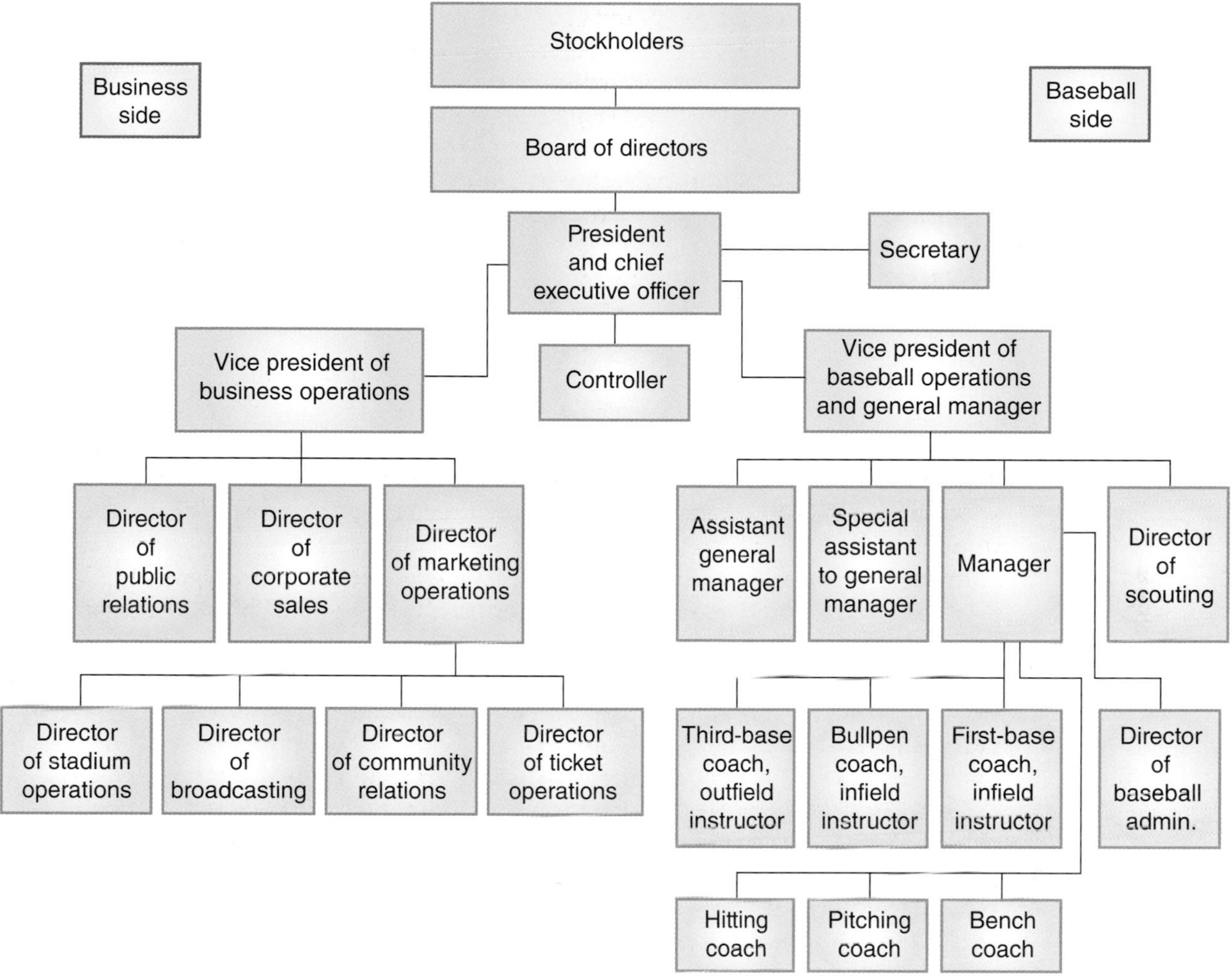

Figure 4.1 Organizational chart of a fictitious professional baseball club.

achieve its goals and objectives. By working collectively, however, organizations can achieve economies of scale and economies of scope.

According to Daft (2010), **economies of scale** represent savings that originate from the mass production of goods and services (i.e., increasing the scale of operations). As an organization produces more goods and services, it can realize savings by buying raw material in larger volume and by maximizing the use of specialized labor or machinery in producing, distributing, and selling these products and services. Economies of scale can result in improved efficiencies within an organization. A greater volume of production and distribution, for example, would enhance the skills of employees in carrying out those tasks. For example, if your sport marketing agency occasionally undertakes market research for professional sport franchises, it will realize economies of scale when it starts to undertake additional market research contracts for other sport organizations. The agency will already have developed the survey tools needed for market research. Refining those tools takes less time than developing them from scratch. In addition, as the employees of the agency undertake more market research contracts from various clients, they will become more knowledgeable, competent, and comfortable with conducting market research.

economies of scale—Savings originating from the mass production of goods and services.

Economies of scope represent savings originating from the maximization of resources used throughout the organization. Scope refers to "the number and variety of products

economies of scope—Maximization of resources used throughout an organization.

The United States Olympic Committee, based in Colorado Springs, Colorado, is an example of a nonprofit sport organization.
Photo courtesy of Paul M. Pedersen.

and services a company offers" and the market it serves (Daft, 2010, p. 213). An organization that has a large scope will be better equipped to realize economies by being able to service more clients in more markets. For example, International Management Group's (IMG) global presence (offices in 30 countries) provides the company with a definite advantage over other marketing, representation, and sport event organizations. IMG's scope allows the organization to service more clients around the globe without expending considerable resources because it is already well established in many countries. In this way, IMG maximizes its resources.

Organizations are vehicles to achieve goals. In their quest to achieve goals, organizations secure inputs and transform them into outputs, like this:

Inputs → Transformation → Outputs

Organizations obtain inputs such as financial resources, human resources, raw materials, expertise, and knowledge from the external environment. They then transform those inputs through technology (e.g., through the use of machinery) and through the skills and abilities of employees to produce outputs, such as goods and services sought by consumers. An organization also produces other outputs such as dividends for shareholders and salaries for employees (Jones, 2010).

There are three types of sport organizations: public, nonprofit, and commercial.

- ***Public organizations.*** The entities that make up this type of organization include federal and state government agencies or units as well as regional and local government departments responsible for the delivery of recreation and sport programs and the maintenance of sport fields, arenas, swimming pools, and parks. The National Park Service, the Los Angeles Department of Parks and Recreation, and the Kansas City Sports Commission and Foundation are examples of public sport organizations.
- ***Nonprofit organizations.*** In the case of nonprofit organizations (also referred to as volunteer or voluntary organizations), volunteer executives are responsible for the operation and management of the organizations. They may hire paid staff to assist in carrying out day-to-day operations, but the volunteer executives are ultimately in charge of making decisions and setting the strategic directions for the organizations.

For example, the United States Olympic Committee (USOC), the International Olympic Committee (IOC), and the US Ski and Snowboard Association are all nonprofit organizations. Their volunteer executive members, often referred to as members of the board of directors or executive committee, make policy decisions about the direction of the sport and often rely on paid staff to implement and evaluate those policies.

- ***Commercial organizations.*** The main goal of commercial organizations is to make a profit. Professional sports are commercial organizations. For example, the New Jersey Devils (NHL), Manchester United (Premier League), and the Boston Celtics (NBA) are commercial organizations. Sport equipment manufacturers are commercial organizations as well. For example, Wilson, Under Armour, and lululemon athletica are commercial organizations. Other examples include sport retailers such as Dick's Sporting Goods and Foot Locker. In addition, organizations that offer sport or sport-related services, such as private golf clubs, downhill ski and snowboard resorts, fitness clubs, tennis and racket clubs, bowling clubs, and bungee-jumping and wall-climbing facilities, also typically operate as commercial organizations.

In the following pages, we introduce a number of management concepts and practices that apply to all three types of sport organizations. These concepts include organizational environment, effectiveness, structure and design, strategic planning, culture, and change.

ORGANIZATIONAL ENVIRONMENT

In the quest to achieve goals, organizations must deal with their environments. Environments can be turbulent and uncertain. To address these uncertainties, leaders of organizations devise strategies to divide labor by area of expertise so that the most qualified employees are in appropriate roles. Organizations also use technology to support the ongoing production of goods and services. Additionally, organizations can manage the external environment by exerting power and control over other organizations (Daft, 2010). For example, executives of professional sport organizations may exert some control over local government officials by requesting a share of the revenues from concessions and parking of the city-owned stadium.

People play an important role in addressing an organization's environment. People can control organizations, and organizations can control people. More specifically, as people create organizations, they can determine what goals they will seek to achieve, how the organizations will be structured, and what processes will be used in the organizations' operations. Conversely, through their rules, processes, and structural elements, organizations can control the behavior of employees.

All organizations operate in an environment. As Daft (2010) explained, the **environment** is composed of "all elements that exist outside the boundary of an organization and have the potential to affect all or part of the organization" (p. 140). The environment can be divided into two categories: general and specific. The general environment includes elements that may not have a direct effect on the day-to-day operations of the organization but may nonetheless influence the organization. Elements in the general environment include the economy, technology, politics, social and cultural forces, and demography.

environment—All elements outside the boundary of the organization that have the potential to affect all or part of the organization.

- Economic conditions affect the way in which a given organization operates. How does inflation affect the organization? For example, are consumers buying expensive sport equipment when inflation rates are high? How do interest rates affect the organization's ability to acquire the inputs necessary for the fabrication of its products?
- Technology has a powerful effect on most organizations. For example, how do computers, software, and the Internet help the organization reach more consumers,

maintain more accurate records of inventory, communicate with suppliers, and monitor purchasing patterns? How does technology help the organization develop more (and better) products?

- The political climate is another element of the general environment. As an example, the development of the North American Free Trade Agreement (NAFTA) between the United States, Canada, and Mexico in the 1990s has facilitated trade among the three countries over the past two decades.
- Social and cultural forces as well as **demography** may affect the organization. The age structure of the population, the level of education, and the standard of living are examples of social, cultural, and demographic elements.

demography—Involves the examination of populations, including such elements as size, births, deaths, migration, and aging.

The specific environment, or task environment, includes stakeholders external to the organizations. Daft (2010) identified stakeholders such as "customers, employees, management, owners and stockholders, unions, creditors, suppliers, community, and the government" (p. 21) as part of the specific environment of the organization. Here are some important questions about elements of the specific environment:

- Who are the consumers? What are their preferences?
- Who are the suppliers? How easy is it for the organization to acquire its resources from suppliers? Does the organization deal with labor organizations or unions for its workforce?
- Who is the competition? Nike, adidas, New Balance, and Asics are all competitors of Puma. But does Puma have other competitors? What about nonsport shoe manufacturers? What about clothing manufacturers who also produce leisure wear?
- What role does the government play in the environment? The government might be an element of the specific environment through its imposition of legislation and guidelines for the treatment of employees and consumers. Organizations must also provide details to government agencies for taxation purposes.

Clearly, the environment significantly influences and represents a major source of uncertainty for the organization. As a result, leaders and managers of organizations must understand the environment and carefully monitor its effects on the organization. Figure 4.2 provides a graphic representation of the general and specific environments.

ORGANIZATIONAL EFFECTIVENESS

effectiveness—The extent to which goals are achieved.

efficiency—The extent to which goals are achieved using the fewest possible resources.

The **effectiveness** of an organization is the extent to which it achieves its goals. A related term, **efficiency**, refers to the achievement of goals using minimum resources. For example, the 2004 Athens Olympic Games were effective because members of the organizing committee achieved their objectives. But did the organizers achieve efficiency? In other words, did they achieve their objectives using the fewest possible resources? Given that members of the organizing committee went down to the wire with the construction of facilities and the training of human resources in advance of the Olympic Games, they were not efficient. They achieved their objectives, but they had to spend more resources (i.e., invest more money than budgeted for facility construction) to ensure the completion of the facilities before the Opening Ceremonies.

Efficiency implies the minimal use of resources to produce outputs (ratio of inputs to outputs). As a result, concepts of cost–benefit, return on investment (ROI), and budget compared with number of customers served are assessed to evaluate efficiency. As you can see, achieving effectiveness is easier than achieving efficiency. In fact, most managers and leaders of organizations rarely achieve efficiency.

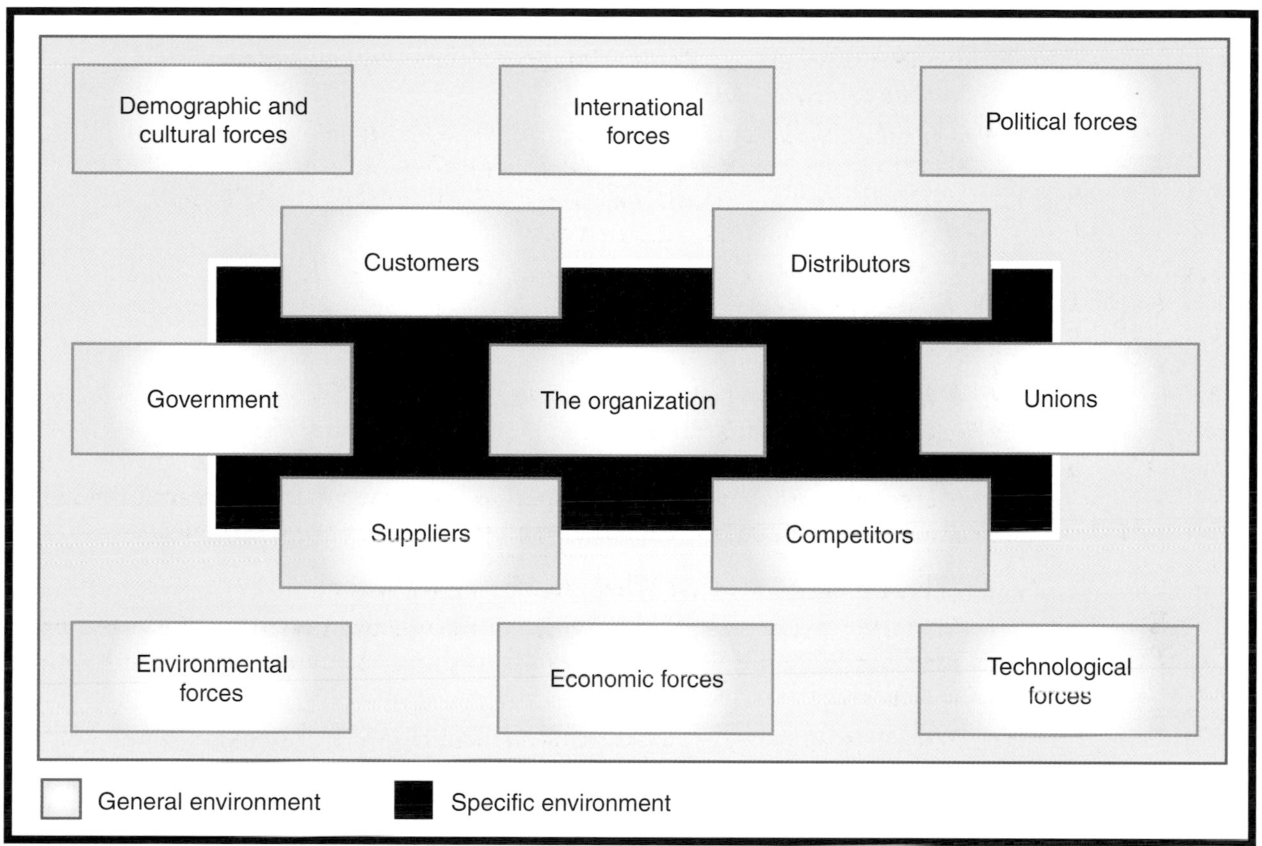

Figure 4.2 Various elements of an organization's environment.

Evaluating Organizational Effectiveness

Ultimately, managers and leaders want to ensure that the goals set out for the organization are met. Assessing organizational effectiveness, however, is not always this simple. Consequently, a number of approaches should be considered to evaluate organizational effectiveness (Jones, 2010). Traditional approaches include the goal approach, the resource-based approach, and the internal process approach. Contemporary approaches include the competing-values approach and the stakeholder approach (Daft, 2010).

- *Traditional approaches.* The goal approach focuses on the outputs side of the organization. The organization is considered effective if it achieves its organizational goal (e.g., maximizing profits, winning the game, successfully teaching sport skills to students, healing patients) (Daft, 2010). The resource-based approach focuses on the inputs side of the organization. With this approach, the effectiveness of an organization is assessed by its ability to acquire resources in order to transform them into outputs. The logic behind this approach is that without inputs or the ability to acquire inputs, an organization will be unable to produce outputs (Daft, 2010). The internal process approach focuses on the transformation side of the organization—the ability to process the inputs while considering the internal well-being of the organization. Focusing on the transformation of inputs into outputs helps ensure the organization's stability and long-term survival (Daft, 2010).
- *Contemporary approaches.* Although the previous approaches all contribute to our understanding of whether or not an organization is effective, the contemporary

approaches to organizational effectiveness presents a more integrated perspective (Daft, 2010). Two approaches are included in this section: competing values and stakeholder. Instead of focusing on single parts of the organization (i.e., inputs, transformation, or outputs), the competing-values approach combines elements of all traditional effectiveness approaches by focusing on the value dimensions of focus and structure. The dimension of focus is represented on a continuum from internal to external, whereas the dimension of structure is represented on a continuum from stability to flexibility. An internal focus means that the organization values the well-being of its employees, whereas an external focus values the well-being of the organization. A stable structure would favor a task-oriented approach, and a flexible structure would favor change and innovation in the organization (Daft, 2010). With the competing-values approach, the assessment of your organization's effectiveness will be based on your values with respect to the dimensions of focus and structure. In the competing-values approach, as a leader or manager you acknowledge that the assessment or interpretation of organizational effectiveness depends on who you are, what interests you represent, and what values you favor for your organization.

The stakeholder approach is based on the premise that several groups, entities, and other organizations have an interest in the focal organization. Various stakeholders will assess organizational effectiveness differently. For example, employees in the organizations might not judge effectiveness in the same manner as executives in the organization do or as customers do. For instance, suppliers may judge the organization's effectiveness by the volume of raw materials that they acquire and sell annually, whereas shareholders may consider the value of the shares as their measure of organizational effectiveness. Furthermore, customers may judge effectiveness by the quality and price of the product they purchased, and employees may consider wages and benefits when they evaluate organizational effectiveness.

Those who subscribe to the stakeholder approach and the competing-values approach believe that the organization must consider the values and interest of the various groups, or stakeholders, in the organization and consolidate these interests and views to achieve effectiveness (Daft, 2010). As explained by Daft, the stakeholder approach and the competing-values approach address the complexities involved in determining whether an organization is effective.

Effectiveness in Sport Organizations

Several sport management researchers have investigated the concept of organizational effectiveness. Wolfe and Putler (2002) examined the perceptions held by various stakeholders (e.g., faculty members, student–athletes, potential students, university students, members of the athletics department, and alumni) about the priorities of the intercollegiate athletics program. These priorities included win–loss record, graduation rates, violations, attendance, gender equity, number of teams, and finances. In a subsequent study, Wolfe, Hoeber, and Babiak (2002) investigated how perceptions of effectiveness differed according to the values of various intercollegiate athletics stakeholders. In a different context, Papadimitriou (2001) evaluated the effectiveness of Greek sport organizations from the athletes' perspectives. Her results showed that athletes perceived their sport organizations' effectiveness to be low because the following factors were poorly addressed: interest in the athletes, long-term planning, caliber of the board, sport science support, and internal and external liaisons. The athletes, as one group of stakeholders of the sport organizations, had different opinions about the sport organizations' levels of effectiveness than did the leaders of those organizations, another group of stakeholders. Papadimitriou concluded that leaders of the organizations should address the concerns of their elite athletes. Given the increasing commitment that athletes make to their sports in training and competition, leaders need to work to improve programs and services to meet the needs of their current athletes as well as their promising athletes.

ORGANIZATIONAL STRUCTURE

Jones (2010) defined **organizational structure** as a "formal system of task and authority relationships that control how people coordinate their actions and use of resources to achieve organizational goals" (p. 7). When addressing the topic of organizational structure, we usually refer to formal organizations, or what we typically see when we examine an organizational chart. As noted earlier in the chapter, figure 4.1 provides an example of a formal organization for a fictitious professional baseball organization. Note, however, that every organization also has an informal dimension. Figure 4.3 illustrates how the formal and informal relationships operate simultaneously within a fictitious sport organization. The solid lines illustrate the official relationships in the formal organization, and the dashed lines illustrate the informal relationships among employees who have lunch together on a regular basis and discuss everything from sports to company politics. These latter relationships are not officially acknowledged in the structure of the organization but are likely to either compete with, or support, the formal organization. Although the formal organization cannot control informal relationships, encouraging a positive organizational culture, a topic discussed later in the chapter, will increase the likelihood of mutual support.

organizational structure—Formal system of task and authority relationships that control how people coordinate their actions and use resources to achieve organizational goals.

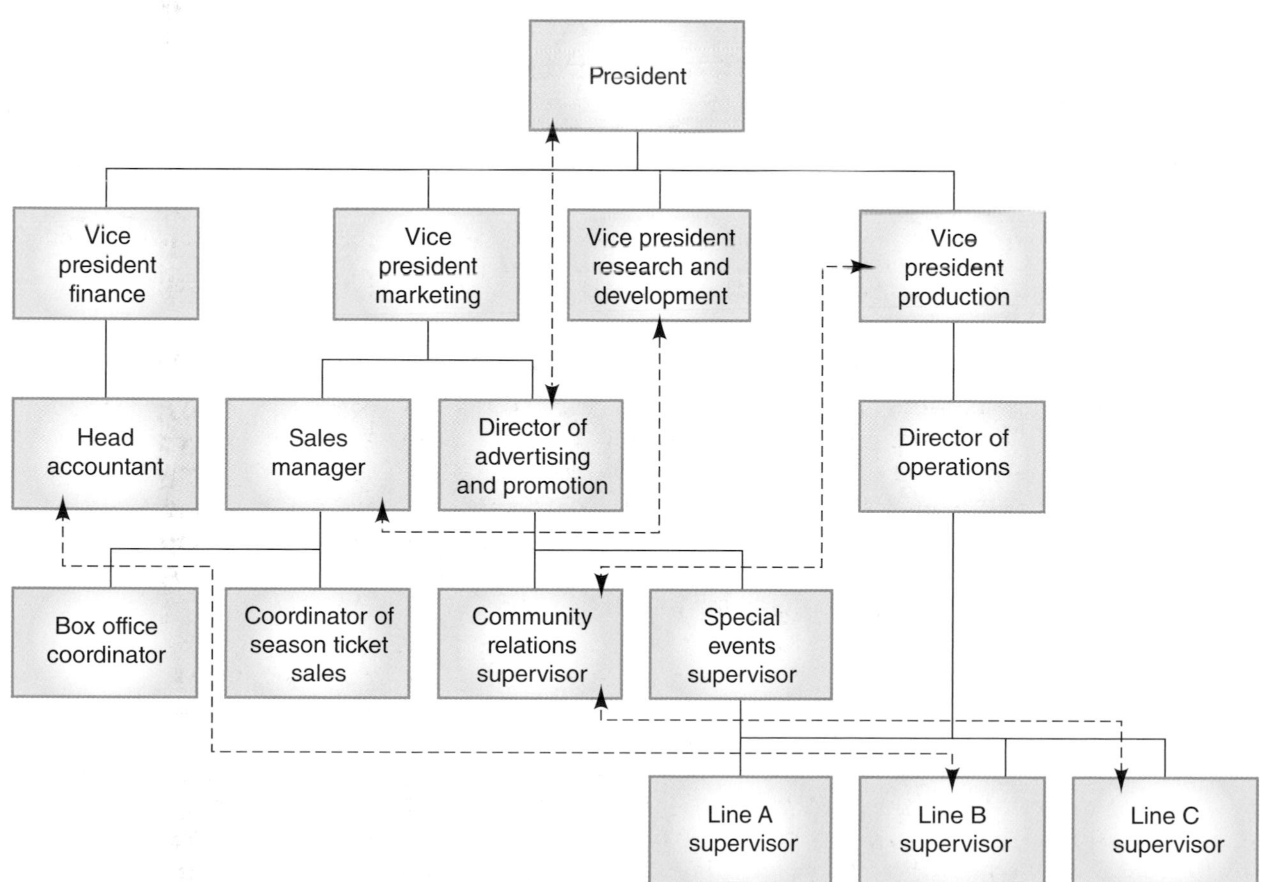

Figure 4.3 Formal and informal groups within a fictitious sport organization.

Dimensions of Organizational Structure

Organizational theorists generally agree on three major dimensions of structure: specialization, standardization, and centralization (Daft, 2010; Jones, 2010). Specialization concerns the division of labor, or the extent to which tasks and duties are divided into separate roles (Daft, 2010). According to Daft, when specialization is high, employees carry out a limited range of tasks and duties, and when specialization is low, individual employees carry out a wide range of tasks. The dimension of specialization is tied to the concept of complexity. There are three levels of complexity: vertical, horizontal, and spatial.

- Vertical complexity is evidenced by the number of levels that exist between the top executive in the organization (i.e., president, chief executive officer) and the lowest positions and units in the hierarchy (i.e., support positions and departments). The more levels there are, the more vertically complex the organization is.
- Horizontal complexity is shown in the number of units that exist across the organization.
- Spatial complexity refers to the number of geographical locations in which an organization operates. An organization situated in a number of locations would be considered spatially complex relative to an organization operating in a single location. For example, the UEFA (Union des Associations Européennes de Football), which includes 53 national football (soccer) associations, is more spatially complex than the CONCACAF (Confederation of North, Central American, and Caribbean Association Football), which has 40 national football associations, or the CONMEBOL (Confederación Sudamericana de Fútbol), which comprises 10 national football associations.

ACTION

Go to the OSG and complete the Learning in Action activity, which will test your understanding of sport management organizational structures.

Organizational Structure Makes a Difference

According to Daft (2010), 11 organizational dimensions are categorized into two broad areas: structural dimensions and contextual dimensions. Daft explained and provided examples of these dimensions. Structural dimensions refer to the labels that describe the "internal characteristics of an organization" (p. 15). The six types of structural dimensions are formalization, specialization, hierarchy of authority, centralization, professionalism, and personnel ratios. The contextual dimensions, he noted, "characterize the whole organization" (p. 15). The five types of contextual dimensions are size, technology, the environment, goals, and strategies.

A recent study in sport management examined the relationship of three structural dimensions—specialization, formalization, and centralization—and job satisfaction in the context of intercollegiate athletics (Cunningham, 2006). Specialization refers to the extent to which sport organizations can be vertically different (i.e., the number of layers in a sport organization) and horizontally different (i.e., in specialized roles to specific persons). Formalization refers to the number of written rules, procedures, written records of employee performance, and job descriptions. Lastly, centralization refers to the hierarchical level that has authority to make a decision.

Associate and assistant athletics directors of NCAA Division I member institutions were surveyed to examine the extent to which the relationships between the three selected elements of organizational dimensions noted earlier were mediated by job satisfaction. The statistical analyses revealed that the relationship of formalization was partially mediated by job satisfaction and that the relationship between centralization was fully mediated by job satisfaction. Although the study did not examine all 11 types of organizational dimensions (e.g., hierarchy of authority, professionalism, personnel ratios, size, technology, environment, goals), the results of the study did demonstrate that for the three organizational dimensions (i.e., formalization, specialization, and centralization) examined in the study, each has a significant effect on subsequent employee work outcomes in the sport industry.

Standardization is another dimension of structure. In the organizational theory literature, the terms *formalization* and *standardization* are often used interchangeably because high levels of formalization result in standardization. Formalization refers to "the amount of written documentation in the organization," (Daft, 2010, p. 15) such as job descriptions, policies, procedures, and regulations. This documentation is often used to control employees' behaviors and activities. A high degree of formalization leads to a high degree of standardization because employees who face similar situations will be expected to act in a similar fashion (Daft, 2010).

Centralization is the third dimension of organizational structure. This concept refers to "the hierarchical level that has authority to make a decision" (Daft, 2010, p. 17). When leaders and managers at the top of the hierarchy handle the decision-making activities, the organization is considered centralized. When decision making is delegated to levels throughout the organization, the organization is decentralized.

Typically, organizations are not completely centralized or decentralized. Some decisions in the organizations may be centralized (e.g., hiring and firing of employees, establishing the strategic direction of the organization), whereas other decisions may be decentralized (e.g., purchasing of organizational supplies, marketing strategies for products and services). Several factors affect whether decisions are centralized or decentralized:

- The cost (i.e., organizational resources) of the decision to the sport organization—the greater the cost, the more centralized the decision will be.
- The timing (how much time a sport manager has to make the decision)—the more urgent the decision, the more decentralized it will be.
- The qualifications of employees—the greater the number of expert employees involved throughout the sport organization, the more decentralized the decision will be.

Relationships Among the Dimensions of Organizational Structure

Specialization and standardization are interrelated. For example, high levels of specialization are typically associated with high levels of standardization. In other words, the greater the number of roles in the organization, the more formalized the organization will be (e.g., more job descriptions, more policies and procedures). In the same way, when an organization has a small number of roles, standardization will be low.

The relationship between standardization and centralization is not as easy to predict. Research in organizational theory has failed to demonstrate a consistent relationship between the two dimensions. As reported by Slack and Parent (2006), research in sport management has not examined the relationship between standardization and centralization. Similarly, research in sport organizations has not analyzed the relationship between specialization and centralization or the relationship between complexity and centralization. In situations where specialization and complexity are high and thus where roles, tasks, and duties within the organization are narrowly defined, one would expect decentralization of decision making. With low levels of specialization and complexity, one would expect centralization of decision making within the organization.

WEB

Go to the OSG and complete the Web search activity, which asks you to examine the organizational structure of three sport organizations.

ORGANIZATIONAL DESIGN

Jones (2010) defined **organizational design** as the process by which leaders "select and manage aspects of structure and culture" (p. 9) so that the organization can undertake its various activities and achieve its objectives. We will address the concept of organizational culture later in this chapter. For the moment, however, consider organizational design as the structural configurations that leaders use to arrange their organization's activities and operations so that it can reach its goals.

organizational design— Process by which leaders select and manage aspects or structure and culture of the organization.

Mintzberg conducted extensive work on organizational design. In a 1979 study he outlined different design configurations for various types of organizations based on the nature of their operations. A sporting goods organization in the business of manufacturing running shoes will be designed differently from a sport marketing agency or an event management business. Mintzberg based his designs on the interplay between five major parts of the organization that have been simplified as the following:

- Top management, which represents the leadership within the organization
- Middle management, which represents the managers who are between the leadership of the organization and the employees who are directly involved with the production of goods and services
- Technical core, which represents the group of employees responsible for the production of goods and services
- Administrative support staff, which represents the employees who provide a support function in the organization
- Technical support staff, which represents the employees who provide technical and technological support to assist in the production of goods and services and the introduction of innovative practices to enhance existing goods and services or create new ones (Daft, 2010)

Based on the relevance and importance of these five parts of the organization, various designs are proposed. Mintzberg (1979) identified several designs, among them the simple structure, the machine bureaucracy, and the professional bureaucracy. Subsequently, new designs have been added to reflect emerging realities for organizations. Among these new designs are entrepreneurial, innovative, missionary, and political designs.

The simple structure is typically a suitable design for small organizations that have only two major parts, top management and the technical core. Simple structures are characterized by low levels of specialization and standardization, and high levels of centralization. A small sport club that operates at the local level might have a simple structure.

Machine bureaucracy is a design appropriate for sporting goods manufacturers that have high levels of specialization, standardization, and centralization. In the machine bureaucracy design, all parts of the organization identified by Mintzberg are important—top management, middle management, technical core, administrative support staff, and technical support staff.

The professional bureaucracy is characterized by an important technical core and administrative support staff along with a limited technical support staff, middle management, and top management. This design would be appropriate for national sport organizations in which professionals (e.g., coaches, sport psychologists, professional administrators) are responsible for the products or services. Decentralization and high levels of specialization and standardization are also characteristics of this design.

Entrepreneurial organizations have a simple design. With a minimal number of staff, the organization has little need for specialization and standardization because the top of the organization coordinates much of the work. As outlined in Sack and Nadim (2002), Starter Corporation, a licensed sport apparel business now owned by Nike, was initially structured as an entrepreneurial organization.

Innovative designs allow greater flexibility than the bureaucratic design while providing decentralization not found in entrepreneurial organizations. Organizations featuring an innovative design emphasize a climate of creativity for the experts responsible for developing the product or the service. As a result, the power in the organization resides in the experts, who might be allowed to work in creative teams or on special projects. A marketing agency or ad agency with several accounts could exhibit an innovative design.

A missionary organization will be designed around its ideology. After employees become indoctrinated into the organization and identify strongly with the organization's ideology, they have the freedom to make decisions. In her research of organizational designs of organizing committees for the Olympic Games (OCOGs), Theodoraki (2001) found evidence of this missionary design.

Organizations with political designs are extremely flexible. They have no definite mechanisms of coordination. Typically, organizations that are temporarily created use this design so that they can address challenging transitions. An organization bidding to host a major sport event such as a World Cup or international championship, for example, might be designed as a political organization as it addresses needs to secure resources (e.g., funding, facilities, volunteers) and support in the hopes of hosting an event. Table 4.1 outlines the structural profiles of all Mintzberg's organizational designs discussed in this chapter.

STRUCTURE AND DESIGN OF SPORT ORGANIZATIONS

Several sport management scholars have investigated or provided an overview (e.g., Slack & Parent, 2006) of the structure and design of various sport organizations. As one example, Theodoraki (2001) applied Mintzberg's organizational design theories to OCOGs. She explained how the organizational design of OCOGs changed over time. The committees are created seven years before the Olympic Games take place, immediately following the IOC's decision about which bid city will host the Olympic Games. These organizations have a life span of eight years and are typically dismantled one year after hosting the Olympic Games. According to Theodoraki, OCOGs initially display a simple structure, Mintzberg's most basic design. She noted that OCOGs eventually display characteristics of the missionary design during the hosting of the Olympic Games and in the year following. In other words, as the members and employees of the OCOG become indoctrinated and socialized into the organization, they start to work collectively toward the organizational goals without the need for high levels of formalization or centralization.

STRATEGY

The managers and leaders of organizations use strategies, or plans, to cope with the environment. A plan refers to a course of action or a direction in which to move the

TABLE 4.1 Characteristics of Organizational Designs and Their Structures

Mintzberg's design types	Specialization or complexity	Formalization or standardization	Centralization
Simple structure	Low	Low	High
Machine bureaucracy	High	High	High
Professional bureaucracy	High	High	Low
Entrepreneurial	Low	Low	High
Innovative	High	Low	Low
Missionary	Low	High	Low
Political	High	Low	Undetermined

Mintzberg 1979; Slack & Parent 2006.

organization from one point to another. The development of a plan involves the following four steps:

1. Identifying the goals, objectives, and mission of the organization. The strategy must be congruent with the goals, objectives, and mission.
2. Determining the strategic objectives. This step involves assessing what the organization wants to achieve with the strategy, and it includes the SWOT analysis. As you will learn in chapter 12, a SWOT analysis consists of an assessment of the strengths and weaknesses of the organization and the opportunities and threats emanating from the organization's environment.
3. Identifying the resources required to implement the strategy. Without adequate resources, the organization will find it difficult to implement the strategy.
4. Establishing a timeline for implementing the strategy and identifying milestones to assess whether the organization is on target to achieve its objectives (Jones, 2010).

Organizations undertake the process of developing a strategy to gain a competitive advantage, or edge, over other organizations. They may achieve this advantage by acquiring scarce resources. For sport organizations, scarce resources may be financial resources, sponsorship opportunities, media visibility, participants or athletes, clients, members and fans, market share, equipment, or facilities. In turn, access to these resources might lead to success in sport competitions or greater profit because of increased fan attendance at games or increased sales of sporting goods. Strategies are extremely important for leaders and managers because they outline the major direction and activities of the organization for the future. As such, strategies serve as the road maps for the organization.

Olberding (2003) investigated the strategies of 33 Olympic sport organizations in the United States. He examined the following elements: each organization's competitive position relative to other US sport organizations, the domestic sport programs, the level of participation in the sport in the country, the costs involved in taking part in the sport, the level of visibility of the sport, the extent to which the sport was entrenched in the grass roots, the opportunities for competitions in the sport, and the new programs being developed within the organization. Using the framework developed by Thibault, Slack, and Hinings (1993) for Canadian sport organizations, Olberding found that US sport organizations used similar strategies (i.e., enhancers, refiners, innovators, and explorers).

Legg (2003) also examined strategies in sport organizations—specifically the Canadian Wheelchair Sports Association over a 30-year period (from the creation of the organization in 1967 until 1997). Legg identified three dominant strategies. Governance strategies included focus on planning, restructuring, recruitment of volunteers, and communications. Fund-raising strategies focused on generating financial resources for the organization's operations, programs, and services. Inclusion strategies included communication and negotiation with other sport organizations to integrate wheelchair sports into the able-bodied system.

Some research on strategy has focused on the development of partnerships (also known as interorganizational relationships or strategic alliances) with other organizations as a strategy to retain or gain a competitive advantage. All types of sport organizations (i.e., public, nonprofit, and commercial) are increasingly involved in alliances with other organizations to capitalize on opportunities and access more resources; to increase programs, services, and products offered to members or clients; and to reduce uncertainty.

In the context of sport, several researchers have applied the work of Oliver (1990) on the organizational motives behind the creation of partnerships. Oliver uncovered six motives: asymmetry, reciprocity, necessity, legitimacy, efficiency, and stability.

- Asymmetry refers to an organization's choice to enter into partnerships to exercise power over, and control of, another organization or its resources.
- Reciprocity refers to the creation of partnerships to achieve common or mutual goals or activities.
- Necessity refers to partnerships created to respond to legal obligations or regulations set by another organization (e.g., government).
- Legitimacy refers to the creation of partnerships to provide credibility or enhance its reputation, image, or authority.
- Efficiency refers to the need for an organization to improve its input–output ratio. As a result, partnerships may be created to decrease the cost of raw materials needed for producing goods and services.
- Stability refers to the development of partnerships to reduce uncertainty and increase predictability for the organization.

Banners that showcase a team's previous successes are representative artifacts of a sport organization's culture.
Photo courtesy of Paul M. Pedersen.

These six motives for partnership creation were featured in the works by Babiak (2007) and Turner and Shilbury (2008, 2010). Babiak studied a training center for high-performance elite athletes and its network of partnerships to achieve its goal of providing the best possible training environment for these world-class athletes. The training center's motives for developing partnerships with other nonprofit organizations, with public organizations, and with private commercial organizations were varied, but these alliances all contributed to the center's strategy to enhance the training environment of the athletes. On a different topic, Turner and Shilbury examined the development of partnerships between clubs of the Australian Football League and the National Rugby League with broadcasters. They found different motives for clubs to undertake strategic alliances with broadcasters. Furthermore, the authors discussed the effect of broadcasting technologies on the establishment of partnerships. Given the increasing importance of broadcasters for sport organizations (e.g., for access to much-needed resources), further studies addressing the relationships between sport leagues and clubs with media are imperative.

ORGANIZATIONAL CULTURE

Edgar Schein (1985), one of the pioneers of research into culture in organizations, defined organizational culture as "a pattern of basic assumptions—invented, discovered, or developed by a given group as it learns to cope with its problems of external adaptation and internal integration" (p. 9). Schein explained that organizations consider this set of assumptions valid and as a result promote them to new members as the appropriate and correct way to act in the workplace. Jones (2010) defined **organizational culture** as "the set of shared values and norms that controls organizational members' interactions with each other and with people outside of the organization" (p. 179).

organizational culture—Set of shared values and norms that controls organizational members' interactions with each other and with people outside the organization.

Culture manifests itself in different ways throughout organizations. These manifestations include stories and myths, symbols, language, ceremonies and rites, physical setting, and symbolic artifacts. Stories and myths are narratives that may be based on truth, fiction, or a combination of the two. Symbols consist of events, objects, or acts that convey meanings for the organization. Organizational logos, slogans, and mission statements are symbols. Language refers to the terminology and jargon that

SPORT ORGANIZATIONS IN THE ISLAMIC REPUBLIC OF IRAN

By Hassan Asadi
University of Tehran, IRAN

Over the past few decades, Iran's sport industry has grown tremendously, particularly in championship and international sports, long- and short-term development plans, and sport facilities and equipment. For example, Iran has hosted a number of international competitions (e.g., the 1974 Asian Games), and it occupied 6th place among the 43 countries that participated in the 2006 Asian Games.

The physical education field was formed in 1938, when the Teacher Training College was established. Today, four subfields (sport management, sport medicine, sport physiology, and motor learning) are offered up to the PhD level at physical education universities. Twelve physical education faculties and 27 physical education professional groups are active throughout the country. In addition, an international journal and 11 national sport journals are published in Iran. Annually, four national conferences and one international conference on sport sciences are held.

The government provides annual budgets to the sport organizations in the provinces, the National Olympic Committee, and the sport federations. Since 2004, the budget allocated to sport has increased 200%; consequently, many sport facilities have been constructed. Student-level and university-level sports are free. At the championship level, private sport clubs and local sport industries are financially autonomous.

The Physical Education Organization began func-

Icon Sports Media.

Iranian body builder Mohsen Ghorannevis competes during the 2006 Asian Games.

organizational members use to communicate with each other. Ceremonies and rites include social events and award and recognition events that leaders organize. These events often reinforce organizational values. Physical setting includes the office space and objects found in the organization. Artifacts are items found in the organization's physical setting. Photographs of past successes or ceremonies; banners; copies of past marketing campaigns; and displays of awards, achievements, and products are examples of artifacts that could be evident in the physical setting. The setting and these artifacts are representative of the organization.

Colyer (2000) investigated organizational culture in nonprofit Australian sport organizations. Her findings revealed the existence of "tensions between two of the main groups of people (employees and volunteers) in sport organizations" (p. 338). She explained that if leaders were to draw cultural profiles of their organizations, they would become aware of tensions and could develop strategies to change the culture

tioning in 1976 and is the largest sport governing organization in the country. The core activities of the Physical Education Organization are facilitating international sport exchanges, promoting Iran's and Asia's sports, as well as sport marketing in Iran and developing youth. The Physical Education Organization has over 50 federations in 31 provinces and a capital district at the provincial level. Through its efforts, the Iranian sport industry receives remarkable attention from people all over the world.

The Physical Education Organization enjoys two strategic plans: the 20-year vision of the country as its long-term goals and the 5-year development plan. In addition, annual action plans are executed and evaluated based on the following criteria: fulfillment of long-term goals, completion of annual action plans, appropriateness of goal setting, and suitability of the strategic plan for achieving goals. These evaluations are designed to keep the organization running effectively.

Another significant sport organization in Iran is the National Olympic Committee (NOC), established as a nonpublic association in 1947. The major business of the NOC is to develop sport, to educate youth, to support Olympic affairs, to promote sport fields as well as the Olympic and Asian Games, and to encourage sport ethics. The NOC has focused on the construction of a healthy society and has performed pivotal roles in expanding the significance of sport and the sport industry to increase the national desire for sport. The NOC will continue to support sport facilities and projects related to the development of youth and to promote the sport industry so that the whole nation will be able to enjoy a healthy and pleasant lifestyle. This support will pave the way to a society that delivers energy and hope to all people in Iran. Because the Physical Education Organization, the NOC, and other sport organizations and federations are active and productive, we are confident that the sport industry has a bright future in Iran.

INTERNATIONAL LEARNING ACTIVITY #1

Many organizations similar to those in Iran exist throughout the world. An example is the Maccabi World Organization (MWO). Explore the MWO Web site at www.maccabiworld.org/. Prepare a paper or a presentation about this organization, including its purpose, history, scope, and events. Many other aspects of the MWO are interesting and pertinent to the world of sport.

INTERNATIONAL LEARNING ACTIVITY #2

Go to the Web site of the North American Society for Sport Management (NASSM) at www.nassm.com/. Click on the link "NASSM Conference Abstract Archive." When you reach the archive, do a search for "organizational culture." You will find the abstracts of papers about organizational culture that have been presented at NASSM conferences in recent years. Read through them and identify at least five that are pertinent to the material in this chapter. Explain how sport organization managers could apply the information in each of those papers.

and thus enhance organizational effectiveness. She also discussed the presence of subcultures—an important element in any examination of an organization's culture.

Other studies have focused on the values held in sport organizations. Because values are central to an organization's culture, they are often the focus of research. Milton-Smith (2002) discussed the scandals, corruptions, and controversies involving the IOC in the late 1990s and early 2000s. He explained how concerns about the Olympic Games mirror concerns about the movement toward globalization. Concerns regarding "winning at any price; commercial exploitation by MNCs [multinational corporations]; corruption; intense national rivalry; [and] the competitive advantage of advanced nations" were identified (p. 132). In analyzing the case of the Sydney 2000 Olympic Games, he drew on the values espoused by the Olympic Movement and demonstrated how members of the IOC and members of the Sydney Organizing Committee for the Olympic Games (SOCOG) violated those values. According to Milton-Smith's analysis, the IOC and SOCOG compromised values such as honesty, transparency, objectivity (i.e., avoiding conflict of interest), fairness, dignity, and loyalty. Although it was not the purpose of his work to discuss the organizational culture of the IOC or the SOCOG per se, Milton-Smith explained that the leadership of the IOC cultivated a culture of excess while overlooking questionable and unethical practices of its members. In other words, the Olympic ideals and the core values of the Olympic Movement were used as marketing tools to showcase the IOC but were never translated into the culture of the organization.

ORGANIZATIONAL CHANGE

Organizational change is defined as "the process by which organizations move from their present state to some desired future state to increase their effectiveness" (Jones, 2010, p. 270). To remain competitive, relevant, and viable, organizations constantly undergo change. Several frameworks have been developed to study organizational change. In the following pages, we will feature two frameworks.

The first framework is identified as the organizational life cycle or the model of organizational growth. This framework is an adaptation of Greiner's (1972) work on the various stages of evolution and revolution that an organization undertakes as it grows and the work of Quinn and Cameron (1983) on the life cycle of an organization. Figure 4.4 provides a graphic illustration of the evolution and revolution stages as an organization grows. There are four stages of growth for organizations (i.e., entrepreneurial, collectivity, formalization, and elaboration) and each of these stages is punctuated by a crisis (i.e., need for leadership, need for delegation with control, need

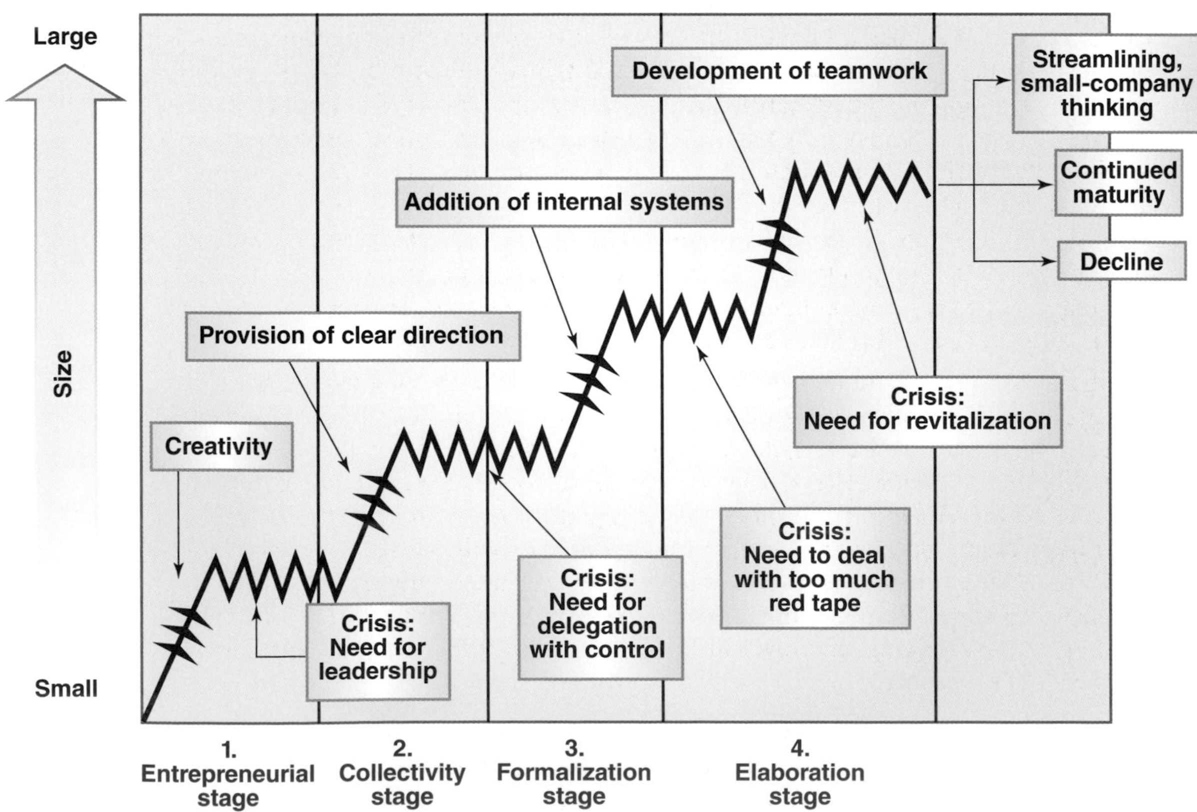

Figure 4.4 Organization stages of development.

Adapted from Greiner 1972; Quinn and Cameron 1983.

to deal with too much red tape, and need for revitalization). These stages and crises are briefly described in the next paragraphs.

- *Entrepreneurial stage:* This stage is based on the vision of the founder of the organization. The founder is investing her or his energies in all aspects of the organization (e.g., management, technical production, marketing, delivery of products or services) to ensure that the organization survives and grows. As a catalyst for progression toward the next growth stage, the organization typically undergoes a crisis identified as *need for leadership*. During this crisis, the founder becomes overwhelmed with the quantity of work involved and with the increasing responsibilities that she or he holds within the organization. As a result, the founder who created the organization needs help.
- *Collectivity stage:* In this stage the leadership crisis has been addressed. The organization is now developing clear goals and establishing its direction. Functional areas, departments, and a hierarchy of authority are created to help divide and assign the work to newly hired employees. Also, formal communication mechanisms are being developed to help in the coordination of the work to be achieved and to address the rapid growth experienced by the organization at this stage. For progression into the next stage, the organization in the collectivity stage will go through a crisis termed *need for delegation with control*. During this crisis, lower-level employees are limited in their ability to make decisions autonomously, and as they gain experience and expertise in their functional areas, they become increasingly frustrated with the strong top-down leadership. During this crisis, leaders develop coordination and control mechanisms within the organization and provide employees with some level of autonomy and decision-making power.
- *Formalization stage:* During this stage, rules and procedures are developed. Job descriptions are created, and communication becomes more formal. Top management executives invest their time in strategic planning and allow middle management the responsibility of managing the operations. During this stage, decentralized units may be created and incentive systems for managers may be introduced to enhance the effectiveness of the organization. As the organization increases its levels of formalization and standardization, the crisis of *too much red tape* will surface. With systems and high levels of formalization in place, middle management may begin to experience some constraints in their ability to do their work within the organization. Specifically, too much bureaucracy may paralyze employees and stifle innovation. The organization is large and complex and will require adjustments to reach the next stage.
- *Elaboration stage:* To address the increasing red tape, leaders and managers within the organization undertake collaboration and teamwork. This collaboration occurs across different hierarchical levels, departments or divisions, and functions. Leaders, managers, and employees work together to solve problems. During this stage, formal systems may be simplified in favor of more collaboration between leaders, managers, and employees. As the organization matures, its crisis woes will be the *need for revitalization*. Renewal may be needed as the organization's alignment with its environment becomes askew. A streamlining of operations may be necessary for the organization to respond better to a changing environment. Also, innovations provide the organization with new energy and spirit.

The various stages involved in an organization's life cycle help us understand the changes that organizations go through as they develop and mature. As reviewed in the previous paragraphs, this life cycle is punctuated with challenges and crises along the way. If a leader responds to these crises, she or he can lead the organization to success.

Another framework to study organizational change is the contextualist approach developed by Pettigrew (1987, 1990). The contextualist approach acknowledges that change does not take place in isolation or in a brief time. Understanding change is important, but it must be accomplished over a long term by considering three elements: content, context, and process. To acquire a full understanding of change, one must first examine the content of change, which is best done by answering the question, What changed? The next element of Pettigrew's framework is the context of change. The focus is on answering the question, Why did the change occur? Context includes two sections: the inner context and the outer context. Inner context consists of internal elements at play within organizations, such as strategy, culture, and the structure of organizations. Outer context refers to general political, economic, and social forces at work within the organizational environment. After content and context of change have been uncovered, the process of change needs to be examined. The process of change is concerned with answering the question, How has change occurred? In uncovering the process of change, leadership is often a key component because change agents often contribute to the adoption of change within the organization. By answering the what, why, and how, leaders are in a better position to understand change in their organizations.

A few studies have applied Pettigrew's contextual approach to organizational change to the sport context. Specifically, Cousens, Babiak, and Slack (2001) investigated changes in the National Basketball Association (NBA) over a 17-year period, focusing on the relationship marketing approach adopted by the league. The scholars discussed the relevance of Pettigrew's approach to understand the need to foster relationships within and outside the NBA. In another example of Pettigrew's work applied to the context of sport, Caza (2000) examined the adoption of innovative practices in a Canadian provincial sport organization. His investigation looked at the extent to which organizational members were receptive to the implementation of two initiatives. Caza found that Pettigrew's framework was useful in understanding challenges related to the implementation of innovations in the sport sector.

Thibault and Babiak (2005) also used Pettigrew's framework to investigate changes in Canada's sport system. They were specifically interested in examining how and why the Canadian sport system changed to accommodate greater involvement from athletes. They found that increased representation by athletes on decision-making boards of sport organizations, greater funding of athletes, the creation of national sport training centers, and the creation of a forum for athletes to resolve conflicts between themselves and sport organizations or coaches all contributed to an athlete-centered sport system. Thibault and Babiak were able to understand the nature of the change that had occurred in light of the context in which Canada's sport system operated. They were also able to examine the leadership role assumed by change agents to bring about the adoption of more athlete-centered change in the sport system.

CRITICAL THINKING IN SPORT ORGANIZATIONS

Critical thinking is important in sport organizations. As introduced in chapter 1, sport leaders, managers, and employees with critical thinking skills are better able to solve problems, make informed decisions, and develop comprehensive plans and strategies for the organization. Given the constant flux in the environment, sport managers must adopt a critical thinking approach whereby they can analyze and evaluate information, facts, evidence, assumptions, ideas, and implications.

Numerous sport management scholars have expounded on the importance of developing critical thinking skills. For instance, Boucher (1998) explained that "a true measure of whether [sport management] graduates are truly prepared is *not* the courses listed on their transcripts but whether they have been educated to *think* intelligently and *make decisions* about issues they will face in the dynamic world of managing a sport enterprise" (p. 81). Similarly, Harris (1993) urged sport management educators to give greater emphasis to students' development of critical and reflective competencies. She surmised that such an emphasis would prepare professionals who would be able to "free themselves from traditional ways of identifying and solving problems, [and] to look at problems from new perspectives" (p. 322). In the same vein, Edwards (1999) suggested that critical reflection should receive more attention than it currently receives in sport management so that we can find "new, less oppressive, and more just ways of creating and managing sport" (p. 79). Furthermore, Frisby (2005) proposed that sport management educators become "versed in critical social science theories" so that they can help students become "strong critical thinkers who will make positive contributions to society" (p. 5). The clear implication of all these suggestions is that, as the managers of the future, you will need exceptional thinking skills to make the necessary decisions to deal effectively and responsibly with the myriad challenges that you will encounter. For instance, sport managers will have to make difficult decisions as they address issues regarding where limited funds are invested (e.g., in high-performance sport or sport for all).

PORTFOLIO

Complete the critical thinking portfolio activity in the OSG, consulting as needed the "Eight Critical Thinking Questions" section in chapter 1.

ETHICS IN SPORT ORGANIZATIONS

Besides applying critical thinking skills, sport organization employees, managers, and leaders will need to act ethically. In recent years, several ethical issues have surfaced in the context of sport. For example, incidents involving drugs and cheating in sport; violence in sport; questionable behaviors from athletes, coaches, and referees on and off the court or field; overtraining of children involved in high-performance sport; eating disorders among athletes; recruitment violations within intercollegiate athletics programs; corruption in decision making; and athlete hazing have all had an effect on sport and sport organizations. As mentioned in the section on organizational culture, the Milton-Smith (2002) study of unethical practices by the members of the IOC and OCOG led to serious negative repercussions for both organizations. Although rules, procedures, and codes of ethics were developed within these organizations, the individuals responsible for upholding the standards of the organizations did not respect them. Managers and leaders of sport organizations are constantly facing situations, events, and issues that challenge their ability to make ethical decisions. In the next chapter, we will provide more details on managers' and leaders' involvement in ethical decision making.

PORTFOLIO

Complete the ethical issues portfolio activity in the OSG, consulting as needed the "Guidelines for Making Ethical Decisions" section in chapter 1.

Summary

The organizational theory topics covered in this chapter—management concepts, organizational environment, effectiveness, structure and design, strategy, culture, and change— are all important to consider and monitor. Left unchecked, problems in these areas can reduce the effectiveness of a sport organization and, ultimately, lead to its demise. Note that these topics are interrelated. For example, the structure and design of the sport organization may affect, or be affected by, the culture of that organization. Similarly, the ability to develop and implement a strategy or to cope with change may affect, or be affected by, the structure and design of the sport organization.

These interrelationships take on even more complexity with consideration of the role that people play in the development and management of organizations in the sport industry. The following chapter addresses the topic of individuals and their roles in organizations.

QUIZ TIME

Did you grasp all the key points in this chapter? Go to the OSG for a short quiz to test your understanding of the material.

Review Questions

1. How would you define the term *organization*? What are three types of sport organizations?
2. What is the difference between effectiveness and efficiency? What is the best approach to the study of organizational effectiveness?
3. Select one sport organization. How would you describe its structure using the three structural dimensions featured in this chapter?
4. What organizational design would be most appropriate for a sporting goods manufacturer? For a sport marketing agency? For an organization bidding for the right to host a major international event?
5. What is the difference between the general environment and the specific environment?
6. Why would sport organizations choose to develop strategies?
7. In what ways can some organizational cultures be positive for a sport organization and in what ways can other cultures be negative for a sport organization?
8. How can you use Pettigrew's contextual approach to study change in a sport organization of your choice?

References

Babiak, K. (2007). Determinants of interorganizational relationships: The case of a Canadian nonprofit sport organization. *Journal of Sport Management, 21*, 338–376.

Barnard, C.I. (1938) *The functions of the executive.* Cambridge, MA: Harvard University Press.

Boucher, R.L. (1998). Toward achieving a focal point for sport management: A binocular perspective. *Journal of Sport Management, 12*, 76–85.

Caza, A. (2000). Context receptivity: Innovation in an amateur sport organization. *Journal of Sport Management, 14*, 227–242.

Chelladurai, P. (2009) *Managing organizations for sport and physical activity: A systems perspective* (3rd ed.). Scottsdale, AZ: Holcomb Hathaway.

Colyer, S. (2000). Organizational culture in selected western Australian sport organizations. *Journal of Sport Management, 14*, 321–341.

Cousens, L., Babiak, K.M., & Slack, T. (2001). Adopting a relationship marketing paradigm: The case of the National Basketball Association. *International Journal of Sports Marketing and Sponsorship, 2*, 331–355.

Cunningham, G.B. (2006). Does structure make a difference? The effect of organizational structure on job satisfaction and organizational commitment. *International Journal of Sport Management, 7*, 327–346.

Daft, R.L. (2010). *Organization theory and design* (10th ed.). Mason, OH: South-Western, Cengage Learning.

Edwards, A. (1999). Reflective practice in sport management. *Sport Management Review, 2*, 67–81.

Fayol. H. (1917). *Administration industrielle et generale.* Paris: Dunod & Pinat.

Frisby, W. (2005). The good, the bad, and the ugly: Critical sport management research. *Journal of Sport Management, 19*, 1–12.

Greiner, L.E. (1972). Evolution and revolution as organizations grow. *Harvard Business Review, 50*(4), 37–46.

Harris, J.C. (1993). Using kinesiology: A comparison of applied veins in the subdisciplines. *Quest, 45*, 389–412.

Jones, G.R. (2010). *Organizational theory, design, and change.* Upper Saddle River, NJ: Prentice Hall.

Legg, D. (2003). Organizational strategy in amateur sport organization: A case study. *International Journal of Sport Management, 4*, 205–223.

Milton-Smith, J. (2002). Ethics, the Olympics and the search for global values. *Journal of Business Ethics, 35*, 131–142.

Mintzberg, H. (1979). *The structuring of organizations.* Englewood Cliffs, NJ: Prentice Hall.

Mullin, B.J. (1980) Sport management: The nature and utility of the concept. *Arena Review, 4*, 1-11.

Olberding, D.J. (2003). Examining strategy content in U.S. Olympic sport organizations. *International Journal of Sport Management, 4*, 6–24.

Oliver, C. (1990). Determinants of interorganizational relationships: Integration and future directions. *Academy of Management Review, 15*, 241–265.

Papadimitriou, D. (2001). An exploratory examination of the prime beneficiary approach of organizational effectiveness: The case of elite athletes of Olympic and non-Olympic sports. *European Journal of Sport Management, 8*, 63–82.

Peters, T., & Waterman, R. (1982). *In search of excellence: Lessons from America's best-run companies.* New York: Warner.

Pettigrew, A.M. (1987). Context and action in the transformation of the firm. *Journal of Management Studies, 24*, 649–670.

Pettigrew, A.M. (1990). Longitudinal field research on change: Theory and practice. *Organization Science, 1*, 267–292.

Quinn, R.E., & Cameron, K. (1983). Organizational life cycles and shifting criteria of effectiveness: Some preliminary evidence. *Management Science, 29*, 33–51.

Sack, A.L., & Nadim, A. (2002). Strategic choices in a turbulent environment: A case study of Starter Corporation. *Journal of Sport Management, 16*, 36–53.

Schein, E.H. (1985). *Organizational culture and leadership.* San Francisco: Jossey-Bass.

Senge, P. (1990). *The fifth discipline: The art and practice of the learning organization.* New York: Doubleday/Currency.

Slack, T. (1997). *Understanding sport organizations: The application of organization theory.* Champaign, IL: Human Kinetics.

Slack, T., & Parent, M.M. (2006). *Understanding sport organizations. The application of organization theory* (2nd ed.). Champaign, IL: Human Kinetics.

Taylor, F.W. (1911). *The principles of scientific management.* New York: Harper.

Theodorakis, E.I. (2001). A conceptual framework for the study of structural configurations of Organising Committees for the Olympic Games (OCOGs). *European Journal for Sport Management*, *8*, 106–124.

Thibault, L., & Babiak, K. (2005). Organizational changes in Canada's sport system: Toward an athlete-centred approach. *European Sport Management Quarterly*, *5*, 105–132.

Thibault, L., Slack, T., & Hinings, C.R. (1993). A framework for the analysis of strategy in nonprofit sport organizations. *Journal of Sport Management*, *7*, 25–43.

Turner, P., & Shilbury, D. (2008). Broadcasting technology and its influence on sport broadcaster inter-organisational relationship formation. *International Journal of Sport Management and Marketing*, *3*, 167–183.

Turner, P.E., & Shilbury, D. (2010). The impact of emerging technology in sport broadcasting on the preconditions for interorganizational relationship formation in professional football. *Journal of Sport Management*, *24*, 10–44.

Wolfe, R., Hoeber, L., & Babiak, K. (2002). Perceptions of the effectiveness of sport organisations: The case of intercollegiate athletics. *European Sport Management Quarterly*, *2*, 135–156.

Wolfe, R., & Putler, D. (2002). How tight are the ties that bind stakeholder groups? *Organization Science*, *13*, 64–80.

Zanger, B.K., & Parks, J.B. (Eds.). (1984). *Sport management curricula: The business and education nexus.* Bowling Green, OH: School of Health, Physical Education, and Recreation, Bowling Green State University.

Zeigler, E.F. (1987). Sport management: Past, present, future. *Journal of Sport Management*, *1*, 4–24.

Zeigler, E.F., & Spaeth, M. (1975). *Administrative theory and practice in physical education and athletics.* Englewood Cliffs, NJ: Prentice Hall.

HISTORICAL MOMENTS

- **1917** Frank Calder named first president of the NHL
- **1920** Kenesaw Mountain Landis appointed first commissioner of MLB and Jim Thorpe appointed first president of the American Professional Football Association (now National Football League [NFL])
- **1946** Maurice Podoloff appointed president of the Basketball Association of America (now NBA)
- **1948** John Wooden became head coach of men's basketball at UCLA
- **1962** Marvin Miller became first executive director of Major League Baseball Players Association (MLBPA)
- **1975** Pat Summitt won first game as head coach of the Tennessee Lady Vols
- **1984** David Stern named NBA commissioner
- **1986** Anita DeFrantz became first American woman and first African American on the International Olympic Committee (IOC)
- **1992** Donna Lopiano became executive director of the Women's Sport Foundation; served until 2007
- **1998** Bud Selig named MLB commissioner and Sepp Blatter elected president of Fédération Internationale de Football Association (FIFA)
- **2001** Jacques Rogge elected president of the IOC
- **2003** Myles Brand became National Collegiate Athletic Association (NCAA) CEO and served until his death in 2009
- **2005** Valerie Ackerman became first female president of USA Basketball; served until 2008
- **2006** Roger Goodell named NFL commissioner
- **2007** Tonya Antonucci named Women's Professional Soccer (WPS) commissioner

Photo courtesy of Paul M. Pedersen.

5

MANAGERIAL LEADERSHIP IN SPORT ORGANIZATIONS

Jerome Quarterman ■ Ming Li ■ Lucie Thibault

LEARNING OBJECTIVES

1. Understand the central roles and functions that people play in sport organizations.
2. Define organizational behavior and its application to the sport industry.
3. Differentiate between the terms *management* and *leadership*.
4. Understand the concepts of decision making, authority, and power.
5. Identify and understand the principles of human resource management.
6. Understand the importance of diversity in the workplace.
7. Explain the critical role that theory plays in the management of people within sport organizations.

GET A JOB!

☑ Continue on your journey in sport management by going to the Online Study Guide (OSG) at www.HumanKinetics.com/ContemporarySportManagement. Check out the job opportunities and consider the skills and experiences that can help you succeed in sport management.

Key Terms

behaviors centered on employees
behaviors centered on tasks
disturbance handlers
figureheads
leadership
management
managerial leadership
monitors
negotiators
spokespersons

In this chapter, we introduce the roles that individuals play in sport organizations. Whereas the previous chapter dealt with structural, design, and environmental features of sport organizations, this chapter examines the roles that individuals play within those organizations. Thus, this chapter is about organizational behavior. Organizational behavior is defined as the study of individuals and groups in organizations (Robbins & Judge, 2008). According to Schermerhorn, Hunt, and Osborn (2008), organizational behavior "is a multidisciplinary field devoted to understanding individual and group behavior, interpersonal processes, and organization dynamics" (p. 5).

This chapter addresses a number of topics related to people in the sport management workplace. The management functions and roles are also introduced, and an examination of leadership and leaders relative to the role of the sport manager follows. The concepts of decision making, authority, and power are then explained. Human resource management, including recruitment and selection of employees, orientation, training, and performance evaluation of these employees, is explained next. The chapter concludes with discussions of diversity in the workplace and the relevance of critical thinking in managing and leading people in sport organizations.

THEORETICAL APPROACHES TO MANAGEMENT

The success of sport organizations ultimately depends on how effectively managers apply their management and leadership skills. Hersey, Blanchard, and Johnson (2008) provided one of the most comprehensive definitions of **management** as "the process of working with and through individuals and groups and other resources (such as equipment, capital, and technology) to accomplish organizational goals" (p. 7). Numerous theoretical approaches to management and managing people in organizations have been developed. We classify these approaches into three basic types: scientific management, human relations management, and the process approach (also known as administrative management). In the following paragraphs, we summarize these approaches.

management—The process of working with and through individuals and groups to accomplish organizational goals.

Scientific Management Approach

Early theorists believed that the primary responsibility of managers was to increase workers' output. Frederick Taylor (1911) developed this approach, in which the major concern was to scrutinize the performance of individual workers. The key was that workers who produced more than others would receive greater rewards. This approach advocated paying people by the number of units produced or sold rather than by the length of time (e.g., hours) that they worked. In the sport industry, this approach is best illustrated when employees work on a commission basis. For example, a game-day salesperson might earn a commission based on the number of programs sold. The sport manager working under such conditions would focus primarily on how effective each individual game-day salesperson was in selling game programs. The scientific management approach considers pay and working conditions to be the most important factors in increasing a worker's performance.

Human Relations Management Approach

The human relations approach grew out of studies conducted at Western Electric's Hawthorne, Illinois, plant during the late 1920s and early 1930s (Mayo, 1933). Mayo's research on more than 20,000 employees found that when employees believed that they were important, they became more cohesive and productive. The researcher's conclusion was that managers' concern for workers would lead to higher rates of job satisfaction, which would result in better performance and higher productivity (Staw, 1986).

Process Approach to Management

The process approach has been the predominant theoretical framework used in the study and practice of management in recent times. Unlike the scientific and human relations management approaches, the process approach focuses on managing the organization as a whole entity. Using the process management approach, we review in the following paragraphs various management functions and roles assumed by managers.

MANAGEMENT FUNCTIONS

The process approach to management uses a set of ongoing, interactive activities—known as the underlying processes of management—to accomplish the goals and objectives of organizations, departments, or work units. Such processes were first introduced more than six decades ago as POSDCORB (Gulick & Urwick, 1937). POSDCORB is the acronym for planning, organizing, staffing, directing, coordinating, reporting, and budgeting. The original seven processes have since been reduced to five functions: planning, staffing, organizing, directing, and controlling and evaluating (Jones & George, 2009). Figure 5.1 illustrates that these underlying processes flow in all directions and that decisions made in each component affect all other components. Ultimately, all the processes revolve around the manager's actions and decisions.

In sport organizations, the management process typically starts with planning and ends with controlling and evaluating. Managers might engage in the activities in various sequences, and sometimes they perform several activities simultaneously as they carry out the responsibilities of their jobs. The element common to all the processes, whenever they are performed, is decision making. Table 5.1 provides definitions of each function, as well as examples of how the manager of a private sport club might practice them. The concepts of decision making, authority, and power will be covered later in this chapter. We now proceed to a discussion of the roles of managers.

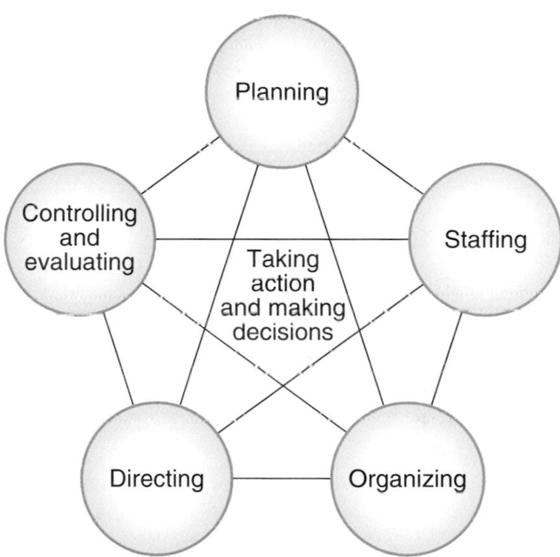

Figure 5.1 The management process approach.

MANAGERIAL ROLES

Besides the various management functions, managers must also assume a variety of roles (Mintzberg, 1973, 1990). Mintzberg defined a role as a set of expected behaviors associated with a managerial position. Based on Mintzberg's theory, the typical manager performs 10 roles, which are classified into three categories: interpersonal, informational, and decisional.

Interpersonal Roles

Figurehead, leader, and liaison are the three specific interpersonal roles that a manager performs. When managers engage in these roles, they are primarily involved in interpersonal relationships with others. As **figureheads,** managers perform a variety of symbolic and ceremonial duties. Managers are engaged in the figurehead role when they welcome visitors to an organization, represent the organization at a public function, or cut the ribbon for a new facility.

figureheads—Managers acting in symbolic and ceremonial ways.

The leader role relates to managers' relationships with their followers. As leaders, managers recruit, select, train, motivate, evaluate, and direct the followers' energies

TABLE 5.1 Management Process of a General Manager in a Private Sport Club

Underlying process	Definition	Example
Planning	Developing and implementing goals, objectives, strategies, procedures, policies, and rules to produce goods and services in the most effective and efficient manner.	The general manager of a private sport club predicts the increase in enrollment at the start of the new year and arranges for the facility to be open 18 hours per day instead of 15 hours per day.
Staffing	Recruiting, selecting, orienting, training, developing, and replacing employees to produce goods and services in the most effective and efficient manner.	The general manager advertises the positions: three teaching pros, one maintenance person, and one administrative assistant. The general manager then holds interviews, checks references, makes job offers, and selects the staff needed for the golf program.
Organizing	Arranging resources (e.g., human, financial, equipment, supplies, time, space, information) to produce goods and services in the most effective and efficient manner.	After conducting an assessment, the general manager establishes a work unit for teaching golf at the club. The general manager appoints a full-time coordinator who will coordinate three teaching pros and a new golf course with an adequate budget.
Directing	Influencing members (e.g., subordinates, peers, supervisors) as individuals and as groups to produce goods and services in the most effective and efficient manner.	The general manager encourages the golf teaching pros to prepare weekend course packages for local executives who have expressed an interest in learning golf skills.
Controlling and evaluating	Evaluating whether the employees are on task and making progress toward achieving the goals and adhering to the guidelines and standards for producing goods and services in the most effective and efficient manner.	After three months the general manager monitors the progress of the new golf program with the pros and discusses ways to make the program more attractive to potential new members.

and efforts toward accomplishing the organization's goals. Leaders are also responsible for coordinating the work of followers. Examples of the leader role are conducting a workshop on computer programming for the support staff and rewarding a staffer for outstanding job performance. The director of ticket sales exhibits the role of leader when providing flexible working hours for the telemarketing staff.

The liaison role refers to a manager's ability to develop and cultivate relationships with individuals and groups outside the work unit or organization. For instance, coordinators of concessions usually maintain contact with vendors to determine when special sales will occur on certain supplies. Directors of campus recreation often meet with peer directors to discuss important issues before official voting sessions. These managers are acting in the liaison role.

Informational Roles

Managers assume informational roles when they exchange and process information. These roles include monitor, disseminator, and spokesperson. As **monitors,** managers scan the environment for information about trends and events that can affect the organization. They collect information from a variety of sources, including subordinates, peers, superiors, contacts, news media, electronic mail, the Internet (e.g., Web sites, Twitter accounts, blogs, message boards), gossip, and hearsay. A supervisor who has a casual conversation with other supervisors about the organization's plans to downsize the support staff is engaging in the monitor role.

monitors—Managers in the role of scanning the environment for information about trends and events that can affect the organization.

As managers collect information, they become the nerve centers of their work areas. When they transmit the information to others, they are disseminators and spokespersons. As disseminators, managers selectively pass on information to others in the organization or work unit. A supervisor who attends an athletic conference meeting and then informs the subordinates of rule changes that were enacted is engaging in the role of disseminator.

As **spokespersons,** managers transmit information to persons or groups outside their organizations or work units. For example, when the director of public relations (PR) of a Major League Baseball (MLB) club speaks to the local Kiwanis Club, she or he might tell the members about the upcoming season and special events. In this situation, the PR director is assuming the role of spokesperson for the baseball organization.

spokespersons—Managers in the role of transmitting information to persons or groups outside the manager's respective organization or work unit.

Decisional Roles

Decisional roles occur in four categories: entrepreneur, disturbance handler, resource allocator, and negotiator. As entrepreneurs, managers search for ways and take risks to effect change and improve their organizations. A manager who provides the latest computer technology for the ticket office is acting in an entrepreneurial role. The general manager of a Canadian Football League (CFL) franchise who makes a decision in player trading is also fulfilling an entrepreneurial role because the decision may come with a certain level of risk.

As **disturbance handlers,** managers respond to unexpected situations that might disrupt the organization's normal operation. Usually, managers must react to such disruptions immediately. For example, if all the support staff of a sport marketing agency become ill with influenza and cannot report to work during the week of a major tennis tournament sponsored by that agency, the normal operations of the tournament will be disrupted. The event manager at the agency would need to hire temporary help and recruit volunteers to handle the disturbance effectively.

disturbance handlers—Managers in the role of responding to unexpected situations that might disrupt the organization's normal operation.

As resource allocators, managers determine how best to allocate resources such as people, money, equipment, supplies, time, and information to each employee, group, or work unit, or to the entire organization. For example, the coordinator of marketing and promotions of a state sport festival must provide the support staff and assistants with adequate office supplies to develop literature for informing the public about upcoming events.

As **negotiators,** managers confer with people inside or outside the work unit or organization to obtain concessions or to agree on pivotal issues. Bargaining and reaching an agreement with subordinates, a regulatory agency, an interest group, or a vendor are examples of the negotiating role. A purchasing manager for a franchise in the Women's National Basketball Association (WNBA) who negotiates with a vendor for lower prices and faster delivery times on equipment and supplies is performing the negotiator role.

negotiators—Managers in the role of conferring with people inside or outside the work unit or organization to obtain concessions or to agree on pivotal issues.

The degree to which managers perform each role described earlier varies with managerial level. For example, Pavett and Lau (1983) found that the disseminator, figurehead, negotiator, and spokesperson roles are closely associated with top-level managers. The leadership, resource allocator, and disturbance handler roles are more closely associated with first-line supervisory managers (Kerr, Hill, & Broedling, 1986). Table 5.2 illustrates the role delineation revealed in a study of NCAA conference commissioners (Quarterman, 1994). To expand our examination of people in sport organizations, we now discuss individual and group behaviors in the workplace.

ACTION

Go to the OSG and complete the Learning in Action activity, which shows how you can apply Mintzberg's managerial roles to different segments of the sport industry.

LEADERSHIP

Hersey et al. (2008) defined **leadership** as influencing people to work individually or collectively towards achievement of a goal. As explained in previous pages, these same authors have defined management as working with individuals and groups while using other resources (e.g., time, money, equipment, facilities) to achieve the goals of an organization. The roles of leaders and managers have both similarities and differences. For

leadership—The process of influencing the activities of an individual or group in an effort to achieve a goal in a given situation.

TABLE 5.2 Adaptation of Mintzberg's Managerial Roles for Intercollegiate Athletic Conference Commissioners

Role	Description of role	Examples
INTERPERSONAL		
Figurehead	Performing ceremonial duties on behalf of the conference	Welcoming dignitaries, greeting visitors, participating in groundbreaking ceremonies
Leader	Influencing subordinates to get the work done at the conference office	Conducting performance evaluations, acting as a role model in the workplace, praising an employee for doing a good job
Liaison	Maintaining a network of outside contacts to gather information for the conference	Attending meetings with peers, listening to the grapevine, participating in conference-wide meetings
INFORMATIONAL		
Monitor	Perpetually scanning the environment for information that may prove useful to the conference	Lobbying for information at an NCAA meeting, staying in contact with other commissioners by telephone, reviewing the athletics literature
Disseminator	Transmitting information received by individuals or groups outside the conference	Sending information to coaches and athletics directors, having a review session on NCAA rules with the athletics directors
Spokesperson	Transmitting information to individuals or groups outside the conference	Speaking at community and professional meetings, briefing the state legislature about athletics
DECISIONAL		
Entrepreneur	Searching for new ideas and implementing changes for the betterment of the conference	Initiating a new marketing concept for increasing revenue, bringing new technology to the conference
Disturbance handler	Making decisions to deal with unexpected changes that may affect the conference	Resolving a conflict among member institutions, dealing with changes in game schedules
Resource allocator	Making decisions concerning resource use—people, time, money, space, or the conference	Making a decision about a tournament site, adding or deleting a sport program
Negotiator	Bargaining with individuals, groups, or organizations on behalf of the conference	Negotiating a television contract, negotiating with vendors

Reprinted, by permission, from J. Quarterman, 1994, "Managerial role profiles of intercollegiate athletic conference commissioners," *Journal of Sport Management* 8(2): 131–132.

WEB

Go to the OSG and complete the Web search, which will help you identify the traits of various sport industry leaders.

example, both roles involve people working with other people. The roles are different with respect to the ways in which leaders and managers accomplish the objectives. Managers are often leaders, but not all leaders are necessarily managers. The term *leader* is broader than the term *manager* because people need not be in management positions to be leaders. Depending on the situation, all employees of the organization can act as leaders. Any time a person influences the behavior of others, regardless of the reason, that person is demonstrating leadership. For example, a sport management intern might have special skills using a specific computer software program to create complex video presentations. When that intern assists the controller or director, she or he is taking the lead during that time. Conversely, when employees in an organization rely on others for direction or guidance, those others are acting as leaders, even if they are not in official decision-making positions. As dynamic and often complex structures, organizations in the sport industry require managers who are skilled in both management and leadership.

Like management, leadership is also conceptualized as an interactive process. The primary goal of leadership is to exert influence on individual and group behaviors, either toward the leader's goals or toward the organization's goals or both. Although the terms *manager* and *leader* are sometimes used interchangeably, the two concepts are not the same. When people function as managers, they are primarily focused on efficiency and *doing things right*. When people function as leaders, they are concerned with effectiveness and *doing the right things*. Differences between management and leadership are further elaborated in table 5.3, which shows that managers cope with complexity in the workplace and that leaders cope with change. In table 5.4, the characteristics of successful leaders are outlined.

Over the years, several approaches to the study of leadership have been developed. Among the most common approaches are (1) theories that attempt to explain why some people are good leaders and others are not and (2) models that represent observed patterns of effective leadership that can be learned. Leadership approaches have identified specific traits and characteristics held by leaders (e.g., honesty, integrity, self-confidence, cognitive abilities); behaviors assumed by leaders (i.e., **behaviors centered on tasks, behaviors centered on employees,** or behaviors centered on both tasks and employees); and leadership based on situations (i.e., where different situations call for different leadership styles). In the following paragraphs, we will present a more contemporary approach to leadership—the full range of leadership model. This model

behaviors centered on tasks—Primarily concerned with the technical or formal aspects of jobs and considering followers primarily as the means for accomplishing the organization's goals.

behaviors centered on employees—Primarily concerned with interpersonal relations, meeting personal needs of followers, and accommodating personality differences among followers.

TABLE 5.3 Comparative Summary of the Management–Leadership Dichotomy

Management (coping with complexity)	Leadership (coping with change)
Planning and budgeting. Setting goals for the future, establishing procedures for achieving the goals, and allocating adequate resources to effectively achieve the goals.	*Setting a direction.* Developing a vision of the future and strategies for producing the changes needed to achieve the vision.
Organizing and staffing. Creating an organizational structure for accomplishing the plan, staffing the organization with qualified workers, delegating responsibility for carrying out the plans, constructing a system to monitor implementation.	*Aligning people.* Communicating the new direction to those who can create coalitions that understand the vision and are committed to its achievement.
Controlling and problem solving. Monitoring results in some detail, both formally and informally, by means of reports, meetings, and other tools; identifying deviations; and then planning and organizing to solve the problems.	*Motivating and inspiring.* Keeping people moving in the same direction, despite confronting major obstacles, by appealing to basic but often untapped human needs, values, and emotions.

Adapted from Kotter 1990.

TABLE 5.4 Characteristics of Successful Leaders

They trust their subordinates.	A good leader will make use of employees' energy and talent. The key to a productive relationship is mutual trust.
They develop a vision.	Employees want to follow a visionary leader. They want to know where they are going and why.
They keep their cool.	Leaders demonstrate their mettle in crisis and under fire. They inspire others to remain calm and act intelligently.
They are experts.	Employees are much more likely to follow a leader who radiates confidence, is intuitive, and continues to master the profession.
They invite dissent.	A leader is willing to accept and integrate a variety of opinions.
They simplify.	Leaders focus on what is important and reach elegant, simple answers to complex problems by keeping the details to themselves.
They encourage risk.	Leaders encourage employees to take chances, readily accept error, and not fear failure.

Adapted from Labich 1988.

SPORT ORGANIZATIONS IN KOREA

By Gi-Yong (Win) Koo • KOREA
University of Arkansas, Fayetteville, UNITED STATES

Over the past few decades, Korea's sport industry has grown tremendously, particularly in the development of international sport. Korea, which hosts the 2011 IAAF World Championships in Athletics, has successfully organized worldwide sport events such as the 1988 Seoul Olympic Games and the 2002 Korea–Japan FIFA World Cup. These events have drawn attention to three sport organizations that are pioneers in the sport business and academic fields: the Korea Sports Council (KSC), the Korea Foundation for the Next Generation of Sports Talent (NEST), and the Korean Society for Sport Management (KSSM).

The KSC is the largest sport governing organization in Korea. Located in Seoul, this organization began functioning in 1920. The core activities of the KSC are to facilitate international sports exchanges, disseminate the Olympic Movement in Korea, and promote sport marketing around the world. The KSC has jurisdiction over 53 sport member associations, 16 state organizations, and 14 international associate branches.

The KSC has a hierarchical organizational structure; therefore, all work units communicate with their immediately superior work units and their immediately subordinate work units. Annually, the Korea Institute of Public Administration evaluates the organizational effectiveness of the KSC based on five criteria: fulfillment of long-term goals, completion of annual business plans, appropriateness of goal setting, suitability of the strategic plan for achieving goals, and potential for obtaining funds.

Another significant sport organization, the NEST, was established as a public foundation in 2007. Its mission involves sup-

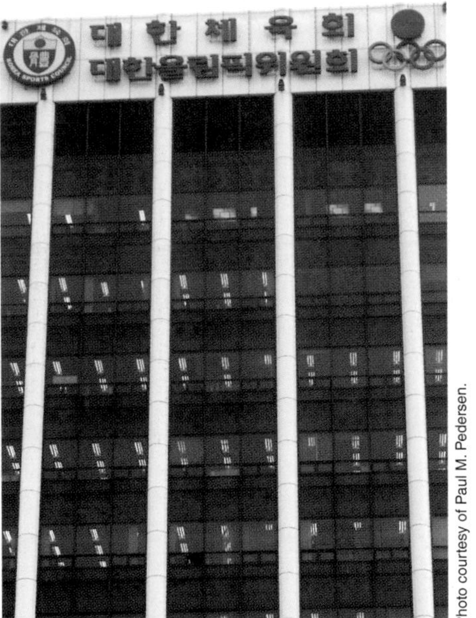

Photo courtesy of Paul M. Pedersen.

The Korea Sports Council (KSC) is the largest sport governing body in South Korea.

includes transactional, laissez-faire, and transformational leader behaviors. As you progress in your sport management curriculum and study leadership in more depth, you will discover additional leadership theories and models. You will also learn that some leader behaviors overlap categories and defy neat classifications. Nonetheless, a brief discussion of this model will provide you with a basic understanding of current thought regarding leadership in organizations.

Full Range of Leadership Model

Bass and Avolio (1994) developed the full range of leadership model based on research investigations of a variety of leader behaviors. An overview of this model, which includes transactional, laissez-faire, and transformational leader behaviors, is presented in table 5.5 on page 104. As shown in this table, the transactional leadership style implies an exchange between leaders and followers whereby they agree on the types of performances that will lead to reward or punishment for followers (Bass & Riggio, 2006). Transactional leadership includes three types of reinforcement behaviors: contingent reward, active management by exception, and passive management by exception. In contingent reward, leaders attempt to be clear about their expectations of followers.

porting "sport talent," which includes elite athletes, coaches, referees, administrators, managers, and scholars in the field of sports. This organization is operated by the profits from a sport lottery called Sport Toto. The major goal of the NEST is to contribute to the development of Korean sport systems by fostering experts for sport diplomacy, building a global human resource in sport business, creating an infrastructure for youth athletes, and supporting retired elite athletes.

Lastly, the KSSM, which has helped develop the sport management academic field in Korea, has established itself as a significant sport organization in Korea. Since its establishment in 1995, the KSSM has played a critical role in lending a scientific hand to the management of sport. The KSSM has focused on the promotion of research and the professional development of sport management. The executive council of the society consists of more than 50 researchers with doctorates in sport management and 20 practitioners from the sport business industry. The KSSM hosts an annual international conference and publishes the *Korean Journal of Sport Management* in both Korean and English. The society has been active in promoting international exchanges. It has played a pivotal role in organizing the Asian Association for Sport Management (ASSM), which includes among its members China, Hong Kong of China, Japan, South Korea, Malaysia, Mongolia, Singapore, Chinese Taipei, and Thailand.

Because the KSC, NEST, and KSSM are active and productive, we are confident that the sport industry has a bright future in Korea.

INTERNATIONAL LEARNING ACTIVITY #1

Identify sport organizations in your country that are similar to the KSC, NEST, and KSSM. Construct a table in which you list various features of these three organizations and the organizations in your country (e.g., history, mission, membership, activities, accomplishments). Compare and contrast these features.

INTERNATIONAL LEARNING ACTIVITY #2

Go to the Web site of the North American Society for Sport Management (NASSM) at www.nassm.com/. Click on the link "NASSM Conference Abstract Archive." When you reach the archive, do a search for "leader" or "leadership." You will find the abstracts of papers about sport leadership that have been presented at the NASSM conferences in recent years. Read them and identify at least five that are pertinent to the material in this chapter. Explain how managerial leaders in sport organizations could apply the information in each of those papers.

When followers' performances are satisfactory, leaders can provide rewards, such as praise or an increase in pay. When followers' performances are unsatisfactory, leaders can respond with notification of the inadequacies and, ideally, with additional clarification. Management by exception (MBE) is a more negative approach. Adherents to this leadership style ascribe to the "If it ain't broke, don't fix it" philosophy (Bass & Riggio, 2006, p. 4). MBE-active leaders keep track of followers' performances. When followers make mistakes, the leaders take corrective action. MBE-passive leaders do not monitor followers' performances. Rather, they wait passively and make corrections only when mistakes occur.

The second leadership style in table 5.5 is characterized as nontransactional. In reality, the nontransactional approach is not a leadership style at all because the people who use this approach are extremely passive. They avoid all forms of leadership. They neither monitor nor correct their followers. Consequently, this style is the least effective.

As shown in table 5.5, the third type of leader behavior is the transformational style (Yukl, 2010). Transformational leaders practice the "four I's": idealized influence, inspirational motivation, intellectual stimulation, and individualized consideration (Avolio, Waldman, & Yammarino, 1991). They are trustworthy, encouraging, risk taking, and considerate. They raise their followers' consciousness about the importance of outcomes

TABLE 5.5 Brief Overview of the Full Range of Leadership

Leadership behaviors	Transactional style
Contingent reward	Gives followers a clear understanding of what is expected of them; arranges rewards for satisfactory performance
Management by exception (active)	Monitors followers' performances and takes corrective action when mistakes are observed
Management by exception (passive)	Waits for mistakes to be made and then corrects them
	Nontransactional style
Laissez-faire	Avoids leadership; is inactive
	Transformational style
Idealized influence	Serves as a good role model; can be trusted to do the right thing
Inspirational motivation	Encourages the optimism and enthusiasm of followers
Intellectual stimulation	Encourages followers to consider new ways of looking at old methods and problems
Individualized consideration	Gives personal attention to followers; listens to them; serves as a coach or mentor

Adapted from Bass 1985; Bass and Avolio 1994.

and explain how followers can reach those outcomes by placing organizational interests ahead of self-interests.

Although most leaders engage in the full range of leadership styles, they do so to differing degrees. Many studies in a variety of organizations have suggested that the leaders who were most effective used the transformational style most frequently, the transactional style occasionally, and the nontransactional (laissez-faire) style rarely, if at all (Bass & Avolio, 1994; Bass & Riggio, 2006).

Managerial Leadership

managerial leadership—The combination of management and leadership into a coherent, integrated concept.

Modern management theorists tend to believe that both management and leadership are essential to the efficient and effective operations of organizations. In concert with this idea, the term *managerial leadership* has emerged to describe the job of the manager–leader. **Managerial leadership** combines the notions of management and leadership into a single construct (see figure 5.2) and expresses the notion that they are two sides of the same coin. As Kotter (1990) observed, good management skills are needed to maintain "a degree of consistency and order," and good leadership skills are needed to "produce movement" in a business (p. 103).

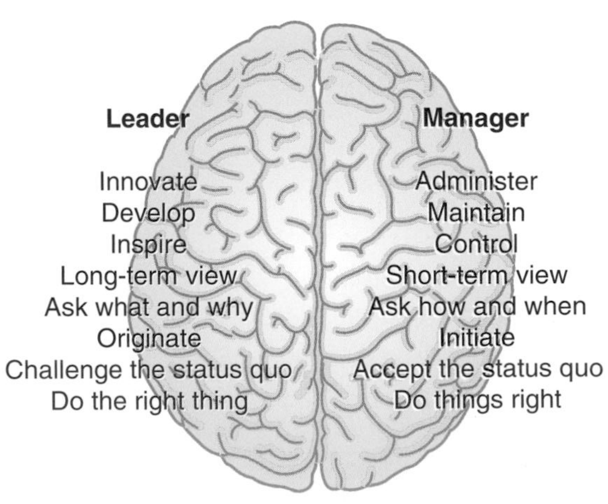

Figure 5.2 The integrative concept of managerial leadership.

Sport management scholars also conceptualized leadership and managerial behaviors as a unified concept. Soucie (1994), for example, suggested that management and leadership are qualitatively different and that each complements the other, resulting in more effective and efficient sport managers. Quarterman (1998) provided further support for this notion when he noted in his study that NCAA conference commissioners used both management and leadership skills, depending on the given situation.

Classifications of Managers

Although all managers have formal authority for directing the work activities of others, managers possess different degrees of authority. In the hierarchy of an organization, managers are usually classified as top level, middle level, or supervisory level.

- *Top-level managers.* The number of managers in this group is small. Also known as executive or senior-level managers, they have the most power and authority. They are usually responsible for the entire organization or a major part of it.
- *Middle-level managers.* Also known as administrative-level managers, these individuals are usually selected by top-level managers. They are, therefore, accountable to top-level managers and responsible for the employees who are below them in the hierarchy. The managers at the middle level are, in general, responsible for (1) managing a department or unit that performs an organizational function, and (2) ensuring that the assigned tasks are done efficiently. To their subordinates, middle-level managers are the source of information and solutions to problems because they know the technical side of the products and services. Middle-level managers are unique because they must be both leaders and followers. They are connected to supervisors and to subordinates, both of whom are also managers.
- *Supervisory-level managers.* These managers, also known as first-line managers or supervisors, report to middle-level managers and are responsible for the employees who work in their units. The employees for whom these managers are responsible can be classified as operatives or technical specialists. Supervisory managers have the least amount of authority. They are primarily responsible for a single area in a work unit, division, or department, in which they supervise the work of the operatives or technical specialists. Their job is to communicate with, inspire, and influence their subordinates to get the job done in the most effective and efficient way. Supervisory managers represent the contact point between the technical specialists (operatives) and middle-level managers. Examples of titles of managers at these different levels in three types of sport organizations are shown in table 5.6 on page 106.

Because many current sport management students will assume supervisory positions relatively early in their careers, we give this level special attention here. Being a supervisory manager can be challenging, rewarding, and stressful. One of the most challenging areas that you will encounter in your first management position is exercising authority over subordinates, especially your former colleagues. Most often, newly promoted managers must distance themselves from their former colleagues and friends and thus contend with being lonely at the top (well, not really the top, but closer to the top than before being promoted). On the other hand, the promotion brings the rewards of elevated status, higher salary, and additional opportunities to make important contributions to the organization as well as to subordinates.

DECISION MAKING, AUTHORITY, AND POWER

The explanations of the three levels of management is a perfect segue into a discussion of decision making, authority, and power. Leaders and managers are consistently called on to make important decisions for the welfare of the organization and its employees. In the following section, we introduce the steps involved in decision making and discuss the concepts of authority and power.

Decision Making

Decision making involves a series of steps. Although authors may disagree on the number of steps, researchers agree on the essence of these steps. For the purposes of our discussion, we present six steps:

TABLE 5.6 Selected Titles for Managers at Different Levels in Three Typical Sport Organizations

Levels of management	Professional baseball organization	Investor-owned health and fitness club	Intercollegiate athletics program
Top-level managers (executive or senior-level)	President Chief executive officer Vice presidents • Business operations • Baseball operations	Owners General managers Regional directors • Corporate wellness • Health promotion	Board of trustees University president Vice president for athletics Athletics director (AD) Senior associate AD
Middle-level managers (administrative-level)	Director of public relations Director of corporate sales Director of marketing operations Team manager Director of scouting	Site managers • Corporate wellness • Health promotion	Associate ADs • Director of development
Supervisory-level managers (first-line)	Director of stadium operations Director of broadcasting Director of community relations Director of baseball administration	Coordinators (supervisors) • Aerobics • Fitness • Golf • Pro shop • Weight training	Assistant ADs Sports information director Coordinator of athletics training Marketing director Academic coordinator Director of event operations Manager of ticket sales Director of compliance Equipment manager

1. ***Defining or framing the problem:*** What is the problem or issue that requires a decision? Does the manager fully understand all that is involved in addressing this problem? For example, if a sport team needs a new stadium, the organization must be in a position to explain the problem (e.g., the current facility is poorly designed and does not meet the needs of the franchise, players, and fans).

2. ***Identifying criteria for decision:*** What criteria must be considered before making the decision? For example, is time of the essence in making the decision about the need for a new stadium (for the next season)? Is there a cost issue to consider? What is the budget for this facility? Are other organizations involved in this decision (e.g., local government, corporate sector, developer)?

3. ***Developing and evaluating alternatives:*** For every problem or issue, various alternatives may be available. Alternatives may include what type of facility will be built (e.g., Should the facility cater to the sport only? Should it be designed to host other sports or other types of events? What will the seating capacity be? What design will be used?) and where the facility will be located (e.g., city center, suburb).

4. ***Selecting an alternative:*** Which alternative will be selected? Which alternative best responds to the problem identified in step 1 and the criteria identified in step 2. The decision is made at this step.

5. ***Implementing the alternative:*** This step involves implementing the decision selected in step 4. Determining who needs to be involved in implementing the decision and how this decision can best be implemented have to be established during this stage.

6. ***Evaluating the effectiveness of the decision:*** Did the decision lead to the intended outcomes? Was it the right decision? Was it the best decision given the circumstances? What were the final costs of building the stadium? Is the stadium in a location that is easily accessible to sport fans?

Decisions are an integral part of the activities that leaders, managers, and employees undertake in their day-to-day work. These individuals must consider all factors involved in the decision and make those decisions within the parameters set out by leaders and by the circumstances. Some decisions are easier to make than others. Decisions involving significant resources—time, personnel, financial resources (as the construction of a stadium would involve)—typically take more time to make than decisions involving few resources. In addition, note that decisions involving several individuals and groups (sometimes beyond the confines of the organization) may take more time because various resources, interests, and values may require more negotiation to reach a decision. Although the process of decision making may appear rational and consensual, power may also be part of this process. In the next section, we present the concept of power and discuss various sources of power.

Power and Its Sources

Power is sometimes defined as the ability to influence others. It has also been defined as control over resources. Individuals within organizations may have power from various sources, ranging from the organizational to the personal. Among the organizational sources, we find legitimate power, reward power, and coercive power. Among the personal sources of power, we find referent, expert, and informational power. In the following paragraphs, we review these sources of power, starting with organizational sources.

Legitimate or positional power is the first source. This source of power comes from the leadership or management position that a person holds in the hierarchy (i.e., top-level manager, middle-level manager, and supervisory-level manager). The manager holds a legitimate source of power as long as she or he occupies the position. Furthermore, the person has power only in the organization in which she or he holds a senior position.

Another organizational source of power is reward power. For this source, the person in the organization who provides rewards to employees has power. In most cases, the individual with legitimate power may also have reward power. Examples of rewards include raises in wages or performance bonuses, promotions, desirable assignments, and training opportunities. Rewards need to be considered valuable by others for the person to have power.

Coercive power is another source of power. The person in the organization who provides sanctions, punishments, or threats to employees has power. Reprimands, demotions, and decreased access to resources are examples of sanctions and punishments. This source of power is often perceived as problematic because it operates in the negative sphere. As in the case of reward power, this form of power is also often tied to legitimate forms of power.

Let us now review the personal sources of power starting with referent power. This source of power stems from charisma, charm, and appeal. Referent power is based on people's perception of the person with power because of personality characteristics, respect, and admiration. The person with power does not have to do anything to "deserve" the power. Note that this source of power can be abused. For example, someone who is charming and likeable but lacks integrity and honesty may rise to power and may use this power for evil.

Another source of personal power is expert power. This source is based on knowledge and skills that are perceived as valuable in a particular situation. Generally,

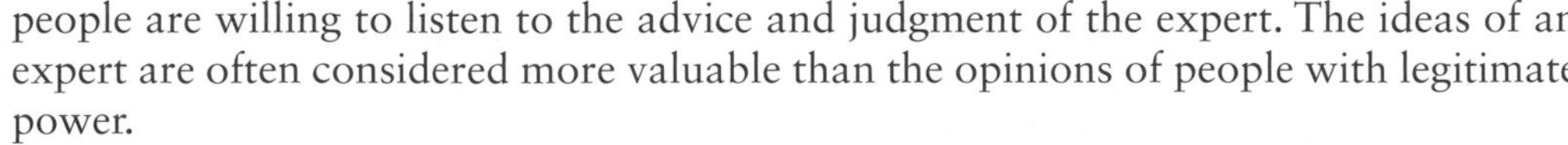

John Wooden's status as the coach of 10 NCAA national championship teams gave him expert power.
Photo courtesy of Paul M. Pedersen.

people are willing to listen to the advice and judgment of the expert. The ideas of an expert are often considered more valuable than the opinions of people with legitimate power.

The last source of power was subsequently added to the original list developed by French and Raven (1959). This source of power involves information. Although this source of power is along the same lines as expert power, the difference is that the person with the power has access to information (not expertise). Access to this information may be a result of the position held in the organization. For example, the support staff of organizational leaders may be privy to valuable information (e.g., promotions, demotions, terminations, budget cuts). Office location may be another circumstance in which a person can have access to information (e.g., by overhearing information that may be considered valuable). Relationships with other people in the organization may be another way in which information can be accessed.

When considering these sources of power, note that people often rely on more than one source of power. Recognize as well that organizational sources of power can be revoked by the organization (e.g., the person in the power position can be demoted or terminated) but that personal sources of power can be held for long periods (in the case of referent power, potentially forever). With exercising power, the ultimate goal is to influence others (e.g., subordinates, peers); individuals who exercise power will typically rely on the source of power that is most likely to achieve their goal of influencing.

Distinction Between Power and Authority

The literature on organizations has often addressed authority and power as two distinct concepts. Authority is defined as the power to enforce rules and to expect subordination from those who have no authority. In terms of French and Raven's (1959) sources of power, authority would fall under legitimate power. Those with legitimate power in organizations have authority.

Power is often perceived at the individual level of analysis where organizational actors, through various sources (e.g., position, personality, resources), have power that can be exercised in decision-making processes. In the absence of such sources of power, influencing decisions in the organization is difficult. Lukes (1974) suggested that power can be viewed beyond the individual level of analysis. He argued that although individuals' behaviors are visible manifestations of power, there are less visible dimensions of power in organizations. These involve collective actions and social interactions among individuals, including "subjective and real interests" and "observable (overt or covert) and latent conflict" (p. 25).

HUMAN RESOURCE MANAGEMENT

One of the most basic activities of sport industry leaders and managers is to plan the needs of their particular sport organizations in terms of the labor force. How many people need to be hired to achieve the objectives of the sport organization? What jobs will these human resources perform within such an organization? What special training will they require to do their jobs better? How will the quality of their work be evaluated at the end of the year? Human resource planning may also involve making difficult decisions (e.g., firing employees if necessary). As such, human resource management is an important responsibility for sport leaders and managers.

Several elements should be considered in the management of human resources. The most basic step before hiring people is to determine what human resources are needed and in what role. After leaders and managers have established the need for more employees in the organization, they will be involved in the recruitment and selection of personnel (Schwind, Das, & Wagar, 2007).

Recruitment involves the development of job ads posted in various outlets (e.g., Web sites, trade publications, professional journals, newspapers) to generate interested and qualified applicants. On each job ad, a position title, along with a summary of work responsibilities and required qualifications will be outlined. Recruitment may also entail active involvement of leaders and managers who contact potential candidates whom they know to inform them of the position and encourage them to apply. After applications are received, a screening of potential candidates takes place, and the selection process follows. Selecting the right candidates involves reviewing résumés or curricula vitae, interviewing the candidates, and verifying the references of those candidates.

After the "right" person has been hired, a process commences whereby this individual is introduced to the operations and practices in the organization. This process is often called orientation. During the orientation, new employees are introduced to coworkers. They become familiar with the organization and their work environment. Policies, procedures, and the employee handbook will be presented to the new employee so that she or he can become familiar with the operations within the workplace (Schwind et al., 2007). During this stage, new employees are often provided with a resource person to whom they can go for answers to their questions. Orientation is an important process in human resource management because it allows full integration of employees into the workplace.

As new employees become integrated into the workplace, they may from time to time require specialized training so that they can be better prepared for the work that they do within the organization. Training may include workshops about new procedures or new computer software or courses to improve sales and promotion skills. Training is always part of a strategy to enhance the effectiveness of both the individual and the organization. New skills acquired during training may also serve to motivate employees and lead to their satisfaction as they learn new things and apply this learning in their work. Training may also lead to employees' mobility within the organization. As employees become better prepared, their responsibilities in the workplace may change or increase, and these employees may be called on to undertake new roles in the organization (e.g., working with different clientele).

Another important area to consider in human resource management is performance appraisal, or the evaluation of an employee's performance in the workplace. The work of each employee in the organization should be assessed on a regular basis (typically, once a year). This evaluation serves many purposes: to improve performance, to adjust compensation, to establish career plans and development for employees, to determine training needs, to assess deficiencies in staffing and job designs, and to assess organizational and environmental challenges affecting employees (Schwind et al., 2007). In a formal meeting, the manager and employee have an opportunity to review the employee's performance during the previous year. This discussion may entail a self-assessment on the part of the employee and an assessment from the manager. Strengths and weaknesses of the employee may be discussed and areas of improvement and strategies to meet productivity targets and performance expectations may be developed. The employee may be asked to propose areas of improvement for the manager to create a better work environment for the employee. Performance appraisals are important because people are the most important resources of an organization. Within the sport industry, the appraisal provides leaders and managers with an opportunity to enhance human resources in the sport organization.

ORGANIZATIONAL DIVERSITY

As noted in chapter 2, leaders and managers of sport organizations are working with an increasingly diverse workforce. Although some may believe that the existence of diversity in the workforce is not important, others understand that a diverse workforce represents an advantage for organizations. A diverse workforce can better respond to consumers' needs and can provide consumers with better goods and services. Diversity can also improve organizational effectiveness by improving managerial decision making. Diversity, therefore, is an important resource for organizations.

Diversity can represent variations in age, gender, race and ethnicity, religion, sexual orientation, socioeconomic status, and ability. Managing diversity in organizations can be challenging, but leaders should not be deterred from ensuring that the workplace is diverse. Although managing diversity effectively is good for business (Jones & George, 2009), diverse employees are often subjected to unfair treatment. Jones and George identified three factors that may lead managers and employees to treat diverse employees unfairly:

- Biases: systematic use of information about others that lead to inaccurate perceptions
- Stereotypes: inaccurate beliefs about characteristics of groups of people
- Overt discrimination: denying diverse individuals' access to opportunities and outcomes

Dass and Parker (1999) proposed four strategies that leaders use to manage organizational diversity: reactive, defensive, accommodative, and proactive. Leaders usually adopt reactive strategies when they do not value diversity. In some cases, reactive strategies have been used to maintain and protect the status quo. Although reactive strategies are often used to resist diversity in the workplace, a reactive strategy may be appropriate in some cases. For example, the Ladies Professional Golf Association (LPGA) Tour might consider using a reactive strategy if male golfers wanted to join a tournament.

Defensive strategies typically emerge from a discrimination and fairness perspective. In this context, leaders are interested in leveling the playing field for members of diverse groups. Legislation (e.g., affirmative action policies, equal opportunity for employees) may force organizations to adopt this strategy.

With the adoption of accommodative strategies, leaders have embraced the notion that a diverse workforce is beneficial for the organization. Differences are celebrated. This strategy ensures that a diverse workforce results in access to more consumers, often from diverse groups.

The last strategy, proactive, represents a more ingrained perspective about diversity in organizational activities compared with accommodative strategies. Proactive strategies originate from the idea that educating managers and employees of the organization will result in the complete adoption of diversity. In this case, diversity is central to the core operations of the organization. Ideally, all leaders would choose to adopt the proactive strategy.

To protect diverse employees, equal employment opportunity initiatives and affirmative action programs have been developed in the United States. Matton and Hernandez (2004) conducted a study of the successes and challenges of diversity and compliance initiatives in 10 organizations. The authors examined training, goal setting and targets for gender and race, equal employment opportunities and affirmative action initiatives, and mentoring and succession planning. Their findings revealed that several factors in the organization favored the success of diversity initiatives:

How to Improve the Organizational Diversity of a Sport Organization

Organizational diversity is a concept used to address diversity-related issues in organizations. To address such issues, a sport organization needs to value diversity at both the managerial and organizational levels, and to promote and increase diversity through initiatives and actions.

Why do sport organizations need to improve their organizational diversity? Although this chapter examines this question in some detail, the following are some specific answers to this question. First, the population is diversifying, racially and ethnically; cultural diversity is a fact of life in today's, and tomorrow's, society. Second, a sport organization can function more smoothly and be more beneficial to society if a set of stakeholder rights and responsibilities can be established and applied meaningfully (Carroll & Hannan, 2000). Furthermore, there is a strong relationship between a commitment to diversity and organizational effectiveness (Wheeler, 2003). Therefore, understanding diversity is a crucial ability, if not a requisite, for managers to succeed in their business dealings.

Building diversity in sport organizations is not simple. It is a multiphase process. According to scholars in diversity research (Carnevale & Stone, 1994), organizations need to improve their organizational diversity with strategies in several areas.

Area I: Governance

- Reexamining its mission statement to determine whether a diversity element is present
- Ensuring that the bylaws of the association refer to the inclusion of all individuals

Area II: Strategic Planning

- Aggressively tracking trends in the sport industry relative to diversity and disseminating the information to stakeholders
- Identifying the diversity issues in the sport organization
- Establishing meaningful goals by adding inclusiveness as one of the sport organization's key goals
- Strengthening management commitment and ensuring that inclusiveness receives organizational attention

Area III: Communication and Promotion

- Adding a periodic diversity column or feature to the in-house organizational newsletter
- Developing a communication and promotion plan that builds awareness of the sport organization's diversity initiatives among employees, customers, and other stakeholders

Area IV: Membership Involvement

- Infusing diversity elements into the sport organization's management structure

Work–Family Conflict Among NCAA Coaches

Marlene A. Dixon and Jennifer E. Bruening conducted a two-part study (Bruening & Dixon, 2007; Dixon & Bruening, 2007) that examined the role conflict experienced by women NCAA Division I coaches in balancing their work and family responsibilities. Multilevel factors such as individual, organizational, and sociocultural have been found to affect the work–family role conflict. For the first part of their research, the authors investigated these multilevel factors and examined the extent to which they affected NCAA female coaches. In the second part, the authors focused on the consequences of this conflict and on the mechanisms developed by coaches to manage the work–family conflict. Forty-one coaches took part in online focus groups.

In the first part of the study, coaches identified a number of elements that contributed to the conflict that they experienced between their coaching and family responsibilities along three factors: individuals, organizational, and sociocultural. Among individual factors, the coaches identified their competitive drive (their expectation to experience success in both coaching and motherhood), the importance that they attributed to both family and work (and trying to balance the need to spend more time with family with the need to spend more time at work), and family being located at a distance (few close family members at hand to help

continued ▶

continued

with childcare, with emergencies, and with travel plans) as all contributing to this work–family conflict. Among organizational factors, the coaches identified the number of work hours, the travel obligations associated with the job, and the level of autonomy in the coaching job (coaches felt pressured, usually by the administration, to spend "face time" in the office during regular work days). From the perspective of sociocultural factors, coaches identified the male-dominated nature of the workplace, women's typical home and family responsibilities, and society's expectations of mothers.

In part two of the study, Bruening and Dixon reported on the mechanisms used by the coaches to deal with the stress of addressing the work–family conflict. These mechanisms included stress release (e.g., playing with their children, getting a massage, retail therapy), self-awareness, organization and time management, sacrificing some aspects of work, and support networks (e.g., family, friends, staff, assistant coaches). Coaches also discussed organizational strategies in place to help them manage the conflict. These strategies included flexibility with work hours, family-friendly policies, and family-friendly culture in the workplace.

- Leadership: commitment, passion for diversity, and sustained involvement from the leaders in the organization
- A diversity or compliance professional: creation of a position within the organization and the hiring of a strong person to implement diversity efforts in the workplace
- Employee involvement: the role of employees in communicating with leaders and informing, assisting, and recruiting diverse employees
- Ties to performance evaluation and reward system: connection to performance evaluations and rewards to middle managers and diversity officers to encourage them to meet their diversity goals
- Availability and communication of data: information allowing leaders and employees in the organization to monitor patterns, problems, and opportunities for diversity in the organization

Matton and Hernandez (2004) noted that the organizational culture was among the challenges associated with the successful implementation of diversity initiatives. Organizational culture was also tied to the difficulty that some organizations had in generating buy-in from current employees and middle managers. Achieving diversity initiatives is extremely difficult when the culture and the employees are not open to diversity in the organization. In 2006 the *Journal of Sport Management* featured a special issue on the topic of diversity in the sport industry. In their introductory article for this special issue, guest editors George Cunningham and Janet Fink (2006) discussed the major diversity issues facing sport organizations. These issues include differences in the quality of the work experience for employees who are judged to be different. Elements of power, inequality, and conflict often emerge in the workplace. Some studies on the work experiences of employees have focused on the effect of diversity on organizational commitment and turnover (e.g., Cunningham & Sagas, 2004). Other studies have investigated the issue of diversity from the perspective of consumption patterns (e.g., Armstrong, 2002; Armstrong & Stratta, 2004).

These studies and several others clearly suggest that diversity can promote the success of organizations. If a sport organization does not have strategies in place to embrace a diverse workforce, consumers, members, and clients may choose to buy their products and services from a competing organization that better understands their interests and responds more effectively to their needs. Using a hand analogy, Chelladurai (2005) clearly demonstrated the value of diversity in the workplace—all the fingers of the hand are different, but each plays an important role, particularly in concert, to open a door, to give a handshake, to hold, to throw a ball, and to write a note.

CRITICAL THINKING IN ORGANIZATIONAL BEHAVIOR AND HUMAN RESOURCE MANAGEMENT

As introduced in chapter 1, critical thinking skills are important for the management of human resources in the sport industry. Leaders and managers should base their decisions and actions on rational, factual, and objective information. Caring about others and considering their opinions, concerns, and interests are important elements for the critical thinker. Steps discussed in decision making and the management of human resources in the workplace offer good strategies to ensure a systematic evaluation of alternatives based on objective criteria to enhance the well-being of employees in the workplace and as such attain the objectives of the organization. Critical thinking ensures sound reasoning about appropriate decisions and behaviors surrounding the most important resource in organizations—human resources.

PORTFOLIO

Complete the critical thinking portfolio activity in the OSG, consulting as needed the "Eight Critical Thinking Questions" section in chapter 1.

ETHICS IN THE LEADERSHIP OF SPORT ORGANIZATIONS

As briefly mentioned in chapter 4, employees, managers, and leaders are expected to act ethically as they undertake their duties and responsibilities within the sport organization. Unfortunately, as many incidents in the recent past have demonstrated, people in organizations do not always act ethically. In a study on ethical decision making and practical morality for compliance officers of US university athletics departments, Kihl (2007) demonstrated that these sport leaders drew from various sources to make ethical decisions. The sources included their personal moral codes, professional codes of conduct, and their organization's standards, rules, and procedures. Decisions made often involved a manager's ability to balance these three sources. To illustrate the challenges of decision making, a modified version of the scenario presented by Kihl is detailed in the next paragraph.

The scenario involves the International Basketball Federation (FIBA) and its decisions related to an under-18 world basketball game. Because of agreements with organizational sponsors and the television company broadcasting the game, the leaders of FIBA wanted to abide by their policy that sought the optimal time to reach the largest audience. Therefore, the leaders decided to go with an 11:00 p.m. local start for the final contest of the tournament. Besides adhering to the prior television and sponsorship agreements, a late start produced the most potential global viewers for the television broadcast. An increase in potential viewership would provide the opportunity for the organization and its stakeholders to reap the economic benefit (e.g., increased revenue through ad sales). But the coaches and leaders of the teams involved believed that the late start could negatively affect the players' performance. Thus they disagreed with the organizational policy.

PORTFOLIO

Complete the ethical issues portfolio activity in the OSG, consulting as needed the "Guidelines for Making Ethical Decisions" section in chapter 1.

This scenario, which is frequently played out in the sport industry (e.g., agreements between television companies and universities regarding the start of college football games), highlights the often conflicting and competing values and interests of the various stakeholders involved in sport. These varying values and interests lead to important challenges that managers and leaders must carefully consider in making the best (i.e., most ethical) decisions.

Summary

People play an important role in sport organizations. In this chapter, we provided an overview of some of the concepts involved in the management of these people and the relevance of leadership in guiding their activities toward the achievement of organizational goals. As outlined in the chapter, management and leadership are two distinct yet complementary functions. Management refers to the process of working with, and through, individuals and groups to accomplish organizational goals. Leadership is the process of influencing individual and group behavior for some desired result.

Contemporary management theorists have cited five underlying functions that guide the concept of management: planning, staffing, organizing, directing, and controlling and evaluating. Managers in sport organizations commonly assume three basic roles: interpersonal, informational, and decisional. When managers perform the interpersonal role, they are primarily involved in interpersonal relationships with others. When they participate in exchanging and processing information, they are engaging in the informational role. When executing the decisional role, managers search for ways to effect change and improve their organization, respond to unexpected situations that might disrupt their organization's normal operation, or determine how best to allocate resources.

Several theories have been developed to explain leadership. In this chapter, we briefly covered traits, behaviors, and situational theories of leadership, and we then focused on a more contemporary leadership model—the full range of leadership model. Parallels between management and leadership behaviors were addressed in the section on managerial leadership. The roles of top-level, middle-level, and supervisory-level managers were explained.

As part of their responsibilities, managers and leaders are constantly involved in making decisions. Steps in decision making include defining or framing the problem, identifying criteria for the decision, developing and evaluating the alternatives, selecting an alternative, implementing the alternative, and evaluating the effectiveness of the decision. The concepts of power and authority are integral to decision making. Power is defined as the ability to influence others or as control over resources. Power can originate from different sources—organizational and personal. Organizational sources of power include legitimate, reward, and coercive power. Personal sources of power include referent, expert, and informational power. Authority is defined as the power to enforce rules and to expect subordination from those who have no authority. Collectively, decision making, power, and authority are important concepts for managers and leaders to understand and carefully wade through to achieve the goals of the sport organization.

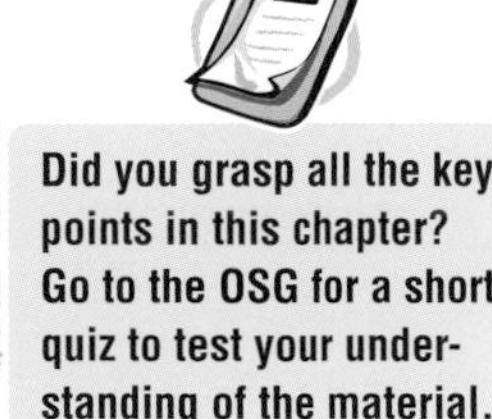

QUIZ TIME

Did you grasp all the key points in this chapter? Go to the OSG for a short quiz to test your understanding of the material.

Human resource management is about addressing the needs of the sport organization in terms of its labor force. More specifically, recruitment and selection of employees, their orientation within the organization, their training, and the appraisal of their performances within the workplace are all important. The management of human resources also includes addressing diversity in the organization. Diversity can represent variation in age, gender, race and ethnicity, religion, sexual orientation, socioeconomic status, and ability. Managing diversity in organizations can be challenging, but leaders should not be deterred from ensuring that the workplace is diverse.

Review Questions

1. Why do sport management majors need to understand management theory? What are three theoretical approaches to management and managing people in sport organizations?

2. What are the five management functions? What are the various roles assumed by managers? Contrast the five management functions with Mintzberg's 10 managerial roles?
3. What is the difference between management and leadership? What are the major features of the full range of leadership model?
4. What is the distinction between management and leadership? Explain the distinction using examples from sport organizations.
5. What steps are involved in the decision-making process?
6. What is the difference between power, authority, and leadership? Provide an example of each.
7. What are the sources of organizational power? What are the sources of personal power? How do these sources of power affect decision making?
8. What elements are involved in the management of human resources? How can diversity enrich the operations and effectiveness of sport organizations?

References

Armstrong, K.L. (2002). An examination of the social psychology of Blacks' consumption of sport. *Journal of Sport Management, 16*, 267–288.

Armstrong, K.L., & Stratta, T.M.P. (2004). Market analyses of race and sport consumption. *Sport Marketing Quarterly, 13*, 7–16.

Avolio, B.J., Waldman, D.A., & Yammarino, F.J. (1991). Leading in the 1990's: The four I's of transformational leadership. *Journal of European Industrial Training, 15*, 9–16.

Bass, B.M. (1985). *Leadership and performance beyond expectations*. New York: Free Press.

Bass, B.M., & Avolio, B.J. (1994). *Improving organizational effectiveness through transformational leadership*. Thousand Oaks, CA: Sage.

Bass, B.M., & Riggio, R.E. (2006). *Transformational leadership* (2nd ed.). Mahwah, NJ: Lawrence Erlbaum Associates.

Bruening, J.E., & Dixon, M.A. (2007). Work-family conflict in coaching II: Managing role conflict. *Journal of Sport Management, 21*, 471–496.

Carnevale, A.P., & Stone, S. (1994). Diversity: Beyond the golden rule. *Training & Development, 48*(10), 22–39.

Carroll, G.R., & Hannan, M.T. (2000). *The demography of corporations and industries*. Princeton, NJ: Princeton University Press.

Chelladurai, P. (2005). *Managing organizations for sport and physical activity* (2nd ed.). Scottsdale, AZ: Holcomb Hathaway.

Cunningham, G.B., & Fink, J.S. (2006). Diversity issues in sport and leisure. *Journal of Sport Management, 20*, 455–465.

Cunningham, G.B., & Sagas, M. (2004). Racial differences in occupational turnover intent among NCAA Division I-A assistant football coaches. *Sociology of Sport Journal, 21*, 84–92.

Dass, P., & Parker, B. (1999). Strategies for managing human resource diversity: From resistance to learning. *The Academy of Management Executive, 13*(2), 68–80.

Dixon, M.A., & Bruening, J.E. (2007). Work-family conflict in coaching I: A top-down perspective. *Journal of Sport Management, 21*, 377–406.

French, J.R.P., & Raven, B. (1959). Bases of social power. In D. Cartwright (Ed.), *Studies in social power* (pp. 150–167). Ann Arbor, MI: University of Michigan Press.

Gulick, L., & Urwick, L. (1937). *Papers on the science of administration*. New York: Institute of Public Administration.

Hersey, P., Blanchard, K.H., & Johnson, D.E. (2008). *Management of organizational behavior: Leading human resources* (9th ed.). Upper Saddle River, NJ: Prentice Hall.

Jones, G.R., & George, J.M. (2009). *Contemporary management* (6th ed.). Toronto, Ontario, Canada: McGraw-Hill Ryerson.

Kerr, S., Hill, K.D., & Broedling, L. (1986). The first line supervisor: Phasing out or here to stay? *Academy of Management Review, 11*, 103–117.

Kihl, L.A. (2007). Moral codes, moral tensions, and hiding behind the rules: A snapshot of athletic administrators' practical morality. *Sport Management Review, 10*, 279–305.

Kotter, J.P. (1990). What leaders really do. *Harvard Business Review, 68*(3), 103–111.

Labich, K. (1988). The seven keys to business leadership. *Fortune, 118*(9), 58–62, 64, 66.

Lukes, S. (1974). *Power: A radical view*. London: Macmillan.

Matton, J.N., & Hernandez, C.M. (2004). A new study identifies the "makes and breaks" of diversity initiatives. *Journal of Organizational Excellence, 23*, 47–58.

Mayo, E. (1933). *The human problems of an industrial civilization*. New York: MacMillan.

Mintzberg, H. (1973). *The nature of managerial work*. New York: Harper & Row.

Mintzberg, H. (1990). The manager's job: Folklore and fact. *Harvard Business Review, 68*(2), 163–176. (Reprinted from *Harvard Business Review, 53*(1), 49–61, 1975).

Pavett, C.M., & Lau, A.W. (1983). Managerial work: The influence of hierarchical level and functional specialty. *Academy of Management Journal, 26*, 170–177.

Quarterman, J. (1994). Managerial role profiles of intercollegiate athletic conference commissioners. *Journal of Sport Management, 8*, 129–139.

Quarterman, J. (1998). An assessment of the perception of management and leadership skills by intercollegiate athletics conference commissioners. *Journal of Sport Management, 12*, 146–164.

Robbins, S.P., & Judge, T.A. (2008). *Organizational behavior* (13th ed.). Upper Saddle River, NJ: Prentice Hall.

Schermerhorn, J.R., Hunt, J.G., & Osborn, R.N. (2008). *Organizational behavior* (10th ed.). Hoboken, NJ: Wiley.

Schwind, H.F., Das, H., & Wagar, T. (2007). *Canadian human resource management: A strategic approach* (8th ed.). Toronto, Ontario, Canada: McGraw-Hill Ryerson.

Soucie, D. (1994). Effective managerial leadership in sport organizations. *Journal of Sport Management*, *8*, 1–13.

Staw, B.M. (1986). Organizational psychology and the pursuit of the happy/productive worker. *California Management Review*, *2*, 40–53.

Taylor, F.W. (1911). *The principles of scientific management*. New York: Harper.

Wheeler, M.L. (2003). Managing diversity: Developing a strategy for measuring organizational effectiveness. In M.J. Davidson & S.L. Fielden (Eds.), *Individual diversity and psychology in organizations* (pp. 57–75). West Sussex, UK: Wiley.

Yukl, G. (2010). *Leadership in organizations* (7th ed.). Upper Saddle River, NJ: Prentice Hall.

PART II

SELECTED SPORT MANAGEMENT SITES

The sport industry offers a wide variety of career opportunities to aspiring sport managers. The purpose of the chapters in this section is to introduce you to six sites within the sport industry in which job possibilities exist for you. These six sites are representative of settings in which you could find careers in sport, but they do not constitute a complete inventory of sport-related job possibilities. If you take advantage of the additional resources included in the reference lists in each chapter and the "For More Information" section in each of this book's part openers, you will discover many more opportunities available to you in the world of sport.

In chapter 6 Jay Gladden and Bill Sutton define professional sport and discuss its history and growth in the United States. The authors address the unique characteristics of professional sport, such as its governance structure and the relationship between labor and management. The significant influences of television and the new media are also presented, as is a discussion of the major revenue sources for professional sport teams. After describing the future challenges facing leaders in professional sport, Gladden and Sutton conclude their chapter with a discussion of the various employment categories associated with professional sport. The international sidebar addresses the association between Giorgio Armani and professional basketball in Italy. Giorgio Gandolfi, editor-in-chief of *FIBA Assist Magazine*, contributed this essay.

Intercollegiate athletics is the topic of chapter 7. First, Ellen Staurowsky and Robertha Abney present an overview of the history of intercollegiate athletics in the United States. Then the authors describe several governing bodies associated with intercollegiate athletics and discuss unique financial aspects of college sport. Staurowsky and Abney conclude their chapter by examining various administrative positions and related responsibilities within intercollegiate athletics departments and governing bodies. In the international sidebar, Isaac Mwangi Kamande of Strathmore University (Nairobi) examines the Kenya Universities Sports Association (KUSA) and discusses the challenges facing university sport in Kenya.

In chapter 8 Warren Whisenant and Eric Forsyth discuss interscholastic athletics, a segment of the sport industry that is often overlooked yet offers numerous career opportunities. The authors first examine the historical and governance foundation of interscholastic athletics. Next they detail the structural and operational differences for high school sports affiliated with public and private educational institutions. After identifying the careers available at all levels of interscholastic athletics, Whisenant and Forsyth conclude their chapter by discussing key issues facing interscholastic athletics. The international sidebar for their chapter is a Canadian perspective of high school sports. The authors of the sidebar are two leaders, Morris Glimcher and John Paton, based in Canada. Glimcher is affiliated with the Manitoba High School Athletic Association and Paton works for the Alberta Schools' Athletic Association.

Sport management in community and youth settings is the topic of chapter 9. In their chapter, Marlene Dixon and Jennifer Bruening present an overview of the operational, strategic, and sociocultural aspects involved in the design and delivery of sport at the youth and community levels. First, the authors illustrate historical aspects of community and youth sport. After providing a clear definition, Dixon and Bruening next examine the size and scope of this segment of the sport industry. They conclude their chapter with a thorough analysis of the managerial challenges and unique offerings associated with community and youth sport. The international sidebar—written by Xiaoyan Xing, a native of China who teaches sport management at Laurentian University (Canada)—is about the development and unique aspects of youth sport in China.

In chapter 10 Bill Sutton, Nicole Fowler, and Mark McDonald define sport management and marketing agencies and present valuable information about the 12 possible functions performed by these sport organizations. The authors then differentiate among four types of agencies—full service, general, specialty, and in-house—and explain the evolution of each. In conclusion, Sutton, Fowler, and McDonald discuss career opportunities associated with sport management and marketing agencies. In the international sidebar, Li Li Leung (Beijing, China)—the managing director for Helios Partners, a strategic sport consulting company with offices in Atlanta, Beijing, and London—discusses the marketing efforts of Helios Partners in connection to the Beijing Olympic Games.

Chapter 11 addresses the unique aspects and career opportunities affiliated with sport tourism. Heather Gibson and Sheranne Fairley first describe tourism and the tourism industry and then explain the intersection of tourism and sport. The authors provide a thorough explanation of the different types of sport tourism: active sport tourism (e.g., traveling to participate in physical activities), event sport tourism (e.g., traveling to watch sporting events), and nostalgia sport tourism (e.g., traveling to sport museums or halls of fame). Gibson and Fairley conclude with a discussion of the sociocultural, economic, and environmental impacts of sport tourism. In the international sidebar, Deakin University's (Australia) Pamm Kellett discusses the interest in sport heritage and sport museums by stakeholders affiliated with Melbourne, Australia.

An understanding of the wide variety of career opportunities available in the sport industry will enable you to plan your professional life more realistically. Rather than concentrating only on the chapters that address the careers in which you are currently interested, we hope that you will study the material in each of these six chapters and reflect on the possibilities that each site might hold for you. Who knows? As you learn more about the possibilities that exist, you might develop new interests and revise your career goals!

For More Information

Professional and Scholarly Associations

American Association of Adapted Sports Programs: www.adaptedsports.org/
Canadian Sport Tourism Alliance: www.canadiansporttourism.com/portal_e.aspx
Canadian Tourism Commission: www.canadatourism.com
Coalition on Intercollegiate Athletics: coia.comm.psu.edu/
Committed to Green Foundation: www.committedtogreen.com/
The Drake Group: www.thedrakegroup.org/
International Alliance for Youth Sports: iays.org/
National Alliance for Youth Sports: www.nays.org
National Association of Intercollegiate Athletics: naia.cstv.com/
National Association of Sports Commissions: www.sportscommissions.org
National Association of Sports Officials: www.naso.org/
National Christian College Athletic Association: www.thenccaa.org/
National Collegiate Athletic Association: www.ncaa.com
National Federation of State High School Associations: www.nfhs.org/
National Interscholastic Athletic Administrators Association: www.niaaa.org/default.asp
National Junior College Athletic Association: www.njcaa.org/
Travel Industry Association of America: www.tia.org
World Tourism Organization: www.world-tourism.org
World Travel and Tourism Council: www.wttc.org

Professional and Scholarly Publications

Academic Athletic Journal
Amusement Business
Annals of Tourism Research
Athletics Administration
Chronicle of Higher Education
Current Issues in Tourism
Interscholastic Athletic Administration
Journal for the Study of Sports and Athletics in Education
Journal of Community Psychology

Journal of Contemporary Athletics
Journal of Hospitality, Leisure, Sport and Tourism Education (JoHLSTE)
Journal of Issues in Intercollegiate Athletics
Journal of Leisure Research
Journal of Sport & Tourism
Journal of Vacation Marketing
Journal of Youth Sports
Leisure Sciences
Leisure Studies
Managing Leisure
National Aquatics Journal
NCAA News
New Directions for Youth Development
NISR Journal of Sport Reform
Sporting News
Sports Business Daily
Sports Illustrated
Sports Travel
Street & Smith's SportsBusiness Journal
Tourism Recreation Research
Visions in Leisure and Business

Additional Internet Resources

AF2: (arena football2): www.af2.com/
American Hockey League: www.theahl.com
Amateur Softball Association of America: www.asasoftball.com
Arena Football: www.arenafootball.com/
Audubon International's Cooperative Sanctuary System, Golf Program: www.audubonintl.org/programs/acss/golf.htm
Austin Sports and Social Club: www.austinssc.com/
Basketball Hall of Fame: www.hoophall.com/
British Tourism Authority Sport Tourism Initiative: www.visitbritain.us/things-to-see-and-do/interests/sports/index.aspx
The Royal Canadian Legion: www.legion.ca/About/youth_e.cfm
Catholic Youth Organization: www.nationalcyosports.org
College Sport Research Institute: www.unc.edu/depts/exercise/csri/
Diverse Issues in Higher Education: diverseeducation.com/
Disney's Wide World of Sports: dwws.disney.go.com
East Coast Hockey League: www.echl.com
Husky Sport: www.huskysport.uconn.edu
Independent Women's Football League: www.iwfl-sports.com/
Intrawest Ski Company: www.intrawest.com/
Little League Baseball and Softball: www.littleleague.org
LPGA Hall of Fame: www.lpga.com/content_1.aspx?mid=2&pid=184
Minor League Baseball: www.minorleaguebaseball.com
National Baseball Hall of Fame: www.baseball-halloffame.org
National Basketball Association: www.nba.com
National Football League: www.nfl.com
National Hockey League: www.nhl.com
Norwegian Cruise Line: www.ncl.com
Olympic Museum, Geneva, Switzerland: www.olympic.org/en/content/The-Olympic-Museum/
Pinehurst Resort, North Carolina: www.pinehurst.com/
Playworks: www.playworksusa.org/
Police Athletic League: www.palnyc.org
Pop Warner Football and Cheerleading: www.popwarner.com
Sport Management and Marketing Agencies: www.business.com/directory/media_and_entertainment/sports/agencies_and_management/
United Football League: www.ufl-football.com/
Up2Us: www.up2us.org/
US Olympic Committee: www.teamusa.org
Women's Basketball Hall of Fame: www.wbhof.com/
Women's National Basketball Association: www.wnba.com
Women's Professional Soccer: www.womensprosoccer.com/
World Golf Hall of Fame, World Golf Village: www.wgv.com
YMCA: www.ymca.net
YWCA: www.ywca.org

HISTORICAL MOMENTS

1903	MLB World Series held
1917	NHL established
1919	Black Sox scandal in MLB erupted
1920	American Professional Football Association formed; renamed National Football League (NFL) in 1922
1920	Negro National League formd
1934	First Masters Golf Tournament held
1941	Ted Williams compiled .406 batting average
1946	Basketball Association of America (BAA), forerunner of NBA, formed
1947	Jackie Robinson became first African American to play in modern MLB
1950	Ladies Professional Golf Association (LPGA) founded
1967	Super Bowl I held—AFL v. NFL World Championship Game (January 15)
1989	Pete Rose banned from baseball
1995	Cal Ripken broke Lou Gehrig's record of playing in 2,130 consecutive games
2006	Effa Manley became first woman elected to the National Baseball Hall of Fame
2009	Martin Brodeur won 557th career game; owns NHL career wins record

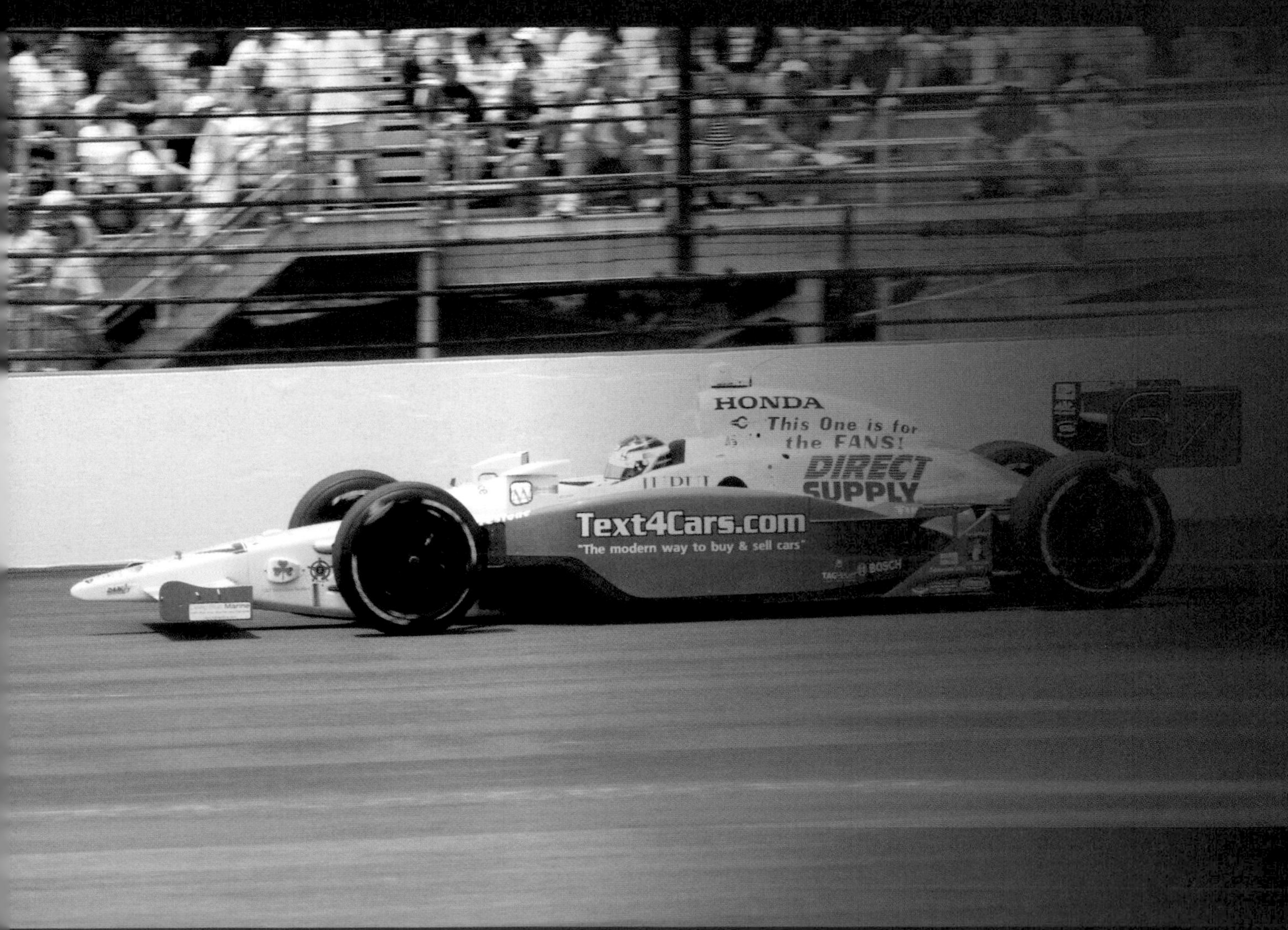

Photo courtesy of Paul M. Pedersen.

6

PROFESSIONAL SPORT

James ("Jay") M. Gladden ■ William A. Sutton

LEARNING OBJECTIVES

1. Define, explain, and discuss the development of professional sport.
2. Describe the unique facets of professional sport, including its governance and the labor–management relationship on which professional team sports depend.
3. Document the significance of the relationship between media and professional sport.
4. Describe the major revenue sources for a professional sport team.
5. Identify the types of employment opportunities available in this segment of the sport industry.
6. Apply ethical reasoning and critical thinking skills to issues in professional sport.

GET A JOB!

☑ Continue on your journey in sport management by going to the Online Study Guide (OSG) at www.HumanKinetics.com/ContemporarySportManagement. Check out the job opportunities and consider the skills and experiences that can help you succeed in sport management.

Key Terms

collective bargaining
labor
league think
LED signage
local television contracts
luxury tax
management
salary caps
sponsorship
virtual signage

Professional sport is any sport activity or skill for which the athlete is compensated. Compensation can be in the form of salary, bonuses, reimbursement for expenses, or any other type of direct payment. The activity that the athlete performs can be a team sport such as basketball, a dual sport such as tennis, an individual sport such as figure skating or skateboarding, or a sport entertainment performance such as World Wrestling Entertainment (WWE). A representative list of some professional sports in North America includes the following:

Baseball	Golf	Skateboarding
Basketball	Hockey	Skiing
Billiards	Horse racing	Snowboarding
Bodybuilding	Ice skating	Soccer
Bowling	Mixed martial arts	Surfing
Boxing	Motocross	Tennis
Curling	Racquetball	Triathlon
Football	Rodeo	Volleyball

Professional sport events such as the Super Bowl, World Series, Masters Golf Tournament, Indianapolis 500, Wimbledon Championships, Kentucky Derby, and X Games now occupy the heart of North American sport. Although we have mentioned both team sports and sports featuring the individual, this chapter concentrates on professional team sport because of its profound economic effect and the number of job opportunities available in this segment of the sport industry. Most jobs associated with professional individual sports are found in sport management and marketing agencies (see chapter 10). The purpose of this chapter is to provide information and insight about four primary aspects of North American professional team sport—its historical development, its unique aspects, its revenue sources, and the variety of career opportunities associated with professional sport.

NATURE OF PROFESSIONAL SPORT

Novelist David Guterson (1994) described professional sport this way: "Like money, it is something we love, a first waking thought and a chronic passion, as well as a vast sector of the economy, a wellspring for myth and totem, and a media phenomenon of the highest order." He added in his *Harper's Magazine* commentary, "Our sports can fend off the brute facts of existence, temporarily arrest the sadness of life, briefly shroud the inevitability of death and provide the happy illusion of meaning through long enchanted afternoons." Guterson then explained, "Sport is a language we all speak. Sport is a mirror. Sport is life. Through sport we might know ourselves" (p. 38).

Guterson's description accurately portrays the powerful role that professional sport occupies in the everyday lives of many people. Professional sport exemplifies sport at its highest level of performance, and it generates the majority of coverage devoted to sport through the print, electronic, and new media. As packaged events, professional team sports (e.g., men's and women's football, men's and women's ice hockey, men's and women's soccer, men's baseball, women's softball, men's and women's basketball) provide considerable entertainment and pleasure for spectators. As such, demands on the three principals that form the professional sport industry—labor, management, and governance—are complex, diverse, and ever changing. **Labor** aggressively continues to protect and procure additional resources for its membership, which is made up of the professional athletes. Management, or the owners of professional teams, is trying to win back some leverage and control lost to labor over the past few decades.

labor—A collective group of athletes in team sports who unionize so that they can bargain collectively with the league owners (i.e., management). Labor is typically represented by a union head in negotiations with management.

Finally, governance, made up of the professional sport leagues, attempts to regulate, but not completely control, both labor and **management.** In professional team sport, governance is the league structure that exists to oversee both the competitive and business elements of the sport. For example, the National Football League (NFL), Major League Baseball (MLB), National Hockey League (NHL), and the Women's National Basketball Association (WNBA) are all forms of governance.

management—When referring to the collective bargaining process, management refers to the collective group of ownership that is negotiating with the players, or labor. Management is typically represented by a league commissioner, who is technically an agent for the owners, in negotiations with labor.

HISTORY OF MAJOR AMERICAN PROFESSIONAL SPORTS

Professional sport can be traced to ancient Greece where, beginning with the Olympic Games in 776 BCE, a class of professional sportsmen known as athletai existed. These athletai were well-paid men recruited from mercenary armies and trained exclusively for brutal competition (Freedman, 1987). In exchange for competing and winning, athletai often received remuneration in the form of prizes and money.

Although baseball is often considered America's national pastime, it was not the first sport that professionals played. Boxers, jockeys, and runners were paid for their prowess during the early and mid-19th century. Baseball, however, was the first team sport to employ professionals. In 1869 the Cincinnati Red Stockings became the first professional baseball team. Their appearance was closely followed in 1871 by the National Association of Professional Base Ball Players (NAPBBP), the first professional sport league (Rader, 2009). In 1876 William Hulbert formed the National League, the precursor to MLB as we know it today.

A recognized professional league in another sport did not form until after the turn of the 20th century. In 1917 the NHL emerged after the National Hockey Association of Canada Limited suspended its operations. This was closely followed in 1921 with the creation of the NFL. The National Basketball League (NBL), founded in 1937, was the first professional basketball league. In 1949 the NBA resulted from a merger between the NBL and the Basketball Association of America (BAA) (Staudohar & Mangan, 1991).

Inclusion (and Exclusion) in Professional Sport

Although professional team sport has been in existence for more than 100 years, only in the past 70 years have professional sport opportunities been available to many minority segments of the American population. Professional sport opportunities were segregated until 1947, when Jackie Robinson broke baseball's modern color line with the Brooklyn Dodgers. Although Fleetwood Walker broke baseball's color barrier in the 1880s, for the most part before 1947 African Americans played in separate, segregated professional leagues. The National Colored Baseball League was founded in 1887 as an outlet for African American baseball players, who were not allowed to play in the all-White major leagues. This league failed because of lack of attendance. But in 1920 the Negro National League was formed. This league and others, such as the Eastern Negro League and Negro American League, afforded players such as Satchel Paige, Josh Gibson, and even Robinson an opportunity to play (*Negro League Baseball*, 2005). In addition, most owners, club managers, reporters, and umpires in the Negro leagues were also African American.

Professional sport outlets for women have also arisen only in the past 70 years. In the 1940s the first women's professional league, the All-American Girls Professional Baseball League (AAGPBL), was formed. Created in 1943 in response to decreased player quality in MLB during World War II and the popularity of women's amateur softball, the AAGPBL played 11 seasons before folding in 1954 because of poor management

April Priest (no. 87) is the tight end, linebacker, and co-owner of the Indiana Speed, a professional football team affiliated with the Women's Football Alliance.

Photo courtesy of Paul M. Pedersen.

(Browne, 1992). Since 1954 a number of other women's professional leagues have operated, mainly in the sport of basketball. From 1979 to 1991 there were four attempts to capitalize on the growing participation and interest of women in basketball, but each league was unsuccessful because of financial difficulty.

In the mid-1960s women began playing semipro tackle football, and by the 1970s teams were competing in Ohio, New York, Michigan, and Pennsylvania. In 1974 the Women's Professional Football League (WPFL) was established with teams in Dallas, Fort Worth, Columbus, Toledo, Los Angeles, and Detroit. During the ensuing years, a number of leagues emerged as women expressed interest and ability in tackle football. Examples of these women's professional football leagues include the Women's American Football League (WAFL), American Football Women's League (AFWL), United Football League, Independent Women's Football League (IWFL), National Women's Football Association (NWFA), Women's Football League, Women's Spring Football League, and Women's Football Alliance (WFA).

The past two decades have seen a resurgence of interest in women's professional sport. In 1996 two women's professional basketball leagues were formed: the American Basketball League (ABL) and the WNBA. The ABL played over two seasons before folding because of financial difficulties, which were at least partially because of competition from the NBA-sponsored WNBA (which still exists today). In June 1997 the Women's Professional Fastpitch (WPF) softball league began. During the summer of 2001 the Women's United Soccer Association (WUSA) began play, but it folded in 2003 because of financial difficulties. In 2009 Women's Professional Soccer (WPS) marked the second formal attempt for women's soccer.

Factors Affecting the Growth of Professional Sport

As professional sport progressed throughout the 20th century, its success was largely tied to the media, which both promoted and financed professional sport. As early as the 1920s baseball games were broadcast on the radio. By the mid-1930s radio networks were paying US$100,000 for the rights to carry the World Series (Rader, 2009). The popularity of professional sport (mainly baseball) on the radio reached its apex in the 1940s and 1950s. During the 1950s televised sporting events became commonplace.

After Congress passed the Sports Broadcasting Act in 1961, the relationship between the media and professional sports changed dramatically. Until that time, antitrust law had prohibited leagues from negotiating network television contracts on behalf of their members. But the leagues believed that they needed to negotiate a collective (on behalf of all league teams) agreement to ensure the financial viability of their member teams. This rationale suggested that the major television networks (i.e., ABC, CBS, and NBC) would pay significantly larger sums of money to obtain leaguewide rights rather than rights to individual teams. As a result, the NFL successfully led a lobbying effort to create an exemption in antitrust law. The Sports Broadcasting Act gave sport leagues an exemption from antitrust law, granting them the right to negotiate fees collectively with the networks. This legislation paved the way for the highly lucrative leaguewide television deals that pervade professional sports today.

UNIQUE ASPECTS OF PROFESSIONAL SPORT

Four aspects of professional sport distinguish it from other industries: interdependence, structure and governance, labor–management relations, and the role of the electronic and new media.

Interdependence

The central premise that differentiates professional team sport from any other business is the need for teams to compete and cooperate simultaneously (Mullin, Hardy, & Sutton, 2007). In other words, the teams depend on one another to stage the games that constitute the product. In his classic work on the NFL, *The League*, David Harris (1986) described this unique situation as **league think.** When teams function together collectively, some teams sacrifice the potential for higher revenue in the interest of league stability. For example, the Dallas Cowboys and Oakland Raiders typically sell a disproportionate amount of NFL-licensed merchandise. This money, however, is pooled and shared equally among all 32 NFL teams. The presence of the Cowboys and Raiders in the collective bargaining agreement increases the revenue generated for all NFL member teams. Because of their location in large television markets, the New York Giants and Chicago Bears function in much the same way during television negotiations. The key is that all members make sacrifices and concessions for the long-term benefit and growth of the league.

league think—Pioneered and most effectively implemented by the NFL, this term represents the notion that teams must recognize the importance of their competition and share revenues to ensure that their competitors remain strong.

Although major professional sport leagues differ in the extent to which they share revenues, each league pools its revenues to some extent. For example, NFL teams all share equally in their national media contracts (e.g., cable, satellite, network) and cannot negotiate separate local media contracts, whereas baseball teams share only their national contracts and keep all revenue from their local agreements. These local agreements can vary significantly in the amount of revenue produced. Large-market teams (clubs located in heavily populated cities that have the potential to negotiate lucrative local media contracts), such as the New York Yankees, have local broadcast packages that are significantly larger than those of small-market teams (clubs in midsize or smaller markets whose potential for local media contracts is not that high), such as the Kansas City Royals. Over the past 15 years the disparity in local media revenues has created significant discrepancies in the amount of money that MLB teams are able to pay their players. Such revenue disparities led MLB to implement a **luxury tax** on teams that had the highest payrolls. Teams with disproportionately high payrolls pay a tax to MLB, and the collected luxury tax money is then shared among teams with lower payrolls.

luxury tax—Device used by MLB and the NBA to tax the teams that spend the most (or spend too much as defined by the collective bargaining agreement [CBA]) on player payroll and those taxes are then shared with teams that do not have high payrolls.

Structure and Governance

Each professional sport has its own structure and system of governance, typically referred to as the league office, which usually involves the following components:

1. League commissioner
2. Board of governors or committee structure composed of the team owners
3. A central administrative unit that negotiates contracts and agreements on behalf of the league and assumes responsibility for scheduling, licensing, record keeping, financial management, discipline and fines, revenue-sharing payments, marketing and promotional activities, developing and managing special events, and other functions such as coordinating publicity and advertising on behalf of the teams as a whole

For example, MLB is composed of 30 teams situated in two leagues (National and American—see table 6.1). Each league consists of three divisions (i.e., East, Central, and West). The MLB commissioner is responsible for representing the interests of all parties associated with professional baseball. These parties include owners, players, fans, television networks, corporate sponsors, host cities and venues, and the minor leagues. Contrast this organizational structure with mainstream business. For example, no authority governs the actions of candy manufacturers Hershey's and M&M Mars in their attempts to make money.

TABLE 6.1 Organization of Major League Baseball

National League East	National League Central	National League West	American League East	American League Central	American League West
Atlanta Braves	Chicago Cubs	Colorado Rockies	Baltimore Orioles	Chicago White Sox	Los Angeles Angels of Anaheim
Florida Marlins	Cincinnati Reds	Los Angeles Dodgers	Boston Red Sox	Cleveland Indians	Oakland A's
Washington Nationals	Houston Astros	San Diego Padres	New York Yankees	Detroit Tigers	Seattle Mariners
New York Mets	Milwaukee Brewers	San Francisco Giants	Tampa Bay Rays	Kansas City Royals	Texas Rangers
Philadelphia Phillies	Pittsburgh Pirates	Arizona Diamondbacks	Toronto Blue Jays	Minnesota Twins	
	St. Louis Cardinals				

Baseball is unique in having an extensive minor league system, which provides an elaborate way of preparing players to participate in the major leagues. Each major league team has at least four affiliate teams in the minor leagues. As long as they meet certain standards in terms of the size of their facilities, owners of minor league teams can enter into contractual relationships with major league clubs whereby the minor league team becomes an affiliate of a major league team. The cultivation of minor league systems is increasingly popular among the other major professional sport leagues. For example, the NBA Development League commonly referred to as "NBA–D," or just the "D League," began play in 2001 and in 2010 the league had 17 teams playing in 14 states. The purpose of the league is to provide a training ground for players, referees, coaches, front-office personnel, and other operational staff who want to prepare for a possible career in the NBA. Each D-League team has one or more NBA affiliates. For example, the Bakersfield Jam is affiliated with both the Los Angeles Clippers and the Golden State Warriors. The 2009-2010 champion, the Rio Grande Valley Vipers, has an affiliate relationship with the Houston Rockets.

Labor–Management Relations

Five unique circumstances and conditions are related to the labor–management relationship in North American professional sport: baseball's antitrust exemption, collective bargaining, free agency, salary caps, and player draft. Some aspects are the opposite of common, traditional business practices and philosophies. But the participating parties consider such idiosyncrasies essential to preserving the financial stability of the professional sport product. In the following sections we will examine each element and explain its uniqueness and significance to professional sport.

Baseball's Antitrust Exemption

Perhaps the most exceptional condition in professional sport is MLB's exemption from the rules and regulations of the Sherman Antitrust Act. This antitrust legislation was created to prohibit companies from dominating their respective markets in interstate commercial activity, thus creating a monopoly in which consumers have only one product choice rather than several. But as a result of the US Supreme Court's ruling in the *Federal Base Ball Club of Baltimore, Inc. v. National League of Professional Base Ball Clubs* (1922), MLB was granted an exemption to antitrust law. In its decision, the court deemed that baseball was local in nature, did not involve the production of a tangible good, and thus was not subject to interstate commerce law. In effect, this ruling granted MLB the right to undertake strategies that would prevent the establishment of competitive leagues. This exemption gives professional baseball team owners significant leverage over the cities in which they operate. In some cases, owners have threatened to leave their host cities if new stadia are not built. Although MLB's exemption from antitrust regulations has been challenged on several occasions, the courts have not overturned the decision.

Collective Bargaining

Workers involved in interstate commerce, which includes all professional team sport (except MLB because of its antitrust exemption), are covered by the National Labor Relations Act (NLRA). The NLRA provides three basic rights that are at the center of labor relations policy in the United Sates: (1) the right to self-organize, form, join, or assist labor organizations; (2) the right to bargain collectively through agents of one's own choosing; and (3) the right to engage in concerted activities for employees' mutual aid or protection (Staudohar, 1989). In professional team sport, the NLRA provides players the right to join a union, to have a basic player contract (establishing a minimum salary, benefits, and working conditions) negotiated collectively by union representatives, and to strike or conduct other activities that help achieve objectives. The term **collective bargaining** is used because all active league players are in the bargaining unit and thus form a collective unit (labor) for negotiating and bargaining with the owners (management). Teams join as a league in bargaining with the players union so that in each league the negotiated contract applies to all teams uniformly. Some of the issues that are subject to collective bargaining include salary (minimum and maximum), drug testing, and discipline procedures.

collective bargaining—Process used to negotiate work terms between labor and management. All active league players are in a bargaining unit and thus form a collective unit (i.e., labor) for negotiating and bargaining with the owners (i.e., management).

Free Agency

Free agency is the ability of players, after fulfilling an agreed-upon (through a collective bargaining agreement [CBA]) number of years of service with a team, to sell their services to another team with limited or no compensation to the team losing the players. Thus the terms *free agent* and *free agency* have evolved to signify the relative freedom that all professional team sport players have to move from one team to another. Professional team sport, however, still imposes significant restrictions on its labor. For example, players do not immediately become free agents. Instead, free agency is a negotiated item in the CBA of all professional team sport leagues. The CBA recognizes the investment that the team has incurred in developing the player, while also recognizing the fair market value of the player in the open market. Thus, the CBA provides free agency after the player has played an agreed-upon (by both labor and management) number of years.

The implementation of free agency in the mid-1970s had a profound effect on the economics of professional sport. After professional athletes gained the freedom to negotiate with the highest bidder, their salaries escalated astronomically. In 1976, when the players first earned the right to become free agents, the average salary in professional baseball was US$46,000. In 2009 (based upon opening day rosters) the average salary in MLB was US$3.26 million, which represents a 4% increase over 2008 (Kendrick, 2009). Similar salaries exist in the other men's major professional sport leagues (i.e., NHL, NFL, and NBA) while currently the average salaries for women's professional sport teams are much lower. See table 6.2 for information on the average salaries in professional sports. The heightened power of the players unions and increased salaries of players contributed to an increase in labor stoppages in the professional sport leagues. With player salaries continuing to rise, owners of professional sport teams are facing the challenge of generating sufficient revenue to match those increased costs.

TABLE 6.2 Average Salaries for Select Professional Sport Leagues*

League	Average salary (US$)
Major League Baseball (MLB)	$3.26 M
Major League Soccer (MLS)	$115,432
National Basketball Association (NBA)	$5.36 M
National Football League (NFL)	$904,522**
National Hockey League (NHL)	$1.9 M
Women's National Basketball Association (WNBA)	$55,000

*Compiled from a variety of sources including *USA Today*, *Street & Smith's SportsBusiness Journal*, and various player association Web sites.

**The NFL figure does not account for the wide range of bonus payments. Bonuses are usually given as a lump sum. For example, in 2008 Pittsburgh Steelers quarterback Ben Roethlisberger received compensation in the amount of US$27.7 million, of which $25.2 million was a one-time bonus payment (Weisman, 2008).

Such concerns have led owners to take an increasingly tough stance during collective bargaining negotiations. Because of management–labor salary disputes, work stoppages have become a frequent occurrence.

Salary Caps

With the onset of free agency in the 1970s, the professional segment of the sport industry allowed players who became unrestricted free agents (those who had fulfilled the terms of their contracts) to sign with the highest bidder or whomever they chose. Consequently, spending on player salaries increased significantly, particularly among teams with greater resources. In response, **salary caps** that set a ceiling on player payrolls were created to protect the owners, essentially from themselves, from overbidding for talent. Salary caps are agreements collectively bargained between labor and management that establish a leaguewide team payroll threshold that cannot be exceeded in most cases. The salary cap is typically set using a percentage of league gross revenues as a starting point. Pioneered by the NBA in 1983 and implemented for the 1985–86 season, the salary cap guarantees that players will receive an established percentage of all gross revenues. The initial NBA salary cap established this percentage at 53%, and the latest CBA implemented in 2005 set the percentage at 57% of all gross revenues.

salary caps—Agreements collectively bargained between labor and management that establish a leaguewide team payroll (i.e., salaries, bonuses, and incentive clauses) threshold that cannot be exceeded in most cases. The salary cap is typically set using a percentage of league gross revenues as a starting point.

Salary caps were designed to ensure parity between large- and small-market teams as well as between owners whose resources may vary considerably. In addition to the NBA, the NFL, the NHL, and MLS have all adopted a salary cap structure, and of the four major pro sport leagues in the United States only MLB does not have a cap. The NBA salary cap is referred to as a soft cap because it has exceptions that in some cases allow teams to exceed the cap. The most notable exception is the "Bird Rule," which was designed to help teams retain their most famous and marketable players by permitting them to pay a higher salary to that player if he elects to stay with that original team. The NFL salary cap is a hard cap. There are no exceptions in a hard cap; teams are allowed to spend only to the ceiling of the salary cap.

Player Draft

In accordance with the principles of league think, the player draft is designed to be an equitable system for distributing new talent among all league members. The draft provides each professional sport league with a mechanism for the teams with poor records to have an advantage over teams with winning records in acquiring talented new players. Through the draft, teams voluntarily agree to restrict competition for new talent. As a result, the team that drafts a player determines the player's destination and salary. Phenomena such as the player draft do not exist in other areas of the labor market. Imagine a scenario in which top sport management graduates were restricted as to whom they could work for and where they could work by an annual draft held by sport businesses throughout the country! Collective bargaining agreements in men's basketball and men's football have sought to limit the number of rounds of the draft. This limitation results in fewer players being drafted and more players being free agents to sign with any team that offers them a contract.

Role of the Electronic and New Media

The electronic and new media—network television, cable and satellite television, terrestrial and satellite radio, and the Internet—play a critical role in driving the popularity of professional sport and generating additional revenue for associated teams. Although radio was the first electronic medium to bring professional sport to the masses, television (e.g., network, cable, satellite) has had a profound effect on the development of professional team sport over the past 50 years. As we move into the second decade of the 21st century, new media sources such as satellite television and the Internet could be the next important horizons in broadening the reach of professional team sport and the enhancement of league revenue streams.

Importance of Television

No single factor has influenced the popularity of sport, the escalation in player salaries, free agency, and the growth and increase of corporate involvement in professional sport more than television. TV has helped elevate professional sport beyond competition and athleticism into the realm of entertainment. *Monday Night Football* (*MNF*), which is now on ESPN, was a pioneering effort to package professional sport as entertainment. Although there were popular televised spectacles for other sports (e.g., boxing, roller derby, bowling), the prime-time extravaganza of *MNF* sought to reach more than just traditional football fans by adding analysis, commentary, special guests, additional camera angles, video replays, graphics, and highlights to enhance the event and broaden its appeal to women and other nontraditional viewing groups (Roberts & Olson, 1995). Concurrent with the success of *MNF*, the ultimate TV sport spectacle, the Super Bowl, was created. Born from the rivalry and merger of the NFL and the American Football League (AFL), the Super Bowl has become one of the most successful televised events of all time, viewed by millions around the world.

WEB

Go to the OSG and complete the first Web search activity, which will help you investigate how *Monday Night Football* has affected many areas of professional sport.

Leagues associated with professional sport need TV for three reasons. First, as already discussed, the leagues and member teams receive significant revenue outlays from network, satellite, and cable TV agreements. Second, TV enhances the enjoyment associated with watching professional sport events. Third, TV helps increase the amount that teams and leagues can charge for sponsorships because of the increased exposure that TV provides.

Emerging Sources of Media Coverage

Imagine that you grew up in Chicago and now live on the East Coast. Because of where you were raised, you are an ardent follower of the Chicago professional sports teams (the Bulls, Red Stars, Bears, Sky, Cubs, Fire, White Sox, and Blackhawks). Unless these teams make the playoffs, however, you are rarely able to follow your team through radio or cable television broadcasts. Millions of fans worldwide face this dilemma. But solutions are becoming increasingly available to such fans. Most notably, satellite television and the Internet have greatly increased the access of sport fans to a full menu of sport events.

Satellite technology and satellite television providers such as DirecTV have worked with the leagues to create packages whereby the average sport fan can access any game during the season either by paying an up-front fee for season-long access or by subscribing (paying a one-time fee) on a game-by-game basis. For example, in 2009, for US$299, owners of a satellite television system received NFL Sunday Ticket, which provided them access to all regular season games. Satellite radio providers such as XM and Sirius also allow displaced fans an opportunity to follow their favorite teams on a regular basis for a monthly fee. The Internet is affording fans increased access to games of interest. Fans can now listen (radio) and view various online sporting events and broadcasts, typically through league-run Web sites. For example, in the scenario described earlier, the Chicago fan living on the East Coast could watch every Cubs game on MLB.com.

REVENUE SOURCES FOR PROFESSIONAL SPORT TEAMS

Revenue sources for sport organizations will be discussed in more detail in chapter 14. We will discuss here some unique aspects of revenue generation in professional sport.

Media Contracts

The details of the national media contracts for a variety of professional sport leagues are presented in table 6.3. One major distinction is found with respect to media revenues in professional sport. Namely, MLB, the NBA, and the NHL all permit their member teams to negotiate **local television contracts** for regular season games, whereas the NFL does not. This arrangement results in great disparity in revenue among teams. For example, the Yankees generate significantly more income from the local television contract with the Yankees Entertainment and Sports (YES) Network than do the Pittsburgh Pirates through their agreement with Fox Sports Pittsburgh.

local television contracts—Agreements made between professional teams and local television stations and regional sport networks. These agreements provide teams with additional media revenue beyond what they receive from the national television contract.

In reality, these dollar amounts listed in table 6.3 may represent the zenith of media rights fees. Although the next NFL agreement may be larger, it may be based on 18 regular season games, not the 16 games required in the current contract. Why are we projecting national and cable media rights fees to decline?

TABLE 6.3 Media Agreements for Four Professional Sport Leagues

League	Network TV	Cable TV	Satellite or other provider	Total TV-related revenue
NFL	$11.6 billion	$8.8 billion	$3.5 billion	$23.9 billion[a]
NBA	$2.4 billion	$2.2 billion	n.a.	$4.6 billion[b]
MLB	$1.5 billion	$1.755 billion	n.a.	$3.255 billion[c]
NHL	Revenue share	$72.5 million	n.a.	$72.5 million[d]

Note: All figures are in US$.

[a]Although the dollar figures include the network agreement through 2011, cable through 2013, and DirecTV through 2014, they do not include revenue from the NFL Network (Joyner, 2004).

[b]These figures do not include revenue from DirecTV NBA League Pass or the NBA Network (*NBA TV Contracts*, 2009).

[c]Does not include revenue from DirecTV Extra Innings Package or from the newly formed MLB Network (Bloom, 2006).

[d]The contract with Versus was for the 2008–09 season only; revenue does include NHL Center Ice package with DirecTV or the NHL Network (*NHL, Versus Negotiate*, 2008).

n.a.—not applicable.

- Each league now has its own network (e.g., MLB Network, NHL Network) and is broadcasting games on those networks; hence, the leagues are becoming limited competitors as well as partners.
- Sponsorship dollars that are a large part of television rights fees have been affected by the economic crisis of 2008–2010 and will decline.
- Television is becoming fragmented, and alternative entertainment options are emerging.

Gate Receipts

As late as 1950, gate receipts and concessions accounted for more that 92% of the revenue of professional teams (Gorman & Calhoun, 1994). With the increasing importance of media revenues, professional sport teams have become less reliant on gate receipts, although gate receipts remain the major source of revenue for NHL and MLS teams as well as minor league baseball. In addition, gate receipts have historically been the most important source of revenue for newer professional leagues such as the WNBA and WPS. The home team retains the majority of the gate receipts, but to varying degrees, depending on the league, a portion of the gate receipts is given to the league (to cover league operating expenses) and a portion of the proceeds may be given to the visiting team. This is not to say that gate receipts are not of consequence to MLB, the NBA, and the NFL. For example, in 2007 the Yankees grossed a US$188 million in gate receipts (Brown, 2008). Table 6.4 provides a sampling of attendance information from a variety of professional sport leagues.

Licensing and Merchandising Revenues

Licensing revenues are generated when leagues and teams grant merchandise and apparel manufacturers the right to use their names and logos. In return for that right, the leagues and teams receive a royalty (i.e., a percentage of the selling price) for each item sold by the manufacturers. These agreements have been an increasingly lucrative source of revenue for professional teams. Licensing programs, administered by the league offices, distribute the revenue equally among the teams. Domestic licensing revenues, however, have begun to plateau as the market for such merchandise has become saturated. The ability to continue to increase licensing revenues depends partly on the growth and demand for league-licensed video games and the demand for league-licensed products overseas. Although leagues continue to seek new opportunities for revenue growth, this revenue stream appears to have leveled off during the 2000 through 2010 period.

TABLE 6.4 Attendance Information from Select Professional Sport Leagues*

League	Average attendance	Percent of capacity	Number of teams at 90% of capacity or greater
NFL (2008)	68,241	97.3%	29 out of 32
NBA (2008–09)	17,385	90.4%	18 out of 30
NHL (2008–09)	17,460	94.8%	20 out of 30
MLB (2008)	32,543	73.2%	8 out of 30
MLS (2008)	16,402	59.9%	3 out of 14
WNBA (2008)	7,917	72.2%	1 out of 14

*Some attendance figures include only partial seasons because of the publication schedule of this textbook.

Adapted from Turnstile Tracker 2008a, 2008b, 2009a, 2009b, 2009c.

sponsorship—The acquisition of rights to affiliate or associate directly with a product or event for the purpose of deriving benefits related to that affiliation or association (Mullin, Hardy, & Sutton, 2007).

Sponsorship

Consider for a moment the magnitude of these sponsorship agreements:

- Prudential Insurance is paying an average of US$5.27 million over 20 years to have its name on the new arena in Newark, New Jersey, which is the home to professional hockey (New Jersey Devils), collegiate basketball (Seton Hall University), and professional soccer (New Jersey Ironmen) ("Naming Rights Deals," 2007)
- Major League Soccer (MLS) and adidas signed off on a 10-year, US$150 million agreement (Warfield, 2005).

Given Mullin, Hardy, and Sutton's (2007) definition of **sponsorship**, these associations and affiliations could be quite lucrative.

LED signage—Signage located in the arena bowl and primarily found on the fascia below the upper bowl. This signage is computer generated and has the capability to add sound, animation, and other visual effects to present a colorful eye-catching message. LED, which stands for light emitting diode, signage is usually sold in 30-second increments with a predetermined number of rotations per game.

virtual signage—Signage that is generated by digital technology and placed into a sport event telecast so that it appears as though the sign is part of the playing surface or adjacent to the playing surface.

Most leagues and teams have more than 100 sponsorship agreements in place and are always looking for more. Revenue per agreement has dropped in recent years, putting more pressure on teams and leagues to find additional sponsors to make up the revenue shortfall. The benefits provided to sponsors through the associations and affiliations often include signage that is visible in the sport venue as well as on television (local broadcasts only). The demand for signage location visible to both attendees and television viewers has led sport marketers to seek new and innovative display techniques such as rotational signage (stationary signage placed on scoreboards and around the playing surfaces that rotates the advertisements shown, usually in 15- to 30-second intervals), **LED signage** (computer-generated signage that can be animated, is much more visual, and is typically found above the lower bowl and below the upper bowl in arenas and stadiums), and **virtual signage** (also computer-generated but imposed over an existing space, such as the wall behind home plate on telecasts during baseball games).

FUTURE CHALLENGES FACING PROFESSIONAL SPORT

As teams in professional sport move to the future, they face a variety of challenges, many of which we have already discussed in this chapter. Although all the challenges are too many to enumerate in this section, we have isolated four major challenges that professional teams face in the future: maintaining reasonable labor–management relations, developing new revenue streams, managing new technology, and dealing with globalization.

- ***Maintaining labor–management harmony in the face of rising salaries.*** First, given the history of acrimony between the players (labor) and the owners (management), and the history of work stoppages (i.e., strikes or lockouts), a continual challenge for professional sport will be ensuring that the games go on. As evidenced by the NHL lockout that cancelled the entire 2004–05 season, accomplishing this goal is not always easy. Although typically a variety of issues create tension between labor and management, the most visible conflict is associated with the owners' desire to manage costs, mostly tied to players' salaries. At the same time, the players are seeking their fair share of the ever-increasing revenues generated by teams and their owners. For this reason, labor disputes are likely to keep occurring.

All eyes have been on the latest round of NFL negotiations with the NFLPA, which commenced in 2009. Early speculation is that league leadership and ownership supported by the television partners will seek to convince the players to agree to an 18-game regular season schedule (up from the current 16 games) to generate additional revenue. Such an agreement would probably avoid a work stoppage in the NFL. The NBA, NHL, and MLB will all monitor this situation closely if any attempt is made to lower player compensation and monies allocated to player salaries. This will be an issue in the other leagues, especially the NBA. For further discussion of this topic, refer to the critical thinking scenario presented later.

- ***Developing new revenue streams.*** Table 6.2 provides the average salaries in professional sport. The size of those salaries has clearly had an effect on the business of sport. To fund continued increases, team owners are looking for new revenue streams or ways to enhance existing revenue streams. Technological advances, such as the virtual signage and satellite television opportunities examined earlier, have already provided significant new revenues to leagues and teams. Such quests for revenue enhancement are likely to continue in the future, and technology will probably be involved. Think for a minute about how our world is shrinking because of technology. Professional sport crosses international barriers with increasing regularity. The Manchester United professional football (soccer to North Americans) team is so popular in Asia that the franchise can operate merchandise stores there. The sales of professional sport products globally, whether through broadcasts or apparel, will continue to be a focus for professional sport organizations.

  One of the more intriguing new revenue stories of late is the formation of Legends Hospitality Management by the Yankees, Cowboys, and equity partner Goldman Sachs. Legends manages regular concessions, suite catering, and team stores at the new Yankees and Cowboys stadiums that opened in 2009. Legends plans to pursue other accounts in the major leagues, as well as college athletics and international sports (Kaplan & Muret, 2008). If this joint effort proves successful, watch for similar models involving successful brands in various leagues to try other ventures.

- ***Meeting the challenges created by technology.*** The same technologies that have helped spread the popularity of professional sport and increase revenues have also created the most competitive entertainment and leisure landscape ever. Twenty-five years ago people could access four or five TV channels. Today they can access hundreds of channels and choose from a wide variety of entertainment without leaving their homes. Further, think about all the other leisure options that compete with the consumption of sporting events. Video games, movies, numerous outdoor activities, e-mail, instant messaging, and other activities occupy people's time as never before. Couple this with the fact that new sports and sporting genres such as action sports appear to be here to stay, and you can clearly see how professional teams have to compete for consumers' attention and money as never before. This competition is likely to continue in the future. Technology will also present challenges to the traditional business models employed by professional sport. For example, digital video recorders (DVRs) such as TiVo allow people to consume sporting events and shows at their leisure and more quickly because they can skip through commercials. This practice may significantly affect the broadcast advertising models that are currently in place. Similarly, the streaming of video content to handheld devices such as cell phones creates a new way for athletes, teams, and leagues to deliver broadcasts. The challenge is to determine what consumers want and how to provide it. Further, at the league level, the emergence of such new sources of revenue will challenge traditional league revenue-sharing concepts.

WEB

Go to the OSG and complete the second Web search activity, which shows you how emerging technology can help you find information and view sporting events.

- ***Dealing with globalization.*** New technologies are also helping spread professional sport across international boundaries as never before. Thanks to technology, Japanese fans can watch Ichiro Suzuki play for MLB's Seattle Mariners and Chinese fans can watch Yao Ming play for the NBA's Houston Rockets. Similarly, new means to facilitate the spread of sport across international boundaries are emerging every day. The NFL has played exhibition and regular season games in Mexico City, London, Toronto, Tokyo, and Berlin, and in the future two regular season games could be played abroad in the

A UNIQUE MATCH-UP: GIORGIO ARMANI AND PROFESSIONAL BASKETBALL

By Giorgio Gandolfi, editor-in-chief
***FIBA Assist Magazine,* ITALY**

Giorgio Armani. His name evokes a sense of style, class, and elegance, which befits the well-respected Italian clothing empire that is his namesake. The name *Armani* also means big-time basketball in Italy. That's because the Armani Jeans label sponsors Olimpia Milan, one of the most successful teams in the Italian professional basketball league. In 2008, after sponsoring the team for four years, Mr. Armani purchased the fabled club that had already won 25 national championships. Olimpia Milan immediately repaid Armani's belief in them, reaching the finals of the 2008–09 Italian league championship before falling to the team from Siena, which captured its fourth title.

Mr. Armani explained his interest in basketball:

> I have always admired the world of sports, and basketball particularly, because I am tied to my memories [his sister, Rosanna, played basketball]. Sport is very important because it helps people grow. It also offers ideal challenges that people can meet, build strength, and develop discipline, which molds the body and gives power to the mind.

AJ | ARMANI JEANS
MILANO

Photo courtesy of Giorgio Armani S.P.A.

Olimpia Milan players wearing their Armani Jeans-sponsored uniforms.

same year. Similarly, MLB has held season-opening games in other countries, as has the NBA. MLB has been an integral part of the World Baseball Classic, which was played in 2006 and 2009. The NBA sent the Orlando Magic and the Cleveland Cavaliers to China in 2007 to participate in the China Games, and in 2009, the Denver Nuggets and Indiana Pacers played an exhibition game in China. These efforts have been geared toward increasing the global popularity of the sports as a way to generate more revenue. One obvious decision facing the leagues is whether to put a professional team outside North America. This issue raises several challenges, such as how to deal with cultural differences and account for exchange rates. At a league-specific level, NFL Europe, the NFL's former development league that played games in the spring and summer, never was profitable, and its long-term viability was always in question. These issues are just a few of the challenges facing professional sport in the future.

> I recognize all these character traits when I watch the young players. I can read it on their faces, on and off the court. They have ambition, great motivation and passion, which magically generate excitement and capture the hearts of the fans. I have the same reaction, and for these reasons, as a Milanese, I decided to donate this beloved team to the city of Milan.

Mr. Armani's sporting interests extend far beyond his Armani Jeans team. He has also turned his attention to the youth of Milan. Livio Proli, the Olimpia team president, has launched the Armani Junior Program with the help of Gianmarco Pozzecco, one of Italy's most beloved basketball players. Professor William Sutton, a former vice president with the National Basketball Association in the United States, is a marketing consultant for the program.

Fifty youth teams from Milan and the surrounding area are affiliated with the program, learning not only the rudiments of basketball but also what it takes to be a true sportsperson. In collaboration with the Milan City Hall, summer day camps for 5,000 youth between 6 and 14 years of age were organized last summer. Other Armani-sponsored events aimed at young athletes are on the drawing board and set to launch over the next few years. The overriding goals are to develop new players for the Armani Jeans team and to help all people involved in local basketball, including coaches, team officials, doctors, trainers, and conditioning coaches.

Although Giorgio Armani calls Piacenza his birthplace, the city of Milan is where he has grown as a fashion icon and where he continues to be an avid promoter of sport as a way of life for the young people of the city. He has given Milan a top basketball team and is helping to secure the team's future success by bringing top-level instruction to young athletes who want to learn to play basketball. That is surely a legacy that the city of Milan will never forget.

INTERNATIONAL LEARNING ACTIVITY #1

Using information posted at www.eurobasket.com, write a report on both men's and women's professional basketball in a country or continent other than your own. Focus on one or two specific aspects that you find interesting (e.g., numbers of teams, competitive schedules, summer camps, national age group teams, news items).

INTERNATIONAL LEARNING ACTIVITY #2

Go to Web sites of five professional sport leagues or teams and explore ways in which they give back to their communities and societies (e.g., WNBA Cares, WizardsCare, Florida Marlins Community Foundation, Chicago Red Stars Charitable Foundation, and Euroleague for Life). Write a paper describing the grassroots efforts of these organizations.

CAREER OPPORTUNITIES IN PROFESSIONAL SPORT

Like any business, a professional sport organization constantly attempts to upgrade its efficiency through its personnel. In searching for new employees, management often looks to sport management and administration programs, to other professional sport organizations, and to people working in the corporate sector who may have skills essential to the sport industry.

Common Categories of Work Responsibility

The types and existence of positions in professional sport organizations vary from team to team and sport to sport. For example, MLB teams, because of their extensive

Photo courtesy of Jeff Ianello.

In Profile: Jeff Ianello

Toward the end of my senior year of college I had little idea where my career was going to begin. I had learned that breaking into the world of sport was going to be difficult. Every job I was being interviewed for was a sales position (in retrospect, I realized that companies were seeking help in sales because they always need people who can produce revenue). Ultimately, I was recommended for an entry-level ticket sales program with the NBA's Hornets, who were just moving from Charlotte to New Orleans. The job entailed selling season tickets as well as ticket packages and group sales. If not for the relationships and advice that my professors had given me, I would not have been recommended for the position, nor would I have accepted it.

My first month as an inside sales representative for the New Orleans Hornets was a rollercoaster ride. Sales consultants recommended by the NBA were sent in to train the staff of 10 new hires. Considering that I had minimal sales experience, the consultants' word was gospel to me. After training we were thrust into the fire of making sales calls. We did most of this by phone, attempting to contact decision makers at businesses, with an occasional face-to-face appointment mixed in. Dealing with rejection, both soft and harsh, was new to me. I quickly identified two things that could give me a competitive advantage—my call volume (it seemed logical that more opportunities would produce more sales) and my technique (the more I worked at it, the better I would be on every call). These two factors paid off as I rose to the top of my inside sales class. After six months in New Orleans I accepted a job as a season ticket account executive on the senior staff with the Phoenix Suns.

I have been in Phoenix for about six and a half years. The basic principles that I learned in New Orleans and the tutelage that I received from my managers in Phoenix led me to become one of the top producers on a senior level and someone who has been fortunate enough to ascend to inside sales manager, director of sales and development, and now senior director of sales. I always feel refreshed when I go to work in the morning because my office is inside a sports arena! My workday begins sometime between 6:45 and 7:15 a.m., because I have found that the best time to get busy work done is before and after hours. Developing great sales people is a pillar of my management philosophy, so I usually send out an e-mail to rally the troops by setting goals for the day or providing a tip on sales technique or sales strategy. I also like to set the pace and lead by example for our current sales staff and managers so they are aware of the importance of work ethic and time management. I have found it is a much better message to do as I say *and* as I do than to simply do as I say.

minor league systems, employ more people in player personnel than do teams in the NBA or the NFL. In addition, minor league organizations (e.g., International Hockey League [IHL], East Coast Hockey League [ECHL]) typically employ fewer people than do major league organizations (e.g., NHL, MLS). This section highlights positions that may be available within any professional sport organization. Major professional sport teams typically have several executives on board:

- Chief executive or operating officer (CEO or COO)—responsible for the day-to-day functioning of the entire organization, both on the field (performance) and off the field (revenue generation)
- Chief financial officer (CFO)—responsible for the organization's accounting and financial planning
- Chief marketing officer (CMO)—responsible for coordinating the marketing mix among communications, ticket sales, and corporate sponsorship and partnership sales

- General counsel—responsible for overseeing all legal matters associated with the team including, but not limited to, player contracts, liability issues, and marketing contracts
- General manager—typically responsible for acquiring, developing, trading, and releasing talent, as well as creating a development system for young players

Beyond these executive positions, jobs with professional sport teams typically fall into two categories:

1. Player personnel positions
2. Business positions

Player Personnel Positions

Numerous jobs focus on player personnel. These jobs involve putting the best possible team on the field or court. Descriptions of these jobs follow. Before you examine the individual jobs on this side of the professional sport organization, recognize the difficulty and competitiveness associated with these positions. Because many of the positions require intricate knowledge of the sport, being a former athlete, or even a former professional athlete, in the particular sport may be a prerequisite for success.

- ***Player personnel.*** This department is involved in identifying, evaluating, and developing potential and current players. In baseball, this department would also be involved in observing players assigned to the minor leagues. Typical jobs in this area include being a scout, in which researching potential draft picks and upcoming opponents are central responsibilities. The pinnacle position within the player personnel side of the organization is typically the general manager position. The general manager is the final decision maker on drafting and trading decisions.

- ***Medical, training, and team support.*** These people assume responsibility for the physical (and sometimes mental) preparation and readiness of the players. Responsibilities include medical care, treatment of injuries, rehabilitation, dental care, nutrition, strength training and conditioning, career counseling, and after-care programs.

- ***Coaching staff.*** This group concentrates on all activities occurring between the lines. In other words, these professionals are primarily concerned with coaching, managing, and training the players on their rosters.

- ***Player education and relations.*** People in these positions are typically responsible for educating players on issues like financial management, substance abuse, nutrition, image management, and additional higher education. Other responsibilities may include working as a liaison between the team and players with respect to player appearances in the community.

- ***Video support staff.*** Responsibilities of the video support staff include producing and editing videos, purchasing and maintaining video hardware and software products, supervising and coordinating satellite feeds, and coordinating all broadcasting that originates at the home facility. The video support staff also is responsible for filming games and maintaining the team's library of game films and player-evaluation videos.

- ***Stadium and facility staff.*** This group is responsible for the maintenance, upkeep, and repair of the playing surface. They are also responsible for preparing the team's offices, locker rooms, training facilities, practice facilities, and playing fields. In terms of playing surfaces and related areas, these people are the liaisons between the venue management team and the professional franchise.

Case Study

The phone rang in Tonya Mertz's apartment. As a senior in the sport management program at Smithson University, Tonya was hoping that this would be a return phone call about an internship for summer.

"Hi, Tonya, this is Kristin Carter of the Raleigh Flyers. I'm calling to offer you an internship in our community relations department. Your responsibilities will include assisting with all of our charitable efforts and events in the community. Your background working in the community with your team at Smithson is what convinced us that you were right for this internship. What do you think?"

"Ms. Carter, I am flattered by your offer," said Tonya. "Would it be possible to think about this over the weekend?"

"No problem, Tonya. I will look forward to hearing your response on Monday," concluded Carter.

Tonya was excited as she hung up the phone. As a four-year starter on the Smithson basketball team, Tonya's career had just ended. Knowing that she was not quite good enough for the WNBA, Tonya decided to parlay her passion for basketball into a career in professional basketball. This opportunity with the Flyers could provide the start she was looking for . . . until the phone rang again.

"Hello, Tonya. This is Paul Butterworth of the Topeka Trackers [a new team in the NBA Development League]. I'm calling to offer you an internship position in marketing. As you know, we are a new organization. So, while this is an internship, we are poised to integrate you into the workings of our ticket sales, corporate sales, and promotions efforts."

Tonya was stunned, but she collected herself enough to say, "Wow, Mr. Butterworth, that sounds great. But would you mind if I took the weekend to think about it?"

"No problem, Tonya. I will wait for your call on Monday." With that Butterworth hung up.

Tonya did not know what to do. She was stunned. Five minutes ago, she was all but headed for the Raleigh-Durham area. Now another company was offering her an internship. What should she do?

Based on what you learned in this chapter, and in chapter 2, and what you can garner from outside research, consider the following questions:

1. What does Tonya need to consider before making a decision?
2. What are the advantages and disadvantages of each opportunity?
3. What are the opportunities for growth with each opportunity?

Business Positions

Unlike the player personnel side of the organization, the business side does not have any control over team performance issues. But people in these positions play an important role in the organization because they are responsible for generating revenue, marketing the product, developing a fan base, and working with customers and other stakeholders.

- *Ticket sales.* One of two types of sales representatives within the organization, ticket sales people typically focus on selling season tickets, partial season tickets, and group tickets. They target not only individual ticket purchasers but also groups and corporations that can buy either a larger number of tickets or expensive season tickets. Working in ticket sales is a good first position in professional sport. Many openings are available in this area because teams must sell a large number of tickets to maximize team revenues.
- *Corporate sales.* In contrast to those who primarily sell individual tickets, corporate salespeople target corporations exclusively. Corporate salespeople may sell corporate sponsorships, luxury suites, or club seats.
- *Game experience.* Responsibilities for these positions focus on enhancing the experience of people who attend games. Specific tasks may include overseeing the music, video boards, and public address messaging during a game. Opportunities in

this area have increased as stadia and arenas have become more sophisticated and as teams have increasingly focused on providing an entertaining experience both on and off the field, court, or ice.

- ***Advertising.*** Responsibilities in advertising include designing and writing advertising copy and identifying, securing, and placing advertisements in a variety of media. The sport organization may handle this responsibility in-house or outsource it to an advertising agency that specializes in ad creation and placement.
- ***Promotions.*** Like the game experience area, promotions offers increasing opportunity as organizations focus on providing an optimal experience to spectators. Responsibilities in promotions typically include overseeing all promotional activity that occurs on the field of play or in the stands during the game.
- ***Community relations.*** This department may be part of the public relations or marketing department. The community relations staff is responsible for creating and administering grassroots functions, such as clinics and other charitable events that the team sponsors. Staff members are also responsible for implementing leaguewide programs, such as the NBA's Read to Achieve program.
- ***Media relations.*** This department is involved in assisting and working with the media by providing information necessary for game coverage and publicity. This job includes ensuring that the needs of the media are met at every sporting event. People in media relations positions are also responsible for all publications, such as media guides, yearbooks, and game programs.
- ***Database marketing coordinator.*** People in this area focus on building databases of information about the team's customers so that the team can more effectively serve its customers and better meet their needs. This position may also include overseeing the marketing research efforts of the professional sport organization.
- ***Hospitality coordinators.*** Hospitality coordinators are responsible for the game-related needs of corporate clients, club seat holders, and luxury box owners. This responsibility includes coordinating the provision of food, beverages, and any other special needs (e.g., Internet connection) required by corporate clients.
- ***Ticketing.*** This department may or may not include the ticket sales staff. Ticketing personnel manage the ticket inventory. They are responsible for ticket distribution, printing, accounting, game-day box office sales, complimentary tickets, and the financial settlement for the visiting team.

ACTION

Go to the OSG and complete the Learning in Action activity, which tests how well you remembered some of the key terms and their definitions used throughout this chapter.

CRITICAL THINKING IN PROFESSIONAL SPORT

Assume that you work for a major professional sport league that is establishing a league-controlled cable network (e.g., NBA TV, MLB Network, NFL Network, NHL Network). The success of these networks depends on your ability to (a) gain distribution through all the cable carriers (e.g., Comcast) and (b) attract enough viewers to be able to sell advertising during programming at a price that will generate a profit. Central to meeting this goal is the quality and attractiveness of the programming offered on the network. Although you can control rebroadcasts of your games, your past practice has been to sell the rights to televise your games to networks and cable channels. That said, if you carried live games, you could sell the advertising in-house (using league resources) and attract a broad audience interested in watching your games. You are now approaching the point where you need to decide whether and how much of the current content (e.g., games) you do not allow the networks and cable channels to use so that you can use the live games to attract viewers.

PORTFOLIO

Complete the critical thinking portfolio activity in the OSG, consulting as needed the "Eight Critical Thinking Questions" section in chapter 1.

ETHICS IN PROFESSIONAL SPORT

The topic of professional athletes' use of performance-enhancing drugs has been at the forefront of conversations about professional sport for the better part of the last 20 years (including in 2010 when former slugger Mark McGwire admitted steroid use during his playing days and Floyd Landis admitted to using performance-enhancing drugs during his professional career as a cyclist). Interestingly, the collective bargaining process has played an important role in this issue. Taking MLB as an example, some argue that management was aware that the gaudy batting statistics posted after 1995 were due to the use of steroids or other illegal supplements and that management ignored this circumstance because of the marketing benefits that accrued from high-scoring games, record-breaking performances, and more towering home runs than ever. Finally, in the past decade, management sought to implement a drug-testing program. Yet this issue is part of the collective bargaining agreement. Therefore, the Major League Baseball Players Association (MLBPA) was not willing initially to agree to a drug-testing program unless management was willing to give concessions in other areas of the collective bargaining process (e.g., more flexibility with free agency, lessening of the luxury tax). Further, the MLBPA could argue that they were acting in the best interests of their players to resist a drug-testing program. Not until the last five years did societal and governmental pressure become so significant that both labor and management agreed on a drug-testing program. Even then, the program was enacted only after a year of confidential testing whereby the volume of positive drug tests had to exceed a certain level for a program to be implemented.

PORTFOLIO

Complete the ethical issues portfolio activity in the OSG, consulting as needed the "Guidelines for Making Ethical Decisions" section in chapter 1.

Summary

Professional sport is a large part of the entertainment, social, political, economic, legal, and cultural fabric of North America. The continued growth of the media and related technology, particularly television and the Internet, ensures that professional sport is prevalent and highly accessible, regardless of the demographic characteristics of its audience. Because of this accessibility and prevalence, the importance of the roles that labor, management, and governance play often seem out of balance when compared with their roles in other forms of business. For the most part, reserve clauses, free agency, league think, and antitrust exemptions exist only in the context of professional sport. These concepts are not essential in conducting the traditional activities of mainstream business operations, but they appear to be essential to the survival of the business of professional sport. Further, these concepts will be crucial for those involved in new professional sport leagues, such as Women's Professional Soccer (WPS), to understand if they are to be successful. By understanding the unique limitations and opportunities of professional sport as well as the revenue sources and the influence of the media, you will be able to appreciate the career challenges and possibilities in the field.

QUIZ TIME

Did you grasp all the key points in this chapter? Go to the OSG for a short quiz to test your understanding of the material.

Review Questions

1. Since 1850, what have been the three most significant developments affecting the growth of professional sport?
2. How is the management of professional sport different from the management of Microsoft?
3. Why is league think important to professional sport?
4. What has been the effect of the Sports Broadcasting Act of 1961? How does it affect media rights agreements today?

5. Can professional sport continue to grow its revenues? Identify the revenue sources that can be enhanced.
6. What would you consider three future challenges that will face the professional sport segment of the sport industry?
7. What are the two general categories of jobs within a professional sport organization?

References

Bloom, H. (2006, July 13). *Going inside MLB's latest $3 billion TV agreements.* Retrieved June 12, 2010, from www.sportsbusinessnews.com/_news/news_347260.php

Brown, M. (2008, May 18). *Papers show Yankees had $188M in gate receipts.* Retrieved January 31, 2010, from www.bizofbaseball.com/index.php?option=com_content&task=view&id=2194&Itemid=42

Browne, L. (1992). *Girls of summer.* Toronto: HarperCollins.

Federal Base Ball Club of Baltimore, Inc. v. National League of Professional Base Ball Clubs, 259 U.S. 200 (1922).

Freedman, W. (1987). *Professional sports and antitrust.* New York: Quorum.

Gorman, J., & Calhoun, K. (1994). *The name of the game: The business of sports.* New York: Wiley.

Guterson, D. (1994, September 1). Moneyball: On the relentless promotion of pro sports. *Harper's Magazine,* pp. 37–46.

Harris, D. (1986). *The league: The rise and decline of the NFL.* New York: Bantam.

Joyner, J. (2004, November 9). *NFL signs new television contract.* Retrieved January 31, 2010, from www.outsidethebeltway.com/archives/nfl_signs_new_television_contract/

Kaplan, D., & Muret, D. (2008, October 20). A sports brand dream team gets into concessions game. *Street & Smith's SportsBusiness Journal,* pp. 1, 7.

Kendrick, S. (2009). *2009 Baseball team payrolls.* Retrieved May 16, 2009, from http://baseball.about.com/od/newsrumors/a/09teamsalaries.htm

Mullin, B.J., Hardy, S., & Sutton, W.A. (2007). *Sport marketing* (3rd ed.). Champaign, IL: Human Kinetics.

Naming rights deals. (2007, December 24). *Street & Smith's SportsBusiness Journal,* p. 27.

NBA TV contracts. (2009). Retrieved January 31, 2010, from www.insidehoops.com/nba-tv-contracts.shtml

Negro league baseball: Timeline of events in professional black baseball. (2005). Retrieved May 16, 2009, from www.negroleaguebaseball.com/timeline.html

NHL, Versus negotiate a 3-year extension. (2008). Retrieved January 31, 2010, from www.cbc.ca/sports/hockey/story/2008/01/22/nhl-versus-extension.html

Rader, B.G. (2009). *American sports: From the age of folk games to the age of televised sports* (6th ed.). Upper Saddle River, NJ: Pearson/Prentice Hall.

Roberts, R., & Olson, J. (1995). *Winning is the only thing: Sports in America since 1945.* Baltimore: Johns Hopkins University Press.

Staudohar, P.D. (1989). *The sports industry and collective bargaining.* Cornell, NY: ILR.

Staudohar, P.D., & Mangan, J.A. (1991). *The business of professional sports.* Urbana: University of Illinois Press.

Turnstile tracker. (2008a, September 22). WNBA. *Street & Smith's SportsBusiness Journal,* p. 17.

Turnstile tracker. (2008b, December 1). NFL. *Street & Smith's SportsBusiness Journal,* p. 12.

Turnstile tracker. (2009a, March 30). NBA. *Street & Smith's SportsBusiness Journal,* p. 20.

Turnstile tracker. (2009b, April 20). NHL. *Street & Smith's SportsBusiness Journal,* p. 14.

Turnstile tracker. (2009c, May 4). MLB and MLS. *Street & Smith's SportsBusiness Journal,* p. 12.

Warfield, S. (2005, March 21). Selling soccer. *Street & Smith's SportsBusiness Journal,* p. 32.

Weisman, L. (2008, November 14). NFL salaries '08: Big Ben smiling as highest-paid player. *USA Today.* Retrieved June 12, 2010, from www.usatoday.com/sports/football/nfl/2008-11-05-salaries_N.htm

HISTORICAL MOMENTS

1852	First intercollegiate sport competition held: Yale–Harvard Regatta
1906	Intercollegiate Athletic Association of the United States (IAAUS) formed; name changed to National Collegiate Athletic Association (NCAA) in 1910
1912	Central Intercollegiate Athletics Association founded, oldest Black athletics conference, comprising 12 institutions of higher education
1935	First presentation of Heisman Trophy took place
1939	First NCAA Men's Basketball Championship game held: University of Oregon over Ohio State University, 46-33
1942	Eddie Robinson became head football coach of Grambling State University; retired in 1997
1951	Walter Byers appointed first executive director of NCAA
1971	Association for Intercollegiate Athletics for Women (AIAW) formed; disbanded in 1982
1973	NCAA split its membership into Divisions I, II, and III
1987	NCAA levied "death penalty" on SMU football program because of repeat violations of NCAA rules
1989	Knight Commission formed by the Knight Foundation in response to scandals in college sports
1994	Equity in Athletics Disclosure Act (EADA) established
1998	Bowl Championship Series (BCS) established
2002	CBS TV signed 11-year rights deal with NCAA for US$6 billion
2009	Pat Summitt reached 1,000 career wins; became all-time wins leader in NCAA basketball history

Photo courtesy of Bowling Green State University.

7

INTERCOLLEGIATE ATHLETICS

Ellen J. Staurowsky ■ Robertha Abney

LEARNING OBJECTIVES

1. Define intercollegiate athletics.
2. Demonstrate an understanding of the events surrounding the development of intercollegiate athletics.
3. Describe the purposes of intercollegiate athletics governance organizations.
4. Identify key administrative personnel within intercollegiate athletics departments.
5. Identify the roles and responsibilities of personnel working in intercollegiate athletics departments.
6. Discuss several current challenges facing intercollegiate athletics administrators.
7. Identify key associations, organizations, and publications related to intercollegiate athletics.

GET A JOB!

☑ Continue on your journey in sport management by going to the Online Study Guide (OSG) at www.HumanKinetics.com/ContemporarySportManagement. Check out the job opportunities and consider the skills and experiences that can help you succeed in sport management.

Key Terms

academic progress rate (APR)
Equity in Athletics Disclosure Act (EADA)
executive search firm
HBCUs
licensing royalty
outsourcing
senior woman administrator
TCUs
ticket operations
ticket scalping

From the intrigues of the Bowl Championship Series (BCS) to March Madness, college sport occupies a prominent place not only within the sport culture of the United States but also within broader society. ESPN's coverage of President Barack Obama's NCAA men's tournament bracket in March 2009 and the national media coverage of his attendance at the Georgetown vs. Duke basketball game in January 2010 illustrate the point vividly.

Whether one is the leader of the Free World or just an average citizen of "fan nation," the fate of favored and favorite teams is the subject of much attention. Bloggers churn out speculation as to which team will come out on top and which shoe company has reached an agreement with which university for a multiyear, big-money sponsorship deal. Fans, as avid in their watchfulness as those following the stock market, fervently monitor the prospects of high school recruits on Rivals.com while following coaches on Twitter. Through sport media coverage, which relies on multimedia platforms including television, radio, print, and Web-based publications, players and coaches become celebrities, and the games themselves entertain millions of fans around the country.

There is much more to college sport than meets the eye. The financial stakes are high, as evidenced by the 13-year, US$10.8 billion agreement that the National Collegiate Athletic Association (NCAA) reached with CBS and Turner Broadcasting in 2010 for the broadcast rights to the men's Division I basketball tournament, which expands to 68 teams in 2011 (Sandomir & Thamel, 2010). In turn, the Bowl Championship Series (BCS) negotiated a new 4-year deal in 2009 (which will go into effect in 2011) worth US$125 million per year (Frommer, 2009). Of equal importance are the reputations of the schools that sponsor these athletics programs. The purpose of this chapter is to provide an overview of contemporary US college athletics and to create a snapshot of what goes on behind the scenes. After reading this chapter, you should have a better understanding of the organizations that govern and regulate college sport, the way that college athletics programs operate, and the kinds of careers that you might wish to pursue in this segment of the sport industry.

ORIGINS OF INTERCOLLEGIATE ATHLETICS GOVERNANCE

According to most historical accounts, college sport as we have come to know it started with a challenge that would "test the superiority of the oarsmen" of Harvard University and Yale University (Veneziano, 2002, ¶ 1). Harvard prevailed in a 2-mile (3.2 km) race proposed by executives from the Boston, Concord, and Montreal Railroad as a way of boosting tourism and travel. According to Edes (1922), "The race was supposed to be a frolic and no idea was entertained of establishing a precedent" (p. 347). As much of a lark at it appears to have been, the event held in 1852 may have been more significant than quaint depictions suggest. Democratic presidential nominee Franklin Pierce, who would eventually win the White House later that same year, attended, as did other dignitaries who would play an important role in pre–Civil War America as lawyers, politicians, and educators.

The fact that the students brokered the deal with the Boston, Concord, and Montreal Railroad, however, reflects how times have changed. During the latter half of the 1800s, college sport was essentially run by students, sometimes as social occasions, at other times as highly competitive contests, and often as a form of protest against boring recitations and a curriculum that did not match their aspirations and goals. By the early part of the 1900s, a shift toward "professional" coaches, overspecialization, and an emphasis on winning against perennial rivals was well underway. As Harvard football coach Bill Reid would document in his diary in 1905, coaches of the age were negotiating with faculty to keep players eligible, developing strategies to subvert an inquisitive press, and clashing with college presidents over the role of sport on college campuses (Smith, 1994).

Prompted by deaths and charges of brutality in college football, President Theodore Roosevelt hosted two White House conferences on football in 1905. Roosevelt summoned coaches, faculty, and alumni representatives from Harvard, Yale, and Princeton universities to the conference. The purpose of the conference was to encourage the representatives to carry out both the letter and the spirit of the football rules. Roosevelt's decree led to the formation of the Intercollegiate Athletic Association of the United States (IAAUS), which was officially constituted on March 31, 1906, and became known as the National Collegiate Athletic Association (NCAA) in 1910 (Crowley, 2006).

National Collegiate Athletic Association (NCAA)

The NCAA is the largest and most influential college sport governing body in the United States. Its membership includes more than 1,288 colleges and universities, conferences, and sport organizations. NCAA rules and regulations focus on amateurism, recruiting, eligibility, playing and practice seasons, athletically related financial aid, championships, and enforcement (*Composition*, n.d.).

The NCAA membership is separated into three competitive divisions, generally referred to as Divisions I, II, and III (see figure 7.1). Several factors determine the divisional classification for NCAA member institutions. These include the number of sports sponsored, the type of sport sponsored (team or individual), the size of the athletics department budget, attendance at games and seating capacity in stadia and arenas, and whether the program offers athletics grants-in-aid. Among football-playing institutions in Division I, subdivisions formerly referred to as Division I-A and I-AA are now referred to as the Football Bowl Subdivision (FBS) and the Football Championship Subdivision (FCS).

The divisional structure within the NCAA is a reflection of how the association has grown and changed over time. At its inception in 1906, the NCAA had 28 members. Expansion in the 1950s and 1960s led to the creation of what were then called the University and College divisions. The three-division system in place within the NCAA arose in the 1970s as the membership continued to expand and become increasingly diverse. By 2007 overall membership had increased from 665 to 1,288. To control membership so as to ensure delivery of quality championships and other services, the NCAA has implemented a series of moratoriums on the acceptance of new members during the past two decades. Division III experienced the greatest influx of new schools, and approximately 20 Division II institutions have sought reclassification at the Division I level. In summary, as more institutions become NCAA members, questions regarding how to manage that growth arise as well (Copeland, 2007). Numerous questions linger.

At present, Division III is the largest of all three divisions, comprising 40% of the NCAA membership. Given the variety of institutions represented within Division III, will the policies governing playing and practice seasons, awarding of financial aid, recruiting, and academic eligibility adequately address the concerns of those members, or will a point come when a Division IV will be created? For Division II, viewed by some institutions as a stepping-stone to Division I, how will it retain membership in a way that allows it to remain competitively viable? And for Division I, although it has implemented a moratorium on future growth through 2011, will it be able to mediate the interests of approximately three dozen institutions attempting to move from a lower division to Division I in the next few years while effectively managing the interests of the division's constituents?

Go to the OSG and complete the Learning in Action activity, which tests how well you recall some facts about the NCAA.

ACTION

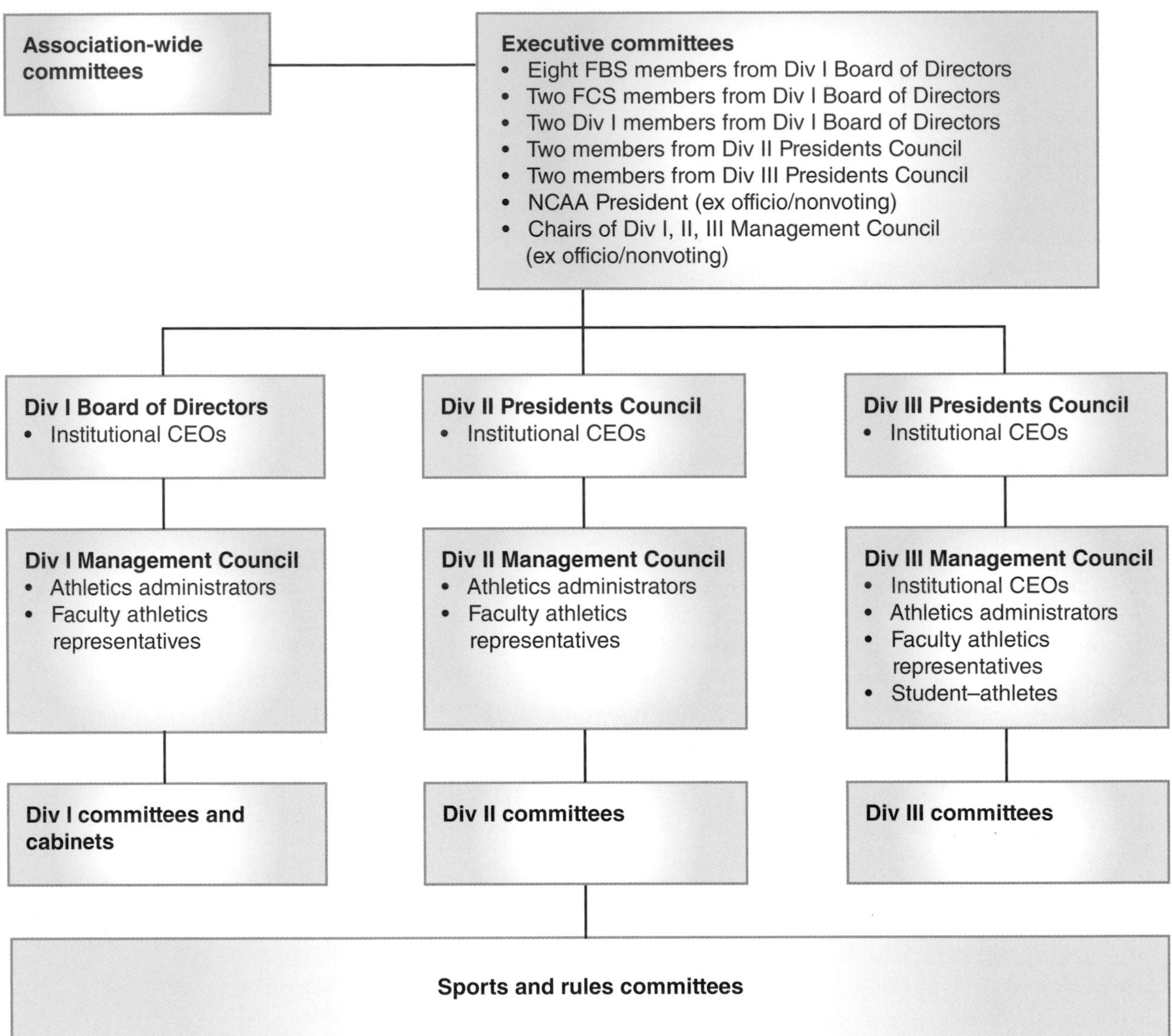

Figure 7.1 NCAA organizational chart and governance structure.

Other National Governing Bodies

Established in 1940, the National Association for Intercollegiate Athletics (NAIA), located in Olathe, Kansas, is composed of 291 member institutions. The NAIA is open to four-year and upper-level two-year colleges and universities in the United States and Canada. With an emphasis on academic achievement, the NAIA is also dedicated to respect, integrity, responsibility, servant leadership, and fair play. In 1948 the NAIA was the first national organization to offer postseason opportunities to Black student–athletes. It was also the first national organization to sponsor both women's and men's intercollegiate athletics, and in 1980 it became the first to offer athletics championships for women's sports. Historically Black institutions were voted into the NAIA in 1953.

At its most powerful in the early 1970s, the NAIA had a membership of 588 institutions and was considered a realistic competitor of the NCAA. The relationship today, however, is markedly different. As Wolverton (2008) pointed out, "In sports lingo, they're David and Goliath—one a struggling organization few people have heard of, the other a money-making machine whose teams vie for championships on national television" (¶ 1). Speculation abounds about the future of the NAIA. There are rumors that the NCAA may buy out the NAIA, whereas others argue that there is still a niche for NAIA schools on the college sport landscape.

Nevertheless, in 2008, shortly after the NCAA backed away from creating a fourth division for the time being, NCAA leaders pursued discussions with the NAIA more earnestly to explore relaxing NCAA ratings that deter member schools from playing against NAIA competitors. They have also engaged in discussions on cost-sharing initiatives to reduce health insurance costs and other administrative expenses. A proposed partnership between the NCAA and NAIA would result in the creation of an NAIA eligibility clearinghouse that would be run through the NCAA's Eligibility Center (Dannelly, 2009).

Another organization that governs intercollegiate athletics is the National Christian College Athletic Association (NCCAA). Incorporated in 1968 and located in Greenville, South Carolina, the NCCAA focuses on "maintenance, enhancement, and promotion of intercollegiate athletic competition with a Christian perspective" (*About the NCCAA*, n.d., ¶ 1). The NCCAA has a membership of just under 100 institutions in two divisions. Division I consists of 47 liberal arts institutions, and Division II consists of 49 Bible colleges.

Although the NAIA does provide a membership option for two-year institutions, governance of intercollegiate athletics within two-year institutions is managed primarily by four organizations: the American Indian Higher Education Consortium Athletic Commission (AIHEC—36 schools representing 1,000 athletes), the National Junior College Athletic Association (NJCAA—517 schools representing approximately 50,000 athletes), the California Community College Commission on Athletics (COA—103 schools representing 25,000 athletes), and the Northwest Athletic Association of Community Colleges (NWAACC—35 schools representing 3,614 athletes) (Staurowsky, 2009). Nearly half of all two-year institutions offer intercollegiate athletics programs to their students (Staurowsky, 2009).

The state of California, with an extensive community college system that educates over 25% of the entire US two-year student population, has long been committed to supporting athletics participation at the two-year level (*Commission*, n.d.). In 1929 the California Junior College Federation was founded, creating a single administrative entity for establishing policies and rules governing athletics participation among its member institutions (Winters, 1982).

Emerging out of the Golden Age of Sports (1920–1930), athletes from California's community college system rose to distinction in sports such as track and field. When the NCAA refused to allow community college programs to compete in the NCAA track and field championship in 1937 (Winters, 1982), the National Junior College Athletic Association (NJCAA) was conceived in Fresno, California, and became a functioning organization in 1938.

Although tribal colleges (**TCUs**) may be members of the COA, NAIA, National Intercollegiate Rodeo Association (NIRA), or the NJCAA, the AIHEC created the Athletic Commission in 2003 to formalize and govern AIHEC intercollegiate sporting events (Talahongva, 2009). This commission oversees the running of the AIHEC men's and women's basketball tournaments as well as other events throughout the year (Woodenlegs, 2009).

TCUs—The 37 Tribal Colleges and Universities (www.aihec.org) in the United States and Canada.

One of the common features in all these associations, with the exception of the AIHEC, is that, at one time, they governed only male sports. Before these associations incorporated women's sports into their rules and championships structures, the Association for Intercollegiate Athletics for Women (AIAW) was established by female physical educators from colleges and universities in 1971 (Wushanley, 2004).

UNIVERSITY SPORTS IN KENYA

By Isaac Mwangi Kamande
Strathmore University, NAIROBI (Kenya)

The Kenya Universities Sports Association (KUSA) is the body mandated to run university sports in Kenya. The association was formally registered in 1979 with the mission of creating opportunities and developing the environment for university students to participate in sports and physical activities at all levels. The object of KUSA is to act as the national authority for the promotion, conduct, and support of university sport in Kenya. KUSA has a membership of 16 universities, and more than 1,000 students take part in the National University Championships. The national association is affiliated with the National Olympic Committee–Kenya (NOC–K), the Kenya National Sports Council (KNSC), the East Africa University Sports Federation (EAUSF), the Federation of African University Sports (FASU), and the Fédération Internationale du Sport Universitaire (International University Sports Federation, or FISU).

Although Kenya is a sporting nation, university sports in Kenya face several challenges. For example, the academic calendar is very tight and does not favor sports. Also, universities have different academic calendars, making it difficult to run fixtures (schedules) to support league competitions. Modern methods of training and coaching are inadequate, so university teams and players cannot perform at top-level competitions. Only one university in Kenya offers programs in physical and health education, exercise science, sports science, and leisure and recreation studies. The other institutions offering physical education are

Photo courtesy of Kenya Universities Sports Association.

The 2008 FASU gold-medal winning rugby team from Kenya.

During its 10-year existence, the AIAW provided many opportunities for female athletes, coaches, and administrators. The organization also offered several national championships, many of which received television coverage. Eventually, however, the NCAA and other college sport governing bodies expanded their structures to include women's athletics.

Athletic Conferences

Picture the scene. The Palmer House in Chicago, 1895. Seven university presidents from the Midwest talking about problems in college football and baseball, contemplating how to prevent athletes-for-hire not enrolled as full-time students from playing for or against their teams. With a motion to restrict "eligibility for athletics to bona fide, full-time students who were not delinquent in their studies," a conference that would later become the Big Ten was formed (*Big Ten History*, 2009, ¶ 3).

teacher-training colleges. Consequently, the professional preparation of coaches, physiotherapists, sport managers, trainers, and officials is inadequate.

Many universities in Kenya rely on student activity fees. This amount is normally insufficient to fund major sports programmes, so many institutions are restricted to intramural competitions. Few corporate sponsors are willing to support university sports, and Kenya suffers from the belief that sport is meant for pastime. Also, universities have little land allocated for sport and other recreational facilities. There is a lack of professional and technical bodies for sport personnel and administrators to lobby for the interests of physical education and sport. Kenya does not have a sports act to guide the operations and administration of sport.

Despite these formidable challenges, a fierce competitive tradition exists amongst university teams. Throughout the year, KUSA holds competitions in many sports within leagues (i.e., conferences). Then, national championships are held as a mini–Olympic Games, where all the athletes camp in an Olympic-type village at the host university for the period of the games. Kenyan universities also participate in the East Africa University Championships, Africa University Championships, and the World University Games, all of which are held every two years. The National University Championships are awarded to universities on a rotating basis.

In the FASU games that were held in Kampala in July 2008, Kenya won a gold medal in rugby and two silver medals and a bronze in athletics. Kenya also took part in the FISU games in Bangkok, Thailand, in 2006 and won a silver medal in athletics. In the World University Games in Belgrade, Serbia, in July 2009, Kenya won three medals in swimming—gold in the 100-meter butterfly, silver in the 50-meter butterfly, and bronze in the 100-meter freestyle.

INTERNATIONAL LEARNING ACTIVITY #1

Identify similarities and differences between the intercollegiate athletics system in Kenya and the intercollegiate athletics system in your country. Note the instances in which you prefer the Kenyan system and those in which you prefer the system in your country. In each case, give reasons for your preference.

INTERNATIONAL LEARNING ACTIVITY #2

Search the Internet for information on intercollegiate athletics systems in countries other than Kenya and your country. Construct a table of their most salient features. Which features do you prefer and why?

In many respects, the work of a conference is much like it was when the Big Ten was founded. The basic function of a conference is to establish rules and regulations that support and sustain a level playing field for member institutions while creating in-season and postseason competitive opportunities. As Grant, Leadley, and Zygmont (2008) pointed out, however, "In the modern era, they also negotiate television contracts and distribute the proceeds and any other revenue they agree to share" (p. 41). With the exception of a few institutions that opt to remain independent, the vast majority of colleges and universities seek membership in conferences that will enhance the prestige and status of their programs and provide competition with peer institutions that are similarly situated financially, academically, geographically, and philosophically.

Although no official agency classifies conferences into major, mid-major, and small-college categories, fans as well as sportswriters routinely use these designations. Thus, the Atlantic Coast Conference (ACC), Big East, Big Ten, Big 12, Conference USA, Pacific-10 (PAC-10), and Southeastern Conference (SEC) are recognizable as major conferences. From year to year, there is some flexibility in the designation of NCAA Division I conferences on the basis of power, influence, and ratings; nevertheless the mid-major list typically includes America East, Atlantic 10, Atlantic Sun, Big Sky, Big South, Big West, Colonial, Horizon League, Ivy Group, Metro Atlantic, Mid-American, Missouri Valley, Mountain West, Northeast, Ohio Valley, Patriot League, Southern, Southland, Southwestern Athletic, Summit League, and West Coast conferences.

The distinction between major and mid-major for Division I conferences, however, is the dividing line between those that have automatic bids in the BCS and those that do not. When understood in this way, the decision-making process behind the college sport enterprise becomes clearer. For example, within the NCAA committee structure, representatives of each of the BCS conferences with automatic bids have guaranteed seats on the Division I Board of Directors and seven seats are available to the remaining 20 conferences (*NCAA Division I*, n.d.).

This lock on decision making is fueling some of the recent investigations on the part of members of the US Congress into the business practices of the BCS, which some allege may be anticompetitive in nature and in violation of antitrust regulations.

Despite the high profile of NCAA FBS and FCS conferences, most conferences are more familiar at a regional and local level. The Eastern College Athletic Conference (ECAC), for example, is the largest conference in the United States, distinctive because of the fact that its 319 members from 16 states include schools associated with NCAA Divisions I, II, and III (*Membership*, n.d.).

In turn, the Central Intercollegiate Athletic Association (CIAA) and the Mid-Eastern Athletic Conference (MEAC) have a different history when compared with major conferences. The CIAA is the nation's oldest Black athletic conference, founded in 1912. Today, the membership of the CIAA and the MEAC are composed exclusively of Historically Black Colleges and Universities (HBCUs).

HBCUs—Historically Black Colleges and Universities (e.g., Alabama State University, Albany State University, Bethune-Cookman College, Florida A&M University, Grambling State University, Howard University, Tuskegee University).

BASICS OF COLLEGE SPORT FINANCE

The college sport industry is like any other sector of the sport industry worldwide. Those expecting to work in it, whether in the capacity of an athletics director or even as a coach, must be aware of the financial considerations that drive the business. An easy way to begin to gain an understanding of the revenue streams that contribute to a college or university athletics budget is to go to reports filed in compliance with what is called the **Equity in Athletics Disclosure Act (EADA)**. To determine whether spending on men's and women's intercollegiate athletics programs is equitable and in conformance with Title IX of the Education Amendments Act of 1972, the EADA requires institutions receiving federal financial assistance to submit a report documenting expenditures for each fiscal year. This information is publicly available on a Web site (www.ope.ed.gov/athletics/) hosted by the US Department of Education Office of Postsecondary Education. The database is searchable, so you can look up individual institutions, institutions by division and association, or institutions by athletic conference.

Equity in Athletics Disclosure Act (EADA)—Provides public information about the spending patterns of athletics departments in terms of men's and women's programs. Information about EADA may be found at www.ope.ed.gov/athletics/

Being able to determine the difference between the capacity of an athletics department to generate revenue versus turn a profit is an important skill for an athletics administrator. According to EADA data for the 2007–2008 academic year, Ohio State University brought in nearly US$118 million in revenue, and the University of Texas at Austin generated just over US$120 million. More important, the revenue generated by OSU and UT exceeded their expenses, in both cases by several million dollars.

Most athletics programs, however, are not profitable. In 2006 OSU and UT were 2 of just 19 schools that turned a profit (Weinbach, 2007). Depending on the year and the comprehensiveness of the analysis, the number of schools that generate revenue in

Corporations such as adidas, Nike, Reebok, and Under Armour can provide an athletics department with a multimillion-dollar revenue stream, in addition to apparel outfitting, when they sign on as an official sponsor.
Photo courtesy of Paul M. Pedersen.

excess of expenses may be as low as 10 (Zimbalist, 2007). An NCAA report on revenues and expenses for Division I intercollegiate athletics programs for the academic year 2005–2006 (Fulks, 2008) revealed the following (all money amounts in US$):

- The median deficit in Division I programs increased to $7,265,000 in 2006 from $5,902,000 in 2004.
- There is a large gap in the capacity of programs in Division I to generate revenue, as seen in the median reported revenue generated being $26 million and the second highest revenue generated by a single program being $105 million.
- Although the largest total expense for a Division I program was $101,805,000, the median total expense for Division I programs was $38,605,000.

WEB

Go to the OSG and complete the Web search activity, which asks you to investigate how equitably your institution is spending resources on men's and women's athletics programs.

Intuition leads many outside observers of college sport to believe that spending more money will lead to greater program success. But in a 2009 study of FBS athletics financing, only the top programs (those ranked in the top 25 in recent years) realized a benefit from spending more. Despite the trend to award multiyear, multimillion dollar contracts to head coaches of football and men's and women's basketball, the researchers further found no significant relationship between winning and high coaching salaries (Hosick, 2009).

From a gender equity perspective, these reports can offer insight into potential problems as well as existing shortfalls. For example, as Grant (2009) pointed out, "It is clear that the athletic budget of men's basketball and football at many institutions in the Football Bowl Subdivision (FBS) are increasing at an alarming rate" (¶ 1). After comparing data from the NCAA's financial reports for 2004 and 2006, she found that spending on men's sports increased during that two-year span by 14% compared with an increase of just 6% for women's sports. Additionally, 78% of men's athletics budgets are consumed by football and men's basketball.

Finally, depending on the division, the issue of whether a program is profit making is an important philosophical issue as well as a monetary one. In NCAA Division III, for example, athletics programs are intended to encourage participation with a focus on the athletes' experience, not spectator appeal. As a consequence, the Division III infrastructure is not designed to generate revenue. The question for Division III institutions then becomes how much to invest in varsity athletics programs and how to justify those investments.

INTERCOLLEGIATE ATHLETICS ADMINISTRATORS

As a student, you may want to find a definitive answer to the question of what athletics administrators do. To some degree, athletics administrators resemble managers in other business settings and industries. Athletics administrators must be able to execute the fundamental managerial functions of planning, organizing, staffing, directing, coordinating, reporting, and budgeting. The sections that follow will expand on the types of management positions found in intercollegiate athletics programs and conferences and outline general responsibilities associated with each position.

In chapter 5 you learned about top-level (i.e., senior) managers, middle-level (responsible to top-level managers and oversee supervisory and technical personnel) managers, and supervisory level, or first-line, managers (report to middle-level managers and oversee nonmanagerial employees). You can find all three types of managers in most intercollegiate athletics departments. An important point to remember is that many administrators have assistants. Novice athletics administrators often pursue and occupy these assistant positions at the beginnings of their careers.

As a rule, the more prominent the athletics department is, the larger the annual operating budget will be; and the more complex the organizational structure is, the larger the full-time and part-time athletics department staff will be. Thus, administrators working in FBS colleges and universities occupy positions with narrowly defined responsibilities. In contrast, administrators in athletics departments in Division II, in Division III, and at the junior and community college levels may be responsible for a wider array of responsibilities. Consequently, people employed in those settings might have to perform duties other than those related to their athletics management role, such as teaching in sport-related areas, coaching, or working in an area related to student life.

The size of the school and the scope of the athletics department are not the only factors that can affect the approach that athletics administrators take to their jobs. Most of what we know about intercollegiate athletics management today pertains to traditionally White institutions. Although management functions overlap significantly in every athletics department, we cannot assume that what we know about intercollegiate athletics management based on that information can be uniformly generalized and applied to HBCUs, such as Tennessee State, Mississippi Valley State, Howard, South Carolina State, Florida A&M, Tuskegee, and Grambling State universities. In fact, historically Black colleges are among the nation's leaders in FCS football attendance (Johnson, 2009).

The notion that not all athletics programs fit the dominant model of college sport management is born out not only by the HBCUs but also by women's college athletics programs. Located in small liberal arts institutions and governed by the rules of Division III, the women's athletics programs in schools such as Smith, Bryn Mawr, Mt. Holyoke, and Mills colleges employ management models that are consistent with single-sex women's education institutions. Because of the variability of the college sport marketplace, no two positions are identical nor are the job titles used to describe them the same. As you explore careers in college sport, spend some time reading position descriptions to gain a better understanding of job expectations and requirements.

Director of Athletics

An athletics director (AD) assumes oversight of numerous areas within the athletics department. Some of these, depending on the structure of the department, may include budget and finance, facilities, risk management, television contracts, compliance with laws and regulations of national and conference governing bodies, academic progress of college athletes, communication with the media, scheduling, marketing games and other events, corporate sponsorships, ticket sales, community relations, alumni relations, campus relations, fund-raising, and personnel management, including the hiring and termination of coaches. A definitive answer to the question of what ADs do is elusive, however, because of the unique nature of athletics departments and how they are structured within specific colleges and universities. On one hand, the business of college sport is big business. As Dave Hart, former AD at Florida State University noted, the job of an AD "is now much like that of a CEO. I don't know where else you find the complexity that exists with the job of an athletics director today" ("Q&A," 2008, ¶ 20).

Villanova University director of athletics Vince Nicastro acknowledged the growing business demands associated with his position, estimating that he spent at least half of his time dealing with issues related to budget, finance, and human resources (Robinson, 2009). Being able to execute what famed entrepreneur Donald Trump refers to as the art of the deal is an essential skill for an athletics director (Harris & Lowry, 2008).

At the same time, an athletics director at a Division III institution or junior college, with responsibility for a budget of perhaps US$2 million, faces different job demands and responsibilities. In many respects, the difference in these situations resembles the distinction between a major corporation and a locally owned business. Both require managerial skills and experience, but the demands on the leaders of the enterprises vary markedly.

Candidates for AD positions are increasingly scrutinized in terms of their business credentials and recruited because of them. In 2009, for example, Tim Pernetti, former vice president of CBS's College Sports Network, was hired to head up the Rutgers University athletics department. At the University of Michigan former Wolverine football player turned chief executive officer of Domino's Pizza, David Brandon, was named to the athletics director position in 2010 (Associated Press, 2010).

As a reflection of the changing stature and status of the athletics director role on campus, it has been elevated to one significant enough to warrant the use of **executive search firms.** Once used by institutions to fill major positions such as chancellors, presidents, and provosts, college and university administrators are now turning to executive search firms to identify and vet qualified athletics administrators for open positions.

executive search firm—An organization that identifies talented administrators for positions as college presidents, chancellors, provosts, athletics administrators, and coaches.

Not surprisingly, when asked about qualities that they find most important when hiring athletics directors, college presidents across all three divisions identified a solid foundation in budget and finance along with skills in management and leadership, marketing, and communication (Schneider & Stier, 2005). A key element of success for ADs who wish to move up the ranks is mastering the art of networking (Whisenant & Pedersen, 2004).

Associate or Assistant Athletics Director

Associate and assistant ADs are clearly middle-level managers. These titles generally represent either the level of administrative responsibility assigned to the person in the role or the level of seniority and experience that the person has. In many respects, the associate or assistant AD supports the AD in achieving the overall mission of the department by working closely with the AD and overseeing specific areas, such as marketing, fund-raising, event management, facilities management, or athletics communications. In large athletics departments, several people are designated as associate or assistant ADs. Senior associates usually serve as the second in command within an athletics department and assume responsibility for the overall operation of the department in the absence of the AD. As mentioned previously, to determine what people in these positions do, you have to read their job descriptions or speak with them directly.

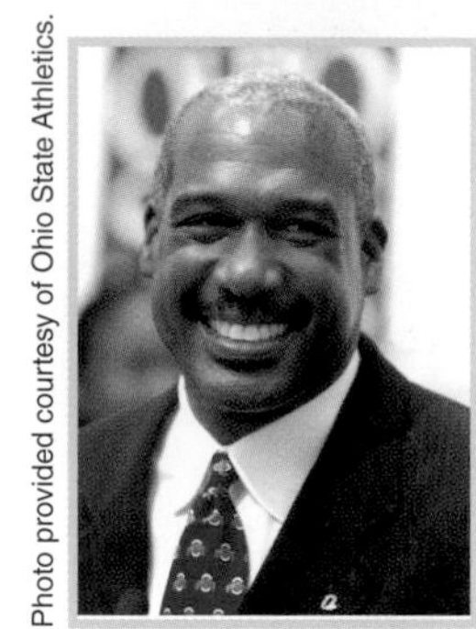
Photo provided courtesy of Ohio State Athletics.

In Profile: Gene Smith

If there is a prototype for the 21st century athletics director, Gene Smith, associate VP and director of athletics at Ohio State University, might well be it. Growing up in Cleveland, Ohio, Smith attended Chanel High School, where he distinguished himself in football, basketball, and track and received the football team's most valuable player award. Smith went on to pursue a bachelor's degree in business administration at the University of Notre Dame, where he played defensive end for the Irish, achieving distinction as a member of the Associated Press 1973 national championship team.

Smith made the successful transition from player to coach at Notre Dame. During the famed 1976–1977 season when Notre Dame emerged as the undisputed national champion, Smith was on staff as an assistant coach. Following his coaching experience, Smith chose to make a career move, becoming a marketing representative for IBM, a decision that would eventually lead to his being hired as the director of athletics at Eastern Michigan University, Iowa State University, and Arizona State University.

In 2005 Smith was appointed the eighth director of athletics at Ohio State University. In his role as director of athletics at Ohio State, he must demonstrate command of an array of organizational management skills in running an FBS athletics department that is a member of the Big Ten Conference. Smith is responsible for providing the vision and direction for one of the most comprehensive and successful university athletics programs in the United States. Overall, Smith oversees an athletics program that sponsors 36 fully funded teams, provides for over 1,100 athletes, has a staff of close to 300, and operates with a US$118 million budget. Smith took over when Ohio State was nearing the end of a major campaign that had resulted in the renovation of existing facilities and new construction, including renovation of historic Ohio Stadium and completion of the largest arena in the Big Ten, the Jerome Schottenstein Center.

Information for this profile was drawn primarily from Gene Smith biography (March 25, 2009). Retrieved May 23, 2010, from www.ohiostatebuckeyes.com/ViewArticle.dbml?DB_OEM_ID=17300&ATCLID=1051911.

First-Line Managers

First-line managers are responsible for specific work groups in the athletics department. These managers typically report to an associate or assistant AD. Many of these positions have emerged or have been expanded only within the past two decades. Positions include academic coordinator, business and finance manager, compliance officer, development and public relations director, event and facility manager, marketing and promotions director, sports information director, ticket manager, senior woman administrator, and equipment manager. Brief descriptions of these jobs follow.

Academic Coordinator

According to the National Association of Academic Advisors for Athletes (N4A), fewer than 10 full-time academic advisors for athletes existed in 1975. As of 2009 the N4A had a membership of over 1,100, an increase of 500 members over the preceding four years (Meleney, 2009). This phenomenal growth resulted from the passage of NCAA bylaw 16.3.1, which requires all Division I programs to offer academic support and tutoring services to athletes, and the existence of the Academic Enhancement Fund Program, which allocates US$62,438 per year to each Division I athletics program in support of these programs.

Athletics academic advisement services are designed to assist athletes in addressing the dual and sometimes conflicting demands of being both a student and an athlete. As with all areas that we have addressed, the structure of these offices and the range of services that they provide can vary from one institution to another. In general, athletics academic offices assist athletes in the broad areas of admission, academic orientation, academic standards, registration, financial aid, housing, and student life. The academic coordinator monitors the academic activities of athletes and maintains records on their academic progress. To do their jobs effectively, academic coordinators work closely with coaches, faculty, the compliance officer, and other administrators.

To address concerns about academic progress and performance among athletes in Divisions I and II, the NCAA adopted a series of rules and initiatives during the past decade. In brief, these include the following:

- Freshman eligibility standards for Division I (16 core high school courses, a sliding scale for test score and grade-point average); for Division II (14 core courses, minimum SAT of 820 or an ACT sum score of 68, minimum of a 2.0 GPA) (*NCAA Eligibility Center*, 2008)
- **Academic progress rate,** more commonly referred to as the APR
- The 40/60/80 rule, which requires an athlete, by the end of the second year, to have completed at least 40% of his or her degree; by the end of the third year, at least 60%; by the end of the fourth year, at least 80%

academic progress rate (APR)—According to the NCAA, this is a measure of how successful athletics programs on individual campuses are in ensuring that college athletes are making appropriate progress toward their degrees.

In the case of the APR, penalties for failure to meet the threshold standards of 900 to 925 per team range from public warning to loss of scholarships to restricted membership in Division I. The academic support staffs associated with athletics departments play a key role in helping athletes remain eligible and in assisting programs in meeting APR requirements (*NCAA Backgrounder*, n.d.).

People interested in working as athletics academic advisors need to understand the business of college sport and the regulations that affect athletes. They must be equally familiar with the processes of social adaptation and human development, academic performance assessment, and career guidance strategies. In large athletics programs, the athletics academic support services staff might include several academic counselors, mentors, and tutors, some of whom will be undergraduate and graduate students.

Business and Finance Manager

The business and finance manager for an intercollegiate athletics department recommends and implements policies, procedures, and methods of accounting that ensure strict compliance with sound business practices in accordance with the rules and regulations of the institution, the conference, and the national governing body. Brown (2008) noted, "Presidents, athletics directors and other campus leaders rely on business managers a great deal for athletics budget projections, comparisons with peer groups and other trend analyses that give those leaders more information on which to base decisions" (¶ 9). He added that business managers are also typically responsible for the business processes of accounting and reporting, contract management, human resources, purchasing, travel, and ticketing operations.

The professional organization for this group of athletics department personnel is the College Athletic Business Management Association (CABMA). With athletics spending progressing at a rate that is three times the rate of spending overall on college and university campuses (Brown, 2007), greater emphasis has been placed on finding ways to reduce expenses. Business managers have been called on to contribute in significant ways to implement what the NCAA refers to as the dashboard indicator project. This project is designed to allow schools to compare budget information that will better inform decision making about athletics spending.

Compliance Officer

Compliance with NCAA regulations is not solely the responsibility of the person designated in an athletics department to serve as the compliance officer or coordinator.

Compliance is technically a shared responsibility among all parties who come in contact with the athletics program, including the AD, coaches, current athletes, prospective athletes, boosters, and alumni, as well as representatives from various campus offices (e.g., admission, financial aid, residence life, health services). The process of compliance in its contemporary form evolved in the 1990s in conjunction with the development of the NCAA program certification process.

Broadly stated, the role of compliance coordinators is to develop educational processes that help everyone directly or indirectly involved with the athletics program understand and comply with the rules of the institution, the conference, and the national governing body. The span of responsibilities to which compliance officers may be assigned includes assessment of student initial eligibility, continuing eligibility, and transfer eligibility as well as adherence to regulations that govern athlete recruitment. Because of the complexity of rules, compliance coordinators often have the task of developing and implementing record-keeping methods to demonstrate that compliance in various areas is monitored. Much of this record keeping is done with computer software programs. Compliance officers play a crucial role in the formulation of compliance reports that institutions must submit to the NCAA on a regular basis.

Those interested in working in the compliance area must be detail oriented and have an exhaustive understanding of NCAA and conference rules and regulations along with the management and communication skills necessary to explain rules and regulations effectively. Although a law degree is not a requirement for this type of position, the nature of the job lends itself to someone with this kind of interest and background.

Development and Public Relations Director

Depending on the institution, the process of raising money from friends of an athletics program is called athletics fund-raising, development, or advancement. Athletics fund-raising organizations may be called fan clubs, booster clubs, friends associations, alumni clubs, or athletics foundations. Athletics development officers are responsible for raising funds to support various aspects of the athletics department by identifying and implementing fund-raising projects and cultivating potential and current donors.

In athletics fund-raising, several basic principles apply. The fund-raiser wants to encourage people who donate to the program to continue to donate and ideally to donate more over time, while searching out and contacting new donors to expand the program's financial base. The importance of development efforts to college athletics programs cannot be underestimated; alumni and booster contributions often involve both individually and collectively millions of dollars in support. The fund-raiser position requires a combination of marketing, management, and media relations skills.

One extremely important element in this area is vigilance with regard to the donors involved with the program. The potential for rules violations in this area has proved to be high. Donors and friends of athletics programs may offer athletes under-the-table payments, improper gifts, and other benefits that violate NCAA rules. Athletics development officers are required to show the steps that they take to educate friends of the program about rules and regulations that govern athletics programs so as to avoid problems in this area.

Event and Facility Manager

In recent years, a marked expansion of athletics facilities on college campuses has occurred. Because of limitations of space and resources, athletics departments must find ways to use facilities to serve the multiple needs of campus constituencies and generate income through the rental and use of multipurpose facilities for special events, such as concerts. The position description for an event and facility manager reflects this trend. Facility scheduling, maintenance, improvements, and contest management are the major duties assigned to event and facility managers. Because many people use athletics facilities, and for many different activities, facility and event managers must be attentive to the reduction of risk and liability while finding ways of being user friendly by creating as much availability and accessibility as possible. One of the major responsibilities of the event and facility manager is game management for home athletics events. This task entails arranging for appropriate levels of security at games; hiring, training, and supervising ushers; marking and lining fields and courts; making arrangements for ticket sellers and ticket takers; managing the time schedule of the game, including such things as the national anthem, bands, and halftime shows; and attending to the needs of game officials. A more detailed description of event and facility management is presented in chapter 15.

Marketing and Promotions Director

In the summer of 2001 the University of Oregon bought a 10-story billboard in New York City's Times Square, on which it displayed a picture of its Heisman Trophy nominee, quarterback Joey Harrington. The cost of that billboard was a tidy US$250,000—a quarter of a million dollars! Although the amount of money invested in the Harrington campaign was exceptionally high, the promotion itself was not unusual; schools routinely invest thousands of dollars in the promotion of their Heisman candidates. Marketing and promoting the contemporary college athletics program happens at all levels and is motivated by the need to generate interest in the program through enhanced visibility, increased attendance, and expanding revenue streams. Marketing and promotions directors may be responsible for promoting ticket sales for individual games, nonrevenue sports, season packages, and championship events along with a complete line of apparel, fan support merchandise, and items for retail sale by direct mail and through the university's bookstore and concessions area. Marketing and promotions directors are also responsible for identifying potential corporate sponsors, developing sponsorship proposals, and ensuring that proposals are implemented according to agreements reached with sponsors (Irwin, Sutton, & McCarthy, 2008). In an age in which product branding, merchandising, and licensing (i.e., **licensing royalty**) have become integral parts of the marketing of intercollegiate athletics programs, marketing and promotions directors must have a comprehensive understanding of trademark licensing and be familiar with trademark principles, terms, and definitions used in trademark law (Pitts & Stotlar, 2007).

Traditionally, the job of marketing an athletics program at the college and university level has been done in-house. During the past decade, however, in an effort to maximize existing revenue and access new revenue streams, Division I athletics departments are **outsourcing** their marketing to firms that specialize in college sport marketing. Companies such as CBS Collegiate Sports Properties, IMG College, the Collegiate Licensing Company (a subdivision of IMG), ISP Sports, Learfield, and Nelligan purchase rights to college properties and share the revenue from the sale of those properties with athletics departments.

licensing royalty—The earnings paid to the sport property, or licensor (e.g., athletics department), by a licensed manufacturer in return for the right to produce and sell merchandise bearing a logo or other mark associated with its sports program (Irwin, Sutton, & McCarthy, 2008).

outsourcing—In the context of this chapter's section on the marketing of college programs, it refers to the use of outside sport marketing firms to maximize revenues for athletics programs.

Sports Information Director

Sports information directors (SIDs)—also referred to as athletics communications specialists, sport publicists, and college sport public relations directors—are responsible for both technical and management functions. As a public relations practitioner, a sports information director must be adept at developing an array of publication materials, including media guides, press releases, recruiting brochures, game programs, feature stories, and newsletters. They also do the background work (e.g., research, interviews with coaches and players) to support those publications.

John Humenik, executive director of the College Sports Information Directors Association (CoSIDA) argues that the college sport industry needs to reconceptualize the role of media relations professionals. Although the title *information director*

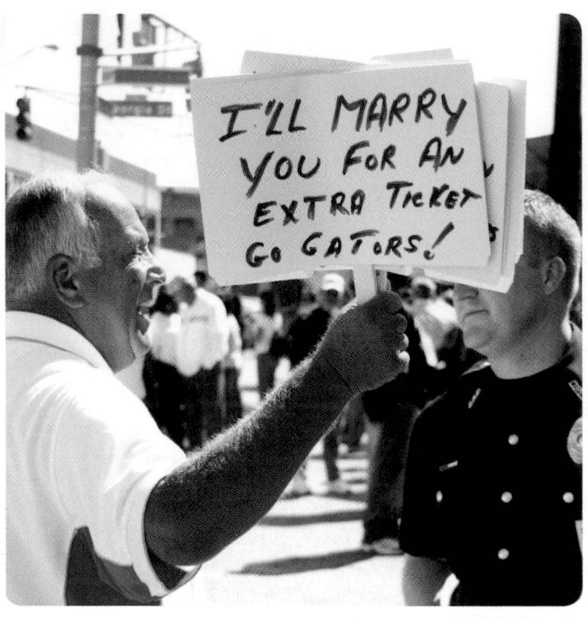

Ticket scalping is an issue that all ticket managers will deal with during their careers.
Photo courtesy of Paul M. Pedersen.

refers to a person "who is involved mostly in keeping stats, preparing basic news releases, working on publications, setting up interviews and managing the press box," according to Humenik, the title *communications director* refers to a person who "is viewed more in a strategic and visionary capacity" (Stoldt, 2008, p. 460). Besides executing the technical demands of the job, sports information directors are also responsible for managing budgets, organizing events, and supervising personnel. Successful sports information directors need to have excellent writing and research skills, a firm understanding of mass communication and media technologies, an awareness of and ability to appeal to internal and external audiences, and a capacity to maintain a calm demeanor while working in high-stress, high-pressure situations. Practicing sports information directors offered this advice for students who want to pursue careers in this field: "Get as much writing experience as possible," "Gain as much experience as possible as an undergraduate," "Be prepared to work long hours," and "Plan on a career with little pay and little appreciation, but also plan on it being a lot of fun" (Hardin & McClung, 2002, p. 38).

Ticket Manager

ticket operations—Process by which tickets are distributed to customers (season ticket holders and fans) coupled with attention to a high level of customer service (Reese, 2003).

ticket scalping—Selling a ticket for a price in excess of the price printed on the ticket.

The primary responsibilities of the ticket manager are coordinating all **ticket operations**, designing the ticketing plan, and accounting for all money expended and received for tickets. Responsible for a major area of revenue generation and customer service, ticket managers are called on to assist in setting the price of tickets, determining staffing, ensuring that ticket distribution is handled in a secure manner, and understanding state laws that pertain to **ticket scalping** (Reese, 2003). A major resource for the ticket manager is the International Ticketing Association (INTIX). Members of INTIX include an array of businesses and organizations in sport and entertainment fields around the world (e.g., amphitheaters, ballet and opera companies, festivals, sport teams, state fairs, theaters, universities). Ticketing software and hardware development workers, ticket agents and printers, and Internet-based ticketing companies also belong to INTIX. This organization sponsors an annual conference as well as an intensive certification program to help people in the industry stay current on trends and techniques to provide the best service possible to consumers.

Senior Woman Administrator (SWA)

senior woman administrator—The highest ranking female administrator involved in the management of an NCAA institution's intercollegiate athletics department.

When you read biographies of people working in intercollegiate athletics, you may come across the term **senior woman administrator** (SWA). The term is not a position title per se. In Divisions I and III it designates "the highest ranking female administrator involved with the management of a member institution's intercollegiate athletics program" (NCAA, 2008, p. 18). At the Division II level it refers to a member of the institution's senior management team (Brown, 2009). The purpose of the SWA concept is to ensure that women have a role in the decision-making process in college sport and that women's interests are represented at the campus, conference, and national levels.

Courtesy of Sideline Photos LLC/ Greg Carroccio.

In Profile: Bernadette McGlade

How do you as a college student, with a glimmer of an idea in your head that you want to play a significant role in college sport administration, begin to map out a plan to become a director of athletics or conference commissioner? Bernadette McGlade's profile provides some useful lessons to help you get started.

As is the case with approximately 60% of athletics conference commissioners, McGlade, who is the Commissioner of the Atlantic 10 Conference, competed as a scholarship women's basketball player at the University of North Carolina at Chapel Hill. After earning both her undergraduate and graduate degrees at UNC at Chapel Hill, McGlade became the youngest Division I women's basketball coach in the country, serving as the first full-time female to coach at Georgia Institute of Technology (Georgia Tech) in 1981.

McGlade initially assisted in developing the women's athletics program at Georgia Tech. Within two years of her arrival, she was handling the coordination of women's sports. By 1985, with a promotion to assistant athletics director for Olympic Sports, McGlade was assigned responsibility for internal operations within the department of athletics at Georgia Tech. Moving full time into athletics administration in 1987, and assuming the role of associate director of athletics, McGlade's responsibilities expanded to include oversight of all sport programs, including football and men's basketball, continued oversight of NCAA compliance, and operations of the Bill Moore Tennis Center.

With each move forward, McGlade expanded her skill sets, areas of expertise, professional network, and knowledge base. During the decade of the 1990s two major roles shaped future opportunities for McGlade. In 1993 she served as the tournament director for the 1993 NCAA Women's Final Four. This tournament was historic in that it sold out in advance of the event. During this period McGlade also served as the 1996 Olympic Games liaison for the Georgia Tech Athletic Association. In that capacity she developed and coordinated the association's strategic plan.

Positioned well to move on into the role of an assistant commissioner with the ACC in 1997, she was initially responsible for overseeing women's basketball. Characteristic of her career path throughout, McGlade quickly grew into that role and was soon promoted to the level of associate commissioner. By the time she was approached to take over as Atlantic 10 commissioner, McGlade's management background included conference scheduling, overseeing the ACC tournament, television oversight and selection, budget management, and serving as conference liaison with the women's basketball coaches.

Information for this profile drawn primarily from the Atlantic 10 Conference. (June 2, 2008). Retrieved May 23, 2010, from www.atlantic10.com/genrel/060208aab.html.

Research about SWAs reveals that 79% of Division I SWAs serve in some administrative role within their departments, occupying assistant, associate, or senior associate athletics director positions (Claussen & Lehr, 2002). Tiell noted (as cited in Brown, 2009) that in Division II over half of those designated as SWAs did not have jobs that positioned them to be members of the department's senior management team, and in Division III 47% of SWAs were not members of a senior management team.

The intention of the SWA designation to integrate women in the decision-making process of athletics departments has not been realized. Comparisons between the perceptions of athletics directors and SWAs regarding the role of SWAs in decision making at the senior management level reveal a disconnect. Whereas ADs perceived that SWAs were instrumental in advancing the interests of the athletics department, SWAs perceived that they encountered barriers because of the limits placed on their assignments or authority (Claussen & Lehr, 2002; Tiell & Dixon, 2008). Many SWAs are not satisfied with the level of participation that they have in operations, budgeting, capital outlay, salary considerations, media broadcast contracts, and sponsorship and advertising (Grappendorf, Pent, Burton, & Henderson, 2008).

Although some SWAs are assigned sole responsibility for women's athletics programs and teams, the range of responsibilities assigned to SWAs can encompass all that goes on in a coeducational athletics department. SWAs have been found to perform roles and tasks that are gender neutral, meaning that they have administrative assignments that support both men's and women's programs. According to McDermott and Lynch (2008), SWAs should contribute to decision making in the following areas: program supervision, budget management, fund-raising and marketing, compliance and governance, human resource management, gender equity monitoring and implementation, and advocacy for women within the athletics program. In recent years, steps have been taken to designate an SWA within athletics conferences as well.

Equipment Manager

According to the Athletic Equipment Managers Association (AEMA) (*What Is Certification*, 2008), equipment managers purchase equipment; fit equipment such as football helmets; check, clean, and inspect uniforms and equipment to reduce wear and risk of injury while preserving the life of the equipment and garments as part of the budget management process; and establish a comprehensive accountability system that includes inventory (pre- and postseason), reconditioning, and storage. As with all other positions mentioned in this chapter, an equipment manager's job includes a significant management component. As Dale Strauf (2002), equipment manager at Cornell University noted, "Equipment managers play a major role in the decision-making process for all aspects of equipment administration" (¶ 2). Effective communication with top-level, middle-level, and other first-line administrators is essential. Since 1991 AEMA has promoted a certification program for equipment managers to ensure a high standard of performance and professional preparation. According to Dorothy Cutting at the AEMA (personal communication, May 7, 2009), in 2009 there were more than 979 certified athletics equipment managers in the United States.

Administrators in Governing Bodies

Recent research on the profiles and career paths of conference commissioners suggests that some distinctly different skill sets and backgrounds may set commissioners apart from other athletics administrators. As a case in point, conference commissioners appear to be more likely to hold degrees in journalism and communication while exhibiting a broader range of experiences. A pattern similar to that seen in individual school settings is the underrepresentation of women and minorities in conference offices (Davis, 2008).

As you learned in chapter 5, conference commissioners in all NCAA divisions perform their duties within three major role classifications: interpersonal, informational, and decisional. Examples of these functions are shown in table 5.2 in chapter 5. Notice that these functions are similar to those of an AD, except that an AD is acting on behalf of a university whereas the commissioner is acting on behalf of member institutions. The organizational chart in figure 7.1 identifies additional positions in the NCAA.

CRITICAL THINKING IN INTERCOLLEGIATE ATHLETICS

Consider this critical thinking scenario: If you were a college or university president, what stance would you take on the issue of whether an FBS football playoff should be established? Do the business practices of the BCS result in a contrived champion that artificially suppresses competition while yielding financial benefits for the BCS schools with automatic bids? Or are BCS schools positioning themselves appropriately in a free marketplace to draw the most fans and the highest television ratings, and therefore are deserving of the benefits that accrue from this system?

PORTFOLIO

Complete the critical thinking portfolio activity in the OSG, consulting as needed the "Eight Critical Thinking Questions" section in chapter 1.

ETHICS IN INTERCOLLEGIATE ATHLETICS

In recent years, the financial stakes in college sport have risen rapidly. In 2009 IMG struck a deal with Ohio State University that will guarantee the Buckeyes US$110 million over 10 years (Berkowitz, 2009). In turn, the NCAA itself in 2009 reorganized the seating plan for the Men's Final Four to accommodate tens of thousands more ticket buyers, resulting in a US$7 million increase in gate receipts (Wieberg & Berkowitz, 2009).

Although corporate entities capitalize on the games played by college athletes, using their performances and likenesses to market everything from television air time to jerseys to video games, the athletes themselves are prevented from receiving compensation beyond the limits of their scholarships. As a study released by the National College Players Association in 2009 documented, athletics scholarships do not cover the full cost of attendance because of NCAA regulations. As a result, even athletes on full scholarship often have to cover an average financial shortfall of US$2,500 per year, meaning that over five years, a full scholarship athlete will have a debt of approximately US$12,500 (Huma & Staurowsky, 2009).

PORTFOLIO

Complete the ethical issues portfolio activity in the OSG, consulting as needed the "Guidelines for Making Ethical Decisions" section in chapter 1.

Although the NCAA argues that its rules of amateurism are designed to protect athletes from commercial and professional exploitation, the question of how the NCAA defines the term *exploitation* has been raised most recently by the Knight Commission on Intercollegiate Athletics (2009). As commercial interests in college sport have escalated, so too has been the real possibility that college athletes will start to seek more compensation for the work that they do.

Summary

Intercollegiate athletics has come a long way from the days when students ran their own practices, devised their own training programs, and negotiated the terms of the contests in which they played. As the business of college sport continues to expand, job opportunities for aspiring young professionals are no longer limited to college campuses. Students can look to media outlets (e.g., CBS Sports, CSTV, Fox College Sports, the Big Ten Network, ESPNU), new and emerging media, as well as numerous sport marketing firms (e.g., IMG College Division, ISP Sports) to find work. The overall structure of intercollegiate athletics extends far beyond the bounds of the BCS and the FBS. Although the challenges are different, numerous opportunities to work in college sport exist in institutions as varied as tribal colleges, NCAA Division III institutions, and NCCAA schools.

One thing that an examination of intercollegiate athletics reveals is that the leaders of tomorrow must be prepared to face challenges ethically and to exercise critical thinking skills in examining what has become standard operating procedure. Intercollegiate athletics has the potential to be a valuable asset to institutions of higher learning and to the students who participate in it. At the same time, to be blind to the persistent problems that have plagued the college sport enterprise is to endanger its future and the future of those who work in it. Thus, students are uniquely positioned to devise new ways of addressing old problems. In this sense, the intercollegiate athletics system is in your hands. What will you make of it?

QUIZ TIME

Did you grasp all the key points in this chapter? Go to the OSG for a short quiz to test your understanding of the material.

Review Questions

1. What is thought to be the first college sport contest, and in what year did it occur?
2. What role did President Theodore Roosevelt play in the development of college sport in the United States?
3. What was the relationship between the NCAA and the NAIA in the 1970s? How has that relationship changed today?
4. How do BCS conferences exert influence and control over decision making within the NCAA?
5. Why is the ECAC such an unusual conference?
6. How many Division I athletics departments make a profit?
7. What is the relationship between winning and high coaching salaries, at least according to one study noted in the chapter?
8. Why is there concern about the rate of spending in men's sports at the Division I level compared with the rate of spending in women's sports? On average, what percentage of Division I men's sport budgets are consumed by football and men's basketball?
9. What possible penalties may be assessed to a school if a team fails to meet the APR standards?
10. What are the possible rules violations that athletics development officers need to be aware of, and how do they try to reduce the likelihood that those violations will occur?

References

About the NCCAA. (n.d.). Retrieved May 23, 2010, from www.thenccaa.org/about.html

Associated Press. (2010, January 5). Michigan names Brandon as AD. *ESPN.com*. Retrieved May 12, 2010 from www.espn.com.

Berkowitz, S. (2009, May 1). IMG jolts campus scene to give schools a cash boost. *USA Today*. Retrieved February 1, 2010, from www.usatoday.com/sports/college/2009-04-01-img-cover_N.htm

Big Ten history. (2009). Retrieved February 1, 2010, from www.bigten.org/trads/big10-trads.html

Brown, G.T. (2007, October 22). Division I budget trends get dashboard treatment. *NCAA News*. Retrieved February 1, 2010, from www.ncaa.org/wps/ncaa?key=/ncaa/ncaa/ncaa+news/ncaa+news+online/2007/division+i/division+i+budget+trends+get+dashboard+treatment+-+10-22-07+-+ncaa+news

Brown, G.T. (2008, May 2). A look at the role business managers play in intercollegiate athletics. *NCAA News*. Retrieved February 1, 2010, from www.ncaa.org/wps/ncaa?key=/ncaa/ncaa/ncaa+news/ncaa+news+online/2008/assocation-wide/cabmaqa+-+05-02-08+ncaa+news

Brown, G.T. (2009, January 21). GLIAC strengthens role of league SWAs. *NCAA News*. Retrieved February 1, 2010, from www.ncaa.org/wps/ncaa?key=/ncaa/ncaa/ncaa+news/ncaa+news+online/2009/division+ii/gliac_strengthens_role_of_league_swas_01_21_09_ncaa_news

Claussen, C.L., & Lehr, C. (2002). Decision making authority of senior woman administrators. *International Journal of Sport Management*, *3*, 215–228.

Commission on athletics. (n.d.). California Community College Athletic Association. Retrieved May 23, 2010, from www.coasports.org/COA.pdf

Composition & sport sponsorship of the NCAA. (n.d.). Retrieved June 3, 2009, from www.ncaa.org/wps/ncaa?key=/ncaa/NCAA/About+The+NCAA/Membership/Our+Members/

Copeland, J. (2007, December 17). A simple question, a difficult answer. *NCAA News*. Retrieved February 1, 2010, from www.ncaa.org/wps/ncaa?key=/ncaa/ncaa/ncaa+news/ncaa+news+online/2007/association-wide/a+simple+question%2C+a+difficult+answer+-+12-17-07+-+ncaa+news

Crowley, J. (2006). *In the arena: The NCAA's first century*. Indianapolis, IN: NCAA.

Dannelly, J. (2009, February 24). *The future of the NAIA: Part 3 of 3*. Retrieved June 3, 2009, from www.collegefanz.com/blogs/jasondannelly/2009/02/24/the-future-of-the-naia-part-3-of-3

Davis, G.K. (2008). *NCAA athletic conference commissioners profiles and career paths*. Unpublished master's thesis. Raleigh: North Carolina State University.

Edes, G. (1922). *The annals of the Harvard class of 1852*. Cambridge, MA: Author.

Frommer, F.J. (2009, May 2). Game-changing call from congress to college football: Playoff. *ABC News*. Retrieved May 23, 2010, from http://thecabin.net/stories/050209/spo_0502090034.shtml

Fulks, D. (2008). *2004–2006 NCAA revenues and expenses of Division I intercollegiate athletics programs report*. Indianapolis, IN: NCAA.

Grant, C. (2009, February 23). Football Bowl Subdivision athletics budgets increase at alarming rate. *Sport Management Resources*. Retrieved February 1, 2010, from www.sportsmanagementresources.com/node/207

Grant, R.R., Leadley, J., & Zygmont, Z. (2008). *The economics of intercollegiate sports*. Mountain View, CA: World Scientific.

Grappendorf, H., Pent, A., Burton, L., & Henderson, A. (2008). Gender role stereotyping: A qualitative analysis of Senior Woman Administrators' perceptions regarding financial decision making. *Journal of Issues in Intercollegiate Athletics*, *1*, 26–45.

Hardin, R., & McClung, S. (2002). Collegiate sports information: A profile for the profession. *Public Relations Quarterly*, *47*(2), 35–40.

Harris, A., & Lowry, J. (2008). The powerful negotiator. *Athletic Business*, 102–107.

Hosick, M.B. (2009, May 1). Board tackles financial issues. *NCAA News*. Retrieved February 1, 2010, from www.ncaa.org/wps/ncaa?ContentID=49508

Huma, R., & Staurowsky, E.J. (2009). *An examination of the financial shortfall for athletes on full scholarship at NCAA Division I institutions*. Retrieved June 5, 2009, from www.ncpanow.org/research?id=0016

Irwin, R., Sutton, W., & McCarthy, L. (2008). *Sport promotion and sales management* (2nd ed.). Champaign, IL: Human Kinetics.

Johnson, G.K. (2009, February 11). Football attendance continues to rise amid economic uncertainty. *NCAA News*. Retrieved June 5, 2009, from www.ncaa.org/wps/ncaa?ContentID=45320

Knight Commission on Intercollegiate Athletics. (2009, February). *2009 NCAA Convention—Future of commercial activity*. Retrieved on February 1, 2010, from www.knightcommission.org/index.php?option=com_content&task=view&id=263

McDermott, E., & Lynch, M. (2008, April). *Enhancing the role of the SWA*. 2008 NCAA Gender Equity & Issues Forum, Boston.

Meleney, M. (2009, February 16). President's message. *NAA News*. Retrieved May 7, 2009, from www.nfoura.org

Membership. (n.d.). Retrieved February 1, 2010, from www.ecac.org/membership/index

NCAA. (2008). *2008–2009 NCAA Division I manual*. Indianapolis, IN: National Collegiate Athletic Association.

NCAA backgrounder on academic reform. (n.d.). Retrieved June 3, 2009, from www.ncaa.org/wps/ncaa?ContentID=339

NCAA Division I committees homepage. (n.d.). Retrieved February 1, 2010, from www.ncaa.org/wps/ncaa?key=/ncaa/ncaa/legislation+and+governance/committees/division1.html

NCAA eligibility center. (2008, May 7). NCAA freshman-eligibility standards quick reference sheet. Retrieved June 3, 2009, from www.ncaa.org/wps/wcm/connect/af238a804e0b869285bcf51ad6fc8b25/Quick_Reference_Sheet_for_IE_Standards-5-2-08.pdf?MOD=AJPERES&CACHEID=af238a804e0b869285bcf51ad6fc8b25

Pitts, B.G., & Stotlar, D.K. (2007). *Fundamentals of sport marketing* (3rd ed.). Morgantown, WV: Fitness Information Technology.

Q&A with Dave Hart Jr. (2008, May 29). *Athletic Management*. Retrieved February 1, 2010, from www.athleticmanagement.com/2008/05/qa-with-dave-hart-jr.html

Reese, J. (2003). Ticket operations. In U. McMahon-Beattie & I. Yeoman (Eds.), *Sport and leisure: A service operations approach* (pp. 167–179). London: Continuum.

Robinson, M. (2009). SMQ profile/interview: Vince Nicastro. *Sport Marketing Quarterly*, *18*, 3–5.

Sandomir, R., & Thamel, P. (2010, April 22). TV deal pushes NCAA closer to 68 team tournament. *The New York Times*. Retrieved May 12, 2010, from www.nytimes.com.

Schneider, R.C., & Stier, W.F. (2005). Necessary education for the success of athletics directors: NCAA presidents' perceptions. *Sport Journal*, *8*(1). Retrieved June 5, 2009, from www.thesportjournal.org/article/necessary-education-success-athletics-directors-ncaa-presidents-perceptions

Smith, R. (1994). *Big-time football at Harvard 1905: The diary of Coach Bill Reid*. Urbana: University of Illinois Press.

Staurowsky, E.J. (2009). Gender equity in two-year college athletic departments: Part II. *New Directions for Community Colleges*, *147*, 63-73.

Stoldt, G.C. (2008). Interview with John Humenik, executive director of the College Sports Information Directors of America. *International Journal of Sport Communication 1*, 458–464.

Strauf, D.L. (2002, October 28). Days of the "towel jockey" are long gone. *NCAA News*. Retrieved February 1, 2010, from www.ncaa.org/wps/ncaa?key=/ncaa/ncaa/ncaa+news/ncaa+news+online/2002/editorial/days+of+the+_towel+jockey_+are+long+gone+-+10-28-02.

Talahongva, P. (2009). Counting coups on the courts. *Tribal College Journal 20*(3), 14–20.

Tiell, B., & Dixon, M.A. (2008). Roles and tasks of the Senior Woman Administrator (SWA) in intercollegiate athletics: A role congruity perspective. *Journal for the Study of Sports and Athletes in Education*, *2*(3), 339–361.

Veneziano, J. (2002). *America's oldest intercollegiate athletic event*. Retrieved June 5, 2009, from www.hcs.harvard.edu/~harvcrew/Website/History/HY/

Weinbach, J. (2007, October 19). Inside college sports' biggest money machine. *Wall Street Journal*. Retrieved February 1, 2010, from http://online.wsj.com/article/SB119275242417864220.html

What is certification, what is its importance, and how do I become certified? (2008). Athletic Equipment Managers Association. Retrieved June 3, 2009, from www.aema1.com/

Whisenant, W.A., & Pedersen, P.M. (2004). The influence of managerial activities on the success of intercollegiate athletic directors. *American Business Review*, *22*(1), 21–26.

Wieberg, S., & Berkowitz, S. (2009, May 1). NCAA, colleges pushing the envelope with sports marketing. *USA Today*. Retrieved February 1, 2010, from www.usatoday.com/sports/college/2009-04-01-marketing-cover_N.htm

Winters, M. (1982). *Professional sports: The community college connection*. Los Angeles: Winmar.

Wolverton, B. (2008, May 23). 2 athletics associations consider joining forces. *Chronicle of Higher Education*. Retrieved February 1, 2010, from http://chronicle.com/weekly/v54/i37/37a01501.htm

Woodenlegs, T. (2009, March). CDKC Warriors head to AIHEC tourney. *Tseokeameehese*, p. 2. Retrieved May 23, 2010, from www.cdkc.edu/March%20Newsletter.pdf

Wushanley, Y. (2004). *Playing nice and losing: The struggle for control of women's intercollegiate athletics 1960–2000*. Syracuse, NY: Syracuse University Press.

Zimbalist, A. (2007, June 18). College athletics budgets are bulging but their profits are slim to none. *Street & Smith's SportsBusiness Journal*, p. 26.

HISTORICAL MOMENTS

- **1888** Massachusetts established the Interscholastic Football Association
- **1904** Georgia became the first state to establish a high school athletics association
- **1921** Midwest Federation of State High School Associations founded
- **1971** National Conference of High School Directors of Athletics founded
- **1974** *Interscholastic Athletic Administration* magazine launched
- **1977** National Interscholastic Athletic Administrators Association (NIAAA) formed
- **1979** Minnesota Adapted Athletics Association (MAAA) established—first high school athletics conference for students with disabilities
- **1981** National Federation Interscholastic Coaches Association (NFICA) formed
- **1982** National High School Sports Hall of Fame established
- **1990** National Federation Interscholastic Spirit Association (NFISA) formed
- **1993** Robert F. Kanaby named the National Federation of State High School Associations (NFHS) executive director
- **1996** American Association of Adapted Sports Programs (AAASP) founded—first interscholastic athletics governing body for students with physical or visual impairments
- **1996** Becky Oakes named first female president of the NFHS
- **2005** Athletics participation topped 7 million for first time
- **2008** NFHS developed its National High School Spirit of Sport Award

8

INTERSCHOLASTIC ATHLETICS

Warren A. Whisenant ■ Eric W. Forsyth

LEARNING OBJECTIVES

1. Identify the historical and governance foundations of interscholastic athletics.
2. Explain the differing critical views of the role that interscholastic athletics plays in society.
3. Discuss the operational differences between public and private schools.
4. Explain the benefits and restraints of athletics departments that are centralized and those that are dispersed.
5. Identify careers available in interscholastic sports at the national, state, district, and local levels.
6. Explain the unique and similar issues that face athletics directors at private schools and public schools.
7. Discuss the associations related to interscholastic athletics at the national and state levels.

Key Terms

athletics administrator
centralized organizational structure
decentralized organizational structure
interscholastic athletics
interscholastic sport governance
National Federation of State High School Associations
National Interscholastic Athletic Administrators Association
private schools
public schools
state athletics or activity associations

GET A JOB!

☑ Continue on your journey in sport management by going to the Online Study Guide (OSG) at www.HumanKinetics.com/ContemporarySportManagement. Check out the job opportunities and consider the skills and experiences that can help you succeed in sport management.

Interscholastic athletics is a segment within the sport industry that seems to draw the least amount of attention within the realm of sport management studies and academia. Scholars have tended to focus their research agenda toward collegiate and professional sport. Students entering the profession also tend to envision themselves as key players within a Division I athletics department or working in the front office of a professional sport team or even working as an agent negotiating multimillion dollar contracts. The attention toward those segments is understandable considering the dominant national media exposure of the professional and collegiate segments within the sport industry provided by cable outlets such as Fox Sports and ESPN. If the lead story on SportsCenter dealt with a rift between the Bulldogs' athletics director and head football coach, viewers would expect to see a story involving Damon Evans and Mark Richt from the University of Georgia, not Poppy Rodriquez and Tony Harris at McAllen High School (McHi) in McAllen, Texas. A story concerning the job security of the head coach of the Cowboys would draw attention to Dallas, not LaBelle High School in Hendry County, Florida. The many issues facing interscholastic administrators seldom draw widespread attention or interest.

Although the national media may not cover high school athletics, this segment of the sport industry should not be overlooked in terms of growth, career opportunities, and economic impact. The US Bureau of Labor Statistics (2007) suggested that the employment opportunities within sport were expected to grow more than 15% from 2006 to 2016, exceeding the growth rate of most other occupations. A significant portion of that growth will occur in the more than 24,000 athletics departments at the high school level, both public and private. Employing over 300,000 coaches and administrators, as a business segment, **interscholastic athletics** contributes over US$15 billion to the sport industry in the United States.

interscholastic athletics—Combination of sport offerings whereby boys and girls can elect to participate in athletics at the high school level.

The potential influence interscholastic athletics administrators have over the lives of young adults can be significant. Over 7.4 million of the 14.9 million (49.7%) high school students who attended public schools during the 2007–2008 school year participated in athletics. As such, interscholastic administrators have a deep responsibility and obligation to meet a wide range of needs to their constituents, the youth of America. For many kids, the manner in which their schools' athletics programs are managed and delivered will shape their perceptions about success and failure, organizational fairness, and other social norms. Although sport management professionals at both collegiate and professional levels are typically tasked with delivering a quality entertainment product for their fan base, interscholastic athletics administrators play an important role in the educational and social development of the students who are involved with the school's athletic program.

ARRIVAL OF INTERSCHOLASTIC ATHLETICS

The first intercollegiate athletics competition can be traced back to August 3, 1852, when Harvard and Yale matched their crew teams on the waters of Lake Winnepesaukee in New Hampshire (Dealy, 1990). The details of the first interscholastic athletics competition are less certain. But students from various public and private high schools in Massachusetts formed the Interscholastic Football Association in 1888 (Hardy, 2003; Wilson, 1994). As such, it may well have been among those Boston-area schools that the first interscholastic athletics competition occurred. At the turn of the century, interscholastic sport had become the largest sector in the entire sport enterprise (Robinson, Hums, Crow, & Phillips, 2001). No other level of sport has as many participants, sport teams, or athletics programs as interscholastic sport does. In addition, each school and each state provides an array of sporting options to meet the interests of their students. Both traditional sports and niche sports are offered across the country. A sampling of the sports offered by schools can be found in table 8.1.

TABLE 8.1 List of Most Common School-Sponsored Sports for Both Boys and Girls

TRADITIONAL SPORTS		
Baseball	Golf	Tennis
Basketball	Soccer	Track and field
Cross country	Softball	Volleyball
Football	Swimming and diving	
NICHE SPORTS		
Adapted floor hockey	Field hockey	Orienteering
Alpine skiing	Flag football	Power lifting
Badminton	Gymnastics	Rifle
Bowling	Heptathlon	Rodeo
Canoeing	Hockey	Sailing
Competitive cheer	Indoor track and field	Skiing
Crew	Judo	Snowboarding
Dance	Kayaking	Synchronized swimming
Decathlon	Lacrosse	Water polo
Equestrian	Nordic skiing	Wrestling

GOVERNANCE OF INTERSCHOLASTIC ATHLETICS

Individual state associations started developing and giving interscholastic athletics a more formalized governance structure in the early 1900s. The associations developed broad and sport-specific standards, rules, and policies. The first state to establish a high school athletics association was Georgia in 1904 (*Georgia High School Association*, 2010). During the early years when state associations were being established, colleges, universities, nonschool clubs, and promoters were organizing many interscholastic athletics competitions. As a result, little attention was given to the eligibility rules that were being established by the state high school athletics associations (*NFHS Handbook*, 2008).

After concerns were raised regarding the welfare of student–athletes, representatives from Illinois, Indiana, Iowa, Michigan, and Wisconsin met to discuss common concerns arising out of collegiate and nonschool publicity of high school athletics contests. As a result of this historic meeting that took place in May 1920, the Midwest Federation of State High School Athletic Associations (MFSHSA) was created in 1921. The mission of the federation was "to protect the athletic interests of high schools belonging to the various state associations and to promote pure amateur sport" (*NFHS Handbook*, 2008, p. 16). This mission still applies today. Not long after the formation of the MFSHSA, other state high school associations began expressing an interest in joining.

Interest grew nationally, and by 1923 it was fitting to change the name to the National Federation of State High School Athletic Associations. By 1930 there were 28 state athletics associations establishing membership. Ten years later, the state athletics association membership had grown to 35. In 1969 all 50 state associations and the association for the District of Columbia had become members of the national association. By the 1970s selected fine arts activities were sanctioned by the national federation, thereby dropping *athletic* from its name entirely. Today, the **National Federation of State High School Associations** (NFHS) consists of 22 additional members outside the

National Federation of State High School Associations—Also known as NFHS, this national governing body provides leadership for the administration of education-based interscholastic sport and nonsport activities.

HIGH SCHOOL SPORT—THE CANADIAN PERSPECTIVE

By Morris Glimcher
Manitoba High School Athletic Association, CANADA
By John Paton
Alberta Schools' Athletic Association, CANADA

Over 750,000 student athletes, 52,000 volunteer teacher coaches, and 3,200 schools are part of the Canadian School Sport Federation (CSSF). The Canadian system operates as a school-based model. Promoting good sportsmanship and ethical behavior is a key objective.

The Canadian philosophy is that school athletics are complementary to the curricular programs. Teachers are encouraged to contribute to the school in capacities such as coaches, supervisors, choir leaders, student council advisors, and other roles. All Canadian school coaches are volunteers. Depending on the province, 65 to 85% of these volunteer coaches are teachers, but this number is declining. As a result, schools and school athletics associations must deal at times with differing philosophies of teacher versus nonteacher coaches regarding issues such as playing time, cut policies, focus on winning, recruiting, and athletic eligibility.

In Canada, most schools and school districts do not have paid athletics directors (ADs). Some schools are able to structure timetables to give a teacher a few slots each week to look after the many athletics

AP Photo/The Canadian Press, Andrew Vaughan.

Bathurst High School, with a student population of approximately 750, is a part of the Canadian School Sport Federation. In 2009, the boy's basketball team won the provincial AA championship.

United States. Associations are located in Bermuda, Guam, St. Croix, St. John and St. Thomas, 10 provinces and three territories in Canada, and seven affiliated associations for defense, forensic, and music (*NFHS Handbook*, 2008). Additional information on each state, including a recap of the history, mission, and beliefs of each state association, may be found on the Web sites of the individual state associations. Summaries of three state associations and the national association follow.

Florida High School Athletic Association

The Florida High School Athletic Association (FHSAA) was founded in 1920 by a group of 29 high school principals. During its nine-decade history, the association has shown steady growth and currently has 748 member schools. For its first 77 years in operation, the association served as a voluntary governing body. Not until 1997 did the Florida State Legislature recognize the association as the official governing body for interscholastic athletics in Florida. The principal aim is to promote, direct, supervise,

issues. This practice is more common in urban areas than in rural areas. Many schools have a physical education coordinator who looks after the curriculum as well as the interschool sport programs.

Although Canada does not have legislation similar to Title IX, gender equity has always been a high priority, and the school athletics programs reflect that position. Litigation relating to school athletics typically occurs through the provincial court system. In some cases, Provincial Human Rights Commissions have dealt with concerns raised by parents and schools, and school athletics associations have modified eligibility policy to comply with their decisions.

Adequate financial support for athletics is not assured because the budgets are school based. Where booster clubs exist, they contribute to a variety of school programs, not just athletics.

Most students pay a participation fee that ranges from C$50 to C$300 or more per sport. Local school sport sponsorships are necessary to keep costs affordable for participants.

Coaches' certification programs are not mandatory for schools in Canada, but many programs are available to coaches. The Coaching Association of Canada (CAC) offers courses to coaches, and the CAC is working with the CSSF on a specific coaching module that will teach them the basics such as ethical decision making, dealing with parents, and understanding provincial athletic association rules.

The CSSF and the Canadian provinces have positive relationships with the National Federation of State High School Associations (NFHS) and the National Interscholastic Athletic Administrators Association (NIAAA) in the United States. Because there is much commonality in what athletics administrators do, we work positively with and between provincial, state, and national organizations to offer the best opportunities for student–athletes. Sometimes we share resources, and at other times we enjoy cross-border (i.e., province to province or province to state) athletics competition. We have many opportunities to share ideas and philosophies among provinces and with the United States. It is all part of the educational process of school sport.

INTERNATIONAL LEARNING ACTIVITY #1

Identify similarities and differences between the interscholastic athletics system in Canada and the interscholastic athletics system in your country. Note the instances in which you prefer the Canadian system and those in which you prefer the system in your country. In each case, give reasons for your preference.

INTERNATIONAL LEARNING ACTIVITY #2

Search the Internet for information on interscholastic athletics systems in countries other than Canada and your country. Construct a table of their most salient features. Which features do you prefer and why?

and regulate high school athletics programs. The association's members are committed to the ideal and belief that education does not begin or end in the classroom but continues outside the classroom. The association asserts that through their participation in interscholastic athletics, high school student–athletes also learn teamwork, sportsmanship, and citizenship as they become future leaders (*Florida High School Athletic Association*, 2010).

Minnesota State High School League

The Minnesota State High School League (MSHSL) was organized in 1916 as the State Interscholastic Athletic Association, and in 1929 the association broadened its scope by including nonsport activities. The inclusion of speech and debate under the association's domain led to a name change to the Minnesota State High School League. The MSHSL's principal aim is to provide educational opportunities for students through athletics and nonsport programs, and to provide leadership and support for its nearly 500 member schools (*Minnesota State High School League*, 2010).

University Interscholastic League

The University Interscholastic League (UIL) governs the largest number of high school athletes in the nation. Since its inception in 1909 the UIL has provided the leadership and guidance to public schools in Texas and has become the largest interschool organization of its kind in the world. The UIL provides oversight to the state's high school extracurricular activities associated with academics, athletics, and music. The goal of the organization (*University Interscholastic League*, 2010) is to "provide healthy, character building, educational activities carried out under rules providing for good sportsmanship and fair play for all participants" (¶ 3).

National Federation of State High School Associations

The NFHS was founded in 1920 to serve as the national leadership organization for high school sport and fine arts activities. Its principal aim is to support academic achievement, good citizenship, and equitable opportunities for boys and girls in high schools (as well as middle schools) by enhancing interaction among its member state associations. The national organization is also dedicated to developing and maintaining the playing rules for athletics contests at the high school level. Through its member state associations, the NFHS serves approximately 19,000 high schools and approximately 11 million participants in high school activities, over 7.4 million of whom are participating in athletics (*NFHS Handbook*, 2008). Table 8.2 lists the year in which each state association joined the national federation.

TABLE 8.2 State Associations and Year Joining the National Federation of State High School Associations

Association	Year	Association	Year	Association	Year
Alabama	1924	Kentucky	1941	North Dakota	1923
Alaska	1956	Louisiana	1925	Ohio	1924
Arizona	1925	Maine	1939	Oklahoma	1924
Arkansas	1924	Maryland	1946	Oregon	1931
California	1940	Massachusetts	1944	Pennsylvania	1924
Colorado	1924	Michigan	1920	Rhode Island	1952
Connecticut	1926	Minnesota	1923	South Carolina	1947
Delaware	1945	Mississippi	1924	South Dakota	1923
DC	1958	Missouri	1926	Tennessee	1925
Florida	1926	Montana	1934	Texas	1969
Georgia	1929	Nebraska	1924	Utah	1927
Hawaii	1957	Nevada	1939	Vermont	1945
Idaho	1926	New Hampshire	1945	Virginia	1948
Illinois	1920	New Jersey	1942	Washington	1936
Indiana	1924	New Mexico	1932	West Virginia	1925
Iowa	1920	New York	1926	Wisconsin	1920
Kansas	1923	North Carolina	1949	Wyoming	1936

VALUE OF INTERSCHOLASTIC ATHLETICS PROGRAMS

According to the NFHS (*Case*, n.d.), three central premises indicate the value of offering interscholastic activities: (a) athletics support the academic mission of schools, (b) athletics are inherently educational, and (c) athletics foster success in later life. Many of the supporters of high school sport draw on these attributes to promote the importance of athletics in the educational mission of public and private schools.

Athletics Support the Academic Mission of Schools

When compared with the general student population with regard to several components (e.g., grade-point averages, attendance, dropout rates, discipline), student–athletes tend to exceed students who do not compete in interscholastic athletics programs. Therefore, athletics should be viewed as an extension of a good educational program.

Athletics Are Inherently Educational

Through athletics participation students learn such things as teamwork, the value of fair play, winning and losing, the benefits associated with hard work, self-discipline, self-confidence, and skills to handle competitive situations. Parents, guardians, and the public typically expect schools to instill such qualities in students during their years in high school.

Athletics Foster Success in Later Life

By collecting exit surveys of participants at the state level, the NFHS has documented over the years the successes of student–athletes. Some of the documented successes are such markers as attending college, earning a degree, and having a higher socioeconomic status within society. Note that nonathletes also attend institutions of higher education, receive degrees, and attain prominent status within their respective communities. Overall, however, the professional success rate is higher for those who participated in interscholastic athletics programs than for those who did not.

Conflicting Views

Some people, however, hold conflicting views of the value in offering interscholastic sport programs within the education setting. Scholars such as Coakley (2009) and Eitzen and Sage (2009) present a critical perspective with respect to interscholastic sports and its place within society. Some critical views include the following:

- Participation in athletics programs distracts students from their academics.
- Athletics programs distort educational values within the school culture.
- Athletics programs turn students into passive spectators.
- Many injuries are associated with athletics competitions.
- Athletics goals are unrelated to educational goals.
- Athletics programs deprive educational programs of resources needed to survive.
- Athletics programs create too many additional pressures on athletes.
- Student–athletes tend to be privileged over other students.
- Athletics prepare students to be disciplined cogs in the industrial world.

Regardless of which lens through which you view high school sport, its presence is well entrenched within the American school system. Although athletics departments and participation rates grew throughout the 1900s, sports were not readily accessible to all students until the early 1970s. Not until the passage of Title IX legislation did girls earn equal access to the sport experience.

PARTICIPATION NUMBERS

Title IX of the Educational Amendments of 1972 was a landmark legislation that banned sex discrimination in public and private schools. The act, covered in detail in chapters 7 ("Intercollegiate Athletics") and 17 ("Legal Considerations in Sport Management"), applies to the activities of educational institutions that receive federal funding. At the time of its passage, fewer than 8% of the 3.9 million student–athletes participating in interscholastic athletics were girls (see table 8.3). At the end of the 2008–2009 school year, girls accounted for 41% of the 7.5 million high school students playing sports. Some critics of the application of Title IX to sport have argued that to be compliant with the legislation, boys' sports were cut, thus diminishing opportunities for boys to participate in sport. That position may be disputable because, as indicated in table 8.3, the number of boys participating in high school sport is at an all-time high, at over 4.4 million.

Texas continues to have the most participants (with 781,000 athletes, or 10.4% of all the high school athletics participants in the United States). The remaining top 10 states are California (771,465 athletes), New York (380,870 athletes), Illinois (341,763 athletes), Ohio (330,056 athletes), Pennsylvania (321,324 athletes), Michigan (311,277 ath-

TABLE 8.3 Participation Among Boys and Girls Since the Enactment of Title IX

Year	Boys	Girls	Year	Boys	Girls
1971–72	3,666,917	294,015	1991–92	3,429,853	1,940,801
1972–73	3,770,621	817,073	1992–93	3,416,389	1,997,489
1973–74	4,070,125	1,300,169	1993–94	3,472,967	2,130,315
1975–76	4,109,021	1,645,039	1994–95	3,536,359	2,240,461
1977–78	4,367,442	2,083,040	1995–96	3,634,052	2,367,936
1978–79	3,709,512	1,854,400	1996–97	3,706,225	2,474,043
1979–80	3,517,829	1,750,264	1997–98	3,763,120	2,570,333
1980–81	3,503,124	1,853,789	1998–99	3,832,352	2,652,726
1981–82	3,409,081	1,810,671	1999–2000	3,861,749	2,675,874
1982–83	3,355,558	1,779,972	2000–01	3,921,069	2,784,154
1983–84	3,303,599	1,747,346	2001–02	3,960,517	2,806,998
1984–85	3,354,284	1,757,884	2002–03	3,988,738	2,856,358
1985–86	3,344,275	1,807,121	2003–04	4,038,253	2,865,299
1986–87	3,364,082	1,836,356	2004–05	4,110,319	2,908,390
1987–88	3,425,777	1,849,684	2005–06	4,206,549	2,953,355
1988–89	3,416,844	1,839,352	2006–07	4,321,103	3,021,807
1989–90	3,398,192	1,858,659	2007–08	4,372,115	3,057,266
1990–91	3,406,355	1,892,316	2008-09	4,422,662	3,114,091

Data from 2008–09 high school athletics participation survey, 2010, (Indianapolis, IN: National Federation of State High School Associations). Available: http://www.nfhs.org/content.aspx?id=3282&linkidentifier=id&itemid=3282

letes), New Jersey (257,798 athletes), Florida (242,356 athletes), and Minnesota (224,220 athletes). In rank order, the 10 most popular sports in terms of the number of participants for boys are football, track and field, basketball, baseball, soccer, wrestling, cross country, tennis, golf, and swimming and diving. For girls, the 10 most popular sports in terms of the number of participants are track and field, basketball, volleyball, softball, soccer, cross country, tennis, swimming and diving, competitive spirit squads, and golf (*2008–09 High School Athletics*, 2010).

Kassy McCarthy was the starting kicker for the 2009 Waunakee (Wisconsin) state champion football team. According to the most recent data *(2008–09 High School Athletics*, 2010), there are 822 girls on high school football teams.

Photo by Michelle Stocker. Copyright *Wisconsin State Journal*. Reprinted with permission.

OPERATING MODELS

One of the most challenging aspects of managing any organization is establishing an organizational structure that best fits the needs of the organization's employees (e.g., teachers, coaches, officials, administrators) and constituents (e.g., parents, students, athletes). One significant consideration when structuring an athletics department is the size of the school district. Small districts or private schools—such as Newfound Area School District in New Hampshire, which serves seven cities and has 1,400 students, one high school, and two middle schools, or Storm Lake Community Schools in Iowa, which has 2,000 students, one high school, and one middle school—have a **centralized organizational structure.** Centralized structures tend to have vertical reporting relationships often characterized as a chain of command (figure 8.1 illustrates the difference between a centralized and a **decentralized organizational structure.** The athletics director (AD) may work at the high school and report to the high school principal while overseeing the athletics administrative duties for the entire district. The AD may also serve as a coach, a teacher, or in some instances be the high school principal. In a centralized structure, the AD typically hires all the district's coaches and has a campus coordinator at each middle school to oversee daily athletics administrative duties. This type of structure is most often used by **private schools.** For larger school districts—such as the Miami–Dade County Public Schools, which has more than 362,000 students in over 90 high schools and middle schools, or the Houston Independent School District, which has more than 200,000 students and over 70 high schools and middle schools—a centralized athletics department would not be feasible or manageable. In these mega athletics programs, administrative responsibilities are often decentralized through a matrix management template. This type of structure allows dual reporting relationships. The district might have a district athletics director who coordinates athletics activities within the district with staff level authority in the schools and school-based athletics directors who report directly to the school principals for implementing the district programs. These high school ADs would most likely supervise feeder school campus coordinators as well as one or more assistant ADs and a business manager.

centralized organizational structure—An operational model whereby all decisions are controlled by a central administration unit and carried down through the chain of command within an organization.

decentralized organizational structure—An operational model whereby respective units of an organization are given autonomy to control and carry out decisions, although each unit is expected to operate within the organization's guiding principles.

private schools—Schools that operate on monies received through various forms of funding and giving (e.g., personal, religious, corporate).

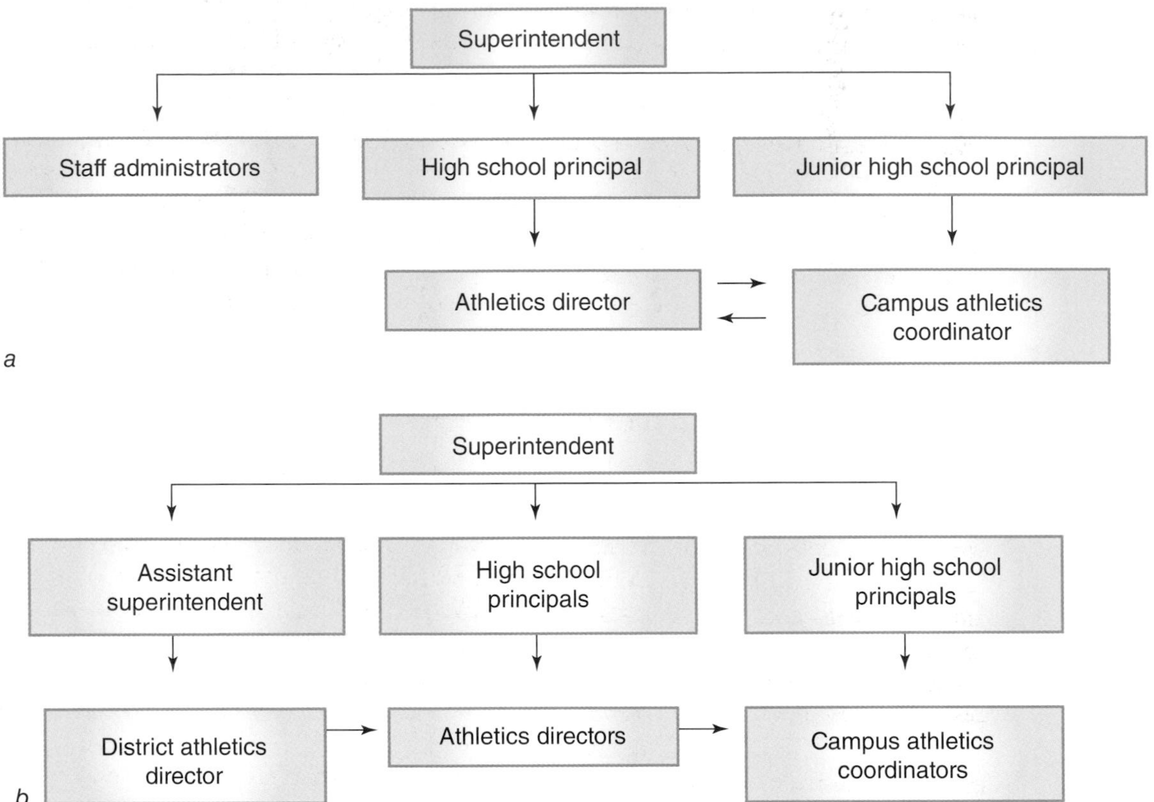

Figure 8.1 Organizational structures: *(a)* centralized structure and *(b)* decentralized structure.

public schools—Schools that operate on monies received largely through local property taxes.

Although athletics budgets may differ from school to school, the primary expenses tend to be similar. Most budgets will be composed of the following categories: salaries and benefits, equipment, supplies, transportation, professional development, awards, and other miscellaneous costs. Typically, insurance and facility costs are held back at the district level for **public schools.** ADs at private schools or smaller public school districts may also be responsible for facility expenditures. School budgets allocated to athletics vary greatly from 1 to 3% of operating budgets to as much as 6 to 8%. As operating costs continued to rise during the 2008–09 school year, the economic downturn across the country had a detrimental effect on overall school funding and, in turn, on athletics. The primary source of funding for most school districts is through property tax assessments. Because the economy grew throughout the 1990s and into 2007, property values increased, providing additional revenues to school districts. In 2008, however, when the real estate market collapsed, many school districts and athletics departments found themselves with significant revenue shortfalls. The Miami–Dade school district, for example, reported an estimated operational deficit in excess of US$200 million, requiring spending cuts in all facets of the education system.

ADs across the country were forced to adapt to the decline in revenues and stretch their budgets to meet the growing needs of student–athletes. Numerous options were available to ADs. Although some programs drastically reduced the number of contests in which their athletes competed, others eliminated sports completely, particularly in middle schools. Additional attempts to resolve funding concerns included replacing some individual contests or matches with tournaments, implementing pay-to-play policies, reducing the frequency of uniform purchases, increasing fund-raising activities, and seeking greater support from booster clubs. Athletics administrators have also reduced transportation costs by restricting competition to schools in proximity to the home school, discontinuing courtesy bus service to transport parents to and from away events, and scheduling contests on the same nights for both the boys' team and the girls' team or the varsity and junior varsity teams so that teams can travel together.

Unlike public schools, which derive most of their funding from district property tax revenues, private schools rely on donations, tuition allocations, or participation fees. When faced with budget issues, private schools can raise tuition or seek donations from companies or individuals. Because public schools tend to be public bureaucracies, ADs must operate within a rigid bureaucratic structure. Private schools tend to be leaner in their management structure, allowing greater flexibility in making decisions.

CAREERS IN INTERSCHOLASTIC ATHLETICS

Career opportunities in high school sport cover a wide array of disciplines at the grassroots level. The nature of the job requires professionals to work long and often irregular hours. Typically, practices and competitive events occur outside the regularly scheduled school day, taking place in late afternoons, evenings, and weekends.

Besides positions in coaching, in officiating, and as athletics directors, people are needed in administrative support, as coordinators at the middle school and junior high level, and in various associate athletics director positions to oversee facilities and transportation, event management, and business operations. Beyond the school district level, professionals play a large role in **interscholastic sport governance** and in the management of the various state and national professional associations. A brief list of full-time professional positions available in interscholastic athletics with their common job accountabilities follows.

interscholastic sport governance—High school athletics competition that is governed by state athletics or activity associations.

Positions Within Professional Associations

- *Executive director.* This person serves as the chief executive officer (CEO) for an association. As the CEO, she or he is accountable for the daily operations of the organization, supervises the staff, carries out the agenda of the organization's membership and officers, and oversees the organization's legal affairs and legislative interests.

- *Chief financial officer.* The CFO is accountable for all financial transactions of the organization affiliated with interscholastic athletics. The financial transactions include business operations, payroll, and accounts payable. Besides overseeing the various transactions required, the CFO prepares all financial reports and the annual operating budget.

- *Director of media relations and marketing.* The person who holds this position serves as the public liaison for the interscholastic athletics organization. Besides maintaining a Web site, this person oversees sponsorships and other revenue-generating ventures such as broadcasting rights, licensing, and merchandising.

- *Director of membership services.* Professionals who hold this position maintain the interscholastic athletics membership database. Furthermore, they manage services and benefits for the membership as well as lead the interscholastic athletics association's membership recruitment efforts.

Positions at the Local School Level

- *Athletics director.* An athletics director (AD) serves as the school's senior administrator for athletics. The primary function is to provide the leadership and management of the interscholastic athletics program. In research that we have conducted we found that ADs spend the greatest amount of their time (39%) engaged in traditional

Photo courtesy of Bruce Whitehead.

In Profile: Bruce Whitehead

Bruce Whitehead is the executive director for the National Interscholastic Athletic Administrators Association. He received his undergraduate and graduate (master's) degrees in mathematics from Purdue University. After completion of his graduate education Whitehead became a high school educator and coach. Eight years later he became an athletics administrator. After 25 years as an athletics administrator he became an assistant with the National Interscholastic Athletic Administrators Association (NIAAA). In 2004 he was hired as the executive director of the NIAAA. The following are his comments about his career and the interscholastic athletics segment of the sport industry:

My career has evolved into a leadership position with the national organization that serves athletics administrators. My position requires many common skills including leadership, organization, financial expertise, and oral and written communication skills.

The biggest overall issue that I face is making the NIAAA voice known to all athletics administrators nationally and internationally. It is very rewarding when athletics administrators tell you that your efforts benefited them and made their program a better program for the students they serve.

An athletics administrator in a local school might start at a salary in the range of US$50,000 to US$75,000 with insurance benefits and a retirement plan. An executive position with the NIAAA would start around US$90,000 with insurance benefits and a qualified retirement plan.

Turnover among athletics administrators is between 25 and 30% per year. Reasons for the turnover include individuals' moving to other administrative positions within the school (for instance, someone moving up to a principal position), the large number of hours required to perform the job adequately, and the high level of stress.

The job market for high school and middle school athletics administrators is readily available. Because of the increasing complexity of the position, previous experience and a demonstration of certification are becoming increasingly important factors. The NIAAA provides a job opening and résumé posting site through the NIAAA member database. In addition, most local schools list position openings each spring with state universities.

An important issue today is keeping high school athletics as an education-based program administered in our schools and available to all students as a purely amateur program. If interscholastic athletics is going to survive as an education-based program serving all students in our schools, the NIAAA must be the leader to ensure that outcome.

The two biggest factors for an individual seeking a position of athletics administrator are to have a keen interest in high school athletics and a sincere, intense desire to help young people have participation opportunities. I would further recommend that a person begin to take the NIAAA's leadership training courses and obtain the NIAAA certification level of registered athletics administrator.

managerial activities. They deal with human resource issues for 27% of their time. The balance of their time is spent engaged in either communication-based activities (24%) or networking (10%). The AD position calls for extensive levels of interaction with students, parents, coaches, faculty, and members of the community. Specific duties and responsibilities include the following:

- Prepare a master budget for capital expenditures and ongoing operations of each school-sponsored sport
- Ensure that all sport programs operate within the guidelines (e.g., eligibility) established by the appropriate governing bodies
- Coordinate and schedule use of all athletics venues

- Hire all officials, coaches, trainers, and athletics department support staff
- Oversee the scheduling of all athletics events
- Provide oversight to athletics booster club activities and fund-raising activities
- Ensure compliance of the athletics program with Title IX

Most ADs begin their careers as teachers or coaches. Although in the past ADs tended to hold two positions (i.e., AD and coach), at larger schools the AD has become more of an administrator with no additional duties. At most smaller schools, however, the AD continues to have multiple collateral duties in addition to athletics administrative activities. The credentials required for ADs vary from state to state and between public and private schools. Typically, the minimum qualifications for the position in a public school system are a bachelor's degree and a valid teaching certificate. Additional requirements may include a master's degree in education administration, educational leadership, or sport administration. In some states, such as Texas, a midmanagement certification may also be required. Private schools have the flexibility to waive teacher certification and other credentials. The **National Interscholastic Athletic Administrators Association** (NIAAA) provides professional certification and development for athletics administrators through its Leadership Training Program. The organization (*NIAAA*, 2005, ¶ 1) noted that the program was developed in 1996 to

- promote the professional growth and prestige of **athletics administrators,**
- provide an opportunity for athletics administrators to participate in the nation's largest professional organization whose activities are directed exclusively to high school and middle school athletics administrators,
- provide education programs as a resource tool for athletics administrators, and
- promote quality in all programs conducted at the national, state and local level.

The organization has three levels of certification: the registered athletic administrator (RAA); the certified athletic administrator (CAA); and the master athletic administrator (CMAA).

National Interscholastic Athletic Administrators Association—This organization, known as the NIAAA, is a national governing body that serves as a liaison between individual state high school athletics associations and state athletics administrator associations.

athletics administrator—A person who provides administrative support to the school's various athletics programs.

Job titles that share similar duties with varying levels of responsibility include associate and assistant athletics director and campus coordinator. Many ADs also serve as coaches or teachers or have additional collateral duties. For example, in Texas, while studying AD job announcements, Whisenant (2005) found that approximately 73% of the advertised AD positions also required the person to serve as the head football coach. Because men outnumber women as coaches and often the AD must also coach, men hold approximately 86% of the AD positions across the United States (Whisenant, 2003).

- *Athletics business manager.* The business manager often oversees a wide range of activities including the implementation of the athletics budget and all business-related affairs of the athletics department. Specific duties and responsibilities include the following:
  - Monitor expenditures and budgets
  - Negotiate contracts and oversee departmental purchases
  - Develop, prepare, distribute, and interpret the financial data for the department and each sport team
  - Perform other duties as assigned by the athletics director

WEB

Go to the OSG and complete the Web search activity, which asks you to investigate the representation of women in leadership roles in high school athletics.

People in this role are often required to have a strong grasp of accounting principles and procedures, be proficient with computers and financial software, and be able to interpret numerical data. Because the athletics business manager serves in a staff position reporting directly to the athletics director, she or he should have strong interpersonal and communication skills that allow effective exchange of information with coaches and other athletics department personnel.

- *Coach.* Most coaches are full-time teachers who coach part time either for the love of the game or to supplement their income. Coaches are responsible for
  - complying with the rules and regulations governing interscholastic athletics and their specific sport;
  - teaching appropriate fundamentals and techniques, rules, and strategies of the sport;
  - scheduling practices and competitions;
  - supervising student–athletes while they participate in school-sponsored activities;
  - teaching fair play and other appropriate social behaviors;
  - ensuring player safety and responding to player injuries;
  - maintaining school equipment, uniforms, and facilities; and
  - maintaining effective communications with parents and booster clubs.

ACTION

Go to the OSG and complete the Learning in Action activity, which lets you participate in a roundtable discussion with high school coaches of various sports.

The credentials required to coach vary between public and private schools. A couple common qualifications, however, are knowledge of the assigned sport and previous coaching experience. Most public schools hire full-time teachers from their own faculty to serve as coaches. Such individuals will hold a bachelor's degree and have a valid teaching certificate. If the school is unable to find a suitable coach within its full-time faculty, a person from outside the school may be hired as a part-time employee to

Photo courtesy of Holly Farnese.

In Profile: Holly Farnese

I am the athletics director at Upper Darby High School. I received my bachelor's degree in Spanish from Bloomsburg University and have a German certification from Villanova University. Throughout my 33 years in education, I have taught Spanish and German, and coached field hockey, gymnastics, and track and field. Furthermore, for 27 of those years I have been an athletics and activities director for the Upper Darby School District in Drexel Hill, Pennsylvania. I have also gained athletics administration knowledge through the NIAAA Leadership Training Program and the American Sport Education Program.

As athletics director of a 4,000-student high school that has 25 interscholastic sport programs and a staff of 75 coaches, I provide leadership, mentorship, organization, and vision for the athletics program. The athletics program is the "front porch" of the school. I hope to set a professional example for the program, high school, and school district to the community.

I have the opportunity to celebrate excellence and make memories each day by keeping high school interscholastic athletics in the proper perspective as an amateur program for all interested athletes. The rewards occur when you least expect them, from the most surprising sources.

Most athletics administrators in Pennsylvania are either teachers or administrators. Teaching salaries range from a low of $41,100 to a high of $90,000, depending on the teacher's degree and years of experience. Administrator salaries range from a low of $80,000 and move up based on degrees and experience.

There will always be a need for teachers and athletics as an extension of the classroom. The challenge is to provide the finest leadership development possible so that educators can best serve our youth. I believe that the NIAAA and individual state associations have been at the forefront of that leadership in the field of athletics.

I always look to hire the most qualified interscholastic athletics administrators to administer the best quality athletics programs. Success is finding a passion in life and educating yourself to be the best that you can be to fulfill that passion. If your passion is interscholastic sports, then perhaps you have a future in athletics administration.

coach a sport. Some states require some type of coaching certificate to coach, whereas others do not. Both the National High School Athletic Coaches Association and the NFHS Coaches Association are actively engaged in professional development activities for high school coaches and have established and recognized certification programs.

Most states provide certification through their own state coaches association. For example, in Texas the Texas High School Coaches Association (THSCA) provides a professional development certification (PDC) program for coaches. The basic qualifications include an undergraduate bachelor's degree and active membership in the THSCA. Requirements for certification are to *(a)* attend a minimum of eight PDC lecture hours at the THSCA's annual coaching school, *(b)* hold current CPR and AED certifications, and *(c)* have a current first aid certificate. The certification is valid for a two-year period. Private schools have the flexibility to waive teacher certification and other credentials.

- ***Athletics trainer.*** Athletics trainers (ATs) are usually the first medical personnel on the scene when a sport-related injury occurs. Because their primary duty is to prevent and treat injuries, their work day is often longer than most other personnel in the athletics department. Before and after practice or competitive events, they treat the athletes' injuries, provide rehabilitation treatment, and apply protective devices to help prevent injuries. For those ATs who are also teachers, the typical work week may exceed 60 or 70 hours. An AT's primary responsibilities include such aspects as providing athletic training services to student–athletes, being accessible at all sporting events in the event of an injury, and serving as a liaison between the school district, physicians, student–athletes, and parents.

Because ATs deal with the physical and psychological well-being of the athletes, the credentials required to work at public and private schools are similar. An athletics trainer should have a bachelor's degree and be certified by the National Athletic Trainers Association (NATA). She or he must also be certified in first aid and CPR before becoming certified as an athletics trainer by the NATA.

- ***Officials.*** Although most of the positions noted previously are full-time positions, officiating in interscholastic athletics is a part-time job. Most states require officials to register with the state's governing agency and pass a competency exam. States also have minimum age requirements, and state interscholastic athletics supervisors conduct a background check to ensure that the prospective official is of sound moral character.

ISSUES FACING INTERSCHOLASTIC ATHLETICS

A recent headline—"School Sport Now a Luxury"—was printed in the *Minneapolis-St. Paul Star Tribune* (Millea, 2009, p. B1). Being eliminated from the team has a whole different meaning as school districts struggle during the current economic crisis. Athletics administrators across the country are making hard decisions to keep their athletics programs afloat. Reducing game contests, cutting back on transportation and equipment, eliminating teams, and raising participation fees are just a few decisions being made by administrators to curtail budgets. The current financial crisis is only one challenging issue that administrators are dealing with today. In a study conducted by Forsyth (2007), athletics administrators identified several challenging issues that face high school athletics.

Experienced and Certified Athletics Administrators

Matching an athletics administrator's responsibilities to the person chosen to fill a vacancy has been a recurring challenge. According to the executive secretary of the

Minnesota Interscholastic Athletic Administrators Association, an administrator's position that becomes vacant is often filled internally by a coach who does not have the necessary knowledge or experience (P. Veldman, personal communication, March 30, 2009). As noted earlier, to help bridge this gap, the NIAAA developed the certified athletics administrator program to assist athletics administrators in their new role. This program consists of leadership training courses that include content such as supervision and decision making, management strategies and organizational techniques, marketing and promotions, budget and finance, mentoring and problem solving, assessing programs and personnel, legal issues, field and equipment management, and contest management. Certification, however, is often not mandated by school principals or district superintendents. Those wishing to pursue a career as an athletics administrator need to take it upon themselves to obtain the necessary credentials to succeed in this complex but exciting position.

Budgetary Constraints

Although some athletics departments may account for as much as 8% of their schools' operating budgets, the NFHS (*Case*, n.d.) reported that most athletics departments receive only 1 to 3% of the total allocation given to schools. Many schools throughout the Midwest, South, and West receive even less. For example, data for the 2007–2008 school year illustrate how some school districts have allocated their budgets:

- Chicago's public schools education budget was US$4.6 billion, and activity programs received US$36.2 million, which amounts to one-seventh of 1%.
- Charlotte-Mecklenburg's public schools education budget was US$1.2 billion, and activity programs received US$4.7 million, which amounts to one-third of 1%.
- Seattle's public schools education budget was US$339.7 million, and activity programs received US$3.2 million, which amounts to one-ninth of 1%.

Although the millions of dollars allocated to high school athletics appear to be a substantial amount to support programs, these figures and percentages fail to represent the true operating costs, particularly as costs continue to escalate year after year. The budgets allocated for athletics fail to keep pace with the annual rising costs. The result requires athletics programs to continue working with less.

An example would be the Albuquerque Public School's (APS) District in New Mexico. According to the budget director for APS, in 1985 the total education budget for the school district was US$247.7 million and the athletics department received US$2.4 million (T. Osborn, personal communication, March 30, 2009). Five years later when the total APS education budget rose to US$279.7 million, the portion allocated to the athletics department decreased to just over US$2 million. After 10 years the total education budget almost doubled to $554.7 million, whereas the athletics department continued to decline to about $1.8 million. APS athletics went from receiving 9/10 of 1% of the total education budget to 3/10 of 1% during this 10-year period. Working with less meant that by 1995 APS lost 24 athletics teams and 62 coaching positions. Student participation also decreased substantially. Over the last five years (2004–2008), money allocated for APS athletics ranged between 2/10 and 5/10 of 1%.

Coach Turnover and Exiting

Another challenging issue is retaining coaches. Many coaches leave coaching after just a couple years on the job. Athletics administrators are finding it more difficult to retain coaches as problems arise with athletes, parents, and fans, adding to the daily personal demands on coaches' time. Under the NFHS umbrella, the National Coaches Association (NCA) has taken initiatives to help athletics administrators retain coaches through its coaches' education and training program. Some of those initiatives are developing positive relationships with parents or guardians and administrators, dealing with challenging personalities, understanding the fundamentals of coaching in specific sports, safety and first aid, and so forth. Unfortunately, these initiatives are not mandatory for coaches to complete. Likewise, those wishing to pursue a career in coaching need to take it upon themselves to pursue the necessary education and training so that they can handle problems that may arise on the job.

Recruitment and Retention of Officials

When it comes to challenging issues with interscholastic sport officials, athletics administrators typically find that the issues are the same as those with their coaches: A shortage exists, and recruiting and retaining quality officials is extremely time consuming. Surveys conducted by the National Association of Sport Officials (NASO) sought to gain: *(a)* the views of high school state association executive directors (*NASO Officials*, 2001) and *(b)* the views of officials (*Accountability*, 2003). The results give a glimpse into why recruiting and retaining officials is challenging:

- Ninety percent of executive directors reported a shortage of qualified officials.
- Seventy-six percent reported lack of fair play by spectators as being the reason that officials quit.
- Sixty-eight percent reported lack of fair play by participants as being the reason that officials quit.
- Forty-nine percent of officials reported lack of respect shown by athletes, coaches, and spectators.

The NASO is committed to helping athletics administrators improve their recruitment and retention of sport officials through consultant programs, newsletters and magazines, Web site services, officiating resources, and performance evaluations. Those wishing to become practicing interscholastic sport officials need to take it upon themselves to take advantage of NASO's offerings and expertise.

Participation Options

Although participation rates have consistently increased from year to year for boys and girls (refer to table 8.3), the athletes' commitments to their schools' athletics program have become another challenge. More students are electing to compete on nonschool athletics teams as well. By competing on a school-sponsored team and a non-school-sponsored team at the same time, athletes are faced with demands from two coaches. Students become torn between their commitments to both teams, and some end up choosing to compete on the non-school-sponsored team only. The reason for this decision is that nonschool programs such as those associated with AAU and the Junior Olympics often have traveling teams and compete year round. Such opportunities entice athletes to choose their nonschool athletics program over their school athletics program. Rather than forcing an athlete to choose, representatives from both school and nonschool programs should work together for the student–athlete's well-being.

Fair Play

Many of the ugly issues apparent in college and professional sport are appearing in high school gyms. Students and parents must be constantly reminded that competition is just a game rather than a war. Fair play is as much a concern for fans as it is for athletes. Because fans and players view poor sport behavior on TV (in collegiate and professional sports), enforcing fair play expectations at the prep level has become extremely difficult. The need to teach fair play through high school sport is apparent.

Is running up the score fair play?
Photo courtesy of Paul M. Pedersen.

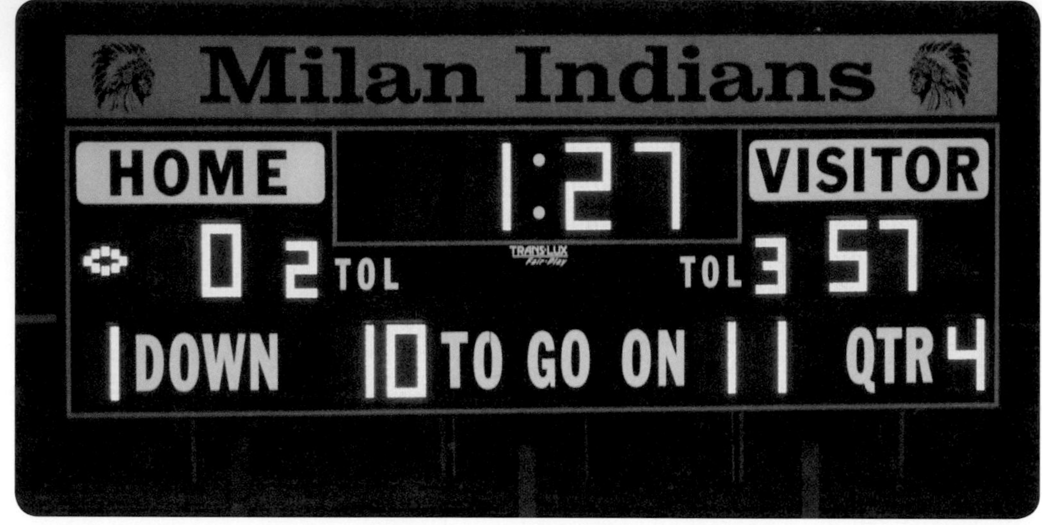

The NFHS is trying to combat poor sporting behavior issues through its program "Citizenship and Asset Building Through Athletics." Also, the NIAAA offers specific courses titled "Student Centered Educational Athletics" and "Coach Centered Educational Athletics" in its certified athletics administrator program curriculum. Perhaps these character-building models are being practiced. At a Texas high school girls' basketball contest, a private school beat a public school by a score of 100-0. After reflecting on the victory, representatives from the winning school not only apologized for the blowout (there are no mercy rules in Texas for such mismatches) but also are trying to have the game forfeited as well (*School Seeks*, 2009). Representatives from both schools appear to have learned a great deal from this experience.

Transfers

Historically, Minnesota permitted open enrollment for high school student–athletes, allowing them to participate at the school of their choice. That changed at the beginning of the 2007–2008 school year, when the Minnesota State High School League's (MSHSL) executive board voted to discontinue open enrollment, with the exception of waivers for special circumstances. Many parents and student–athletes did not agree with this new policy, so they took their complaints to their local legislators. Before legislators could attempt to overrule the new policy, the MSHSL conducted a public relation push through the media to explain their rationale for the change. The tactic, according to the executive director of the MSHSL, inevitably won favor and the legislators' efforts ended (D. Stead, personal communication, March 30, 2009).

state athletics or activity associations—Governing body that sets rules and policies for high school sport eligibility, competitions, and state championship tournaments.

Most **state athletics or activity associations** require a waiting period for transfers to be eligible to compete. Transfers often are athletically motivated (Smith, 2005). Many say that private schools have an unfair advantage over public schools, because private schools recruit athletes and eligibility rules do not apply to transfers who attend private high schools (Popke, 2006). Athletes and parents have stretched the truth to the breaking point to bring about transfers; changes of address, divorces, separations, illnesses, and the like have been claimed, although later it was found out that none of those had occurred.

These issues challenge administrators to adapt to a constantly changing environment involving school policies and the rules governing sport. Each issue is often unique in the minds of the people involved, so the administrator must be consistent when dealing with them. Coaches, parents, players, officials, and members of the community all may have a sense of involvement that the administrator must balance.

CRITICAL THINKING IN INTERSCHOLASTIC ATHLETICS

Balancing the needs and interests of the student–athletes and the educational mission of a high school often requires the athletics administrator to reach some form of compromise. If the decision is fair and ethical, all the affected constituents should be satisfied or at least willing to accept the decision. Maintaining fairness in the decision-making process, involving the associated parties some degree of participation in the process, and treating everyone with dignity and respect throughout the process will often result in acceptance of the decision. The following paragraphs present two issues that require critical thinking by athletics administrators.

Proponents of high school sport stress the importance of athletics as an extension of the classroom learning experience. As covered earlier in this chapter, sport offers some unique benefits that are certainly laudable. For example, many argue that participation in sport builds character, teaches teamwork, and encourages fair play. Participants learn the rewards of hard work, self-discipline, and self-confidence. Participation often improves social adaptability. Students involved in extracurricular activities often have lower dropout rates, higher attendance rates, higher grade-point averages, and fewer discipline problems in school. Furthermore, students engaged in extracurricular activities are often less likely to use drugs or become teen parents. Using the critical thinking questions from chapter 1, examine the argument that through the benefits offered by participation, athletics is an extension of the classroom learning experience.

Yet another critical thinking exercise could involve the monetary aspect of interscholastic athletics. For example, we noted earlier in the chapter that because of declining property values many communities and school districts face revenue and budget shortfalls. Many schools have embraced outsourcing as a means of controlling their expenses. Typical services being provided by private sector companies include school transportation, food services, custodial services, and substitute teachers. Why not expand the services to athletics? Schools could outsource their athletics departments either to one company or to a variety of private club sports. Another option might be to provide vouchers so that kids could play the sport that they prefer in a club-sport setting year round.

PORTFOLIO

Complete the critical thinking portfolio activity in the OSG, consulting as needed the "Eight Critical Thinking Questions" section in chapter 1.

ETHICS IN INTERSCHOLASTIC ATHLETICS

As issues arise in interscholastic athletics, appropriate resolutions require high school administrators to make decisions consistent with the goals and aspirations of their programs, teams, and various stakeholders. The various options to be considered require constant consideration to ensure that ethical conduct is maintained. Two examples of the myriad issues that require ethical reasoning in interscholastic athletics follow.

Department Action and School Mission

One junior high school had as its mission statement the following:

> ABC Junior High School is committed to creating and maintaining an environment whereby each student is given the opportunity and encouragement to grow intellectually, physically, emotionally, and socially in order to assume a responsible role in today's ever-changing world. Students, teachers, parents, and the community will work collaboratively so that all students will achieve a quality education.

The school's enrollment was approximately 1,100 students (55% girls and 45% boys). The athletics department at the school fielded six football teams each fall. Three teams were for seventh-grade boys, who practiced in the morning before school. The other

PORTFOLIO

Complete the ethical issues portfolio activity in the OSG, consulting as needed the "Guidelines for Making Ethical Decisions" section in chapter 1.

three teams were for eighth-grade boys, who practiced in the afternoons after school. Each team had a roster of approximately 45 boys. No teams cut players, so all boys who wanted to play could be on a team. For the girls, the major fall sport was volleyball. The school had one girls' volleyball team that had a roster of 12 girls. Over 200 girls tried out for the team each fall.

Funding Interscholastic Athletics

As noted earlier in this chapter, athletics administrators face difficult decisions to keep their athletics programs afloat during times of economic hardships. The money is simply not available to operate athletics programs at their current capacity. Therefore, athletics administrators are trying to make reductions that will have the least negative effect on their schools and programs. One direction that athletics administrators may take to support their programs is to market talented athletes.

Let's consider a prediction made by sport marketers. Because of the growth of national and regional television outlets looking for sport programming and the money that those outlets can offer, Mullin, Hardy, and Sutton (2007) predicted that such enticements "will begin having a noticeable effect on top-tier high school athletics programs, which will schedule athletics contests on a national scale and 'rent' athletes for one- or two-year terms to become attractions" (p. 466). These scholars wonder whether talented high school athletes will be more motivated to transfer to showcase their abilities, whether booster clubs will become more motivated to raise funds on the talents of selected athletes rather than the athletics programs and their purpose, and whether the marketing of athletes might trickle down to high school, middle school, and even youth programs.

Summary

This chapter has provided an overview of interscholastic athletics, which is one of the largest, yet relatively understudied, segments of the sport industry. From a human development and sociological perspective, high school athletics affects 50% of all high school students. As a segment of the sport industry, interscholastic athletics contributes billions of dollars to the economy and provides full-time and part-time jobs for more than half a million people. School-sponsored athletics programs shape or influence in some form the lives of more than 14 million people (e.g., students, family members, coaches, administrators) in the United States. Although supporters and detractors may have differing views of the role that interscholastic athletics should play in the educational process, both would agree that athletics is tightly woven into the culture and society of the United States.

QUIZ TIME

Did you grasp all the key points in this chapter? Go to the OSG for a short quiz to test your understanding of the material.

Review Questions

1. In what year did high school sport governance begin, and why was a governing body needed?
2. How has the passage of Title IX affected participation rates in high school sport?
3. What are the major operational differences between public school and private school athletics departments?
4. In relation to other levels of sport competition, where does interscholastic athletics rank in size and scope?
5. What are some of the underlying factors that caused interscholastic sport to become part of the educational system?

6. What are some of the perceived benefits that students receive by participating in interscholastic sport programs?
7. How are career paths similar and different at the national, state, district, and local levels?
8. Would a school voucher program affect low-income students and middle-class students differently? Explain your answer.

References

2008–09 high school athletics participation survey. (2010). Indianapolis, IN: National Federation of State High School Associations. Retrieved June 1, 2010, from http://www.nfhs.org/content.aspx?id=3282&linkidentifier=id&itemid=3282

Accountability in officiating survey. (2003). National Association of Sports Officials. Retrieved February 1, 2010, from www.naso.org/surveys/Acct.Survey.pdf

Case for high school activities. (n.d.). Indianapolis, IN: National Federation of State High School Associations. Retrieved February 1, 2010, from http://www.osaa.org/osaainfo/08CaseForHSActivities.pdf

Coakley, J. (2009). *Sports in society: Issues and controversies* (10th ed.). New York: McGraw-Hill Higher Education.

Dealy, F.X. (1990). *Win at any cost*. New York: Carol.

Eitzen, D.S., & Sage, G.H. (2009). *Sociology of North American sport* (8th ed.). Boulder, CO: Paradigm.

Florida High School Athletic Association. (2010). Retrieved February 1, 2010, from www.fhsaa.org/about

Forsyth, E. (2007). *Current issues surrounding interscholastic sports: Survey report*. Indianapolis, IN: National Interscholastic Athletic Administrators Association.

Georgia High School Association. (2010). Retrieved February 1, 2010, from www.ghsa.net/general

Hardy, S. (2003). *How Boston played: Sport, recreation, and community, 1865–1915*. Knoxville: University of Tennessee Press.

Millea, J. (2009, January 19). School sports now a Minnesota luxury? *Minneapolis-St. Paul Star Tribune*, p. B1.

Minnesota State High School League. (2010). Retrieved February 1, 2010, from www.mshsl.org/mshsl/aboutmshsl.asp?page=2

Mullin, B.J., Hardy, S., & Sutton, W.A. (2007). *Sport marketing* (3rd ed.). Champaign, IL: Human Kinetics.

NASO officials shortage survey results. (2001). National Association of Sports Officials. Retrieved February 1, 2010, from www.naso.org/surveys/shortage.html

NFHS Handbook. (2008). Indianapolis, IN: National Federation of State High School Associations.

NIAAA. (2005). Retrieved February 1, 2010, from www.niaaa.org/Leadership_Training/leadership_training.asp

Popke, M. (2006). Public notice: Schools in Kentucky claim unfair advantages for private schools. *Athletic Business*, *30*(4), 106–110.

Robinson, M., Hums, M., Crow, R., & Phillips, D. (2001). *Profiles of sport industry professionals: The people who make the games happen*. Gaithersburg, MD: Aspen.

School seeks to forfeit 100-0 win. (2009). Retrieved February 1, 2010, from http://highschool.rivals.com/content.asp?CID=903780

Smith, L. (2005). A tough game: Dealing with athletically motivated transfers. *Athletic Management*, *17*(6), 26–33.

University Interscholastic League. (2010). Retrieved on June 1, 2010, from www.uil.utexas.edu/about.html

US Bureau of Labor Statistics. (2007, December 18). *Occupational outlook handbook, 2008–09*. Retrieved June 27, 2009, from www.bls.gov/oco/ocos251.htm

Whisenant, W. (2003). How women have faired as interscholastic athletic administrators since the passage of Title IX. *Sex Roles*, *49*(3/4), 179–184.

Whisenant, W. (2005). In Texas it's football: How women have been denied access to the AD's office. *International Journal of Sport Management*, *6*, 343–350.

Wilson, J. (1994). *Playing by the rules: Sport, society, and the state*. Detroit: Wayne State University Press.

HISTORICAL MOMENTS

- **1807** The Montreal Curling Club organized the first curling contests in North America
- **1844** Young Men's Christian Association (YMCA) founded; Ladies Christian Association founded in 1858 (the term *YWCA*, for Young Women's Christian Association, was first used in 1866)
- **1888** Amateur Athletic Union (AAU) formed
- **1898** Canadian Amateur Athletic Union (CAAU) formed
- **1906** Federated Boys Clubs in Boston formed; later renamed Boys and Girls Clubs of America
- **1914** Police Athletic League (PAL) began in New York City
- **1929** Pop Warner Football began
- **1939** Little League Baseball began
- **1961** Fitness and Amateur Sport Act passed in Canada
- **1964** American Youth Soccer Organization (AYSO) founded
- **1978** Amateur Sports Act of 1978 adopted by United States Congress
- **1981** National Alliance for Youth Sports (NAYS) founded
- **2002** Canadian Centre for Ethics in Sport released a report specifically addressing issues in youth sport
- **2003** International Alliance for Youth Sports (IAYS) established
- **2009** President Obama established White House Office of Olympic, Paralympic, and Youth Sport

Photo courtesy of Paul M. Pedersen.

9

YOUTH AND COMMUNITY SPORT

Marlene A. Dixon ■ Jennifer E. Bruening

LEARNING OBJECTIVES

1. Define youth and community sport.
2. Identify different sectors and key providers of sporting opportunities at the youth and community levels.
3. Identify and explain challenges regarding access to youth and community sport.
4. Explain key challenges in managing youth and community sport and propose solutions for those challenges.
5. Differentiate the outcomes and goals associated with various types of sport offerings and the management implications thereof.
6. Identify career opportunities within youth and community sport.

Key Terms

community sport
national regulatory association
professional human resource management model
quality of life
social capital
sport-based youth development model
sport league
sport tournament
volunteer sport organization (VSO)
youth sport

GET A JOB!

☑ Continue on your journey in sport management by going to the Online Study Guide (OSG) at www.HumanKinetics.com/ContemporarySportManagement. Check out the job opportunities and consider the skills and experiences that can help you succeed in sport management.

Many people around the world have participated in sport in their communities either as children, as adults, or perhaps throughout their lives. Because of familiarity with this sport participation structure, participants may tend to think that their experiences are similar to the experiences of most participants in other localities in North America or around the world. In so doing, however, they may take for granted the unique organizational and structural challenges surrounding the management of community and youth sport. This chapter introduces the history of community sport in North America as well as its current forms. It also presents an overview of some of the operational, strategic, and sociocultural challenges and opportunities inherent in the design, delivery, and future direction of youth and community sport.

ORIGINS AND HISTORY OF COMMUNITY SPORT IN NORTH AMERICA

The history of sport in North America is difficult to condense because it varies widely by place of residence, gender, social class, race and ethnicity, and family background. In other words, not everyone's experience in sport was the same. But some general trends in this sport history can help us understand the place of community sport in our society and the way that **community sport** is organized and delivered today.

community sport—Organized physical activity that is based in community, school, and local sport organizations.

In North America, sport and games were part of communities and cultures long before the arrival of Europeans. Emerging histories of native communities in North America showed rich and varied traditions of sport and physical contests. The contests ranged from the races, wrestling, and rites-of-passage contests of the North American Dene and Inuit peoples, to moose-skin ball of the Athapaskan women, to perhaps the most influential game, lacrosse, among the Iroquoian, Algonquian, Sioux, Chickasaw, Choctaw, and Cherokee nations (Morrow & Wamsley, 2005). In native communities, sport and contests often served the purposes of training youth for adult experiences; displaying the strength, skill, and prowess of community members; or celebrating the

Native American communities participated in many forms of sports and games, as illustrated in this engraving showing native youths shooting arrows, throwing balls at a target placed on a tall pole, and running races.

Courtesy of the Library of Congress, LC-USZ62-37992.

culture and religion of the community. Although much of the original meaning and symbolism of community sport from these native peoples has been lost or redefined, these peoples and games have had a lasting influence on the structure, form, and meaning of community sport in North America.

Before the 1800s, European North Americans rarely engaged in physical contests that could be labeled as sports as we know them today (Rader, 2009). Much time was spent simply surviving and establishing new towns, cities, and industries. The folk games played at this time were usually simple and had no written rules; they were legitimated by custom and often changed to fit the circumstances of play (e.g., space or time available). In the early 1800s in rural Canada and America, these games often sparked contests between citizens or towns that formed the basis of early sport experiences. For example, fishing, hunting, snow shoeing, rowing, archery, throwing, running, and rail-splitting were activities that could be contested between men, often serving as a source of pride and identity for the family or village (Morrow & Wamsley, 2005; Rader, 2009).

At the same time, a sporting fraternity of sorts emerged in urban centers such as New York, Philadelphia, Montreal, and Toronto where men would gather to play sports and wager on billiards, horse racing, prize fighting, or footraces. For example, the Great Race of 1835 offered a prize of $1,000 to anyone who could run 10 miles in less than an hour. Over 20,000 spectators watched as one man, Henry Stannard, a farmer from Connecticut, finished in 59 minutes and 48 seconds (Rader, 2009). In Canada, curling contests, races, and hunting contests between fur traders and frontiersman thrived through local taverns and military garrisons (Morrow & Wamsley, 2005). The races and spectacles continued across the continent, yet sport remained largely unorganized and unregulated.

In the early 1800s, however, voluntary sport clubs emerged for sports such as curling, rowing, cycling, snowshoeing, quoits, cricket, track and field, and baseball. These clubs were mostly the domain of upper- and middle-class men who could afford the time and membership dues required to belong to the sporting clubs. Contests were arranged first within clubs for the benefit of the club members and then later between clubs. The sponsoring club provided the rules, the facilities, the prize money, and the social events surrounding the contests. For example, the Montreal Curling Club, established by the Scots in 1807, organized the first curling contests in North America exclusively for the benefit of its 20 elite citizens (Morrow & Wamsley, 2005). The Montreal Snowshoe Club, Montreal Bicycle Club, and Montreal Lacrosse Club also served as important clubs for the early foundation of regulated amateur sport in Canada. In the United States, the New York Athletic Club (established in 1850) built the first cinder track for track and field and sponsored the first national amateur track and field championship in 1876. This club also sponsored the first national amateur championships for swimming (1877), boxing (1878), and wrestling (1878). The various sport clubs in the United States and Canada represented the beginning of a larger sport movement in the countries that spread both in types of sport offered and the delivery and governance thereof. As sport clubs expanded, battles ensued over who would provide and regulate community sport, and who would define its guiding principles.

In the early 1900s sport and physical activity continued to grow. In the United States, for example, under the presidency of Theodore Roosevelt, local, state, and national funding was committed to the growth of parks and recreation facilities and spaces, and the Playground Association of America (which eventually became the National Parks and Recreation Association) was born. At this time, parks and recreation activities were more focused on play and leisure, not necessarily on organized sport. Sport was in the domain of private clubs, schools, and the Amateur Athletic Union (AAU), which represented the United States in international competition. After World War II much debate occurred during the ensuing decades about America's lack of prominence in international sport, which led to the passage of the Amateur Sports Act in 1978 and the creation of national sport governing bodies (e.g., USA Swimming, USA Track and Field). These governing bodies have been given the task of sport development in the United States, and they govern US representation in international sport, but they do not necessarily have enforcement powers to become the sole sport providers or governors of amateur sport within the country.

In Canada the governance of community sport took a slightly different route. The formation of the Canadian Amateur Athletic Union (CAAU) in 1898 gave Canada a unified structure for the regulation of amateur sport. This body also "vowed to advance and improve all sports among amateurs and stated an even loftier goal, that is, to encourage systematic physical exercise and education in Canada" (Morrow & Wamsley, 2005, p. 76). The CAAU, along with the passage of the Fitness and Amateur Sport Act of 1961, has kept Canada's sport and recreation systems more coordinated and unified than those in the United States. Thus, in Canada sport is delivered on a local level but typically is coordinated under the auspices of the national governing body (i.e., a **national regulatory association**).

national regulatory association—A national sport governing body that makes eligibility and playing rules and sponsors competition according to its rules.

In summary, the history of North American sport in the 19th and 20th centuries has highlighted the emergence of two very different community sport systems in the United States and in Canada. Neither system is superior, and both present challenges to sport managers in the design and delivery of community-level sport. For example, although many parks and recreation centers in the United States have adopted sport programming, debate continues to this day about whether sport is complementary or contradictory to the mission and goals of parks and recreation. This debate is not seen in Canada (or in most other countries in the world) and often creates ongoing tension over the meaning and purpose of public recreation centers. In the United States, furthermore, because no single body governs amateur sport, sport structures and systems vary widely across states, cities, and local communities. In Canada, although sport is seemingly more uniform and coordinated, some sport organizations struggle for more control and voice in their local sport governance. Today, community sport in North America is a widely varying experience that offers both challenges and opportunities to sport managers.

YOUTH SPORT HISTORY

As Americans began to understand the effect of children's social interactions and activities on their development, organized sport emerged as a means to provide interactions, friendships, and learning experiences transferrable to life outside these activities. Since the late 19th century when the Young Men's Christian Association (YMCA) began offering boys competitive sporting opportunities (Koester, 2000; Marten, 2008), sport has been a part of the landscape for children. The Boys Clubs also began in the 1800s with a mission of providing safe spaces for boys to play. The charter was expanded in 1990 to represent its current participants as the Boys and Girls Clubs (Halpern, 2002). The Young Women's Christian Association (YWCA) began in 1898, although sport programming today exists at only about 24% of US facilities (Hopkins, 1951; Murphy, 2005).

Other notable beginnings include the Police Athletic League (PAL), Pop Warner Football, the Catholic Youth Organization (CYO), and Little League. The PAL, created in 1914 in New York City, had the goal of providing safe places to play for children who lived in the city. Pop Warner Football, started in 1929, is still the only youth football organization that requires participants to maintain academic standards. The CYO commenced in 1930, followed by Little League Baseball (1939) and Little League Softball (1974). The Canadian Royal Legion began in the 1940s with the Foster Fathers

Job Opportunities in Youth Sport

Two organizations are highlighted in this sidebar. First, Up2Us (www.up2us.org) is a growing association currently composed of 172 youth programs from across the United States. The goal of Up2Us is to bring together community sport programs that share common missions emphasizing the health, life skills, and social change benefits of sports. One function of the coalition is to share opportunities for jobs that exist at its member organizations in order to assist in expanding the workforce for youth sport programs.

Next, an example of an Up2Us member organization is Playworks. Playworks (www.playworksusa.org/) is a nonprofit that focuses on low-income schools by providing opportunities for play with the aim of fostering a positive environment for both learning and teaching. Playworks has set out to "rescue recess" at more than 170 schools across the country. The youth sport organization hires city directors, among other staff, who are responsible for managing all aspects of their programs in a particular city. Part of their duties includes the implementation of the Playworks comprehensive school-based programming at as many as eight schools per year. The city director is Playworks' senior staff person in a particular city and oversees up to 11 staff people in the first year of operations and then builds the staff each year moving forward.

Program for boys left fatherless by World War II. The program originated as an effort to teach boys leadership skills through sport. This philosophy, as evidenced by the focus on boys in these original youth sport organizations, is supported by Howard Chudacoff's (2007) history of children at play in the United States. The historian traces the origins and evolution of community-based youth sport from the male-centered model aimed at building character and preparing young boys and men for their futures in the workplace. Over time, community-based **youth sport** has evolved to include more girls, particularly after the passage of Title IX in 1972 and its enforcement beginning in the 1980s. Today, in the United States close to 20 million children of both genders between the ages of 6 and 16 participate in organized sport (Coakley, 2009).

youth sport—Organized physical activity for children and adolescents offered through schools, community organizations, or national sport organizations.

Organized youth sport has a broad definition in North America ranging from the community organizations highlighted earlier to both interscholastic and club programs. The variations on sport that exist on a town, region, state or province, and national level are grounded in both the philosophy and the financial situation of the specific location. Shortly after the turn of the century, the Canadian Centre for Ethics in Sport (2002) released a report that specifically addressed issues in youth sport. The results included discussion that the increasing economic influence of youth sport, particularly at the club level of competition, and the "Americanization of sport" (p. 1) are leading youth sport away from its beginnings as a means to educate children and build leaders to a source of revenue and entertainment. With the growing privatization and specialization of organized youth sport (Coakley, 2009; Engh, 1999), some community-based teams and leagues are finding themselves with fewer participants from which to draw.

Consider a recent development in youth basketball in the United States that speaks to the issues discussed in the Canadian Centre's report. The National Collegiate Athletic Association (NCAA) is stepping into the youth arena because of its concern that school-based basketball is not as essential to children as it once was. The club system has taken over the role of developing young basketball players and according to the NCAA is missing the educational and sportsmanship aspects that the organization believes are necessary. So, in 2009 the NCAA announced an initiative to provide more structure to the club system. The NCAA added that although the organization wishes to have a positive influence on all children who participate in nonscholastic basketball, a second aspect of the initiative is to identify and develop elite players (Brown, 2009) who could eventually play at NCAA institutions.

Service Learning Through UConn's Husky Sport

Bringle and Hatcher (1995) collected multiple definitions of service learning across disciplines and across universities. From these definitions, they derived three general characteristics of service learning on college campuses:

1. It is designed to meet the needs of the communities in which it takes place.
2. It includes both reflection and academic learning.
3. It develops or accentuates students' interest in and understanding of community life.

The Husky Sport program at the University of Connecticut uses a service learning model to expose students to an urban community in need of nutrition, life skills, and sport and physical activity opportunities for its children. The UConn students mentor the community children in these areas during both in-school and after-school hours at seven sites (four schools, one YMCA, one recreational center, and one faith-based community program) in one neighborhood. Visit the Web site www.huskysport.uconn.edu to learn more about service learning and the Husky Sport program.

The NCAA initiative is but one example of the ongoing tension in youth sport in North America. In youth sport, should the focus be education or elite sport development? Who should govern youth sport? Who has access to the various kinds of sport opportunities? Remember that throughout the history of North American sport, not everyone has agreed on the purpose or process of youth sport, which continues to present significant challenges to sport managers in this context.

DEFINITION OF COMMUNITY SPORT

In defining community sport we take a broad approach wherein community sport is conceptualized as organized physical activity that is based in community, school, and local sport organizations. Thus, this definition—drawn from the work by Stewart, Nicholson, Smith, and Westerbeek (2004)—encompasses both recreational and competitive sport but does not include exercise and fitness facilities or programs. Further, community sport may, but does not necessarily have to, culminate in high-performance sport that takes place at the college, professional, Olympic, national, or international level. Table 9.1 provides examples of community and youth sport organizations mentioned throughout this chapter.

Emphasis on the Participant

In professional sport (see chapter 6), management's concerns are often focused on people as spectators and consumers of sport for entertainment. In contrast, the emphasis in community sport is on people as participants. Therefore, management's concerns in this area focus on continuing to attract new participants and keeping them involved in the programs. Management's concerns include the types of programs or sports offered, the time and place of activities, the organization and delivery of programs, and cost and pricing considerations. Concern for the financial performance of the organization coincides with a focus on high quality of service as well as sport development. By keeping participant needs and wants central, managers can ensure the short- and long-term viability of their organizations. In terms of youth community sport, in particular, these needs and wants include participation and education on the rules and strategies of the game as well as the related social and ethical development of the children (Hedstrom & Gould, 2004; Larson, Walker, & Pearce, 2005; Le Menestrel & Perkins, 2007).

TABLE 9.1 **A Sampling of Community Sport Organizations in North America**

Organization	Web Site
YMCA	www.ymca.net
YWCA	www.ywca.org
Police Athletic League	www.palnyc.org
Little League Baseball and Softball	www.littleleague.org
The Royal Canadian Legion	www.legion.ca/About/youth_e.cfm
Catholic Youth Organization	www.nationalcyosports.org
Pop Warner Football and Cheerleading	www.popwarner.com
Women's Sports Foundation	www.womenssportsfoundation.org
GoGirlGo	www.womenssportsfoundation.org/GoGirlGo.aspx
National Alliance of Youth Sports	www.nays.org
International Alliance of Youth Sports	www.iays.org
Canadian Fitness Tax Credit	www.cra-arc.gc.ca/fitness/
Lakewood (CO) Recreation Department	www.lakewood.org/comres
Hartford (CT) Recreation Department	www.hartford.gov/Human_services/html%20files_06/Recreation.htm
United States Tennis Association	www.usta.com
West Suburban YMCA, Newton (MA)	www.ymcainnewton.org/main/programs/sports/instructional_programs/super_sports
City of Burbank Youth Sports	www.ci.burbank.ca.us/index.aspx?page=323
American Softball Association	www.asasoftball.com
United States Volleyball Association	www.usavolleyball.org
United States Field Hockey Futures	www.usfieldhockey.com/futures/
United States Youth Soccer	www.usyouthsoccer.org
Amateur Athletic Union	www.aausports.org
United States Swimming	www.usaswimming.org
YMCA of Greater Toronto	www.ymcatoronto.org
Sugar and Spikes Softball Club	www.eteamz.com/sugarnspikes91/
Fitz Urban Youth Sports	www.sportinsociety.org/uys/index.htm
Husky Sport	www.huskysport.uconn.edu
Playworks	playworksusa.org/
Up2Us	www.up2us.org

Benefits of Sport Participation

Numerous benefits are associated with sport participation. Some of these positive aspects include physical benefits, improved family well-being, a sense of community, and increased social capital for families and other groups. Although much focus has been placed on physical benefits, the broader benefits to individuals, families, and communities have sometimes been overlooked (Chalip, 2006; Dixon, 2009).

Quality of Life

The physical benefits of sport participation include increased cardiovascular health, decreased stress, and increased functioning of the musculoskeletal system (US Department of Health and Human Services, 1996). One benefit of sport participation for children specifically is helping to maintain a healthy weight; sport participation can reduce weight in obese children (Stanford University Prevention Research Center, 2007).

In addition, people who participate in recreation and sport report better concentration, task persistence, disposition, and analytical ability. These gains can lead to higher work productivity and lower absenteeism. People also report psychological benefits of participation such as increased self-esteem and social belonging (Dixon, 2009; Koltyn & Schultes, 1997). Children, in particular, benefit from being physically active through sport. Physical activity improves psychological health and helps cognitive, physical, social, and emotional development. Sport participation and physical activity can delay the onset of many chronic diseases (Government Accountability Office, 2006; Stanford University Prevention Research Center, 2007). Overall, there is general agreement that sport participation can positively affect a person's **quality of life** and that childhood physical activity through sport increases the likelihood of maintaining an active lifestyle as an adult.

quality of life—The degree of well-being felt by an individual or a group of people.

Note, however, that these benefits are not experienced universally or to the same degree across all groups. In 2008 the Women's Sports Foundation (WSF) published findings revealing that a gender gap continues to be present in youth sport participation and that girls from both urban and rural communities are disproportionately not participating in sport. Additionally, the data show that interest in being physically active in both sport and exercise results not from biological inheritance but rather from the opportunity and encouragement of influential others in a child's life. The WSF also reports that physical education classes, indicative of other sport and exercise participation, are even further unequal on the basis of both gender and geography. Urban girls, rural girls, and low-income boys and girls, in that order, are underrepresented as students in school physical education classes. More positively speaking, girls have expanded their participation to include a larger variety of sports and activities than boys do, although boys' sports tend to fall more often under the umbrella of school or community sport. Lastly, according to the data, girls have a shorter time frame in which to participate than boys do. Girls typically start later (i.e., age 7.4 compared with 6.8 for boys) and exit organized sport sooner, usually during middle school (i.e., between the ages of 12 and 14) (Sabo & Veliz, 2008).

Family Life

Benefits of sport participation extend beyond the individual because participation often includes improved family well-being. Families report a greater sense of belonging and increased bonds through sport and recreation participation (Henderson & Hickerson, 2007). Many parents report enjoyment from participating in recreational activities with their children, in coaching their children's sport teams, or in attending sporting events together with their families (Dixon, 2009). Children's athletic participation was associated with higher levels of family satisfaction (Government Accountability Office, 2006; Sabo & Veliz, 2008).

Sense of Community and Social Capital

Finally, sport participation can create a sense of community and create **social capital** for families and other groups of people (Putnam, 2000). Social capital could be defined as a "contextual characteristic that describes patterns of civic engagement, trust, and mutual obligation among individuals" (Cuskelly, Hoye, & Auld, 2006, p. 8), or more simply as the glue that helps communities stay together (Badcock, 2002). People who participate in sport together along with those who volunteer together to deliver a community sport program develop social networks, shared norms, and understandings that can lead to greater cooperation and cohesiveness in a community. Chalip (2006) maintained that one of the main outcomes that legitimizes sponsoring sport at its various levels is community development and the building of social capital within and across communities.

social capital—Contextual characteristics of communities that describe how people develop trust and social ties. Social capital is also described as the glue that holds communities together.

SIZE AND SCOPE OF COMMUNITY SPORT

Although counting the exact number of people in North America who participate in sport is difficult, recent reports indicate that sport participation in general continues to grow in both the United States and Canada and that millions of people in both countries participate in sport at both the recreational and competitive levels. In Canada more than 33,000 volunteer sport organizations serve participants of all ages in their communities. In the United States recent data from the Sporting Goods Manufacturers Association (2008) show trends and actual participant numbers in a myriad of sports ranging from billiards and darts to waterskiing. Table 9.2 reports the most popular participant sports in 2008. For example, 18 million Americans aged six and above participated in basketball at least 13 times over the past year, and 25 million played at least once. Bowling had over 15 million regular participants, baseball had 11.6 million, and another 7.9 million played tennis on a regular basis. Some of the fastest growing sports over the past eight years (2000–2008) in the United States include lacrosse (104% increase), triathlon (35% increase), running (30% increase), tennis (30% increase), and cheerleading (25% increase). Sports that report declining participation include boxing (44% decrease), roller skating (32% decrease), ice hockey (24% decrease), badminton and racquetball (20% decrease), and wrestling (11.5% decrease). Individual conditioning and exercise has seen the largest gains in participant numbers over the past eight years. For example, participation in Pilates has increased 490%, participation in elliptical training has increased 200%, and participation in yoga has increased 125%. It is not clear, however, whether these participants are in addition to sport participants or have shifted from sport to exercise.

Thus, in the United States most traditional sports continue to have strong participation rates, indicating a continued demand for community sport offerings. But sport managers should note trends in increasing or decreasing demand so that new sports can be added or old programs dropped if they are no longer relevant to sport consumers.

TABLE 9.2 Most Popular Sports (Based on Participation Numbers) in the United States

Sport	Number of core participants
Basketball	18.0 million
Bowling	15.4 million
Baseball	11.6 million
Tennis	7.9 million
Football (touch)	6.4 million
Soccer (outdoor)	6.3 million
Softball (slow pitch)	6.0 million
Martial arts	5.4 million
Football (tackle)	4.2 million
Volleyball (court)	4.15 million
Track and field	2.7 million

Note: A core participant is one who participates in the sport 13 or more times in a given year. Respondents may participate in more than one core sport. Includes community and school providers (Sporting Goods Manufacturers Association, 2008).

TYPES OF COMMUNITY SPORT ORGANIZATIONS

ACTION

Go to the OSG and complete the Learning in Action activity, which helps reinforce your understanding of the popularity of community sports.

In this section we examine types of community sport organizations in North America. We first examine Canadian sport organizations before turning our attention to sport organizations in the United States. Although the two sport systems have some similarities in the ways that community sport is designed and structured, there are also distinct differences.

Although sport is offered through primary and secondary schools and in colleges and universities in Canada, community sport is almost exclusively offered through local and regional sport clubs (Cuskelly et al., 2006). These club-sport offerings are in addition to recreational sport (e.g., outdoor sports) and exercise and fitness (e.g., yoga, aerobics) opportunities in both public (e.g., community centers) and private health clubs in Canada (e.g., Goodlife Fitness Clubs). Community sport clubs, also known as

volunteer sport organization (VSO)—Nonprofit local sport organization that provides organized sport opportunities for community members. VSOs are governed and supported through volunteer management and coaching.

volunteer sport organizations, or **VSOs,** provide myriad sport opportunities including curling, hockey, cross-country skiing, basketball, and soccer. Typically, these organizations work in conjunction with a network of organizations including their provincial and national counterparts (e.g., a local soccer club will be a member of the provincial soccer association, and this provincial association will be a member of the Canadian Soccer Association). This network of organizations oversees and governs the various elements of the sport system. VSOs are all not for profit and are run by volunteers. In this system, therefore, it is not unusual for a sport participant to serve in some volunteer capacity for the organization (Cuskelly et al., 2006).

In the United States, sport at the community level is offered through a wide range of organizations, both public and private. Private facilities include organizations such as the YMCA and YWCA, in which sport is one of many programs or services offered. Participants pay membership dues to join the organization and receive access to the programs and facilities. A paid staff manages the organization and provides the services. Community sport is also provided at private country clubs, which typically offer sports such as swimming, golf, and tennis. Sport is also offered at private, for-profit clubs such as soccer centers and running clubs. Again, in this model, members usually pay a fee in exchange for the opportunity to play in the club's sport leagues, receive professional training or coaching, and have access to the organization's facilities. As the number of private sport organizations continues to grow in the United States, sport management students have found more employment opportunities in community sport. (See the sidebar "Career Opportunities: Austin Sports and Social Club" for more information.)

Community sport in the United States is also offered through public entities such as schools and parks and recreation facilities and programs. Unlike in most countries throughout the world in which sport for school-aged children is sponsored by community organizations, in the United States youth sport is not only offered by public schools but often is considered central to the middle and high school experience (Hartmann, 2008). In school-sponsored sport, communities pay taxes to support the schools, which then provide the coaches and sport opportunities. In some school settings (e.g., Texas) coaches are also expected to teach an academic subject, whereas in other settings (e.g., Colorado, Ohio) coaches can be part-time professionals hired only to coach. As noted

Career Opportunities: Austin Sports and Social Club

The Austin Sports and Social Club (www.austinssc.com) was founded in 2005 to provide sporting opportunities for adults in the Austin, Texas, metropolitan area. The club has since expanded operations to San Antonio and Dallas. In the beginning, the club was owned and operated by a single person who maintained the office, organized the leagues, and hired part-time officials to manage the games. As the club has expanded, opportunities have grown for administrative positions such as financial officer, Web site manager, league coordinator, and tournament coordinator. These individuals work to promote the club and manage team entries, progress, and so on. One critical position that has been created is a director of market research. This person explores the needs of people in the target markets so that the sports offered in the club meet those needs. This person also explores the expansion possibilities for new markets, ensuring that the population to support an expansion is viable. Finally, this person works with sponsors to ensure that the club is reaching the appropriate target market for the sponsors so that they are achieving the desired results from their sponsorship dollars. Other positions are more directly involved with the sports themselves. One person manages all the officials, which involves recruitment, training, and scheduling. Another person is in charge of facilities and scheduling. This person works with public recreation facilities to lease playing fields for the club and to ensure that the fields are safe and clean. Thus, positions are available for marketing, finance, operations, and risk management.

earlier, sport opportunities through the public schools are largely subsidized by local tax dollars. Some schools, however, now charge a participation fee to students to help offset costs of providing the sports. For more information on such arrangements, see chapter 8 ("Interscholastic Athletics").

Publicly supported parks and recreation centers also offer sport and recreation opportunities at the community level. These centers are usually supported financially by a combination of local tax dollars and user fees, depending on the governmental unit involved. People who live within the tax district are able to participate in the program or use the facilities at a discounted rate, and some programs are limited only to people who live within the defined tax district (so that the taxpayers are also the beneficiaries of the programs). For example, the City of Lakewood, a suburb of Denver, Colorado, provides sport and recreation facilities and programs for its citizens. They offer everything from pay-as-you-use recreation facilities to organized **sport leagues** for participants age five and older. From a management perspective, public parks and recreation facilities operate much like private clubs—with paid management and operations staff, although many still rely heavily on volunteer coaches for the delivery of their youth and adult organized sport programs. An example of a different model would be that in the city of Hartford, Connecticut. Hartford's six recreation centers as well as its four swimming pools are open to residents of the city at no cost. The city also provides free swimming lessons at these pools to its residents, space permitting. Children in Hartford are also eligible for free, eight-week summer camps at one of the city's parks. The free camps include transportation to and from any of the city's recreation centers. In most cases children can participate in any structured program offered at the city's recreation centers at no cost. A nominal charge for basketball leagues is the exception. The city, whose residents have a much lower average socioeconomic status (SES) than those in Lakewood, subsidizes these programs rather than tapping its citizens for additional fees.

sport league—An organization that exists to provide ongoing regulated competition in a specific sport.

Yet another example of how models of community sport opportunities are managed comes from Canada. In 2005 then member of parliament (MP) Stephen Harper, now the prime minister, proposed a tax break for families who enrolled their children in organized sport (Leitch, Bassett, & Weil, 2006). The strategy of the proposal, packaged with a childcare and general sales tax credit, was to provide economic relief, particularly to middle-class citizens, and to encourage children to be active in sports. The proposal went into effect in 2007. Children under the age of 16 were eligible in certain sports, and children under the age of 18 who had disabilities were also eligible. Although the motivation of the Canadian government was to promote physical activity and fitness through this legislation, it has been criticized because only certain activities qualify for the tax credit and the initial amount of the credit (C$500 per child) is not what families receive after their marginal tax rate is taken into account (Taber, 2008).

Finally, in 2007 the Mexican government dedicated $100,000 over two years to assist in the implementation of the Game On! Youth Sports program for children in Queretaro, Mexico. The goals of the program are to address issues (e.g., inadequate funding, facilities, equipment, transportation) associated with access to and participation in youth sport. The initiative has proven effective because the International Alliance for Youth Sports, who created Game On! Youth Sports has located an office in Queretaro, translated the program's materials into Spanish, and begun plans to duplicate the Mexican program across Latin America (International Alliance for Youth Sport, 2007a, 2007b).

MANAGEMENT CHALLENGES

Community sport presents a unique challenge concerning management because its structure and delivery system is varied and nonprescriptive (Cuskelly et al., 2006).

YOUTH OLYMPIC SPORT DEVELOPMENT IN CHINA

By Xiaoyan Xing • CHINA
Laurentian University, CANADA

Chinese youth recruited to the sport development system are often instilled with the goal of representing China at the Olympic Games. A systematic feeder system of sports training for programs, teams, and events at the county, city, provincial, and national levels is in place to facilitate the Olympic pathway. Schools with traditions in designated sports and sports schools are two sites where the Olympic dreams of many Chinese young people start.

Sports commonly included in sports schools and schools with traditions in designated sports are (1) sports with large numbers of medals such as swimming and track and field, (2) sports that Chinese athletes dominate in international competitions such as weightlifting and table tennis, and (3) team sports popular at the grassroots level such as basketball and soccer. Across different regions in China, the sports portfolio varies based on socioeconomic, geographic, and climatic factors. Sport programs in diving and sailing are more common in the economically advanced Guangdong province in the southeast of China. The cold climate in China's northern provinces such as Heilongjiang, Jilin, and Liaoning makes that region a powerhouse for winter sports such as speed skating and figure skating.

Schools with traditions are regular elementary, middle, and high schools that have teams specializing in selected sports. In elementary schools, students who show interest or talent are recruited to the schools' sports teams. In middle and high

Photo courtesy of Paul M. Pedersen.

Yao Ming, the product of a Chinese sports school, is one of the most popular athletes in China.

That is, some organizations are highly professional, using paid staff to govern, manage, and deliver the sport offering. Others are loosely organized, informal volunteer groups that form more of a cooperative coalition to provide sport for themselves and a small network of community members. In many cases, the community sport organization is governed by a volunteer board of directors that sets policy for the organization. The board's wishes are carried out by a paid executive director, who employs a small paid staff and a larger cadre of volunteers, especially volunteer coaches. Although volunteers have long been a mainstay of community sport delivery, pressure is increasing to make sport programs more professional because of legal issues and government policy. This circumstance can create tension in management styles between professional, standardized, and clearly defined procedures and volunteers' desire to have freedom over their volunteer experience (Cuskelly et al., 2006). Still, most experts agree that volunteers are a critical component of community sport, and managing volunteers is essential to organizational functioning and survival.

schools, students may be admitted to the sports team based on their athletic performance. These student–athletes attend regular classes and train after school. In 2004 there were 11,477 schools with traditions throughout China.

Sports schools usually have full-time coaching and support staffs. Students at county and city levels attend regular elementary and middle schools but spend substantial time in training. In sports schools at the provincial level, students typically spend half the day studying and half the day training. In 2008, 1,703 sports schools existed at various levels.

When Yao Ming was nine years old, he learned to play basketball at a sports school in Shanghai. His parents sent him to this school in hopes that his basketball skills would improve his chance to attend university. Yao stayed in the sport development system and became one of the most popular athletes in China while playing in the NBA in the United States.

In the 1970s parents in rural families sent their children to sports schools for the chance at jobs in the city. In the 1980s a major motive of joining the school sports teams was to gain a competitive advantage in applying to universities. In the 1990s some parents invested in their children's sports training in hopes that the children would become professional athletes and make big money. The commonality across these decades is the parents' desire for their children to have a bright future, either in or out of the sport system. A future trend is to achieve greater integration of the Chinese youth sport Olympic training systems into the education systems so that athletes who exit sport at an early age can continue their education uninterrupted and uncompromised.

INTERNATIONAL LEARNING ACTIVITY #1

Did the sports training schools described in this sidebar accomplish their goals relative to China's performance in the Olympic and Paralympic Games? What was China's medal count in the last five Summer and Winter Olympic and Paralympic Games? Do you believe that there is a connection between the sports schools and the medal counts? Why or why not?

INTERNATIONAL LEARNING ACTIVITY #2

Write a paper describing the youth sport development systems in a country other than China. Include information on the history, mission, and activities of the program. What was the medal count of that country in the last five Summer and Winter Olympic and Paralympic Games? Is there a connection between the medal count and the mission of the program? Why or why not?

Although a **professional human resource management (HRM) model** can sometimes be a hindrance in completely volunteer-run sport organizations, it can be helpful in providing guidelines, structure, and accountability for community sport organizations (Meijs & Karr, 2004). Establishing HRM procedures and guidelines for worker (paid or volunteer) recruitment, selection, training, and development can help organizations streamline program delivery and make better transitions as people come and go through the organization. The basic HRM functions and their relationship to volunteer management are described next.

professional human resource management (HRM) model—A model that describes scientific methods for staffing, training, developing, and managing human resources. Although well suited for paid employees, it does not often fit for volunteers.

Personnel management begins with planning, a task that involves examining the organization's strategies, goals, and resources. As the organization's managers plan their programs and services, they can then begin to think through their personnel needs to deliver the programs. In planning for volunteers, organizational managers may ask the following questions: Does the organization have the resources to provide paid personnel, or will it rely on volunteers? What work will be performed by volunteers, and what activities will receive compensation? How many volunteers will be necessary to perform essential functions? From where will volunteers be recruited? How many hours will volunteers need to commit? What skills or training will volunteers need? How can we ensure participant safety (e.g., child protection laws) and privacy protection (e.g., participants' personal information that can be accessed by volunteers)?

After these questions are answered, the organization can develop a plan for recruiting and selecting volunteers and paid personnel. Recruitment can involve informal word-of-mouth contacts, advertisements, or broader search mechanisms. In local communities, volunteers are often the members themselves or parents of members. For example, a player on an adult soccer club team may volunteer to organize the league's schedule and book fields through the local community center. Selection of volunteers involves completing background checks (to ensure child safety) and matching volunteer skills and desires with organizational needs.

Next, volunteers often need to undergo training and development to understand the organization's goals, policies, and procedures and to help them be competent and successful in their volunteer duties. Much training is focused on volunteer coaches, because they are often at the forefront of sport delivery and participant experience in sport largely depends on the quality of coaching (Wiersma & Sherman, 2005). If children, in particular, do not enjoy their sport experience, they are unlikely to continue to participate. Coach training should include ethical standards, proper child safety (if coaching children), education in the particular sport coached in terms of techniques and tactics, and education in motivation and behavior management (Cuskelly et al., 2006).

Although quality HRM is essential to community sport delivery and volunteers in particular need guidelines and training to ensure a quality experience for themselves and the participants, community sport managers must also ensure that volunteers enjoy the experience, see it as valuable and worthwhile, and do not become overburdened with procedure at the expense of experience.

ADULT COMMUNITY SPORT OFFERINGS

Community sport opportunities in North America are often provided through three basic structures: classes, leagues, and tournaments. Classes are defined as instructional sessions provided to enhance the skill or fitness level of the participants. For example, a person may want to participate in golf classes (individual or group) to enhance her or his golf skills for either recreational or competitive play.

Leagues are organized forms of ongoing sport competition in a given sport. They may be as simple as a few teams at a community recreation center that play each other on a rotating basis, or as complex as a professional sport league (e.g., the Pacific Baseball League in Mexico, National Football League in the United States, Canadian Hockey League). Leagues define the playing season, rules, and participant eligibility, and usually provide a system to determine a champion. Although usually thought of in terms of team sports (e.g., soccer, basketball, hockey), leagues can also be formed for primarily individual sports (e.g., golf, tennis, archery).

Tournaments are organized forms of sport that usually extend over several days or weeks, starting with a large pool of participants and narrowing down to an eventual champion. Again, these can be as simple as a local three-on-three basketball charity fund-raiser to as complex as the annual US Tennis Open Championships. For example, the United States Tennis Association (USTA) sponsors tournaments around the country nearly every weekend. The tournaments are managed and sponsored by local tennis clubs, or facilities, but are conducted under USTA rules and regulations.

YOUTH SPORT OFFERINGS

Community youth sport offerings and the rate at which children take advantage of those offerings vary by demographic factors (e.g., socioeconomic status, race and ethnicity), cognitive and behavioral factors (e.g., attitudes, family influences, beliefs, perceptions, social influences, sedentary behaviors), and community factors (e.g., general safety, built environment, availability of venues for sport, school-based sport) (Government Accountability Office, 2006). These factors are important to consider when planning, implementing, and managing youth sport. Organized activities affiliated with youth sport are typically structured as classes, as instructional leagues, as competitive leagues, and through after-school programs.

Many youth activities are offered in organizations around the world, often in venues such as this YWCA located in Seoul, South Korea.

Photo courtesy of Paul M. Pedersen.

Classes

Youth sport classes can range from beginning sport instruction at facilities such as community recreation centers or through organizations such as the YMCA or YWCA. From a young age, even infancy in the case of swimming lessons, children can enroll to learn skills, rules, and strategies with an emphasis on enjoyment. The classes can be sport specific or composed of a variety of sports, emphasizing development. For instance, the West Suburban YMCA in the Boston suburb of Newton, Massachusetts, offers a program called Super Sports for children ages four through nine. In the seven-week program, children play a different sport each week. Typically, the offerings include kickball, soccer, Wiffle ball, basketball, floor hockey, flag football, and an occasional game of dodgeball or capture the flag to facilitate the children's learning of sports while maintaining a fun environment.

Instructional Leagues

The goal of instructional leagues is to provide information and knowledge to children as they begin to play sports or are introduced to new sports. Youth sport programs build basic motor skills (e.g., eye–hand coordination, footwork, balance) and provide children positive instruction in the basic skills, rules, and strategies associated with a specific sport. Children are also provided with the opportunity to scrimmage or play the sport to put into practice what they have learned. At the younger levels, most leagues have at least an instructional component and others are strictly instructional with no scores or standings being kept.

In Burbank, California, the city recreation department provides to children instructional leagues for several sports (e.g., soccer, baseball, softball, volleyball, flag football). The philosophy of both the offerings and the instruction is based in several national models. The city of Burbank is a member of the National Alliance for Youth Sports (NAYS), which adheres to the provision of positive and safe sports and activities for children. The city does this through its application of the NAYS National Standards for Youth Sports to its coaches, officials, administrators, and young athletes. In addition, the parents of participants complete the Parents Association for Youth Sports (PAYS) orientation program to assist them in understanding how sport plays a role in the development of their children. Specifically, Burbank's softball league offers noncompetitive T-ball divisions for grades K through 2 and then transitions into competitive leagues for grades 3 through 8. The instructional league provides motor skill and fundamental development and concludes the season with its annual jamboree during which children participate in a parade and skill events to highlight what they have learned during their season.

Competitive Leagues

Continuing with the city of Burbank, after children enter third grade they transition into competitive spring and fall leagues guided by American Softball Association (ASA) standards and rules. Children can continue in the competitive leagues until they graduate from high school and enter adult leagues. These ASA national standards and rules provide the structure for what is still a positive environment with quality instruction that adds the competitive aspect of standings and the opportunity to enter the ASA district **sport tournament** and progress to a national championship. The ASA has more than 90 national championships, starting with age 10 and under fast pitch. Annually, more than 40,000 players from children to adults participate in ASA national championships.

sport tournament—A competition involving a relatively large number of competitors. It can be offered over a set period at a single venue or can be a set of matches or competitions that culminate in a single champion.

Similar to the ASA model, other competitive sports progress from the local level to national championship events. The United States Volleyball Association (USAV) sponsors junior leagues beginning at 10 years of age and under. At the younger levels more emphasis is given to instruction and development, and at the older levels the emphasis shifts to competition. Teams play at local and regional tournaments, and based on finishes at those events they can qualify for national tournaments and even the Junior Olympic Championships. USAV also sponsors outdoor leagues (e.g., Junior Beach Programs) and a Junior Beach Tour. Other examples of youth club-sport opportunities include the United States Field Hockey Futures, the Amateur Athletic Union (e.g., track and field, basketball, gymnastics), and United States Swimming.

After-School Programs

Historically, after-school programs have been viewed as beneficial to children for the personal enjoyment that they experience, the safety and supervision provided, the academic enrichment and improvement in social skills that may occur, and the emphasis on physical health and fitness (Afterschool Alliance, 2008). The hours immediately after school ends are considered a crucial time in the development of children (Bruening, Dover, & Clark, 2009; Noam, 2002). But according to the *America After 3pm* report (Afterschool Alliance, 2008), only 11% of children in the United States in grades K through 12 are in after-school programs of any kind. Typically, younger children are more likely to be enrolled in after-school programs than older ones are; as many as 66% of participants are from grades K through 5. The number drops to 15% for grades 5 through 8. Furthermore, as many as 11% of children in grades K through 5 are identified as taking care of themselves after school with no adult presence. In particular, African American and Hispanic youth spend more time unsupervised than other children do, so the demand for after-school programs is much higher in those families.

In the United States, public schools provide the largest number of general after-school programs. YMCAs and Boys and Girls Clubs are within the top five of providers of after-school programs even when sports are not specified in the rankings. For example, the YMCA of Greater Toronto offers after-school programs for children in grades K through 8 at more than 125 facilities across the metro area, making it the largest provider of after-school programs and care for children in Canada. Through these programs, children receive affordable after-school care centered on healthy character development and team building with the benefits of the facilities and trained staff of the YMCA.

Other private and nonprofit organizations also offer after-school sports programming, and like the YMCA, this programming typically uses sport as a means to learning larger life lessons. Such programming subscribes to the **sport-based youth development model.** For example, The Center for the Study of Sport in Society at Northeastern University in Boston provides the Kevin W. Fitzgerald Urban Youth Sports (FitzUYS) program focusing on physical activity and programming. The program reports that it

sport-based youth development model—Programs that use sports in general, or a particular sport, to facilitate learning and life skill development.

has served more than 14,000 children and has created more than 1,600 new sport and recreation opportunities in the last two years alone. The unique approach of FitzUYS is to build relationships between community health centers and families who are eligible to use their facilities. Health professionals and researchers develop programming that emphasizes physical activity as a means to improve the health of the children in the communities. Sport programming paired with life skills training and healthy development initiatives are the means to achieve FitzUYS's goal of widespread change not just in the Boston area but in urban communities regionally, nationally, and internationally.

WEB

Go to the OSG and complete the Web search activity, which asks you to research five organizations that use a youth development model to provide sport opportunities for youth.

CRITICAL THINKING IN COMMUNITY SPORT

In a 12-and-under girls travel soccer game, the Cheetahs and the Sharks meet to determine which one will advance to the national tournament. The teams faced each other earlier in the season, and the game was close and competitive. In particular, the midfielders of the two teams played a rough game against each other. As this game is nearing the end of the first half, the Cheetahs' midfielder is called for a tackling foul against the Sharks' midfielder. At the beginning of the second half, the Sharks' midfielder makes a remark to her opponent in response to the foul call. The tension continues between the two players throughout the remainder of the game until, as the horn sounds to end the game with a 2-1 victory for the Cheetahs, the Sharks' midfielder runs at the Cheetahs' midfielder and shoves her forcibly from behind so that she falls to the ground. The Sharks' player runs off the field to join the rest of her team on the sidelines. The Cheetahs' player is visibly injured.

PORTFOLIO

Complete the critical thinking portfolio activity in the OSG, consulting as needed the "Eight Critical Thinking Questions" section in chapter 1.

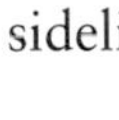

ETHICS IN COMMUNITY SPORT

One of the persistent questions in community sport involves asking whether sport should be equally accessible to all people. Consider the case of Sondra, a single mother of four children who lives in a suburban area in the midwestern United States. Sondra would like her two older children to play baseball in the youth league offered at her local public recreation center. The fee for the league is US$75 per child with a US$25 discount for multiple children. Thus, Sondra and her family would have to pay US$125 for the two children to play in the league. Although this fee may not be substantial for some, it is burdensome for Sondra in her financial situation. Sondra went to see the director of the recreation center. She was told that because of recent budget cuts no financial assistance would be available for her children to participate. She was also told that sport participation is a privilege, not a right, and that the recreation center was therefore under no obligation to provide such financial support. Sondra was frustrated. She thought that sport participation would be beneficial for her children but also believed that she could not afford the US$125 participation fee.

PORTFOLIO

Complete the ethical issues portfolio activity in the OSG, consulting as needed the "Guidelines for Making Ethical Decisions" section in chapter 1.

Summary

Youth and community sport in North America is offered in a variety of settings including schools, private sport clubs, and public recreation centers. The different types of sport structures create various management challenges including access, management of volunteers, financial viability, and conflicts over the mission and goals of the organization.

Although sport participation continues to grow in both Canada and the United States, participation opportunities vary widely based on geography and gender; rural areas and girls still lag behind in access to sport participation. Individuals, families, and communities benefit from sport and physical activity participation. These benefits include improved physical and psychological health, increased family time together, and increased social capital. Because sport can be beneficial, sport managers should identify ways to attract and retain participants in the local community.

Youth and community sport opportunities also take a variety of forms ranging from instructional classes to after-school programs to competitive tournaments and leagues. Understanding the structure and goals of a participation opportunity helps managers determine the organizational needs and strategies for meeting those needs among the various constituents. Sport managers in this sector must continually monitor participant needs and wants so that they can provide the kinds of sports and formats that serve their community best.

Review Questions

1. How would you define youth and community sport?
2. What are the various sectors of youth and community sport?
3. What are the goals and outcomes associated with each youth and community sport sector?
4. What are some key providers to the youth sector? To the community sector?
5. How is access to youth and community sport a complex issue in different communities?
6. What challenges exist in managing youth and community sport? How would you meet those challenges?
7. What career opportunities within youth sport can you identify?
8. Which career opportunities in community sport are most attractive to you and why?

QUIZ TIME

Did you grasp all the key points in this chapter? Go to the OSG for a short quiz to test your understanding of the material.

References

Afterschool Alliance. (2008). *America after 3pm: A household survey on afterschool in America key findings*. Retrieved on February 1, 2010, from www.afterschoolalliance.org/documents/AA%203%20pm_Key_Findings.pdf

Badcock, B. (2002). *Making sense of cities: A geographical survey*. London: Arnold.

Bringle, R., & Hatcher, J. (1995). A service learning curriculum for faculty. *Michigan Journal of Community Service Learning*, 2, 112–122.

Brown, G. (2009, January 9). NCAA and NBA look to change youth basketball culture. *NCAA News*. Retrieved February 1, 2010, from www.ncaa.org/wps/ncaa?ContentID=43661

Bruening, J.E., Dover, K.M., & Clark, B.S. (2009). Preadolescent female development through sport and physical activity: A case study of an urban after-school program. *Research Quarterly in Exercise and Sport*, *80*, 1–18.

Canadian Centre for Ethics in Sport. (2002). *Public opinion survey on youth and sport final report*. Ottawa, Ontario, Canada: Decima Research.

Chalip, L. (2006). Toward a distinctive sport management discipline. *Journal of Sport Management*, *20*, 1–21.

Chudacoff, H. (2007). *Children at play: An American history*. New York: New York University Press.

Coakley, J. (2009). *Sport in society: Issues and controversies* (10th ed.). New York: McGraw Hill.

Cuskelly, G., Hoye, R., & Auld, C. (2006). *Working with volunteers in sport: Theory and practice*. London: Routledge.

Dixon, M. (2009). From their perspective: A qualitative examination of physical activity and sport for working mothers. *Sport Management Review*, *12*, 34–48.

Engh, F. (1999). *Why Johnny hates sports: Why organized youth sports are failing our children and what we can do about it*. Garden City Park, NY: Avery.

Government Accountability Office. (2006). *Childhood obesity: Factors affecting physical activity*. GAO-07-260R. Washington, DC: Author.

Halpern, R. (2002). A different kind of child development institution: The history of after-school programs for low-income children. *Teachers College Record*, *104*, 78–211.

Hartmann, D. (2008). *High school sports participation and educational attainment: Recognizing, assessing, and utilizing the relationship*. Retrieved February 1, 2010, from www.la84foundation.org/3ce/HighSchoolSportsParticipation.pdf

Hedstrom, R., & Gould, D. (2004). *Research in youth sports: Critical issues*. East Lansing, MI: Institute for the Study of Youth Sports.

Henderson, K.A., & Hickerson, B. (2007). Women and leisure: Premises and performances uncovered in an integrative review. *Journal of Leisure Research*, *39*, 591–610.

Hopkins, C.H. (1951). *History of the YMCA in North America*. New York: Association Press.

International Alliance for Youth Sport. (2007a). *IAYS Latin American regional representative visits national headquarters*. Retrieved February 1, 2010, from www.iays.org/fullstory.cfm?articleid=10043

International Alliance for Youth Sport. (2007b). *Mexican municipal government allocates $100,000 for Game On!* Retrieved on February 1, 2010, from www.iays.org/fullstory.cfm?articleid=10050

Koester, M. (2000). Youth sports: A pediatrician's perspective on coaching and injury prevention. *Journal of Athletic Training, 35*, 466–470.

Koltyn, K., & Schultes, S. (1997). Psychological effects of an aerobic exercise session and a rest session following pregnancy. *Journal of Sports Medicine and Physical Fitness, 37*, 287–291.

Larson, R., Walker, K., & Pearce, N. (2005). A comparison of youth-driven and adult-driven youth programs: Balancing inputs from youth and adults. *Journal of Community Psychology, 33*, 57–74.

Leitch, K., Bassett, D., & Weil, M. (2006). *Report of the expert panel on the children's fitness tax credit.* Ottawa, Ontario, Canada: Canadian Department of Finance.

Le Menestrel, S., & Perkins, D. (2007). An overview of how sports, out-of-school time, and youth well-being can and do intersect. *New Directions for Youth Development, 115*, 13–25.

Marten, J. (2008). A new view of the child: Children and youth in urban America, 1900–1920. *Romanian Journal of Population Studies, 1*, 67–81.

Meijs, L., & Karr, L. (2004). Managing volunteers in different settings: Membership and programme management. In R. Stebbins & M. Grahem (Eds.), *Volunteering as leisure/leisure as volunteering* (pp. 177–193). Wallingford, Oxfordshire, UK: CABI.

Morrow, D., & Wamsley, K. (2005). *Sport in Canada: A history.* Toronto, Ontario, Canada: Oxford University Press.

Murphy, K.P. (2005). Hallelujah lads and lasses: Remaking the Salvation Army in America, 1880–1930; Making men, making class: The YMCA and workingmen 1877–1930. *Labor, 2*, 112–114.

Noam, G. (2002). Youth development and after-school time. *New directions for youth development, 94*, 1–2.

Putnam, R. (2000). *Bowling alone: The collapse and revival of American community.* New York: Simon & Schuster.

Rader, B.G. (2009). *American sports: From the age of folk games to the age of televised sports* (6th ed.). Upper Saddle River, NJ: Prentice Hall.

Sabo, D., & Veliz, P. (2008). *Go out and play: Youth sports in America.* East Meadow, NY: Women's Sports Foundation.

Sporting Goods Manufacturers Association. (2008). *Sports participation in America.* Washington, DC: Author.

Stanford University Prevention Research Center. (2007). *Building "generation play": Addressing the crisis of inactivity among America's children.* Palo Alto, CA: Author.

Stewart, B., Nicholson, M., Smith, A., & Westerbeek, H. (2004). *Australian sport: Better by design? The evolution of Australian sport policy.* London: Routledge.

Taber, J. (2008, September 29). Harper offers tax credit for children's arts programs. *The National*, p. A13.

US Department of Health and Human Services. (1996). *Physical activity and health: A report of the surgeon general.* Atlanta, GA: US Department of Health and Human Services, Centers for Disease Control and Prevention, National Center for Chronic Disease Prevention and Health Promotion.

Wiersma, L., & Sherman, C. (2005). Volunteer youth sport coaches' perspectives of coaching education/certification and parental codes of conduct. *Research Quarterly for Exercise and Sport, 76*, 324–338.

HISTORICAL MOMENTS

1905	Honus Wagner signed first baseball bat endorsement contract with Hillerich & Bradsby, Co.
1921	Sports agents arrived—Christy Walsh began ghostwriting columns for Babe Ruth
1960	Mark H. McCormack started International Management Group (IMG)
1972	Host Communications founded
1985	Sponsorship measurement agency Joyce Julius and Associates formed
1995	First Summer X-Games held (first called Extreme Games)
1998	Bill Duffy founded BDA Sports Management, became Yao Ming's NBA agent in 2002
1999	SFX Sports Group and Octagon sports agencies founded
2002	First Battle at Bighorn: Sergio Garcia defeated Tiger Woods
2004	Ted Fortsmann acquired IMG after founder Mark McCormack's death in 2003
2005	Women's Tennis Association (WTA) signed US$88 million six-year title sponsorship deal with Sony Ericsson, largest sponsorship deal in history of women's sport
2007	IMG College formed
2009	Women's National Basketball Association (WNBA) Phoenix Mercury signed US$1 million team jersey sponsorship deal
2009	NBA team owners reversed ban on courtside advertising by spirits brands
2009	Ohio State University signed US$110 million 10-year marketing and media rights deal with IMG College

Photo courtesy of Paul M. Pedersen.

10

SPORT MANAGEMENT AND MARKETING AGENCIES

William A. Sutton ■ Nicole Fowler ■ Mark A. McDonald

LEARNING OBJECTIVES

1. Explain the role, scope, and influence of sport management and marketing agencies as they relate to the business of sport.
2. Differentiate between the types of agencies to determine which are most appropriate for particular tasks and assignments.
3. Describe the evolution and growth of sport management and marketing agencies.
4. Define the functions performed by sport management and marketing agencies.
5. Examine ethical issues associated with the work of agencies in the sport industry.
6. Use critical thinking skills to evaluate issues facing sport management and marketing agencies.
7. Appraise career opportunities associated with sport management and marketing agencies.
8. Detail the key challenges facing agencies in the sport industry in the second decade of the 21st century.

GET A JOB!

✓ Continue on your journey in sport management by going to the Online Study Guide (OSG) at www.HumanKinetics.com/ContemporarySportManagement. Check out the job opportunities and consider the skills and experiences that can help you succeed in sport management.

Key Terms

downsizing
entitlement
gatekeepers
grassroots programs
inventory
procurement
solicitation
turnkey
value added
venue

A sport management and marketing agency is a business that acts on behalf of a sport property. This sport property can be a person, a corporation, an event, a team, a place, or even a concept. The actions undertaken on behalf of the property may include one or more of the following: representation, negotiation, sales, licensing, marketing, or management. The agency represents or controls the rights to affiliate or associate with the sport property. Given the scope of potential activities that encompass the arts, festivals, sport events, resorts, and music, a more appropriate term to describe these agencies is *sport and lifestyle management and marketing agencies*.

The first sport management and marketing agencies were formed primarily to represent athletes in contract negotiations and to seek endorsements and other revenue streams for these athletes. Honus Wagner of the Pittsburgh Pirates was the first professional athlete compensated for endorsing a product—Louisville Slugger baseball bats. The International Management Group (IMG), established in 1960 by the late Mark H. McCormack in Cleveland, Ohio, was the first agency dedicated to representing professional athletes. In the company's own words, "IMG leads the sports marketing industry it pioneered over 40 years ago" (IMG, 2010, ¶ 1). As time has passed and the marketplace and opportunities have changed, sport marketing and management agencies have become more diverse in scope and focus. Today, sport management and marketing agencies are involved not only in contract negotiations but also in numerous other functions.

The purpose of this chapter is to provide an overview of sport management and marketing agencies and to introduce career opportunities within this rapidly growing segment of the sport industry. We will shed light on these unique and multifaceted companies by classifying the many agencies into four categories: full service, general, specialty, and in-house. Examples of each type of agency will help delineate the similarities and differences. After providing information about career opportunities and challenges, the chapter will conclude with some examples of ethical and critical thinking applications in sport management and sport marketing agencies.

FUNCTIONS OF SPORT MANAGEMENT AND MARKETING AGENCIES

Sport management and marketing agencies perform a vast scope of functions. As you read the following list, you can appreciate the degree of specialization necessary to discharge each duty. Although an agency might perform several or perhaps only one function, some agencies, such as IMG and Octagon, perform all of them.

- Client management and representation
- Client marketing and product endorsement and placement
- Event creation and development
- Event management and marketing
- Property representation and licensing
- Television development and production
- Negotiation of media contracts
- Sponsorship solicitation and consulting
- Hospitality management services
- Grassroots and participatory programs
- Research and evaluation
- Strategic and financial planning and management

- *Client management and representation.* Client management and representation involves representing a client in contract negotiations and making marketing decisions to manage the client's income potential and earnings. The contract negotiations could be between player and team, licensee and licensor, or product and endorser. The management function involves the agency in a strategic planning process for its client that may involve any of the following: financial planning, investment and management, marketing, personal appearances, and other forms of revenue production and management.
- *Client marketing and product endorsement and placement.* Similar to the management function, client marketing involves the agency in the promotion and total marketing of the client. For a professional athlete, this may involve securing endorsement opportunities, product endorsements (e.g., Philadelphia Eagles quarterback Donovan McNabb's deal with Campbell's Chunky Soup), personal appearances, product placements, book contracts, movie and television roles, interviews and feature stories, video games, and so on. IMG, for example, secures Tiger Woods' endorsements for Nike, EA Sports, and more (although some endorsements have been lost after the revelations of Woods' marital infidelity).
- *Event creation and development.* The growth of sport television in the 1970s, the proliferation of sport networks over the past 20 years, and the development of new satellite technology such as DirecTV have led to fiscally rewarding opportunities to create new sports and events. Examples of emergent ways in which sport managers have capitalized on these opportunities include sport leagues (e.g., AF2, Major League Lacrosse), an increase in the number of college football bowl games, and a wider array of collegiate basketball doubleheaders. Some television entities such as ESPN, ESPNU, Fox Regional Sports Networks, and Turner Broadcasting have created events to fill their **inventory.** For example, ESPN created the Great Outdoor Games and the X Games for this purpose.

inventory—The assets that a sport property has to sell, including not only its quantity but also its characteristics and traits.

Sport Marketing as Part of a Communication Strategy

It's a Tuesday morning at First National Bank in River City, USA. At a staff meeting, Ms. Smith, the regional president, states that First National is continuing to lose customers to Second City Federal—a bank that seems to appeal to younger and more upscale clients. Ms. Smith believes that First National's attempts to communicate with its market through traditional outlets such as advertising and direct mail have become too routine and consequently that customers are not receiving the message. "It is for that reason," says Ms. Smith, "that I have asked Sport Properties Ltd., an international sport marketing agency, to assist us in developing a new communication strategy through sports and special events to help us retain our current customer base and, we hope, attract new customers."

The room begins to buzz with questions: What is a sport marketing agency? What type of sport or special event is best associated with a bank? What services should we promote through the event? What exactly will the agency do?

At the same time, in the regional offices of Sport Properties Ltd., Mr. Brown, regional vice president, is meeting with his staff members to discuss their upcoming presentation to First National Bank. "We have an excellent opportunity to use some of our existing properties, such as snowboarding, kayaking, and an array of action sports, to create grassroots programs that appeal to younger, more upscale individuals in each of First National Bank's primary markets." At that point, Ms. Perez, senior project director, asks about developing a tie-in with participants from each grassroots venue competing in a championship or finals at the headquarters of First National in River City. "Excellent concept, Ms. Perez!," says Mr. Brown. "Perhaps we should also consider finding other sponsors who might want to become part of this opportunity with First National. Let's begin preparing our agenda."

- ***Event management and marketing.*** Given the high cost of personnel (i.e., salaries and benefits), the need for specific expertise, the seasonality of some events, and the geographic scope of the activities, many sport organizations now hire outside agencies to manage, activate, and market their events. Event management and marketing agencies are involved in activities such as golf and tennis tournaments, festivals, bowl games, and other sport and lifestyle special events. Event management may involve any of the following areas: tournament operations, hospitality and entertainment, sponsorship and ticket sales, licensing and merchandising, television production, public relations, and promotion.

- ***Property representation and licensing.*** Sport management and marketing agencies often represent sport properties in promotional licensing and sponsor solicitation and **procurement.** A sport property can be defined as any sport or lifestyle entity that has name or event recognition, desirability, and perceived value, and that chooses to offer itself for some type of affiliation. Examples of sport and lifestyle properties include the Rose Bowl, the Rock and Roll Hall of Fame, the San Antonio Spurs, Fenway Park, the Rolling Stones, the US Tennis Open, Ohio State University, NBC's Dew Action Tour, and the Taste of Cincinnati. The property can be a facility, event, team, athletics program, band or concert tour, and so on. Property representation can result in the sales of rights fees, promotional licensing opportunities, sponsorship sales, signage and advertising agreements, and endorsements. Go to the section "Ethics in Agency Activities" for more information regarding revenue sources in the sport industry.

procurement—Successful solicitation of financial or other resources on behalf of the sport property.

- ***Television development and production.*** The growth and proliferation of cable, satellite, and pay-per-view have created many opportunities and outlets for developing and producing programming for television. Host Communications (which was acquired by IMG in 2007) and Raycom Sports are agencies that have been involved in packaging rights fees for college football and basketball and the subsequent sales of these rights to networks such as CBS, NBC, ABC, ESPN, and TBS. The revenue potential of such television programming and the interest of the networks and their sponsors have had an effect on the traditional conference structure in collegiate sport, resulting in the emergence of 12-team conferences such as the Big Ten Conference, the Atlantic Coast Conference (ACC), and the Southeastern Conference (SEC). For these new conferences, the result has been a lucrative market for a televised conference championship matching the winners of the two 6-team divisions. In 2004 the Big East Conference lost three football powerhouses—Boston College, the University of Miami (FL), and Virginia Tech to the ACC—but added five schools well known for prowess in men's basketball—Louisville, Cincinnati, DePaul, Marquette, and South Florida. This conference reconfiguration led to an amended broadcasting contract with ESPN (Bernstein, 2005). The SEC made history in August 2008 by inking 15-year contracts with network giant CBS and cable powerhouse ESPN. CBS will pay the conference an average of US$55 million annually for most football and basketball rights, and ESPN will shell out about US$2.25 billion total through 2023 to televise sporting events that were not included in the deal with CBS. The agreements will end the SEC's long affiliation with Raycom Sports but will establish the SEC as the most widely distributed conference in the United States and effectively end talks to launch a separate SEC network. The deals could end up paying each SEC school around $15 million per year (Smith & Ourand, 2008). Traditional sport management and marketing agencies have recognized the opportunities that television presents and have aggressively moved to capitalize on them. IMG has long had its own television production division, Trans World International (TWI), so that it could maximize the revenue derived from the properties that it represents. Beginning more than 25 years ago with a made-for-TV competition among athletes from various sports, *The Superstars*, IMG continues to add similar events such as the TELUS World Skins Game.

▪ ***Sponsorship solicitation and consulting.*** The most common functions of sport management and marketing agencies, regardless of the size or scope of the agency, are consulting about solicitation and securing corporate sponsorships. Corporations were expected to increase sponsorship spending by less than 2% in 2009, the smallest increase since 2002. Sponsorships grew almost 15% in 2008 up to US$11.4 billion. Still, according to the *IEG Sponsorship Report* (as cited in Toms, 2009), sport will comprise 68%, or US$11.6 billion, of the US$17 billion spent on North American sponsorships. Although many properties (e.g., teams, sport events, festivals) handle these functions in-house, most seek outside assistance in determining value and identifying and obtaining appropriate sponsors. Similarly, corporations and other potential sponsors often employ a sport management and marketing agency to identify properties that may assist them in achieving their corporate goals and objectives. Vivid Marketing in Atlanta describes itself as a "strategic 'mobile' experiential marketing shop delivering turnkey solutions to a roster of blue chip clients 365 days a year" (*Vivid Marketing*, n.d., ¶1). As detailed on its Web site (*Vivid Marketing*, n.d.), the agency works to connect the customer to the brand, usually mobilizing the "brand experience," allowing potential consumers to see, touch, taste, hear, and smell the products. Each experience is customized to the particular brand and company, making the consumer's experience unique and setting the brand apart from its competitors. The agency develops and implements the entire experiential package, executing a memorable on-site interaction to increase product trial through innovative sampling. Vivid Marketing's goal is to create deep brand relationships, allowing the client to see their return on investment (ROI) in action and leave a lasting impression on the consumer.

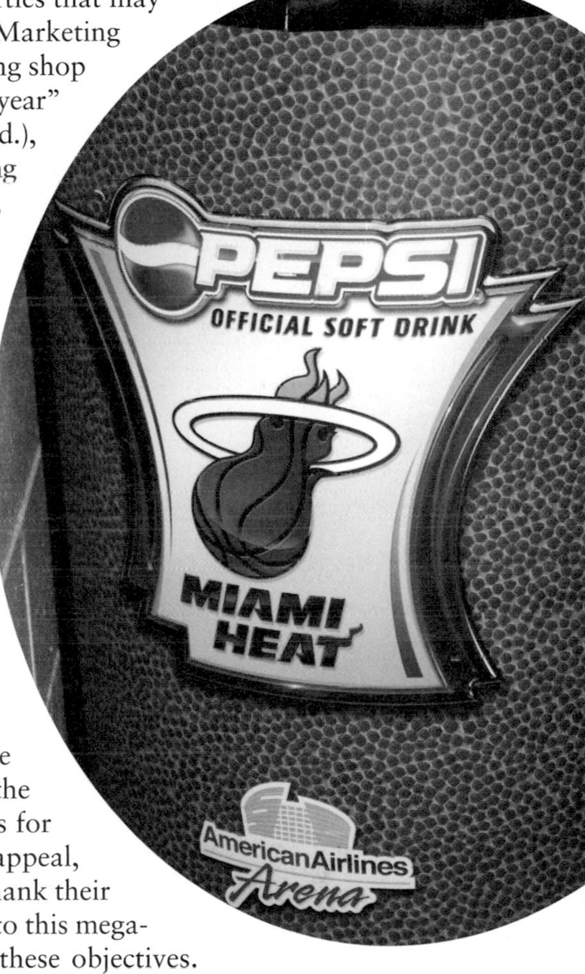

Pepsi is a major corporate sponsor, and the official soft drink provider, of the NBA's Miami Heat and the team's home, AmericanAirlines Arena. Sponsorship acquisition, solicitation, and consultation are major activities for sport management and marketing agencies.
Photo courtesy of Paul M. Pedersen.

▪ ***Hospitality management services.*** A frequently overlooked function of a sport management and marketing agency is that of creating, arranging, and managing hospitality management services. Hospitality management services include, but are not limited to, transportation and other logistical issues; menu and food service planning and management; corporate sponsor entertainment; special auxiliary event creation and management; housing; and awards, gifts, and recognition programs. As with most events and activities, the type and scope of these services vary greatly according to the event. In the United States, the Super Bowl is one of the most coveted destinations for hospitality packages in all of sport because of geographic location, appeal, and ticket demand. Corporations reward their best sales personnel, thank their highest volume customers, and court new clients through invitations to this mega-event. The Super Bowl offers a prestigious opportunity to achieve these objectives. Agencies such as Party Planners West (PPW) arrange transportation; accommodations; meals; auxiliary events such as cruises, golf tournaments, and postevent parties; gifts; and spouse programs (Conrad, 1995). PPW produces the NFL Experience, the fan interactive event in association with the Super Bowl that attracts more than 100,000 attendees annually (Colon, 2009).

▪ ***Grassroots and participatory programs.*** Grassroots programs are designed to build a following for a product, service, or organization. Although they may not pay immediate benefits, they contribute to long-term growth by creating interest among potential consumers. Most **grassroots programs** are aimed at children and adolescents who may or may not be consumers of the product, service, or organization in question but who possess the qualities, abilities, and potential to become consumers in the future. Grassroots programs are often designed to involve participants in activities and

grassroots programs—Programs targeted to people at the primary level of involvement, usually participants rather than spectators.

events that are held at local sites, which could be thousands of miles or kilometers from the headquarters of the sponsoring organization. These local events and activities are often targeted to certain demographic groups and ethnic markets. For example, Major League Baseball's RBI Program targets inner-city youth, and the National Basketball Association's Basketball Without Borders is a global program that targets youth.

- ***Research and evaluation.*** Evaluation and documentation are critical factors in determining the success of the various types of sport management and marketing programs discussed throughout this chapter. Several concepts (e.g., **downsizing, value added**) stress a high degree of relevance and accountability, for both the sport organization and the agency or program delivering the services. One such example is the concept of reengineering, whereby a sport organization changes its structure or philosophy to capitalize on existing opportunities. Another concept, postevent impact analysis, involves research conducted (usually by a third party but commissioned by a sponsor or the event itself) after the event ends to determine the effect that the event had on the sponsor's product (i.e., image, awareness, or sales) or on the community in general (e.g., economic growth through spending associated with the event). Research, through mail surveys, on-site surveys, personal interviews, pre- and postevent impact analyses, focus groups, and other methods, is essential to assist the decision maker in justifying a program's cost, value, and relevance to the client. Most corporations involved in sponsorship or licensing activities perform some type of assessment, either through an in-house department or by contracting with an agency that offers research and evaluation services. The research agency selected is typically not involved in the sponsorship and licensing sales process to ensure that it does not have a stake in the findings. Thus, the research agency selected should be a specialist in evaluating sponsorship and licensing programs or perhaps in sport consumer behavior. Joyce Julius and Associates, Performance Research, and Navigate are examples of research or consulting companies that specialize in such services. The type of research to use and the best agency to employ will vary with the scope and magnitude of the event, whether the event is televised, the types of sponsorship and licensing activities that take place at the event, the budget, and the commitment of the organization to undertake a sound research approach (see the sidebar "*Sponsors Report* and the NTIV Analysis").

downsizing—Becoming a smaller organization by reducing personnel or departments, often because of a change in the mission or direction of the organization.

value added—The perception, by the consumer, of added or augmented product or service benefits.

- ***Strategic and financial planning and management.*** This highly specialized service involves accountants, financial planners and advisors, and investment specialists and portfolio managers. Few sport management and marketing agencies specialize in financial planning and management. IMG offers this service as part of its client management

Sponsors Report and the NTIV Analysis

The services provided by Joyce Julius and Associates are among the most used and reputable in the industry (Liberman, 2005). Through their primary products—*Sponsors Report* and the National Television Impression Value (NTIV) Analysis—Joyce Julius and Associates arguably set an industry standard. *Sponsors Report* is a publication that focuses on the value of the exposure received directly from national television broadcasts. Value is determined by calculating clear, in-focus exposure time during the broadcast. Exposure time is the amount of time given to logos, signage, displays, and audio mentions during the broadcast. Clear, in-focus exposures are the exposures that television viewers can readily see. These exposures are measured and converted to advertising costs per 30 seconds for the actual advertising costs on that specific broadcast. The NTIV Analysis determines the gross impressions from varied exposure sources and assigns a value to those impressions using a single factor that reflects the comparative cost of national television media purchases (Schreiber, 1994).

services. Several of IMG's clients have benefited well enough from the investing and planning services that they have started their own companies or have entered limited partnerships with IMG to create new ventures. The success of both Arnold Palmer and Jack Nicklaus in creating their own companies and ventures is testament to the performance of IMG in discharging its fiscal planning duties. But except for IMG and a few others, sport management and marketing agencies usually contract financial and investment services out to reputable financial planners and accountants whose primary function is related not to sport but to fiscal management and planning.

WEB

Go to the OSG and complete the Web search activity, which has you research current or upcoming internship or part-time employment opportunities with the top sport management and marketing agencies.

TYPES OF SPORT MANAGEMENT AND MARKETING AGENCIES

More than 1,000 agencies identify themselves as sport management and marketing agencies (Gottlieb, 2009). This figure does not include city or state sport commissions, corporations such as Anheuser-Busch and MasterCard, or divisions of leagues such as NBA Properties, Inc. If these quasi-agencies were included, the figure would exceed 3,500. A few of the top agencies are listed in table 10.1.

TABLE 10.1 Top Sport Marketing Agencies

Top sport marketing agencies	Founded	Office locations	Services or functions	Key clients or projects
International Management Group (IMG)	1960	Cleveland; New York; London (overall, 58 offices in 30 countries)	Representation, event management, sponsorship, event hospitality and promotion, consulting, licensing, market research	Tiger Woods, Roger Federer, Maria Sharapova, Peyton Manning, John Madden
Octagon	1999	McLean, VA; Norwalk, CT; Los Angeles; Charlotte, NC; Richmond, VA; Atlanta; New York; Cary, NC; Chicago; Minneapolis, MN; Naples, FL; Ormond Beach, FL; Portland, ME; Rogers, AR; San Diego; San Francisco; multiple offices in Canada, Europe, China, Japan, Australia, and South Africa	Consulting group, athlete and talent representation, media rights, promotions, public relations, product sampling, research, contract negotiations, activation, event creation, strategic planning and sponsorship, asset valuation, endorsements, financial planning, event management	Sprint Nextel, Michael Phelps, John Elway, Chris Paul, Marvin Lewis, foremost Olympic marketing company in the world
Host Communications (Purchased by IMG in 2007)	1972	Lexington, KY	College athletics representation	Universities of Kentucky, Texas, Tennessee, and Florida
Wasserman Media Group (WMG)	1998	Los Angeles; Raleigh, NC; New York; Bethesda, MD; Carlsbad, CA; Coral Springs, FL; Fort Worth, TX; Beijing; Mumbai; London	Full-service agency	Tracy McGrady, Derrick Rose, Travis Pastrana, Dave Mirra, Nokia, Wachovia, Nationwide Insurance
Momentum Worldwide	1988	New York; Atlanta; Chicago; Cincinnati; Detroit; Los Angeles; San Francisco; St. Louis; San Juan; Toronto; Vancouver; Calgary; 63 other offices worldwide	Sponsorship, promotion, retail and event marketing, public relations, organizes and promotes music events	American Express, Anheuser-Busch, Coca-Cola, Intel, Microsoft, Nestle

(continued)

TABLE 10.1 *(continued)*

Top sport marketing agencies	Founded	Office locations	Services or functions	Key clients or projects
GMR	1998	New York; Dallas; Charlotte, NC; Los Angeles; San Francisco; Milwaukee, WI; Chicago; Detroit; Beijing; Paris; London; Vancouver; Toronto	Music and entertainment strategy and consulting, talent procurement and licensing, experiential live activation, entertainment partnerships, brand integration and product placement, digital consulting and marketing	Miller, Major League Baseball, Green Bay Packers, Visa, Major League Soccer, Microsoft, National Basketball Association, Apple, Bank of America
Velocity Sports & Entertainment	1999	Norwalk, CT; Charlotte, NC; London; Atlanta; San Francisco; Washington, DC	Strategic consulting, brand promotions, retail marketing, event management, customer entertainment, property alliances, research ad evaluation	*Sports Illustrated*, FedEx, IBM, Toyota, AT&T
Millsport	1975	Darien, CT; Charlotte, NC; Los Angeles; Dallas; Chicago; New York; Boston; London	Sports asset strategy and acquisition, sports platform strategy and management, promotional concepts and activation, event on-site and field activation, media and PR leveraging, sports hospitality, ROI and program analysis	Visa, Taco Bell, Gatorade
Premier Partnerships	2003	Los Angeles; New York; Dallas; Moreland Hills, OH; Durham, NC	Naming rights, corporate consulting, sales representation, revenue optimization	ESPN, Pizza Hut, JetBlue, Oakland Athletics, Rose Bowl Stadium
Creative Arts Agency (CAA)	1975	Los Angeles; New York; Nashville, TN; Chicago; St. Louis; London; Beijing; Calgary; Stockholm	Talent (film, television, music, theater, literature) and athlete representation, strategic counsel, financing and consulting, licensing, endorsements, broadcast rights, corporate marketing, sales and sponsorship services, consumer behavior research	Peyton Manning, Eli Manning, Derek Jeter, LeBron James, Dwayne Wade, Sidney Crosby, LaDainian Tomlinson, Tony Romo, David Beckham, David Letterman, Brad Pitt, Steven Spielberg, Oprah Winfrey, Bruce Springsteen, Mariah Carey, Justin Timberlake

A portion of this information from: Ranking the agencies. (2006, October 16). *Street & Smith's SportsBusiness Journal*, pp. 16, 32.

These agencies vary in size, budget, type of clientele, and scope of services. Some agencies perform a variety of services for one client, whereas others work for many clients but perform only one function. Examining the various types of agencies (i.e., full service, general, specialty, and in-house) illustrates the variety and scope of sport and entertainment management and marketing agencies.

Full-Service Agencies

solicitation—Requesting support or assistance on behalf of a sport property from a potential sponsor.

These agencies offer the full range of services, including client management, event creation, television development, sponsorship **solicitation,** hospitality services, research and evaluation, and financial planning, and they perform the functions in-house. Attorneys, accountants, sales personnel, public relations personnel, creative personnel, and management information services personnel are all contained in-house. Full-service agencies include IMG, Octagon, and Wasserman Media Group (WMG). An examination of IMG provides an excellent overview of a full-service agency.

IMG, the first completely dedicated sport marketing agency, was initially created to represent the interests of golfer Arnold Palmer. As times changed and marketing forces such as television gained greater influence on the sport scene, the roles of sport marketing agencies expanded to include managing not only athletes but other sport properties and events as well. IMG owes much of its early success to being visionary and recognizing the opportunities that the Golden Age of Sport Television (1958–1973) offered.

The diversity of IMG's endeavors reflects how successful the company has become. IMG represents athletes, performing artists, writers, fashion models, broadcasters, speakers, world-class events, corporations, resorts, cultural institutions, and most recently college athletics programs, under the umbrella IMG College. IMG has evolved into the largest sport marketing agency in the world, with 58 offices in 30 countries (IMG, 2010). Mark McCormack, founder of IMG, died in 2003. In 2004 buyout firm Forstmann Little & Co. bought IMG for $750 million ("Stories," 2008). IMG has four core businesses: client management, event management and marketing, television, and corporate marketing (see figure 10.1). Examining each core business is essential in comprehending the entire scope and magnitude of IMG.

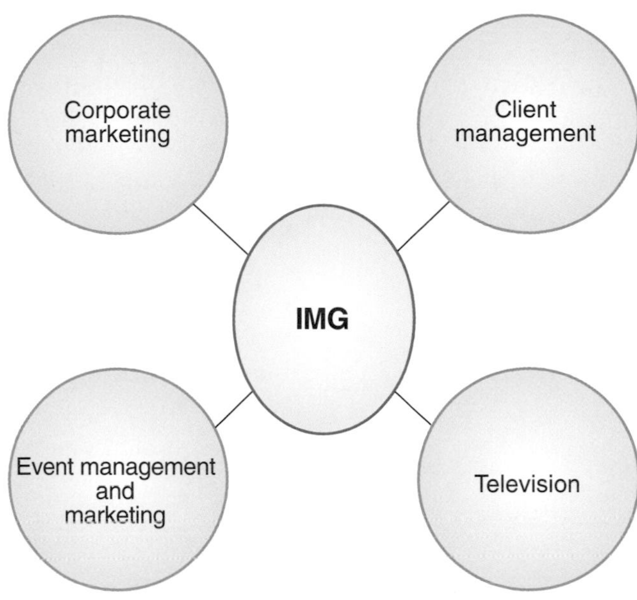

Figure 10.1 IMG's four core businesses.
Data from IMG Corporate Reports 2001.

Client Management

IMG's client management activities encompass contract negotiation, personalized strategic planning, endorsement marketing, corporate and resort affiliation, personal appearances, broadcasting, publishing, licensing, and merchandising (IMG, 2010). Because of the size and scope of IMG, as well as the many relationships that it has constructed during the past four decades, IMG may enjoy an advantage over competitors in attracting clients and providing services. Here is a partial listing of IMG clients:

- Annika Sorenstam (golf)
- Arnold Palmer (golf)
- Brett Hull (hockey)
- Carlos Moya (tennis)
- Jeff Gordon (auto racing)
- Lindsay Davenport (tennis)
- Itzhak Perlman (music)
- John Madden (broadcasting)
- Julie Foudy (soccer)
- Serena Williams (tennis)
- Peyton Manning (football)
- Tiger Woods (golf)
- Tommy Moe (skiing)
- Tyra Banks (modeling)
- Maria Sharapova (tennis)
- LaDainian Tomlinson (football)
- Tom Coughlin (coach)
- Roger Federer (tennis)
- Rafael Nadal (tennis)
- Vijay Singh (golf)
- Michelle Wie (golf)
- Steve Nash (basketball)
- Justin Timberlake (music)

One key to successful client management is to have satisfied, highly successful, and visible clients involved in a variety of sport and lifestyle activities. The success of the clients ensures successful negotiations and endorsements, and the visibility helps attract new clients, who create a cyclical effect. Given the labor unrest in professional sport in the second decade of the new millennium, having a client base that ensures income, stability, and diverse sports or activities is extremely valuable.

Event Management and Marketing

IMG is involved in creating, developing, and managing sport and lifestyle activities and events. The company also manages licensing, sponsorship, and broadcast rights for many of the oldest and most distinguished events on the international sport and event calendar. These events include Wimbledon, the America's Cup, the Australian Open, World Championship of Women's Golf, Snowboarding World Championships, and Escape from Alcatraz Triathlon. Given the diverse nature and varying demands of these properties, as well as the combination of rights, duties, and obligations associated with these events, the complexity of the event management and marketing industry becomes clear.

Television

As noted earlier in the chapter, the television appendage of IMG is TWI. This organization is the largest independent source and distributor of sport programs in the world. The main function of TWI is to provide programming to major television networks around the world and to represent the entities owning the rights to those events (Parascenzo, 1993). TWI is able to accomplish this in three ways:

1. By serving as an advisor and consultant to rights holders
2. By negotiating the sale of television rights
3. By creating and producing television series and events for sale or distribution

Overall, TWI and related IMG media subsidiaries package, produce, and distribute more than 18,000 hours of programming content (IMG, 2010).

Corporate Marketing

In much the same way that IMG capitalized on the opportunities afforded by television in the 1960s, it recognized the clutter of television advertising in the 1980s and sought an effective strategy for assisting corporations in communicating to their target markets. IMG decided that the most effective way for corporations to communicate was through sport event and lifestyle marketing.

General Agencies

16W Marketing is a generalist type of agency that uses an integrated approach in the development of client programs. Led by partners Steve Rosner and Frank Vuono, 16W Marketing provides the following business components:

- Athlete, coach, and broadcaster marketing and representation: full-service representation for all off-field and off-court business and marketing endeavors, including licensing, endorsements, broadcaster contract negotiation, media placement, promotions, speaking engagements, and personal appearances. The company specializes in seeking "ownership" for athletes and celebrities, gaining equity positions with affiliated companies to provide mutual incentives to grow.
- Team and **venue** services: helps professional teams, universities, and organizing bodies and sport authorities in franchise acquisition, management, marketing, and integrated sponsorship sales, including venue **entitlement,** stadium development, merchandising (including e-commerce), concessions, and retail sales.
- Corporate consulting and property marketing: comprehensive strategic planning and implementation of integrated marketing programs for consumer products or service corporations, online or e-commerce fulfillment companies, manufacturers, retailers, and sport and entertainment management organizations. Services include sponsorship negotiations and evaluation, value-added media packages, licensing, merchandising, and cross-promotional ties.
- Hospitality and event management: **turnkey** hospitality, event management, promotion coordination, and television packaging for top sport and entertainment events (including the Super Bowl, Masters, US Open, and so on), sponsorship sales, and licensing and merchandising, both on-site and at retail. (See the sidebar

venue—A facility or site where a special event or sport activity takes place.

entitlement—Associating the name of a sponsor with the name of an event or facility in exchange for cash or other considerations (e.g., the AT&T Cotton Bowl Classic).

turnkey—A program or product that the vendor executes without further involvement from the client.

Turnkey Sport and Entertainment Team Brand Index: Measurement That Is Easy to Understand, Applicable, and Actionable

Although all teams do research, it is not often used to answer core brand questions (e.g., who do fans think we are as opposed to what do fans like or dislike). Furthermore, research is rarely maintained consistently enough to sort out the ebbs and flows of a good or bad week, month, or season (King, 2007). "We have campaigns for marketing and selling tickets," stated Charlie Jacobs, executive vice president of the Boston Bruins, "but branding is more about how customers feel about you" (¶ 24).

The basic premise of the *Turnkey Team Brand Index* (2010) is to assess the strength of each of the 122 professional team sport brands in football, baseball, basketball, and hockey in each of their respective local markets. This objective is achieved through a survey of 200 to 500 fans in each pro sport market for the aforementioned leagues (the actual number of surveys is based on the number of teams in each of those markets).

Perhaps the most important element of the *Turnkey Team Brand Index* (2010) is that it measures and maps a team's brand in its own hometown, not across North America, by surveying the fans who know the team best (e.g., fans in Atlanta rate the Atlanta teams and fans in Baltimore rate the Baltimore teams). Thus the other elements of the *Index*—including the Sponsor Loyalty Index (SLI), the most admired sponsor and the preferred sponsors, and finally the Value Quadrant—are based only on what is important and related to that specific market. This approach is similar to the market-specific data generated by organizations such as Scarborough. The data are highly relevant to both the teams and their sponsors because such data provide a snapshot of how their respective target markets perceive them. Both the teams and the sponsors can then capitalize on identified strengths as well as address perceived weaknesses within that target market. This type of research not only establishes a benchmark of where teams are but also identifies the key areas in which they need to work to improve their brand and, ultimately, their rankings.

"Turnkey Sport and Entertainment Team Brand Index" for more information on turnkey hospitality.)

Specialty Agencies

A specialty agency specializes in the types of services that it provides or in the scope of its clientele. For example, Velocity Sports & Entertainment, headquartered in Norwalk, Connecticut, specializes in sponsorship and event marketing. According to Brian Phillips, vice president of US marketing, "What sets them apart is that they are a marketing agency that happens to specialize in sports and entertainment sponsorship, as opposed to a sports and entertainment agency that dabbles in marketing" (Lefton, 2003, ¶ 24).

SportsMark Management Group Ltd. of San Rafael, California, is a specialty agency solely involved in event management and hospitality. SportsMark has entertained 27,000 guests at 50 Olympic hospitality events since the 1992 Winter Games in Albertville, France. Hospitality services include arranging hotel rooms and transportation, obtaining hard-to-get event tickets, and providing food and beverage services. Using the Olympic Games as a platform, the firm has been able to build strong business relationships with Fortune 500 corporations such as Xerox, Visa, General Motors, and AT&T (Schwartz, 2000).

In-House Agencies—Professional League Departments

In-house agencies are departments of companies (e.g., Anheuser-Busch, MasterCard) that perform sport functions on behalf of the products and divisions of the parent company. In-house agencies have only one client—themselves—and function as **gatekeepers** in reviewing opportunities presented to them by other entities. Besides performing this gatekeeping function, in-house agencies work with other units of the corporation, such as brand or product managers, advertising departments, public relations departments, and

gatekeepers—Individuals or groups responsible for controlling the flow of proposals or solicitations to the decision maker.

MARKETING THE BEIJING OLYMPIC GAMES

By Li Li Leung
Helios Partners, Beijing, CHINA

The People's Republic of China has just recently been able to sit back and take a deep breath after playing host to a historically monumental sporting event, the Beijing 2008 Olympic Games. For years to come, these Olympic Games will influence the sporting landscape in Beijing and the rest of China. Helios Partners, an Olympic consulting company, was fortunate to be able to play a part in that event.

Helios Partners is a strategic sport consultancy that was appointed by several Olympic sponsors to help with various aspects of the marketing mix such as contract negotiations to secure sponsorship rights, planning to create a marketing roadmap, and implementation to assist in making everything come to fruition. Among the sponsors with whom we worked were adidas, Lenovo, Volkswagen, and Snickers.

To illustrate our role, let us use the personal computer manufacturing company Lenovo as a mini case study. Lenovo executives first came to Helios Partners asking for help to analyze the Olympic opportunity. Should they sponsor? If the answer was yes, should they pursue a global or a domestic (China-based) sponsorship? After analysis, we suggested that they should pursue an Olympic sponsorship. In our view, how could they pass up the unique opportunity of being able to leverage an Olympic Games right in their own backyard? Given the fact that Lenovo wanted to become

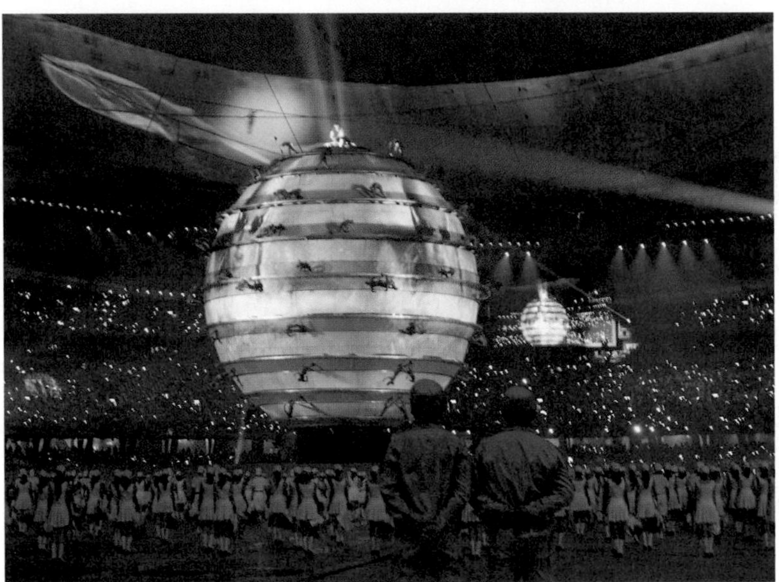

Photo courtesy of Li Li Leung.

The Opening Ceremonies of the 2008 Olympic Games showcased the host country of China. Agencies such as Helios Partners worked with several sponsors affiliated with the Beijing Olympic Games.

community affairs departments, to create or implement sport and lifestyle programming useful in achieving corporate objectives.

Professional league departments are one example of in-house agencies. Each professional sport league and most sport organizations have departments that focus their marketing and promotional efforts on the entire league or unit. For example, NBA Events and Attractions, an NBA division, markets and promotes the NBA as a holistic product through special events and activities such as NBA Jam Session, the NBA draft, and international tours and activities. NBA Events and Attractions personnel work with the marketing departments of individual teams to promote the growth and development of the league itself. In many cases, these departments, along with their respective corporate partnership divisions, are charged with creating and implementing the activation programs that corporate partners have purchased as part of their sponsorship or licensing agreements. To do so, these personnel must understand the uniqueness and complexities of each team's market and must be prepared to assist teams in maintaining their identity while promoting the image of the whole league.

ACTION

Go to the OSG and complete the Learning in Action activity, which will test your understanding of the different types of sport management and marketing agencies.

an internationally recognized brand, we also recommended that the company pursue a global sponsorship.

After the agreement was successfully negotiated, Helios assisted the Lenovo executives in several other aspects of their sponsorship programming such as strategic planning, resource planning, and program implementation, as well as return on investment (ROI) evaluation. To be more specific, we helped develop Lenovo's overarching Olympic sponsorship objectives in all parts of its sponsorship such as the torch relay, hospitality program, and employee initiatives, as well as online and on-site initiatives. We identified and facilitated copromotional opportunities with sponsors such as Visa and Coca-Cola. Helios also helped Lenovo identify and sign Olympic athletes to the Olympic Ambassador program. During the Games, we helped manage Lenovo's stakeholder hospitality program and on-site implementation of the Lenovo i.lounges (Internet lounges), which were located on the Olympic Green, in the Media Press Center, and in the Athletes' Village.

The Beijing 2008 Olympic Games were certainly a success in many aspects, and Lenovo was able to capitalize on the Olympic platform. As a result of the company's Olympic sponsorship, Lenovo enjoyed a 2008 sales revenue increase of almost 11%. From June 2007 to June 2008, sales in Europe, the Middle East, and Africa regions increased 26%. Between 2004 and 2006, Lenovo's global brand recognition increased 75%. *Dow Jones Insight* and *Global Language Monitor* ranked Lenovo as having one of the best three sponsorship campaigns associated with the 2008 Olympic Games. Looking forward, we hope that future sponsors enjoy similar results and wish the London Organising Committee of the Olympic and Paralympic Games the best of luck as they embark on their 2012 Olympic Games adventure.

INTERNATIONAL LEARNING ACTIVITY #1

Conduct an online search for international sport marketing and management agencies. Make a list of the agencies that you find. Describe and evaluate each company. What advice would you offer to your classmates regarding each of these agencies?

INTERNATIONAL LEARNING ACTIVITY #2

The National Basketball League (NBL) in Australia started in the late 1970s. Compare and contrast sponsorship in the NBL with the US-based National Basketball Association (NBA) and Women's National Basketball Association (WNBA). How do the respective leagues and corporate sponsors address concerns such as player drain to other countries, players' conduct on and off the court, and media coverage? The NBL Web site is www.nbl.com.au/.

CAREERS AND CHALLENGES

The following section provides an overview of careers in sport management and marketing agencies and some of the challenges currently facing these agencies. Careers in this segment of the sport industry are diverse, requiring a wide range of skills and abilities. Furthermore, mergers, acquisitions, and labor unrest in professional sport leagues have created added levels of uncertainty for people working in agencies.

Careers

Careers in sport and lifestyle event management and marketing are challenging and varied. Many sport management and marketing agencies do not hire entry-level personnel. Instead, they bring in experienced people from other industry segments who have a network in place that they can use to generate new clients. A critical consideration in the hiring process, particularly in smaller agencies, is an assessment of a candidate's ability to get along, communicate, and be productive in a working environment with

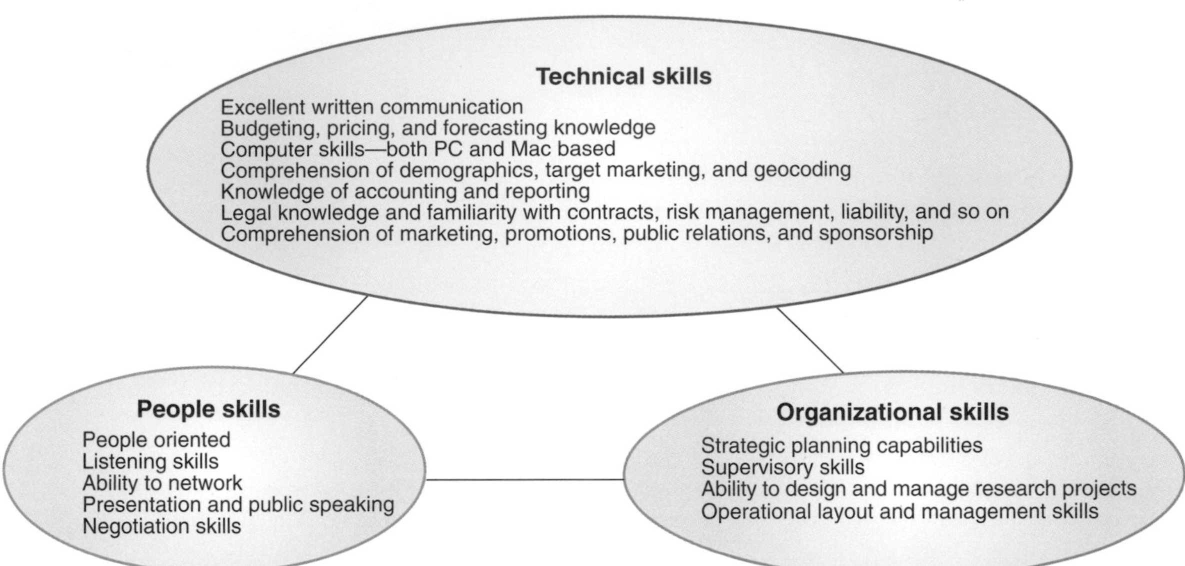

Figure 10.2 Organizational, technical, and people skills essential for sport management and marketing agency personnel.

few staff members who must interact daily. In these smaller agencies, staff members must be compatible because they must act as a team. The ability of a team to work together harmoniously is often called chemistry.

In terms of educational background, a business degree with a marketing background is preferable. A sport management degree, with several electives in business, is also desirable. An advanced degree in business, law, or sport management is an advantage for the applicant.

Clearly, the sport management and marketing agency segment of the sport economy is diverse and contains both generalists and specialists. Although the personnel in larger sport management and marketing agencies are more likely to function as specialists, those employed in smaller agencies must have a variety of skills and knowledge to perform their duties effectively. Skills essential to working in sport marketing and management agencies can be classified as organizational, technical, and people. Essential skills under each classification are provided in figure 10.2.

Challenges Facing Sport Management and Marketing Agencies

Although the sport management and marketing agency segment of the sport industry is growing in number of firms and job opportunities, agencies still face several difficult challenges as we move into the second decade of the 21st century. These challenges are similar to those encountered by advertising agencies, public relations firms, and similar enterprises. We can categorize them as follows.

- ***In-house versus outsourcing.*** After benefiting from high-level performance by a sport management and marketing agency for several years, a client may believe that he or she knows the functions that the agency performs and decide to dismiss the agency to bring that function in-house. The agency then faces a challenge because it might have to cut personnel and budgets because of losing the account. The agency also may have lost a key staff member to the client, who has hired that person for his or her expertise and familiarity with the organization. This practice is becoming more prevalent in professional sport leagues, such as the NBA and NHL, and in collegiate athletics departments because of the need to maximize revenues. By bringing sponsorship, licensing, and broadcasting in-house instead of outsourcing them to agencies or hiring an outside agency to perform functions on their behalf, organizations believe that they will have more control and generate more income while cutting expenses (agency fees). For a more detailed examination of outsourcing, refer to the critical thinking section later in this chapter.

- ***Conflicts of interest.*** With the growth of full-service agencies, the potential for conflicts of interest has increased. Firms such as IMG represent the interests of leagues, teams, athletes, events, and corporate sponsors. The interests of these parties occasionally come into conflict. For example, an agency may be under contract with both a free-agent basketball player and several NBA teams, resulting in a potential conflict of interest. Additionally, as noted earlier in this chapter, agencies create and own events in which their athletes participate. Given the charge to maximize profits on agency-owned events, will the agency pay fair market value for the participation of athletes under its representation?

- ***Mergers and acquisitions.*** Agencies have traditionally grown organically in size and scope, but the current trend is toward growth through aggressive mergers and acquisitions. Three firms that have used this growth strategy are WMG, IMG, and Octagon. Since 2005 WMG has acquired SFX Sports, OnSport, Reich & Katz baseball representation, RAM Sports and Entertainment (UK), SportsNet, Arn Tellern's athlete management business, and Champion Sports Group. WMG has emerged as a global leader among sport management and marketing agencies. Regarding IMG, as noted earlier in the chapter, this agency acquired Host Communications in 2007, which now operates as a division of IMG College. Lastly, Octagon, as a division of advertising conglomerate Interpublic Group, expanded rapidly by acquiring firms such as Advantage International; Flammini Group, an Italian motor sports producer; CSI, a large UK-based television rights and production firm; Koch Tavares, a Brazilian sports agency; and IMS Sports, an agency that represents action sports athletes. Octagon now represents over 500 athletes and manages over 3,000 events ("Labor and Agents," 2008). The acquisitions strategy allows agencies to reach critical mass quickly and provide a full range of services to clients. A downside of this strategy is the challenge of assimilating new parts into the overall culture of the agency.

- ***Labor unrest.*** After the resolution of the NHL's labor issues in 2005, the four major sports leagues—the NHL, MLB, NBA, and NFL—seem to be back on track. The NFL's current collective bargaining agreement (CBA) expires after the 2010 season; the 2009 season was the last under the salary cap under the current deal. This means that NFL owners and the NFL Players Association (NFLPA), with its relatively new executive director (DeMaurice Smith), need to work toward labor peace. The former head of the NFLPA, the late Gene Upshaw, stated that if there is even one season without a salary cap, the players will never go back to a capped salary structure. The owners' priorities are for players to recognize the costs associated with building and operating stadia and to agree to rookie salary caps. Owners believe that the previous CBA favored players too heavily and cite the need to keep expenses down, labor being just one of them. Costs need to be kept down to keep ticket prices affordable for fans. Players currently are compensated with about 60% of team revenues.

The NFL is not the only league facing potential labor issues. The NBA's current CBA expires on July 1, 2011. The main issues at hand are the division of revenues, the institution of hard salary caps, and guaranteed contracts. NBA players currently collect 57% of basketball-related income. NBA team owners would like to reduce their costs (mainly player salaries) in order for teams to be more profitable. Additionally, team owners would like a hard salary cap, similar to the NFL. This could curb the potential bidding wars and skyrocketing contract offers for elite players during free agency—which produces a domino effect for many other players—and reduce overall operating costs per team. Lastly, NBA players' contracts are almost fully guaranteed under the current CBA, meaning that even if a high salaried player's talent and production decline in the middle of his contract, he will still earn top money through the length of his contract. At the time of publication, there has not been a resolution for any of these issues; however, the National Basketball Players Association (NBPA) and the NBA team owners are in negotiations, trying to avoid a potential lockout or work stoppage for all or part of the 2011-2012 season.

Economic Challenges Facing Sport Marketing Agencies

Sport management and marketing agencies face unique challenges in the second decade of the 21st century. To remain competitive and profitable, they must address the following 10 issues.

- The current need of the banking and automotive sectors to improve their business models and satisfy a high level of accountability and public scrutiny will force some companies to reduce sponsorship activities, thus reducing the pool of sponsorship partners for marketing opportunities and platforms.
- The factors mentioned in the first challenge will result in a move back to return on investment (ROI) and away from return on objective (ROO) and return on experience (ROE), in some cases eliminating the need for a sport marketing agency because of a shift away from sponsorship and toward traffic-building ideas and couponing.
- The sport management and marketing agency will need to become more creative in terms of activation and more responsible in terms of accountability and results.
- New revenue models featuring revenue sharing may become more common because of the economy. Agencies will have less up-front money but more of an upside in terms of revenue sharing. This approach will require different strategies and forms of accountability and documentation.
- Sport management and marketing agencies and their clients (e.g., properties, teams) will need to become more focused on creating business solutions using marketing platforms.
- Sport management and marketing agencies must become more nimble in making quick adjustments to capitalize on new and emerging opportunities and markets. The time available to wait and react is limited.
- Deal terms will be shorter and contract amounts will be smaller, requiring each agency to have more clients to achieve the same financial success.
- Companies that have been off-limits in sport, such as alcohol purveyors, are now back in play. Agencies need to identify new opportunities for products and brands that have limited or no previous sport marketing experience.
- Sport management and marketing agencies must become well versed in global thinking and understanding different cultures. This knowledge will provide them with an accurate way of assessing international marketing opportunities and provide them the best chance of experiencing success outside the United States.
- Sport products such as sponsorships and premium seating (e.g., suites) may be sold in different incremental offerings (e.g., monthly, quarterly) than they were in the past. Agencies must be able to visualize how to use sport in a more constricted time basis that might lead to a better ROI and expanded marketing opportunities.

CRITICAL THINKING IN AGENCY ACTIVITIES

For over two decades collegiate athletic departments have made a common practice of outsourcing their rights fees in several areas, most notably in the area of radio and television rights fees but also in the area of their corporate partnerships. Purchasing the rights fees from collegiate athletic departments was a practice developed by Host Communications, which originated in Lexington, Kentucky, in 1972 and was acquired by IMG in 2007 to form IMG College.

These rights fees, which can be limited to a single college or university or an entire conference, can include all or multiple elements of the following services: corporate sponsorships, radio and television programs, publishing, printing, creative design, marketing, Internet, national advertising and signage sales, and numerous lifestyle and event marketing platforms ("IMG to Acquire," 2007). The reasons for the popularity of outsourcing are multifaceted. First, it provides a guaranteed revenue stream of a set amount regardless of team performance and the economy. Second, it eliminates the headcount issue for athletics departments who are not equipped to structure the types of compensation and benefit packages available to secure the services of people to sell their inventory. Third, it lets athletics directors and departments focus on what they do best. Finally, it allows the bundling of athletics departments by the outsourcing agencies to generate a higher price for premier properties.

In 2009 IMG College entered into a record US$110 million agreement with Ohio State University. This contract is the largest ever in this marketing area and is even more impressive because it does not include any TV rights (which are owned by the Big Ten Conference) except the coaches' television shows. The deal also excludes the current licensing agreement with Nike, which will continue to be managed in-house (Smith, 2009). IMG's rights will include corporate sponsorships and stadium and arena signage, on-site marketing, coaches' endorsements and television shows, publishing rights, and a partnership with RadioOhio, the broadcast company that has held the Buckeyes' radio rights since 1984.

According to senior associate athletics director Ben Jay, "My concern, with the economy, is how many of our sponsorship deals were going to get renewed." Jay added, "(H)ow many of those sponsors are going to be looking for a reduction" (Smith, 2009, ¶ 15). The 10-year agreement gives OSU peace of mind on both accounts. Conversely, the length of the agreement provides IMG College with a sufficient length of time to develop its relationships and grow the business. OSU athletics director Gene Smith, when asked why the Buckeyes, one of the last programs to hold its rights in-house, was willing to make a change, stated

> When you project our revenue in future years, IMG's bid is almost double what we were looking at had we kept the rights in-house. This deal gives us guaranteed long-term stability for the next 10 years that we might not have had. (Smith, ¶ 16)

PORTFOLIO Complete the critical thinking portfolio activity in the OSG, consulting as needed the "Eight Critical Thinking Questions" section in chapter 1.

Only time will tell how the current economy will affect the ability of IMG College not only to meet the obligations and expectations of this agreement but also to generate profit from the relationships. Needless to say, IMG College's competition and potential future clients will be watching with great interest.

ETHICS IN AGENCY ACTIVITIES

In 2009 NBA team owners reversed a long-time ban on courtside advertising by spirits brands in an effort to increase revenue during the current economic downturn. Before this decision, alcoholic spirits signage was limited to premium clubs and related signage that was not on camera during telecasts. The NBA decision followed that of MLB, the

National Hockey League (NHL), and NASCAR in allowing spirits advertising within camera view.

This ownership vote opens new revenue sources for all NBA teams who have observed the ban on such advertising since 1991. According to Chris Granger, senior vice president of team marketing and business operations for the NBA, "We are always trying to find ways to drive more revenue and this falls in line with that." Granger added, "We are working too on what other opportunities will exist" (Lombardo & Lefton, 2009, ¶ 5).

Over the past decade, various ad restrictions at sport properties regarding formerly off-limit categories have been loosened. For example, casino resorts are a fixture at many big sport venues and on sports telecasts, as are state lotteries. Gary Stevenson, a principal of WMG stated, "I don't have an issue with this because I don't see a lot of difference between hard liquor and beer when it comes to advertising" (Lombardo & Lefton, 2009, ¶ 12). Given the state of the global economy, what comes next? Will tobacco be given consideration under a set of narrow and restrictive guidelines for messaging? One thing that remains clear is that as some categories and businesses cut back on their sport spending, those revenues need to be replaced. The list of potential replacements is not a long one at this point. Stay tuned.

PORTFOLIO

Complete the ethical issues portfolio activity in the OSG, consulting as needed the "Guidelines for Making Ethical Decisions" section in chapter 1.

Summary

A sport management and marketing agency is a business that acts on behalf of a sport property. Although these agencies initially represented athletes, they have evolved to serve myriad functions, such as representation, negotiation, sales, licensing, marketing, and management. More than 1,000 companies are classified as sport management and marketing agencies. If quasi-agencies such as city and state sport commissions, divisions of leagues, and corporations such as Gatorade are included, the number of marketing and management firms exceeds 3,500. We can classify these agencies into the following four categories:

1. Full-service agencies (e.g., IMG)—provide a full range of services performed by in-house personnel
2. General agencies (e.g., 16W Marketing)—provide a variety of services to clients but are not involved in all potential agency functions
3. Specialty agencies (e.g., WMG)—specialize in providing particular types of services or serving certain kinds of clients
4. In-house agencies (e.g., NBA Events and Attractions)—departments of existing companies that perform many sport marketing functions on behalf of the products or divisions of the parent company

QUIZ TIME

Did you grasp all the key points in this chapter? Go to the OSG for a short quiz to test your understanding of the material.

Personnel at larger sport marketing and management agencies tend to function as specialists, whereas those in smaller agencies need to have a greater variety of skills and knowledge. Degrees in business and sport management are preferred, and a background in marketing is essential. Careers in sport and lifestyle management and marketing agencies are challenging and varied. Sport management and marketing agencies face several challenges in the coming years—in-house versus outsourcing; labor unrest; conflicts of interest; mergers and acquisitions; and legislative and judicial review.

Review Questions

1. What are the functions performed by sport management and marketing agencies?
2. Why is research and evaluation a crucial role performed by agencies?

3. How are specialty agencies different from full-service sport management and marketing agencies?
4. What are some of the benefits of bringing functions such as sponsorship in-house instead of outsourcing to agencies?
5. Founded in 1960, IMG benefited from being the first and best known sport management and marketing agency. Which events reviewed in this chapter have affected the competitive situation faced by IMG?
6. What are some examples of how you can apply ethical decision making and critical thinking skills to the activities of sport management and marketing agencies?
7. What are the most pressing challenges facing agencies in the second decade of the 21st century?

References

Bernstein, A. (2005, February 7). ESPN, Big East end long disagreement over change in rights fees. *Street & Smith's SportsBusiness Journal*, p. 13.

Colon, D. (2009, January 20). Get in the game: Your guide to the NFL Experience. *St. Petersburg Times*. Retrieved June 13, 2010, from www.tampabay.com/features/events/article969093.ece

Conrad, E. (1995, January 10). NFL experience: Super Bowl-related bazaar will be running right next to JRS. *Sun Sentinel*, p. 10.

Gottlieb, R. (2009). *Sports market place directory*. Millerton, NY: Grey House.

IMG. (2010). Retrieved February 1, 2010, from www.imgworld.com/home/default.sps

IMG to acquire Host Communications. (2007, November 12). *Marketwire*. Retrieved February 1, 2010, from www.marketwire.com/press-release/Img-NASDAQ-TCMI-791612.html

King, B. (2007, November 5). The top team brands. *Street & Smith's SportsBusiness Journal*, p. 1.

Labor and agents. (2008, April 28). *Street & Smith's SportsBusiness Journal*, p. 75.

Lefton, T. (2003, September 8). Client-centric culture breeds growth at a rapid velocity. *Street & Smith's SportsBusiness Journal*, p. 1.

Liberman, N. (2005, September 26). Agencies roll out new measurement tools as sponsors seek to justify their investments. *Street & Smith's SportsBusiness Journal*, p. 23.

Lombardo, J., & Lefton, T. (2009, January 19). NBA cans ban on liquor ads. *Street & Smith's SportsBusiness Journal*, p. 1.

Parascenzo, M. (1993, May 3). Prime time. *Business Week*, pp. 100–103.

Ranking the agencies. (2006, October 16). *Street & Smith's SportsBusiness Journal*, pp. 16, 32.

Schreiber, A.L. (1994). *Lifestyle and event marketing*. New York: McGraw-Hill.

Schwartz, D. (2000, May 29). Super concierge to the Olympics, SportsMark claims its niche. *Street & Smith's SportsBusiness Journal*, p. 33.

Smith, M. (2009, March 30). Ohio State lands $110M deal. *Street & Smith's SportsBusiness Journal*, p. 1.

Smith, M., & Ourand, J. (2008, August 25). ESPN pays $2.25B for SEC rights. *Street & Smith's SportsBusiness Journal*, p. 1.

Stories of the decade. (2008, April 28). *Street & Smith's SportsBusiness Journal*, p. 10.

Toms, P. (2009, March 5). *Sport marketing is the recession's new whipping boy*. Retrieved June 13, 2010, from www.bizofbaseball.com/index.php?option=com_content&view=article&id=3039:sports-marketing-is-the-recessions-new-whipping-boy&catid=67:pete-toms&Itemid=155

Turnkey team brand index. (2010). Turnkey Sports & Entertainment. Retrieved February 1, 2010, from www.turnkeyse.com/ttbi.html

Vivid Marketing. (n.d.). Retrieved June 13, 2010, from www.vividsport.com

HISTORICAL MOMENTS

1895	Pinehurst Golf Resort founded
1897	First Boston Marathon held
1912	Inaugural Calgary Stampede held
1936	Sun Valley Ski Resort opened
1939	National Baseball Hall of Fame dedicated
1963	Pro Football Hall of Fame opened
1975	First General Assembly of World Tourism Organization held in Madrid, Spain
1978	First Ironman Triathlon held
1987	First National Senior Olympic Games held in St. Louis, Missouri
1992	National Association of Sports Commissions (NASC) founded
1997	Disney's Wide World of Sports opened
2001	First World Conference on Sport and Tourism held in Barcelona, Spain
2006	FIFA World Cup hosted in Germany
2008	Beijing Summer Olympic and Paralympic Games held
2010	Vancouver Winter Olympic and Paralympic Games held

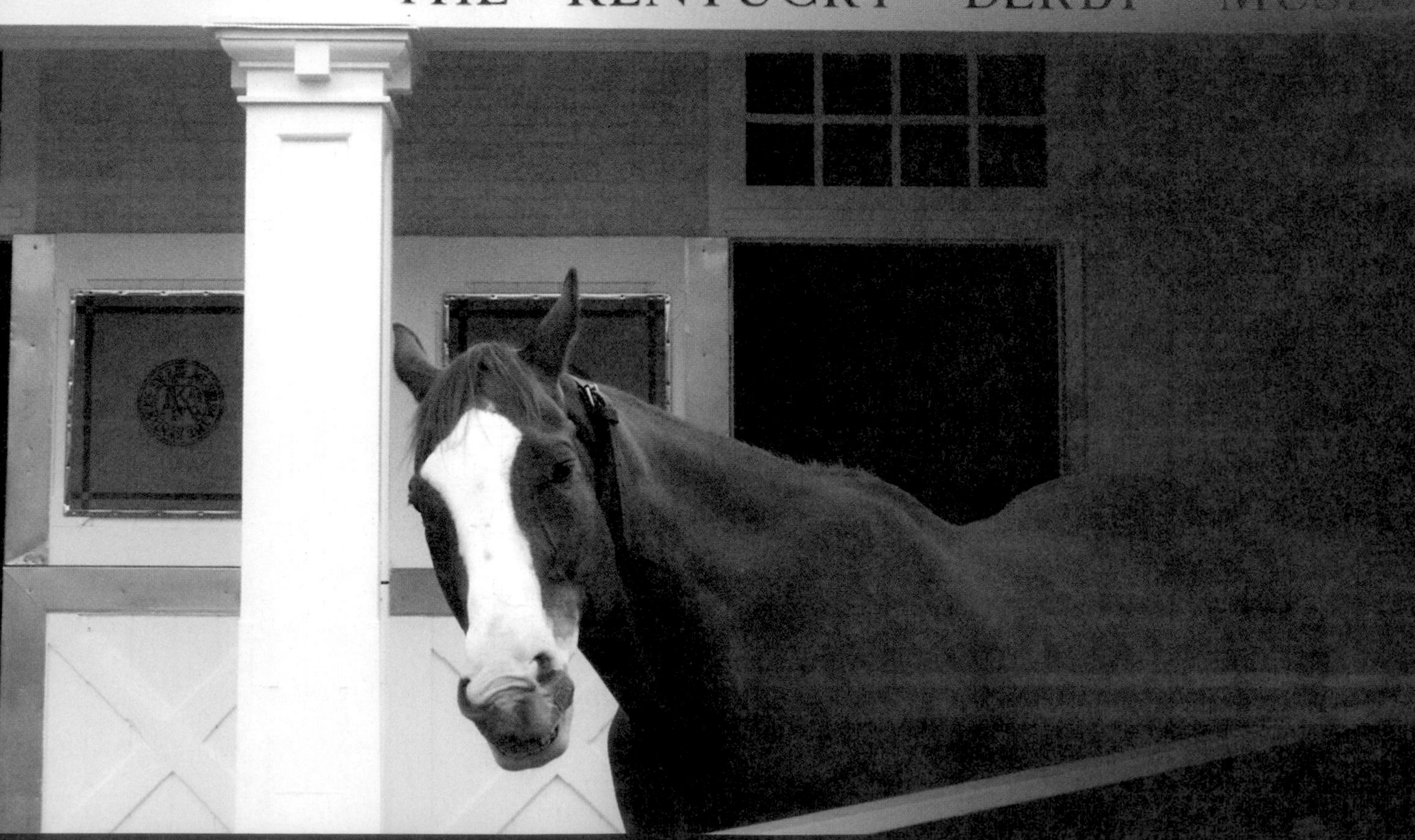

Photo courtesy of Paul M. Pedersen.

11

SPORT TOURISM

Heather Gibson ■ Sheranne Fairley

LEARNING OBJECTIVES

1. Explain tourism and the tourism industry.
2. Describe the intersection between sport and tourism.
3. Distinguish among the three types of sport tourism: active, event, and nostalgia.
4. Discuss the sociocultural, economic, and environmental effects of sport tourism.
5. Understand the basic premises of sustainable development and how they relate to sport tourism.

Key Terms

casuals
convention and visitors bureau (CVB)
destination image
displacement effect
leverage
psychic income
seasonality
sports commission
synergy
time switchers

GET A JOB!

- ☑ Continue on your journey in sport management by going to the Online Study Guide (OSG) at www.HumanKinetics.com/ContemporarySportManagement. Check out the job opportunities and consider the skills and experiences that can help you succeed in sport management.

Since the mid-1990s, sport-related travel has received more attention from both academics and the sport and tourism industries. The Travel Industry Association of America (TIA), one of the foremost research agencies for tourism in the United States, estimated that between 1994 and 1999, 75.3 million US adults traveled to take part in an organized sport event either as spectators or as participants (Travel Industry Association of America [TIA], 1999). Moreover, two of the world's most influential agencies for sport and tourism, the International Olympic Committee (IOC) and the United Nations World Tourism Organization (UNWTO), have cooperated since 1999 and recognized the mutually beneficial relationship that sport and tourism can have as a tool for sustainable economic growth.

Sport-related travel stretches back over the centuries. The Greeks traveled to take part in the ancient Greek Games from as early as 900 BCE, and the Romans regularly staged popular sport competitions that drew large crowds of spectators from various localities (Coakley, 2009). In recent years, the term *sport tourism* has become widely used to describe this type of travel and involvement, and sport-related travel has gradually become a specialized sector of the sport and tourism industries. Sport tourism as defined by Gibson (1998a; 1998b) encompasses three main types of travel and sport participation:

- Active sport tourism, a trip in which the tourist takes part in a sport such as golf
- Event sport tourism, a trip in which the tourist watches a sport event such as the Super Bowl
- Nostalgia sport tourism, a trip in which the tourist visits a sport-themed attraction such as the Baseball Hall of Fame in Cooperstown, New York

The purpose of this chapter is to explore the relationship between sport and tourism, to examine the three types of sport tourism, and to recognize some of the environmental, economic, and sociocultural effects of sport tourism within a framework of sustainable development. The intent is to provide future sport managers with an understanding of the symbiotic (i.e., mutually beneficial) relationship between sport and tourism and to present some of the issues related to this growing industry.

TOURISM AND THE TOURISM INDUSTRY

In the first decade of the 21st century, the tourism industry experienced some rocky times. Economic uncertainty, the terrorist attacks of September 11, 2001, the bombing of a nightclub in Bali (Indonesia), the SARS outbreak in Asia and Canada, and the swine flu epidemic in 2009 all affected the confidence of the traveling public. Despite the increased risks associated with travel, people have often returned to travel again in even greater numbers after various incidents. In 2007 the UNWTO reported that tourism generated US$856 billion and is the largest industry in the world. The onset of global recession in 2008, however, led to declining numbers of travelers and caused concern for event organizers (Gleeson, 2008).

The enormous size of the tourism industry is partly attributed to the range of services and products associated with it from airlines to rental cars, cruise ships to bus tours, campsites to five-star resorts, and theme parks to national parks. Indeed, Goeldner and Ritchie (2009) proposed that any definition of tourism must include four components:

1. Tourists
2. Businesses that provide goods and services for tourists
3. The government in a tourist destination
4. The host community, or the people who live in the tourist destination

The travel and tourism industry also encompasses a wide range of traveler types—leisure travelers, business travelers, those visiting friends and relatives, and those traveling for a range of other reasons. Over 15 years ago the World Tourism Organization (1994) developed a standardized definition of tourism to alleviate some of the inconsistencies that had been occurring around the world in measuring tourism: "Tourism comprises the activities of persons traveling to and staying in places outside of their usual environment for not more than one consecutive year for leisure, business and other purposes" (p. 9).

WEB

Go to the OSG and complete the Web search activity, which has you research and compare the government sport tourism strategies of at least two countries.

If tourism constitutes the "activities of persons traveling," it would follow that a tourist is the individual who actually does the traveling outside his or her home community. At the simple level this is correct, but the defining characteristic of a tourist is not just the travel component. Attributes also include the reason or the motivation for the trip, the length of the trip, and even the distance traveled.

In terms of motivation or reason for the trip, Cohen (1974) argued that people who travel for leisure are tourists and that business travel is a related but separate segment of the travel industry. In the realm of sport tourism, it makes sense to adopt the idea that a tourist is a leisure traveler because most sport-related trips constitute our everyday understanding of leisure as occurring in nonwork time, that is freely chosen and enjoyable (Roberts, 2006). Consequently, examples of a sport tourist would be someone who travels to play golf, to watch a favorite team play football, or to visit a sport hall of fame.

DEFINING SPORT TOURISM

Most existing definitions of sport tourism distinguish between two types of behavior: active, in which a person travels to take part in a sport, or passive, in which a person travels to watch a sport (Standeven & De Knop, 1999). Redmond (1991) recognized the growing popularity of sport-themed destinations such as sport halls of fame, cruises in which tourists have the opportunity to meet their favorite sport personalities, and sport stadia as tourist attractions. Like Redmond, we argue that this type of sport tourism constitutes a third type of behavior—one motivated by nostalgia or a chance to pay homage to a sport personality or stadium associated with a great team or event. This third type is called nostalgia sport tourism.

Thus, the working definition of sport tourism for this chapter will be "leisure-based travel that takes individuals temporarily outside of their home communities to participate in physical activities [active sport tourism], to watch physical activities [event sport tourism], or to venerate attractions associated with physical activities [nostalgia sport tourism]" (Gibson, 1998b, p. 49).

Active Sport Tourism

The first type of sport tourism is travel to take part in sport, or active sport tourism. With a growing focus on active living, more people are choosing to be active while on vacation (Fluker & Turner, 2000). Mintel (2006) estimated that sport and adventure travel in the United States generates US$328 billion annually and constitutes 19% of all domestic leisure trips in the United States.

Taking a lead from one scholar's discussion about the growth of active sport tourism (De Knop, 1987), we can identify a number of recent trends that might explain the increased popularity of active sport vacations. These trends include an increase in the range of sports offered to include nontraditional sports such as mountain biking and snowboarding, more people choosing to take active sport vacations, and a growing awareness of active vacations around the world (Mintel, 2006). A review of some of the specific types of active sport tourism illustrates the growth in opportunities for the active sport tourist.

Cruises

Sport-themed cruises, part of the cruise industry since the 1990s, provide opportunities for both nostalgia sport tourism and active sport tourism. For example, Royal Caribbean ads show groups of men playing golf on board the ship and a mother indicating that she had taken a spinning class. The invention of the golf simulator has been credited with creating a close relationship between golf and the cruise industry. Many cruise ships such as the *Queen Mary 2* have multiple golf simulators on board. Some cruise lines also pair their on-board golf offerings with itineraries that promise passengers a chance to play a different course every day as the ships visit various ports (Finney, 2007).

Amateur Sports

Amateur sport events, which encompass both active tourism and event sport tourism, have grown in recent years. Many community organizations host running road races that attract not only local residents but also runners from outside the community, both sport excursionists and active sport tourists (Nogawa, Yamguchi, & Hagi, 1996). Of course, major races such as the New York Marathon and Boston Marathon are international events in which professional and amateur runners race side by side. But even lesser-known races, such as the Manchester Road Race—a Thanksgiving Day run in Manchester, Connecticut—attract runners from all over the world, including Europe and Africa.

Amateur sport events are held in a wide range of sports, including archery, cycling, soccer, volleyball, swimming, and rugby. Some of these events are multisport competitions that are targeted at various population segments. For example, the Junior Olympics holds regional and national events for young athletes, the Special Olympics has events for people with mental disabilities, and the Transplant Games are for participants who have undergone transplant surgery. Since 1987 when the first National Senior Games Association (2010) competition was held, thousands of athletes aged 50 and older have participated at local, state, and national levels in a variety of sports.

Golf and Skiing

Over the past century two of the most popular forms of active sport tourism have been golf and snow sports, notably alpine, or downhill, skiing. Indeed, US Airways alters its route structure to accommodate golfers and skiers during the appropriate seasons (Zachary, 1997).

The United States has 29.5 million golfers (age six and over), and 15,970 golf courses, many of which are located in southern resort destinations (National Golf Foundation, 2009). The National Golf Foundation estimates that golfers spend US$26.1 billion on golf-related travel and favor such destinations as Florida, North and South Carolina, and Arizona. Moreover, when golfers live in areas with harsh winter climates or a lack of facilities, they are more likely to travel to pursue their sport. Many harbor a dream to play a round at the ultimate mecca of golf, the Old Course at St. Andrews in Scotland.

The development of downhill skiing in the United States resulted in tourism activities similar to those that occurred with golf. Sun Valley, Idaho, the first all-inclusive ski resort in the United States, was designed as a way of increasing passenger volume on the new westward expansion of the railroad. Subsequently, ski resorts in Aspen and Vail, Colorado; Park City, Utah; and Lake Tahoe, California, among others, followed. Like the regions of the United States associated with golf, these towns became synonymous with skiing.

seasonality—The variable patterns of tourist visitation throughout the year at a destination. Most destinations have three seasons: a peak season, a shoulder season (which occurs just before and just after the peak), and an off-season.

Like those in other segments of the tourism industry, resort managers realized that to maintain profitability they had to combat **seasonality**, or the variable pattern of visitation throughout the year at a destination. Most destinations have three seasons: a peak season, a shoulder season (which occurs just before and just after the peak), and an off-season. Ski resorts have a definite season (winter), and fall and spring skiing occurs on either side. With the decline in the number of skiers, operators of ski areas realized at the start of the 1990s that they had to combat the effects of seasonality to remain profitable. Many ski areas added all-weather indoor and outdoor activities and facilities and actively targeted the convention market and nonskiing vacationers (US Travel Data Center, 1989). As an article in the Delta Airlines magazine *Sky* proclaimed, "If you only think winter when you think about ski resorts, you're missing out on some serious opportunities for fun" (Ebisch, 2005, p. 42).

For many family-owned resorts, becoming a year-round destination was not enough. Faced with increasing costs because of aging lift equipment, rising liability insurance rates, and the need for snowmaking equipment, many independent resorts merged with or were acquired by larger ski corporations in the 1990s.

Thus, to maintain its profitability as we move into the second decade of the 21st century in the face of a decline in the absolute number of skiers, the ski industry has actively targeted the destination skier, the active sport tourist who spends more than a day at the resort, buying accommodation, food, and transportation as well as lift tickets. Moreover, golf and skiing continue to forge a closer relationship. Ski resorts use golf to combat seasonality and have begun to diversify their holdings. Intrawest, for example, owns a golf resort in Sandestin, Florida.

Event Sport Tourism

The second type of sport tourism pertains to sport events as tourist attractions and the sport tourists who travel to watch them. To combat seasonality and create or enhance their **destination image**, towns and cities around the world are increasingly hosting sport events that draw spectators as well as active sport tourists. These can be hallmark events such as the Wimbledon Championships and the Super Bowl, megaevents such as the Olympic Games and World Cup, regional events such as PGA golf tournaments and NCAA-sanctioned college sports, or amateur events such as road races and the Senior Games. The competition among communities to host these events is intense because community leaders focus on the economic impact from event patrons, sponsorship deals, and, for the major events, television rights (Ritchie, 1999). In recent years, as community leaders have recognized the **synergy** between sport and tourism (Standeven, 1998), they are increasingly looking to generate tourism by developing a destination image by hosting sport events. In examining event sport tourism, it is useful to think about two levels: the major events that draw international attention, such as a hallmark event or megaevent, and the small-scale sport event (Higham, 1999).

destination image—The impression that people (especially potential tourists) hold of a certain location.

synergy—The interaction between two components, such as tourism and sport.

Hallmark Events

Ritchie (1984) defined hallmark events as

> major one-time or recurring events of limited duration, developed primarily to enhance the awareness, appeal and profitability of a tourism destination in the short and/or long term. Such events rely for their success on uniqueness, status, or timely significance to create interest and attract attention. (p. 2)

Hallmark events include carnivals and festivals such as Mardi Gras in New Orleans, important cultural or religious events such as a British royal wedding, and major sport events such as the Super Bowl or the Calgary Stampede. Ritchie (1984) further added the criteria of relative infrequency, uniqueness of the event, aura of tradition, excellence in participants, and international attention. Jago and Shaw (1998) suggested that hallmark events are one of two types of major international-level events. They proposed that the Olympic Games and the FIFA World Cup football tournament constitute megaevents because they are large-scale events that garner international-level participation from athletes, spectators, and the world's media.

SPORT MUSEUMS: HARNESSING THE VALUE OF AN INTERNATIONAL HERITAGE COLLECTION

By Pamm Kellett
Deakin University, AUSTRALIA

Sport organizations, governments, and tourism providers recognize sport museums as key tourist attractions for domestic and international consumers. Increasingly, sport museums are becoming essential elements in the tourism portfolios of many destinations. For example, the Museo del Fútbol Club Barcelona is the most visited museum in Barcelona, Spain, surpassing the Picasso Museum. In London, Lord's Cricket Museum and the Wimbledon Lawn Tennis Museum are important components of the city's tourism strategy. The Lawn Tennis Museum is second only to the London Eye as the most visited attraction in the city (Kellett & Hede, 2008). In general, sport museums have been created to celebrate the sporting history of cities and nations, which adds further value to the brand of destinations for tourism purposes.

In Melbourne, Australia, sport heritage is an important component of the city's tourism portfolio. The federal government recently invested A$15 million to assist the development of the National Sports Museum located at the Melbourne Cricket Ground (MCG). The MCG is a 100,000-seat football and cricket stadium that was the main stadium for the 1956 Olympic Games in Melbourne. In 2005 it was included on the Australian National Heritage List. The National Sports Museum is the permanent home of the Sport Australia Hall of Fame, the Australian Gallery of Sport and Olympic Museum, the Australian Cricket Hall of Fame, and the Melbourne Cricket Club Museum. This multisport museum is

PA Photos.

The "swift suit" that Olympic 400m gold medalist Cathy Freeman wore when she won gold at the Sydney Olympic Games is now part of the collection of the National Sports Museum.

Increasingly, the mega sporting events have become as much a media spectacle as they have a sporting competition. Cities around the world regard the Olympic Games and the FIFA World Cup as a chance to reimage themselves with the aim of boosting their tourism industry and attracting new businesses (Essex & Chalkley, 1998). When the United States held the men's FIFA World Cup final tournament in 1994, the expressed intent was to bill it as a tourist event and not just a sport event ("World Cup Soccer," 1993). Likewise, the Australian Tourist Commission actively worked to **leverage** the tourism associated with the 2000 Olympic Games in the years following by inviting the international travel media to visit and showcase various aspects of Australia in their travel writing and television coverage. Following the IOC's announcement that London would host the 2012 Olympic Games, VisitBritain, the UK's tourism authority, estimated that over a period of 7 to 10 years between 50 and 75% of the economic benefit of hosting the Olympic Games would be generated from tourism,

leverage—Using strategies to optimize the benefits or outcomes associated with an event.

designed to celebrate the unique contribution of sport to Australian culture through athletes, event sites, and the like.

Tennis Australia, the national tennis governing body, has its own heritage collection that it proposes to house at Melbourne Park, which is only a few hundred meters from the MCG. The Tennis Australia heritage collection, purchased in 2004, is international in scope and includes memorabilia from European and American tennis clubs dating back hundreds of years. The collection comprises a variety of specific items directly related to the sport (e.g., equipment, clothing) as well as artifacts related to the game of tennis. For example, the collection includes a grandfather clock with a ceramic insert of a hand-painted tennis club scene, tennis-themed brooches and jewelry, tennis-themed statues and ornaments, and items once used at French tennis clubs such as crockery and children's building blocks with various tennis-related scenes painted on them. The collection also embraces a large assortment of tennis artwork.

Interestingly, the US Tennis Association (USTA) declined an offer to buy this international collection before its purchase by Tennis Australia. Some of the strategic questions the USTA may have been grappling with include the following: What are people's motives for visiting sport museums? How could the international Tennis Heritage Collection be presented to appeal to such motives? From the perspective of the host destination, what are advantages and disadvantages of having a single-sport, international collection such as the Tennis Heritage Collection as part of the destination portfolio? After studying this chapter, you may be able to provide answers to these and other questions.

INTERNATIONAL LEARNING ACTIVITY #1

Find the Web sites of three sport heritage museums in your country. Describe each museum, including information such as its purpose, exhibits, documents, photographs, and other items of interest. What is the value of these museums to their sports and what is their value as tourist destinations?

INTERNATIONAL LEARNING ACTIVITY #2

Go to www.london2012.com and investigate strategies that the London Organising Committee of the Olympic Games and Paralympic Games (LOCOG) has outlined for a sustainable hallmark event. Describe how the LOCOG plans to build a sustainable Olympic Games. Do you think that the committee's plans for sustainability are achievable? Explain why or why not. How does the idea of legacy relate to the overall proposed sustainability of the London 2012 Olympic Games? Go to www.sochi2014.com and answer the same questions about the 2014 Winter Games in Sochi, Russia.

a figure predicted to be over £2 billion (US$3.5 billion) ("Olympics Could Breathe," 2005).

The concept of destination image drives many communities to invest significant resources in hosting one event. It is generally thought that the international media coverage associated with a megaevent will increase awareness of the host city and lead to increased tourism and business investment in the years to follow (Ritchie & Smith, 1991). A host city, however, cannot always expect the media coverage to be positive. For example, in the months leading up to the 2004 Olympic Games in Athens, Greece, the media focused consistently on the construction delays of the venues. Beijing, the host city of the 2008 Olympic Games, hoped that the event would constitute China's coming-out party, announcing to the world that the country was an emerging superpower (Steinmetz, 2008). Although staging the Olympic Games went relatively well, China received a lot of negative press before the Olympic Games about the poor air quality in Beijing and the protests about the country's relations with Tibet, which were a constant part of the Olympic torch relay (Streets, Fu, Jang, Hae, & He, 2007). Nonetheless, studies of previous Olympic Games showed that hosting this hallmark event can raise awareness and the image of a country around the world (Kim & Morrison, 2005; Ritchie & Smith, 1991). For maximum benefit to occur, however, an organizing committee needs to implement strategies to encourage the media to showcase the sights of the city and country beyond the sport venues (Chalip, 2004; Green, Costa, & Fitzgerald, 2003).

Unfortunately, such hallmark events, as Roche (1994) observed, "are short-term events with long-term consequences for cities that stage them" (p. 1). For example, the 1998 Olympic Games cost Nagano, Japan, US$10 billion, and the city was in debt (ABC, 2002). The facilities cost US$12 million in operations and maintenance per year, and the revenue generated from renting them out for events brought in only 10% of those costs. The bullet train built so that spectators could easily access the Olympic Games meant that skiers were now going to Nagano on day trips and not staying overnight in hotels, which resulted in a loss of revenue for the community. A Nagano resident said, "The Olympics made things great for a while, but it's been downhill since" (ABC, 2002).

Stories such as this are more common than not in the aftermath of megaevents. As a result, over the past five years there has been a call by the IOC and others to encourage organizing committees to identify and plan for the legacies associated with hosting the Olympic Games. Preuss (2007) defined legacy as "all planned and unplanned, positive and negative, intangible and tangible structures created for and by a sport event that remains for a longer time than the event itself" (p. 86). Subsequently, the

Events such as the Special Olympics contribute to the growth of the sport tourism segment of the sport industry and are important to the host communities. They are also important to participants, as evidenced in these comments by Wood County, Ohio, Special Olympian Amanda Gump.

Photo courtesy of Steven Garner. Letter reprinted by permission of Amanda Gump.

I want to thank everyone for being here today. Special olympics has been a great oppertunity for me. in the past I tryed to play with the regular kids my age. I was the one always picked last or the one they made fun of for having something wrong with them.

Since I have been in special olympics I have been able to acheive my dream of playing sports. Here I am treated as an equal. The people with in the special olympics does not look at your disabilities. They look at you as a person.

I have been in sports for five years now. I play, softball, basket ball, and I run track. my teammates have helped me and taught me alot about the person I want to be. They wellcome me in their life win or lose. And because of this I have made so many friends. I consider them my other family.

I want to take the time to thank my family and coaches. My coaches for being there for me and teaching how to play sports, even through I have a disability. You guys do a wonderful job. my family for taking me to my practice and sitting through my games, and supporting and loving me.

Special olympics has given me a chance to do something that I love. it is where any one with a disibility can be accepted, and acheive their dreams. it has built my confedence and made me a better person.

2010 Vancouver–Whistler Winter Olympics had a legacy committee responsible for recognizing and facilitating the long-term legacy of the Olympic Games. The London 2012 Olympic Games bid document mentioned the word *legacy* more than 150 times. Despite such thinking, host cities are often left with empty buildings and huge debts. Five months after the close of the 2008 Beijing Olympic Games, the iconic Bird's Nest (the Olympic Stadium) was "searching for a new purpose." It had yet to have any big events scheduled, and the government was worried about recouping the US$450 million required to build it. It has become a tourist attraction, drawing about 10,000 visiting tourists per day (Steinmetz, 2009).

Although communities continue to vie with one another to host these megaevents, the realization is growing that hosting smaller scale events might be more beneficial. Indeed, Ritchie (1999) suggested that recurring events such as the Boston Marathon or the Calgary Stampede might be more valuable to a community than one-time events such as the Olympic Games. The long-term effects of hosting megaevents may lie in improved infrastructure and community pride rather than increased tourism (for more information on this topic, read the later section on social dimensions).

Small-Scale Event Sport Tourism

Although megaevents such as the Olympic Games are regarded as the pinnacle for a community in terms of hosting a sport event, Higham (1999) suggested that small-scale sport events provide communities with more benefits and fewer burdens than the short-lived hallmark events. He defined small-scale sport events as "regular season sporting competitions (ice hockey, basketball, soccer, rugby leagues), international sporting fixtures, domestic competitions, masters or disabled sports, and the like" (p. 87). He suggested that small-scale sport events usually operate within the existing infrastructure of a community, require minimal investment of public money, are more manageable in terms of crowding and congestion, and may minimize the effects of seasonality for a destination. Indeed, following the failed bid of Dallas–Fort Worth to host the 2012 Olympic Games, one reporter (Wood, 2001) suggested that the US$8 billion generated from hosting amateur sport events each year might be more lucrative than the Olympic Games in the long run.

Many sport events around the United States fit the definition of a small scale event, from professional and collegiate sports to amateur sport events such as the Senior Games and Special Olympics, which represent the crossover between active and event sport tourism discussed earlier. One form of small-scale sport tourism with much untapped potential is college sports. In an interview with the owner of a clothing and souvenir shop in Gainesville, Florida, home of the University of Florida Gators, Fisher (2001) found that the shop averaged 1,500 sales on a home football game day compared with 25 sales per day in the off-season. The football game between the University of Texas and the University of Oklahoma in October 2001 was seen as a godsend for the Dallas area tourism industry following September 11, 2001. Dave Whitney, president of the Dallas Convention and Visitors Bureau, said that the 100,000 visitors "will spend between $15 million and $17 million" (Alm, 2001, p. D1). Other communities around the United States experience similar economic effects from hosting college sport events. Thus, community tourism agencies need to work closely with universities to market sport events and provide information about the destination to potential tourists (Irwin & Sandler, 1998). Two such agencies are the **convention and visitors bureau** (CBV) and the **sports commission.**

Communities around the United States and the world are recognizing that although hosting the Olympic Games may be out of the question, hosting small-scale sport events is a possibility. Even Walt Disney World in Florida recognized the value of the tourism potential associated with sport tourism by opening Disney's Wide World of Sports in 1997, which caters to both active and event sport tourism.

convention and visitors bureau (CVB)—A community agency funded by the "bed tax," the local taxes paid for stays in commercial lodging facilities such as hotels. A CVB promotes tourism in a community and acts as a centralized source of information about events, accommodations, and other visitor-related information.

sports commission—Local or state agency responsible for attracting and organizing sport events to help communities capitalize on the potential benefits of sport tourism.

Walt Disney World Wide World of Sports: The Ultimate Sport Tourism Destination

Photo courtesy of Paul M. Pedersen.

Since 1997 Walt Disney World (WDW) in Orlando, Florida, has become an important venue for sport tourism with the opening of its Disney's Wide World of Sports Complex (in 2008 it was announced that the name would change to the ESPN Wide World of Sports). The area contains world-class facilities for hosting a range of sport events from baseball and beach volleyball to basketball and gymnastics, and hosts about 170 professional and amateur events per year. The Milk House, the indoor venue, has over 30,000 square feet of space for competitions and seating for 5,500 spectators. Similarly, the tennis complex has 10 courts and room for 1,000 spectators. Seating can be expanded to accommodate 7,500 people when hosting a professional event. The baseball stadium is the spring-training venue for the Atlanta Braves. But most of the sport events held at Disney's Wide World of Sports are youth and adult amateur competitions. These include the Special Olympics, high school field hockey championships, Amateur Athletic Union (AAU) wrestling competitions, the annual Walt Disney World Marathon, and the Orlando International Dragon Boat Festival. The strategy behind Disney's Wide World of Sports is to use sport tourism to promote its core product, the theme parks. Athletes and spectators are actively encouraged to visit the parks during their stay. Theme park tickets are packaged with tournament fees and on-site hotel accommodations.

The complex uses volunteer sports enthusiasts to help run the larger events. On event days, guests can participate in the NFL Experience, a simulated football training camp. Boston's Northeastern University has a branch of its Center for the Study of Sport in Society housed within the complex, thereby providing research resources for use by the Center and WDW. Moreover, on the WDW resort properties as a whole, many opportunities are available for guests to take part in sports including golf, tennis, and jet boat racing. The Richard Petty Driving Experience helps guests realize the dream of being a NASCAR driver. WDW annually hosts the Danskin Orlando Triathlon for women, which entails swimming across the lagoon and biking and running around Fort Wilderness. The complex's auditorium hosts forums in which fans get a chance to listen to and interact with their favorite athletes. At the end of the day guests can watch their favorite athletes on the TV screens of the ESPN Zone restaurant. In its diversity of sport tourism offerings, WDW provides opportunities for active, event, and nostalgia sport tourism in conjunction with visiting the four theme parks.

Nostalgia Sport Tourism

The third type of sport tourism is nostalgia sport tourism. Redmond (1991) identified this type of sport tourism as involving travel to visit sport halls of fame, taking sport-themed vacations on cruise ships or resorts, attending fantasy sport camps, and touring famous sport stadia. In spring and summer 2001, the credit card company MasterCard ran an advertising campaign that showcased the journey of two friends in a Volkswagen bus who visited the 30 Major League Baseball (MLB) parks in the United States. This type of trip for a nostalgia sport tourist might be regarded as a dream vacation, a once-in-a-lifetime trip. Other nostalgia sport vacations might be more commonplace and involve such activities as visiting Cooperstown (home of the National Baseball Hall of Fame and Museum), the LPGA Hall of Fame, or the sport venues for the 2008 Beijing Olympic Games as discussed earlier.

Most Olympic and major sport stadia provide tours so that visitors can see behind the scenes from the locker rooms to the press boxes and the VIP seating. Somebody who can provide in-depth information about the venue and the history behind it generally guides these tours. In the United Kingdom, soccer fans of a particular team can visit the football grounds, meet the players, and relive significant events in the history of the team. In the United States, an example of a company that specializes in sport vacations is Sports Travel and Tours. The company's baseball tour itineraries usually include four or more MLB games and a side trip to the Baseball Hall of Fame, thereby combining both event and nostalgia sport tourism.

Another trend over the past 15 years or so has been adult fantasy sport camps. Michael Jordan hosts Michael Jordan's Senior Flight School. This basketball fantasy camp in Las Vegas provides fans a chance to play basketball with him (*Upcoming Camps*, 2009). Golf, baseball, football, and NASCAR all have fantasy sport camps where fans can spend a week or a weekend celebrating the sport of their choice.

Nostalgia sport tourism is a relatively underdeveloped area of study, yet the growing popularity of this type of tourism suggests that researchers need to pay more attention to it. Nearly four decades ago Redmond (1973) suggested that "the ultimate raison d'être for a sports hall of fame, like the ancient Greek statuary, is the glorification of sporting heritage" (p. 42). Gammon (2002), in an examination of the nostalgia sport tourism associated with the sport fantasy camp, suggested, "Fantasy camps provide both the opportunity to relive the past and the propensity to rewrite it" (p. 69). Introducing another way of understanding nostalgia sport tourism, Fairley (2003) presented the idea that nostalgia may be associated not only with physical artifacts such as stadia or sports equipment housed in halls of fame but also with the social interactions of the group. While traveling by bus with a fan group, the scholar found that the fans reminisced about trips that they had previously taken together and enacted ritual activities as a way of reliving the nostalgia associated with those trips. Similarly, Kulczycki and Hyatt (2005) focused on the nostalgic feelings among Hartford Whalers hockey fans

ACTION

Go to the OSG and complete the Learning in Action activity, which has you identify different types of sport tourism.

The World Golf Hall of Fame: A Case Study in Nostalgia Sport Tourism

The World Golf Hall of Fame, part of the World Golf Village, is located 15 minutes from St. Augustine, Florida. Since it opened in 1998, more than one million visitors have walked through the 18 thematic areas that emulate an 18-hole golf course. Visitors go on a guided or self-guided tour through the history of golf from its beginnings in Scotland to its introduction and development in the United States to the technology now required to broadcast the top tournaments to viewers around the world. Each of the themed areas provides photos and narrative about historical developments in the game of golf. An 1880s-style putting green complete with replica putters of the time allows visitors to try their hand at sinking a shot without the aid of modern high-tech equipment. A video golf swing analysis enables visitors to match their technique to the top player whom they most resemble. Tourists can have their photos taken atop a replica of the Swilkern Bridge on the 18th hole at St. Andrews or feel the pressure of television cameras and a crowd in the viewing gallery as they try to sink the championship putt. Shell Hall contains 126 crystal spheres commemorating the men and women who have been inducted into the Hall of Fame. Along the opposite wall are computer terminals where visitors can spend hours accessing databases that document the careers of each of the 126 inductees. Before leaving, visitors can ascend the 190-foot (60 m) memorial tower, which offers a panoramic view of the World Golf Village, which includes shops, the Murray Bros. Caddyshack Restaurant, an IMAX theater, resort hotels, golf courses, and homes for golf enthusiasts. Finally, tourists can try their hand at the 18-hole putting course or the 132-yard challenge hole, which offers the opportunity to experience hitting a shot to the Island Green hole number 17 at the famed Tournament Players Club. Although the Hall of Fame certainly captivates the nostalgia sport tourist, the golf courses and the PGA Tour Golf Academy provide opportunities for active sport tourism as well. As a print advertisement for the World Golf Village says, "Built for those of you who think about golf morning, noon and night."

who traveled to watch NHL hockey games because their own team (the Whalers) had relocated to Raleigh, North Carolina.

SUSTAINABILITY AND SPORT TOURISM

Over the past five years the concept of sustainable development has become more commonplace. In general terms, sustainability takes the approach of balancing the needs of today with those of the future. Much of the focus has been placed on the environment and the conservation of natural resources. But the environment is only one prong of the three-pronged approach to sustainability, the other two being economics and social (cultural) well-being. The phrase "triple bottom line" is frequently used to describe the interrelationship among the three prongs of sustainability. In the tourism realm, the topic of sustainable development has been receiving a lot of attention in recent years (*From Davos to Bali*, 2007). Without paying attention to the long-term sustainability of a tourism destination, the effects of a large number of visitors can quickly destroy the attractiveness of a destination. In the realm of sport, less attention has been paid to sustainability, and we argue that it is time to start thinking about the long-term sustainability of sport, particularly for those sports that rely on certain climate conditions such as skiing or golf or those that can have negative effects on the environment or local communities, both socially and economically. Thus, as sport tourism continues to grow in popularity, we need to be aware of the potential negative and positive effects of this sector on the sport and tourism industries and to work on the sustainable development of this particular niche. We will now look at each of the three prongs of sustainable development in turn.

Social Dimensions

Tourism studies have produced abundant evidence that tourism can have both positive and negative effects on a host community. Some of the positive effects relate to economic benefit or community pride and excitement among residents (Garnham, 1996). This pride in community results in what Burgan and Mules (1992) called the **psychic income** associated with hosting an event. Tourism has also been shown to open societies to new ideas and even bring about a liberalization of values in more rigid or closed cultures (Dogan, 1989). Tourism may provide the funding and the impetus to preserve historic buildings, traditional practices (e.g., dances, crafts), and natural settings.

psychic income—The pride that people have in their community, generated by hosting a sport event.

In recent years, there has been a growing focus on the social benefits of event sport tourism for communities. Many believe that the social benefits are the true legacy of hosting a megaevent. Waitt's (2003) study of the social impacts of the 2000 Sydney Olympic Games found that despite protests and negative attitudes in the lead-up to the event, during the 16 days of the Games there was "a reason to celebrate rather than protest" (p. 200) and residents reported an increased sense of community. In a similar study of the 2002 FIFA World Cup in South Korea, Kim and Petrick (2005) found that although the fervor does seem to diminish after the event, it does not disappear totally.

Another social benefit of hosting sport events is the legacy of urban regeneration. Indeed, hosting the America's Cup in 1987 has been credited as being the catalyst for the renovation of the downtown area in Fremantle, Australia (Longley, 2001). Soutar and McLeod (1993) found that the fears about congestion and crowds were unfounded. Instead, residents thought that infrastructural improvements and potential for increased tourism would contribute to the increased quality of life in the years after the event.

Positive outcomes, however, may not always result from sport events. In a study of the potential costs associated with the 2000 Sydney Olympics, Hall and Hodges

(1996) found that a megaevent affected different segments of a host community unequally. Low-income residents often suffer the most because they are frequently displaced from their homes by plans to redevelop their neighborhoods with high-priced residences. This displacement of low-income residents has been a common practice in relation to the Olympic Games, as host cities face decisions over where to build stadia, athletes' villages, and so forth (Whitson & Macintosh, 1993). For more information on this topic, see the later section on ethics and the Vancouver 2010 Olympic Games.

Event sport tourism is not the only type of tourism to have an effect on a host community. The crowding and congestion experienced by small ski towns or golf resort areas such as Myrtle Beach, South Carolina, also need attention. In most tourism regions, host communities experience a love–hate relationship with tourists. On the one hand residents realize that their economic well-being often depends on tourists, yet the high prices, traffic congestion, and sometimes increased crime that accompany living in a tourist destination may lead to resistance and even hostility among community members (Dogan, 1989; Fredline, 2005). All these effects need to be carefully thought through in any proposed tourism development. But as many of us argue, emphasis is too frequently placed on the potential economic benefits. The voices of the community are often unheard, and the social legacies are often ignored. The sustainability of most events may lie in the social dimensions, particularly enhanced community spirit, increased patriotism, and even an experienced event volunteer labor force that has the skills necessary to help with future events hosted by the community.

Sport Volunteer Tourism: Traveling to Volunteer at Sporting Events

Because many sport events are not fixed to a particular location, volunteers must often travel some distance to the host venue. The travel requirement creates a sport tourism opportunity. An example of volunteer sport tourists are the members of the Sydney Olympic Volunteer (SOV) Social Club. The SOV Social Club was established as a Web-based community in September 2000. The stated purpose of the club was to "keep the [Olympic] spirit alive" and to coordinate a concerted effort to volunteer at future Olympic Games and other sporting events. The Web site initially served as the primary communication medium for club members. A discussion section was posted on the Web site to facilitate dialogue among people interested in volunteering at the 2004 Athens Olympic Games. The discussion section included information about volunteering in Athens, a link to the official Athens 2004 Web site, and a suggestion that interested people should meet regularly to learn about Greek culture and to organize the trip to Athens collectively.

To prepare for volunteering in Athens, the SOV Club met every three months at a Greek restaurant in Sydney. At these meetings they shared stories about their experiences at the 2000 Games; heard from guest speakers who were key to the Olympic subculture; learned about Greek culture through language, food, and trivia; and exchanged information about logistical issues associated with travel to the Athens Olympic Games. The main reasons people chose to travel to Athens to volunteer included nostalgia (i.e., wanting to relive volunteer experiences at the Sydney Olympic Games), camaraderie, being part of the Olympic subculture, and wanting to use the knowledge and skills that they had acquired while volunteering at the Sydney Olympic Games.

After arriving in Greece, group members used various means of accommodation, including staying with family or friends, participating in a Greek Homestay program (i.e., living with a local family in Athens), or staying in a community facility that had been converted into a discount accommodation venue for the Olympic Games. Although some club members chose to stay only for the duration of the megaevent, others extended their stay and explored other parts of Greece and Europe. After returning from Athens, the group changed its focus to the 2008 Olympic Games in Beijing, China, and subsequently met at a Chinese restaurant in the lead-up to the Beijing Olympic Games. After the closing of the 2008 Olympic Games, the focus shifted to the 2012 London Olympic Games.

Economic Dimensions

When community leaders attempt to raise money to build a new stadium, secure a professional franchise, or host a sport event, they often point to the projected economic benefits arising out of these projects. But research has shown, particularly in relation to professional sport, that as many as 70% of spectators come from within the metropolitan area (Crompton, 1995) and therefore are not event sport tourists according to any definition of a tourist. Thus, although using sport as a tourist attraction is a valuable strategy for economic and community development, we need to be sure when we read studies about the tourism-related impacts accruing from sport events that locals were not included in the people surveyed or the economic estimates generated.

We also need to be clear about how economic impact is measured. As Crompton (1995) explained, at least 11 common mistakes can occur when communities estimate economic impact, including using the wrong multiplier, measuring **time switchers** and **casuals,** and including people whose primary motivation was not to attend the event but who happened to be in the vicinity or switched the timing of their visit to coincide with the event. Another phenomenon that appears to be associated with hosting the megaevents is the **displacement effect.** Some potential visitors avoid a host city and region in the years leading up to, and during, the event, dissuaded by fear of congestion, construction-related hassles, and terrorism. Mules and Dwyer (2005) suggested that there is no accurate way to estimate how many visitors are displaced. But in conversations with various business owners, we have been told that "regular tourism" disappeared in Victoria, British Columbia, when the city hosted the 1994 Commonwealth Games. Similarly, in 2008, in the lead-up to the Beijing Olympic Games, hoteliers in the host city were already reporting a decline in the number of visitors compared with previous years. High prices, the difficulty of obtaining visas, and fears about terrorism were cited as reasons for the downturn in number of visitors (Steinmetz, 2008). This scenario is more common in the months leading up to most megaevents and exemplifies the displacement effect noted earlier, although since 2001 perceived risks associated with megaevents appear to have heightened the displacement effect (Neirotti & Hilliard, 2006).

time switchers—Visitors who had been planning to visit the destination and then switched their visit to coincide with the event; their spending cannot be attributed to the event.

casuals—People who happened to be visiting the destination and chose to attend the event instead of doing something else. Their attendance at the event was not their prime reason for visiting the destination.

displacement effect—The process whereby potential tourists are discouraged from visiting a destination because of perceptions of such hassles as crowding and construction or fear of terrorism.

Studies associated with the 2002 men's FIFA World Cup (Kim & Chalip, 2004; Toohey, Taylor, & Lee, 2003) have documented perceptions of risk associated with attending an event. As a result of the perceived risks involved, security costs associated with hosting an event have become a major part of an event budget. But in a study of the perceived risks associated with the 2008 Beijing Olympic Games, Qi, Gibson, and Zhang (2009) found that among their respondents there was less perceived risk associated with attending the Olympic Games than with visiting China as a regular tourist. Similarly, Taylor and Toohey (2006) found that attendees at the Rugby World Cup in Australia tended to downplay safety and security issues. Thus, the issue of perceived risk and event sport tourism needs more study. Refer to chapter 15 for more information about how strategies to manage security threats are a major part of contemporary event planning.

Nonetheless, the lure of the potential economic impacts associated with sport tourism will continue to grow as countries around the world rely more heavily on tourism to boost their gross national product. Members of the Cooperative Research Centre for Sustainable Tourism in Australia suggested from their studies of the 2000 Olympic Games that conducting a cost–benefit analysis may be more appropriate than emphasizing economic impact (Chalip & Green, 2001; Mules & Dwyer, 2005). Indeed, some of the preliminary lessons learned from hosting a hallmark event have been not to focus on the effects of an event but to use strategic leveraging to maximize the legacies and thus the sustainability of the event (Chalip, 2001).

Environmental Dimensions

As the popularity of sport vacations increases, we must consider the effects on the environment. Over the past 15 years, those in the tourism industry have begun to realize that the environment is the core of the tourism product. The growth in ecotourism has been one outcome of this environmental concern. More recently, however, there has been a push toward extending sustainable development practices to all segments of the tourism industry. This new focus includes adopting a more comprehensive approach to sustainability that not only includes the social and economic dimensions (as discussed earlier) but also recognizes that forces such as global climate change may in turn affect the long-term viability of some tourism activities such as snow sports and scuba diving (*From Davos to Bali*, 2007).

Take, for instance, scuba diving. The growing popularity of the sport and recreational activity has resulted in increasing pressure on the environment (Tabata, 1992). Pollution of the water, littering, anchor damage, trampling, and specimen collecting by divers can destroy the natural resource base. Moreover, from the perspective of global climate change, as temperatures increase, the health of the coral reefs is declining because of the increasing intensity and frequency of major storms, coral bleaching events, and other occurrences (Wilkinson, 1999). Hence, the long-term viability of many diving locations around the world is being questioned.

Controversies surrounding skiing provide another example. Tensions have grown between environmentalists and the alpine skiing industry in recent years. In Vermont environmentalists have raised an alarm over the amount of water being taken from rivers for snowmaking. In Colorado an activist group called the Ski Area Citizens' Coalition produces a scorecard that ranks resorts on their environmental friendliness so that skiers can choose to ski at mountains that employ sustainable practices (Janofsky, 2000; *Ski Area*, 2009). Yellowstone National Park has limited the use of snowmobiles because of the noise and air pollution that they cause and because conflicts have arisen between snowmobilers and cross-country skiers in the western part of the park.

Around the world, ski resort development is causing alarm among environmentalists (Hudson, 1996). As Buckley, Pickering, and Warnken (2000) explained, ski resorts are

Sport tourism and industry leaders are increasingly embracing sustainability practices. An example of this was the decision to install solar energy panels on the roof of this professional soccer facility (Schuco Arena) in Bielefeld, Germany.

Photo courtesy of Paul M. Pedersen.

among the most intensive forms of development in mountain regions, requiring tree clearing for ski runs and water for snowmaking and servicing the resorts. A longer season may reduce the economic effects of seasonality, but it leaves little time for grass and plant regeneration and relief from the noise and air pollution caused by the sheer number of people using the mountain roads to access the resorts. From the global climate change perspective, warmer winters and less snowfall may cause many of the lower-elevation ski resorts to close within 30 to 50 years (Connor, 2003; *From Davos to Bali*, 2007).

Some of the same concerns have been raised in relation to the golf industry (Palmer, 2004; Pleumarom, 1992). Golf courses are land intensive, and the use of chemicals on the greens and the use of water in desert areas have been of particular concern. Some golf courses have adopted strategies to protect the ecological balance of their courses with programs to protect wildlife sponsored by partnerships between the United States Golf Association and the Audubon Society, among others (*Audubon Cooperative*, 2010). More needs to be done in this area, particularly in the lesser-developed countries where national governments have identified golf tourism as a source of much-needed foreign currency while ignoring the severe socioeconomic and environmental consequences that golf courses have for their citizens (Palmer, 2004). On a more positive note, Scott and Jones (2007) noted that some golf courses could benefit from global warming. With less snow and cold weather some golf courses may have longer playing seasons.

The IOC has charged host countries with implementing environmentally friendly practices in relation to the Olympic Games. The 1994 Winter Olympic Games in Lillehammer were called the first Green Games (Chernushenko, 1996). The Norwegian Parliament mandated Project Environment Friendly Olympics to protect the fragile ecology surrounding the small host city. Chernushenko argued that the Lillehammer Olympic Games provided a good example of event sport tourism and environmentalism that future events could copy to produce not only a better event but also satisfied tourists and a reputation as a clean and attractive destination.

Although the Sydney Olympic Games were also called the Green Games, Sparvero, Trendafilova, and Chalip (2005) contended that Sydney did not keep all its promises, citing the failure to detoxify Homebush Bay, where the main Olympics complex was located. The scholars questioned the traditional approach of using environmental guidelines mandated by sport governing bodies. They suggested that consensus-building approaches in which the local organizing committees and host communities are integrally involved in establishing environmental policies and practices for their events might be more successful.

CRITICAL THINKING IN SPORT TOURISM

PORTFOLIO

Complete the critical thinking portfolio activity in the OSG, consulting as needed the "Eight Critical Thinking Questions" section in chapter 1.

Certainly, there is evidence of a growing realization of the need for sustainable development in tourism of all kinds. The question becomes this: How do we balance the growing popularity of tourism in general and sport tourism in particular, along with the potential for greater economic profitability, with the need to protect the natural and sociocultural environments? A unified policy between sport and tourism agencies might be one way of balancing sustainability with profitability, in line with the three-pronged approach to sustainability.

ETHICS IN SPORT TOURISM

Winning a bid to host a megaevent takes a lot of time, energy, and money. As noted earlier, megaevents can bring many benefits to the host communities. For example,

Vancouver raised its global profile considerably after hosting the 1986 World's Fair, Expo 86, and was looking for another event. When the Vancouver–Whistler, British Columbia, sites were awarded the 2010 Winter Olympic and Paralympic Games, much celebration and excitement ensued.

But not everyone was pleased. Even before being awarded the Winter Olympic Games, there was controversy about how much it was going to cost to host the event and how that money could have been better spent on improving health care for residents of the province. Protests against seeking the Olympic bid were vocal, strong, and creative. For instance, the protests included a "Health Care Before Olympics" bumper sticker campaign and satire in the form of a logo contest using that slogan, the winner of which was used to sell T-shirts (*Local Artist's Graphic*, 2009). A plebiscite was held for Vancouver and Whistler residents to determine whether they wanted the Olympic Games. When 64% said yes, they did want the Olympic Games, the bid went ahead and was ultimately successful. Government funding for the 2010 Winter Olympic Games came from federal, provincial, and municipal sources. A question to consider here is whether it is ethical to ask members of the host city about hosting the Olympic Games without asking residents of the entire province, who will share the debt load and the impacts of more visitors.

Canada may be a little hesitant about hosting mega sport events because in the past cost overruns from infrastructure construction led to a debt load carried by locals for decades. For example, Montreal's 1976 Olympic Stadium was finally fully paid for in 2006, 30 years after the city hosted the Summer Olympic Games (*Montreal's Olympic Stadium*, 2006). Construction for the 2010 Olympic village ran over budget by $45 million (CAN) and now the city is having a hard time filling the apartments (Cernetig, 2010). With any large project seeking use of vast amounts of money, opinions will differ about appropriate ways of doing business. Mega sport events are no exception and probably have more than their fair share of ethical issues.

Heather L. Bell from the University of Florida wrote this section on ethics.

PORTFOLIO

Complete the ethical issues portfolio activity in the OSG, consulting as needed the "Guidelines for Making Ethical Decisions" section in chapter 1.

Summary

You should now have a good overview of sport tourism in terms of both academic knowledge and some practices around the world. We started the chapter by analyzing the sport and tourism connection. The focus was on understanding tourism and the tourism industry. Tourism, the world's largest industry, is composed of many segments, including transportation; accommodation; attractions; and the government and nongovernmental agencies responsible for planning, setting policy, and marketing. A tourist is defined in this chapter as a leisure traveler. Sport tourism is defined as travel to participate in sport (active sport tourism), to watch sport (event sport tourism), or to venerate (e.g., honor, revere) something or somebody associated with a sport (nostalgia sport tourism).

In reviewing the three types of sport tourism, we discussed some possible explanations for the increasing popularity of active sport tourism over the past 15 years or so. Some of this popularity may be related to increased awareness of the benefits of an active lifestyle coupled with increased opportunities to take part in sport on vacation at resorts, on cruises, and at amateur sport events. We examined golf and skiing as the most popular types of active sport tourism. Golf is increasing in popularity as the population ages, whereas the alpine skiing industry has experienced some difficulties in sustaining its market share. All sectors of event sport tourism, on the other hand, are increasing in popularity. Cities around the world compete vigorously to host megaevents such as the Olympic Games and the World Cup. But communities around the United States and Canada are coming to realize that small-scale sport tourism events may be more manageable and beneficial than megaevents. As a result, many communities now have sports commissions whose task is to attract sport events to their towns or cities. Sports commissions, coupled with convention and visitors bureaus, are helping many towns and cities throughout North America develop sport tourism. The third type of sport tourism we discussed, nostalgia sport tourism, is the least well developed in terms of research and attention from tourism professionals. Nonetheless, in the United States and around the world, sport halls of fame, museums, and sport-themed events are becoming more popular. Even the cruise industry has developed a niche in the nostalgia sport tourism realm by offering cruises with various sport personalities.

Besides providing sections on critical thinking and ethical considerations, we ended the chapter by addressing the issue of sustainable development as it relates to sport tourism. We adopted the three-pronged approach to sustainability and looked at the social, economic, and environmental dimensions of sustainability. We concluded with the idea that all three dimensions are interrelated and must be addressed to ensure not only the sustainability of sport tourism but also the overall sustainable development of communities. As communities around the world examine strategies for economic development, we need to urge governments and community leaders to think about the long-term effects of their decisions. One way of doing this is to pay attention to the triple bottom line of sustainable development. The economic impacts of sport and tourism always garner much attention. Closer cooperation between sport and tourism agencies at all levels may be one way of reaping both the economic benefits and the social benefits of sport tourism while decreasing the negative impacts on the physical and social environment.

QUIZ TIME

Did you grasp all the key points in this chapter? Go to the OSG for a short quiz to test your understanding of the material.

Review Questions

1. What are the major dimensions of sport tourism and the sport tourism industry?
2. If sport tourism is leisure-based travel, is a professional athlete a sport tourist? Why or why not?
3. Why has golf tourism continued to grow, whereas winter sport tourism has been uneven in its growth?
4. What strategies might you suggest to your community to leverage the tourism associated with college sports?
5. What are the arguments for and against a city's hosting of the Olympic Games?
6. Why has nostalgia sport tourism become popular in recent years?
7. How might we implement a sustainable development approach to future sport tourism ventures?
8. In what ways do you think sport tourism will grow over the next 10 years?
9. What sorts of career opportunities are available in sport tourism for sport management majors?
10. Do we need to offer a separate degree in sport tourism at the university level? If your answer is yes, explain why a specialist sport tourism degree would be beneficial. If your answer is no, suggest how we might better prepare students for a career in sport tourism from within existing degree programs.

References

ABC. (2002, February 10). *ABC evening news*. Report on Nagano, Japan.

Alm, R. (2001, October 5). Area tourism industry hopes for a big score from Texas–OU game. *Dallas Morning News*, p. D1.

Audubon Cooperative Sanctuary Program for Golf Courses. (2010). Retrieved February 1, 2010, from http://acspgolf.auduboninternational.org/

Buckley, R., Pickering, C., & Warnken, J. (2000). Environmental management for alpine tourism and resorts in Australia. In P. Godde, M. Price, & F. Zimmermann (Eds.), *Tourism and development in mountain regions* (pp. 27–45). Wallingford, UK: CAB International.

Burgan, B., & Mules, T. (1992). Economic impact of sporting events. *Annals of Tourism Research, 19*, 700–710.

Cernetig, M. (2010). Time for the city to make a tough decision: Rent the Olympic village at market rates. *Vancouver Sun*, Apr 12, 2010. Retrieved from www.vancouversun.com/sports/Vancouver+2010+Olympic+costs+million/2911884/Time+city+make+tough+decision+Rent+Olympic+village+market+rates/2791270/story.html

Chalip, L. (2001, February). *Leveraging the Sydney Olympics to optimize tourism benefits*. Paper presented at the International Conference on the Economic Impact of Sports, Athens, Greece.

Chalip, L. (2004). Beyond economic impact: A general model for sport event leverage. In B. Ritchie & D. Adair (Eds.), *Sport tourism: Interrelationships, impacts and issues* (pp. 226–252). Clevedon, UK: Channel View.

Chalip, L., & Green, B.C. (2001, June). Leveraging large sports events for tourism: Lessons learned from the Sydney Olympics. *Supplemental Proceedings of the Travel and Tourism Research Association 32nd Annual Conference*, Fort Myers, FL.

Chernushenko, D. (1996). Sports tourism goes sustainable: The Lillehammer experience. *Visions in Leisure and Business, 15*, 65–73.

Coakley, J.J. (2009). *Sport in society: Issues and controversies* (10th ed.). Boston: McGraw-Hill.

Cohen, E. (1974). Who is a tourist? A conceptual clarification. *Sociological Review, 22*, 527–555.

Connor, S. (2003, December 3). Global warming to kill off Europe's top ski resorts, says UN. *The Independent*. Retrieved April 30, 2009, from http://findarticles.com/p/articles/mi_qn4158/is_20031203/ai_n12723340/

Crompton, J. (1995). Economic impact analysis of sports facilities and events: Eleven sources of misapplication. *Journal of Sport Management, 9*, 14–35.

De Knop, P. (1987). Some thoughts on the influence of sport tourism. In *Proceedings of the International Seminar and Workshop on Outdoor Education, Recreation and Sport Tourism* (pp. 38–45). Netanya, Israel: Wingate Institute for Physical Education and Sport.

Dogan, H. (1989). Forms of adjustment: Socio-cultural impacts of tourism. *Annals of Tourism Research, 16*, 216–236.

Ebisch, R. (2005, July). Cool mountains: You want peak experiences? We'll give you peak experiences! *Sky Delta Airlines Inflight Magazine*, pp. 42–51.

Essex, S., & Chalkley, B. (1998). Olympic Games: Catalyst of urban change. *Leisure Studies, 17*, 187–206.

Fairley, S., (2003). In search of relived social experience: Group-based nostalgia sport tourism. *Journal of Sport Management, 17*, 284–304.

Finney, P.B. (2007, August 21). Golf a hit on cruise ships. *The New York Times*. Retrieved February 1, 2010, from http://travel.nytimes.com/2007/08/21/business/21golf.html?fta=y

Fisher, J. (2001). *The Gator Shop: In-person interview*. Unpublished manuscript, University of Florida, Gainesville.

Fluker, M.R., & Turner, L.W. (2000). Needs, motivations, and expectations of a commercial whitewater rafting experience. *Journal of Travel Research, 38*, 380–389.

Fredline, E. (2005). Host and guest relations and sport tourism. *Sport in Society, 8*, 263–279.

From Davos to Bali: A tourism contribution to the challenge of climate change. (2007). World Tourism Organization. Retrieved February 1, 2010, from www.unwto.org/climate/current/en/pdf/CC_Broch_DavBal_memb_bg.pdf

Gammon, S. (2002). Fantasy, nostalgia and the pursuit of what never was—but what should have been. In S. Gammon & J. Kurtzman (Eds.), *Sport tourism: Principles and practice* (pp. 61–71). Eastbourne, UK: Leisure Studies Association.

Garnham, B. (1996). Ranfurly Shield Rugby: An investigation into the impacts of a sporting event on a provincial city, the case of New Plymouth, Taranaki, New Zealand. *Festival Management and Event Tourism, 4*, 145–149.

Gibson, H. (1998a). Active sport tourism: Who participates? *Leisure Studies, 17*, 155–170.

Gibson, H. (1998b). Sport tourism: A critical analysis of research. *Sport Management Review, 1*, 45–76.

Gleeson, M. (2008, November 24). Soccer-FIFA worried economic downturn will affect World Cup fans. *Reuters UK*. Retrieved February 1, 2010, from http://uk.reuters.com/article/worldFootballNews/idUKLO70144620081124

Goeldner, C., & Ritchie, J.R. Brent. (2009). *Tourism: Practices, principles, philosophies*. New York: Wiley.

Green, B.C., Costa, C., & Fitzgerald, M. (2003). Marketing the host city: Analyzing exposure generated by a sport event. *International Journal of Sports Marketing & Sponsorship, 4*, 335–353.

Hall, C., & Hodges, J. (1996). The party's great, but what about the hangover? The housing and social impacts of mega-events with special reference to the 2000 Sydney Olympics. *Festival Management and Event Tourism, 4*, 13–20.

Higham, J. (1999). Commentary—sport as an avenue of tourism development: An analysis of the positive and negative impacts of sport tourism. *Current Issues in Tourism, 2*, 82–90.

Hudson, S. (1996). The greening of ski resorts: A necessity for sustainable tourism or a marketing opportunity for skiing communities? *Journal of Vacation Marketing, 2*, 176–185.

Irwin, R., & Sandler, M. (1998). An analysis of travel behavior and event-induced expenditures among American collegiate championship patron groups. *Journal of Vacation Marketing, 4*, 78–90.

Jago, L., & Shaw, R. (1998). Special events: A conceptual and definitional framework. *Festival Management and Event Journal, 5*, 21–32.

Janofsky, M. (2000, December 3). Environmental groups' ratings rile ski industry. *New York Times*, p. 30.

Kellett, P., & Hede, A.M. (2008). Developing a sport museum: The case of Tennis Australia and the Tennis Heritage Collection. *Sport Management Review, 11*, 93–98.

Kim, N., & Chalip, L. (2004). Why travel to the FIFA World Cup? Effects of motives, background, interest, and constraints. *Tourism Management, 25*, 695–707.

Kim, S., & Morrison, A. (2005). Change of image of South Korea among foreign tourists after the 2002 FIFA World Cup. *Tourism Management, 26*, 233–247.

Kim, S., & Petrick, J. (2005). Residents' perceptions on impacts of the FIFA 2002 World Cup: The case of Seoul as a host city. *Tourism Management, 26*, 25–38.

Kulczycki, C., & Hyatt, C. (2005). Expanding the conceptualization of nostalgia sport tourism: Lessons learned from fans left behind after sport franchise relocation. *Journal of Sport & Tourism, 10*, 273–293.

Local artist's graphic "statements" about 2010 Olympics. (2009, January 27). Retrieved February 1, 2010, from www.no2010.com/node/715

Longley, J. (2001, July 2). *Opening session*. ANZALS Conference, Fremantle, Australia.

Mintel. (2006). *Sports and adventure travel–US–November 2006*. Retrieved May 1, 2009, from http://academic.mintel.com/sinatra/oxygen/display/id=168019

Montreal's Olympic Stadium finally paid off. (2006, December 19). Retrieved May 1, 2009, from www.ctv.ca/servlet/ArticleNews/story/CTVNews/20061219/oly_stadium_061219/20061219?hub=Canada

Mules, T., & Dwyer, L. (2005). Public sector support for sport tourism events: The role of cost-benefit analysis. *Sport in Society*, *8*, 338–355.

National Golf Foundation. (2009). *Frequently asked questions*. Retrieved May 1, 2009, from www.ngf.org

National Senior Games Association. (2010). *History of NSGA*. Retrieved February 1, 2010, from www.nsga.com/DesktopDefault.aspx?tabname=&sidebarname=History%20of%20NSGA&Params=454b04071756557a401a0c0b7b625a000000037f

Neirotti, L., & Hilliard, T. (2006). Impact of Olympic spectator safety perception and security concerns on travel decisions. *Tourism Review International*, *10*, 269–284.

Nogawa, H., Yamguchi, Y., & Hagi, Y. (1996). An empirical research study on Japanese sport tourism in Sport-for-All Events: Case studies of a single-night event and a multiple-night event. *Journal of Travel Research*, *35*, 46–54.

Olympics could breathe life into London economy. (2005, July 6). *USA Today*. Retrieved February 1, 2010, from www.usatoday.com/money/economy/2005-07-06-olympics-benefits-london_x.htm

Palmer, C. (2004). More than just a game: The consequences of golf tourism. In B. Ritchie & D. Adair (Eds.), *Sport tourism: Interrelationships, impacts and issues* (pp.117–134). Clevedon, UK: Channel View.

Pleumarom, A. (1992). Course and effect: Golf tourism in Thailand. *The Ecologist*, *22*, 104–110.

Preuss, H. (2007). FIFA World Cup 2006 and its legacy on tourism. In R. Conrady & M. Buck (Eds.), *Trends and issues in global tourism 2007* (pp. 83–102). Berlin: Springer.

Qi, C., Gibson, H., & Zhang, J. (2009). Perceptions of risk and travel intentions: The case of China and the Beijing Olympic Games. *Journal of Sport & Tourism*, *14*, 43–67.

Redmond, G. (1973). A plethora of shrines: Sport in the museum and hall of fame. *Quest*, *19*, 41–48.

Redmond, G. (1991). Changing styles of sports tourism: Industry/consumer interactions in Canada, the USA, and Europe. In M.T. Sinclair & M.J. Stabler (Eds.), *The tourism industry: An international analysis* (pp. 107–120). Wallingford, UK: CAB International.

Ritchie, J.R. Brent. (1984). Assessing the impact of hallmark events: Conceptual and research issues. *Journal of Travel Research*, *23*, 2–11.

Ritchie, J.R. Brent. (1999). Lessons learned, lessons learning: Insights from the Calgary and Salt Lake Olympic Winter Games. *Visions in Leisure and Business*, *18*, 4–13.

Ritchie, J.R. Brent, & Smith, B. (1991). The impact of a mega-event on host region awareness: A longitudinal study. *Journal of Travel Research*, *30*, 3–10.

Roberts, K. (2006). *Leisure in contemporary society*. Wallingford, UK: CABI.

Roche, M. (1994). Mega-events and urban policy. *Annals of Tourism Research*, *21*, 1–19.

Scott, D., & Jones, B. (2007). A regional comparison of the implications of climate change for the golf industry in Canada. *Canadian Geographer*, *51*(2), 219–232.

Ski Area Environmental Report Card 2009/2010. (2009, November 23). Retrieved February 1, 2010, from www.skiareacitizens.com/

Soutar, G., & McLeod, P. (1993). Residents' perceptions on impact of the America's Cup. *Annals of Tourism Research*, *20*, 571–582.

Sparvero, E., Trendafilova, S., & Chalip, L. (2005, June). *An alternative approach to environmental dispute resolution in sport contexts*. Poster presented at the North American Society for Sport Management Conference, Regina, Saskatchewan, Canada.

Standeven, J. (1998). Sport tourism: Joint marketing—A starting point for beneficial synergies. *Journal of Vacation Marketing*, *4*, 39–51.

Standeven, J., & De Knop, P. (1999). *Sport tourism*. Champaign, IL: Human Kinetics.

Steinmetz, T. (2008, July 7). *Hosting Olympics can damage tourism*. Retrieved February 1, 2010, from www.eturbonews.com/print/3530

Steinmetz, T. (2009, January 13). *Beijing stadium fights "tourist trap" status*. Retrieved April 30, 2009, from www.eturbonews.com/print/7185

Streets, D., Fu, J., Jang, C., Hae, J., & He, K. (2007). Air quality during the 2008 Beijing Olympic Games. *Atmospheric Environment*, *41*(3), 480–492.

Tabata, R. (1992). Scuba diving holidays. In B. Weiler & C. Hall (Eds.), *Special interest tourism* (pp. 171–184). London: Belhaven Press.

Taylor, T., & Toohey, K. (2006). Impacts of terrorism-related safety and security measures at a major sport event. *Event Management*, *9*, 199–209.

Toohey, K., Taylor, T., & Lee, C. (2003). The FIFA World Cup 2002: The effects of terrorism on sport tourists. *Journal of Sport Tourism*, *8*, 167–185.

Travel Industry Association of America. (1999). *Profiles of travelers who attend sports events*. Washington, DC: Author.

Upcoming camps. (2009). Retrieved July 25, 2009, from www.basketballfantasycamps.com/

US Travel Data Center. (1989). *Discover America 2000: The implications of America's changing demographics and attitudes on the US travel industry*. Washington, DC: Author.

Waitt, G. (2003). Social impacts of the Sydney Olympics. *Annals of Tourism Research*, *30*, 194–215.

Whitson, D., & Macintosh, D. (1993). Becoming a world class city: Hallmark events and sport franchises in the growth strategies of western Canadian cities. *Sociology of Sport Journal*, *10*, 221–240.

Wilkinson, C. (1999). Global and local threats so coral reef functioning and existence: Review and predictions. *Marine and Freshwater Research*, *50*, 867–878.

Wood, S. (2001, November 4). Fort Worth, Texas, area aims for smaller sporting events after losing the Olympics. *Fort Worth Star-Telegram*. Retrieved February 1, 2010, from www.accessmylibrary.com/coms2/summary_0286-7829916_ITM

World Cup soccer games finally come to America. (1993, May 17). *Business America*, pp. 2–6.

World Tourism Organization. (1994). *Recommendations on tourism statistics*. Madrid, Spain: Author.

Zachary, J. (1997, March). *Assembling the most attractive sport tourism packages*. Panel session at Teaming for Success: A Forum on Sport Tourism, Arlington, VA.

PART III

SELECTED SPORT MANAGEMENT FUNCTIONS

The four chapters in this section present valuable information about sport marketing and promotion; communication, public relations, and community relations; finance and economics; and facility and event management. These functions are universal in sport in that they are performed at most sport-related sites, including those discussed in the previous section—professional sport, intercollegiate athletics, interscholastic athletics, youth and community sport, sport management and marketing agencies, and sport tourism.

In chapter 12 Wayne Blann and Ketra Armstrong define sport marketing and explain the unique aspects of this key sport management function. Next, the authors present the elements of the marketing mix and show how a marketing plan addresses those elements. They discuss the elements of a SWOT analysis and explain how to use it to assess present and future market climates. Blann and Armstrong then present information on the various dimensions of sport products and events, define product positioning and market niches, and explain the communication of product images. They also cover branding, market segmentation, pricing and promotion strategies, distribution channels, and the packaging and selling of sport products. The theme of socially responsible sport marketing runs throughout the chapter. In the international sidebar, Sungho Cho examines the sport sponsorship activities and partnerships of Samsung Electronics, the consumer electronics company based in South Korea. Cho, a native of Korea, teaches sport management at Bowling Green State University.

Clay Stoldt, Steve Dittmore, and Paul Pedersen address the broad segment of sport communication in chapter 13. After presenting basic and definitional information about communication in the sport industry, the authors explain the concepts (i.e., genres, context, process, elements, and effects) upon which the theoretical framework of sport communication is established. The remainder of the chapter involves an in-depth examination of the strategic sport communication model (SSCM). Within this model are three major components: personal and organizational communication, mass media, and sport communication services and support. Stoldt, Dittmore, and Pedersen explain each of these components in detail, but they pay particular attention to that last component because it contains the areas of sport public relations, media relations, and community relations. Finally, they discuss careers in media relations and community relations by delineating the responsibilities involved and the skills needed for each. Matthew Goltz—a staff writer, translator, and content editor for Realmadrid.com—contributed the international sidebar for this chapter. Goltz describes the financial and customer relationship benefits that have been realized through Real Madrid's focused and proactive facilitation of its popular Web site.

In chapter 14 Tim DeSchriver and Dan Mahony introduce basic information about finance and economics within the sport industry. After explaining the size and scope of the sport industry in economic terms, the authors describe the current financial situation of the US professional and intercollegiate segments of the sport industry. They then present principles of the economics of sport. A discussion of microeconomics follows, addressing supply and demand and the economic impact of sport. Next, DeSchriver and Mahony further explain the business structure of sport organizations and introduce basic tools of financial management. They conclude the chapter with advice for students who aspire to careers in financial management of sport organizations. The international sidebar contains an essay on the financial aspects of professional rugby in Wales. John Harris, a native of Wales who teaches the sociology and administration of sport at Kent State University, contributed the essay.

Rob Ammon and David Stotlar address sport facility and event management in chapter 15. First, the authors note the current state of sport facility construction and the impact that the current economic climate has had on this segment of the sport industry. Ammon and Stotlar then differentiate among several types of facilities and explain the current trend toward the privatization of facilities. A discussion of ways in which sport managers can minimize risks associated with facilities and events follows. The final sections of the chapter provide in-depth information on facility management personnel and responsibilities as well as examples of event personnel assignments. Real-life scenarios illustrate the importance of proper planning for sporting events. In the international sidebar, Babs Surujlal, who teaches sport management at Vaal University of Technology in South Africa, examines stadium disasters and the need for a sound risk management plan at sporting events in South Africa.

For More Information

Professional and Scholarly Associations

Academy of Marketing Science: www.ams-web.org/

The American Communication Association: www.americancomm.org/

American Marketing Association: www.marketingpower.com/Pages/default.aspx

American Sports Data, Inc.: www.americansportsdata.com

Associated Press Sports Editors: apsportseditors.org/

Association for Education in Journalism and Mass Communication: www.aejmc.org/

Association for Women in Sports Media: www.awsmonline.org/

College Sports Information Directors of America (CoSIDA): www.cosida.com

Direct Marketing Association: www.the-dma.org/index.php

Female Athletic Media Relations Executives (FAME): www.personal.psu.edu/staff/m/j/mjh11/FAME/index2MJ.html

Football Writers Association of America: www.footballwriters.com

International Association of Assembly Managers: www.iaam.org/

International Association of Business Communicators: www.iabc.com

International Facility Management Association: www.ifma.org

International Licensing Industry Merchandisers' Association (LIMA): www.licensing.org/

National Association of Collegiate Directors of Athletics (NACDA): nacda.cstv.com/

National College Baseball Writers Association: www.sportswriters.net/ncbwa/

National Recreation and Park Association: www.nrpa.org/

Public Relations Society of America: www.prsa.org

Society of Professional Journalists: www.spj.org/

Sport Marketing Association (SMA): www.sportmarketingassociation.com/

United States Basketball Writers Association: www.usbwa.com

Professional and Scholarly Publications

Advertising Age

American Journalism Review

Athletic Business

Business Journalist

CoSIDA Digest

Editor & Publisher

ESPN The Magazine

Facility Manager

International Journal of Sport Communication

International Journal of Sport Finance

International Journal of Sports Marketing and Sponsorship

Journal of Communication Management

Journal of Marketing

Journal of Marketing Research

Journal of Public Relations Research

Journal of Quantitative Analysis in Sports

Journal of Sponsorship

Journal of Sports Economics

Journal of Sports Media

Journal of Venue & Event Management

Marketing Communications

PR Week

Psychology and Marketing

Public Relations Strategist

Special Events Report

Sponsors Report

Sport Marketing Quarterly

Sporting News Magazine
Sports Market Place
Team Marketing Report Newsletter

Additional Internet Resources

Crowd Safety: www.crowdsafe.com/reports.html
Investigative Reporters and Editors: www.ire.org/
Migala Report: www.migalareport.com/
National Sports Forum: www.sports-forum.com/
National Sports Journalism Center: sportsjournalism.org/
Poynter Institute for Media Studies: www.poynter.org/

HISTORICAL MOMENTS

1877	Pittsburgh team accused of "pirating" Louis Bierbauer from Philadelphia A's so the team adopted a new name—Pirates
1928	Coca-Cola began marketing partnership with the Olympic Games
1934	Lou Gehrig became first athlete to appear on a Wheaties box
1949	Babe Didrikson Zaharias landed first major endorsement deal for a female athlete
1951	Eddie Gaedel, at 3 feet, 7 inches (110 cm), pinch hit for St. Louis Browns
1960	CBS paid US$50,000 for the rights to televise the Winter Olympic Games in Squaw Valley, California
1964	Blue Ribbon Sports founded; renamed Nike in 1972
1973	Battle of the Sexes: Billie Jean King defeated Bobby Riggs in tennis
1974	Ali defeated Foreman in the Rumble in the Jungle
1979	Mike Veeck put on Disco Demolition Derby Night during Chicago White Sox doubleheader
1989	NBA initiated global marketing campaign
1993	"Got Milk?" ad campaign launched
1997	MasterCard MLB "Priceless" campaign launched
2004	Social networking site Facebook launched
2008	NBA China formed
2010	Sun Life Stadium hosted the New Orleans Saints and Indianapolis Colts in Super Bowl XLIV

Photo courtesy of Paul M. Pedersen.

12

SPORT MARKETING

F. Wayne Blann ■ Ketra L. Armstrong

LEARNING OBJECTIVES

1. Recognize how a marketing plan is linked to a sport organization's mission statement and core values.
2. Assess the present and future market climate for a sport or event by conducting a SWOT analysis.
3. Analyze the dimensions of a sport product.
4. Describe the process of positioning a product to appeal to specific groups of consumers.
5. Define market segmentation and identify viable target audiences.
6. Discuss how sports are distributed to consumers.
7. Define packaging and selling a sport product.
8. Evaluate the effectiveness of a sport marketing plan.
9. Apply ethical guidelines and critical thinking skills to challenges confronting sport marketers in the second decade of the 21st century.

GET A JOB!

☑ Continue your journey in sport management by going to the Online Study Guide (OSG) at www.HumanKinetics.com/ContemporarySportManagement. Check out the job opportunities and consider the skills and experiences that can help you succeed in sport management.

Key Terms

branding
external factors
internal factors
lifestyle marketing
marketing mix
marketing plans
place
sport marketing
sport sponsorship
SWOT analysis

Marketing is a complex function that is extremely important to the overall success of sport organizations. You probably have heard the term *sport marketing* in many contexts, and you might be wondering exactly what it means. Some corporate executives might describe sport marketing as selling goods and services to generate a profit. But sport marketing is more than selling. People who work in advertising and public relations might consider sport marketing as obtaining Super Bowl XLVI tickets for clients or entertaining a corporate sponsor at the 2011 US Open Golf Championship at the Congressional Country Club in Maryland. But sport marketing is more than advertising and public relations. Those who provide services for professional athletes might view sport marketing as arranging for athletes to attend the grand opening of a shopping mall or arranging to have corporate executives play tennis with Rafael Nadal or Serena Williams. But sport marketing is more than community relations.

sport marketing—The process of designing and implementing activities for the production, pricing, promotion, and distribution of a sport product or sport business product to satisfy the needs or desires of consumers and to achieve the company's objectives (Pitts & Stotlar, 2007, p. 69).

Pitts and Stotlar (2007) defined **sport marketing** as "the process of designing and implementing activities for the production, pricing, promotion, and distribution of a sport product or sport business product to satisfy the needs or desires of consumers and to achieve the company's objectives" (p. 69). Balancing a company's business objectives with consumer wants and needs is a challenge in any industry, but sport marketing is particularly complex because sport has certain characteristics that make it unique. A brief examination of sport's unique combination of characteristics proposed by Mullin, Hardy, and Sutton (2007) will show how sport differs from other products, goods, and services and therefore why the approach to marketing sport is unique.

- Aspects of sport are intangible. For example, you cannot touch the actual competition that takes place between two football teams.
- Sport involves emotions. Some spectators become emotionally attached to their teams and are referred to as fanatics or fans. Other consumers might buy licensed products with team logos and uniform replicas as a way of identifying with their teams. Consumers do not often display such heightened emotions or psychological attachment to other goods or products, such as vacuum cleaners.
- Sport is subjective and heterogeneous because the impressions, experiences, and interpretations about the sport experience may vary from person to person. Because sport marketers cannot easily predict the impressions, experiences, and interpretations that consumers will have about the sport consumption experience, it is often challenging to ensure that consumers will have satisfying sport experiences.
- Sports are inconsistent and unpredictable for a variety of reasons. A few of the many factors that influence the sport experience include injuries to players, the emotional state of athletes, team momentum, and the weather.
- Sport is perishable because the sport experience is simultaneously produced and consumed. For example, as the athletes are competing (i.e., producing the action and experience), the spectators are watching the competition (i.e., consuming the action and experience). Based on the perishability of sport competitions, sport marketers often offer tangible items (e.g., T-shirts, souvenirs) that serve as lasting reminders of the perishable sport experience.

Sport's unique combination of characteristics provides marketers with some interesting challenges and opportunities. Given these characteristics, what factors should we consider in making decisions about packaging, promoting, and delivering sport? Who will be attracted to certain sport events, and how will the packaging, promoting, and delivering of the event influence the consumers' perceptions, desires, and experiences? What changes will we need to make in the packaging, promoting, and delivering of sport in the future? This chapter addresses these questions.

DEVELOPING A SPORT MARKETING PLAN

Marketing plans serve as road maps or game plans for an organization's marketing activities. Having a well-developed marketing plan is essential to the marketing success of sport organizations. The four primary elements of a marketing plan—product, price, place, and promotion—make up the **marketing mix.** These elements are well established in the marketing industry and are universally known as the *four Ps.*

marketing plans—Comprehensive strategic frameworks for identifying and achieving a sport organization's marketing goals and objectives.

marketing mix—The elements of product, price, place, and promotion, which sport marketers manipulate to achieve marketing goals and objectives.

- Product—a tangible good (object), a service, or an intangible quality that satisfies consumers' wants or needs
- Price—the value of the product and the costs that the consumer must accept to obtain the product
- Place—the distribution channels that allow consumers to access or obtain the product
- Promotion—the integrated communication and public relations activities that communicate, inform, persuade, and motivate consumers to purchase the product

To maximize their success, sport marketers develop strategic plans to manipulate the four Ps in a variety of ways depending on the mission of the organization and the fluctuations of the market (Pitts & Stotlar, 2007). This manipulation is critical to carrying out a successful marketing plan. But to devise a comprehensive plan for achieving marketing goals and objectives, sport marketers must consider factors beyond the four Ps. In this chapter we present a 10-step process for developing a sport marketing plan. This process consists of the 10 Ps—purpose, product, projecting the market, position, players, package, price, promotion, place, and promise. This process, shown in figure 12.1, illustrates that although the four Ps are central to the marketing plan, they must be integrated with other elements to achieve optimal sport marketing success.

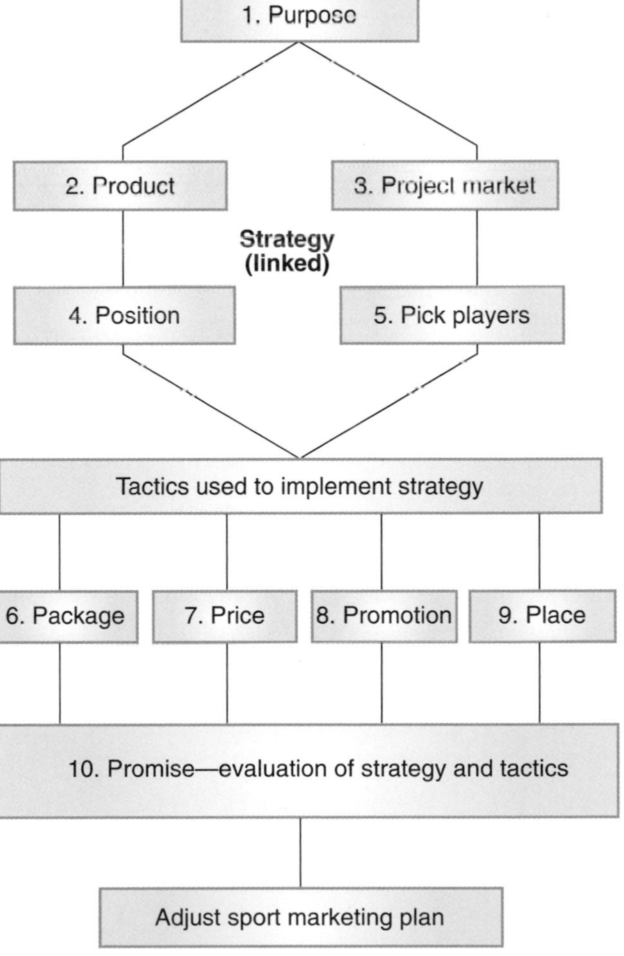

Figure 12.1 Steps in developing a sport marketing plan.

Adapted, by permission, from B.G. Pitts and D.K. Stotlar, 2002, Sport marketing theory. In *Fundamentals of sport marketing*, 2nd ed. (Morgantown, WV: Fitness Information Technology, Inc.), p.87. © Fitness Information Technology & West Virginia University.

Step 1: Identify the Purpose of the Sport Marketing Plan

The first step in the process involves clarifying the purpose of the sport marketing plan and linking the plan to the organization's mission and core values. Before packaging, promoting, and delivering can occur, sport marketers must establish a context to provide a direction for what they are trying to accomplish and how they expect to do so. "An organizational mission statement is important because it creates in people's hearts and minds a frame of reference, a set of criteria or guidelines by which they will govern themselves," noted Covey (1989). "They have bought into the changeless core of what the organization is about" (p. 143). Every sport organization exists for a purpose. The organization defines this purpose in its mission statement. The mission statement of a sport organization must reflect the values and beliefs that are prevalent in the environments in which it operates. The mission statement answers two questions: Why does the organization exist, and what is the organization striving to achieve? Answering these questions establishes a context that enables sport managers to select the best option from alternative choices and make appropriate and right (ethical) decisions that are consistent with the organization's mission and core values. The National Basketball Association's (NBA) mission, presented in figure 12.2, provides a good example of a mission statement with core values.

Besides allowing the mission statement to guide the marketing planning process, sport marketers must also have clearly defined and measurable goals and objectives. Goals are general summary statements of expected outcomes. Examples of sport marketing goals might be to increase attendance by 5% and to increase youth participation in community relations programs by 10%. Objectives are the specific activities that enable the sport marketer to obtain the expected outcomes. Examples of objectives linked to the earlier mentioned goals might be to increase preseason ticket sales by offering discount prices, adding game promotions giveaway items for youth, and offering youth sports clinics and camps. When the goals and objectives are achieved and are aligned with the mission of the sport organization, the marketing plan is deemed a success.

The NBA's mission is to be the most respected and successful sports league organization in the world.

We aim to achieve our mission, and thereby continue to enhance the economic value of our teams, by

working to make basketball the most popular global sport and to maintain the NBA's position as the best in basketball; creating and maximizing business opportunities and relationships arising from basketball; and capitalizing on our key assets and strengths—our people, skills, experience, reputation, and innovative and entrepreneurial spirit—to expand beyond basketball into related activities worldwide.

We have a commitment to excellence

We do every task as well as it can be done, reflecting quality and attention to detail at every stage—from inception, to planning, to execution.

We strive at all times to live by and act in accordance with the following core values:

Innovation We encourage entrepreneurship and innovative thinking. We create opportunities and do not merely react to those that come our way. We aim always to be on the cutting edge and ahead of all competition.

Integrity We conduct ourselves in accordance with the highest standards of honesty, truthfulness, ethics, and fair dealing.

Respect We value our individuality and diversity. We are civil and respectful to each other, to our fans, customers, and business associates. We take pride in our success, but we are not arrogant.

Social responsibility We recognize and embrace our responsibility—as a corporate citizen in the world, in the United States, and in local communities to support causes that help people to achieve an improved quality of life.

Teamwork We work hard together in a true cooperative spirit and without regard for departmental lines or individual goals. Our priority is always to provide the best possible service to all our constituencies.

Workplace environment We believe in equal opportunity, the importance of job satisfaction, and that each employee has an important role in achieving our mission. We empower each employee to make job-related decisions commensurate with the employee's experience and level of responsibility. We promote and reward our employees solely on the basis of merit, and we evaluate not only achievement but also whether the employee's conduct reflects conformity with our mission and values.

Figure 12.2 Mission statement of the National Basketball Association (NBA).

Reprinted, by permission, from the National Basketball Association.

Step 2: Analyze the Sport Product

The second step requires the sport marketer to analyze the dynamic and complex nature of the sport product. The sport product is three-dimensional (Pitts, Fielding, & Miller, 1994), composed of tangible goods, support services, and the game or event itself. Sport goods include tangible items such as clothing and equipment. Support services include activities or programs ancillary to sport but necessary for its operation (e.g., game officials, athletics trainers, sport psychologists). The game or event itself is composed of two dimensions: the core product and product extensions (Mullin, Hardy, & Sutton, 2007).

The core product of the event is the actual competition (e.g., the players and coaches on the competing teams, the sport activity itself, the facility in which the competition takes place). Brooks (1994) proposed the following tangible elements in the core sport product:

- Type of sport—football, basketball, gymnastics, and so on
- Participants—athletes (e.g., beginner, elite, professional), coaches (e.g., volunteer, part-time salaried, full-time professionals), and the environment (e.g., challenging golf courses, difficult mountains)
- Team—University of Notre Dame, Dallas Cowboys, Detroit Shock

Product extensions are the ancillary items, such as the mascot, music, halftime entertainment, concessions, bands, and cheerleaders associated with the overall sport experience. Because of the flair and excitement of product extensions that are created around the core product, sport events are often viewed as a form of entertainment (e.g., the NBA All-Star Game, the World Series, the NCAA Final Four). Marketers must understand and appreciate the elements of the core product of sport as well as the core product extensions before they can develop an appropriate and effective marketing plan.

Step 3: Project the Market Climate

As mentioned previously, sport does not exist in isolation; market conditions have a profound influence on it. Therefore, the third step in the process of developing a sport marketing plan is an analysis of the past and current market climate. This step is needed to project and forecast the future market climate, which will affect marketing practices. Assessing the sport climate requires an examination of internal and external factors as they affect marketing efforts. For example, **internal factors** affecting the climate of Major League Baseball (MLB) include players, owners, team management, and staff personnel. The media, corporate sponsors, advertisers, spectators, and the federal government represent examples of **external factors** that affect the climate of MLB.

Assessing the past market climate enables sport managers to identify factors associated with successful or failed marketing efforts. On the other hand, forecasting the future market climate requires reexamination of the organization's mission. An assessment of the internal strengths and weaknesses of a sport organization or sporting event and the external opportunities and threats faced by the organization or event is called a **SWOT analysis.** A SWOT analysis includes four elements: (1) *strengths* are internal factors that are advantageous to the sport organization's ability to achieve its marketing goals and objectives; (2) *weaknesses* are internal factors that are disadvantageous and may prevent a sport organization from achieving its marketing goals and objectives; (3) *opportunities* are external factors or conditions in the environment that may enhance a sport organization's ability to achieve its marketing goals and objectives; and (4) *threats* are the unfavorable factors or conditions in an environment that could interfere with a sport organization's ability to achieve its marketing goals and objectives. Marketing

internal factors—Factors inside a sport organization that affect the sport marketing climate (e.g., players, owners, team management, staff personnel).

external factors—Factors outside of a sport organization that affect the sport marketing climate (e.g., media, corporate sponsors, advertisers, spectators, federal regulations, regulations of sport governing bodies).

SWOT analysis—A management technique available to sport marketers to help them assess the strengths and weaknesses of an organization and the opportunities and threats that it faces.

plans should be designed to maximize the strengths and opportunities and minimize the weaknesses and threats identified in the SWOT analysis. The sidebar on this page presents an example of a SWOT analysis applied to women's professional basketball.

Remember, the key to marketing success is for a sport organization's strengths and opportunities to outweigh its weaknesses and threats. Applying the SWOT analysis to the Women's National Basketball Association (WNBA) and the American Basketball League (ABL) illustrates why the WNBA is still in existence and why the ABL suspended operations and eventually disbanded. Like the marketers of the WNBA, sport marketers should continuously examine market conditions and develop strategies that will enable them to maximize their products' or events' strengths and opportunities and minimize their weaknesses and threats.

Step 4: Position the Sport Product

According to Shank (2008), positioning refers to the process of establishing a sport entity in the minds of consumers in the target market. The objective of positioning is to differentiate the sport product from competing products by creating a distinctive image of the product. Distinctive images are created in consumers' minds based on (1) the types of consumers who buy the product, (2) the design of the product as well as the benefits offered by the product, (3) the price of the product, and (4) the place where the product is available or where the event occurs (e.g., arena, ice rink). Sport marketers often position products by means of verbal and nonverbal communications to consumers. Sport images can be communicated through logos, symbols, and messages through such avenues as TV and radio advertisements, public service announcements, jingles, press releases, and news articles.

There are numerous cases of positioning in sport marketing. For example, the Paralympics does an excellent job in communicating positive images of elite athletes who are physically challenged by showing that they can compete in athletic events just

SWOT Analysis of Women's Professional Basketball

A SWOT analysis for two professional women's sport leagues, the Women's National Basketball Association (WNBA) and the now defunct American Basketball League (ABL), provides another illustration of the manner in which internal and external factors can influence marketing success. The major strength of the WNBA was that it was a product of the National Basketball Association (NBA); a weakness of the ABL was its ownership by a small group of private investors. Consequently, the WNBA had the financial backing (from the NBA) to absorb deficits (a condition that was a strength), whereas the ABL had a limited budget and did not have the financial resources to absorb the financial losses incurred (a condition that was a weakness). The WNBA teams were located in large cities that were considered major US markets (a condition representing an opportunity); the ABL teams were located primarily in midsize, medium-market cities (a condition representing a threat). The WNBA games were held in NBA arenas (a strength), whereas the ABL games were held in collegiate and other smaller venues within their respective cities (somewhat of a weakness). Another major strength of the WNBA was its national media distribution (i.e., NBC, ESPN, and Lifetime); a major weakness of the ABL was its regional media distribution (i.e., regional sports channels, Prime Network, and Black Entertainment Television). The ABL did not allow its players to participate in other professional women's basketball leagues (a weakness that limited players' appeal and exposure), whereas the WNBA allowed its players to participate in other leagues (a strength that maximized the players' appeal and exposure). The WNBA season of competition was held during the summer months and did not compete with other girls' or women's basketball leagues (an opportunity), whereas the ABL season of competition was held during the winter months, competing with girls' high school basketball and women's college basketball games (a threat).

Renaming the Washington Bullets

The name Bullets was associated for several decades with professional basketball, beginning in the 1960s as the Baltimore Bullets, who then became the Capital Bullets in the early 1970s and eventually the Washington Bullets in 1974. This was the name of the team before the arrival of the team's stars such as Gilbert Arenas (who in 2010 was suspended for the season for a locker room gun incident), Caron Butler, and even Michael Jordan, up through the mid-1990s. During the 1995–1996 season, however, Abe Pollin, owner of the Bullets, decided that the team nickname conveyed a negative image because bullets had nothing to do with basketball but everything to do with people being injured or killed by shooting incidents in Washington, DC, and the surrounding communities. The actions by the team throughout the renaming process illustrate the four steps of effective communication practices (detailed in the text).

First, Pollin communicated openly and honestly with the public about the need to change the team's nickname (step 1). Second, Pollin involved the public in a promotional contest to determine a new team nickname, one that would convey a positive and socially responsible image of the team (step 2). Third, the contest was an example of how an organization should work cooperatively with the public and respond to the public's interest (step 3). Fourth, a corporate sponsor contributed prizes for some contestants, thus generating interest and publicity and establishing a good-faith relationship with the public (step 4). Moreover, an antiviolence campaign was launched in conjunction with the team nickname contest. This campaign communicated the message that the NBA franchise was a responsible corporate citizen that wanted to help the community solve an important social problem. The promotional contest resulted in a new name—the Washington Wizards.

like athletes who are not physically challenged. Another example is the New Orleans, Louisiana, State Farm Bayou Classic (the largest and most popular Black college sport event in America), which has been successfully positioned as a sociocultural and festive entertainment event that contains market features particularly salient to the Black community. Many Black consumers who are not football fans attend because the event has an image of excitement and cultural relevance (Armstrong, 1998, 2002).

WEB

Go to the OSG and complete the Web search activity, which has you analyze the Web site for the State Farm Bayou Classic.

In their landmark work on public relations theory, Grunig and White (1992) suggested that effective communication practices consist of four key elements:

1. Open and honest communication with the public
2. Images and messages that are socially responsible
3. Cooperation with the public and response to their interests
4. Good faith relationships with the public

The sidebar on this page presents a story of an NBA team's name change from the Washington Bullets to the Washington Wizards, a classic application of the four steps in effective communication practices.

To respect the sacred values and customs of American Indians, a number of colleges and universities have replaced nicknames of their mascots and eradicated promotional routines that reflected aspects of American Indian traditions and practices. Moreover, as a measure of respect for the many values of its diverse consumers, the National Collegiate Athletic Association (NCAA) announced that it would not allow universities that contained hostile, abusive, and offensive American Indian mascot nicknames to host NCAA postseason tournaments. Because of the special circumstances and unique relationships that exist between some American Indian tribes and some NCAA universities, the approval of the use of Native American nicknames and mascots by American Indian tribes will be factored into the NCAA's decision.

Based on the increasing diversity of sport participants and consumers, the best way to position a sport product in the market is to do so by using honest and nonoffensive verbal and nonverbal communication that creates a distinctive and socially responsible image of a sport product.

branding—The process of using a name, design, symbol, or any combination of the three to help differentiate a sport product from the competition.

The positioning of the sport product in this way is called branding. **Branding** is the process of using a name, design, symbol, or any combination of them to help differentiate a sport product from the competition. According to Shank (2008), the branding process consists of several elements:

- Brand awareness—The consumers' recognition and recollection of the brand name
- Brand image—The consumers' perceptions and set of beliefs about a brand which, in turn, shape their attitudes
- Brand equity—The value that the brand contributes to a product in the marketplace
- Brand loyalty—The consistent purchase or repeat purchase of one brand over all others in a product category

The favorable positioning of a product that results from successfully branding is critical to sport marketing success because it leads to a preference and positive affinity for consuming the product. In sport marketing, brands such as Nike athletic shoes and apparel, Louisville Slugger baseball bats, Titleist golf balls, and Penn tennis balls are just a few products that have achieved this status.

Step 5: Pick the Players: Analyze and Target Consumers

In this fifth step, the sport marketer targets or selects particular consumers who will allow for sport marketing success. This process of selecting consumers can be envisioned as "picking the players." This approach involves grouping consumers according to common characteristics (wants and needs) relative to the sport product or sporting event being promoted and delivered. Selecting the right consumers for sport marketing is a challenge because sport consumers are very heterogeneous (different). So, to appeal to the uniqueness of sport consumers, marketers must have information about consumers that will provide some insight into how they may be grouped.

The process of breaking large populations of sport consumers into smaller identifiable groups with similar wants and needs is referred to as market segmentation. Sport marketers use this process to identify target audiences. They often do so by grouping or segmenting consumers in four areas: demographics, psychographics, media preferences, and purchasing behavior. Demographic segmentation refers to clustering sport consumers based on their age, gender, income, race or ethnicity, education, and place of residence. Psychographic segmentation refers to appealing to consumers' attitudes, interests, and lifestyles. Market segmentation based on media preference would cluster consumers based on their sport media (e.g., TV, radio, Internet) preferences. Purchasing behavior as a means of market segmentation refers to grouping sport consumers according to the frequency of usage behavior (e.g., how often they attend basketball games, how frequently they purchase sport drinks).

Market segmentation allows the sport marketer to identify smaller clusters of sport consumers who may exhibit similar wants, needs, and interests regarding sport. Rather than attempting to sell products to all consumers, the process of market segmentation assists marketers in zeroing in on specific consumers who are most likely to find the product appealing. For example, a sport equipment manufacturer might identify the primary target audience as 12- to 16-year-old males who are interested in in-line skating and who watch MTV.

The economic power and sport interests among ethnic minorities represent a huge opportunity for sport organizations. Sport marketers have also realized the importance of devising marketing strategies to appeal to female consumers. Until recently, women were not considered a viable target market segment for men's sports. But with increased buying of men's sport teams' merchandise by women, women's increased spectatorship of men's sports (e.g., the National Football League [NFL], NBA, MLB, National Hockey League [NHL]), the growth of women's sports, the financial gains that women have made as consumers, and the general influence that women exert over family purchases and consumption decisions, women have become an important target market for sport marketers (Sutton & Wattlington, 1994). Moreover, the Title IX generation (women and girls born after 1972) is young and relatively affluent, two desirable attributes sought by sport marketers. Other groups of consumers that have attracted the attention of sport marketers are Generation X (people born from 1964 through 1978) and Generation Y (people born from 1979 through 1990) consumers. Consumers from different generations exhibit unique behaviors that illustrate how demographics (age) and psychographics (attitudes and interests) interact to influence sport consumer behavior. For instance, sport events such as the X Games, the Dew Tour, and the Gravity Games illustrate that the latest generations (i.e., X, Y) are target markets to be reckoned with. In addition, consumer characteristics such as race and ethnicity, age, and gender may be integrated or combined to create specific target markets within the Generation X and Generation Y categories.

As mentioned previously, sport marketing success requires that sport marketers target the right groups of consumers. Criteria for selecting the viable target markets include factors such as the size of the target group, the amount of resources available to the target group, and whether the target group is accessible to the organization. The determination of whether a target market is viable varies among sport organizations, based largely on the organization's marketing goals and objectives. For example, a target market of 100 students for a football event that attracts over 100,000 consumers may not be of sufficient size to warrant specific marketing attention. On the other hand, a target market of 100 students for a fitness club with a membership of approximately 200 is an acceptable size and may have a significant effect on the overall marketing success of the fitness club.

After marketers have identified the target consumers for their product, they must engage in a number of strategies that will help draw the targeted consumers to the sport organization or event. The remaining five steps of the development of a sport marketing plan describe tactics that help marketers attract their target audiences.

Step 6: Package the Sport Product

The sixth step in the process involves packaging the sport product. This step includes presenting the product in the best possible manner to encourage selected target audiences to purchase it. Because consumers differ, sport marketers must present the product in different ways. Packaging tangible or industrial sport products involves explaining the benefits of the products, such as the strength and longevity of metal bats, the comfort and safety of helmets, and the expanded sweet spot of oversize tennis rackets. Packaging the core product of sport (the game or event itself), however, involves communicating the expectations of the product and providing information before the point of purchase (POP). For example, sport marketers might package the game or event as family entertainment and offer family ticket plans. Or marketers might package sport as a good place to make business contacts and offer business ticket plans. A sport organization that wants to be seen as one that cares about the community might offer group discount ticket plans for social service and charitable organizations.

SAMSUNG ELECTRONICS AND SPORT: A SPONSORSHIP SUCCESS STORY

By Sungho Cho • KOREA
Bowling Green State University, UNITED STATES

Sport sponsorship is a primary advertising vehicle for many conglomerates because sporting events provide corporate sponsors with avenues of marketing communication and dynamics for brand image enhancement. South Korea's Samsung Electronics, the largest consumer electronics company in the world, is one of the most active players in the global sponsorship market. Samsung's first sport sponsorship effort was as a local sponsor of the Seoul 1988 Olympic Games. This sponsorship was established in response to a strategic guideline set forth by former CEO and major shareholder Kun-Hee Lee, who had directed the company to create strategies that would raise Samsung's brand value at the global level.

In 2005 Samsung initiated a partnership with Chelsea FC, a professional English soccer club with a stylish heritage and a reputation for class and success. Although Chelsea FC is based in West London, England, it boasts 25 international players from 14 countries. According to Paul Smith, Chelsea's business affairs director, during the 2004–2005 season when the team won the league title, the fan base increased by 300% to 2.9 million, and its worldwide fan base was approaching 20 million.

Samsung's partnership with Chelsea demonstrates how companies anticipate benefits from sport sponsorship. First, given Chelsea's enormous fan base, the sponsorship effort should provide a valuable avenue of marketing communication for

Photo courtesy of Hallie S. Pedersen.

One of Samsung Electronics' major sponsorship partnerships is with Chelsea Football Club (Chelsea FC).

Another aspect of product packaging is the manner in which product extensions (discussed in step 2) are included in the overall sport experience. For instance, music, halftime promotions, and entertainment contribute to the overall packaging of a sport event. Some consumers may not be specifically attracted to the core product (e.g., the basketball game), but they may be attracted to the way in which the core product is packaged (e.g., music, fun, entertainment).

Another aspect of the sport product is the associated licensed merchandise. Many sport teams and events offer goods such as hats, T-shirts, and jackets as well as nonapparel items such as watches, novelty items, memorabilia, and decorative items that consumers perceive as extensions and representations of the teams or events.

sport sponsorship—The acquisition of rights to affiliate or associate with a sport product or sporting event in order to derive benefits from the affiliation or association (Mullin, Hardy, & Sutton, 2007).

Packaging the sport product to secure financial support from corporations is an especially important aspect of the marketing plan called **sport sponsorship.** Sponsorship involves an agreement between a sport organization or event and a corporation wherein the corporation pays a fee to the organization or event to acquire the rights

Samsung. Additionally, Samsung would expect a halo effect from Chelsea's image of rich history and recent success. Samsung hoped that Chelsea's strong image would spill over onto its own brand image during the course of sponsorship. The Samsung–Chelsea case epitomizes why many corporations are pursuing partnerships with high-profile sport teams (i.e., accessibility to consumers and brand image enhancement). In the words of In-Soo Kim, president of Samsung European,

> Chelsea is making its mark on the world stage as one of the rising stars of football, and the association with the club will not only drive and enhance Samsung's image on a global scale but also allow us to get even closer to our customers. Samsung is an equally ambitious company, and we are looking forward to sharing that drive and momentum to build on our success and boost brand awareness. (*Chelsea Football Club,* 2005)

According to Interbrand, the world's largest brand consulting company, after Samsung began its worldwide marketing campaign with an array of high-profile sport sponsorships (e.g., Olympic Games, National Football League, English Premier League), its brand value grew more than fivefold from US$3.1 billion in 1999 to US$16.2 billion in 2006. Not a company to rest on its laurels, Samsung is currently considering replacing insurance company AIG as the shirt sponsor for Manchester United, the 2009 Carling Cup winner, when the AIG contract expires in 2010. In addition, the company has entered into a three-year, multipound contract with International Association of Athletics Federations (IAAF). Samsung Electronics, which maintains the coveted TOP (the Olympic Partner Programme) status, stands as a prime example of how a company can employ sponsorships to capitalize on the worldwide passion for sport.

INTERNATIONAL LEARNING ACTIVITY #1

Go to www.olympic.org/en/content/The-IOC/Sponsoring/Sponsorship/?Tab=1 and identify The Olympic Partner (TOP) Programme sponsors for the next two Olympic and Paralympic Games. Then read two of the posted articles about the marketing of the Olympic and Paralympic Games and report your findings to your classmates.

INTERNATIONAL LEARNING ACTIVITY #2

In your campus library or online, locate the *International Journal of Sport Management and Marketing* or the *International Journal of Sports Marketing and Sponsorship*. In one of these journals, find an article that interests you and write a report on it, including reasons that the information in that article would be useful to sport marketers working in an international marketplace.

to affiliate with it. Sponsorships can help corporations increase sales, change attitudes, heighten awareness, and build and maintain positive relationships with consumers.

The way that a product is packaged either directly or indirectly influences or is influenced by every other aspect of the 10 Ps process outlined in this chapter, such as who will be attracted to the product or event, how it is relevant to the current market climate, what its price should be, how it should be promoted, and how it will be delivered. Therefore, sport marketers must understand how all the elements that contribute to product packaging influence the success of the marketing plan.

Step 7: Price the Sport Product

The seventh step is determining the value of the product by assigning it a price. Price is the most visible and flexible element because of discounts, rebates, and coupons. According to Pitts and Stotlar (2007), marketers should consider four factors when developing a pricing strategy:

1. Consumer—Analyze all aspects of the consumer, including demographics, psychographics, purchasing behaviors, and media preferences.
2. Competitor—Analyze the consumer's perception of the product value compared with all competing products and analyze the competitors' prices.
3. Company—Analyze the costs involved in producing the product (e.g., materials, equipment, salaries, rent) and set a minimum price to cover the costs.
4. Climate—Analyze external factors (e.g., laws pertaining to pricing, government regulations, the economic situation, the political situation).

Normally, consumers exchange money for products. In sport marketing, however, trading is a common practice. For example, marketers of a tennis tournament might make trades with corporate sponsors, such as tickets for tennis balls, stadium signage for food and beverages for a hospitality tent, and scoreboard advertisement for the use of vehicles to transport players and officials.

Factors other than price help determine the value of a product. Each consumer has attitudes, preferences, beliefs, and a certain amount of expendable money. These factors, along with price, influence how people determine the value of a product. Because the value of a product is unique to each consumer, the pricing strategy must appeal to as

Billboards lining the walls of a subway entry are an unique form of outdoor advertising.
Photo courtesy of Paul M. Pedersen.

many different consumers as possible. For example, sport franchises set different prices for corporate season ticket holders, charitable organizations, group ticket purchasers, miniseason ticket purchasers, family ticket purchasers, and single-ticket purchasers. Prices are generally differentiated based on the consumer's interest, ability, and willingness to commit time and money to participate in the sport experience.

Consumers tend to equate price with value. Therefore, a new sport franchise should price tickets to be comparable with competing products (e.g., other sporting events, movies) rather than set a lower price. Consumers might equate a lower price with an inferior product.

Lead time is important to sport pricing. More day-of-the-game or walk-up sales occur at MLB games than at NBA games because many more games and seats are available at lower prices in baseball than in basketball (Mullin, Hardy, & Sutton, 2007).

Sport pricing is complex and critical to the success of the marketing plan. Price, however, is one aspect of the marketing plan that may be readily changed (i.e., increased or decreased slightly). For example, sport organizations often alter their prices to attract different consumers (e.g., students may pay a different price for event tickets than that paid by the general public). Sport organizations may also change prices according to the market environment (e.g., lowering prices during a recession or economic downturn) or the team's performance (e.g., increasing prices as a team's performance dramatically improves). In the final analysis, sport marketers must determine how consumers perceive the value of the product compared with all competing products and use that information to set an appropriate price. Additionally, sport marketers should seek to offer consumers a satisfying experience with perceived benefits that surpass the personal and financial costs that consumers incur.

Step 8: Promote the Sport Product

The eighth step involves communicating the image of the product to the selected target audiences. Promoting sport products involves implementing a mix of activities that will best (1) communicate the desired image of the product to the target audiences, (2) educate and inform the target audiences about the product and its benefits, and (3) persuade the target audiences to buy the product.

Elements that compose a promotion strategy are referred to as the promotional mix and include advertising, publicity, activities and inducements, public relations (including community relations and media relations), personal selling, and sponsorship.

- ***Advertising.*** One-way paid messages about the sport product. The messages can come through outlets such as newspapers, magazines, TV, radio, direct mail, scoreboards, in-arena signage, pocket schedules, game programs, posters, outdoor advertising, and the Internet.
- ***Publicity.*** Nonpaid communication about a sport product in which the sponsor is usually not identified and the message reaches the public because it is newsworthy. Such publicity typically comes through news releases and TV and radio public service announcements.
- ***Activities and inducements.*** Promotions to encourage consumers to purchase the sport product. These come in the form of giveaways, coupons, product samples, cash refunds, contests, raffles, and so on.
- ***Public relations.*** Activities and programs, especially those associated with community and media relations, that help the sport organization develop positive relationships with its target audiences. For example, through their Be Fit campaign, the WNBA seeks to communicate the importance of being physically active. Moreover, WNBA players, coaches, and administrators are involved in a number

of public relations activities that promote awareness of breast cancer and the need for women to take an active role in early detection.

- *Community relations.* Activities and programs, such as the NBA Cares initiative, designed to meet the interests and needs of the public and, by so doing, establish good-faith relationships with the public. This area includes activities and programs such as youth sport clinics, athlete autograph-signing opportunities, and the collection of food items at sport arenas to help people in the community. With the growing need for sport organizations to be socially responsible, community relations activities that garner favorable relationships with the public are essential for marketing success.
- *Media relations.* Maintenance of networks and positive relationships with people in the media to obtain positive media exposure for a sport product. This goal can be accomplished by providing the media with press releases, having news conferences, hosting media-day events, and providing media guides.
- *Personal selling.* Direct face-to-face communication with individuals, groups, or organizations to sell tickets, luxury suites or boxes, or sponsorships. Personal selling is unique and highly effective because it allows salespeople to adapt messages based on feedback, communicate more information to the target audience, guarantee that the target audience will pay attention to the message being delivered, and develop a long-term relationship with the target audience.
- *Sponsorship.* A form of promotion that involves a partnership between sport organizations or events and corporate entities. Business partnerships are based on exchange theory. Corporations provide money, products, or services to sport organizations or events, and in return sport organizations or events provide rights and benefits of association such as use of the sport organization or event logo, name, or trademark; exclusive association with the event or facility; exclusive association within a product or service category; use of various designations or

Step 8 focuses on the promotion of the sport product. Here, marketing executives of a professional basketball team (the Cleveland Cavaliers) are using advertising on a mass transit vehicle to communicate the image of their product (e.g., the history of the team, the celebration of an anniversary) to pedestrians in downtown Cleveland.

Photo courtesy of Paul M. Pedersen.

phrases in connection with the product, event, or facility, such as "official sponsor," "official supplier," "official product," or "presented by"; exclusive use of the product; and authorization to conduct particular promotional activities such as contests, advertising campaigns, or on-site product sales. Corporations make significant investments in sport for a number of reasons, such as to (1) establish or improve their image through association with high-visibility events, (2) promote their products, thereby increasing sales, (3) display goodwill, and (4) obtain access and exposure to the target audiences of events.

Step 9: Place the Sport Product

The ninth step is analyzing the place of the sport product. **Place** refers to the location of the sport product (e.g., stadium, arena), the point of origin for distributing the product (e.g., ticket sales at the ice rink, sales by a toll-free telephone number), the geographic location of the target markets (e.g., global, national, regional, state, communities, cities), and other channels that are important to consider regarding how target audiences may access the product (e.g., time, day, season, or month in which a product is offered; media distribution outlets that consumers may use). Factors related to the physical location of the sport can have a favorable or unfavorable effect on the marketing plan. To ensure a favorable effect, the sport facility must be easily accessible (e.g., highway systems, parking, walkways, ramps); have an attractive physical appearance (e.g., well maintained, painted); have a pleasant, convenient, and functional environment (e.g., quick and easy access to concessions, clean restrooms, smoke-free and odor-free environment); and have safe and pleasant surroundings (e.g., adequate public safety and security personnel, attractive neighborhood).

place—The comprehensive manner in which sport is distributed to consumers.

Sport is unique in the way that it is distributed to consumers. The production and consumption of the product occur simultaneously for spectators attending sport events in stadia or arenas. The sport product is also distributed to consumers, nationally and globally, through the electronic media of television (regular cable and pay-per-view), radio, Internet broadcasts, social networking endeavors, mobile technology, and a host of other forms of new media.

Ticket distribution is another critical aspect of sport distribution. The objective of a ticket distribution system is to make consumer purchases easy, quick, and convenient. Some approaches adopted by sport organizations include using outside companies such as Ticketmaster; ticket outlets at local banks, shopping malls, and grocery stores; mobile van units that transport ticket personnel and operations to various locations throughout the community; on-site stadium and arena ticket sales with expanded hours of operation; toll-free telephone numbers; and will-call pickup arrangements.

The overall objective of distributing the sport product is to facilitate consumers' ability to take part in the sport experience, or purchase the sport product, in a timely and convenient manner, thereby promoting marketing success.

Step 10: Promise of (Evaluating) the Sport Marketing Plan

The last step in the process of sport marketing plan development is the evaluation of the plan. Therefore, this step involves evaluating the extent to which the marketing plan met its promise to help achieve the sport organization's mission. This evaluation requires obtaining feedback about the marketing plan from inside and outside the sport organization. Some inside sources of feedback are ticket sales; merchandise sales; and customer inquiries, complaints, and suggestions. Some outside sources of feedback include consumers, corporate sponsors, advertisers, and media personnel. The sport marketer must analyze and evaluate the feedback. The evaluation should focus on determining the extent to which the plan helped the organization achieve

ACTION

Go to the OSG and complete the Learning in Action activity, which tests how well you recall the 10 steps of creating a sport marketing plan.

its mission by acting in accordance with its core values. For example, to evaluate the effectiveness of the marketing plans for some of the Black college sport events that specifically seek to empower the Black community sociologically and economically, marketers may evaluate the number of students who attended the event, examine the financial contributions that the event made to the respective HBCU (Historically Black Colleges and Universities) institutions, and examine the economic contributions of the event to the local economies.

Implementing a sport marketing plan in accordance with the sport organization's stated core values helps to ensure that the plan will be socially responsible. Sport marketers who develop marketing plans linked to the organization's mission and core values are being proactive. "Reactive people are driven by feelings, by circumstances, by conditions, and by their environment," noted Covey (1989). "Proactive people are driven by values—carefully thought about, selected, and internalized values" (p. 72). Proactive sport marketers will achieve the promise of the marketing plan because their actions will be socially responsible and will help fulfill the mission of the organization.

CRITICAL THINKING IN SPORT MARKETING

Another trend in sport marketing is an infusion of hip-hop nuances into the marketing plan. The term *hip-hop* is grounded in and reflects the burgeoning African American youth-oriented culture that originated in the Bronx, New York, during the 1970s (McLeod, 1999). Hip-hop symbolizes the voice of many urban Black youth and is reflected in the culture of their music, clothes, language, and overall way of life (Midol, 1998). The hip-hop genre has spawned a cultural revolution, and this trendsetting market has exerted a formidable influence on mainstream consumption patterns worldwide. Many companies and industries have made concerted efforts to capitalize on the popularity of hip-hop, and the sport industry is no exception. The overall appeal of the hip-hop culture has not been lost on sport marketers. Hip-hop artists frequently (1) provide the pregame, postgame, and halftime entertainment of sport events, (2) are featured in sport promotions and advertisements, and (3) are often used as sport product endorsers. The challenge of infusing cultural nuances of hip-hop into marketing practices is to be sensitive to the authenticity and social responsibility needed to reach urban consumers and the markets of consumers that they influence (McLeod, 1999). Sport marketers must obtain and demonstrate a sincere responsiveness and respect for the cultural essence of hip-hop. The NBA has made concerted efforts to capitalize on the popularity and appeal of hip-hop to improve the league's overall market share. Some argue that the NBA's image and reputation is jeopardized because hip-hop often glamorizes violence, sexism, and consumerism, and it often depicts Black urban life in a negative manner.

PORTFOLIO

Complete the critical thinking portfolio activity in the OSG, consulting as needed the "Eight Critical Thinking Questions" section in chapter 1.

ETHICS IN SPORT MARKETING

In many segments of the sport industry, sport marketers are pressured to increase their product sales to generate increased revenues for their organizations. This pressure poses a challenge. Because sport marketers are involved in persuading consumers to buy, they run the risk of exaggerating or misrepresenting their products and misleading their consumers in an effort to sell their products. Today, and in the future, sport marketers should recognize this risk and monitor their marketing strategies to ensure that they communicate honest images and messages about their products and to their consumers. These images and messages should be consistent with the core values of their organizations.

A new culture of technology has emerged and has had a dramatic effect on sport marketing practices and on consumers' wants and needs. Technology affects every phase of the marketing process (e.g., the product features, the channels of media and ticket distribution, sponsorship leverage). Technology bells and whistles have had a pervasive influence on the entertainment appeal of sport. In the future, sport marketers will have to decide how best to use technology to make the sport product and experience more entertaining for consumers without negatively affecting the true nature of sport. Overemphasizing the entertainment aspects that surround sport runs the risk of undermining sport or, worse, transforming sport into what Hall (2002) called sportainment. According to Hall, sportainment is a marketplace reaction to consumers' increasing demand for greater human excellence and the desire to feel a sense of escape from ordinary life. Sportainment represents combining sport and entertainment in ways that will fulfill these consumer expectations. Although technology has allowed a number of improvements in the overall appeal of sport, sport marketers will need to guard against the temptation to overuse technology (e.g., the overuse of pop-ups and scrolls of statistical information can be distracting and detract from the game) simply to meet the entertainment expectations of fans without considering its effect on the game or event itself. Failing to do so might jeopardize the integrity of sport and undermine its inherent value.

Increasing consumer diversity may be the trend that will have the greatest influence on the success of sport marketing plans. Sport, like other businesses, operates in a global market and must respond to the rapidly changing racial and ethnic demographics in the societies in which it operates. A person's race or ethnicity generally exerts a profound influence on that person's thoughts, attitudes, and behaviors, including those that pertain to sport consumption. Racial and ethnic influences are often difficult to discern because they may be internal (factors within individuals that may influence sport consumption behaviors) or external (factors prevalent in a sport setting or environment that may influence sport consumption behaviors) (Armstrong, 2001, 2008). Sport consumers' wants and needs may also differ based on a variety of other factors such as gender (e.g., the unique tastes of females compared with males) and age (e.g., the interests of senior consumers compared with Generation Y consumers). Developing marketing strategies and promotional tactics that respond to particular groups of consumers (i.e., target audiences) who exhibit certain lifestyles is referred to as **lifestyle marketing.** Sport events play a critical role in the culture of most consumers, and many sport events have ethnocultural symbols, rituals, and emblems that may be more salient to some ethnic groups than others (Pons, Larouche, Nyeck, & Perreault, 2001). As the consumer base for sport continues to increase in ethnic diversity so will the need for marketing plans that reflect the multicultural nature of that base.

lifestyle marketing—A means of promoting products to particular groups of consumers (target audiences) who exhibit certain lifestyles (e.g., Generation X, Generation Y, hip-hop).

To help you think about the connection between ethics and sport marketing, consider the following hypothetical example. As the director of marketing for a minor league baseball team located in a city with a 15% Hispanic–Latino population base, you decide to plan three games during the season that focus on the Hispanic–Latino culture. Furthermore, you provide special pricing and promotions benefits to Hispanic–Latino fans who attend the games. Following the first Hispanic–Latino promotional game the organization is confronted with negative media reaction to the event. Comments on radio and TV sports talk programs and in newspaper articles criticized the perceived special treatment offered to a particular ethnic group. The general manager schedules a meeting with you to discuss the situation and get your recommendations about whether to proceed with the next two Hispanic–Latino cultural game days.

Complete the ethical issues portfolio activity in the OSG, consulting as needed the "Guidelines for Making Ethical Decisions" section in chapter 1.

PORTFOLIO

The changing demographic and psychographic characteristics of sport consumers will increase the overall diversity that sport marketers must respond to as they seek to develop successful marketing plans. The trend toward increased diversity in the national and global markets will pose both a special challenge and a unique opportunity for sport managers and marketers in the second decade of the 21st century. The increased diversity in the environments in which sport operates will require sport marketers to be equipped with not only the marketing fundamentals but also the skills to adapt them to multicultural sport consumers. Sport marketers will have to develop appropriate and acceptable intercultural communications, packaging features, positioning strategies, and distribution channels to reach culturally diverse consumers in domestic and international environments (Armstrong, 2008).

Summary

This chapter outlined a 10-step process that you can use to develop a sport marketing plan. Although the core of this process is the marketing mix, traditionally known as the four Ps, the process also includes factors such as organizational, environmental, and consumer-related considerations. A sport marketing plan will most likely succeed when marketing is viewed as a comprehensive process of packaging, promoting, and delivering sport to consumers in a manner that satisfies consumers' wants and needs and simultaneously meets the sport organization's marketing goals and objectives. Therefore, tactical marketing mix strategies should communicate a distinct, positive, and honest image of a product and the consumers to whom it is targeted. Such strategies will enable the sport organization to establish a favorable position among its targeted consumers in the market and will subsequently fulfill the promise of socially responsible marketing that is linked to and consistent with the mission and core values of the organization.

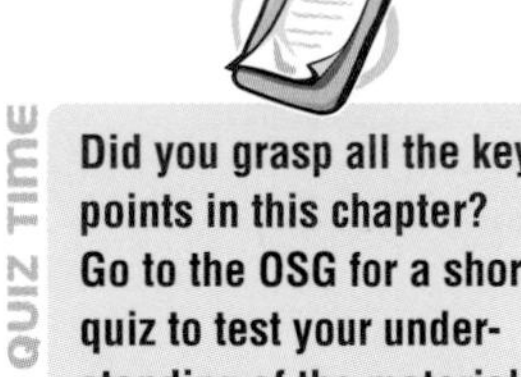

QUIZ TIME

Did you grasp all the key points in this chapter? Go to the OSG for a short quiz to test your understanding of the material.

Review Questions

1. What is a mission statement and how does it influence the development of sport marketing plans?
2. How is a SWOT analysis used in directing or informing marketing plans?
3. What are the dimensions of a sport product, and in what ways do the unique elements of sport influence sport marketing?
4. How do promotional activities help to position or establish an image of a sport product in the minds of consumers?
5. Why should a sport product or event be promoted in ethical and socially responsible ways?
6. What are the methods used to segment a market in order to identify viable target audiences for a sport product?
7. What are some strategies that can be used to distribute a sport product to consumers?
8. What is the role of packaging in selling a sport product to specific target audiences?
9. What are the two sources used to obtain feedback about a sport marketing plan?
10. What are some ethical challenges confronted by sport marketers in the second decade of the 21st century?

References

Armstrong, K.L. (1998). Ten strategies to employ when marketing sport to Black consumers. *Sport Marketing Quarterly*, *7*(3), 11–18.

Armstrong, K.L. (2001). Creating multicultural sport spectating experiences: Marketing the sociology of sport consumption. *International Journal of Sport Management*, *2*, 183–204.

Armstrong, K.L. (2002). An examination of the social psychology of Blacks' consumption of sport. *Journal of Sport Management*, *16*, 267–288.

Armstrong, K.L. (2008). Consumers of color and the "culture" of sport attendance: Exploratory insights. *Sport Marketing Quarterly*, *17*, 218–231.

Brooks, C.M. (1994). *Sports marketing: Competitive business strategies for sports*. Englewood Cliffs, NJ: Prentice Hall.

Chelsea Football Club announces Samsung as official sponsor. (2005, April 25). Retrieved June 2, 2010, from www.mobiledia.com/news/30099.html

Covey, S.R. (1989). *The seven habits of highly effective people*. New York: Simon and Schuster.

Grunig, J.E., & White, R. (1992). Communication, public relations and effective organizations. In J.E. Grunig (Ed.), *Excellence in public relations and communications management* (pp. 1–30). Hillsdale, NJ: Erlbaum.

Hall, M. (2002, August 19–25). Taking the sport out of sports. *Street & Smith's SportsBusiness Journal*, p. 23.

McLeod, K. (1999). Authenticity within hip-hop and other cultures threatened with assimilation. *Journal of Communications*, *49*(4), 134–150.

Midol, N. (1998). Rap and dialectical relations. Culture, subculture, power, and counter-powered. In R. Genevieve (Ed.), *Sport and postmodern times* (pp. 333–343). Albany: State University of New York Press.

Mullin, B.J., Hardy, S., & Sutton, W.A. (2007). *Sport marketing* (3rd ed.). Champaign, IL: Human Kinetics.

Pitts, B.G., Fielding, L.W., & Miller, L.K. (1994). Industry segmentation theory and the sport industry: Developing a sport industry segmentation model. *Sport Marketing Quarterly*, *3*(1), 15–24.

Pitts, B.G., & Stotlar, D.K. (2007). *Fundamentals of sport marketing* (3rd ed.). Morgantown, WV: Fitness Information Technology.

Pons, F., Larouche, M., Nyeck, S., & Perreault, S. (2001). Role of sport events as ethnocultural emblems: Impact of acculturation and ethnic identity on consumers' orientations toward sporting events. *Sport Marketing Quarterly*, *10*, 231–240.

Shank, M.D. (2008). *Sports marketing: A strategic perspective* (4th ed.). Upper Saddle River, NJ: Prentice Hall.

Sutton, W.A., & Wattlington, R. (1994). Communicating with women in the 1990s: The role of sport marketing. *Sport Marketing Quarterly*, *3*(2), 9–14.

HISTORICAL MOMENTS

1924	The Notre Dame backfield became known as the Four Horseman
1939	First televised MLB broadcast (NBC)—Cincinnati Reds v. Brooklyn Dodgers
1954	NCAA's first PR manual for intercollegiate athletics issued
1954	First issue of *Sports Illustrated* published
1957	College Sports Information Directors of America (CoSIDA) founded
1961	ABC's *Wide World of Sports* made its debut
1963	Instant replay first used—Army v. Navy football game
1970	*Monday Night Football (MNF)* launched on ABC; *MNF* moves to ESPN in 2006
1979	Entertainment Sports Programming Network (ESPN) launched
1985	First all-sports radio station made its debut in Denver
1991	*The National* (daily sports newspaper) folded
1998	*Street & Smith's SportsBusiness Journal* launched
2006	*Journal of Sports Media* launched
2006	Micro-blogging service Twitter launched
2008	*International Journal of Sport Communication (IJSC)* launched

Photo courtesy of Paul M. Pedersen.

Communication in the Sport Industry

G. Clayton Stoldt ■ Stephen W. Dittmore ■ Paul M. Pedersen

Learning Objectives

1. Explain the definition and theoretical elements of sport communication.
2. Identify the components of the strategic sport communication model (SSCM).
3. Recognize the importance of interpersonal and organizational communication in sport.
4. Demonstrate the components and workings of the sport media.
5. Explain how communication technology affects the sport industry.
6. Describe how media relations and community relations professionals serve their sport organizations.
7. Identify ethical issues associated with aspects of and careers in sport communication.
8. Explain how critical thinking skills relate to effective sport communication.

Get a Job!

☑ Continue your journey in sport management by going to the Online Study Guide (OSG) at www.HumanKinetics.com/ContemporarySportManagement. Check out the job opportunities and consider the skills and experiences that can help you succeed in sport management.

Key Terms

community relations
effects
electronic communication
new media
one-way model of public relations
print communication
sport communication
sport public relations
strategic sport communication model
two-way model of public relations

Sport communication is one of the most prominent and exciting aspects of sport management. Sport media personalities such as Bob Costas, Linda Cohn, and Michael Wilbon are often as recognizable as the coaches and athletes whom they cover. Fans often look with envy at sport public relations professionals who are hard at work in some of the best seats in the house as they perform their duties from the press box or press row. Further, technological advancements are allowing sport consumers to interact with the organizations that they support and with one another in new and exciting ways. It is little wonder that so many sport management students are highly interested in communication.

In this chapter you will learn how sport communication is defined and understood using communication theory. You will also be introduced to a model that portrays the various facets of the field. You will see why effective interpersonal and organizational communication is critical to success in the field. You will learn about the various forms of sport media and how sport organizations deal with the media and other key publics in their community. You will see how technological advancements are changing the field, and you will be introduced to some of the key ethical issues confronting communication specialists in sport management.

Communication is such an integral part of our lives that it is easy to overlook just how complex and pervasive it really is. In sport settings, communication includes everything from a conversation between an event manager and a volunteer regarding the logistics of hospitality to the posting of new information on a team Web site to the presentation of a live event on television. Conceptualizing something so multidimensional is challenging, but Pedersen, Miloch, Laucella, and Fielding (2007) offered a helpful definition. They described **sport communication** as "a process by which people in sport, in a sport setting, or through a sport endeavor share symbols as they create meaning through interaction" (p. 196).

sport communication— A process by which people in sport, in a sport setting, or through a sport endeavor share symbols as they create meaning through interaction.

As you will see in the following section, a number of communication theories and concepts influenced the development of this brief definition. Each has important implications for students and practitioners.

THEORETICAL FRAMEWORK OF SPORT COMMUNICATION

Numerous communication models, from basic to sophisticated, have been developed to help explain how we communicate. An examination of the theory base as a whole reveals five key concepts: communication genres, context, process, elements, and effects.

Genres

Communication scholars have used a variety of approaches in studying their subject matter. Littlejohn and Foss (2008) described a number of categories that represent these approaches. They range in focus from the individual (e.g., how people learn, why they behave as they do) to the societal (e.g., how social systems function) to the interpretive (e.g., how meaning is discovered). Students who pursue in-depth study in sport communication will become familiar with these theories. The key point for now is that no single approach to studying communication can adequately address the subject. By recognizing the varied approaches to communication, students can position themselves for better understanding.

Context

Just as there are multiple approaches to studying communication, there are a number of contexts in which communication occurs. Common contexts for communication include interpersonal, group, organizational, and mass mediated. Interpersonal communication occurs between two people (e.g., ticket taker greets a fan). Group communication takes place among three or more people (e.g., focus group interview). Some communication scholars differentiate between small groups and large groups because the dynamics vary based on the number of people involved. Organizational communication occurs both internally (e.g., meetings, memos) and externally (e.g., news releases, Web site). Mass-mediated communication takes place when information is shared with large audiences through print, electronic, or new media channels. Each context is relevant in sport management, and prospective sport managers should build knowledge and develop competencies in regard to each.

Process

As noted in the definition, sport communication is a process. This process involves multiple participants, dynamics, and influences at any given moment. For example, a public address announcer shares information about an upcoming event to a large, noisy crowd, many of whom are distracted by personal conversations that they are having. Some hear; others do not. Of those who hear, some will take note and plan to attend the event. They may even cheer. Others, meanwhile, will ignore the information.

This example conveys just some of the dynamics involved in the process of communication. The complexity of the process becomes even more apparent when we remember the popular game Gossip, or Telephone, that involves whispering a sentence to the person in the next seat, who then whispers it to the next person, and so on until everyone playing the game has passed along the message. The outcome is usually a message that differs radically from the original whispered communication. Although

At a sporting event such as this football game, communication is taking place in various contexts, such as interpersonal interactions among fans, a group meeting between an athletic director and boosters in a luxury box, and media members receiving game notes from the sports information director in the press box.
Photo courtesy of Paul M. Pedersen.

this distortion or miscommunication might be amusing in a game, the results are not as funny when we fail to communicate our message in situations in which accurate communication is important.

Elements

Communication is a process, and the value of communication models is that they help us understand that process. Most people do so by identifying the elements involved in the process. The most basic components are portrayed in a model developed by Lasswell (1948):

- Sender
- Message
- Channel through which the message is delivered
- Receiver

ACTION

Go to the OSG and complete the Learning in Action activity, which lets you dissect the communication process between a coach and an athlete.

Using this model, the communication source could be a speaker at a community relations event, the author of a new company policy, or the writer of a news release. The message in each of these cases is the denotation and connotation of the spoken or written words and pictures that the sender produces. Although we can describe channels literally (e.g., broadcast or cable channels), communication scholars usually use the term to describe the delivery system or the way in which the message gets from the sender to the receiver (e.g., spoken word, gestures, over-the-air broadcast television, film). Thus, the channel through which a message is delivered could be face-to-face spoken words (with accompanying voice, expression, and gesture cues) or printed words (with accompanying graphics and layout). The receiver of the communication could be one person or several people who are listening to a speaker, reading a magazine, or visiting a Web site.

Shannon and Weaver (1949) created a communication model that added two additional elements—encoding and decoding—to this process. The encoding and decoding components of the communication process refer to the inescapable fact that every sender and receiver of communication assigns meaning to the communicated message. This meaning might or might not be readily apparent. Think about the times that you have heard or seen something that did not communicate the intended message. Key words might not have been familiar, or the speaker's language might have been communicating one message while her facial expressions communicated another.

Schramm (1954) expanded on earlier models by including the element of feedback. The resultant model portrayed communication as a two-way, rather than a one-way, process. Feedback helps the communicator understand whether the receiver got the correct message. It provides information for future communication. Phone calls concerning a change in the services offered by a recreation facility, fans erupting in cheers at a spirit rally, or the defeat of a municipal ballot initiative to help fund a team's new sports arena are all examples of feedback.

Another communication concept, noise, refers to elements that can impede successful communication. It can be literal, such as fans' yelling at a sporting event that might drown out the public address announcer. Noise can also be figurative; a poorly printed brochure would certainly hinder communication effectiveness and thus be a form of noise. The goal in communicating is to minimize controllable noise and cut through uncontrollable noise so that as few impediments as possible are present in the communication process.

Schramm (1954) also argued that for communication to exist, the sender and the receiver must share something: a common language, vocabulary, or interest in or understanding of the subject being communicated. The more the sender and receiver share, the easier it is for them to communicate effectively. Schramm's point is a useful one to consider when you communicate. Ask yourself how much you and the receiver of your communication share. If you can increase the level of shared interest, you will increase the likelihood that your communication efforts will be successful.

Effects

One of the questions that has arisen as communication models have evolved over the years is just how much effect communication has on the parties involved in the interaction. More specifically, a number of theories have addressed the **effects** of the mass media on audiences. For instance, an early model of unlimited effects theorized that audiences are highly susceptible to the effects of messages conveyed through the mass media. Unable to resist the power of media messages, audience members are easily influenced, according to the unlimited effects theory. Research, however, did not support this theory, so a number of theories regarding the limited effects of the mass media have taken its place. These theories include the following:

effects—Varied results of communication in regard to its effect on audience members and society in general.

- *Uses and gratification:* According to this theory, audience members self-select which mass media messages to embrace based on their psychological dispositions and needs. They reject messages that they do not find useful or personally gratifying.
- *Agenda setting:* As proposed by McCombs and Shaw (1972), the mass media are not powerful enough to tell people what to think about an issue. But the media do have the power to influence which issues people think about. In other words, the mass media influence the public agenda.
- *Innovation:* This theory recognizes that the mass media may influence audience members by providing information regarding new developments, products, or services. Accordingly, the media play a role in the process by which innovations are adopted.
- *Diffusion of information:* According to this theory, one of the ways that the mass media affect large numbers of people occurs when people who receive a message through the media then share that message with others.
- *Modeling and cultivation:* These two theories address the influence of the mass media on various audiences. Modeling theory proposes that children and young adults in particular may be inclined to alter their behavior based on media messages that they consume (e.g., following role models). Cultivation theory suggests that media messages influence opinions and attitudes based on the media consumption patterns of audiences. For example, audience members who frequently select violent programs may view the world as being more violent than people who do not as frequently select violent programs.

Each of these theories has implications for sport communication specialists. Combined they provide the theoretical foundation on which the **strategic sport communication model** (SSCM [Pedersen, Miloch, & Laucella, 2007]) is built.

strategic sport communication model—A model depicting the dynamics of communication and the various settings in which communication occurs in sport.

STRATEGIC SPORT COMMUNICATION MODEL

The strategic sport communication model (SSCM) provides a framework for us to see how the dynamics of communication and the various settings for communication come together in sport. The model, depicted in figure 13.1, has four primary elements. One element is the sport communication process, which is displayed twice to emphasize that the process, elements, and effects described in the previous section pervade all the settings within the field. The other key elements are the personal and organizational communication in sport component, the sport mass media component, and the sport

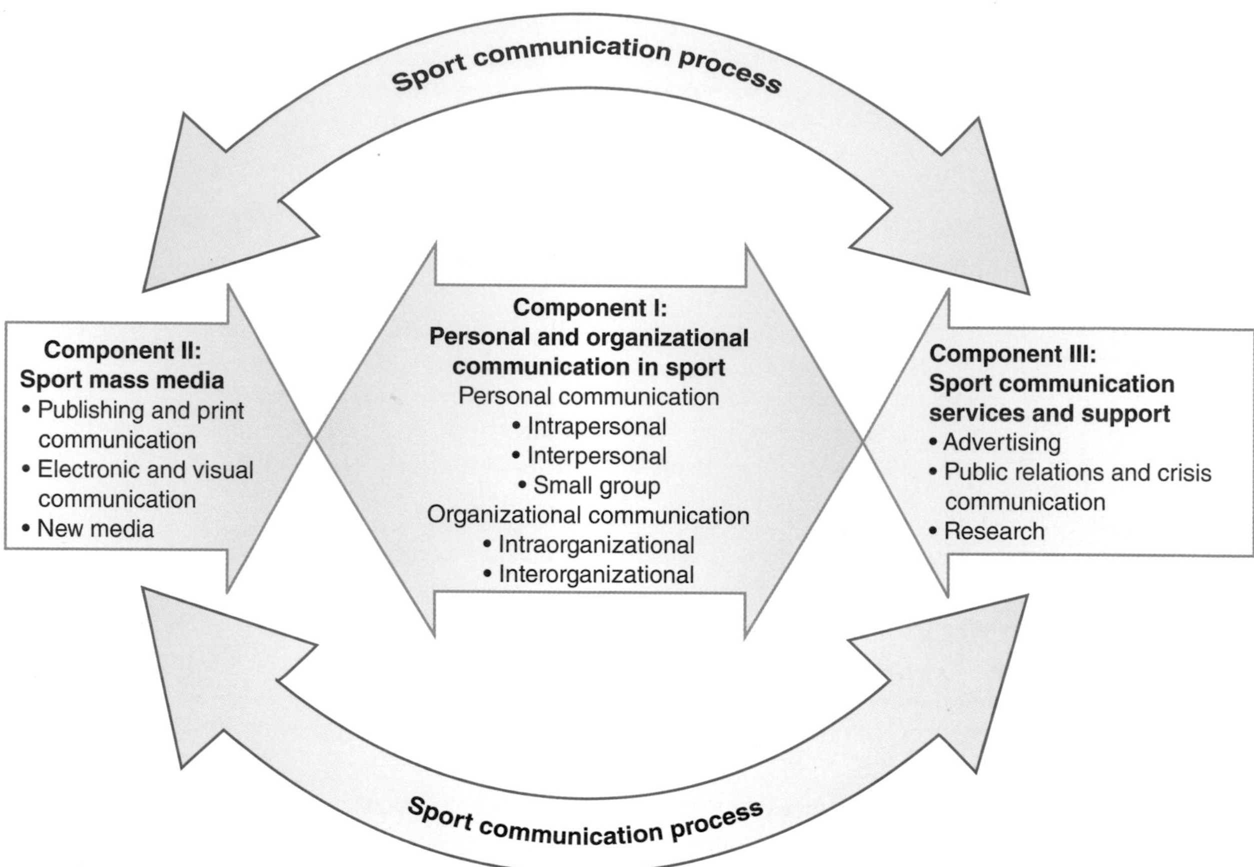

Figure 13.1 Strategic sport communication model.
Reprinted, by permission, from P.M. Pedersen, K.S., Miloch, and P.C. Laucella, 2007, *Strategic sport communication* (Champaign, IL: Human Kinetics), 85.

communication services and support components. Note that these key elements (i.e., components in the model) are related. The arrows pointing to and from component I denote that the types and forms of communication in the central component influence the forms of communication in components II and III, and vice versa.

Personal and Organizational Communication

Component I in the SSCM includes the various forms of personal communication and organizational communication in sport. Each is considered in the paragraphs to follow.

Personal Sport Communication

Personal communication includes intrapersonal, interpersonal, and small-group communication. The prefix *intra* means "within," so intrapersonal communication is the internal communication that each of us experiences. The prefix *inter* means "between," so interpersonal communication is the exchange of messages between two people. Intrapersonal communication is individual in nature but so prevalent that it is arguably the most common type of communication. Intrapersonal communication is by definition private, but many people choose to share their thoughts in forums such as Internet blogs.

Interpersonal communication occurs in face-to-face interactions, may be verbal or nonverbal (e.g., facial cues), and may involve such actions as engaging in telephone conversations and exchanging information through notes, memos, e-mail correspondence, and text messages.

Small-group communication occurs in settings of three or more people. Although more people are involved, the means for small-group communication are identical to those for interpersonal communication. Small-group communication is also like interpersonal communication in that the communication has a shared purpose and the people involved influence one another in the process. It is more complex, of course, because more people are involved. The varying degrees to which people in the group engage in communication and the differing ways in which they respond can make group communication extremely complex.

The following example incorporates each of the three types of personal sport communication. The president of a professional baseball team desires to see her team achieve a greater level of involvement with its community. She engages in an internal dialogue (i.e., intrapersonal communication) regarding the various approaches that the team may take to address the issue. After she identifies a few ideas, she shares them with the team's director of public relations through an e-mail message (i.e., interpersonal communication). The director replies that he will forward the ideas to his staff members at their next meeting and will follow up with feedback after the meeting ends. The staff meeting (i.e., group communication) provides a forum for the discussion of the relative merits of the ideas, and as a result, the best ideas are prioritized for development. The director of public relations then shares those ideas with the president for final approval.

Organizational Sport Communication

The three types of personal communication may occur in either an intraorganizational or an interorganizational setting. Again, because *intra* means "within," intraorganizational communication occurs within a particular sport organization setting. And because *inter* means "between," interorganizational communication occurs when members of a sport organization interact with those outside the organization.

The example in the previous section was of intraorganizational communication in its various forms. To carry that example to its next step, say that one of the community engagement initiatives that the organization develops is a caravan program in which members of the team, its coaches and manager, its broadcast team, and the team mascot make a series of appearances in the organization's surrounding area to promote the upcoming season. As the team representatives make speeches to the fans in attendance, conduct interviews with members of the media, and sign autographs afterward, they are engaging in interorganizational communication. That is, they are communicating with people outside their organization.

Communication Skills

The most basic personal and organizational communication skills that you need to develop are your writing and speaking abilities. To write effectively, you must be able to track down information, organize it, and record it in a way that interests and informs readers. Sentences must be grammatically correct, wording must be succinct, and ideas must flow from one point to another. Speaking effectively also entails organizing information. Strong speakers are able to boil down large amounts of information into key points that they repetitively emphasize, and they are able to build on those points with additional information and humorous or insightful stories. They also connect with their audiences by using appropriate gestures and body language. Because sport communicators must routinely reach a variety of audiences, failure to develop effective communication techniques is usually a prelude to unproductive or even counterproductive efforts.

So how do you become an effective communicator? There's the old joke: How do you get to Carnegie Hall? Practice, practice, practice! When you interview for an entry-level job in the field of sport communication, your prospective employer will expect you to have already developed strong communication skills and gained some related experience. You might get some of this experience through experiential learning activities in your classes, but that kind of practice probably will not be enough to distinguish you competitively. You will likely need to volunteer with a sport organization (e.g., media relations, community relations) or with a mass media outlet (e.g., campus newspaper, local radio station) to get the repetition necessary to hone your skills adequately. Significant volunteer experience will likely position you to gain a high-quality internship in which you can continue to build the skills necessary for a successful career in the field.

Component II of the SSCM includes publishing and print communication, electronic and visual communication, and new media. The three main categories are addressed in the following sections.

Print Communication

print communication—Communication through printed publications, including sport sections in newspapers, sport magazines, and sport books.

The publishing and print communication setting includes sports sections in newspapers, sport magazines, and sport books. Accordingly, the people working in sport **print communication** positions include sports writers, sports columnists, and sports editors.

Although newspaper readership has been in decline, various readership trends reported by the Newspaper Association of America (2010) reveal interesting information. For instance, more than 154 million adults, or 48% of the adult population, read at least a portion of a newspaper each day. Sport coverage draws a significant number of those readers; 55% of newspaper readers report that they usually read that section. Sport magazines are also prevalent in the marketplace. These magazines range in scope from general interest periodicals such as *Sports Illustrated* and the *Sporting News* to more specialized publications such as *Inside Triathlon* and *Golf Digest*.

The print media are also prominent in other nations. For instance, based on a 2008 readership survey by the Newspaper Audience Bank (NADbank), *Toronto Sun* publisher and CEO Kin-Man Lee revealed that "77% of Canadians 18 years and older (are) reading papers, either in print or online" (Robertson, 2009, ¶ 8). In the United Kingdom a national readership survey concluded that a weekday issue of a daily newspaper is read for an average of 40 minutes. An average Saturday newspaper is read for an average of 57 minutes, and 42% of readers spend an hour or more. An average Sunday newspaper is read for an average of 61 minutes, and 50% spend an hour or more (NRS, n.d.).

Electronic Communication

electronic communication—Communication by electronic media, including sports broadcasting on television (e.g., broadcast, cable, satellite), sports radio, sport film (e.g., movies), and sport photography.

The electronic and visual communication setting encompasses sports broadcasting on television (e.g., broadcast, cable, satellite) and radio. **Electronic communication** includes sport film (e.g., movies) and photography.

Electronic media are prevalent. Research indicates that 99% of American homes have radios and 98% have television sets (US Census Bureau, 2006). Moreover, 88% have video recorders of some kind. Serving these households are more than 12,000 radio stations (4,789 commercial AM stations and 8,961 commercial FM stations). There are also 2,218 television stations serving American homes (Central Intelligence Agency, 2009), and 9,339 cable systems are operating in the United States. Most offer 60 or more channels. These organizations would not be in business without a large market for programming. Adult TV viewers watch television for an average of over 353 minutes a day (Council for Research Excellence, 2009).

Broadcast media outlets are prevalent throughout much of the world. Table 13.1 displays the number of TV and radio stations broadcasting in a number of countries. Some TV and radio stations are noncommercial or educational, but most are commercial. TV stations are either affiliated with a broadcast network (e.g., ABC, CBS, NBC, Fox, CW) or operate as independent stations with limited or no network affiliation. Many major network affiliates have local news and thus sport programming. Many broadcast and TV networks have additional sport personnel to cover events on a regu-

TABLE 13.1 Number of Television and Radio Stations

Nation	Number of TV stations	Number of AM radio stations	Number of FM radio stations
Australia	104	262	345
Canada	148	245	582
Japan	211	215	89
Russia	7,306	323	~1,500
United Kingdom	940	206	696

Data based on Central Intelligence Agency, 2008, *The world factbook 2008*. Available: www.cia.gov/library/publications/the-world-factbook/

lar or special basis (e.g., the National Football League [NFL] season, the Wimbledon Championships). Obviously, ESPN and its sister channels require a large number of sport reporters and anchors to handle their all-sport format. Some programs that air on ESPN, however, are sold to the network as a package complete with announcers and commentators under contract to the company that produces the programs, not the network airing them.

New Media

new media—Communication through nontraditional media platforms, most of them Internet based and ranging from traditional Web sites to sport Web logs (i.e., blogs) to e-commerce systems.

New media include a variety of communication platforms, most of them Internet-based. They range from traditional Web sites and social networking Web sites (e.g., Twitter, Facebook, MySpace) to sport Web logs (i.e., blogs) and e-commerce systems. As of 2009 more than 1.7 billion people worldwide were using the Internet (Internet World Stats, 2010). Many of these users go online to access sports information. Sport Web sites such as ESPN.com, SportsLine.com, FoxSports.com, Sports.Yahoo.com, NBCSports.com, SI.com, SportingNews.com, and NFL.com frequently draw heavy traffic. Growth in recent years has been significant. The percentage of the North American population using the Internet was over 74% in 2009, a number that has grown by 134% since 2000 (Internet World Stats, 2010).

The emergence of new media has already had a profound effect on how many sport communication professionals practice their profession, and it seems certain that more changes are on the way. One advantage that many sport organizations have already realized through the Internet is the ability to disseminate messages to a mass audience quickly and inexpensively without having to go through the mass media. Only a few years ago, sport media relations professionals were completely reliant on the mass media to convey messages that originated with the sport organization through news releases. If the media did not use the releases, the information simply was not available to the public. Now, sport public relations practitioners can post that information on organizational Web sites where interested parties can access it at their convenience. Or the public relations professionals can use a distribution list to e-mail the information to interested parties who have previously provided their addresses to the organization. These options offer a level of message control previously unattainable in the field.

Additionally, the Internet provides a forum for a two-way flow of communication with the public. Many sport organizations are only now beginning to take advantage of this opportunity. Some sport managers are doing some simple but important things. For example, a number of prominent sport figures are now using blogs and microblogs (e.g., Twitter) to share information with the public. Others periodically set up chat sessions in which they answer questions and respond to comments from audience members.

Of course, new technology also has a way of making things more complicated, and sport communication professionals are finding this to be true too. Media

REALMADRID.COM

By Matthew Goltz
Realmadrid.com English version, SPAIN

Real Madrid Club de Fútbol is just one of hundreds of sport organizations around the world that have found the use of online content to be an indispensable tool for communicating with their publics. Launched in May 2000, realmadrid.com has undergone continual evolution in concert with the development of Internet capabilities and technological advances in new media.

Over the last three years, realmadrid.com has progressed from a relatively static Web site to an interactive media platform published in Spanish, English, and Japanese that receives over one million unique visits per month from around the world. To reach out to fans of the most successful team in the history of fútbol, Real Madrid seeks to maintain contact with its global fan base at the click of a button. For this reason, the three language versions of the Web site, a number that is likely to increase in the future, are updated on a daily basis. This need to reach global masses can be attributed to the popularity of the sport around the world and the diversity of the team and its fans. This trend is slowly catching on in the United States where, for example, Major League Baseball is experiencing an influx of Latino players, resulting in a fan base including more Hispanics. Similarly, Major League Soccer is trying to capitalize on the ever-increasing Hispanic population in North America.

Unlike US-based teams whose Web sites are operated in conjunction with their respective

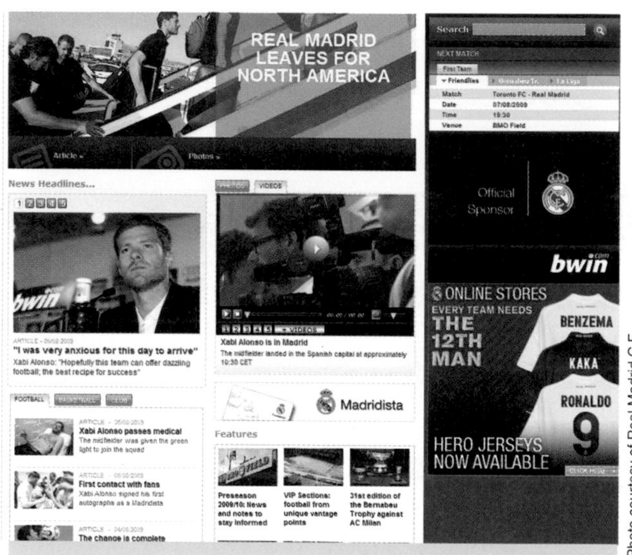

Photo courtesy of Real Madrid C.F.

The Web site for Real Madrid reaches a global audience by being offered in several languages, including English.

relations specialists in particular are dealing with a couple of challenging issues. First, the specialists are receiving more requests from bloggers for media credentials to events and interview access to players and coaches. Another issue that they are facing is the growing amount of noncredible information (e.g., false rumors about a sport organization) and unauthorized credible information appearing on the Internet. These issues, and others, will call on sport public relations professionals to adjust their strategies as new technologies continue to develop.

Given the growing prevalence of technology in the field, one additional concern has begun to receive attention in recent years. Some sport communication professionals have become so reliant on technology that they may underuse the direct communication skills necessary to be effective (Battenfield & Kent, 2007). Although the ability to develop message content for online distribution is a powerful communication tool, informal interactions in the workplace and telephone conversations with members of important publics remain essential for effective sport communication.

Sport Communication Services and Support

Component III of the SSCM includes three elements—advertising, public relations and crisis communication, and research. A powerful form of interorganizational com-

leagues, Real Madrid uses its in-house staff of sports writers, translators, and photographers to keep Madridistas abreast of all news involving the club, including daily training reports, press conferences, game schedules, game reports, and interviews. This approach is an ideal way to disseminate official news such as player signings and significant club developments in a fast and effective manner, and it serves to cross-promote club sponsors and club departments such as the nonprofit Real Madrid Foundation.

Realmadrid.com has gone to great lengths to make the site as interactive as possible without putting the club's name and reputation in jeopardy of being damaged by outside sources. Through the site, readers are able to purchase game tickets, view and download photographs and videos, participate in polls, access the official online store and mobile content, connect to the club through social networking sites, download the official Real Madrid toolbar, and opt to receive RSS content. Initiatives are also undertaken in an attempt to bring the fans from all corners of the world closer to their team. "Madridista Planet," for example, gives supporters the opportunity to express their loyalty and have their pictures published on the site, and articles labeled "News and Opinions" allow fans to speak their mind and exchange thoughts on the piece in question.

Web sites have become an important source of revenue and customer relationship management (CRM) for sport organizations. Real Madrid, therefore, must take a proactive approach in building and sustaining relationships with its stakeholders and publics by engaging them with interactive and informative online content and news in a timely manner.

INTERNATIONAL LEARNING ACTIVITY #1

Go to the Web sites of five sport teams in your country. Compare and contrast the interactive elements of those sites with the same elements on realmadrid.com. If you were to design a Web site for a sport team, what interactive elements would you include? Why?

INTERNATIONAL LEARNING ACTIVITY #2

Go to the Web sites of the 2012 London Olympic and Paralympic Games and the 2014 Sochi Winter Olympic and Paralympic Games. Evaluate the content, design, and usability of these sites. What changes would you recommend?

munication, advertising is primarily a marketing tool, and as such, it is addressed in chapter 12. Similarly, research is addressed in chapter 20. For now, we will simply emphasize that good research serves as the foundation of successful advertising and public relations efforts.

WEB

Go to the OSG and complete the Web search activity, which has you analyze the Real Madrid Web site.

The remainder of this section focuses on public relations. **Sport public relations** has been defined as a "managerial communication-based function designed to identify a sport organization's key publics, evaluate its relationships with those publics, and foster desirable relationships between the sport organization and those key publics" (Stoldt, Dittmore, & Branvold, 2006, p. 2). Accordingly, public relations refers to organizational communication with various groups of people who are affected by the organization. Key publics often include the media, the community, employees, investors, donors, customers, and regulators. We now consider basic models of public relations practice and then address the two most common types of public relations practiced in sport—media relations and community relations.

sport public relations—A managerial communication-based function designed to identify a sport organization's key publics, evaluate its relationships with those publics, and foster desirable relationships between the sport organization and those key publics.

Models of Public Relations Practice

Some prominent public relations scholars have argued that public relations practitioners work under four basic models of communicating (Grunig & Hunt, 1984): two

one-way model of public relations—A communication model focusing exclusively on the flow of information from the sport organization to its publics.

two-way model of public relations—A communication model focusing on communication give and take between a sport organization and its key publics.

one-way models and two **two-way models.** The assumptions made about the communication process and the organization's purpose in communicating usually drives the decision about which model to use.

The first model is a one-way publicity and press agentry model. Organizations using this model do not seek input from their key publics, but they are extremely concerned about having messages disseminated to a wide audience. Sometimes, to get attention, they are willing to stray beyond the boundaries of what would be considered appropriate or ethical. If you have ever watched a news conference promoting an upcoming boxing match turn into a staged melee, you have seen this model in action at its worst. The boxers, and sometimes the promoters, are willing to risk their credibility, not to mention the well-being of anyone caught in the middle of the fracas, in exchange for the buzz that the prematch fight will generate among the public. This model has many ethical applications as well. Note that Grunig and Hunt (1984) suggested that the entertainment industry commonly employs the limited one-way model (one could argue that sport falls into that category much of the time). In such cases, feedback is limited to responses such as ticket sales.

The second one-way model is the public information model. Organizations that use this model are not as extreme in seeking public attention. Instead, they offer useful services to members of the mass media and the public by providing information in a credible manner. For example, they might assist members of the mass media in setting up interviews, or they might provide a variety of other services to members of the media who are covering a sport event. Many professional organizations and college athletics programs have media relations or sports information offices to perform these functions. By offering such services, they hope to receive greater amounts of favorable publicity.

Two-way communication models are based on the assumption that the most effective forms of communication require input from target publics. In other words, communication requires give and take. For example, if the owner of a sport team wants the community to vote in favor of a tax increase to help fund a new stadium, that owner would be smart to gather some information regarding public sentiment toward the team and public projects in general before attempting to craft public relations messages. In such an example, the owner is using the first two-way model, the asymmetrical approach. The goal is to use information about a public in a scientific way to communicate more effectively and induce that public to behave as desired. In the case of our example, the desired outcome would be for the community to vote in favor of the tax increase to fund the new stadium.

The second two-way model is the symmetrical approach. This method also employs planned information-gathering techniques to communicate more effectively, but it recognizes that the outcome of the communication process will likely mean that both the organization and the public will have to change their positions or behavior. In other words, the second two-way model is about negotiating mutually acceptable solutions. In her study of public relations practices in two English cricket clubs, Hopwood (2005) found that one of the clubs made considerable use of two-way symmetrical communication practices whereas the other was less proactive. The more proactive club was at the forefront of public relations practices among the clubs in its league.

MEDIA RELATIONS IN SPORT

The mass media devote considerable attention to sport. Because of that interest, most sport managers find that working with members of the mass media is an important part of their jobs. In many cases, sport organizations hire people specifically to manage media relations. These media relations professionals—or sports information professionals, as they are sometimes called—typically operate in a manner consistent with the public information model.

What Media Relations Specialists Do

Sport media relations professionals who work for a team, facility, or organization are responsible for creating, coordinating, and organizing information about that entity and disseminating it to the public indirectly through the mass media or through direct channels (e.g., organizational Web site). The sidebar "Professional Profile: Larry Rankin" describes the background and work of one such professional. The following sections elaborate on a few of the more common duties assumed by media relations professionals.

Writing News Releases

The goal of a news release is to disseminate information to targeted publics in the most positive light possible. The media usually determine what is and what is not newsworthy. The job of a media relations professional is to get information into the hands of the media and persuade them to use it because it is newsworthy to some segment of the media's audience.

Courtesy of LWS Photography.

Professional Profile: Larry Rankin

When the Wichita State University (WSU) men's basketball team earned national acclaim by advancing to the Sweet 16 of the 2006 NCAA Men's Championship, the team's media relations contact, Larry Rankin, was well prepared. As the assistant athletic director for media relations at WSU, Rankin has worked many high-profile events, and he has seen the profession evolve, particularly in recent years.

Rankin has served in his current position for 10 years, and he has been on the media relations staff at WSU for 17 years. Before that, he worked as a sports information student assistant at Oklahoma State University (OSU) for five years. Besides being the media coordinator for the Sweet 16 team noted earlier, Rankin served as team media coordinator for the 1989 and 1990 OSU national championship wrestling teams, the 1991 Sweet 16 OSU women's basketball team, and the 1996 WSU College World Series baseball team. He was also the event media coordinator for the 1989 NCAA Wrestling Championship in Oklahoma City and the 1995, 1996, 1998, and 1999 NCAA baseball regionals in Wichita, Kansas.

Rankin now manages and oversees media relations for WSU's 15 Division I sports and is the primary contact for men's basketball. He supervises a staff of two full-time assistants, three graduate assistants, and one student administrative assistant who supports the media relations office with specific sport responsibilities. The students working on Rankin's staff are gaining experience that will be critical as they advance their own careers.

"Getting involved in athletics as a student, graduate assistant or volunteer early in your college career will assist you in advancing toward your goals of working in Division I athletics," Rankin explained. He added that the nature of media relations work is changing as social media continue to gain popularity. He said that media relations professionals are now using platforms such as Facebook, MySpace, and Twitter to reach their audiences. Many are also interacting with the public through organizational blogs.

Rankin stated that the Internet is likely to cause fundamental changes in some traditional forms of organizational media. For example, media guides are moving exclusively online, allowing athletics departments to realize significant savings in printing costs.

Planning News Conferences

The goal of a news conference, like a news release, is to disseminate noteworthy information from an organization to its targeted publics. News conferences allow face-to-face interaction with members of the media as an organizational spokesperson offers information or makes a statement. After the spokesperson finishes the statement, reporters usually have the opportunity to ask questions. Key considerations for media relations professionals concerning a news conference include who will speak on behalf of the organization and where the news conference will be held.

Managing the Press Box

The primary purpose of a press box is to provide accredited working members of the media with a place to sit and record the actions of the event. The location of this space varies from sport to sport, but the media generally have an unobstructed view of the competition. Separate booths or rooms are generally provided for broadcast media including TV sportscasters, the home organization's radio broadcasters, and the visiting organization's radio team. Sport organizations usually provide results, statistics, and other publicity information to media working in the press box.

Careers in Media Relations

Competition for jobs in sport media relations is intense. Salaries are not always commensurate with similar communication positions in the corporate world because many people seem willing to work in sport almost for free. In addition, sport media relations professionals are frequently called on to work long hours. "First one to arrive, last one to leave" is a common reality in the profession. Work schedules of 60 to 80 hours per week are not uncommon during a particular season, and for those working at the collegiate level, sport seasons usually run about 10 months.

COMMUNITY RELATIONS IN SPORT

Community relations activities tend to center on promoting charitable initiatives and developing opportunities for face-to-face contact with stakeholders, and as such, they complement media relations. Sport organizations engage in **community relations** activities for many reasons, including demonstrating social responsibility, generating long-term goodwill in the community, and producing new revenue in the short term (Stoldt et al., 2006).

community relations— Often focuses on the promotion of charitable initiatives affiliated with the sport organization and the development of opportunities for face-to-face contact with sport organization stakeholders.

What Community Relations Professionals Do

Sport community relations professionals who work for a team, facility, or organization are responsible for creating, organizing, and executing charitable initiatives and other programs designed to involve the sport entity in community enhancement. The sidebar "Professional Profile: Aprile Pritchet" describes the work of one such practitioner. A common form of sport community relations activity is the donation of money to various charities. Some sport organizations, particularly those at the major professional level, execute a variety of fund-raising events throughout the year and then donate the proceeds to charitable organizations. Other sport organizations may simply contribute autographed merchandise that the charity can then auction off in its own fund-raising activities. A second form of community relations activities that sport organizations commonly employ involves initiatives to better the community through direct contact. For example, some organizations cultivate youth sport participation by constructing sport venues (e.g., ball fields) and sponsoring clinics. Others might engage in partnerships with charitable organizations to advocate important messages (e.g., "stay in school") or generate an important service (e.g., building a home with Habitat for

Humanity). These initiatives take place at multiple levels from the professional sport league to the member franchise to the individual player or coach. In addition, some sport organizations are looking to take their community relations efforts to a new level of effectiveness by creating strategic partnerships with corporate sponsors to serve their communities more effectively. A third form of common community relations activity does not directly benefit charitable organizations but does enable the sport organization to build relationships with various constituents through direct contact. Many community relations professionals coordinate speaking appearances by other members of their organizations. Still others organize promotional events such as the annual winter caravans that many Major League Baseball (MLB) teams stage to rally support during the off-season. Some organizations, particularly those at the minor league level, find that the most popular personality at such appearances is the team mascot.

Careers in Community Relations

Community relations activity is common in a wide range of sport organizations from professional entertainment organizations to colleges and universities to for-profit fitness centers to sporting goods manufacturers. The larger the organization and the greater

Courtesy of DC United.

Professional Profile: Aprile Pritchet

Aprile Pritchet, the community relations director for DC United, knows the value of experiential learning. She began her career with DC United of Major League Soccer (MLS) as an intern, as did many of her colleagues on DC United's staff.

The results have been impressive. Pritchet was the corecipient of the 2008 MLS Community Relations Executive of the Year award, given annually to the MLS community relations executive who guided his or her team to make the greatest contribution in the community (Major League Soccer, n.d.).

Pritchet is responsible for creating and implementing all of DC United's community outreach programs and initiatives. She also oversees staff members involved in the execution of those programs. She generates and coordinates public appearances for players and coaches and develops other off-the-field publicity strategies for the team. Pritchet also serves as the team's liaison with local leaders relative to community affairs activity.

The United Builds program under Pritchet's direction has been recognized as one of the best in MLS (DC United, n.d.). The program secures volunteer opportunities for players, staff, and supporters, and it has resulted in thousands of volunteer hours being devoted to worthy organizations such as Thrive DC, formally known as the Dinner Program for Homeless Women.

DC United Soccer Geography is another team program designed to assist fourth- through eighth-grade students in the DC metropolitan area by providing soccer-related lesson plans for geography teachers. More than 300 classes and 14,000 students have used the program.

Pritchet earned her bachelor's degree in sport management at Hampton University and has a master's degree in sport studies from the University of Massachusetts at Amherst. Her graduate education was supported by a full scholarship awarded by the National Association of Collegiate Directors of Athletics (NACDA), ESPN, and the National Basketball Association's (NBA) Cleveland Cavaliers.

Four years into her professional career, Pritchet notes the importance of building on educational experiences by networking and securing relevant experience. "The best advice I can give for this industry is to meet as many people as you can!" she says. "More often than not, you have to start at the bottom and work your way up. Many people at DC United are former interns and now hold management positions."

its resources, the more likely it is that organization will have one or more employees assigned specifically to community relations.

On balance, fewer full-time positions are available in community relations than in media relations in sport. One primary reason is that hundreds of colleges and universities hire at least one full-time employee in sports information. Many community relations responsibilities are delegated to the student life skills division of the athletics department. Still, community relations is a viable career option in the sport industry.

Other Public Relations Positions

Many sport organizations employ public relations professionals in positions that extend beyond media relations or community relations. Some of the common positions are the following:

- *Corporate communications:* Tasks may include marketing communication such as media placement in support of a promotional effort, employee communications, community relations, investor relations, and customer relations. Corporate communications positions tend to be more common in sport organizations with relatively large public relations staffs.
- *Creative specialists:* These public relations practitioners possess specialized skills in design, layout, graphic arts, and other technical skills.
- *Employee and volunteer relations:* These professionals build strong internal relationships by creating forums for communication and staging special events (e.g., volunteer appreciation day). Volunteer relations positions are more prevalent in settings such as state amateur sport festivals in which a large volunteer workforce is critical to successful execution of the event.
- *Web site manager:* These sport communicators update online information, respond to inquiries from visitors to the Web site, facilitate discussion forums, and serve as liaisons with other staff members whose functions include Web site interests (e.g., sports information, marketing, ticket sales).

Depending on the setting, other public relations jobs in the sport industry may focus on donor relations, government relations, or relations with various governing bodies.

PORTFOLIO

Complete the critical thinking portfolio activity in the OSG, consulting as needed the "Eight Critical Thinking Questions" section in chapter 1.

CRITICAL THINKING IN SPORT COMMUNICATION

Given the rapid ascension of nontraditional forms of communication such as message boards, blogs, social media, and microblogging sites, sport communication professionals have found themselves needing to address ways to develop media policies for dealing with these emerging forms of media.

As potential future sport communication professionals, you will be put in a position to make decisions regarding how, when, and to whom certain information is released. You may also be called on to design communication programs that maximize return to the organization while using a minimal amount of resources.

Additionally, the nature of how sports fans consume sport products such as games is changing. More options are available for television, mobile, and Internet video content. Future sport communication professionals who are creative in ways of distributing content and especially those who can monetize that delivery will be in demand. So, the next time that you are watching a sporting event, either in person, on television, or on the Internet, think about what innovation might improve your experience. Perhaps it is player updates delivered to your cell phone while watching in a stadium. Or maybe it is pausing live television during a play to switch camera angles and watch a replay, much as the director of the broadcast could do.

Although we do not know how the sport mass media will change in the next several years, it is clear that the communication professional who has a firm understanding of how people communicate, ranging from face-to-face interactions to technological interactions such as text messaging, will be well positioned to contribute positively to organizational success.

ETHICS IN SPORT COMMUNICATION

Sport communication professionals are frequently faced with ethical dilemmas. For example, those in sport mass media encounter ethical issues relating to their sources, coverage decisions, objectivity requirements, and so forth. Two examples in the areas of media relations and community relations in sport illustrate the myriad issues involving ethical and unethical actions in sport communication.

Ethical Issues in Media Relations

Media relations professionals frequently deal with a variety of ethics-related issues. Perhaps the most sensitive issues center on privacy. Media relations professionals have access to a great deal of information—much of it personal. If you work in the field, you need to be sensitive to this and release only information that will not compromise people's right to privacy. For example, it is unethical (not to mention illegal) for a college media relations professional to publicly release student–athlete grade-point averages. An exception might be the authorized release of information about a student–athlete who earns academic all-star recognition. The College Sports Information Directors of America (CoSIDA) is a professional organization that has a prescribed code of ethics designed to guide members as they wrestle with privacy-related and other ethical issues. Please review this code (www.cosida.com/About/codeofethics.aspx) and identify the primary issues addressed. Refer to chapter 1 and read the section involving ethical guidelines. How could you use the CoSIDA code of ethics to help you in your application of ethical decision making? How could media relations professionals use the code as a framework by which to evaluate the propriety of one another's actions? For instance, Kant's categorical imperative states that an ethical action taken under a particular set of circumstances could be considered a universal rule of behavior. Kant's mandate is reflected in the CoSIDA code of ethics. For example, the code stipulates that sports information personnel avoid public criticism of their colleagues and support their coaches and student–athletes when they refrain from commenting on a question posed by the media. Both tenets align with the Kant principle.

PORTFOLIO

Complete the ethical issues portfolio activity in the OSG, consulting as needed the "Guidelines for Making Ethical Decisions" section in chapter 1.

Another ethics-related issue relevant to media relations has to do with the one-way and two-way models discussed earlier in this chapter. Many sport managers think that the job is limited to publicity—to generating coverage of a team or event, or practicing damage control when something negative happens or is suspected. But a more complete and sophisticated approach to media relations would classify generating publicity as only one aspect of the work. Sport organizations that rely predominantly on a one-way flow of information might violate the boundaries of ethical relationships with their key constituents.

Ethical Issues in Community Relations

Community relations professionals also confront ethical issues. One ethical issue that they face is the obligation to keep their priorities straight. Sport organizations are in a unique position to capitalize on the publicity that often accompanies their charitable initiatives. For example, visits by sport figures to patients in a children's hospital might make for good press and moving visual images. Publicity for such ventures clearly enhances the reputation of the sport organization within the community. But the service, rather than the publicity, should be the primary motive for the visits, and if at any point the dignity and privacy of the children being served is compromised, a serious ethical boundary has been breached. Imagine how uncomfortable it would be to defend such an action in a TV interview. The audience would be justifiably indignant about the exploitation of sick children.

Summary

Communication is a core skill required of all sport managers, and it presents an exciting array of career options for prospective professionals. As noted earlier in the chapter, sport communication is defined as a process by which people in and through sport endeavors and settings share symbols and through their interactions create meaning. The strategic sport communication model (SSCM) depicts both the dynamic sport communication process and the various settings in which sport communication occurs. The components of the SSCM include personal and organizational communication, the sport mass media, and sport communication services and support.

Personal communication may occur on an intrapersonal, interpersonal, or small-group basis. It includes both intraorganizational communication (i.e., within the organization) and interorganizational communication (i.e., between organizational representatives and external constituents).

The many forms of sport media range from print to electronic to new media. The print media include sports sections in newspapers, sport magazines, and sport books. The electronic media encompass sport on television, on radio, and in the movies. New media include sport on the Internet and as communicated through other relatively recent technological innovations. The Internet is particularly powerful because it provides opportunities to reach constituents directly, instantaneously, and interactively.

Sport communication services and support include both advertising and public relations. The latter topic received considerable attention in this chapter. Sport media relations professionals disseminate information to the public through the mass media or through organizational Web sites. They also manage additional media requests, service the media during games or events, and manage records and statistics. Sport community relations professionals generate goodwill for their organizations. They coordinate organizational participation in charitable endeavors, fund-raisers that benefit various nonprofits, and public appearances by managers and players. By carefully executing these activities, they enhance their communities and the reputations of their organizations within their communities.

QUIZ TIME

Did you grasp all the key points in this chapter? Go to the OSG for a short quiz to test your understanding of the material.

A variety of ethical issues are associated with sport communication. These range from protecting people's privacy to allowing for give and take in communication with key publics. Strong critical thinking skills are also important for sport communicators because they face a rapidly evolving communication environment. New technologies, accompanied by more frequent demand for bottom-line results from communication programs, mean that future professionals will be required to process significant amounts of information, apply appropriate value judgments, and define prudent actions.

Review Questions

1. Why is communication a critical concern to all sport managers whether they are communication specialists or not?
2. What are the primary elements of the SSCM? What kinds of career opportunities pertain to the various elements?
3. What skills and experiences are most important to sport communication professionals?
4. What would you include in an inventory of the sport media that you commonly use?
5. What emerging technologies are affecting sport communication professionals? What do you see as the greatest opportunities and threats that these technologies bring to the profession?
6. Describe the work of sport media relations professionals. What sorts of tasks are included in their job descriptions?
7. How would you describe some of the tasks performed by sport community relations professionals?
8. What are some of the common ethical issues facing sport public relations professionals?
9. What are some of the nontraditional forms of communication now being used by sport managers?

References

Battenfield, F., & Kent, A. (2007). The culture of communication among intercollegiate sport information professionals. *International Journal of Sport Management and Marketing*, 2, 236–251.

Central Intelligence Agency. (2008). *The world factbook 2008*. Retrieved May 15, 2009, from https://www.cia.gov/library/publications/download/download-2008/

Central Intelligence Agency. (2009). *Field listing—television broadcast stations*. Retrieved April 9, 2009, from www.cia.gov/library/publications/the-world-factbook/fields/2015.html

Council for Research Excellent. (2009). *Video consumer mapping study*. Retrieved February 1, 2010, from www.researchexcellence.com/vcmstudy.php

DC United. (n.d.). *United builds*. Retrieved February 1, 2010, from www.dcunited.com/community/united-builds

Grunig, J.E., & Hunt, T. (1984). *Managing public relations*. New York: Holt, Rinehart and Winston.

Hopwood, M.K. (2005). Public relations practice in English county cricket. *Corporate Communications: An International Journal*, *10*, 201–212.

Internet World Stats. (2010). *Internet usage statistics*. Retrieved June 12, 2010, from www.internetworldstats.com/stats.htm

Lasswell, H.D. (1948). The structure and function of communication in society. In L. Bryson (Ed.), *The communication of ideas* (pp. 37–51). New York: Harper.

Littlejohn, S.W., & Foss, K.A. (2008). *Theories of human communication* (9th ed.). Belmont, CA: Wadsworth.

Major League Soccer. (n.d.). *MLS 2007 league awards: Candidates bios*. Retrieved February 1, 2010, from www.mlsnet.com/mls/awards/2007/bios.jsp?award=community

McCombs, M.E., & Shaw, D.L. (1972). The agenda-setting function of mass media. *Public Opinion Quarterly*, *32*(6), 176–187.

Newspaper Association of America. (2010). *Readership*. Retrieved February 1, 2010, from www.naa.org/TrendsandNumbers/Readership.aspx

NRS. (n.d.). *Time spent reading*. Retrieved May 15, 2009, from www.nrs.co.uk/time_spent_reading/time_spent_reading

Pedersen, P.M., Miloch, K.S., & Laucella, P.C. (2007). *Strategic sport communication*. Champaign, IL: Human Kinetics.

Pedersen, P.M., Miloch, K.S., Laucella, P.C., & Fielding, L. (2007). The juxtaposition of sport and communication: Defining the field of sport communication. *International Journal of Sport Management and Marketing*, 2, 193–207.

Robertson, I. (2009, March 25). *The* Sun *shines in readership survey*. Retrieved June 12, 2010, from www.torontosun.com/news/torontoandgta/2009/03/25/8886016.html

Schramm, W. (1954). How communication works. In W. Schramm (Ed.), *The process and effects of mass communication* (pp. 3–26). Urbana: University of Illinois Press.

Shannon, C.E., & Weaver, W. (1949). *The mathematical theory of communication*. Urbana: University of Illinois Press.

Stoldt, G.C, Dittmore, S.W., & Branvold, S.E. (2006). *Sport public relations: Managing organizational communication*. Champaign, IL: Human Kinetics.

US Census Bureau. (2006). *Utilization of Selected Media: 1980 to 2006*. Retrieved May 15, 2009, from www.census.gov/compendia/statab/tables/09s1090.pdf

HISTORICAL MOMENTS

1966	Naming rights granted—Busch Memorial Stadium, St. Louis
1967	NFL Super Bowl 30-second ad cost US$42,500 on CBS and US$37,500 on NBC—the only time the game was broadcast on two networks; in 2010 the cost of some spots rose to more than US$3 million
1971	NFL New England Patriots Stadium became Schaefer Field in US$150,000 deal with Schaefer Brewing Company
1973	Buffalo Bills Stadium became Rich Stadium in US$1.5 million deal with Rich Foods
1985	The Olympic Partner (TOP) Programme created
1990s	Approximately 170 new pro sport teams and 13 new leagues formed during decade of US economic expansion
1999	Enron Corporation agreed to pay Houston Astros US$100 million over 30 years to name the team's stadium Enron Field; after Enron declared bankruptcy the Astros bought back the naming rights in 2002
2001	Alex Rodriguez signed 10-year, US$252 million contract with Texas Rangers
2002	YES Network, joint venture between MLB's New York Yankees and NBA's New Jersey Nets, established
2003	CBS signed TV contract for NCAA Men's Basketball Championship for over US$500 million per year
2004–05	NHL lockout resulted in cancellation of season when collective bargaining agreement (CBA) expired; NHL and NHL Players Association ratifed a new CBA with a salary cap
2005	MLB salary average reached US$2.6 million, up from US$1.07 million in 1995
2007	David Beckham signed US$250 million, five-year contract to play for MLS Los Angeles Galaxy
2008	Five soccer clubs (Manchester United, Real Madrid, Arsenal, Bayern Munich, Liverpool) and 19 NFL teams were worth at least US$1 billion according to *Forbes* calculations
2009	Real Madrid paid Manchester United record US$131 million transfer fee for Cristiano Ronaldo

Photo courtesy of Paul M. Pedersen.

Finance and Economics in the Sport Industry

Timothy D. DeSchriver ■ Daniel F. Mahony

Learning Objectives

1. Explain the basic principles of economics and relate the theories of economics to the sport industry.
2. Discuss the concept of economic impact analysis and its relationship to sport events and facilities.
3. Describe the business structures of sport organizations.
4. Identify the basic principles and tools of financial management and apply them to the sport industry.
5. Recognize the basic elements of balance sheets and income statements for sport organizations.
6. Identify the various professional and career opportunities in the sport industry that are related to economics and financial management.
7. Understand the importance of ethics and critical thinking skills in the areas of sport finance and economics.

Key Terms

demand
economic interaction
law of demand
law of supply
market equilibrium
market shortage
market surplus
scarcity
sport economic impact studies
supply

Get a Job!

☑ Continue your journey in sport management by going to the Online Study Guide (OSG) at www.HumanKinetics.com/ContemporarySportManagement. Check out the job opportunities and consider the skills and experiences that can help you succeed in sport management.

Sport is one of the most diverse industries in the business world. It is composed of subindustries such as professional sports, collegiate athletics, facility management, health and fitness, and sporting goods. This diversity increases the difficulty of measuring the overall economic size of the industry. For example, should the sale of camping equipment be considered sport spending? Should the money that Sprint spends to be an official NASCAR sponsor be considered sport spending?

One unfortunate result of the lack of an exact definition of the sport industry is that few attempts have been made to measure the economic size of the industry. No empirical measurement of the overall size of the sport industry has been completed since the late 1990s. Meek (1997) estimated that the cumulative spending on sport-related goods and services in the United States was US$152 billion in 1995. Based on this estimate, Meek noted that sport was the 11th largest industry in the United States, larger than both the insurance and legal services industries. *Street & Smith's SportsBusiness Journal's* most recent estimate is that the size of the sport industry is US$213 billion ("Advertise," 2009). Although the US Department of Commerce does not estimate the overall size of the sport industry, it does provide some financial information on the size of specific sectors within the sport industry (see table 14.1). For example, in 2006 approximately US$2.23 billion was spent at skiing facilities such as Breckenridge Mountain in Colorado and Camelback Ski Area in Pennsylvania. The most recent numbers also revealed that the skiing industry employed over 73,800 full-time workers (US Census Bureau, 2009). Lastly, the Sporting Goods Manufacturers Association (SGMA) reported that Americans spent almost US$70 billion on the purchase of sporting goods and equipment in 2007 (SGMA, 2008). Although the actual dollar amount that can be attributed to the sport industry might be debatable, all the estimates make it clear that sport contributes a great deal to the US and global economies.

Although the sport industry has shown tremendous growth over the past decade, it is not immune to the fluctuations in the global economy that influence many other industries. The global recession that began in 2008 may have major effects on the sport industry. For example, in 2008 the National Football League (NFL) announced employee layoffs at its league offices in New York City. The league laid off approximately 10% of its 1,100 staff members (Battista, 2008). Other sport properties such as NASCAR and the English Premier League were also affected by the global downturn. For example, NASCAR announced in 2008 that it was eliminating offseason testing on racetracks to save millions of dollars during the tough economic times (Blount, 2008). Meanwhile, English soccer team Manchester United lost AIG as its primary uniform sponsor because of the insurance company's financial troubles (Laurent, 2009).

Another aspect of the global recession was the prevalence of unethical, and in some cases illegal, financial behavior. No case was more public than the alleged Ponzi scheme

TABLE 14.1 Economic Activity of Selected Sport Industry Sectors

Sport industry subsector	2006 sales level (US$)	2005 full-time employees
Skiing facilities	$2.23 billion	73,800
Golf courses and country clubs	$19.27 billion	304,600
Fitness and recreational sports facilities	$18.45 billion	488,800
Professional sport teams and clubs	$15.77 billion	46,700
Racetracks (horse and dog)	$7.76 billion	48,400
Agents and managers for artists, athletes, and public figures	$3.57 billion	19,400

U.S. Census Bureau 2009.

of Bernard Madoff. Through his investment firm, Madoff allegedly swindled investors out of US$50 billion (Creswell & Thomas, 2009). Madoff was not the only financier who allegedly broke the law, and one instance in particular had a direct connection to the sport industry. In 2009 the US Securities and Exchange Commission accused Robert Allen Stanford of stealing about US$8 billion of his investors' money. Stanford's company, Stanford Financial Group, was a major player in the athlete endorsement and sport sponsorship world. Stanford contracted with PGA golfers such as Vijay Singh, Henrik Stenson, Camilo Villegas, and Morgan Pressel to represent the company. Additionally, Stanford has sponsorship deals with sport organizations such as the National Basketball Association's (NBA) Miami Heat, the Sony Ericsson Open in tennis, and the PGA Tour's St. Jude Championship (Rovell, 2009). As you can see, the global economic troubles and financial misdeeds have had a major effect on the sport industry as we move into the second decade of the 21st century.

Recognition of both the growth and possible contraction of the sport industry leads to a discussion of economic and financial concepts. This chapter presents basic principles of economics and financial management, addresses the relationship between these economic and financial principles and the sport industry, and discusses career opportunities related to the financial management of the sport industry.

CURRENT FINANCIAL SITUATION OF US PROFESSIONAL SPORT

One segment of the sport industry that has seen tremendous growth over the past decade is professional sport. For example, the NFL in 2007 had operating revenues of approximately US$7.09 billion, and the league's teams had an overall operating income of about US$789 million ("NFL Team Valuations," 2008). Throughout the last decade, major professional men's sport leagues have seen their revenues increase over 10% annually. Despite this growth in revenue, economic problems remain.

For example, Major League Baseball (MLB) has seen a widening gap between the high- and low-revenue teams. In 2008 *Forbes* magazine estimated that the New York Yankees generated over US$327 million, making the club the highest revenue team in MLB. In the same year the Florida Marlins ranked last in revenue with only US$128 million ("The Business," 2008). This imbalance is an economic concern because all MLB teams, regardless of revenue, compete for the same players. The current revenue disparity makes it difficult for teams that have older stadia or are located in small markets,

Economic Cycles and the Sport Industry

All economies experience cyclical changes. For example, the world economy fell into a recession in early 2008. This recession brought higher unemployment rates and lower sales of consumer goods like automobiles and computers. Historically, most sport economists have believed that the sport industry has been recession proof, in other words, that sales of sport-related products have not fallen during past recessions. This steady demand is most likely due to the need for people, even in bad economic times, to engage in leisure and recreational activities. Also, sport has been considered a relatively inexpensive and affordable type of leisure. But this trend may be changing with the most recent recession. If the sport industry is no longer recession proof, the reasons most often cited are the increases in ticket prices and sport teams' increasing reliance on revenue from corporations in the form of sponsorship, advertising, and luxury suite sales. The recession that began in 2008 may have a larger economic impact on sport organizations than any prior downturn.

such as the Kansas City Royals and Pittsburgh Pirates, to acquire the best players and be competitive on the field. In the long run, this disparity may lead to a decrease in overall fan interest in MLB, particularly for fans of teams that are consistently poor.

To deal with this problem, most professional leagues attempt to equalize the differences in team revenues through revenue sharing. For example, all four of the traditional major men's leagues (i.e., NBA, MLB, NFL, and National Hockey League [NHL]) share revenue from national television rights fees and merchandise sales. Therefore, although an NFL team such as the New York Giants might be more popular than the Cincinnati Bengals, both receive the same amount of money from the NFL's US$3.08 billion annual television deals, the league's largest source of revenues. Revenue sharing equalizes team revenues and allows teams in smaller markets (e.g., the Green Bay Packers) to compete financially with the big-market teams. This equalization is important for professional sport leagues. As you learned in chapter 6, professional teams within a single league both compete and cooperate. Although their teams attempt to beat each other on the field, team managers must cooperate to ensure financial success for all. If some teams struggle financially, the entire league could decline.

As you might have already noticed, professional men's sport leagues rely heavily on the media. For example, teams in the NFL generate more money from their national and local media deals than they do from gate receipts. Table 14.2 shows the amount of money that some professional leagues and college events generate from media rights. Despite the fact that most major professional men's sport leagues have seen media and other revenue sources grow substantially over the past decade, this increase has not guaranteed overall profitability. Note that both revenues and costs determine the profits of a business. The following equation can be used to calculate the profit level for a sport organization:

Profit = Total revenues – Total costs

Although MLB has seen tremendous growth in revenues over the past decade, owners still claim to be losing money. They base this claim on cost increases in areas such as team payroll, travel expenses, and coaching and staff salaries. Shortly after the turn of the century, MLB commissioner Bud Selig released financial information for the league showing that the 30 teams combined lost US$232 million in one season alone ("2001 MLB," 2007). These data are the most current financial information available to the public about the overall finances of MLB. A couple of years after Selig's MLB report, the owners in the NHL claimed that they lost over US$270 million during one season (Bernstein, 2004).

Single-Entity Structure

As discussed throughout this book, the sport industry is unique in a variety of areas. One example is the use of the single-entity structure in professional sport. Although professional sport teams are all members in a particular league and often share certain revenue sources (e.g., national television revenue) and expenses (e.g., league marketing), each team is generally operated as a separate entity. But some sport leagues (e.g., Major League Soccer [MLS]) have gone with a single-entity structure. The advantage of using the single-entity structure is that the league members can work together more efficiently and make decisions that focus more on what is good for the league than what is good for an individual team. In addition, the league can set limits for player salaries in a way that would be illegal if the league were not using the single-entity structure. The long-term success of the single-entity structure is still unknown, but it has become popular for certain sport leagues.

TABLE 14.2 Sports Television Rights Deals

Property	Networks	Annual average (US$)	Length
NFL	CBS, Fox, ABC, ESPN	$3.08 billion	*
NBA	ABC, ESPN, Turner	$930 million	2008–2016
MLB	Fox, TBS, ESPN	$652 million	2006–2013
NHL[1]	NBC, Versus	$73 million	2007–2011
NASCAR	TNT, Fox, ESPN, ABC	$600 million	2006–2013
NCAA Basketball Tournament	CBS	$545 million	2003–2013
Bowl Championship Series[2]	ESPN	$125 million	2011–2014

*Length of contract varies across networks.

[1]The NHL has a five-year contract with the Versus network and a revenue-sharing deal with the NBC in which the two split advertising revenues from the game telecasts, but there are no guaranteed rights fees.

[2]The BCS deal with ESPN does not include the Rose Bowl.

Although many have questioned the accuracy of these numbers, some teams in major professional sport leagues are clearly not profitable because revenue growth has not kept up with the large increases in team operating costs. Specifically, team owners have been unable to control their spending on players. The average player salary in MLB was over US$3.24 million for the 2009 season. In comparison, the average player salary just 10 years earlier in 1999 was US$1.72 million ("MLB Salaries," 2010). The most noteworthy salary is probably that of Alex Rodriguez, the third baseman for the Yankees. The team re-signed him to a 10-year, US$275 million contract beginning with the 2008 season. At US$27.5 million per year, Rodriguez's salary for 2008 was more than the entire roster of the Florida Marlins ("Rodriguez Finalizes," 2007).

As you learned in chapter 6, NHL team owners have also had difficulty controlling player salaries. As stated earlier, this problem has led to substantial losses for teams that have not been able to increase their revenues. The situation in the NHL became a crisis in the fall of 2004. In an attempt to change the economic system in the league, the owners agreed to lock out the players before the start of the 2004–2005 season. The club owners and the players' union (NHLPA) were unable to agree on a new economic system, and an entire season was lost. After more than a year of negotiation, the two groups reached an accord on a new collective bargaining agreement (CBA) in the summer of 2005 and the players returned to the ice for the 2005–2006 season. The NHL is on the road to recovery, helped by the improbable run in 2010 by the Philadelphia Flyers and exciting playoff series such as the 2009 Stanley Cup Finals between the Pittsburgh Penguins and Detroit Red Wings.

In contrast, the NFL and NBA owners have been able to negotiate agreements with players through the collective bargaining process, thus helping to control salaries. For these leagues, the amount of money that owners spend on players' salaries is based on the level of revenues that they produce. Therefore, player salaries will increase only if teams are generating additional revenue. This arrangement reduces the likelihood that NBA and NFL owners will become as financially stressed as some MLB owners are. Team profitability is also more consistent in the NBA and NFL.

CURRENT FINANCIAL SITUATION OF US COLLEGE ATHLETICS

Rising costs are also an important issue in collegiate athletics. Most collegiate athletics programs, even at the Division I level, do not produce enough revenue to cover their costs. A study of the finances in collegiate athletics for 2006 found that only 16% of Division I Football Bowl Subdivision (FBS) athletics departments produced revenues that exceeded costs, and in many cases this profit occurred only because the university provided institutional resources to the athletics department. Furthermore, the percentage of schools at which costs exceed revenues is even greater at the Football Championship Subdivision (FCS) and Division II and III levels (Fulks, 2008).

Many athletics departments face a difficult financial future as costs increase in areas such as team travel, equipment, coaches' salaries, and grants-in-aid. Some colleges and universities have also seen their costs increase as they increase opportunities for women. In response to the financial pressure from rising costs in all areas of collegiate athletics spending, some athletics departments have eliminated sport teams and reduced scholarships. For example, in 2009 the University of Delaware eliminated their men's indoor track program to save money and, according to school officials, to maintain Title IX compliance (Maguire, 2009).

Rising costs have also placed additional emphasis on the need to increase revenues. Athletics administrators have turned to private donations, corporate sponsorship, television, and merchandising for additional revenue. At the Division I level, athletics administrators have used television rights fees and ticket sales to help their financial situation. Within the past decade schools such as the University of Maryland and Ohio State University have expanded their football stadia to increase ticket sales revenue and meet spectator demand. Penn State University generates over US$5 million in ticket revenue from one home football game at the 107,000-seat Beaver Stadium. But not all institutions are able to find additional revenue sources so easily. Many athletics departments are increasingly relying on student fees and other forms of institutional support to avoid large budget deficits. Even Division I institutions are applying this remedy, and it becomes increasingly common at lower-division levels in the NCAA and at NAIA schools where other revenue sources are limited.

The largest single source of revenue in collegiate athletics is the annual men's basketball championship. In 2003 CBS began paying the NCAA an average of over US$500 million per year for the right to televise three weeks of men's basketball in March. The US$500 million will be about 90% of the overall revenues generated by the NCAA. Division I universities have been pleased with this deal because over 75% of this money is distributed from the NCAA to them. The contract provided a sizable increase over the more than US$100 million per year received in the prior contract. This additional revenue has aided big-time college athletics departments as they attempt to pay for their growing expenses, but most programs will likely continue to experience annual deficits.

ECONOMICS OF SPORT

The word *economics* intimidates many people. For some, it brings back memories of studying how intangible items such as widgets and utils are produced and sold. But this example is far from the whole story. Economics is one of the few academic disciplines that can be applied to almost any human action. Within the field of sport management, economics can help us understand issues such as the price paid by consumers for a pair of shorts in a sporting goods store, the escalating salaries of MLB players, and the decision made by an athlete to leave college early and play professionally.

Definition of Economics

scarcity—The basic economic problem facing all institutions, including sport. A sport product is considered scarce if people want more of the product than is freely available for consumption.

The economics of sport can be defined as the study of how people within the sport industry deal with scarcity. This statement leads to the obvious question, What is scarcity? **Scarcity** is present in the world today because resources are insufficient to meet the wants and needs of society. For example, a health club might want 100 machines available to its members. Unfortunately, because of the scarce resources available to club management, the club might be able to provide only 50 machines. Economics helps determine how the health club management will decide to distribute its scarce resources, not only to machines but also to staff salaries, rent, utilities, and office supplies.

Scarcity is an important issue in sport management because all managers encounter it. Managers have a maximum quantity of resources available for their use. Even the ultrarich Yankees have a limited amount of resources that they are willing to devote to players' salaries. The most successful managers are those who make the best use of limited resources. Although the fact that the Yankees have the most resources gives them a greater probability of winning the World Series, it does not guarantee a championship. Indeed, the team's World Series victory in 2009 was its first since 2000, and the Yankees did not even qualify for the postseason in 2008. Their management must make wise decisions about how to allocate resources to be successful.

The limited resources available to managers are used to produce goods and services that are then sold to consumers. Goods are tangible products (e.g., soccer cleats, tennis rackets, mountain bikes), and services are intangible products (e.g., marketing advice, business consulting, financial planning). Goods and services are exchanged through the **economic interaction** of individuals and organizations. For example, the purchase of a new tennis racket at a store is an economic interaction. One product of value, a tennis racket, is exchanged for another product of value, cash. Note that not all economic interactions involve cash. For example, a business might provide free equipment (e.g., computer, tables) or services (e.g., shuttle support, medical personnel) to an event organizer in exchange for advertising space on the event T-shirt.

economic interaction—The exchange of one product of value for another product of value.

Transactions such as those just described occur in markets, which can be defined as arrangements by which economic exchanges among people or business occur. A market could be an actual physical location such as a sporting goods store or a minor league ballpark. It could also be an intangible idea such as a computerized stock exchange or the market for players in the Women's National Basketball Association (WNBA). For teams such as the Washington Mystics and the Los Angeles Sparks, a market exists in which players are bought and sold, but the market is not an actual physical location. These markets are the core of economic activity. Without markets, the exchange of goods and services could not occur.

Economics has been traditionally separated into two areas of study: macroeconomics and microeconomics. For the sport manager, the principles of microeconomics have the most effect on the day-to-day operations of their organization. Therefore, the following section will examine that area of study within economics.

Microeconomics and the Sport Industry

Microeconomics is the study of the behavior of individual businesses and households (Keat & Young, 2009). It uses economic theories to explain specific industries such as sport and recreation, automobile manufacturing, and health care. Microeconomics studies variables such as price, revenues, costs, and profits for individual industries and organizations. For example, microeconomics helps to explain why you might walk into two sporting goods stores and see different prices for the same model of running shoe.

Supply–Demand Model

Microeconomists often use models to explain the behavior of producers and consumers. These models are simplified descriptions of how markets operate. A market comprises two fundamental aspects: demand and supply. The supply–demand model is the most widely used and most powerful model in economics. As you will see, an accurate supply–demand model can provide information on the amount of a product or service that consumers are willing to buy at various prices, the amount that suppliers are willing to produce at various prices, and the final price that consumers will pay.

demand—The relationship between the price of a product and the amount of the product that consumers are willing to buy.

law of demand—Consumers will demand less of a product as its price increases and more of a product as its price falls.

supply—The relationship between the price of a product and the amount of the product that suppliers are willing to produce and sell.

law of supply—Suppliers will increase production as the price of the product increases and decrease production as the price falls.

market equilibrium—The price at which the quantity demanded equals the quantity supplied.

market surplus—A price at which the quantity supplied of a product is greater than the quantity demanded.

market shortage—A price at which the quantity demanded of a product is greater than the quantity supplied.

We will begin by discussing demand. **Demand** is the relationship between the price of a product and the amount of the product that consumers are willing to buy. The amount that consumers are willing to buy at various prices is referred to as the quantity demanded. In general, consumers will demand less of a product as its price increases, and they will demand more of a product as its price falls. This relationship is known as the **law of demand.** Demand can be shown through either a table or a graph. Let's use the example of a hypothetical market for NFL licensed jerseys. Table 14.3 shows the quantity of jerseys demanded by consumers at different price levels. Figure 14.1 illustrates the same relationship graphically. As you can see, the demand curve is downward sloping, as will always be the case because of the law of demand.

The other side of the supply–demand model is supply. **Supply** is the relationship between the price of a product and the amount of the product that suppliers are willing to produce and sell. The amount that suppliers are willing to produce and sell at various prices is known as the quantity supplied. Overall, suppliers will increase production as the price of the product increases and decrease production as the price falls. This relationship is referred to as the **law of supply.** Like demand, supply can be represented in both tabular and graphic forms. Let's continue with the NFL jersey example. Table 14.4 shows the number of jerseys supplied by businesses in the market at various prices, and figure 14.2 presents the information in graphic form. Note that the supply curve will generally have this upward-sloping shape. Again, this relationship occurs because suppliers will increase production as the price that they can charge for their product increases.

The last phase of the supply–demand model is to determine **market equilibrium.** By analyzing tables 14.3 and 14.4, you can determine that at a price of $100 consumers are willing to buy 1,000 jerseys and suppliers are willing to produce and sell 1,000 jerseys. Thus, this point would be the market equilibrium. Graphically, the intersection of the supply and demand curves represents market equilibrium. As shown in figure 14.3, when the supply and demand curves intersect, the equilibrium price and quantity are $100 and 1,000 jerseys, respectively.

You might wonder what would happen if the price of jerseys was $120. Notice that at a price of $120, consumers are willing to buy 800 jerseys and suppliers are willing to sell 1,200 jerseys. Under these circumstances, the market is not in equilibrium. We would refer to this situation as a **market surplus** because producers are willing to sell more jerseys than consumers are willing to buy. Conversely, a **market shortage** occurs

TABLE 14.3 Demand Schedule for NFL Licensed Jerseys

Price	Quantity demanded
$160	400
$140	600
$120	800
$100	1,000
$80	1,200
$60	1,400
$40	1,600

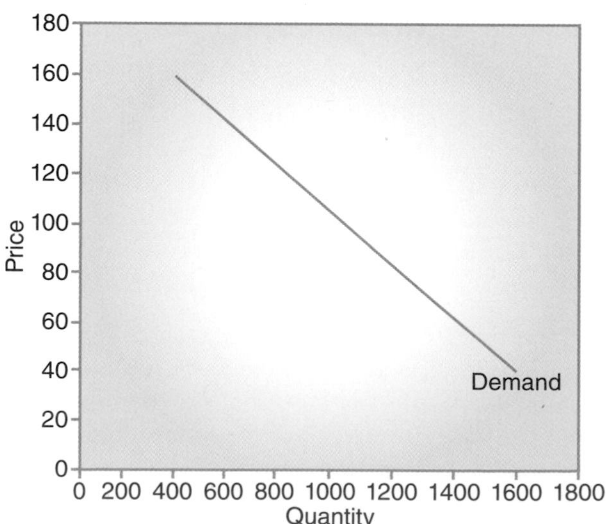

Figure 14.1 Demand for NFL licensed jerseys.

TABLE 14.4 Supply Schedule for NFL Licensed Jerseys

Price	Quantity Supplied
$160	1,600
$140	1,400
$120	1,200
$100	1,000
$80	800
$60	600
$40	400

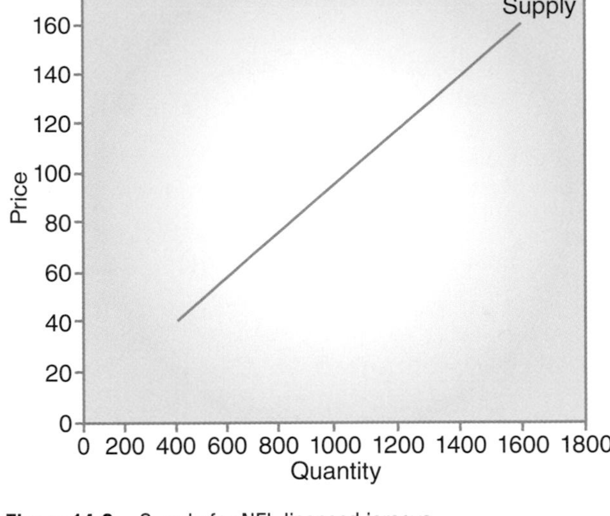

Figure 14.2 Supply for NFL licensed jerseys.

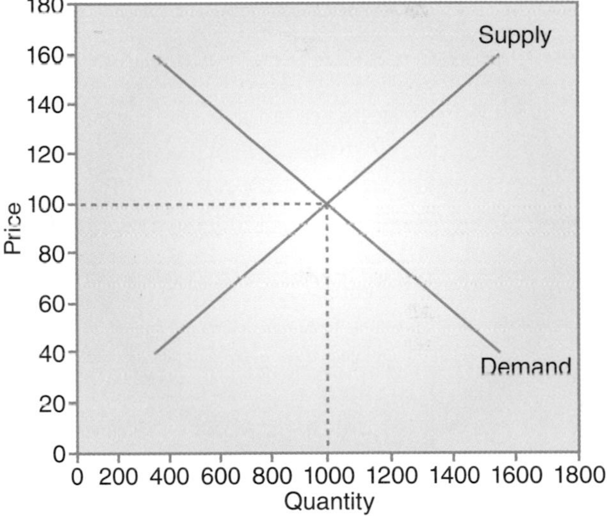

Figure 14.3 NFL licensed jersey market equilibrium.

when consumers are willing to buy more jerseys than suppliers are willing to produce and sell. This condition would occur if the price was $80.

As you can see, the supply–demand model is a powerful tool in microeconomics. The model helps us determine the quantity of a product demanded and supplied at various prices and the equilibrium price and quantity. Additionally, it can show whether the market is in a state of surplus or shortage.

Economic Impact of Sport Events and Facilities

With the growth of the sport industry, major sport events seem to take place every week. Although these events bring enjoyment to a community, they can also bring a substantial amount of economic activity. Community leaders believe that events such as the Olympic Games, the Super Bowl, and the NCAA Final Four will stimulate their local economies because of increased spending by out-of-town visitors. This spending will, in turn, increase local tax revenues and produce jobs (Howard & Crompton, 2004). Although major events such as those mentioned might produce a significant amount of money for a local economy, smaller events such as road races, soccer tournaments, and festivals can also increase economic activity.

Sport economic impact studies are estimates of the change in the net economic activity in a community that occurs because of the spending attributed to a specific sport event or facility (Turco & Kelsey, 1992). These studies are helpful in measuring the increase in revenues, tax dollars, and jobs attributable to a sport event or facility. For example, Phoenix, Arizona, hosted the 2008 Super Bowl. A study conducted by Arizona State University estimated the overall economic impact of the Super Bowl to be US$500 million (*Economic Impact Study*, 2008).

sport economic impact studies—Analyses of how expenditures on sport teams, events, or facilities economically affect a specific geographic region.

Researchers conduct economic impact studies by collecting information on the spending patterns of visitors to a sport event or facility. A researcher might distribute survey instruments to event spectators to determine how much they spent on things

Financing Professional Rugby Union in Wales

By John Harris • WALES
Kent State University, UNITED STATES

Following the 1895 split that led to two different codes (i.e., rugby league and rugby union), rugby union remained an amateur sport for more than a century. During the 1970s Wales was a dominant power in the game, and the team became an important signifier of the nation. Before the open professionalization of the sport in 1995, many leading Welsh rugby union players had "gone North" to England to play professional rugby league. The loss of many players was widely cited as a reason for the sharp decline in the performances of the national team during the 1980s and early 1990s. But to say that rugby union had remained strictly amateur for a hundred years would be a stretch. Although players were not always paid in cash, "shamateurism" would be a more apt descriptor to convey the fact that many of them received some form of payment. Boot (under-the-table) money was commonplace, and many leading players were provided jobs and received other perks to remain in Wales.

The open professionalization of rugby union changed the power dynamics of the game

PA Photos.

The Welsh Rugby Union plays its home matches at Millennium Stadium, a multimillion dollar facility.

WEB

Go to the OSG and complete the first Web search activity, which has you research the results of an economic impact study conducted for a sport event or facility.

such as hotels, rental cars, food, game tickets, and merchandise. These data are then used to determine the overall new economic activity. Most often, researchers use computer software packages such as RIMS II (Regional Input-Output Modeling System) and IMPLAN to calculate the final economic impact.

Experts disagree about the potential of sport events and facilities to generate economic activity. A study completed by the Maryland Department of Fiscal Services concluded that M&T Bank Stadium, home of the NFL's Baltimore Ravens, generates only about US$33 million per year in economic benefits for the state of Maryland. In addition, the stadium produced only 534 additional full-time jobs for the state. In comparison with other projects in the state, the new job creation was small. For example, Maryland's Sunny Day Fund for economic development cost taxpayers US$32.5 million and produced 5,200 full-time jobs (Zimmerman, 1997). Proponents of the public financing of sport facilities argue that the facilities and teams generate intrinsic benefits for a community that cannot be measured in monetary terms. Unlike the Ravens, the Sunny Day Fund cannot produce a Super Bowl–winning team.

As you can see, economic impact analysis is an important topic in the economics of sport. Economic impact studies have received a significant amount of media attention

and its relationship with rugby league. Top exiles were tempted back to union, and some high-profile league players were also recruited as the various national unions flexed their financial muscle. In 1998 the Welsh Rugby Union (WRU) appointed New Zealander Graham Henry as its national coach for a salary five times that of the previous coach. When he arrived in Wales, Henry was amazed to see players at the lower levels of the game being paid. Few of those involved in the governance of rugby union really understood the wider financial aspects of the game. Many clubs tried to buy success and soon found themselves in serious financial trouble because the revenues did not cover the increasing costs.

The WRU had also incurred significant debt in building the Millennium Stadium in time to host the 1999 World Cup Finals. This project cost approximately £114 million (US$163,248,013) and left the WRU with debts totaling more than half this amount early in the new millennium. A significant change occurred in 2003 when the nine leading Welsh club sides were merged into five regional teams (which became four the following year). These regions compete in the Magners League, the EDF Energy Cup, and the European Rugby Cup competitions. Leading Welsh players are now paid by their region and by the WRU. Although national squad members are under pressure to remain in Wales and are now paid better, some players are still tempted by the salaries offered by clubs in England and France.

As with many other sports around the globe, debate continues concerning the number of overseas players in the domestic game. Many of these are amongst the highest paid players in the sport, earning about £175,000 (US$250,600) a year. Whilst a few elite rugby players are well paid, this pales in significance when compared with the salaries in the leading US sport leagues or the top European soccer leagues.

INTERNATIONAL LEARNING ACTIVITY #1

Using information posted on the Internet, identify some high-profile players who changed codes. Explain why these individuals could earn more money playing rugby union rather than rugby league.

INTERNATIONAL LEARNING ACTIVITY #2

Go to the Web site of the European Rugby Cup at www.ercrugby.com and examine the performance of Welsh teams in the competitions. What factors might explain the greater success of teams from England, France, and Ireland?

because civic leaders and team owners have used them to justify the use of public funding for new sport facilities. Any economic impact study is only as good as the methods used to generate its results. Educated readers should always ask two questions when seeing the results of an economic impact study:

1. Who conducted the research?
2. How was the research conducted?

Unfortunately, economic impact studies can be manipulated to generate a variety of results. A proponent of a new facility might greatly overestimate the economic impact, but a critic of the same facility might underestimate the economic impact. For example, a study done by PricewaterhouseCoopers (PwC) estimated the direct spending impact of the 2009 Super Bowl in Tampa to be about US$150 million ("Study," 2009). This finding is in stark contrast to a study completed by economist Philip Porter on the economic impact of the last Super Bowl hosted by Tampa in 2001. At that time Porter estimated the impact of the Super Bowl to be around zero (Porter, 2001). Ironically, the two sides might be using the same statistical information; they are simply analyzing it in very different ways.

OVERVIEW OF FINANCIAL MANAGEMENT

Generally, the functions of financial management fall into two broad areas—determining what to do with current financial resources (i.e., money) and determining how to procure additional financial resources. For example, in a given year the NFL's Cleveland Browns might earn a profit of US$20 million. The question for the financial manager is what the Browns should do with that money. The franchise owner (Randy Lerner) and executives (e.g., Mike Holmgren) could decide to use the money to sign a high-priced free agent, renovate their practice facility, or increase the salaries of current employees. They could also decide to invest the money or distribute it among themselves.

Even after the organization decides how to use the money, the financial manager must choose the method for distributing the money. For example, if the Browns decide to spend the money on a free agent, they still must structure the player's contract. The financial manager would try to determine the difference in cost between giving the player a large signing bonus up front and structuring the deal in such a way that the player would receive most of the contract money in the future. Choosing what to spend the money on and how to spend it has significant long- and short-term implications for the team. For example, an MLB team that loads much of the contract on to later years might face financial difficulties when it is paying the player more when he might be generating less fan interest. In addition, the team could have more difficulty trading the player because of the large amount of money that it still owes him. When the MLB's Texas Rangers decided to trade Alex Rodriguez and his large contract, only a few teams were interested. More recently, the NBA's New York Knicks had to buy out the contract of Stephon Marbury because no teams believed that his value was equivalent to the amount of his large contract. Soon after the buyout, the Boston Celtics signed Marbury for a much lower amount.

Although the example of the Browns described earlier may generate an interesting discussion, few sport organizations have the luxury of deciding how to spend excess money. Because many sport organizations were struggling financially even before the recent financial crisis (Howard & Crompton, 2004), two of the key roles of the financial manager are determining how much money the organization will need to meet long-term obligations and how they will procure those funds. Although most involved with sport immediately think of selling tickets or merchandise as ways to increase available funds, a number of other means have potential. For example, good investments can produce significant income. Also, some sport teams have sold stock in their organizations to raise funds, and many leagues have collected large fees from expansion teams.

Financial Statements

To allow both internal and external parties to monitor its financial situation, a sport organization develops financial statements on a regular basis. The limited scope of this chapter does not permit discussion of every detail included in financial statements and all the ways in which one might examine those statements to understand an organization's current financial situation. We will, however, provide an overview of the major financial statements and the useful information that they provide.

Balance Sheet

Figure 14.4 is the balance sheet for a fictional professional football team, the Springfield Stars. In this example, the Stars are co-owned by Robert Goldstein and Connie Shumake. Connie owns 60% of the team, and Robert owns the remaining 40%. The balance sheet reflects the financial condition of the organization on a particular date. Although the balance sheet is generally reported at the end of a given financial period (e.g., the end of a year), a financial manager could generate a balance sheet any time

Springfield Stars
Balance Sheet (in thousands)
March 31, 2011

Assets	
Current assets	
Cash and cash equivalents	$33,365,586
Marketable securities	58,132,669
Other short-term investments	95,558,465
Accounts receivable	3,213,175
Notes receivable	5,678,695
Prepaid expenses	2,616,407
Other current assets	5,900,586
Total Current Assets	$204,465,583
Long-Term Assets	
Land	$52,495,823
Facilities	45,895,631
Equipment	1,689,954
Long-term investments	6,028,318
Total long-term assets	$106,109,726
Total assets	$310,575,309
Liabilities	
Current liabilities	
Accounts payable	$19,714,620
Deferred revenue	28,610,372
Ticket refunds payable	150,908
Long-term debt, current portion	14,365,096
Deferred compensation, current portion	16,209,896
Total current liabilities	$79,050,892
Long-term liabilities	
Long-term debt, noncurrent	$75,000,000
Deferred compensation, noncurrent	48,850,057
Total long-term liabilities	$123,850,057
Total liabilities	$202,900,949
Owners' Equity	
Paid-in-capital, Connie Shumake	$30,000,000
Paid-in-capital, Robert Goldstein	20,000,000
Retained earnings, Connie Shumake	34,604,616
Retained earnings, Robert Goldstein	23,069,744
Total owners' equity	$107,674,360
Total liabilities and owners' equity	$310,575,309

Figure 14.4 Springfield Stars balance sheet.

such information is needed. The balance sheet includes three categories—assets, liabilities, and owners' equity. Assets are the financial resources of the company and include both current assets and long-term assets. Current assets are generally items that are cash or expected to be converted into cash within the next year and will be used to meet current obligations. Long-term assets are items that are not expected to be turned into cash during the next year. Some examples include land, buildings, and equipment. All these items are initially recorded at the price paid for them, and some are reduced as their value declines (i.e., depreciation). Long-term assets also include the long-term investments, which might include government bonds that will not be converted to cash for a number of years.

Liabilities are obligations to pay money or provide goods or services to another entity. In other words, liabilities are money, goods, or services owed to others. Current liabilities are those that are due to be paid in the next year, and long-term liabilities are those that are due sometime after the current year. The owners' equity is Connie's and Robert's shares of the resources of the business. It includes both the money that they have personally put into the company (i.e., paid-in-capital) and their earnings from the Stars that they have decided to leave in the company (i.e., retained earnings). As you can see in figure 14.4, total assets are equal to liabilities plus owners' equity. This relationship is always true. Logically, all the resources (i.e., assets) either belong to the owner or owners (i.e., owners' equity) or are owed to another entity (i.e., liabilities).

Income Statement

In figure 14.5 you will see the income statement for the Springfield Stars. The income statement provides the financial results of the organization's operations over a specific period. As with the balance sheet, the income statement is often reported at the end of a year but can be generated at any point and for any period. For many people, the income statement is the most important financial statement because it presents the organization's bottom line (i.e., the net profit or net loss). Although developing a complete understanding of the organization's financial situation requires a thorough examination of all the financial statements, the bottom line gives the user a quick assessment of the organization and its success in achieving the primary goal of profit-oriented companies—profitability.

The income statement includes two categories—revenues and expenses. Revenue is the inflow of value to the business. Note that revenue is the inflow of value, not the inflow of cash. Therefore, revenue is recorded when the good or service is delivered to a customer, not when the cash is received for that transaction. For example, when the NHL's New York Rangers sell a ticket to a December hockey game in July, the revenue from that sale is not recognized until the game is played in December. Likewise, if a customer receives a ticket for the December game for the promise that payment will be made in January, the revenue is recognized in December, not when the cash is received in January.

At the top of the income statement for the Stars is the organization's operating income. This figure represents the amount of revenue generated by the Stars from the team's main business. Note that some other revenue items (e.g., interest income) appear toward the bottom of the income statement. These items are separate from operating income because most financial analysts are more concerned with revenue from the company's main business, which is generally more useful for predicting future revenue.

The expenses are generally broken up into four categories—direct expenses (or cost of sales), operating expenses, other expenses, and income tax expense. Again, the income statement is more useful to analysts if the expenses are reported in this way. Direct expenses, or cost of sales, are expenses that can be directly matched to the main sources of revenue. For example, the cost of sales for a sporting goods company is the

Springfield Stars
Income Statement
For the Period Ending March 31, 2011

Operating income	
National television	$95,425,375
Road games	13,919,710
Other NFL revenue	15,075,968
Home games	30,451,440
Private box income	12,289,395
Marketing and sponsorships	37,789,075
Local media	7,721,250
Concessions and parking	5,932,282
Miscellaneous	3,393,293
Total operating income	$221,997,788
Operating expenses	
Salaries	$115,868,020
Team expenses	37,233,957
Marketing expenses	4,854,095
Operations and maintenance	13,838,354
General and administrative	25,883,773
Total operating expenses	$197,678,199
Net operating income	$24,319,589
Other income (expenses)	
Interest and divident income	$6,231,027
Interest expense	(859,333)
Gain (loss) on sale of assets	3,253,365
Net taxable income	$32,944,648
Income tax expense	$12,100,000
Net income	$20,844,648

Figure 14.5 Springfield Stars income statement.

total cost to produce or manufacture all the items sold during the year. You will note that there are no direct expenses on the income statement for the Springfield Stars. Although it is relatively easy to tie the cost of a pair of shoes to the revenue produced from selling those shoes, it is not practical to directly tie the costs of a sport team to the revenue that is generated. Operating expenses are other normal business expenses, such as salaries, rent, and utilities, that cannot be directly matched to specific revenue items. Other expenses are those that occur outside normal business operations for a given company. Items such as interest expense and unusual losses are often recorded here. For example, if the Stars lost $500,000 in a lawsuit, the company would report that loss under other expenses. Finally, income tax expense is the amount that the company pays to the Internal Revenue Service (IRS), the state, or the city related to the profits for the year. After subtracting all the expenses from all the revenue, the

WEB

Go to the OSG and complete the second Web search activity, which has you identify sources of expenses and revenues for three sport organizations.

income statement provides the user with the net income (or loss) at the bottom of the statement; this number is, literally, the bottom line.

SOURCES OF REVENUES AND EXPENSES FOR SPORT ORGANIZATIONS

Organizations in the sport industry have various types of revenues and expenses, depending on the type of organization. In this section we will briefly discuss some of the business types in the sport industry and examine some sources of revenues and expenses in those businesses.

Types of Sport Organizations

As previously discussed, sport organizations can take many forms and have varied goals. Some organizations are geared toward encouraging sport participation. These include youth sport organizations, community recreation programs, and high school sports. Other organizations seek to make a profit by providing participation opportunities not offered by, offered by, or not offered as well as, nonprofit organizations. These include sport organizations that rent their facilities to participants (e.g., bowling alleys, health clubs), organizations that seek to train people (e.g., those that provide personal trainers, others who provide lessons in a particular sport), and organizations that provide the equipment necessary to participate in a certain sport (i.e., sporting goods companies).

Many companies focus more on sport spectators. These include both professional sports (e.g., WNBA, NASCAR, PGA Tour) and big-time college sports. Although these organizations receive a large portion of the money generated by sport spectators, other entities also benefit from sport spectating, including independent sport facilities that host sporting events, the sport media that bring sport events and information related to sport events to the consumer (e.g., television, radio, newspapers, magazines, the Internet), and companies that sell products licensed by these professional and college sport organizations. The diversity of the sport industry produces a variety of revenue and expense sources. The next two sections focus on types and aspects of revenues and expenses that are unique in the sport industry.

Sources of Revenues

Some of the sources of revenue unique to sport are items related to game attendance (e.g., concessions, personal seat licenses, luxury suite rentals, booster club donations), media rights, sponsorships, and licensed merchandise. Although the ticket price is generally the major source of revenue related to attendance at events outside sport, this is not always true in sport. The total price of attendance is often much greater than the cost of the ticket. Consider the following:

1. Most sport organizations charge fans an additional fee for parking during the event.

2. Fans typically spend money on concessions at the stadium. Purchasing hot dogs, beer, soda, and so on is considered by many fans to be an important part of the game experience. Some sport teams and facilities maintain complete control over the concessions at the stadium, but many prefer to hire a company with expertise in handling concessions. In the latter case, the contract outlines how these organizations share the profits from concessions.

3. Some professional and college sport teams now charge fans for personal seat licenses (PSLs), which give a fan the right to buy a particular seat. For example, a fan may buy a 10-year PSL for $10,000. The fan must then pay for season tickets each year

for the next 10 years. If the season ticket price is $1,000 per year, the fan will end up paying $20,000 [$10,000 + ($1,000 × 10)] over 10 years to watch games from that particular seat.

4. A fan who wants a more exclusive setting for watching games might decide to rent a luxury suite or pay for a club seat. As with the PSL, the fan must still buy tickets for the game after paying the cost of renting the luxury suite. In the NBA, for example, an average annual lease price for a luxury suite would be around US$200,000 while an average price for club seat would be around US$7,500.

5. College sport fans often donate money to an athletics department so that they can buy better seats or, in some cases, so that they can buy any seat. For example, a college sport fan might have to donate $4,000 each year for the right to buy two $400 season tickets. In this case, the fan is actually paying $4,800 ($4,000 + $400 + $400) for the season tickets, or $2,400 per seat. Overall, donations to college athletics departments have increased from 5% of athletics department revenue to 17% of revenue over last four decades (Fulks, 2008).

Because of the increasing cost of attending games, many sport spectators watch or listen to games at home. This large audience for sport beyond those who attend games means that many sport teams make a large percentage of their revenue from media contracts. For example, the NFL signed six-year contracts with CBS and Fox in 2004 worth US$8 billion for the television rights. In 2005 the NFL negotiated an eight-year contract with ESPN for the Monday night games worth an average of US$1.1 billion annually and a six-year contract with NBC for Sunday night games worth US$650 million annually. In addition, big-time college sports receive large amounts of money for their broadcasting rights. As noted earlier in the chapter, the NCAA's contract for the men's basketball tournament is at the top of the list with an 11-year contract that began in 2003 and is worth US$6.2 billion, a 252% increase from the previous contract. Because the tournament takes place on only 10 days, the NCAA receives an average of over US$50 million per day for the broadcast rights. In many cases television networks make little or no money directly from the broadcast of sporting events. The networks believe, however, that broadcasting games will be beneficial because they can use the broadcasts to promote other programming, and they believe that they will benefit from a positive association with sport.

Corporations also seek to take advantage of positive associations with sport events, leagues, teams, and players. Spending by corporate sponsors now exceeds US$15 billion in North America, and worldwide sport sponsorship exceeds US$40 billion (Chipps, 2008). Companies invest heavily in sport sponsorship because they believe that association with these sport organizations will create a positive image of their company and influence people to buy their products or services. The largest sums of money, such as the US$300 million paid by Reliant Energy to the NFL's Houston Texans, have generally been paid for naming rights of stadia.

Nike's contract with LeBron James is estimated to be worth more than US$90 million.
Photo courtesy of Paul M. Pedersen.

Likewise, corporations pay large amounts of money to athlete endorsers to promote their products and services. For example, Nike became the dominant force in the athletics footwear industry just as the career of its top endorser, Michael Jordan, was taking off. Nike, like other corporations, continues to sign large endorsement deals with athletes, including the deal with the back-to-back NBA MVP, LeBron James.

Also looking to take advantage of the positive feelings that sport spectators have about teams and players are the sellers of licensed products. Once a rather small industry, sales of sport licensed products became big business during the 1980s. Although most people immediately think of players' jerseys and team hats, the licensed products industry includes a variety of items such as video games, blankets, framed pictures, and sport equipment. Although most of the money from these sales goes to the producers of the products, sport organizations receive a percentage of the sales revenue.

Sources of Expenses

Two critical sources of expenses for most sport organizations are the cost of sport facilities and the cost of salaries. Sport facilities can be extremely expensive. Most sport organizations try to persuade local communities to pay for stadia, but many are finding that they have to pay at least part of the cost. This arrangement results in long-term payments, which can affect the financial stability of the organization for many years. Sport facilities are also costly to maintain, particularly large open-air facilities that might not be used for much of the year but must be maintained year round. In addition, sport facilities tend to become obsolete fairly quickly. If an organization has to make payments for 30 years, it could end up making payments on a facility that it is no longer using. In fact, some large sport facilities have been torn down before reaching their 30th birthdays. Combined, these factors require organizations that decide to build a new facility to proceed carefully and explore all options. For example, some sport organizations have been able to pay for some of the cost of a new facility by collecting PSL and rental fees for luxury suites before the opening of the stadium.

Salaries in both professional and college sport have increased dramatically during the last 40 years (Howard & Crompton, 2004). Players' and coaches' salaries often make up more than 50% of the expenses in professional sport, and big-time college coaches (e.g., John Calipari at the University of Kentucky) are often by far the highest paid employees on campus. Alex Rodriguez' US$275 million deal with the Yankees is an astonishing contract, but many other annual contracts are above US$20 million. Average salaries in each of the four highest paid men's team sport leagues in the United States exceed US$1.5 million per year. Some college coaches are also signing deals worth over US$2 million per year, and salaries above US$1 million are not unusual. Although many argue that the salaries are justified because of the revenue that players and coaches generate for an organization, some have questioned this assumption. Zimbalist (1999) suggested that even the best college coaches are worth much less than their annual salaries, and it is hard to explain how one player is capable of generating an additional US$25 million per year. Therefore, although profits are important to these organizations, some of these salaries are not related to the bottom line. Some organizations might pay more than they can afford because the owner or university official cares more about winning than about profits. The strong desire to win has probably led many sport organizations to make unwise financial decisions.

CAREERS IN FINANCIAL MANAGEMENT FOR SPORT ORGANIZATIONS

An increasing variety of jobs relate to financial management in sport. In the past, financial management jobs in sport were generally not complicated. Many organizations had business managers who were basically bookkeepers. They recorded receipts and distributions of money and made sure that organizational financial records were in order. Although these jobs still exist, many jobs today require far more sophisticated financial management skills. For example, the decision of MLB's Cleveland Indians to issue public stock required sophisticated financial skills that the typical bookkeeper would not possess. Likewise, negotiation of a player's contract requires both the team and the player to hire representatives who have a strong understanding of financial management. As the sport industry becomes more sophisticated at all levels, the need for people with sophisticated financial skills will become increasingly important.

A number of jobs are available for people who are interested and have ability in the area of financial management. Because sophisticated financial management skills are needed for some activities, many professional teams and other large, for-profit sport organizations have people with such skills in positions of assistant general manager or vice president for financial operations. This arrangement is particularly common if the general manager or president does not possess the skills necessary to make complicated financial decisions. To help them make particularly complicated financial decisions, some sport organizations hire consulting firms. A number of companies provide such advice and have people who specialize in sport consulting.

ACTION

Go to the OSG and complete the Learning in Action activity, which tests how well you remembered some of the key terms and their definitions used throughout this chapter.

As a student of sport management, you must understand that the skills needed for many of these jobs, particularly those that require highly sophisticated financial skills, require the student to take coursework beyond that required for a typical undergraduate degree in sport management. One course in sport finance will not prepare you to handle a public stock offering.

CRITICAL THINKING IN SPORT FINANCE AND ECONOMICS

Critical thinking plays a key role in the financial management of a sport organization. Sport managers must be continually developing new strategies to be financially efficient in the operation of their organizations. For example, an NFL general manager must critically analyze the players' abilities in comparison to their contracts. The signing of draft picks (e.g., the US$41.7 million deal that Matthew Stafford signed with the Detroit Lions), the extension of current contracts (e.g., the US$45 million deal that Manny Ramirez signed with the Los Angeles Dodgers), or the signing of new free-agent players (e.g., Albert Haynesworth's US$100 million deal with the Washington Redskins) can have considerable short-term and long-term ramifications for the overall financial success of the sport organization. Additionally, team managers must critically analyze the sometimes competing organizational motives of maximizing wins versus maximizing profits. These two goals often come into conflict with one another.

In another example, representatives from companies such as Nike, Under Armour, and Reebok must critically analyze the markets in which they compete to ensure long-term financial success. Market changes such as shifting consumer tastes may have a significant influence on financial decisions related to such issues as expanding production, hiring additional staff, and increasing marketing and promotional budgets. Failure to incorporate critical analysis into these financial decisions can have a significant negative effect on a sport organization.

PORTFOLIO

Complete the critical thinking portfolio activity in the OSG, consulting as needed the "Eight Critical Thinking Questions" section in chapter 1.

One of the most discussed issues related to sport finance is the compensation of professional athletes. Athletes such as Kevin Garnett and Mark Teixeira are paid in excess of US$20 million annually. There are ongoing debates as to whether or not player salaries are too high and what the ramifications would be of lowering high salaries.

ETHICS IN SPORT FINANCE AND ECONOMICS

You read earlier in this chapter about the illegal financial behavior of Bernard Madoff. The Madoff case, as detailed by Creswell and Thomas (2009), is an excellent example of unethical financial behavior. Ethics can play a significant role in the financial management of a sport organization. Sport managers have a responsibility to act ethically, and legally, with respect to the organizations that they manage. Unfortunately, some people connected to the sport industry have violated this ethical responsibility. Earlier in the chapter we examined the case of Robert Allen Stanford. This person, a major player in athlete endorsements and sport sponsorship (Rovell, 2009), was accused by the US Securities and Exchange Commission of stealing US$8 billion of his investors' money. Another example is from the 1990s. In this case, John Spano lied about his personal net worth to obtain bank loans to acquire the New York Islanders of the NHL. Federal authorities eventually uncovered Spano's financial misdeeds, and he was convicted on six counts of fraud (Fried, Shapiro, & DeSchriver, 2008).

PORTFOLIO

Complete the ethical issues portfolio activity in the OSG, consulting as needed the "Guidelines for Making Ethical Decisions" section in chapter 1.

Although the Spano case is an example of ethical conduct that resulted in legal action, in other situations financial conduct may be legal but not necessarily ethical. For example, is it ethical for a sports agent who represents several star athletes in a single sport to use his or her knowledge of the contract situation of one client to enhance the bargaining position of another? Could this agent be damaging the financial future of one client to enhance the financial future of another? Sports agents such as Drew Rosenhaus, Scott Boras, and Leigh Steinberg must continually face this situation.

Summary

This chapter has introduced the basic concepts of economics and finance. Sport economics is the study of how people within the sport industry deal with scarcity. Ideas such as supply, demand, and price equilibrium are important for sport businesses such as professional teams, sporting goods manufacturers, and sport facility operators.

QUIZ TIME

Did you grasp all the key points in this chapter? Go to the OSG for a short quiz to test your understanding of the material.

Financial management is the application of skills in the manipulation, use, and control of funds. Students need to have a thorough understanding of financial information available through financial statements. Balance sheets and income statements contain a plethora of data that are vital to the successful management of a sport organization. Lastly, students must have knowledge of the different types of revenues and costs that are present for sport organizations.

Review Questions

1. What does the term *economic impact* mean? Provide an example of how it can be used in sport.
2. How would you construct the supply and demand curves from the table on the right to show the supply and demand for basketballs?
3. From the table, how would you determine the market equilibrium price and quantity for basketballs? What would happen if the price level were $10?

Supply and Demand for Basketballs

Price	Quantity demanded	Quantity supplied
$50	30	180
$40	60	160
$30	90	140
$20	120	120
$10	150	80
$5	180	20

4. What are the different types of business structures in the sport industry? Give examples of each.
5. What is the main purpose of each of the financial statements?
6. What type of useful information does each financial statement provide?
7. What are the major sources of revenues and expenses in the sport industry? How are they different from or similar to revenues and expenses of nonsport organizations?
8. What types of positions are available in financial management in the sport industry?

References

2001 MLB profits and losses. (2007). *ESPN.com*. Retrieved February 2, 2010, from http://assets.espn.go.com/mlb/s/2001/1205/1290765.html

Advertise with us—the sports industry. (2009). *Street & Smith's SportsBusiness Journal*. Retrieved June 8, 2009, from www.sportsbusinessjournal.com/index.cfm?fuseaction=page.feature&featureId=1492

Battista, J. (2008, December 9). Feeling pinch, N.F.L. will cut about 150 jobs. *New York Times*. Retrieved February 2, 2010, from www.nytimes.com/2008/12/10/sports/football/10nfl.html?_r=1&scp=1&sq=nfl%20will%20cut%20about%20150%20jobs&st=cse

Bernstein, A. (2004, February 23). Daly: Shutdown blots red ink. *Street & Smith's SportsBusiness Journal*, p. 43.

Blount, T. (2008, November 14). With economy hurting budgets, NASCAR bans testing to save money. *ESPN.com*. Retrieved February 2, 2010, from http://sports.espn.go.com/rpm/nascar/news/story?id=3702207

Chipps, W. (2008, January 18). *Sponsorship spending to total $16.78 billion in 2008*. Retrieved February 2, 2010, from www.sponsorship.com/About-IEG/Press-Room/Sponsorship-Spending-To-Total-$16.78-Billion-In-20.aspx

Creswell, J., & Thomas, L. Jr. (2009, January 24). The talented Mr. Madoff. *The New York Times*. Retrieved February 2, 2010, from www.nytimes.com/2009/01/25/business/25bernie.html

Economic impact study: Phoenix scores big with Super Bowl XLII. (2008, April 23). Retrieved June 21, 2009, from Arizona State University, W.P. Carey School Web site: http://knowledge.wpcarey.asu.edu/article.cfm?articleid=1597

Fried, G., Shapiro, S.J., & DeSchriver, T.D. (2008). *Sport finance* (2nd ed.). Champaign, IL: Human Kinetics.

Fulks, D.L. (2008). *2004–2006 Revenues and expenses of Divisions I intercollegiate athletic programs report*. Indianapolis, IN: National Collegiate Athletic Association.

Howard, D.R., & Crompton, J.L. (2004). *Financing sport* (2nd ed.). Morgantown, WV: Fitness Information Technology.

Keat, P.G., & Young, P.K. (2009). *Managerial economics: Economic tools for today's decision makers* (6th ed.). Upper Saddle River, NJ: Prentice Hall.

Laurent, L. (2009, January 21). AIG leaves Manchester United in the lurch. *Forbes*. Retrieved February 2, 2010, from www.forbes.com/2009/01/21/manchester-united-aig-markets-equity-cx_ll_0121markets09.html

Maguire, P. (2009, February 17). Indoor track demoted to club team. *The Review*. Retrieved June 8, 2009, from http://media.www.udreview.com/media/storage/paper781/news/2009/02/17/Sports/Indoor.Track.Demoted.To.Club.Team-3632559.shtml

Meek, A. (1997). An estimate of the size and supported economic activity of the sports industry in the United States. *Sport Marketing Quarterly*, *6*(4), 15–21.

MLB salaries. (2010). *CBSsports.com*. Retrieved February 2, 2010, from www.cbssports.com/mlb/salaries/avgsalaries

NFL team valuations. (2008, September 10). *Forbes*. Retrieved June 8, 2009, from www.forbes.com/sports/lists/2008/30/sportsmoney_nfl08_NFL-Team-Valuations_Income.html

Porter, P. (2001, January 15). Super Bowl impact figures a super stretch. *Street & Smith's SportsBusiness Journal*, p. 31.

Rodriguez finalizes $275M deal with Yankees. (2007, December 13). *ESPN.com*. Retrieved February 2, 2010, from sports.espn.go.com/mlb/news/story?id=3153171

Rovell, D. (2009, February 17). Stanford Financial's big play in sports. *CNBC.com*. Retrieved October 9, 2009, from www.cnbc.com/id/29243340

Sporting Goods Manufacturers Association. (2008, June 9). *US sports industry: Nearly a $70 billion business*. Retrieved February 2, 2010, from www.sgma.com/press/3/U.S.-Sports-Industry:-Nearly–a-$70-Billion-Business

Study: Economy lessens Super Bowl economic impact. (2009, January 21). *Tampa Bay Business Journal*. Retrieved June 21, 2009, from www.bizjournals.com/tampabay/stories/2009/01/19/daily32.html

The business of baseball. (2008, April 16). *Forbes*. Retrieved June 8, 2009, from www.forbes.com/lists/2008/33/biz_baseball08_The-Business-Of-Baseball_Rank.html

Turco, D.M., & Kelsey, C.W. (1992). *Conducting economic impact studies of recreational and parks special events*. Arlington, VA: National Recreation and Park Association.

US Census Bureau. (2009). *Statistical abstract of the United States: 2009*. Retrieved June 8, 2009, from www.census.gov/compendia/statab/

Zimbalist, A. (1999). *Unpaid professionals: Commercialism and conflict in big-time college sports*. Princeton, NJ: Princeton University Press.

Zimmerman, D. (1997). Subsidizing stadiums: Who benefits, who pays? In R.G. Noll & A. Zimbalist (Eds.), *Sports, jobs and taxes* (pp. 119–145). Washington, DC: Brookings Institution Press.

HISTORICAL MOMENTS

1863	First covered skating rink in Canada opened in Halifax
1879	The first Madison Square Garden opened
1912	Fenway Park opened; Wrigley Field opened two years later
1912	First electronic timers introduced at Stockholm Olympic Games
1931	Maple Leaf Gardens opened in Toronto
1935	Cincinnati Reds played seven games under the lights
1959	First Daytona 500 held at Daytona International Speedway
1965	Astroturf developed; first used in the Houston Astrodome, which opened in 1965
1989	California earthquake caused 10-day interruption in A's v. Giants World Series
1999	Columbus Crew stadium opened—first soccer-specific stadium in the United States
2000	Pacific Bell Park (now AT&T Park) opened—first privately funded MLB stadium built since 1962
2005	Ski Dubai opened—world's largest indoor snow park
2006	Cardinals Stadium (now University of Phoenix Stadium) opened—first retractable grass playing surface in the United States
2008	Beijing National Stadium (Bird's Nest) opened—world's largest steel structure
2009	US$1 billion NFL Cowboys Stadium opened
2010	Stampede at Makhulong Stadium in South Africa injured 15 fans before World Cup

Photo courtesy of Paul M. Pedersen.

SPORT FACILITY AND EVENT MANAGEMENT

Robin Ammon, Jr. ■ David K. Stotlar

LEARNING OBJECTIVES

1. Distinguish between the various types of venues that hold sport and entertainment events.
2. Recognize the necessary steps in managing a facility.
3. Identify the differences between public assembly facilities and those managed by private companies.
4. Discuss the similarities and differences between event and facility management.
5. Demonstrate an understanding of the procedures, principles, ethical practices, and current trends in planning and managing an event or facility.
6. Recognize the importance of crowd management and identify critical elements for a proper crowd management plan.
7. Use critical thinking skills to describe several major problems currently facing facility and event managers.

Key Terms

Americans with Disabilities Act (ADA)
boilerplate
booking
cost analysis
documentation
in-house
privatization
settlement
split
work order

GET A JOB!

☑ Continue your journey in sport management by going to the Online Study Guide (OSG) at www.HumanKinetics.com/ContemporarySportManagement. Check out the job opportunities and consider the skills and experiences that can help you succeed in sport management.

The number of sport and entertainment facilities constructed or renovated in the United States has increased dramatically during the past 10 to 15 years. For example, during 2008 three major league stadia, six minor league ballparks, seven minor league arenas, and three college arenas were constructed. Estimates of total cost were almost US$2.4 billion ("Highs," 2008). This surge in construction is by no means specific to the United States. The Chinese spent an estimated US$43 billion developing new, state-of-the-art venues for the 2008 Summer Olympic Games. Note as well that funding is needed to keep the facilities operational after the Olympic Games. For example, the yearly maintenance cost for the new Beijing National Stadium (known as the Bird's Nest) is estimated to be nearly US$9 million (Demick, 2009). Acknowledging the cost overruns that previous Olympic committees have experienced, the Vancouver Organizing Committee sought to ensure that the 2010 Winter Olympic Games stayed within its C$1.34 billion projected budget (Lee, 2009).

Because of the deteriorating US economy, professional teams are experiencing problems securing the necessary financing to complete their megaprojects. Two such examples include the proposed US$950 million Barclay's Center (new home for the National Basketball Association's [NBA] New Jersey Nets) in Brooklyn, New York, and the proposed $1.2 billion Chargers Stadium for the National Football League's (NFL) San Diego franchise. The Chargers had hoped to stay in San Diego County but shifted the stadium's location from San Diego to Chula Vista. Because of the state of California's financial crisis, however, those plans have been put on hold ("Sports," 2009). The struggling economy, however, does offer some advantage for teams with the necessary funding. For example, prices for steel, copper, and aluminum have decreased to the extent that the associated construction bids have also declined. The bids for the Orlando Magic's US$480 million arena and Kansas City's Arrowhead Stadium's US$375 million renovations have all diminished from original estimates. Some experts believe that prices will continue to fall and that venue stakeholders may benefit by waiting to begin construction (Muret, 2009).

Professional positions in these facilities provide students from a variety of majors, including sport management, with opportunities to work with facility operations, schedule events, oversee facility finances, equip facilities with TV and video connections, supervise maintenance and custodial services, conduct facility marketing and promotions, engage in event merchandising, and direct risk management services. The distinction between sport and entertainment has blurred to the point that sport and entertainment events are more similar than they are different. The events are similar, and the skills and competencies required to manage the facilities that host the events are comparable.

TYPES OF FACILITIES

Types of sport and entertainment facilities are as diverse as the events that they host (see table 15.1). Some facilities are designed for only one sport. Citi Field (home of

TABLE 15.1 Types of Sport Facilities

Type of facility	Examples
Single purpose	Softball complex, bowling alley, Oriole Park at Camden Yards
Single purpose, specialized	Ice arena
Multipurpose	Large stadium (e.g., Rogers Centre [Toronto]), high school field house
Nontraditional	Skateboard park, convertible indoor–outdoor facility

Major League Baseball's [MLB] New York Mets) is an example of a new single-purpose facility. Golf courses and skate parks are also single-purpose facilities. Swimming pools, bowling alleys, motorsport tracks, and water parks exist for a single purpose. Other facilities are built for specialized events but might not be single-purpose facilities. For example, ice arenas can be used for instructional and recreational skating, figure-skating competitions, ice hockey, and curling, but not for rugby matches.

Other facilities, called multipurpose facilities, host a variety of events, such as concerts, truck pulls, motocross races, home and garden shows, and recreational vehicle shows. In addition, these facilities might be home to intercollegiate and professional sport competitions. For example, Lucas Oil Stadium (home of the NFL's Indianapolis Colts), named by *Street & Smith's SportsBusiness Journal* as the Sports Facility of the Year in 2009, hosted the NCAA Men's Final Four in 2010 and will host the NCAA Women's Final Four in 2011. Originally, many types of events were held in large outdoor stadia, going as far back as the chariot races in ancient Rome. In recent years, many stadia and large arenas, some of them covered, have been built. Stadium capacity has increased greatly in the last century and in the first decade of the 21st century. Two of the largest stadia in the world are home to collegiate football teams in the United States. The University of Michigan's stadium ("The Big House") was built in 1927. The stadium's original capacity was 72,000, but it has since been increased to 106,201. Penn State University's Beaver Stadium has a slightly larger capacity at 107,282. International stadia have also become much larger. The original seating capacity of San Siro in Milan, Italy, was 10,000 when it was built in 1926. Its capacity has since been expanded to 85,700. Rungrado May Day Stadium in Pyongyang, North Korea, built in 1989, is the largest stadium in the world and has a seating capacity of 150,000. The stadium also has an indoor swimming pool.

Not all sport and entertainment facilities are restricted to spaces that are roofed and walled. Golf courses, ski areas, and amusement parks are classified as sport and entertainment facilities. Another mistake would be to think that all facilities contain seating areas for large numbers of spectators. A fitness center might provide activity spaces for gymnastics, a swimming pool, tennis and racquetball courts, jogging trails, a cardiovascular area, fitness machines, and free weights. Finally, in some situations, the mission of a facility is broad, and the facility will incorporate many sports or activities. For example, a multipurpose high school gymnasium might be designed for interscholastic sport practices and competition, physical education classes, school plays, and graduation ceremonies.

Regardless of the size or type of the facility or the kinds of events that it hosts, one factor remains consistent: To maintain a safe and enjoyable environment, proper management of the facility and events is crucial.

During the past 20 years, many sport and entertainment facilities have turned to private companies to handle their management tasks. **Privatization** is the term used to describe this move from public to private management. Either private owners or municipalities still own the facilities, but they outsource, which is the process of subcontracting services to an independent contractor, the management of their facilities to professionals who specialize in facility management (Steinbach, 2004).

privatization—Moving the management of facilities from the public sector to private companies or organizations.

The trend toward privatization began with US professional team facilities and spread to intercollegiate facilities, the minor professional leagues, and sport and entertainment facilities in other countries. Some high schools and municipal recreation centers in the United States have also privatized. Often, the owners of private sport and entertainment venues and the managers of public facilities are not prepared to engage in the facility management business. In such cases, poor management can lead to less than optimal operational efficiency, and venue operations become a drain on financial resources. In public facilities, variables such as political red tape and even patronage (i.e., hiring people in repayment for political favors) have caused financial difficulties. In most of these cases, gross operating expenses exceed gross revenues, causing the facilities to operate at a deficit. As you can imagine, this situation has led to reductions in services and the elimination of events, which in turn has led to privatization (Ammon, Southall, & Blair, 2004).

FACILITY MANAGEMENT

WEB

Go to the OSG and complete the Web search activity, which has you research staff positions at various sport venues.

The number of managers in a given facility, as well as their specific titles and duties, varies depending on the size and purpose of the facility. Consequently, those interested in working in facility management need to read job descriptions carefully to determine the precise duties associated with particular titles. In the sections to follow, we will describe several management positions and accompanying responsibilities with the caveat that specific situations may differ. In general, however, three positions that exist in most facilities are the facility director, the operations manager, and the event coordinator.

The *facility director* (also called the facility manager or the chief executive officer) has overall responsibility for the entire facility. This person is mainly responsible for the creation and proper administration of the facility's standard operating procedures.

The *operations manager* reports directly to the facility director and is responsible for all personnel, procedures, and activities related to the facility. This manager has a variety of duties, such as defining the roles, responsibilities, and authority of facility staff; recruiting personnel to coordinate the various areas of the facility; coordinating personnel, policies and procedures, and activities within the facility; evaluating facility operations; and making recommendations to the facility director.

The *event coordinator*, who also reports to the facility director, is responsible for managing individual events held in the facility. These events can vary from concerts to ice shows and from political rallies to sport events. The event coordinator's responsibilities usually include transporting, assembling, erecting, and storing equipment; establishing a control system for venue and equipment logistics; recruiting, training, and supervising specific personnel; assisting in maintaining venues and equipment during the event; facilitating ticketing and ticket distribution at venue sites; and evaluating venue and equipment operations.

EVENT MANAGEMENT

Every event is a product, an outcome, and an occurrence. An event occurs in a specific year and month, on a specific date, and at a specific place. All preparation must be completed before the event begins. The total effort is much like the preparation of an actor who is waiting in the wings for the cue to go on stage. The pressure for perfection in event management is high. Many students in the United States think that obtaining a 90% (A) grade for academic work constitutes excellent performance. But if you are managing an event for 70,000 people and the satisfaction level is 90%, you will have 6,300 unhappy patrons.

Events come in many shapes and sizes, from a small corporate 5K run to the New York City Marathon, from an 18-hole community golf tournament fund-raiser to the Masters, from a Little League Baseball game to the World Series. Event management includes the planning, coordinating, staging, and evaluating of an event. Most events have similar components, regardless of their scope.

Whether the event is a small golf tournament or the NFL Super Bowl, the planning of many components is crucial to its success. The components involved depend on the nature of the event, the time, the place, and the clientele. For example, a ticket to an event such as the Super Bowl is a prized possession, so serious attention is paid to

Courtesy of Kroenke Sports Enterprises.

Professional Profile: Mike Rock

Named to his present position in October 2007, Mike Rock, general manager of venue operations at Kroenke Sports Enterprises (KSE) in Denver, Colorado, is familiar with the operations of the Kroenke Sports Enterprises organization, having previously overseen event coordination, concessions, guest services, and security operations as the senior director of event operations at the Pepsi Center from 2002 to 2005. The Pepsi Center is home to the Denver Nuggets of the NBA, the Colorado Avalanche of the National Hockey League (NHL), and the Colorado Mammoth of the National Lacrosse League (NLL).

As the senior director of development from 2005 to 2007, Rock led the KSE development team in building an 18,000-seat Dick's Sporting Goods Park in Commerce City, Colorado, which includes a sports and entertainment complex with 24 fully lit sports fields. The stadium is home to the Colorado Rapids of Major League Soccer (MLS). The field complex is home to the Mile High Music Festival and a variety of youth and adult sport leagues, tournaments, and clinics.

Before joining KSE in 2002, Rock served as the director of guest services for MLB's Colorado Rockies from 1995 to 2001 and assisted in the opening of Coors Field. He began his career in the sport and entertainment industry in 1988 as an intern at the Oakland–Alameda County Coliseum and Arena, where he was an event manager and event coordinator until 1995. Born in Boston, Massachusetts, and raised in Davis, California, Rock is a 1983 graduate of the University of Arkansas.

ticketing in the NFL. Likewise, think of the preparation of the stadium maintenance crew for an NFL playoff game. Events like NCAA postseason championships present unique challenges because teams do not know where they will play until a few days before the competition.

Event Management Personnel

Because of the varied nature of events, no two events will have identical organizational structures. Many elements, however, are common across the industry of event management. Figure 15.1 shows a typical event management personnel structure for a moderately large (2,000 to 3,000 participants) sporting event. As you study the figure you will notice that the executive director is at the top of the hierarchy, division managers are in the second tier, and the remaining positions are primarily coordinators. For the sake of brevity, we will discuss only three of the positions identified in figure 15.1: executive director; operations division manager; and the public relations, marketing, and hospitality division manager.

- *Executive director.* The executive director is responsible for the overall administration of the event. Some of the responsibilities include developing operational and strategic plans, preparing the financial statements and budgets for approval, anticipating problems, and implementing solutions. The director is responsible for hiring and recruiting division managers and coordinators, and defining their roles, responsibilities, and authority. The director also needs to provide administrative support for division managers and coordinators in the overall planning for each area. The executive director also must prepare an event manual with guiding principles, policies and procedures, roles and responsibilities, and so on. The manual should clearly define the roles, responsibilities, and authority of each division manager and facilitate communication

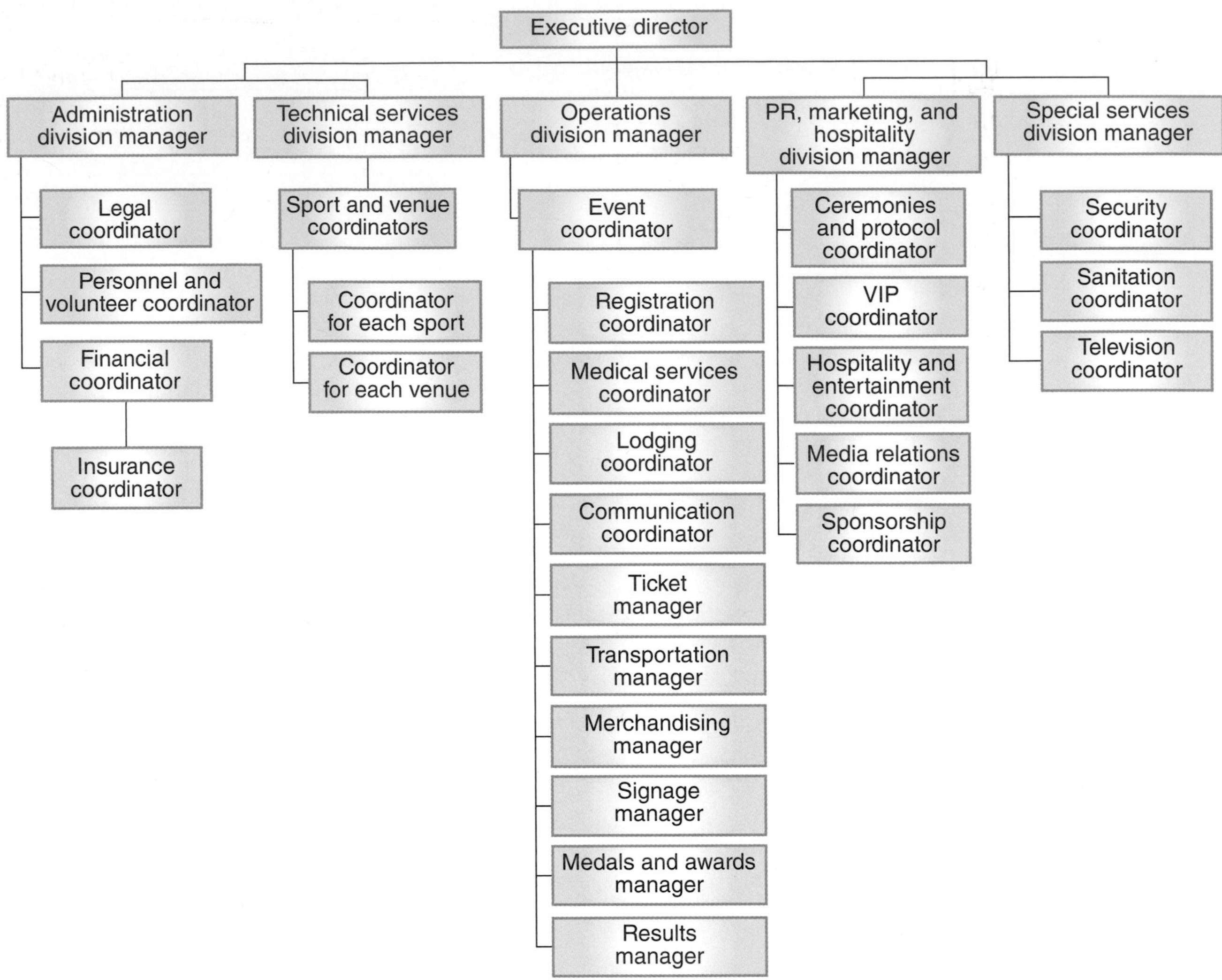

Figure 15.1 Event management structure.

among the divisions. The director assumes responsibility for organizational duties not specifically assigned to division managers or coordinators. The director approves overall plans, strategies, and budgets while at the same time monitoring the financial and human resources (e.g., budget, revenues, expenditures, staff, volunteers). The director is ultimately accountable for all aspects of the event.

- ***Operations division manager.*** The operations division manager is responsible for all personnel, procedures, and activities contained in the operations division. These items include registration, lodging, medical services, communications, merchandising and concessions, transportation, signage, medals and awards, and results. The operations division manager is also responsible for clearly defining the roles, responsibilities, and authority of each coordinator and manager while recruiting personnel to coordinate each operations area. The person in this position helps coordinators and managers complete their assigned tasks and assists them in the overall planning for each area. He or she coordinates personnel, policies and procedures, and activities within the operations division and facilitates communications among all operations coordinators and managers and among other division personnel as needed. The operations division manager communicates with other division managers while supervising personnel and approving policies. Finally, he or she evaluates the operations division and makes recommendations to the executive director, to whom he or she reports directly.

- *Public relations, marketing, and hospitality division manager.* The public relations, marketing, and hospitality division manager works at the direction of the executive director in all matters pertaining to public relations (PR), marketing, and hospitality. This person is responsible for personnel, procedures, and activities contained in this division, including, but not limited to, ceremonies and protocol, sponsorship, VIP services, media and PR, and hospitality entertainment. He or she recruits personnel to coordinate each activity and helps staff complete assigned tasks and responsibilities. While coordinating personnel, policies, procedures, and activities within the division, this manager also assists other divisions with PR, marketing, and hospitality needs. The PR, marketing, and hospitality division manager develops, implements, and manages the overall event marketing plan and facilitates communications among personnel in other divisions as needed. He or she reports directly to the executive director. In addition, he or she evaluates the PR, marketing, and hospitality division and makes recommendations.

ACTION

Go to the OSG and complete the Learning in Action activity, which has you participate on a panel to guess the event management personnel mystery guest.

An effective organizational structure facilitates effective event planning. All events—from a local tennis tournament to the Wimbledon Championships at the All England Lawn Tennis Club—need effective event management plans. A management plan should include seven basic steps: scheduling, negotiating, coordinating, staging, settling with the promoter, cleaning up, and evaluating. The executive or facility director is ultimately responsible for developing this plan.

Preevent Tasks

The major tasks to be done before the event comprise scheduling the event, negotiating the details with the organization involved, and coordinating the management of every aspect of the event.

Scheduling the Event

Scheduling an event entails a reservation process in which events are planned according to the philosophy of the facility. Because most facilities maintain a profit-oriented philosophy, a facility director tries to schedule the largest possible number of events without overburdening the facility or employees. Securing and contracting one specific event or attraction is known as **booking** an event.

booking—Securing and contracting one specific sport or entertainment event.

Scheduling may involve difficult decisions about what events are acceptable to the owners and management of the facility. For example, a Harley-Davidson motorcycle rally or an Ultimate Fighting Championship (UFC) competition might be considered too controversial for some constituents, or might be distasteful to owners or managers. But these types of events might produce a large profit from significant ticket sales and the accompanying concession and merchandise revenues. The facility builds its reputation on how its directors handle such conflicts.

Negotiating the Event

After making the decision to schedule the event, the facility director (or his or her representative) negotiates the terms of the contract with a representative of the event, usually the promoter. Most facilities use a **boilerplate** contract that addresses the specific terms (e.g., cost of facility, division of revenue) agreed on by the facility and the promoter. This type of document uses standard language and a fill-in-the-blank format (similar to most apartment leases) to describe the various clauses in the contract. Normally a prearranged percentage known as a **split** is used to divide revenue from the sale of tickets, merchandise, and sometimes concessions. These financial negotiations are critical factors

boilerplate—Generic document that uses standard language and a fill-in-the-blank format.

split—A prearranged percentage used to divide various sources of revenue between the promoter and the facility.

Stormy Weather

It was a dark and stormy Friday night in April, and the "Big Band" had just finished playing a rock concert at the World Arena in Colorado Springs, Colorado. The group was scheduled to perform on Saturday night at the Budweiser Events Center in Loveland, Colorado. The performers decided to sleep in and relax on Saturday instead of traveling to their Loveland hotel. The roadies left early to set the stage and lighting for the Saturday 7:00 p.m. show.

Spring weather in Colorado is notoriously unpredictable. On Saturday afternoon a snowstorm blew in over the mountains. Frantically, the band members gathered their belongings and entourage, and the bus departed at 3:30 p.m. for the 125-mile (200 km) trip north. At 4:00 p.m. (three hours before the 7:00 p.m. show) the bus became mired in the snow in one of the mountainous areas along the route. It seemed that the trip would not be completed as planned.

The managers of the Budweiser Events Center got the call at 4:15 p.m.: "Our bus is stuck on Monument Hill, and I-25 is closed. We cannot arrive until 8:00 p.m. at the earliest."

What do you do?

Here is the play-by-play of what the Budweiser Events Center managers did.

1. We gathered the crisis management team at the arena and started our action plan. We were confident that the concert would begin only about an hour late based on highway reports from the Colorado State Police.
2. We secured our ticket lists from the Web site database and divided the contact information into groups: e-mail and phone. We had our information technology (IT) people send e-mail blasts to everyone we had an address for and notified them of the problem.
3. All of us were responsible for calling roughly 50 people on the phone contact list. In addition, we created and printed flyers. As people came to the parking lot access gates, we handed them flyers so that they knew they could leave and come back later without getting out of their cars.
4. For patrons who had already arrived, we posted notices on the entry doors.
5. Patrons were allowed into the arena but were confined to the concourse until just before show time.
6. People who requested a refund were assigned a reference number, and all requests were granted.
7. In case too many people desired entry into the building, we readied an adjacent venue (Expo Hall) for overflow from the concourse.
8. The scheduled intermission was cut in half so that the show would not extend too far into the night.
9. Staff members were instructed to deal with complaints right away and be up front and honest; all messages on our phones were to be returned immediately.
10. At 7:20 p.m., the performers showed up and needed a few minutes to warm up.
11. At 8:10 p.m., it was show time at last.

It was a dark and stormy night.

in establishing the cost of an event. If the amount is too high, additional negotiations ensue to determine which costs to adjust and which splits to modify.

Coordinating the Event

cost analysis—An estimation of the revenues and expenses of an event.

After completing the preliminary negotiations with the promoter and calculating the **cost analysis,** the event coordinator sits down and studies all aspects of the event. The event coordinator is responsible for providing specific venue and equipment needs as requested by the promoter or appropriate representatives. An event coordinator needs to transport, assemble, erect, and store equipment while establishing procedures and guidelines for the rental, purchase, storage, and transportation of venue equipment. Securing a warehouse area for equipment storage and distribution as well as establishing a control system for venue and equipment logistics (e.g., inventory management, storage, transportation of equipment) are crucial steps in the process. After completing these tasks, the event coordinator works with the facility director to recruit and hire event personnel who will assist in maintaining the venues and equipment during the event. The event coordinator then trains and supervises these personnel.

The event coordinator designs a plan or **work order** for all employees to follow. The work order is the game plan for the event. It documents all requirements discussed with the promoter or other company representative. Anything not documented will be the responsibility of the event coordinator. The work order also defines the time required to do each assigned task.

work order—A document that illustrates all requirements of the event.

Staging the Event

After much planning and anticipation, the day of the event arrives. During smaller events such as a local golf tournament, the event coordinator makes certain that items such as longest-drive and closest-to-the-pin markers are in place and that each group has received its caddy or electric cart. Finally, refreshments, award tables, and portable toilets should be properly located. For large events such as concerts and ice shows, an entire day is usually allowed for load-in and setup after the trucks carrying the equipment for the event arrive.

At the designated hour on the day of the event, the doors or gates are opened, the crowd flows inside, and the event begins. At this point, the event coordinator discovers whether he or she was effective in planning and coordinating the many facets of staging the event, including parking, seating, alcohol policies, and crowd control.

Seating

Many facilities in the United States use reserved seats for events. This policy has not always been in place in sport stadia around the world. Standing room areas or terraces were permitted in many European stadia until the late 1980s. In April 1989 thousands of football fans flocked to Hillsborough Stadium in Sheffield, England, to watch the FA (Football Association) Cup semifinal between Liverpool and Nottingham Forest. Too many fans were allowed into an already full terrace at one end of the stadium. In the resulting crush, 96 Liverpool fans were killed and many others were seriously injured. As a result, a government report (*The Taylor Report* by Lord Justice Taylor) required reserved seats and phased out the terraces from the Premier League levels of British soccer, although standing room is still allowed in the lower divisions (Warshaw, 2004).

With a reserved ticket, a spectator is assured of a specific seat, in a specific row, in a specific section at the event. With the use of trained ushers and an effective crowd control plan, few problems occur at events with this type of seating. Other types of seating are not as easy to manage. General admission (GA) seating is a first-come, first-served process that sometimes causes fans to line up outside for hours before the facility opens, in the hope of gaining that prestigious front-row seat. Festival seating is a type of GA seating, but it is a misnomer because no actual seats exist. Festival seating allows spectators to crowd together standing shoulder to shoulder in open floor space. Although promoters can sell more tickets by using festival seating rather than reserved or general admission seating, it is a potentially deadly arrangement and continues to be a controversial topic in event management.

A variety of fatal incidents have occurred at entertainment events around the world, including the following:

- December 1979, Cincinnati, Ohio—11 were killed in a crush to get into a concert by The Who.
- January 1991, Salt Lake City, Utah—3 teenagers were killed when the crowd at an AC/DC concert rushed the stage.

RISK MANAGEMENT: STADIUM DISASTERS IN AFRICA

By Babs Surujlal
Vaal University of Technology, SOUTH AFRICA

Sport stadia have the potential to cause a variety of calamities related to their daily operations. In Africa many of the risks are associated with unruly crowds, overcrowding, and incompetent personnel. The poor management of these risks has, in many instances, resulted in disasters.

Stadium disasters are not a new phenomenon in Africa. The causes of fatalities and severe injuries in most of these disasters were stampedes that occurred at overcrowded stadia where security was either inadequate or incompetent:

- In January 1991, 40 fans were trampled to death and 50 were injured in a stampede in Orkney, South Africa.
- In June 1996, 9 soccer fans were crushed to death and 78 others were injured during a stampede in Lusaka, Zambia.
- In April 1997, 5 fans were crushed to death and more than a dozen were injured during a stampede toward a locked exit in Lagos, Nigeria.
- In April 2000, 3 people suffocated as result of thousands of fans forcing their way into an overcrowded stadium in Monrovia, Liberia.

AP Photo.

In March 2009, 19 people died and more than 100 were injured in a stampede ahead of a World Cup qualifying match in Abidjan, Ivory Coast.

- May 1999, Minsk, Belarus—53 were killed when a crowd fleeing a severe rainstorm during a downtown rock concert and beer festival stampeded in an underground passage.
- July 2000, Copenhagen, Denmark—8 were killed in crush of fans trying to get closer to Pearl Jam at an outdoor concert.
- February 2003, Chicago, Illinois—21 died at a Chicago nightclub when guests stampeded to the exits after a security guard used pepper spray to break up a fight.
- February 2003, West Warwick, Rhode Island—100 died after pyrotechnics ignited flammable foam lining the walls of the venue during a Great White concert.
- July 2003, Moscow, Russia—17 people were killed when two explosions went off at a rock festival. Reports were that two suicide bombers set off the blasts in the crowd at the entrance to the festival when security guards prevented them from entering the gates.
- April 2008, Quito, Ecuador—15 people died after pyrotechnics, lit by a band member, ignited a nightclub hosting a rock concert.

- In April 2001, 7 spectators were crushed to death in a stampede in Lubumbashi, Congo.
- In May 2001, more than 120 people died in a stampede after police fired tear gas in reaction to an unruly crowd in Accra, Ghana.
- In October 2004, 4 people were killed and another 8 were injured during a stampede resulting from a power outage that caused crowds to panic and rush towards the exits in Lome, Togo.
- In June 2007, 12 fans were crushed to death in a stampede in Lusaka, Zambia.

These alarming incidents provide compelling evidence that management of risk at sport facilities is an important concern.

In South Africa, Coca-Cola Park, known as Ellis Park Stadium until 2008, is regarded as one of the country's prime stadiums. Located in Johannesburg, it is accredited by both the South African Football Association (SAFA) and the International Federation of Association Football (FIFA) for soccer and by the South African Rugby Football Union (SARFU) and the International Rugby Board (IRB) for rugby. Yet in 2001 one of the worst stadium disasters in South African sport occurred here when 43 people were killed and 160 were injured as football fans tried to barge their way into an overcrowded stadium.

A disaster report on the Ellis Park tragedy identified many precipitating factors that led to the disaster: poor forecasting of match attendance, failure to learn from the lessons of the past, overcrowding, inappropriate and inadequate response of security to screams and signals from spectators, the use of tear gas, failure to identify and designate areas of responsibility, failure to adhere to FIFA and SAFA guidelines, unacceptable spectator behaviour, corruption and dereliction of duty, an inadequate public address system, unsatisfactory attitude of private security companies, poorly managed ticket sales, and failure to use a big screen. A sound risk management plan, based on the knowledge that South African football fans are excessively rowdy, might have prevented this tragedy.

INTERNATIONAL LEARNING ACTIVITY #1

Using information presented in this chapter, construct a risk management plan for Coca-Cola Park. How would this risk management plan differ from one constructed for your university's basketball arena?

INTERNATIONAL LEARNING ACTIVITY #2

Go to the Web site of the Millennium Stadium at www.millenniumstadium.com and look at the various types of events staged in this arena. What other events could be staged in this facility to increase revenue?

- June 2010, Johannesburg, South Africa—Although not fatal, a stampede before a warm-up World Cup soccer match injures 15 fans.

Customer Service

Todd Leiweke, CEO of the NFL's Seattle Seahawks, emphasizes that for any sport or entertainment event to be a success, facility and event managers must concentrate on three fundamentals: brand, audience, and experience. The brand is the venue (the place). The audience comprises all those people driven by a passion for the product (the event), and the experience is the relationship between the ticket buyer and the event itself (Deckard, 2005). Customer service, guest relations, and fan services are all terms used to describe the relationship that exists between the event (or facility) management and the people who attend the event.

The customers, or guests, are the fuel that the sport and entertainment industry relies on. Without patrons there would be neither events nor facilities to house them. But the guests who attend sport and entertainment events are products of a society that has come to expect immediate results or instant gratification. Everyone knows that most businesses must have repeat customers to be profitable. In the same way, event managers depend on repeat customers to produce a profit. Thus, to guarantee repeat customers, event and facility managers must listen to their guests and respond effectively to their concerns. These managers must adopt a customer-centered business philosophy, because, as we all know, putting on an event without an audience is difficult. Although most facility and event professionals would assert that the customer is always right, "more important than serving one person is serving all the people" (Deckard, 2005, p. 2).

Alcohol Policies

A potential liability exists if intoxicated patrons create dangerous situations for themselves and others. Some people argue that revenue generated from beer sales is worth the risk, and some facilities would find it difficult to generate a profit without beer sales. Others have determined that the increased revenue produced by selling alcohol does not outweigh the liabilities. Although the controversy continues, alcohol probably will continue to be a part of many sporting events, and facility managers must continue to devise tactics to reduce the risks created by alcohol consumption.

Fan behavior at stadia has become an increasing concern at all major sport venues. In 2008 the NFL released a fan code of conduct in response to numerous complaints from fans. Unruly fans who cause a disruption at the game can be ejected. Also, intoxicated fans can be asked to leave the game or even be denied access into the stadium. In fact, for certain offenses, season ticket holders can lose their seats if they (or their guests) are ejected (McCarthy, 2008).

Crowd Management

A facility or event manager needs a crowd management plan even when managing an event with a small number of spectators. Whether employed at a small high school basketball game, a local YMCA, or an NCAA Division I Softball Championship, the facility or event manager needs a crowd management plan because the manager must strive to provide a safe and enjoyable environment. The crowd control plan must be an integral element of a larger risk management plan. The components of such a plan are staff training, emergency planning, accessibility for spectators with disabilities, procedures for ejecting disruptive people, an efficient communication system, and effective signage.

- ***Staff training.*** Training competent staff to carry out the plan is the first component of an effective crowd control plan. Management at some facilities choose to use their own staff to conduct crowd control duties. This approach is known as **in-house** secu-

in-house—Services provided by the facility staff.

As part of the risk management preparation for a sport event, the crowd management and emergency planning activities often necessitate visible security and police personnel such as are present here for a professional soccer match in Europe.

Photo courtesy of Paul M. Pedersen.

rity or crowd management. Management at other facilities contract out, or outsource, crowd management services to independent contractors.

- *Emergency planning.* An emergency plan is the second component of an effective crowd control plan. The intent of an emergency plan is to ensure that minor incidents do not become major incidents and that major incidents do not become fatal. Emergencies take many forms, such as medical problems (e.g., life-threatening issues, minor injuries), severe weather (e.g., lightning, tornadoes), natural disasters (e.g., earthquakes, floods), fires, bomb threats, power losses, and, in today's society, terrorist activities. Managers must not only design and implement an emergency plan but also practice it, because the courts will ask for documentation about when the plan was practiced. Because of the terrorist threat, managers at several venues use practice sessions to test the ability of their emergency services during a mock attack. Baltimore's M&T Bank Stadium in 2008 held a mock nuclear weapon terrorist attack. The drill, called Operation Purple Haze, attracted 500 fans. Venue managers released a "bomb" and fans scrambled to escape. The fans' "injuries" were treated by 300 first responders who, along with local hospitals, practiced their emergency response plans (Williams, 2008).

- *Ensuring accessibility for spectators with disabilities.* The third component of an effective crowd control plan should address the procedures necessary to ensure facility accessibility for all citizens. Congress passed the **Americans with Disabilities Act (ADA)** in 1992. The ADA has had a major effect on the design of sport and entertainment venues. Sport and entertainment event managers must be familiar with the ADA because its various requirements pertain to facility features such as signage, restrooms, telephones, parking, and shower stalls. Furthermore, event managers must also develop plans for the evacuation of spectators with disabilities or special needs.

Americans with Disabilities Act (ADA)—Legislation that protects people with disabilities from discrimination. Specific to sport facilities, the law states that managers must provide "reasonable accommodations" for people with disabilities (Ammon et al., 2004, p. 68).

- *Procedures for ejecting disruptive people.* The fourth component of an effective crowd control plan addresses the procedures necessary to eject disruptive, unruly, or intoxicated patrons. The ejection duties should remain the responsibility of trained crowd control staff and, in some jurisdictions, police officers, sheriff's department personnel, or state troopers. These individuals must understand the concepts of the reasonably prudent person and excessive force, and they should understand that they might be sued for negligence if they eject patrons incorrectly. Ushers should not undertake these duties if they are not trained in crowd control procedures. Removing disruptive or intoxicated fans will provide a safer environment for the remaining spectators and help protect the facility or event manager from potential litigation (Ammon & Unruh, 2007).

- *An efficient communication system.* An efficient communication network is the fifth component of an effective crowd control plan. Communication is critical in providing spectator safety, enjoyment, and security. The use of a centralized area for representatives from each group involved in the management of an event (i.e., law enforcement, maintenance, medical, and security) will facilitate communication and improve decision making.

- *Effective signage.* The creation and use of proper signage is the sixth and final component of crowd control. Informational and directional signs build a support network between fans and facility management staff. Spectators appreciate being treated fairly and if previously informed will normally abide by facility directives pertaining to no-smoking sections, alcohol policies, and prohibited items. Directional signs have several important uses. As spectators approach the facility, road signs can indicate the correct exits and provide relevant parking information. Other signs serve to indicate the correct gate or portal and direct ticket-buying patrons to the box office. Signage will help facility patrons locate concession stands, first-aid rooms, telephones, and restrooms. Informational signs regarding prohibited items assist patrons in making decisions before entry (Ammon & Unruh, 2007).

Postevent Tasks

After the event has occurred, several additional items need to be completed before the event becomes history and the event coordinator can go home. The postevent procedures include activities such as event cleanup, **settlement,** and evaluation of the event.

settlement—Reconciling the expenses and revenues of an event and dividing the profits according to a contracted arrangement.

Event Cleanup

After the event is over and the crowd has filed out, the equipment used in the event is gathered up and put away or stored in trucks, and cleanup of the facility commences. Another entire day is usually set aside for the load-out.

Evaluating the Event

Immediately after the event, the management team evaluates the process. **Documentation** of the entire process is critical, not only for protection against subsequent litigation but also for reference in planning future events.

documentation—Completing detailed records that describe the event.

Critical Thinking in Sport Facility and Event Management

PORTFOLIO

Complete the critical thinking portfolio activity in the OSG, consulting as needed the "Eight Critical Thinking Questions" section in chapter 1.

Many aspects of ethical and moral conduct involve consideration and debate of possible actions and outcomes. One feature of critical thinking is the systematic evaluation of various arguments and positions. These discussions help managers weigh possible alternatives and their requisite outcomes. For example, consider the following event and facility management scenario about fans at a university basketball arena. At this university in the southern part of the United States, a fan at a basketball game stands and displays a poster with a Confederate flag. The flag, to some, represents the glory and pride of southern residents. To others, it represents a symbol of slavery and racism.

Ethics in Sport Facility and Event Management

All employee-training programs should include a discussion of the role that professional ethics plays in facility and event management. Ethical behavior is not the sole province of employees. Most sport facilities have standards by which patrons are expected to comply. For example, the Pepsi Center (Denver, Colorado) has established the following code of conduct (*Security*, 2010):

> All Pepsi Center guests are expected to maintain reasonable and appropriate behavior at all times. Any behavior defying the code of conduct as determined by facility management can result in ejection and possible arrest. Ejected guests will not receive a refund for their tickets or be compensated in any way. Inappropriate behavior includes, but is not limited to the following:
>
> - Standing on chairs or seats
> - Drunk and disorderly conduct
> - Fighting or challenging others to fight
> - Interference with the event or participants of the event in any way
> - Throwing, tossing, or discharging any object
> - Using profanity or other offensive words
> - Taunting or using offensive language against the players, referees, or performers
> - Entering a seating area without the correct ticket
> - Disturbing other patrons' enjoyment of the event
> - Failing to comply with facility personnel

- Violating Pepsi Center rules, regulations, and policies
- Violating any local, state, or federal laws

Pepsi Center management reserves the right to deny entry or eject from the facility guests displaying inappropriate behavior, as determined by facility or event management.

PORTFOLIO Complete the ethical issues portfolio activity in the OSG, consulting as needed the "Guidelines for Making Ethical Decisions" section in chapter 1.

Summary

The FIFA World Cup, the Olympic Games, concerts, and high school track meets have two common denominators: They take place in some type of facility, and they are events. All facilities and events need people to manage them.

The management of many sport and entertainment facilities is being outsourced to private management companies. These private entities have been successful in raising the profit margins of many sport and public assembly facilities across the United States.

To ensure a successful event, facility directors must perform several important tasks. They need to know and understand how these tasks relate to the successful completion of every event. Scheduling and booking an event begin the overall process, and a cost analysis is critical in these initial operations. After the facility director has decided that the event will be held, the necessary contracts need to be signed, and the event coordinator must create and communicate a work order to the others on the event management team. Items such as seating arrangements, crowd management, alcohol policies, settlement, and event evaluation must be carried out for an event to be successful.

The number of facilities has grown significantly in recent years, and many of these facilities schedule sport and entertainment events with global implications. Worldwide terrorist attacks have changed the facility and event management industry dramatically. In addition, some areas of sport have downsized because of factors such as changes in the economy, corporate mergers, and business failures. Because of these trends, the future of facility and event management is not as clear as once imagined. Slower revenue growth has affected profit margins. The influence that this domino effect has on facility and event management needs to be continually monitored.

QUIZ TIME Did you grasp all the key points in this chapter? Go to the OSG for a short quiz to test your understanding of the material.

Review Questions

1. What is the nearest major single-purpose facility in your area? List the personnel who would be involved in the management at this type of facility.
2. What are some of the nearby multipurpose facilities in your area?
3. Currently, several companies privately manage more than 300 facilities nationally and internationally. What are some of the companies near you?
4. In reference to the question above, why would a facility choose to contract with one of these companies?
5. What is a work order similar to? What is the purpose of a work order? Who compiles the work order?
6. Why do the management team members need to meet to evaluate the overall production after the event ends? Why should the team complete all the proper documentation at this meeting?
7. Why is employing trained people to reduce facility risks a less expensive alternative than reacting to potential disasters or litigation without such people? How can much of this litigation be avoided?
8. Why is it important for sport event and facility managers to develop proper ethical guidelines and critical thinking skills?

References

Ammon, R. Jr., Southall, R., & Blair, D. (2004). *Sport facility management: Organizing events and mitigating risks.* Morgantown, WV: Fitness Information Technology.

Ammon, R. Jr., & Unruh, N. (2007). Crowd management. In D.J. Cotton & J. Wolohan (Eds.), *Law for recreation and sport managers* (4th ed.) (pp. 334–344). Dubuque, IA: Kendall/Hunt.

Deckard, L. (2005, January 19). Keynoter stresses customer service to ticketing professionals. *VenuesToday*, *4*(3), 2–3.

Demick, B. (2009, February 22). Beijing's Olympic building boom becomes a bust. *Los Angeles Times*. Retrieved May 24, 2010, from www.latimes.com/news/nationworld/world/la-fg-beijing-bust22-2009feb22,0,5564951.story

Highs and lows from 2008. (2008, December 22). *Street & Smith's SportsBusiness Journal*, p. 15.

Lee, J. (2009, January 31). VANOC: Balanced budget on target, but surplus in doubt. *Vancouver Sun*. Retrieved February 2, 2010, from www2.canada.com/vancouversun/news/westcoastnews/story.html?id=01da3995-6171-44b2-9e92-99199f5bc457

McCarthy, M. (2008, August 6). NFL unveils new code of conduct for fans. *USA Today*. Retrieved February 2, 2010, from www.usatoday.com/sports/football/nfl/2008-08-05-fan-code-of-conduct_N.htm

Muret, D. (2009, January 12). Slump sends construction costs lower. *Street & Smith's SportsBusiness Journal*, p. 15.

Security policy. (2010). Pepsi Center. Retrieved May 24, 2010, from www.pepsicenter.com/Facility/Security/Default.aspx

Sports projects play the waiting game. (2009, January 12). *Street & Smith's SportsBusiness Journal*, p. 16.

Steinbach, P. (2004, August). Special operations. *Athletic Business*, *28*(8), 24–28.

Warshaw, A. (2004, March). Making a stand. *Stadia*, pp. 12–14.

Williams, J.J. (2008, August 4). Baltimore disaster drill draws 300 first responders. *Baltimore Sun*. Retrieved May 24, 2010, from www.ems1.com/ems-training/articles/422948-baltimore-disaster-drill-draws-300-first-responders/

PART IV

CURRENT CHALLENGES IN SPORT MANAGEMENT

A critical step in the process of becoming a responsible and effective manager of sport enterprises is recognizing the significance of sport as a major social and increasingly global institution. The first four chapters in this section provide the foundation for understanding the challenges presented by consumer behavior, legal, social, and international aspects of sport. An appreciation of these facets of sport will increase the likelihood that you will make wise managerial decisions within the context of the broad social and global environment in which sporting activities occur. Chapter 20, the final chapter of the book, deals with research. As you progress through the curriculum at your college or university, some of your instructors will require you to write reports on research articles published in the sport management literature. Instructors assign these reports because they know that when you become a practicing professional, one of your obligations to your employer, to your employees, to the consumers of your products, and to the public will involve being familiar with the research in your field. A problem with these assignments, however, is that students are seldom familiar with why people conduct research, how they conduct it, or how to evaluate the published product. Therefore, chapter 20 will give you a basic understanding of these concepts.

Christine Green and Carla Costa address consumer behavior in chapter 16. In the first section the authors examine the individual factors that influence active (i.e., sport participation) and passive (i.e., sport spectation) sport consumption. They explain in detail how consumers are influenced by certain motives, and how perceptions and attitudes influence consumers' involvement and identification with a sport, team, athlete, or sport brand. In their second section Green and Costa discuss group influences on the sport consumer. Within this discussion are analyses of the influence of reference groups and socialization on consumer decision making. Green and Costa conclude their chapter with an explanation of the decision-making process itself. The underlying theme of this chapter is that understanding how people make decisions about their consumption of the sport product will be valuable to sport managers as they compete with a multitude of other diversions for the time and money of consumers. The international sidebar for this chapter contains an essay on the consumer behavior associated with sumo wrestling. Toshiyuki Ogura, a native of Japan who is now at the University of Texas at Austin, contributed this international vignette.

In chapter 17 Anita Moorman and Chris Reynolds introduce basic concepts related to legislation affecting the management of sport in the United States. After presenting a brief introduction to the American legal system, the authors discuss the influence of the federal Constitution on sport management and the effects of federal legislation, explicitly the Americans with Disabilities Act and Title IX of the Education Amendments Act. Then they examine state legal systems, including tort law, negligence, intentional torts, and contracts. Moorman and Reynolds conclude the chapter with a discussion of legal challenges that await prospective sport managers. The topic of this chapter's international sidebar addresses legal and policy matters associated with grassroots and commercial sport in Greece. Anastasios Kaburakis, a native of Greece who is a sport law and policy expert at Southern Illinois University Edwardsville, contributed this essay.

Chapter 18 focuses on the role of sport sociology in the management of sporting activities. Nicole LaVoi and Mary Jo Kane define sport sociology and discuss the social significance of sport. LaVoi and Kane then examine possible benefits of sport, such as its ability to socialize participants and unify people. Next, they present several examples of the darker side of sport, including sexism, homophobia and heterosexism, and racism. LaVoi and Kane conclude the chapter with a discussion of how sport can serve as a vehicle for social transformation and how you can apply your knowledge of sport sociology in the management of sport. The international sidebar in this chapter is an essay on the barriers faced by and opportunities presented to women in their pursuit of sport leadership positions in New Zealand. Sarah Leberman, who teaches management at Massey University (New Zealand), contributed the essay.

In chapter 19 Ted Fay, Luisa Velez, and Janet Parks first define international sport. Next, the authors analyze the unprecedented international growth of sport. They provide five prominent examples to illustrate this growth: changes to the Olympic Games, expanded opportunities for women, the redefinition of international sport, increased recruitment and marketing efforts at the international level, and increased participation in international sport by countries with emerging economies. Included in the last example is a comprehensive discussion of China as the awakening giant of sport in the 21st century. Fay, Velez, and Parks next discuss the relocation of sporting goods manufacturing companies and explain the concerns associated with international sport governance, two of the most pressing issues in international sport. After detailing the knowledge and skills necessary for a successful career in international sport, the authors conclude the chapter with a discussion of several trends that will affect international sport. The importance of Brazil as a new sport power is the topic of this chapter's international sidebar. Ricardo João Sonoda Nunes from the Federal University of Paraná (Brazil) contributed this essay.

Chapter 20 addresses the important topic of research in sport management. We conclude the book with this subject because we know that to perform your sport management job effectively and efficiently, you will need to know how to evaluate research. The better you become at interpreting and evaluating research, the less likely you will be to waste your time and your organization's money on unsound suggestions. If you understand research, you will be able to make decisions grounded in the analysis of relevant data rather than depend on hunches or simply perpetuate tradition. The earlier you learn to evaluate research, the more meaningful those research article assignments will be later on. Moreover, as you develop greater skill in evaluating research, you will be more prepared to make the difficult decisions that surely will come your way as a sport manager. Therefore, chapter 20 provides an introduction to sport management research. Jess Dixon, Wendy Frisby, and Bob Boucher begin their examination of this topic by explaining why asking good research questions and getting accurate answers are critical to the success of sport management ventures. After discussing why sport managers should understand research, the authors explain the academic and commercial aspects of sport management research. Dixon, Frisby, and Boucher then examine several key research concepts—ways of knowing, science and pseudoscience, basic and applied research, quantitative and qualitative data, research design, and validity and reliability of research instruments. The authors next detail the major issues influencing sport management research. They conclude the chapter by discussing the future of research conducted by sport managers, who will need research skills to operate successfully in a knowledge-based economy. The international sidebar in this chapter examines how European soccer researchers and practitioners have applied the research and concepts of *Moneyball*. Bill Gerrard, who teaches sport management in England at the Leeds University Business School, contributed this essay.

For More Information

Professional and Scholarly Associations

Academy of Legal Studies in Business: www.alsb.org

American Sociological Association (ASA): www.asanet.org

Australia and New Zealand Sports Law Association: www.anzsla.com.au/

International Association of Sports Law: iasl.org/pages/en.php

National Association for Girls and Women in Sport (NAGWS): www.aahperd.org/nagws/

North American Society for the Sociology of Sport (NASSS): www.nasss.org

Society of Consumer Affairs Professionals: www.socap.org/

Sport and Recreation Law Association (SRLA): www.srlaweb.org

Sports Lawyers Association: www.sportslaw.org/

Women's Sports Foundation (WSF): www.womenssportsfoundation.org

Professional and Scholarly Publications

Academy of Management Journal

Academy of Management Review

Administrative Science Quarterly

American Business Law Journal

DePaul Journal of Sports Law & Contemporary Problems

Entertainment and Sports Law Journal

Entertainment and Sports Lawyer

European Journal for Sport and Society

Florida Entertainment, Art & Sport Law Journal

Global Sport Management

Harvard Business Review

Human Relations

ICHPER-SD Journal of Research (International Council for Health, Physical Education, Recreation, Sport, & Dance)

International Gambling Studies

International Journal of Sport

International Review for the Sociology of Sport

International Sports Law Journal

International Sports Studies

Journal of Business Research

Journal of Consumer Research

Journal of ICHPER-SD

Journal of the Legal Aspects of Sport

Journal of Sport & Social Issues

Journal of Sport Behavior

Journal of Sports Law & Contemporary Problems

Legal Issues in College Athletics

Marquette Sports Law Review

Michigan State University College of Law Entertainment and Sports Law Journal

Paralympian Online

Quest

Research Quarterly for Exercise and Sport

Seton Hall Journal of Sports and Entertainment Law

Sociology of Sport Journal

Sport in Society

Sport Journal

Sport Psychologist

Sport, Education, & Society

Sports and Entertainment Litigation Reporter

Sports Law Forum at Fordham University School of Law

Sports Lawyers Journal

Sports, Park and Recreation Law Reporter

Strategic Management Journal

Texas Review of Entertainment & Sports Law

University of Miami Entertainment and Sports Law Review

Villanova Sports & Entertainment Law Journal

Virginia Sports and Entertainment Law Journal

Willamette Sports Law Journal

Women in Sport and Physical Activity Journal

Additional Internet Resources

Amateur Athletics Foundation of Los Angeles Sports Library: www.aafla.org/

Centre for Leisure Management Research: www.deakin.edu.au/buslaw/clmr/

Cerebral Palsy International Sports & Recreation Association: www.cpisra.org/

Cornell University Law School: www.law.cornell.edu/

FindLaw: www.findlaw.com/

General Association of International Sports Federations: www.sportcentric.com/home/

Institute for Diversity and Ethics in Sport: www.tidesport.org/

Institute for International Sport: www.internationalsport.com/

International Committee of Sports for the Deaf/Deaflympics: www.deaflympics.com/

International Paralympic Committee: www.paralympic.org/

Maccabiah Games: www.maccabiusa.com/

Olympic Games: www.olympic.org/en/

Pan-American Games: www.guadalajara2011.org.mx/eng/

Research and Markets: www.researchandmarkets.com/

Sport Business Research Network: www.sbrnet.com/

Sport in Society: www.northeastern.edu/sportinsociety/

Tucker Center for Research on Girls & Women in Sport: www.tuckercenter.org

University of Calgary Scholarly Sport Sites: www.ucalgary.ca/lib-old/ssportsite/index.html

HISTORICAL MOMENTS

1894	*Daily Racing Form* made its debut
1908	Pari-mutuel betting introduced at Kentucky Derby
1962	Fantasy football began among beat writers for the AFL Oakland Raiders
1969	Internet established
1976	Basking in reflected glory (BIRGing) concept identified by Robert Cialdini and colleagues
1980	Daniel Okrent started first Rotisserie Baseball League
1993	Electronic Arts launched EA Sports brand
1994	DirecTV founded
1998	Sportvision made its debut of its "1st & Ten" system, a yellow computer-generated line to aid TV viewers
1999	TiVo made its debut
2000	Major League Baseball Advanced Media founded
2003	NFL Network launched
2005	YouTube founded
2006	Wii Sports game launched by Nintendo
2009	US$40 million video board unveiled at the new US$1.15 billion Cowboys Stadium

Photo courtesy of Paul M. Pedersen.

SPORT CONSUMER BEHAVIOR

B. Christine Green ■ Carla A. Costa

LEARNING OBJECTIVES

1. Identify key motives for sport participation, spectation, and sport product purchases.
2. Define consumer perception and its application to the sport industry.
3. Describe the components of consumers' attitudes toward sport.
4. Differentiate between consumer involvement and identification.
5. Explain ways in which groups can influence the consumption behaviors of individuals.
6. Discuss the process of consumer decision making in sport.
7. Identify situational factors that can influence the decision-making process.
8. Apply ethical reasoning and critical thinking skills to sport consumer behavior.

GET A JOB!

☑ Continue on your journey in sport management by going to the Online Study Guide (OSG) at www.HumanKinetics.com/ContemporarySportManagement. Check out the job opportunities and consider the skills and experiences that can help you succeed in sport management.

Key Terms

aspirational reference group
cognitive dissonance
diversion
eustress
extrinsic rewards
intrinsic rewards
market segment
need recognition
situational influence
target market

Imagine that you have developed a new sport. Who will play your sport? Who might watch it? The success of your new sport depends on your ability to attract customers. You need to know all you can about your customers—what they want, what they need, what they think, what they feel, what they know, and what they value. Most important, you want to know *why* they make the choices that they do. The study of consumer behavior enables you to do just that.

Consumer behavior consists of the processes involved in the search, selection, purchase, and use of products, services, and experiences that fulfill consumers' needs or desires. Consumer behavior helps you understand how personal and group factors influence consumer decisions and how people make purchase decisions. A good understanding of current and potential consumers enables an organization to develop products and services that meet the needs of customers and to develop marketing strategies that attract and retain customers.

The purpose of this chapter is to provide an overview of consumer behavior in sport. In the first section, you will learn about individual factors that influence sport consumption. This section describes the motives for active (i.e., sport participation) and passive (i.e., sport spectation) sport consumption, and examines consumers' perceptions and attitudes toward sport. Individuals' motives, perceptions, and attitudes influence their involvement with any particular sport and the ways in which they identify with a sport, team, athlete, or sport brand. The second section examines group influences on the sport consumer. In this section you will examine the influence of direct and indirect reference groups and the socialization process on consumer decision making. The final section introduces you to the decision-making process itself.

UNDERSTANDING THE INDIVIDUAL AS A SPORT CONSUMER

Think for a minute about buying a gift for two of your close friends. Would you buy each one the same gift? Probably not. How, then, do you choose a gift suited to each of your friends? Most likely, you will consider what you know about each friend. The more you know about your friend, the easier it is to choose the perfect gift. The same is true for sport businesses. To sell more tickets, to sell more tennis rackets, or to entice more players and teams to join a league, sport organizations need to know about their customers. The more a sport organization knows about its customers, the better it is able to design products and services to meet the needs of those customers, to design marketing messages that attract new customers and keep existing customers coming back, and to target messages to those most receptive to those messages.

Although no two individuals are the same, people often have some characteristics in common. A standard practice in marketing is to try to group, or segment, people based on common characteristics. In marketing terms, groups that share a number of characteristics are called **market segments.** Marketers then choose to focus their efforts on one or more of the identified market segments. The selected market segments are referred to as **target markets.** Products and services are designed to meet the needs of the target market.

market segment—A portion of the population that is distinctive in terms of its needs, characteristics, or behavior.

target market—Market segment or segments identified as the focus of an organization's marketing efforts.

Marketers often segment sport consumers based on their motives, perceptions, and attitudes. Consumers build these attributes from experiences, which might depend on their interests and opinions. Sport consumers often are emotionally and psychologically involved with their sports. Many athletes and fans define themselves in terms of their sport identity. The following sections describe consumer needs and motivations, perceptions, attitudes, involvement and identification, and loyalty, and then explore the ways that each can be used to understand the sport consumer.

Consumer Needs and Motivation

The fulfillment of needs is the essence of a marketing orientation (Shank, 2008). Everybody has needs. We are born with innate physiological needs—the need for food, water, air, clothing, and shelter. The fulfillment of these needs is required for life. We also have acquired needs such as the need for esteem, affection, or power. These needs are not necessary for life and tend to vary from culture to culture and from person to person. These needs are better described as wants and desires. Motives can be thought of as the reasons that people behave the way they do. This driving force exists in response to an unfulfilled need. The key to the success of a sport organization (e.g., a professional basketball franchise) is to identify and satisfy customers' unfulfilled needs better or faster than the competition (e.g., other professional clubs, college teams, other entertainment options) does. Consequently, successful marketers define their target markets by the needs that they are trying to satisfy. Although individual needs and motives vary, researchers have identified some common participation and spectator motives. We first examine the research involving participation motives and then analyze the research related to sport spectator motives.

Participant Motivation

As Green (1996) revealed, researchers have identified over 100 motives for participating in sport. Fortunately, the reasons that people give to explain their participation can be grouped into three key motives: (1) achievement motivation, (2) social motivation, and (3) mastery motivation (Smith & Bar-Eli, 2007). The need to compete, to win, and to be the best are examples of achievement motivations. These needs nearly always require an element of social comparison. To attract participants motivated by achievement goals, sport marketers emphasize the competitive elements of their programs. A competitive league structure and playoff opportunities would be important to players motivated by achievement. These players might also value **extrinsic rewards** such as MVP awards, all-star games, and trophies.

extrinsic rewards— Rewards given to a person by someone else.

A Swim Club in Crisis

A small suburban swim club was in trouble. Although the club enjoyed moderate success in the local summer swim league, substantial turnover of membership occurred from summer to summer. Each year almost half the families from the previous season did not return. The club conducted a survey at the end of one of its seasons and discovered that families had many different reasons for joining the club. Some wanted their children to win ribbons, medals, and trophies (achievement motivation); some found that the club was a good way to get to know other people in the community (social motivation); and some wanted their children to improve their swimming skills (mastery motivation). The club had always assumed that its primary task was to help children become winning competitive swimmers. The club focused on achievement by helping its swimmers find a specialty event and train to win in that event. All members were required to compete at weekend swimming meets. Although the team had a picnic at the end of the season, the club did little else to foster social interaction among its members.

After the survey, the club changed its policies. Coaches implemented special coaching to help swimmers who wanted to develop swimming skills beyond their primary competitive events (mastery motivation). Members who did not want to compete were not required to enter weekend swimming meets. The club also introduced several social events for members, including pizza parties and midseason picnics (social motivation). Within two years, the club had grown from 62 families to over 300 families, and members typically stayed with the club for several years. By developing its programs to appeal to multiple motivations, the club increased its membership, improved its financial position, and became league champion.

Marketing efforts directed toward participants seeking social opportunities through their sport participation should highlight social interactions among participants. Advertisers of both sport and nonsport products often use images of athletes enjoying themselves during and after competitions. Many clubs offer coeducational sport in an attempt to provide more extensive social interaction between females and males. Running clubs clearly cater to social motivations. Unlike most sports, running does not require participants to train with others, and runners can compete without being part of a team. But that does not mean that people do not run for social reasons or that runners do not value social interactions. Two elements of club membership are important for socially motivated runners: (1) people can run with a group and thus do not have to run alone, and (2) socializing often continues after the run and thus is not limited to the training session itself.

The third key motivational category for participation in sport is mastery motivation. Skill development, learning, and personal challenge appeal to mastery-oriented participants. Programs offering instruction, coaching, or mentoring often appeal to these participants. For a person in this category, competition is for **intrinsic rewards** and is less about winning and more about challenging oneself. Training and instruction take place regularly in elite sport settings and in most sport programs designed for children and teens. But what about programs designed for adults? Although instruction is not the only way to appeal to mastery-motivated participants, it is certainly an underused element of adult sport programs.

intrinsic rewards—Rewards received by a person from the experience itself.

We have identified three fundamental motives for sport participation: achievement, social, and mastery motives. Now think of the things that motivate you to participate in your favorite sport. Chances are that more than one thing motivates you. People usually have multiple motives for participating in sport. Rarely do people take up running just to socialize with others. Nor is it likely that a person would join a volleyball team just to best the competition. In marketing your sport to current and potential participants, you would do well to provide elements to appeal to each of the motives examined earlier and to communicate in ways that highlight benefits that appeal to each motivational segment.

Spectator Motivation

The reasons that people give for watching sport are quite different from their reasons for participating in sport. Like participation motives, spectator motives vary considerably. As we illustrate here, numerous motives have been found to capture the many reasons given for attending sporting events (Wakefield, 2007). For many, watching sport is a way to escape from everyday life, a **diversion** from stress or boredom.

diversion—A distraction from a course or activity.

Others are driven by a desire for drama and excitement. Most of us have felt the glow and satisfaction of a victory by our favorite team. Basking in reflected glory (BIRGing), first labeled by Cialdini and colleagues (1976), is a key driver of attendance for fans seeking to enhance their self-esteem by associating themselves with a successful team or player (Bryant & Cummins, 2010). Fans motivated by **eustress** seek excitement and stimulation. Economic gain is another powerful motive for a small but growing group of people. Although betting on sport is not a new phenomenon, it has become more commonplace since the advent of Internet gambling. Yet another spectator motive for many fans is the innate beauty of athletic performance. The aesthetic motive is most clearly associated with sports such as ice dancing and rhythmic gymnastics, but fans of all sports report being fascinated by the aesthetic elements of the sport. Soccer fans, for example, repeatedly mention the pure beauty of well-executed skills. Another motivation for spectation is that some fans want to be part of something, to feel that they belong. Similar to those who are motivated by the desire for affiliation, some people attend sporting events to spend time with their families. As you can see, people have various motives for attending sport events.

eustress—Positive levels of arousal provided to sport spectators.

Participant and Spectator Markets

Many people believe that the best place to find fans for a sport team is among players of that sport. Although some overlap is present between fans and participants of any particular sport, it varies from sport to sport and is much less common than one might think. For example, youth soccer is ubiquitous in communities all across the country, and it is the second most played sport by working adults. Yet the average attendance for Major League Soccer (MLS) was just over 16,000 fans per game in 2008 (Mickle, 2008). Given the number of soccer players in the United States, you might expect higher attendance figures for professional soccer matches. If you compare the key motives for participation with those for spectation, it is clear that different needs drive playing sport and watching sport.

Spectators have many motives for watching sport, including escapism, drama, excitement, and diversion.

Photo courtesy of Paul M. Pedersen.

Consumer Perceptions

As important as they are, needs and motives do not fully explain consumers' sport choices. The degree to which a consumer perceives sport as meeting a particular need or motive depends on that person's perceptions and experiences. Consumers must recognize the opportunity to watch or participate in a sport as a means to fulfill a need or motive. That recognition depends on experiences and the ways in which consumers perceive those experiences. This section considers the role of consumer perceptions.

Each of us perceives the world in our own way. Many Americans perceive the sport of curling as an unusual and uninteresting winter sport. The 1.5 million curlers throughout the world would surely disagree with that perception. Similarly, you might consider football an exciting, physically challenging game, whereas your friend may think of it as brutish and violent. Whose perception is correct? Although perceptions often do not correspond to reality, people tend to act and react based on perceptions rather than objective reality. In fact, marketers spend enormous sums of time and money trying to alter people's perceptions of specific products and services. So what are the sources of our perceptions and how can sport marketers shape customers' perceptions of certain products?

Perception can be defined as a process by which a person selects, organizes, and interprets stimuli to create a meaningful picture of the world. A stimulus can be any input to any of the senses. Stimuli can be physical inputs from the surrounding environment such as sights, sounds, smells, tastes, sensations, or they can be cognitive inputs such as expectations, motives, and learning as a result of experience.

Consider the following scenario. A group of friends attended a college basketball game. Afterward, the friends discussed the game at the local pizza shop. Dan, a former high school basketball player, regaled Steve with a play-by-play account of what he called "the most beautiful fast break I've ever seen." No one else in the group even recalled seeing the play under discussion, including Steve. Steve is a high school volleyball coach. He had been impressed with the strategy that the visiting team used. David, a musician with little interest in team sports, talked incessantly about the entertainment at the game—the halftime show, the pep band, the cheerleaders, and the crowd chants. It was almost as if the three friends had attended entirely different events. This story illustrates the idea of selective attention: choosing (often subconsciously) to pay attention to elements that are relevant to one's needs, attitudes, and experiences. People tend to be aware of stimuli that meet their needs and interests, and they filter out stimuli that are less personally relevant.

People rarely attend to each stimulus individually. Rather, they group stimuli together and perceive them as a unified whole. Sport teams have taken advantage of the grouping effect by associating their teams with particular images. For example, many teams choose their mascots to imply desired characteristics to the team. As a result, American football teams tend to choose mascots such as Bears, Vikings, and Cowboys in the hope that fans will then associate their teams with strength, aggression, and toughness. Similarly, advertisements for a variety of products and services use sport imagery to associate their products with desired characteristics.

People are selective about the stimuli that they perceive and then organize the stimuli into patterns and groupings. Ultimately, however, perceptions depend on each person's interpretation of the stimuli. The interpretation, and consequently the perception, is uniquely individual. Your experiences help form particular expectations that might provide alternatives that you would use to interpret the stimuli presented. The broader your experiences are, the more interpretations and alternatives you have to draw on.

Consumer Attitudes

As the previous section indicates, experiences and existing attitudes greatly influence our perceptions of various sports, teams, athletes, and other sport products and services. Marketing efforts are often directed at shaping people's perceptions of a particular product, service, or brand. Essentially, this marketing tactic attempts to form or change customers' attitudes about the product or service. But what exactly is an attitude, and how do we form our attitudes? In its simplest form, an attitude can be an expression of a person's inner feelings that reflect whether he or she likes or dislikes something. Attitudes are based on a person's experiences (behavioral component), feelings (affective component), and beliefs (cognitive component) about an object (Shank, 2008). These three components work together to formulate an attitude (see figure 16.1).

Consumer involvement has been characterized as a combination of a person's interest in a sport product (e.g., team, athlete, sport) and the degree to which the person considers the product an important part of his or her life (Wakefield, 2007). Many sport spectators and participants become highly involved with their sports. Correspondingly, they think about, talk about, and read about their sports frequently. They tend to feel more deeply about their sports than do less involved participants and spectators. Sport marketers value involvement because high levels of involvement are associated with increased purchasing and consumer loyalty.

The more a person becomes involved with a sport, a team, or some other sport product, the more it becomes a part of that person's identity. Consequently, involvement and identification are closely related. The process of identification occurs as a person's role (as a participant or as a fan) becomes central to his or her personal sense of self—that is, his or her identity (Shamir, 1992). Hence, the statements "I am a Penguins fan" and "I am a scuba diver" are expressions of identification with a team and with a sport, respectively. Highly identified consumers attend more games, are less sensitive to price, and invest more time and effort in being a fan (Wakefield, 2007). They tend to buy and display licensed products. They also tend to be more tolerant of performance slumps and losing seasons. Because performance

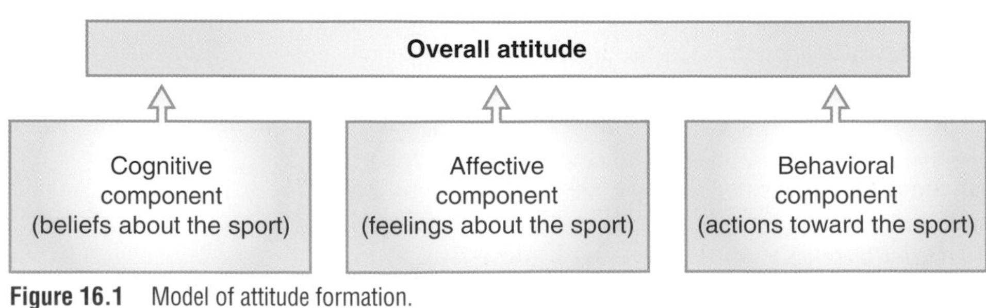

Figure 16.1 Model of attitude formation.

is beyond the control of sport marketers, the desirability of highly identified fans is obvious. These fans are not fair-weather fans; they are loyal.

Loyalty, involvement, and identification vary considerably from person to person. They are functions of individuals' motives for participating in or watching a sport, their previous experiences, and the perceptions and attitudes that they form about the sport, sport service, or product. These are largely internal, psychological processes. But sport consumers rarely make decisions or form attitudes or preferences based solely on their own experience. External groups exert tremendous influence on sport consumption decisions. This influence is sometimes subtle, as in the case of culture and ethnicity, and sometimes blatant, such as when your friends drag you to a local sporting event. We turn next to an examination of group influences on sport consumption decisions.

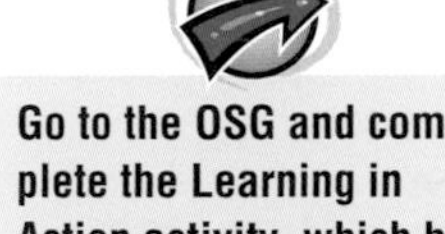

ACTION

Go to the OSG and complete the Learning in Action activity, which has you identify how involved different fans are with a sport team.

GROUP INFLUENCES ON THE SPORT CONSUMER

This section examines external factors that influence sport buying behavior. Each of us is influenced by the people closest to us, by the groups with whom we choose to associate, and by the broader society in which we live. Take a moment to think about choosing to play on an intramural team at your college or university. The types of sports offered are typically those sports valued by your national culture. Consequently, American college and university students might choose to play basketball, British students might choose to play cricket, and Malaysian students might choose to play badminton. Further, your membership in a group can greatly influence your choice whether to play or not play intramural sports. Physical education majors would be expected to value sport participation highly, but music majors might not. If you choose to participate, your close friends might then influence your choice of sport.

Clearly, different people influence each of us, and we value the opinions of different groups. Thus, each of us has our own reference groups. These people and groups influence our values, norms, perceptions, attitudes, and behaviors by providing us with a valued point of comparison. Reference groups can be either direct or indirect. Direct reference groups are groups that require face-to-face interaction. Family and friends serve as reference groups throughout the lifespan. Think about your own sport participation. Who first encouraged you to play a sport? Parents or teachers usually introduce children to a sport. Later, peers play a more powerful role in participation choices. Similarly, you probably shared your first moments as a fan of your favorite team with friends or family members. Furthermore, friends and family usually reinforce your choices. For example, if you are a tennis fan, you might watch the US Open with your family, you might attend a local tournament with friends, or your brother might give you a tennis shirt for your birthday. Each of these actions subtly reinforces your attitudes and behaviors regarding tennis.

Although friends and family can be powerful influences on a person's sport choices and purchases, they are not alone in their influence. Nearly everyone is part of a larger group of some kind. Some of these groups offer formal membership (e.g., sport teams, special interest clubs, service groups), but most do not (e.g., high school sophomores, business majors, residents of a particular neighborhood). The point is that the group shares something and the group's values serve as a point of evaluation for a person's attitudes and behaviors.

Culture is perhaps the largest of the direct reference groups. Each of us is embedded in a national and ethnic culture. You could think of culture as the personality of society. It colors our values, expectations, attitudes, and opinions. It affects our view of the place of sport in society, the sports that we learn to value, and the products and

SUMO WRESTLING AND CONSUMER BEHAVIOR

By Toshiyuki Ogura • JAPAN
University of Texas at Austin, UNITED STATES

Sumo matches are thought to have begun in prehistoric times as religious rituals dedicated to the gods with prayers for an abundant harvest. In the 8th century CE, sumo was introduced into the Imperial Court of Japan as a wrestling festival with music and dancing. During the Kamakura Samurai dictatorship (1185–1333), it became a means of increasing the efficiency of the fighting men. Under the more peaceful Tokugawa Shogunate of the 17th century, professional sumo groups were organized as show business.

The Japanese Sumo Association (JSA), established in 1927, organizes six 15-day Grand Sumo Tournaments every year. Each tournament offers traditional Japanese cultural, entertainment, and hospitality activities and services to meet the needs and motivations of diverse sport consumers. Each day starts at 8:30 a.m. with matches of junior wrestlers and ends with the Bow Ceremony at 6:30 p.m. Between the physical and aesthetic sumo matches, traditional sumo rituals and ceremonies such as sumo dancing, demonstration of basic sumo techniques, hairdressing, and ring entering entertain the spectators.

The Grand Sumo Tournament has something for everyone. Spectators motivated by aesthetics enjoy the traditional architectural design of the Kokugikan, the colorful Japanese aprons of the wrestlers, the costumes of referees and ushers, the bodies of well-trained wrestlers, and kimarite (winning techniques). For ¥40,000 (US$440), customers seeking status or prestige can choose a

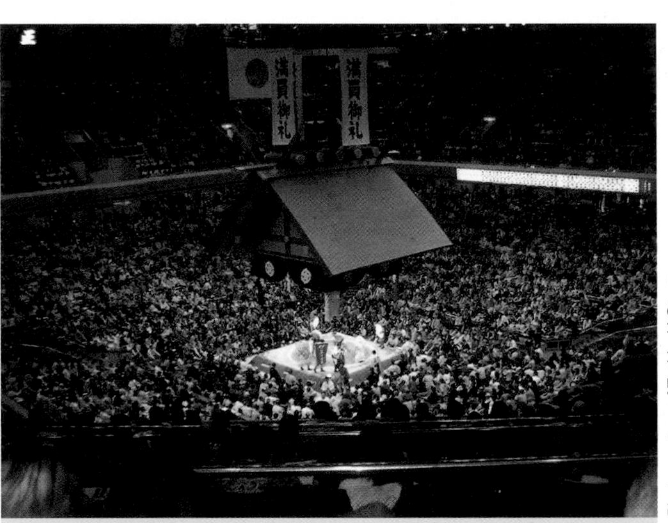

Photo courtesy of Toshiyuki Ogura.

Sumo wrestling has existed in Japan for thousands of years.

services that we seek. Its effects are subtle but powerful. Culture profoundly influences our view of what is normal, or at least what is expected.

Culture affects the sports we choose, as well as the way we choose to become involved with sport. Both Japan and North America support professional baseball leagues, but the values inherent in the sport vary by country. In the United States, the purpose of the game is to do your best by contributing to the team in every way you can. In Japan, the purpose of the game is to contribute to the team by not doing certain things (e.g., showing off, being individualistic). This conduct fits the cultural values of Japanese society. Not surprisingly, fan behavior also differs. In Japan, cheering is largely confined to organized cheering by fans seated behind the outfield; other fans only occasionally join in. In North America, fans cheering for the home team usually fill the home stadium. In Japan, the fans of the home team always sit on the first-base side of the field, and fans of the visiting team sit on the third-base side. Even when the stadium is not crowded, fans adhere to this tradition (Takahashi, 2006).

Social class can sometimes place invisible boundaries on our choices by delineating appropriate and inappropriate behavior. Social class often serves as a referent when choosing to participate (or not participate) in a particular sport. We tend to associate

luxury package of box seats for a group of four, where they sit on a mat and zabuton cushions. Families and younger people might choose seats in the upper deck for as little as ¥2,800 yen (US$31). The concessions offer signature food such as Yakitori (chicken barbecue), Japanese Bendo lunch boxes, and various sumo novelties. Novice fans and those motivated to learn about sumo can listen to the in-house radio broadcast of former sumo wrestlers commenting on each match in Japanese and English. Socially motivated fans often enjoy the matches and then head to a Chanko Nabe restaurant that serves original sumo club recipes.

Although sumo has long been a part of Japanese culture and is respected as a major professional sport, globalization is creating a new debate. The JSA is under pressure to diminish the importance of the traditional cultural values that have characterized sumo for centuries. Many high-ranked sumo wrestlers are not Japanese but are still required to have in-depth understanding of traditional sumo values. In fact, Hakuho and Asashoryu, two of the Yokozuna (highest ranked sumo wrestlers), are Mongolian. Other wrestlers come from Bulgaria, Russia, and Estonia. Some local media report that these wrestlers have extrinsic motives for sumo participation, such as financial rewards and higher status. The different motives and cultural values are reflected in their behavior and sometimes conflict with traditional Japanese sumo culture, which places a high value on intrinsic rewards such as dignity and cooperation. The traditional sumo culture satisfies the aging core market of Japanese fans and is a key factor in the emergence of Grand Sumo Tournaments as one of the most popular tourist attractions for international visitors to Japan.

INTERNATIONAL LEARNING ACTIVITY #1

Go to www.usasumo.com/what_links.html and investigate amateur and professional sumo wrestling in various countries. In which countries do both women and men participate in sumo wrestling? If you were organizing a sumo tournament in your country, which cultural values and motives would you employ to attract consumers? Would these values and motives be the same for both women's and men's tournaments? Why or why not?

INTERNATIONAL LEARNING ACTIVITY #2

Locate a sports bar or a community center that caters to the international soccer crowd and televises soccer games. Attend a televised game there, during the world championship if possible. Observe the behaviors of the fans around you as well as the behaviors of the spectators on television. Compare them to the behaviors that you would expect from North American football and baseball fans.

certain sports with members of a particular social class. Social class tends to serve as a global referent; that is, it affects a person's choices and behaviors across a variety of settings. But not all reference groups have global influence.

Indirect reference groups do not require direct contact, but they can be highly influential. They might consist of people such as athletes, coaches, actors, or politicians; alternatively, they might be groups or subcultures. In either case, the influence of the individual or group is not the result of direct, face-to-face contact. Instead, the influence derives from **aspirational reference groups**—groups in which a person is not currently a member but aspires to be one. Gatorade's legendary advertising campaign featuring Michael Jordan ("Be Like Mike") is perhaps the most unabashed use of an aspirational reference group to sell a product, but numerous, albeit subtler, examples of advertisements use athletes as aspirational referents.

aspirational reference group—A group to which an individual wishes to belong.

Subcultures operate in much the same way as aspirational reference groups do. Let's assume for the moment that you want to be a surfer. Even before you learn to surf, chances are that you will be influenced by what you know about surfers and the surfing subculture. You might enjoy surfing movies such as *Stranger Than Fiction* or *The Endless Summer*. You might buy *Surfing* magazine, watch surfing events, and talk to people who surf. Your knowledge of the surfing subculture, however superficial, might influence the style and brand of clothing that you choose to wear, the music that you listen to, or even the way that you style your hair. Marketers are more than willing to sell you products that help you to look and feel as though you belong to the group.

As a marketer, you can take advantage of the ability of reference groups to change consumers' perceptions, attitudes, and purchase behaviors. But for the reference group to wield its influence, according to de Mooij (2004), it must be able to (1) make the person aware of your product, (2) provide a chance for the person to compare himself or herself with the group, (3) influence the person to adopt attitudes and behaviors consistent with the group, and (4) support the person's decision to use the same product or service as the group does.

Your perceptions and experiences affect your choice of reference groups. Your choice of reference groups can affect your preferences for particular sports and the sport choices that you make. In other words, the reference groups that you choose are based, in part, on what you have learned, and the reference group might affect what you learn subsequently. This process is an effect of consumer socialization.

Consumer Socialization

We have seen that family, friends, teachers, and other reference groups can affect your decisions about participating in sport and about watching sport. Yet the effect of people who are significant in your life reaches even further. Through them you learn not merely *what* you prefer, but also *how* to consume what you prefer. Let's assume that you want to watch a baseball game. You have several choices. You could watch a game played by a local Little League team. You could watch a minor league game. You could watch a Major League Baseball (MLB) game. If you choose an MLB game, you could attend the game or watch it on television. If you attend the game, you could sit in the bleachers, behind home plate, or behind a dugout. The choices that you make will be influenced, in part, by what you have learned about the ways to watch baseball. If when you were first learning to enjoy watching baseball, your family or friends typically preferred to watch on television, you will be more likely to choose to watch on television. On the other hand, if going to the ball game was something that your family or friends treated as a valuable choice, then you are likely to consider going to the game preferable to watching it on television.

As we grow and mature, we learn how to consume the sport that we prefer. Both direct and indirect reference groups influence the ways in which we consume sport. For example, Tom has season tickets to watch the Baltimore Orioles. When he was young, his father took him to watch the Washington Senators. Three things were always part of the baseball experience for Tom. One, he always took his baseball glove to the game; two, his father always bought him peanuts and a hotdog at the ballpark; and three, they always hollered at the umpire. Tom has continued these rituals as an adult. Unintentionally, he has also taught his children that baseball games require a person to bring a glove, eat peanuts and hotdogs, and yell at the umpires. This is an example of socialization through modeling. Just as Tom did as a child, his children watched their father's behavior at baseball games and began to copy his behavior. Prompting and reinforcement can further assist in the socialization process. For example, Tom might prompt his daughter to bring her glove or ask if she would like some peanuts. Similarly, he might reinforce her jibes at the umpire by laughing or praising her comments.

Socialization is a process that often goes unnoticed. Think of your own sport experiences. How did you develop your fan behaviors? Do you remember someone telling you when to clap, at whom you could shout, or how to show your support for a great play? Chances are that your earlier experiences and reinforcement (or lack of reinforcement) by important reference groups shaped your current behavior.

Each of these processes—modeling, prompting, and reinforcing—also occur through indirect reference groups. Spectators seen on television broadcasts and in movies often influence our attitudes and consumption behaviors. In our current global era, people may not even need to attend live events to be aware of the appropriate behaviors or rituals of specific sports. As you learned in chapter 13, the mass media (e.g., sport programming on terrestrial, cable, and satellite television) and new media (e.g., streaming videos on sport Web sites) provide extended and comprehensive broadcasts of global sports and their environments. Advertisements, broadcasts, Web sites, and other types of indirect reference groups can prompt behaviors or reinforce our perceptions of appropriate ways to enjoy a game or a sport. Over time, we are socialized into a way of consuming sport that is shaped by our reference groups, both direct and indirect. Sport marketers are also interested in ways to socialize customers into particular consumption patterns.

SITUATIONAL INFLUENCES ON THE SPORT CONSUMER

In the previous sections we identified key internal factors and external group influences on sport consumers. In practice, isolating influences of either internal or external forces is difficult. Rarely does a single force influence sport consumption decisions. Rather, a person's relationship to a reference group or membership in a particular subculture forms and interprets internal attitudes, perceptions, and experiences. Further, different contexts and situations result in different decisions. A situation is a set of factors outside the individual consumer and removed from the product or advertisement of the product that the consumer is buying. To develop marketing strategies that enhance the purchase of their products, marketers need to know how purchase situations influence consumers.

We can identify five categories of **situational influence.** First, physical surroundings include geographic location, decor, sound, smells, lighting, weather, and crowding. For example, weather would obviously influence the decision to play tennis. Retailing organizations pay particular attention to the physical characteristics of their stores. For example, one Niketown store has a hardwood basketball court in its basketball shoe section and plays recordings of the unique sounds of shoes squeaking during a basketball game. Second, social surroundings refer to the effects of the physical presence of others. For example, if you want to go to a movie but the group that you are with prefers to go bowling, you will probably comply with the group and find yourself at the bowling alley. Third, task requirements speak to the context of the purchase (that is, the intent or requirement of the purchase). Consider the purchase of a pair of running shoes. If you are buying them for yourself, you might be more concerned with performance functions than with price. But if you are buying them as a gift, you might be more concerned with price and attractiveness than with performance. Fourth, time pressures, the time of day, and the season of the year are all examples of potential temporal influences on sport consumption. Fifth, purchasing can be affected by antecedent states such as anxiety, excitement, or even hunger and by momentary conditions such as cash on hand, fatigue, or illness. If you have ever attended a sporting event and wondered, on your return home, why you bought that gigantic foam finger, you have probably experienced the influence of excitement on the purchase decision process. Let's look more closely at the decision process.

situational influence—The influence arising from factors that are particular to a specific time and place and are independent of individual customers' characteristics.

CONSUMER DECISION MAKING IN SPORT

You make hundreds of decisions each day, many of them related to sport. You decide whether to participate in sport, which sports you will try, whether you will watch sport, which sport you will watch, which team or player you will cheer for, whether

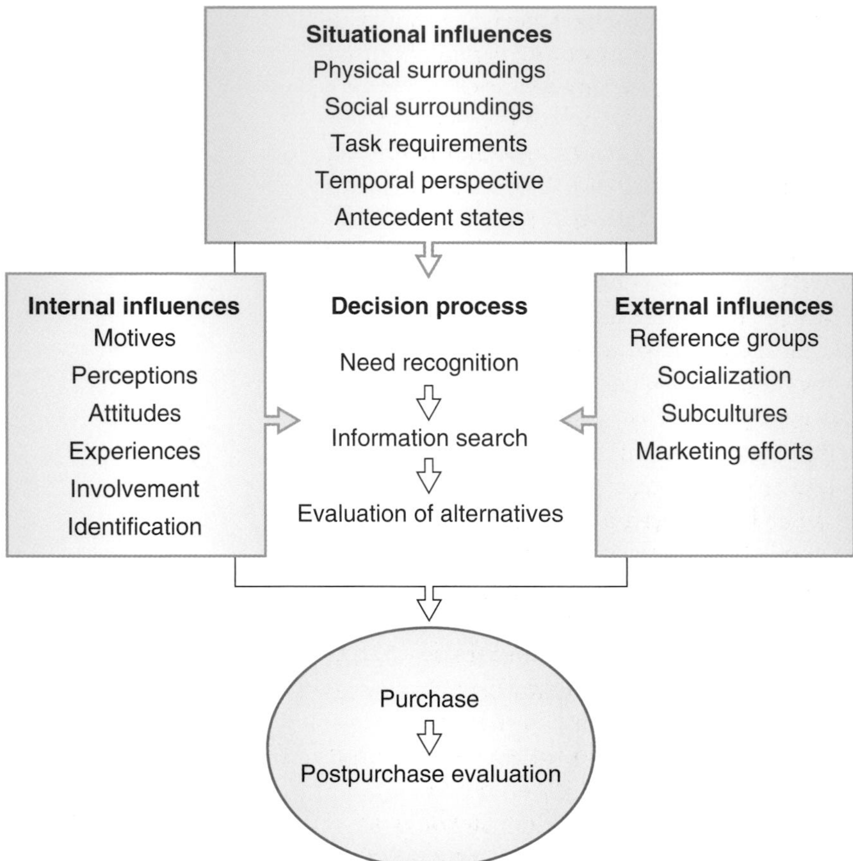

Figure 16.2 Model of the consumer decision-making process.

you will buy season tickets, and whether you will wear your team jersey. The list of decisions seems endless. You make some easily; others require much thought. In any case, the decision-making process has a common progression. It begins with the recognition of a need or problem that spurs you to gather information about potential solutions. You then evaluate alternatives, and the "best" alternative leads to purchase. The purchase experience is followed by a period of postpurchase evaluation that will influence your future purchase decisions (see figure 16.2). Notice that decision making does not happen in a void. Rather, each of the factors already discussed influences the process.

Each of us arrives at a decision in a slightly different way. We begin with motives, perceptions, attitudes, and experiences that are uniquely our own. We are influenced by reference groups and subcultures that are important to us, and we have been socialized in different ways. In fact, we are rarely consistent in the way that we arrive at purchase decisions. We perceive each situation differently. Consumption decisions are not always rational, as can be seen with impulse purchases. As a result, we interpret and react to marketing efforts in varied ways. Despite these differences, the steps in the decision process are remarkably consistent from consumer to consumer.

need recognition—Perception of a difference between a desired state and the actual situation; the first stage of the decision-making process.

Need recognition is the first step in the decision process. This stage is likely to occur when you confront a problem or recognize a difference between an actual state and a desired state. This stimulus can be as straightforward as the need to replace a worn-out softball glove or as complex as a desire to be fit. In the first case, the need is obvious: The equipment no longer works, so you must replace it. In the second case, the need is less straightforward. The desired state is to be fit. In this case, the need emerges from the gap between your current and desired fitness levels.

After identifying the need, the consumer seeks information that helps resolve the problem or fulfill the need. Experience or brand loyalty might provide the consumer with enough information to determine alternatives. For example, Carlos' satisfaction with his old glove might be all the information that he needs to decide to buy the latest model of the same glove. If he is loyal to a particular brand, he might limit his search by collecting information only about products produced by that company. He might ask the opinion of respected members of his reference group or be influenced by the acceptability of a brand or style within his softball subculture. He might search out information on the Internet, in magazines, or at the local sport store. In any case, he will collect enough information to determine his purchase options.

After Carlos has determined his purchase options, he begins the evaluation process. When evaluating purchase options, consumers tend to use two types of information:

(1) a list of the potential products, and (2) the features and characteristics that they will use to evaluate those products (de Mooij, 2004). Price or convenience might be two features important to Carlos. People assess features and characteristics differently based on their values, attitudes, motives, and expectations. Notice that a person's reference groups also influence his or her belief about which features and characteristics are important. Sport marketers need to understand which features are important to their target markets. Using the highest quality of leather for softball gloves is useless if consumers evaluate gloves based on their fit and price. Consumers make their purchase decisions based on personal evaluations of particular products and their attributes.

You might think that the process ends with the purchase, but another step is yet to occur—the postpurchase evaluation (Shank, 2008). As consumers use a product, they evaluate it with respect to their expectations. Let's return to the example of Carlos and the softball glove. Carlos will have developed expectations about the performance of his new glove. He might expect that it will look good, break in easily, and fit his hand well. After using the glove for several practice sessions, he will evaluate its actual performance. If the glove performs as well as or better than expected, Carlos will be satisfied with his purchase. But if the glove does not fit well or is difficult to break in, then he might be dissatisfied with his purchase. From a marketing standpoint, Carlos' satisfaction is important for two reasons. One, his satisfaction will affect his future purchases of the product, and two, it will affect word-of-mouth communication about the product and the brand. He will tell others about his satisfaction or disappointment.

An important part of the postpurchase evaluation is consumers' attempts to reassure themselves that they made the right decision. Feelings of doubt about a decision are called **cognitive dissonance.** Consumers attempt to reduce postpurchase cognitive dissonance in several ways. They might rationalize their decision as being a wise choice (e.g., this is definitely the best softball glove because it fits so well). They might search for marketing materials that confirm their decision and avoid advertisements for competing products. They might try to persuade others to make the same purchase, or they could seek others who are satisfied with their purchase of the same product (e.g., talking with other players after practice or online). Each of these strategies reinforces their satisfaction with the purchase. Reducing consumers' cognitive dissonance in the postpurchase period is a strategy that can increase repeat purchases.

cognitive dissonance—Feelings of anxiety or doubt that can occur after an important decision has been made.

CHALLENGES

Analyzing and understanding sport consumer behavior is a complex endeavor. The challenges facing sport marketers are equally complex. Four issues are becoming increasingly important to understanding and marketing to sport consumers:

1. The meaning and emotion of sport consumption
2. The globalization of sport
3. Virtual consumption
4. Compulsive consumption

We know much about the ways that people think about sport purchases. Yet consumers consistently report emotional attachments to sport products, teams, events, and other sport services. To understand sport consumers, we need to know how they create these emotional attachments, what influences those attachments, and how the attachments vary as a function of culture or subcultural values. The globalization of sport is creating a related challenge for sport marketers. On one hand, consumers worldwide are being presented with the same sports, broadcasts, products, and advertisements. On the surface, sport is much the same across the globe. On the other hand, we know that culture influences the meaning and value inherent in sport consumption. In this respect, the world is made up of a multitude of consumer groups. We need to understand where similarities and differences exist, and work to tailor our sport products and services for optimal sales.

The other two challenges to understanding and reaching sport consumers are emerging forms of sport consumption—virtual and compulsive. The Internet is a multifunctional space for sport consumption. Participants can purchase hard-to-find equipment; fans can buy tickets and licensed products for teams anywhere in the world. But actual purchases are only the tip of the iceberg. Fans can find a community of other fans online (e.g., by joining sport message boards, by posting thoughts on microblogging sites such as MySpace, Facebook, and Twitter). They can participate in online fantasy leagues. Participants can receive or share information about their sport, team, players, and coaches instantly. The list is endless. Wireless technology has made it even easier for fans to stay involved with their teams. Scores and other statistics are routinely delivered to mobile phones. Digital photos and video can be sent by mobile phone. Recently, a college football coach complained that fans were able to see footage of a player getting hurt in practice before he could inform the player's parents. With sport content almost limitless, the challenge for sport organizations is to find ways to use new consumption technologies to reach their fans or participants more effectively.

WEB

Go to the OSG and complete the Web search activity, which asks you to search the Internet to find answers to sport consumption questions.

As you can see from the football coach's complaint, sport consumption is not all positive. As sport consumption opportunities become ubiquitous, compulsive consumption is becoming more prevalent. Compulsive consumption refers to the repetitive consumption of sport such that it is addictive. Sports betting can be one of the most damaging forms of compulsive sport consumption, but there are others (e.g., sport video games). Fantasy leagues can become a compulsion as well; some participants spend astonishing amounts of time and money managing their teams. Compulsive consumption is not limited to fan behavior. Participants might spend well beyond their means traveling to pursue their sport participation. More likely, participants dedicate outrageous amounts of time to their sports. Compulsive consumption is a delicate issue for sport marketers. After all, effective marketing efforts that take advantage of in-depth knowledge of consumers' psychology, in the case of compulsive consumers, feed their addiction. Yet most sport consumption is not destructive. The challenge, then, is to use knowledge of consumers to build effective marketing strategies without feeding consumers' addictions.

Today's sport marketers are grappling with these challenges. Each challenge is representative of the broader society in which sport is embedded. All are interrelated. The emotion elicited by sport might be the high that compulsive consumers seek. Technologies such as the Internet and wireless services provide quick access to sport products and services from all corners of the world, at all times of day and night. Globalization of sport creates content that can be shared, often by technology, with people anywhere in the world. There is much to understand about sport consumers, and many ways to collect information. The challenges identified here also create opportunities for sport marketers to learn more about their consumers.

CRITICAL THINKING IN SPORT CONSUMER BEHAVIOR

Obesity is now considered one of the most serious public health problems in the United States, because the rate of obesity has risen dramatically during the past two decades. Obesity is not merely being overweight; it means that a person is severely overweight. As we move into the second decade of the 21st century, a third of all adult men and over a third of all adult women in the United States have been classified by the Centers for Disease Control and Prevention (CDC) as obese, and one in every six children and

Twitter Stimulates Fan Involvement

The microblogging site Twitter (www.twitter.com) is attracting users at a phenomenal rate. According to comScore, traffic to the Twitter Web site hit 10 million visitors in February 2009. Originally, Twitter was seen as an interesting new form of social media that served no real business purpose. Businesses of all kinds, however, are increasingly seeing the value of tweeting (sending messages through Twitter) to reach customers at a deeper level than traditional marketing and advertising campaigns. Businesses, organizations, groups, and individuals can use Twitter. Sport organizations such as the NFL, NFL Network, NASCAR, FIFA World Cup, and the NCAA have Twitter accounts with regular followers. Coaches, players, and even owners are increasingly using Twitter to engage with fans. Because of their celebrity status, most players and coaches have little direct contact with fans. Twitter allows sportspeople (and others) to connect with fans as often as they wish, with short messages about whatever they want to say. The media's role in shaping, interpreting, and reinterpreting athletes' messages disappears with the directness of Twitter. As you might expect, fans are drawn into the athlete's world through their interactions.

Shaquille O'Neal is an avid tweeter and early adopter of microblogging. He currently has more than 1.3 million people signed up to follow his tweets, and boasts more than 1,800 updates on his site (@the_real_shaq). Besides being able to reach traditional fans, O'Neal has used his humor to reach beyond normal fans to attract a new audience (Bratt, 2009). In this way, microblogging has the capacity to grow the fan base of an athlete, team, or league. Twitter can also encourage offline involvement. For example, tweets can be used to organize a "tweet-up," a gathering of tweeters. The Phoenix Suns hosted a tweet-up in 2009. One hundred and twenty-five fans showed up. The NBA franchise also uses Twitter in its promotions. For example, the Suns invite followers of their Twitter site (@PhoenixSuns) to register for a chance to win tickets to their annual draft party including food, a $10 game card, and appearances by Suns alumni, the Suns Dancers, and the Gorilla. In 2009 they called this event the Dwaft Party Tweet-Up! Athletes, teams, leagues, and other sport personnel are still learning how best to use Twitter to meet the needs of their customers. As a future sport professional, how would you use Twitter?

adolescents was also considered obese. This rate of obesity is a problem for a variety of reasons including the fact that obesity increases the risk for many serious ailments.

The CDC blames the current high levels of obesity on the increasingly sedentary lifestyle of Americans and is consequently seeking means to encourage greater levels of physical activity among Americans of all ages. The organization's approach has included advocacy for mandatory physical activity in the schools (several hours weekly), walking programs for adults, and programs designed to encourage people to take stairs instead of elevators. But the obesity problem persists. At present, the CDC has not implemented or encouraged programs designed to persuade people to participate in sports, although sport would be one means to foster physical activity. One advantage that sport has over many other forms of physical activity (e.g., exercise) is that it can be playful, which is one of its intrinsic rewards. The challenge, then, is to find means to encourage sport participation by Americans who are currently sedentary, to increase the amount of sport being done by those who are engaging in only small amounts of physical activity, and to encourage the few Americans who are very active to stay active.

Complete the critical thinking portfolio activity in the OSG, consulting as needed the "Eight Critical Thinking Questions" section in chapter 1.

PORTFOLIO

ETHICS IN SPORT CONSUMER BEHAVIOR

You are the assistant marketing director for a running-shoe brand. It is the beginning of the third quarter, and sales are down compared with the previous year. The marketing budget has been reduced by one-third. Therefore, you have to come up with innovative yet inexpensive ways to market the running-shoe line. Theo, a bright new employee comes up with a great idea to influence consumers and presents it at a staff meeting. He explains that the best way to persuade clients to buy the product is to infiltrate their existing social networks, whether online or while interacting with other runners, and to find ways that create the impression that spontaneous enthusiasm surrounds the product. Then he highlights how economical, effective, and easy the approach is, especially if the company hires a couple of college students to carry out the strategy. Theo's main point is that consumers tend to trust word-of-mouth references, especially when they believe that the recommendation is coming from real and unbiased users who choose to share their unsolicited positive experiences of the product.

PORTFOLIO

Complete the ethical issues portfolio activity in the OSG, consulting as needed the "Guidelines for Making Ethical Decisions" section in chapter 1.

The whole team seems excited about the idea except Susan, who is uncomfortable with how clients may feel if they figure out that they have been manipulated. You leave the meeting not certain how you feel about the integrity of the process. As the assistant marketing director you must decide whether or not to follow through with the strategy.

Summary

The study of consumer behavior in sport helps you understand your customers. A better understanding of your customers can help you develop products and services that meet their needs and design marketing strategies to attract new customers and retain existing customers. This chapter explored the individual, group, and situational factors that influence sport consumption. Individual factors examined were motives, perceptions, attitudes, involvement, and identification. Reference groups, socialization processes, and subcultures were identified as the primary group factors that affect decisions to attend sporting events, participate in sporting activities, and buy sport products and services.

Rarely, however, does a single force influence sport consumption decisions. Typically, group and individual influences work simultaneously to exert influence over a purchase decision in a given situation. Individual, group, and situational factors exert influence at each stage of the decision process. The recognition of a need or problem is the first step in the process. After identifying a need, the consumer seeks information about potential products and services that can fulfill that need or solve the problem. The consumer then develops a set of possible purchase options and evaluates each before making the purchase.

But the process does not end with the purchase. Customers can evaluate their purchases in two ways. They often evaluate their purchases in reference to prepurchase expectations. If performance meets or exceeds their expectations, then customers are satisfied. Customers tend to reassure themselves that they made the right purchase. This action is an attempt to reduce cognitive dissonance. Sport marketers can help customers feel good about their purchase by providing information after the purchase that highlights the benefits and attributes of the product or highlights the use of the product by valued members of customers' reference groups.

QUIZ TIME

Did you grasp all the key points in this chapter? Go to the OSG for a short quiz to test your understanding of the material.

As a sport marketer, you have the job of enticing customers to buy your products, attend your games, compete in your events, and use your services. The consumer decision-making process identifies the steps leading to purchase. You can use your knowledge of the situational, group, and individual factors that can influence each step in the decision process to design products, services, and marketing campaigns that meet the needs of your customers. Furthermore, from the information that you learned in this chapter, you can rely on ethical guidelines and critical thinking skills to assist you in making marketing decisions and performing actions related to sport consumer behavior.

Review Questions

1. What are the key motives for sport participation? Explain each one and provide an example of each.
2. What are the key motives for sport spectation? Explain each one and provide an example of each.
3. You and a friend attend a basketball game at your university. Why might the two of you have different perceptions of the game?
4. What are the three components of an attitude? Describe each one.
5. What is the difference between consumer involvement and fan identification?
6. What are potential group influences on a person's decision to attend a sporting event? Give an example of the way that each would influence the decision.
7. How would you go about describing the decision-making process of parents who are choosing a youth sport program for their child?
8. What would you do to reduce postpurchase cognitive dissonance?

References

Bratt, E. (2009). *Twitter success stories: How 11 companies are achieving their marketing objectives—140 characters at a time.* Houston, TX: Marketing Profs.

Bryant, J., & Cummins, R.G. (2010). The effects of outcome of mediated and live sporting events on sports fans' self- and social identities. In H.L. Hundley & A.C. Billings (Eds.), *Examining identity in sports media* (pp. 217–238). Thousand Oaks, CA: Sage.

Cialdini, R.B., Borden, R.J., Thorne, A., Walker, M.R., Freeman, S., & Sloan, L.R. (1976). Basking in reflected glory: Three (football) field studies. *Journal of Personality and Social Psychology, 34*, 366–375.

de Mooij, M.K. (2004). *Consumer behavior and culture: Consequences for global marketing and advertising.* Thousand Oaks, CA: Sage.

Green, B.C. (1996). A social learning approach to youth sport motivation: Initial scale development and validation (Doctoral dissertation, University of Maryland, 1996). *Dissertation Abstracts International, 60*, 203.

Mickle, T. (2008, November 3). MLS attendance, TV viewership numbers slip. *Street & Smith's SportsBusiness Journal*, p. 10.

Shamir, B. (1992). Some correlates of leisure identity salience: Three exploratory studies. *Journal of Leisure Research, 24*, 301–323.

Shank, M.D. (2008). *Sports marketing: A strategic perspective* (4th ed.). Upper Saddle River, NJ: Prentice Hall.

Smith, D., & Bar-Eli, M. (Eds.). (2007). *Essential readings in sport and exercise psychology.* Champaign, IL: Human Kinetics.

Takahashi, N. (2006). Voluntary associations formed through sport spectatorship. In J. Maguire & M. Nakayama (Eds.), *Japan, sport and society: Tradition and change in a globalizing world* (pp. 98–112). New York: Routledge.

Wakefield, K. (2007). *Team sports marketing.* Burlington, MA: Butterworth-Heinemann.

HISTORICAL MOMENTS

- **1922** *Federal Base Ball Club of Baltimore v. National League of Professional Base Ball Clubs* established Major League Baseball (MLB) antitrust exemption
- **1938** *Pittsburgh Athletic Co. v. KQV* established baseball clubs' control of broadcast rights to a game
- **1961** Sports Broadcasting Act permitted sport leagues to pool their television rights package
- **1972** *Flood v. Kuhn*—Curt Flood (St. Louis Cardinals) challenged MLB's reserve clause
- **1987** Civil Rights Restoration Act overturned *Grove City v. Bell* (1984) ruling
- **1992** Professional and Amateur Sports Protection Act banned sports betting in all but a few states
- **1995** *Vernonia School District v. Acton*—US Supreme Court upheld constitutionality of random drug testing of student–athletes
- **1996** *Cohen v. Brown University*—class action Title IX lawsuit filed
- **1998** *Fraser v. Major League Soccer*—US District Court ruling found that MLS' single-entity structure did not violate Sherman Antitrust Act
- **2001** *PGA Tour v. Martin*—Supreme Court ruled that Casey Martin could use a golf cart in PGA events
- **2004** *Clarett v. NFL*—court ruled in favor of the NFL's age restriction rule
- **2007** *C.B.C. Distribution and Marketing, Inc. v. MLB Advanced Media*—fantasy sports leagues won right to use MLB player statistics without license
- **2007** *TSSAA v. Brentwood Academy*—US Supreme Court upheld TSSAA rules limiting high school sports recruiting
- **2008** *Borden v. East Brunswick*—court upheld school district policy prohibiting coach's participation in student-led prayer
- **2009** *Van v. VANOC*—female ski jumpers filed lawsuit against Vancouver Olympic Organizing Committee

Photo courtesy of Paul M. Pedersen.

17

LEGAL CONSIDERATIONS IN SPORT MANAGEMENT

Anita M. Moorman ■ R. Christopher Reynolds

LEARNING OBJECTIVES

1. Identify select legal issues affecting sport management stakeholders, operations, and organizations.
2. Explain the American judicial system and its application to the sport industry.
3. Identify situations involving the management or marketing of sport in which legal issues influence the decision-making process of those in leadership positions.
4. Describe legal concepts in a sport context with matters involving Title IX legislation, tort law, and the Americans with Disabilities Act (ADA).
5. Discuss the fundamental elements of contract law and apply them in a sport management context.
6. Engage in critical thinking and problem solving regarding how the law can influence sport management decisions.
7. Apply systematic guidelines to ethical dilemmas involving legal concepts in sport.

Key Terms

common law
constituencies
de minimis
due process
precedent
proximate cause
restatements
stare decisis
statutes
tort

GET A JOB!

✓ Continue on your journey in sport management by going to the Online Study Guide (OSG) at www.HumanKinetics.com/ContemporarySportManagement. Check out the job opportunities and consider the skills and experiences that can help you succeed in sport management.

As you learned in chapter 1, sport managers make numerous decisions each day. These decisions will be of various levels of importance and difficulty. All of them, however, require the sport manager to engage in a process of decision making. The manager's decisions are likely to affect numerous **constituencies**, including coworkers, supervisors, the media, spectators, and participants, just to name a few. All these groups are entitled to hold the sport manager accountable for her or his decisions. Chapter 1 also introduced you to the value of critical thinking skills in responding to constituencies who challenge decisions that have been made and who may demand justification for chosen strategies. Now that you have acquired a fundamental understanding of the importance of critical thinking and have learned to ask the core critical questions, you can move on to a deeper understanding of how the law affects both your decision-making process and the results of your decisions.

constituencies—For purposes of this chapter, constituencies are any people influenced by a particular decision.

This chapter will introduce you to situations that require sport managers to examine how legal principles can influence decisions. We will introduce selected legal issues, discuss the situations in which these legal issues arise, and present questions for you to ponder. This chapter introduces the law and the legal system of the United States. You should keep in mind while reading this chapter, however, that as the sport industry continues to expand into the global marketplace, international law affects many sport organizations. Besides introducing the legal areas noted earlier, the chapter provides analyses of how the law intersects with sport on the amateur (e.g., interscholastic, intercollegiate) and professional levels.

BASICS OF LAW

Interpretations and definitions of the law vary. *Black's Law Dictionary*, a useful resource in legal research, defines the law as "the aggregate of legislation, judicial precedents and accepted legal principles" (Black, 2004). (See the sidebar on this page for the various sources of law.) Moreover, the law is an accumulation of rules and regulations that govern our behavior. Failure to abide by the defined rules of law results in either civil or criminal penalty. In the United States, judges, juries, or congressional representatives do not arbitrarily define the law. Rather, the citizens of the country, in part, define the law. Legislatures (state and federal) enact **statutes**, which create the need for agencies to write or promulgate rules and regulations. The courts are then required to interpret the statutes or rules and fill in any gaps left by legislatures.

statutes—Enactments made by a legislature and expressed in a formal document.

The American judicial system is divided into distinctly separate federal and state systems. The United States Constitution is the supreme law of the land. It governs conduct of the federal and state governments, as well as providing for the fundamental rights of private citizens. Each of the 50 states similarly has a state constitution that governs the conduct of the state government and protects citizens of that state. The United

Sources of Law

- Constitutions: United States Constitution and individual state constitutions
- Statutes: Federal laws enacted by Congress—United States Code (USC), state laws enacted by state legislatures
- Administrative law: Rules and regulations created by federal agencies—Code of Federal Regulations (CFR), rules and regulations created by state agencies
- Common law: Federal and state court decisions

States Congress and 50 state legislatures also enact laws (i.e., statutes) that address issues ranging from enforceability of contracts, to product liability, to the registration of trademarks. Each of the 50 states has its own court system, as does the federal government. These court systems, both federal and state, are hierarchical in structure. The highest court is usually a supreme or superior court. An intermediate appellate court is at a middle level, and a district or trial court is at the bottom. Most cases originate at the trial or district court level and work their way up through the court system. It can take years for a case to move through all levels of the court system.

A fundamental premise of the law includes the concepts of **precedent** and **stare decisis.** The doctrine of stare decisis is the legal principle that compels courts to follow a previous decision or precedent when deciding a subsequent case in the same district or jurisdiction (Connors, 2009). A precedent is simply a decided case that furnishes a basis for determining later cases involving similar facts or issues (Black, 2004). These two concepts, precedent and stare decisis, work together to provide predictability and consistency to judicial decisions. This predictability and consistency are important because those bound by the law are then able to make sound decisions and conduct themselves and their affairs in accordance with the law. For example, consider a situation in which a football player accidentally injures another player during a game and the injured player threatens to sue the first player. If players had to worry about being sued every time another player was injured, many sport competitions would probably never occur. But the majority rule as established by numerous judicial decisions provides that a player is liable to another player for an injury only if the player causing the injury acted recklessly (i.e., with conscious indifference to an extreme risk). The reckless standard is a much higher standard for determining liability than a traditional negligence standard (i.e., failing to act reasonably). Thus, the concepts of precedent and stare decisis would lead to the conclusion that a player is not liable to another player for accidental or negligent injuries. This precedent helps guide how sport participants conduct themselves and how sport organizations manage sport contests. Players, coaches, and event organizers in the sport industry can predict this judicial outcome because courts will rely on precedents when facing the same or a similar situation.

precedent—A legal case establishing a principle or rule that a court may need to adopt when deciding subsequent cases with similar issues or facts. The term may also refer to the collective body of case law that a court should consider when interpreting the law.

stare decisis—Literally means "to stand by things decided." This principle expresses the notion that prior court decisions must be recognized as precedents, according to case law, and followed accordingly.

The law is dynamic and works to bring order to societal norms (Koller, 2006). As a result, legislatures adopt statutes reflecting, in part, the desires of those whom they represent. It should be no surprise that many of these adopted laws affect sport managers, sporting events, and sport organizations either directly or indirectly with the intent of better serving society as a whole. For example, many states have adopted the Uniform Athlete Agent Act (UAAA), which provides protection for student–athletes from unscrupulous sport agents and establishes uniform agent registration and disclosure requirements. Specifically, the UAAA identifies several provisions that must be included in an agency contract. For example, a couple of these provisions are language that requires notice to an educational institution after an agency contract has been entered into with one of its student–athletes and the right of the student–athlete to cancel an agency contract within 14 days after it is signed. Provisions of this kind in the contract between the student–athlete and agent can have the result of protecting institutions from harsh National Collegiate Athletic Association (NCAA) penalties and allowing the student–athlete to terminate an agreement with an agent that effectively exploits the student–athlete. Besides issues such as the illegal actions of agents, other societal influences and behaviors have spawned statutes governing ticket scalping, steroid use, gambling, drug testing, and discrimination in athletics. The law, being as dynamic as it is, can be applied to areas of public life that range from statutes that govern property rights and taxes to issues involving sport.

WEB

Go to the OSG and complete the Web search, which has you look up two court cases related to sporting issues.

The next section of this chapter provides a basic overview of significant legal principles in the United States that have a direct or at least tangential effect on various

SPORT LAW AND POLICY IN GREECE

By Anastasios Kaburakis • GREECE
Southern Illinois University, UNITED STATES

The US distinction between amateur and professional does not apply to the structure, law, and policies of the sport governance systems of other countries. Hence, this essay addresses law and policy that apply to both grassroots and commercial (professional) sport in Greece.

The core of the Greek sport system is the club, the team, and the sport society operating under the rules of the respective sport federation. In this federalized, club-based, sociocultural model of sport, participation starts on the club level. As athletes proceed through the various age levels, age-specific, regional select teams are identified, from which the national team is selected. A major principle in the Greek system is that national team service is the utmost obligation of athletes. Consequently, sanctions for refusal to participate on national teams in international competitions are severe.

The club that contributes to a player's development and training "owns" the player's rights (i.e., the player's athletic eligibility card for national and international competition). According to Greek sport law (2725/1999), the athlete's 18th birthday brings the obligation to sign a one- to five-year contract with that club. According to European Union (EU) Law and European Court of Justice (ECJ) jurisprudence, however, Greek athletes who do not wish to follow the internal market route may sign contracts in other Euro-

PA Photos.

Greece's European Basketball Championship triumph in 1987 was a moment that changed Greek history and many lives. Nick Galis was a member of this historical team.

decisions (e.g., managerial), activities (e.g., marketing), and personnel (e.g., athletics directors) in the sport industry.

US CONSTITUTION

The US Constitution is the supreme law in the United States and is regarded as the document that provides the greatest source of individual rights to American citizens. The Constitution is made up of a preamble, seven articles, and 27 amendments. The first three articles of the Constitution establish and describe the functions of the legislative, executive, and judicial branches of government. The remaining articles address matters pertaining to states' powers and limits (Article IV), process for amending the Constitution (Article V), issues related to public officials taking an oath

pean countries or overseas. Should they wish to return to Greece, sport federations mandate that they first negotiate with and sign a contract with the club that owned their rights. If a returning athlete wishes to join a different club, the original club would be entitled compensation after the athlete's transfer.

Because no contractual relationship exists between the athlete and the club, this practice is incompatible with EU law. Sport clubs, however, have traditionally been exempted from various laws and restrictions imposed by normal legal standards. The theory is that the club is the main entity that contributes to sport development (the proverbial argument for self-regulation of sport by the federations) and, as such, is entitled to some protection. The norm, therefore, has been for European jurisdictions to defer matters to the respective sport governing bodies (i.e., the sport federations) in the name of the sociocultural model of sport.

Not all legal decisions regarding athletes have favored tradition. In concert with EU law, several practices that formerly extended privileges to high-profile Greek athletes have been discontinued. For example, a mechanism by which successful junior athletes were allowed entrance to the university and school or department of their choice was replaced by a fairer system that abides by EU law. Also, government officials have ceased arbitrarily appointing their favorite Greek athletes to prestigious state and civil service positions and have stopped issuing licenses for sport betting offices to star athletes.

In Greece and across the EU, governments have a history of deep involvement in sport. Some public officials object to this involvement and would like to see state appropriations to sport federations reduced or discontinued. The proper role of government regarding sport law and policy remains controversial.

INTERNATIONAL LEARNING ACTIVITY #1

Compare club ownership of Greek athletes' rights to the reserve clause that used to be included in the contracts of all American professional athletes. Who were the three professional baseball players that challenged the reserve clause in American sport? What was the outcome for each of them?

INTERNATIONAL LEARNING ACTIVITY #2

The World Anti-Doping Agency (WADA) is a Swiss private law foundation headquartered in Montreal, Quebec, Canada. It coordinates and monitors the global fight against doping in sport. Go to the WADA Web site at www.wada-ama.org/en/ and take the anti-doping quiz that is posted in the "Education & Awareness" menu. After you take the first quiz, you can take additional versions of it by clicking on "New quiz." Discuss the answers with your classmates. If any of your answers are wrong, find the right answer in the appropriate section of the Web site.

to support the constitution (Article VI), and the steps necessary to ratify the Constitution (Article VII).

Over the years, several amendments have been added to the Constitution. The first 10 amendments to the Constitution, commonly referred to as the Bill of Rights, were added in 1791. In short, the Bill of Rights preserves the basic and fundamental rights of the people. Subsequently, 17 amendments have been added over time. In total, there are 27 amendments to the US Constitution.

Chemerinsky (2006) noted that the US Constitution limits and empowers American government. The legal scholar adds that besides providing a framework for government, the Constitution protects individual rights by limiting governing authority. In the sport industry, such limitations by the US Constitution have been evident. A number of civil rights cases decided in the 1970s and 1980s raised issues of racial discrimination

Photo courtesy of the Big Ten Conference.

In Profile: Jim Delany

Jim Delany, the commissioner of the Big Ten Conference, has served as an athletics administrator since 1975. Delany, as detailed in the Big Ten Conference Web site (www.bigten.org/school-bio/delany-bio.html), completed his undergraduate and law degrees from the University of North Carolina, where he participated as a student–athlete on the basketball team from 1967 through 1970. Delany's legal background consists of working on the North Carolina Senate Judiciary Committee Counsel, as well as serving as a staff attorney for the North Carolina Justice Department from 1974 to 1975.

Following a brief career in the legal system, Delany began his involvement with athletics administration in 1975, where he served as an NCAA enforcement representative. Before securing his current role as the commissioner of the Big Ten Conference, Delany served as the commissioner of the Ohio Valley Conference. Since being appointed as commissioner of the Big Ten in 1989, the conference has experienced a tremendous run of success. Delany's major accomplishments include the creation of the Big Ten Network and the development of the first instant replay system in collegiate football. Moreover, in large part because of his legal training and background, Delany has successfully participated in several media contract negotiations for the NCAA and Big Ten Conference. For example, he helped negotiate the CBS contract with the NCAA that covers an 11-year term and totals US$6 billion. He also participated in the creation of the Bowl Championship Series (BCS). In his role, Delany must always be prepared to communicate with conference presidents and athletics directors on various legal issues and matters such as Title IX and ADA regulations that are prevalent in college athletics.

Delany was also influential in adding Penn State University to the Big Ten Conference. He has served on several boards such as the USA Basketball Executive Committee and the University of North Carolina's General Alumni Association Board of Directors.

Based on www.bigten.org/school-bio-html.

in public recreation areas. Sport management practitioners over the past few decades have witnessed landmark and other important decisions involving the intersection of constitutional, antitrust, and employment law with sport. Throughout this chapter we will refer to some of these cases and issues that involve the sport industry and the US Constitution.

A fundamental purpose of the US Constitution is to protect the people from the government's unwarranted intrusion, discrimination, arbitrary and capricious treatment, and infringement of liberty and property rights without **due process.** The Constitution provides protections for its citizens whenever there is an infringement on a person's basic and fundamental rights. Moreover, an organization's public or nonpublic designation makes a tremendous difference in determining whether its policies and practices are subject to the Constitution.

due process—As it is embodied in the 5th and 14th Amendments to the United States Constitution, due process ensures that a law shall not be unreasonable, arbitrary, or capricious and that the means selected for enforcing a law shall have a reasonable and substantial relation to the objective sought by the government.

Sport organizations governed by the US Constitution include, for example, athletics programs in public schools, state university athletics departments; federal, state, and municipally owned park and recreation departments; and possibly a person or organization that leases state-owned property to host a sporting event. As a result, these public sport organizations must comply with a number of Constitutional requirements in the management of their business activities. Thus, if a state high school athletics association created a rule or regulation limiting or restricting eligibility to participate in high school athletics to males only, this rule or regulation would have to pass Constitutional scrutiny, or "muster," to be enforceable. The 14th Amendment, which provides equal protection, would not permit the state high school association to make impermissible distinctions based on race, ethnic origin, or gender. For example, the 14th Amendment would require the state athletics association to demonstrate what important government interest was being served by a gender-based distinction and that there is a substantial likelihood that the government interest would be achieved by the regulation. Because it is unlikely the state high school athletics association could articulate an important reason to exclude females from high school athletics, this regulation would be an unconstitutional deprivation of equal protection of female students.

The US Constitution was not intended to govern the operation of privately owned and operated sport organizations such as retail sporting goods stores (e.g. Dick's Sporting Goods), fitness clubs (e.g., Urban Active), private golf courses (e.g., Augusta National Golf Club, whose membership is composed completely of males), or professional sports teams (e.g., the National Basketball Association's [NBA] dress code could be perceived as a restriction on how a player may choose to express himself through his manner of dress, but because the NBA is a private organization, no First Amendment [free speech and expression] challenges could be asserted against the league).

Earlier we discussed the US Constitution and its various amendments. Take a closer look at the 14th Amendment, which was also examined earlier. This amendment provides citizens within a given state the same protections against unwarranted actions by state government. The provisions that regulate the acts of the federal government as embodied within the first 10 amendments were passed down to the operations of state governments. Thus, the first 10 amendments to the US Constitution (i.e., the Bill of Rights) prohibit state-related unwarranted behaviors and intrusions on the people. For more on the application of the 14th Amendment, please read the critical thinking section near the end of this chapter. The critical thinking exercise will further illustrate how the protective intent of the US Constitution can be applied to the sport industry.

The US Constitution is an important source of individual rights and guarantees and is the highest legal authority in the United States. No statutes, laws, regulations, or policies may contradict its provisions. The next section introduces you to federal legislation and provides examples of federal laws that have application to sport.

FEDERAL LEGISLATION

The US Constitution empowers Congress to enact legislation in a variety of subject areas (e.g., copyrights, patents, trade and commerce, taxation, securities regulation). Congressionally enacted legislation reflects societal interests regarding future conduct about a variety of issues including, for example, discrimination and business practices (e.g., sports betting, unfair trade practices, ticket scalping). Statutory language may appear general in nature because of its emphasis on governing uncertain future conduct (i.e., situations demanding statutory application that have not yet arisen). In turn, judges, through their written judicial opinions, establish the application and interpretation of a statute. Oftentimes the judiciary is guided by a detailed legislative history that may accompany a statute. On other occasions, the legislative history may be minimal or not specific, so instead the court may have more leeway in interpreting the language used by Congress. For example, Congress may have identified the purpose of a piece of legislation to eliminate discrimination against people with disabilities. In interpreting this legislation, the courts will take into account that the stated purpose is broad. Therefore, the various provisions or remedies contained in the statute may also be interpreted broadly to maximize the reach of the statute and thereby better fulfill the purpose of the law.

Many federal laws affect sport, some specifically and others only indirectly. For example, the Americans with Disabilities Act (ADA) and Title IX, both of which will

Photo courtesy of LA84 Foundation.

In Profile: Anita DeFrantz

Anita DeFrantz is a board member of the International Olympic Committee (IOC) and serves as chair of the Commission of Women and Sports. A native of Philadelphia, Pennsylvania, DeFrantz completed her undergraduate degree at Connecticut College with honors in 1974. While attending Connecticut College on an academic scholarship, DeFrantz became involved in athletics as a rower. After completing her undergraduate degree, DeFrantz enrolled in the University of Pennsylvania law school and continued to row competitively. She led the US women's Olympic team to a bronze medal in the 1976 Games and won a silver medal at the 1978 World Championships. In 1999 *Sports Illustrated for Women* named her the 56th best female athlete of all time. DeFrantz's achievements in athletics and her background in law helped her become the first African American female to be appointed to the International Olympic Committee's executive board in 1992. Before the 1994 reform of the organization, an integral part of the IOC was the Court of Arbitration for Sport, which was created to arbitrate decisions regarding sport-related legal disputes. DeFrantz's familiarity with the law gave her increased ability to work with judiciaries and uphold rulings made by the court.

Immediately following law school, DeFrantz worked as an attorney in a juvenile detention center. She continued to be involved in Olympic endeavors by serving in various roles for the International Olympic Committee. In 1981 DeFrantz was hired as vice president of the Olympic Villages for the Los Angeles Organizing Committee. During the Los Angeles Games, she became a member of the Amateur Athletic Foundation, which was formed to handle the US$94 million surplus that Los Angeles had received for hosting the games. DeFrantz's legal training in negotiations also enabled her to transform the Olympic movement by persuading 43 African nations not to boycott the games because a South African runner was allowed to compete for Great Britain. Upon successfully managing her responsibilities with the Los Angeles Games and the International Olympic Committee, she became the organization's first female vice president in 1997. Besides carrying out her primary responsibilities, DeFrantz currently serves as vice president of FISA, the international rowing federation.

Based on http://usocpressbox.org/usoc/pressbox.nsf/(staticreports)/Breaking+News/$File/AnitaDeFrantz.pdf?Open;http://www.marshall.usc.edu/execed/programs/sbi/sbibios/anita-defrantz-biography.htm

be discussed in the following sections of this chapter, apply to a broad range of individuals and entities. In other words, when Congress enacted these laws, the elimination of discrimination was a broad and sweeping goal, not just in sport programs but also in employment, education, and public places throughout the United States. The legislation has had, and continues to have, a significant effect on the decision-making activities of those in various sport-related leadership and managerial positions. Other federal legislation such as the Ted Stevens Olympic and Amateur Sports Act (2005), the Sports Agent Responsibility and Trust Act (2005), and the Unlawful Internet Gambling Enforcement Act (2006) were enacted to regulate a specific aspect or function within the sport industry. In addition to those legislative acts, two laws enacted by Congress have had a significant effect on the management of sport. A discussion of these two acts follows.

Americans With Disabilities Act

The Americans with Disabilities Act (ADA), which was passed in 1990, prohibits discrimination against people with disabilities as well as people who are perceived to have a disability. Under the ADA, a person is defined as having a disability if he or she has (1) a physical or mental impairment that substantially limits one or more major life activities, (2) a record of a disability, or (3) a perception of possessing a disability. Title I of the ADA prohibits discrimination in employment. Employers cannot discriminate against a person with a disability who meets essential job qualifications with or without reasonable accommodation. Title III prohibits discrimination in places of public accommodation. In other words, people with disabilities must be provided reasonable accommodations that permit them access to places where the public congregates or participates for purposes of recreation or leisure (e.g., bowling centers, health and fitness centers, skating rinks, sport arenas, stadia). An accommodation is not required if accommodating the disabled person poses a direct threat to other participants or if a requested accommodation creates an undue hardship by fundamentally changing the nature of the product offering (e.g., aerobic dance class), represents an excessive financial burden, or disrupts the environment itself.

Driven by the potential for additional revenue, many colleges and universities are expanding their stadia, hoping to generate additional revenue for their athletics departments. Stadia renovated to include suites and club seating attract financial support from alumni and donors. Although athletics facility enhancements throughout the country are being made in revenue-generating sports such as football and men's basketball, athletics directors must be certain that these facilities comply with ADA. Moreover, in sports that have grown in popularity in recent years, updates must be made to their facilities to accommodate the increasing number of spectators. The University of Michigan recently encountered this situation during the US$226 million upgrade of its football stadium. The university characterized its renovation as a repair rather than a renovation, but was sued by a disabled veterans' group. Ultimately, the university settled with the disabled veterans' group and the Department of Justice by increasing the number of wheelchair-accessible seats.

Title IX of the Education Amendments Act

In the United States a law known as Title IX, which was passed in 1972, precludes discrimination based on sex in any educational program or activity that receives federal financial assistance. With regard to sport, compliance with Title IX is generally evaluated in three areas. The first area looks at the school's distribution of financial aid among its women's and men's athletics teams. The second area evaluates other benefits, opportunities, and treatments within men's and women's sports programs. Areas evaluated include, but are not limited to, the following:

1. Provision of equipment and supplies
2. Scheduling of games and practice times
3. Travel and per diem allowances
4. Opportunity to receive coaching and academic tutoring
5. Provision of locker rooms, practice facilities, and competitive facilities
6. Provision of medical and training facilities and services
7. Provision of housing and dining facilities and services
8. Publicity and recruitment procedures
9. Assignment and compensation of coaches
10. Other support services provided (e.g., clerical or administrative)

The third area examines whether the interests and abilities of the underrepresented group have been accommodated.

The Department of Education has identified a three-prong test for examining the extent to which the interests and abilities of the underrepresented group have been

Title IX ensures that women have an equal opportunity as men to participate in sports at institutions that receive federal money. There is still controversy, though, regarding how to ensure this equal opportunity exists.

accommodated. The three-prong test provides three ways to comply with Title IX. A university can demonstrate compliance under any of the three prongs. The first prong is both the most difficult to comply under and the most controversial. This prong compares the proportionality of the university's male and female students to the proportionality of male and female student–athletes. For example, if the population of the student body at State University is 53% female, the percentage of female student–athletes should also be 53% under this first prong. Few college athletics programs meet this challenging standard. Opponents to the first prong have argued that it is an impermissible quota, but the courts have consistently rejected that argument because it is not the only way in which a university can demonstrate compliance.

The second prong allows a school to demonstrate compliance by showing that the school has a history and a continuing practice of program expansion responsive to the interests and abilities of the underrepresented sex. This is a dual requirement, because both a history and a continuing practice are required. The courts have said that the best evidence of expansion is expansion itself; thus, typically, proposals and plans may not satisfy this second prong. Also, a school cannot cite its elimination of men's programs under this prong. The courts have indicated that the action of eliminating opportunities for men is not the equivalent of expanding opportunities for women.

Lastly, the third prong allows a school to demonstrate compliance by proving that it is fully and effectively meeting the interests and abilities of its students with its current athletics programs. In other words, this prong conveys that although a disparity may exist between the percentage of males and females within the general student population versus the percentage of males and females among student–athletes, this inequity is due to legitimate, nondiscriminatory factors. Proving interest levels is not an exact science. Courts have identified several ways that a school may obtain information about interest levels in athletics participation: (1) student requests that a sport be added; (2) requests to elevate a club team to varsity status; (3) participation levels in club or intramural sports; (4) interviews with students, newly admitted students, coaches, administrators, or others regarding interest in a particular sport; (5) results of questionnaires of current and newly admitted students; (6) participation levels in interscholastic sports; (7) discussions with amateur athletics associations or community sports leagues; and (8) inclusion of participation and interest questions on university admissions forms. For more information on this aspect of Title IX, read *Pederson v. Louisiana State University* (2000).

A controversial clarification letter from the Department of Education in 2005 stated that a school could demonstrate effective accommodation of current interest and abilities by conducting an online interest survey of its student body. This letter was widely repudiated as serving to redefine and weaken Title IX rather than to clarify existing law. Because the majority of Title IX litigation has focused on this three-prong analysis (i.e., proportionality, history or continuing practice, and effectively accommodating current interests), acceptance of this "clarification" of Title IX would have had the potential of negatively affecting the access of females to athletics opportunities. As a result, organizations such as the National Collegiate Athletic Association (NCAA), the National Association for Girls and Women in Sport, the Women's Sports Foundation, the National Women's Law Center, the National Coalition for Women, and Girls in Education quickly moved to denounce the letter issued by the Department of Education. But in 2006, based on the recommendations of the Title IX Commission appointed by former US education secretary Rod Paige, the Department of Education's Office of Civil Rights affirmed that e-mail surveys of student interest could satisfy Title IX requirements for compliance. However, in 2010, President Barack Obama rescinded the 2005 and 2006 letters, thus, these surveys are no longer recommended by the Department of Education.

As a result of the passing and enforcement of Title IX, women's athletics has witnessed tremendous growth and popularity. Moreover, recent landmark court rulings in this area have sent a message that discrimination against women in athletics is unacceptable and will be met with serious consequences. Fresno State University has paid out several million dollars as a result of lawsuits brought by its former women's basketball coach, volleyball coach, and associate athletics director (Steeg, 2008). In another case involving high school athletics, millions of dollars have been awarded (Slezak, 2008) in favor of the plaintiffs. Furthermore, in 2009 the US Supreme Court rendered a decision that broadens the protections for females involved in athletics. If a plaintiff files a Title IX claim against a defendant, the plaintiff can simultaneously file a gender discrimination claim against the school under the 14th Amendment of the Constitution (refer to the discussion earlier in the chapter on the 14th Amendment).

As noted earlier, the 10th Amendment to the Constitution empowers Congress to enact legislation that affects the lives of citizens in a variety of ways. But if it is not explicitly stated that the Constitution has the power to impose itself on the lives of US citizens, then each state may legislate its own laws to govern its citizens so long as these laws are not inconsistent with federal law. In the next section we look at state legal systems and their application to the sport industry.

STATE LEGAL SYSTEMS

As mentioned in the previous paragraph, the legislature of each state is responsible for enacting laws to govern its citizens in matters where federal legislation is silent. Each state has a constitution that sets forth the rights of its citizens and the limitations of the state government. Furthermore, each state has a court system to interpret and apply the laws of that state. Two areas of law that are based solely on state law are torts and contracts. Although the concepts of precedent and stare decisis apply within the state court systems, a state court is not compelled to follow a precedent from another state. For example, if Minnesota has already decided a case similar to a case pending in New York, the Minnesota decision would be informative or perhaps even persuasive to the New York court, but the New York court would not be required to follow the precedent established in Minnesota. For example, suppose a suit is filed against a National Football League (NFL) team in New York in a wrongful death case involving a professional football player who dies on the practice field from complications of heat stroke. Furthermore, suppose that the state supreme court in the state of New York renders the decision on the case. The decision in the state of Minnesota cannot serve as legal precedent for arguing a successful case in New York.

Regarding a state legal system, the state's constitution is the highest legal authority in the state. Moreover, its statutes must always be consistent with the federal Constitution. If they are not, the statutes will be deemed invalid by our courts. Again, state laws govern the citizens of a state in matters where federal legislation is silent.

The following section addresses issues involving tort law. Tort law cases can range from cases involving product liability (e.g., head injury because of a faulty helmet) to those associated with medical malpractice (e.g., misdiagnosis of a career-threatening injury).

tort—A civil wrong or injury for which the law permits a recovery. Typically, the wrong or injury is either a negligent act or an intentional act by one person that causes an injury to another person or his or her property.

Tort Law

A **tort** is a civil wrong or injury for which the law permits a recovery. Typically, a wrong or injury is either a negligent act or an intentional act by one person that causes an injury

Photo courtesy of the Atlanta Braves.

In Profile: Greg Heller

Greg Heller is vice president and general counsel for the Atlanta Braves. In this role, he oversees and manages all legal affairs for this Major League Baseball (MLB) club, as well as the organization's minor league affiliates. Heller's responsibilities and duties include providing direction and legal advice on intellectual property, employment, baseball operations, and litigation.

Before serving in his current role with the Braves, Heller was employed for seven years with the TBS sports legal group, which included the Braves, the Atlanta Hawks, the Atlanta Thrashers, Phillips Arena, the Goodwill Games, the Turner Sports television group (and its NBA, NASCAR, PGA, British Open, and MLB properties), and the Turner Sports new media group (and its NASCAR, PGA, PGA Tour properties). Before joining TBS, Heller worked at law firms in Atlanta and Chicago where his work involved sport and entertainment matters among other legal areas.

Heller's educational background commenced at Indiana University (IU). He received a bachelor's degree in sport management from IU and interned with the Peoria Chiefs (a minor league affiliate of the Chicago Cubs) and in the IU athletics department. After graduating from IU, Heller attended law school at Marquette University.

Based on http://law.marquette.edu/cgi-bin/site.pl?2130&pageID=1469; http://atlanta.braves.mlb.com/news/press_releases/press_release.jsp?ymd=20070521&content_id=1977844&vkey=pr_atl&fext=.jsp&c_id=atl

to another person or his or her property. Tort law focuses on whether a particular person (or persons) failed to perform appropriately based on her or his (or their) relationship with the injured plaintiff. The purpose of tort law is to remedy a wrong. Compensatory or punitive damages (or both) can provide a remedy for the wrong. Compensatory damages can reflect monetary damages for medical bills, lost days of work, payment for hired hands, lost earning potential, and pain and suffering. Punitive damages, in comparison, can impose additional monetary damages on the defendant that serve to punish the defendant for his or her wrongdoing and make an example of the defendant's conduct so that others do not engage in similar acts. Punitive damages often greatly exceed the actual costs of the injury and are generally available only for intentional torts.

As mentioned in the preceding paragraph, a person may have a cause of action in tort because of the negligent or intentional acts of another. Unintentional torts encompass claims based on negligence. Claims based on defamation, invasion of privacy, assault, and battery represent intentional torts. The next two sections will provide you with an understanding of the legal aspects of negligence and intentional torts and their application to sport.

Negligence

proximate cause—A cause that directly produces an event and without which the event would not have occurred.

Negligence represents the failure to act as another reasonably prudent person would have acted in a like or similar circumstance. To prove negligence, a plaintiff must prove the following four elements: duty, breach of duty, **proximate cause**, and injury. The duty can be based on (1) relationship with the plaintiff (e.g., coach and student–athlete, teacher and student, manager of a sport facility and spectator), (2) voluntary assumption of a duty (e.g., a volunteer coach who agrees to assist a student–athlete with her or his college application materials), or (3) duty imposed by a statute (e.g., a state law that requires lifeguards at all public swimming pools). Breach of duty, the second element, represents a failure to act as a reasonable, prudent person would have acted it in the same or similar situation. Typically, liability is eminent when an injury is foreseeable by another reasonable, prudent professional or the defendant's actions reflect a disregard for the relevant professional standards. Proximate cause relates to the linkage between the defendant's failure to adhere to the standard of care (breach of duty) and actual injury suffered (Spengler, Anderson, Connaughton, & Baker, 2009). For example, although the defendant may be negligent, the injury may have resulted from some other intervening act. Consider the following example: A swimming pool manager has a duty to provide a lifeguard and fails to do so, and a child is injured when a table umbrella falls on top of him. The failure of the pool manager to provide a lifeguard did not cause the injury. Lastly, an injury must actually occur. For example, a swimming pool operator could fail to provide a lifeguard, but if no one is injured from these acts, a claim for negligence would also fail. Defenses for negligence can include, but are not limited to, assumption of risk, comparative negligence, failure to meet one of the four elements of negligence, failure to meet procedural guidelines (e.g., statute of limitations), governmental immunity, volunteer immunity statutes, and recreational use immunity statutes.

Intentional Torts and Other State Law Rights

Tort claims may also result from intentional rather than negligent conduct. A number of intentional torts provide a plaintiff with a legitimate cause of action. Intentional torts include invasion of privacy, defamation, assault, and battery (see the sidebar "Types of Intentional Torts"). A state law right that is also highly relevant in the sport industry is the right of publicity. Publicity rights evolved from invasion of privacy rights but are now recognized by many states by statute or common law as an independent right.

Invasion of privacy and defamation are closely linked. Invasion of privacy is a tort claim that allows a person to recover for the publication of truthful information and is intended to protect people from unwarranted intrusions into their private lives. Invasion of privacy claims can be based on excessive intrusion into private areas and the unwarranted disclosure of private facts. The fundamental principle underlying invasion of privacy claims is a person's right to be let alone (*Rosenbloom v. Metromedia*, 1971). A three-prong test is used to determine invasion of privacy liability based on intrusion or disclosure. The three prong analysis asks three questions:

1. Did intentional intrusion or disclosure occur regarding private information?
2. Was the intrusion or disclosure something viewed as private to the plaintiff?
3. Would another member of society be reasonably offended?

Invasion of privacy claims are grounded in the right of a person to solitude or to be let alone and protected from unreasonable intrusions. Right of publicity claims are similar to invasion of privacy claims but with a twist. Publicity rights protect the commercial value of a person's name or likeness from intrusion or misappropriation. For example, suppose that you are a sport marketing entrepreneur who is looking for an opportunity to capitalize on the upcoming race of the Indianapolis 500. You decide to

Types of Intentional Torts

- Invasion of privacy: protects against unwarranted privacy intrusions and disclosures
- Defamation: protects against publication of false statements that are harmful to a person's reputation
- Assault: protects against threats that could result in physical harm
- Battery: protects against actual physical harm or offensive touching

print up hundreds of T-shirts that have Danica Patrick's image printed on them. If you went through with your idea and then sold the T-shirts, you would be using Patrick's image for profit and misappropriating her likeness without her permission in violation of Indiana's state right of publicity laws.

Defamation claims are intended to protect a person's reputation and allow him or her to recover from the publication of damaging, false information. A plaintiff who alleges defamation must prove four elements to win a defamation claim: (1) a false communication, (2) communication with a reckless disregard for the facts, (3) communication reported to a third party, and (4) communication causing damage to his or her reputation. These elements can be found in the Restatement (Second) of Torts, § 559 (1963). (**Restatements** are secondary legal research sources that seek to restate the legal rules that constitute the common law in a particular area. The American Law Institute [ALI], a prestigious legal organization composed of noted professors, judges, and lawyers, writes the restatements. The ALI has completed restatements in 15 areas of law including torts, contracts, property, conflict of laws, foreign relations law, and products liability.) The tort of defamation strives to protect a person's right to her or his reputation, pride, and integrity. For example, a coach who is terminated during an ongoing NCAA recruiting scandal investigation would find it difficult to find other employment if information were published implying that he or she had committed or contributed to the violations. Truth, however, is a defense to a defamation allegation. Thus, if the coach did in fact commit the violations, a defamation claim would be inappropriate. The proof required in defamation claims tends to be subjective. Hence, a successful defamation claim is difficult to prove and can require years to litigate.

restatements—Secondary legal research sources that seek to restate the legal rules that constitute the common law in a particular area such as contracts, torts, property, foreign relations, and product liability.

Sport managers are better able to protect themselves and their employers, while also serving their fans, spectators, consumers, clients, and employees, when they understand the distinction between invasion of privacy and defamation, as well as the behaviors that can subject them and the sport entity to liability. Sport managers should know how to insulate themselves from legal claims. As you will see in the next section, a sound understanding of contract law can offer sport managers some protection from being on the losing end of claims of negligence and acts of fraud.

Contracts

The law of contracts is also known as the law of private agreements. Contract law enables private parties to enter into agreements and enforce those agreements legally. A contract represents an agreement between two or more parties to do, or not to do, a particular act. When a contracting party fails to abide by the terms of the agreement, the nonbreaching party has a legal cause of action. Contract law preserves and encourages the right of partics to make and enter into agreements as long as the parties abide by the legal tenants associated with contract law, including, for example, (1) legal subject matter; (2) defined offer, acceptance, and consideration; (3) terms within the realm of acceptable public policy; (4) parties in possession of capacity (i.e., appropriate age and without significant mental disability); (5) no economic duress or exercise of excessive bargaining power; and (6) clear and unequivocal contractual language. An offer, acceptance, and consideration represent the three basic tenets associated with contract law. Consideration refers to the bargained-for exchange (e.g., I'll pay you $75,000 in exchange for your employment as the marketing vice president for my sport management firm; I'll pay you $100 for your vintage rookie baseball card now worth $1,000). In the latter example, the agreed-upon consideration benefits the buyer of the baseball card much more than it does the seller. Common law and statutes that govern contractual agreements do not require that the agreed-upon consideration be equal (or even fair) to both parties as long as the agreement is made without fraud, duress, or deceit. In other words, one party

Waivers can help protect an organization from lawsuits by event participants. For example, if one of these marathon participants sustained an injury because of his own negligence during the race, the organization would not be responsible for compensating the athlete for that injury.

may clearly benefit by the terms of the contract itself. Recourse for breach of contract actions can include court-imposed injunctions, restoring the parties (or a party) to a contract to their (or his or her) precontract condition, reforming the contract so that it better represents the intention of the parties or fairness, or total abandonment of the contract itself (i.e., rescission).

A variety of sport organizations routinely use exculpatory agreements as part of their daily operations. Waivers and releases both reflect exculpatory agreements, that is, agreements used to excuse an organization for its own acts of negligence. For example, health clubs typically require members to sign a waiver before they use the facility's programs and equipment. The signed waiver excuses an organization (e.g., a health club) from ordinary negligence liability even if an employee of the health club is responsible for negligence and a resultant injury.

Exculpatory agreements represent a conflict with the purpose of tort law. As mentioned earlier, tort law seeks to allow a person injured by another's negligence to recover damages as a matter of public policy; that is, the one causing the injury should be responsible to the injured person. On the other hand, contract law seeks to allow the enforcement of agreements entered into between private parties even though the agreed-upon terms may benefit one party more than another. Waivers jeopardize the legal rights of a few so that society may benefit. In sport and physical activity, the realm of possible injuries is extensive, ranging from mild muscle strains to sprains, heat exhaustion, heat stroke, broken bones, and even death. If people were allowed to sue for the minor injuries inherent in sport and physical activity, the expense associated with owning and managing a sport or recreational organization would be exorbitant and likely prohibitive. Insurance costs, litigation-related fees (e.g., discovery, attorney fees, expert witness testimony), and damaged public relations could result in the cessation of the sport and recreational industry. Judicial and legislative approval of the signed waiver, although it denies recovery to an injured plaintiff, benefits society through the continued solvency and sustained profitability of the sport and recreation industry.

If written correctly, waivers can provide legal protection to a sport entity for acts of ordinary negligence. As mentioned earlier, contract law is based on state common law and statutes. Some states permit complete enforcement of waiver agreements; others refuse to enforce waivers at all because they conflict with acceptable public policy. It is always important to review individual state statutes and common law cases regarding the enforceability of exculpatory contracts, as well as state and industry specifications required for a legally enforceable contract.

SUMMARY OF FUNDAMENTAL SPORT LAW COMPONENTS

The law in the United States is composed of a system of rules that are enforced through a variety of prescribed institutions. In the US system of government, the process for interpreting and creating law on the federal level is clearly described in the Constitution. In this system, states are able to govern themselves in matters that do not have federal jurisdiction. The democratic form of government in the United States includes a system of checks and balances so that persons, regardless of their office or position, are held accountable for governing with integrity and respect for the rule of law. The power of the executive branch resides with the president of the United States, who acts as head of state and commander-in-chief. But as powerful as the president is in our form of government, the person who holds this office must work in concert with the judicial and legislative branches. For example, the president is empowered by the Constitution to sign legislation into law or veto bills enacted by Congress. But Congress (which resides in the legislative branch) may override a veto with two-thirds vote of both houses. Federal legislation such as the Education Act of 1972 (Title IX) and the ADA serve to protect citizens that have historically been discriminated against and denied the opportunity to participate in society with the rights and privileges that are extended to all citizens of the United States.

Besides examining the legislative acts and constitutions at the state and federal level, the chapter also examined tort law and contract law. Because accidents and intentional misdeeds inevitably occur, tort law works to determine whether an injured party can receive compensation from someone who is legally responsible for the injury that has occurred. Furthermore, as covered earlier, contract law is instrumental in formalizing agreements between parties. Because we have examined the various fundamental components involved with sport law, we can now turn our attention to applying the legal aspects in sport management.

Earlier in this chapter we discussed the US Constitution. In reference to the critical thinking scenario presented later, let's look at the issue in the context of the language of the Constitution regarding religion. As you read the following paragraphs, consider the extent to which your new knowledge of critical thinking (from your reading of critical thinking in chapter 1) might influence how you would react to the later section "Critical Thinking in Sport Law."

common law—The body of law derived from the judgments and decrees of the courts rather than those laws created by legislatures.

Common law is the body of law derived from the judgments and decrees of the courts rather than those laws created by legislatures. In addressing the issue of school prayer, common law decisions have held that because young students have impressionable minds, what might begin as a tolerance for religious expression can later become coerced indoctrination. With this in mind, consider the following.

In a 6-3 opinion delivered by Justice John Paul Stevens, the Supreme Court held in the *Santa Fe v. Doe* case that the school district's policy permitting student-led, student-initiated prayer at football games violates the establishment clause. The Court concluded

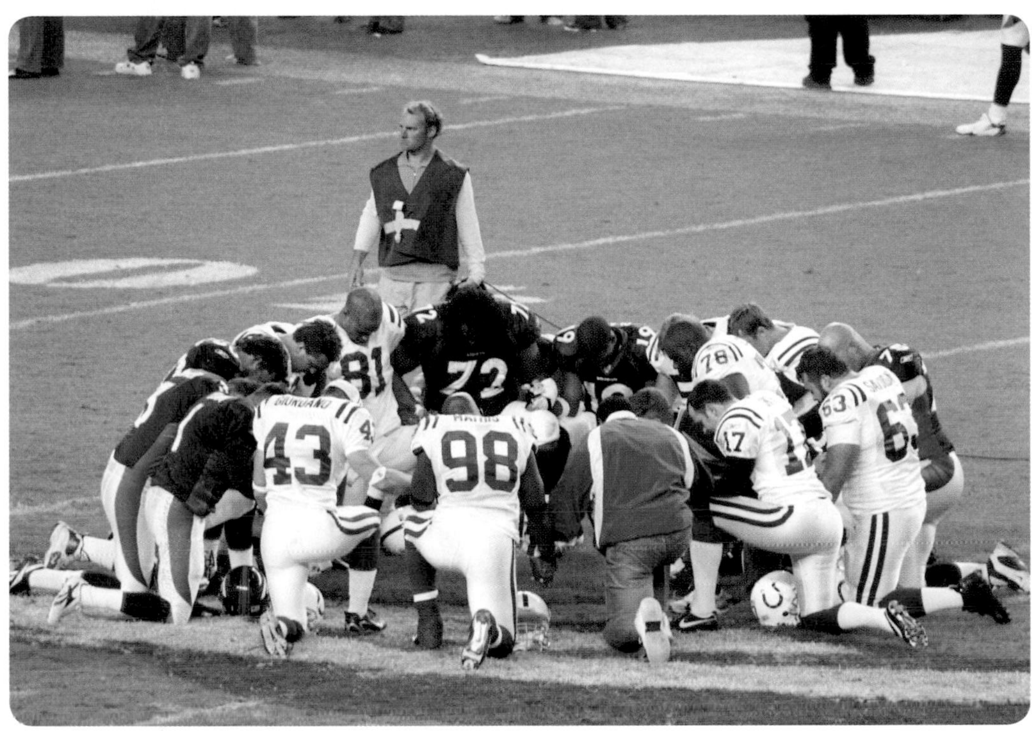

Organized prayer by professional athletes after a sporting event is a common and acceptable practice; however, organized prayer by athletes in public schools and public universities may raise legal issues as to whether the school's or coach's endorsement or control of the activity violates the establishment clause (i.e., the separation of church and state) of the First Amendment.

Photo courtesy of Paul M. Pedersen.

that the football game prayers were public speech authorized by a government policy and taking place on government property at government-sponsored school-related events and that the district's policy involved both perceived and actual government endorsement of the delivery of prayer at important school events.

Even more recently, a federal court has considered the nature of the events at which the prayer is present (e.g., high school football games). In *Borden v. School District of the Township of East Brunswick* (2008) the court concluded that a coach's presence at an event where students are praying is not permissible. The courts posit that when an adult begins to participate in student-led prayer, then the act of prayer is no longer totally voluntary because of the possible existence of pressure for students to participate in the prayer when an adult is present. Because music credit in some cases is given to students for participation in band and because physical education credit is sometimes provided to students who participate on athletics teams, the courts have reasoned that attendance at a high school football game, although not compulsory, is required for some students who want to obtain the overall education experience.

Although only a few students may experience a diminished educational experience because of their unwillingness or inability to participate in events at which a prayer occurs, it is indisputable that the role of the courts includes protecting the rights of the minority. Hence, the establishment clause (i.e., the separation of church and state) of the First Amendment is violated when what may be viewed as **de minimis** (or minimal) religious activity becomes entangled with school activity. A moment of silence has become a common alternative to prayer as a means of preserving the convivial attitudes and respectful behaviors of both the audience and the participants (Deppe, 2009).

de minimis—Literally meaning "about minimal things"; means something that is trivial or seemingly unworthy of the law's attention.

FUTURE CHALLENGES

The daily decisions of sport managers profoundly influence employee and customer recruitment and retention, as well as organizational solvency. Effective and efficient

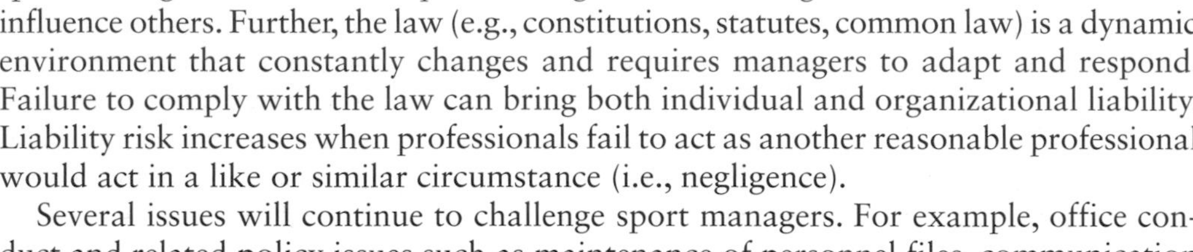

sport management entities require managers who are cognizant of how their actions influence others. Further, the law (e.g., constitutions, statutes, common law) is a dynamic environment that constantly changes and requires managers to adapt and respond. Failure to comply with the law can bring both individual and organizational liability. Liability risk increases when professionals fail to act as another reasonable professional would act in a like or similar circumstance (i.e., negligence).

Several issues will continue to challenge sport managers. For example, office conduct and related policy issues such as maintenance of personnel files, communication with the media, and inspection of employee e-mail communication can subject an organization to invasion of privacy or defamation litigation. Contract negotiation is becoming a vital skill for sport managers as the sport industry continues to expand. Compensation for an average NCAA Division I coach is often in the millions of dollars and flows from a variety of sources (e.g., salary, media shows, perks, endorsements, licensing opportunities, sport camps, personal appearances, performance bonuses), all of which must be provided for in a clear and enforceable contractual agreement. Sport managers in leadership positions today must thoroughly understand contract law and be prepared to make challenging decisions regarding the retention and hiring of coaches and administrators. Lastly, advances in technology continue to create legal issues that challenge sport managers. For instance, the increase in new media technology (e.g., Facebook, Twitter) has affected the sport industry with numerous legal challenges. The increasing influence of the Internet in the marketing and promotion of sport has led to a number of new legal challenges such as Internet domain disputes (e.g., recent suits filed over Web sites such as vancouver2010.org, steffigraf.com, chicago2016.com), ambush marketing, and defamatory blogging.

ACTION

Go to the OSG and complete the Learning in Action activity, which tests how well you remembered some of the key terms and their definitions used throughout this chapter.

CRITICAL THINKING IN SPORT LAW

Earlier in the chapter we discussed the US Constitution. As you read in chapter 1, being able to apply critical thinking skills to the field of sport management is important to future sport managers. For example, an issue that requires sport managers to use critical thinking skills to evaluate a constitutional issue is the question of prayer at public school sporting events. This controversy, which is particularly prominent in the United States, presents an excellent opportunity for you to practice critically evaluating an issue of great concern to the public while also learning about how the law, specifically the US Constitution, can be interpreted.

Assume that you were recently named to the position of athletics director at a public high school that had a long tradition of offering prayers over the public address system at athletic contests. Recently, following the Supreme Court decision in *Santa Fe Independent School District v. Doe* (2000), which held that such practices violated the establishment clause in the First Amendment, the practice of offering prayers over the public address system had been halted. But some students and parents have inquired about whether a moment of silence or reflection could be used to replace the prayer before athletic contests. You are not sure what to do.

PORTFOLIO

Complete the critical thinking portfolio activity in the OSG, consulting as needed the "Eight Critical Thinking Questions" section in chapter 1.

ETHICS IN SPORT LAW

Sport law often intersects with ethics. The following are two illustrations of ethical dilemmas associated with the legal aspects of sport management. After you read each dilemma, return to chapter 1 and read the section on ethical guidelines. After you read that section, apply the ethical guidelines to each of the problems presented below.

The first ethical dilemma involves the NCAA's use of a student–athlete's image or likeness. As graphic design becomes more realistic and the popularity of college sports video games rises, concern is growing over the use of the likenesses of student–athletes in video games. The NCAA has long proclaimed that its primary interest remains in preserving amateurism, yet there is a sense that the organization's commercial interests cannot be denied. Former University of Nebraska and Arizona State University (ASU) quarterback Sam Keller is suing both the NCAA and its corporate partner EA Sports, claiming that they are using the likenesses of amateur players who are prohibited from sharing in the profits of any games ("Keller Sues," 2009). According to Keller, the EA Sports NCAA video game accurately portrays his character's height, weight, jersey number, and position. Furthermore, after transferring from ASU to Nebraska, Keller switched his jersey number from 5 to 9, and the video game incorporated the same number switch. The former quarterback is seeking a damage award for himself and believes that each athlete who is accurately depicted should be compensated for his or her respective likeness. Disputing Keller's assertions, EA Sports issued a statement claiming that EA Sports and the NCAA have "reviewed the complaint, and do not believe that the claims have merit" (Wieberg, 2009, ¶ 9). The NCAA maintains the standpoint that because the various college players' likenesses are not being used as a tool to sell the video game, there is no reason to believe that a problem exists. This situation presents a legal and ethical dilemma because the NCAA reaps profits from its sponsorship agreements with companies like EA Sports. At the same time, current NCAA legislation prohibits student–athletes from receiving compensation from the NCAA in exchange for their participation in athletics. Some believe that student–athletes should receive compensation in exchange for their participation in college athletics.

The second ethical dilemma involves one amateur sport organization's ban on lawyers for its student–athletes (Schwarz, 2009). The National Collegiate Athletic Association (2008) states in its bylaws (12.3.2.1) that a lawyer may not be present during discussions of a contract offer with a professional organization or have direct contact with a professional sport organization on behalf of a student–athlete. According to NCAA rules, a lawyer's presence during such discussions is considered representation by an agent. The NCAA emphasized this point by suspending Oklahoma State University pitcher Andrew Oliver following his hiring of a representative to assist in contract discussions with the Minnesota Twins. Following the suspension, Oliver promptly filed and won a lawsuit against the NCAA. The court found that the NCAA bylaw had not been enforced consistently and that the bylaw itself was contributing to the exploitation of student–athletes.

The ethical dilemma in the Oliver case revolves around a lawyer's involvement in contract negotiations on behalf of a person with NCAA eligibility remaining. The NCAA outlines in its bylaws that it wants to separate professional sport involvement and participation in intercollegiate athletics. It can be argued that when a student–athlete hires a sport agent or sport lawyer to represent him or her in contracts talks with a professional team, then the NCAA's line of demarcation has been crossed. Consider whether a student, such as a highly touted college basketball player, should be permitted to retain college eligibility after hiring an attorney and involving the attorney in contract negotiations with a professional basketball team.

PORTFOLIO

Complete the ethical issues portfolio activity in the OSG, consulting as needed the "Guidelines for Making Ethical Decisions" section in chapter 1.

Summary

This chapter has discussed how to identify legal issues that affect sport management operations and has introduced many basic legal concepts that affect sport managers. It has also identified and explained a number of ways in which legal issues influence the sport industry and has emphasized how important it is for sport managers to make effective decisions when confronting legal issues. To recognize and respond to legal issues successfully, effective sport managers must engage in critical thinking and prudent problem solving.

An effective sport manager must have a basic familiarity with the court system (e.g., constitutions, state law, federal law), legislative acts (e.g., Title IX, ADA), and myriad legal topics and issues (e.g., negligence, defamation). Moreover, because employment and sponsorship contracts are an integral part of professional sport and college athletics, sport managers and athletics administrators must be knowledgeable of and adept at working with the critical components of these agreements. Lastly, because of the increased litigiousness of our society, people are increasingly looking to the US Constitution for protection in asserting fundamental rights in issues related to sport. This chapter has introduced you to these and other legal issues that affect sport managers, sporting events, and sport organizations.

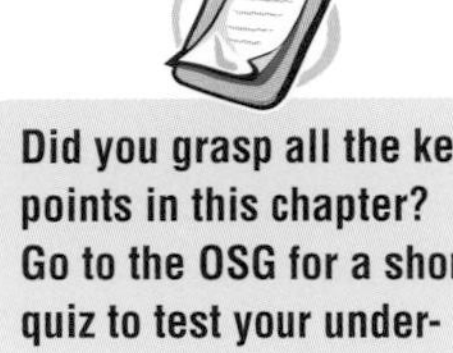

QUIZ TIME

Did you grasp all the key points in this chapter? Go to the OSG for a short quiz to test your understanding of the material.

Review Questions

1. Why does society need laws that govern behavior?
2. What are the four elements of negligence that the plaintiff must successfully prove?
3. What guarantees included in the US Constitution affect sport?
4. Can legal precedent of a sport issue in the state court of Ohio be used as the basis of a decision in the state court of Nevada? Please explain your answer.
5. Why is the concept of invasion of privacy based on intrusion, disclosure, and misappropriation? Provide an illustration of why a plaintiff may sue for invasion of privacy.
6. How have the ADA and Title IX legislative acts influenced the sport industry?
7. How has the establishment clause influenced prayer before competitive events or practices?
8. What are the benefits of contracts for sport organizations (e.g., athletics departments), nonsport entities that deal with sport (e.g., event sponsors), and sport personnel (e.g., coaches)?
9. What applications does tort law have to sport?

References

Americans with Disabilities Act of 1990, 42 USCA § 12101 et seq. (West, 1993).

Black, M.A. (2004). *Black's law dictionary* (8th ed.). St. Paul, MN: West.

Borden v. School District of the Township of East Brunswick, 523 F.3d 152 (3rd Cir. 2008).

Chemerinsky, E. (2006). *Constitutional law: Principles and policies*. New York: Aspen.

Connors, J.W. (2009). Treating like subdecisions alike: The scope of stare decisis as applied to the judicial method. *Columbia Law Review*, *108*(3), 681–715.

Deppe, G. (2009). *Not a prayer in protecting the reasonable observer: Borden shows the endorsement test is just not working*. Unpublished manuscript, Chicago-Kent College of Law.

Keller sues EA Sports over images. (2009, May 8). *Associated Press*. Retrieved February 2, 2010, from http://sports.espn.go.com/ncf/news/story?id=4151071

Koller, P. (2006). The concept of law and its conceptions. *Ratio Juris*, *19*(2), 180–196.

National Collegiate Athletic Association. (2008). *NCAA (2008–09) Division I manual*. Indianapolis, IN: NCAA.

Pederson v. Louisiana State University, 213 F.3d 858 (5th Cir. 2000).

Restatement (Second) of Torts (1963).

Rosenbloom v. Metromedia, 403 U.S. 29 (1971).

Santa Fe Independent School Dist. v. Doe, 530 U.S. 290 (2000).

Schwarz, A. (2009, February 12). N.C.A.A. ban on lawyers for athletes ruled illegal. *The New York Times*. Retrieved February 2, 2010, from www.nytimes.com/2009/02/13/sports/baseball/13ncaa.html

Slezak, J. (2008, April 10). *Judge rules against MHSAA*. Retrieved June 30, 2009, from www.bellevilleview.com/stories/041008/spo_20080410014.shtml

Spengler, J.O., Anderson, P.M., Connaughton, D.P., & Baker, T.A. III. (2009). *Introduction to sport law*. Champaign, IL: Human Kinetics.

Sport Agent Responsibility and Trust Act, 15 USC § 7801–7807 (2005).

Steeg, J.L. (2008, May 13). Lawsuits, disputes reflect continuing tension over Title IX. *USA Today*. Retrieved February 2, 2010, from www.usatoday.com/sports/college/2008-05-12-titleix-cover_N.htm

Ted Stevens Olympic and Amateur Sports Act, 36 USC § 220501 et seq. (2005).
Title IX of the Education Amendments of 1972, 20 USC § 1681–1688 (1990).
Unlawful Internet Gambling Enforcement Act, 31 USC § 5361–5367 (2006).
Wieberg, S. (2009, May 7). Ex-QB sues NCAA, EA Sports over use of athletes' likenesses. *USA Today*. Retrieved February 2, 2010, from www.usatoday.com/sports/college/2009-05-07-keller-ncaa-easports-lawsuit_N.htm

HISTORICAL MOMENTS

1926	Gertrude Ederle became first woman to swim the English Channel
1936	Jesse Owens won four gold medals in athletics at Berlin Olympic Games
1943	All-American Girls Professional Baseball League (AAGPBL) formed; disbanded in 1954
1957	Althea Gibson became first African American woman to win Wimbledon singles title and appear on *SI* cover
1968	At Olympic Games in Mexico City, Tommie Smith and John Carlos raised black-gloved fists on medal stands
1972	Title IX passed
1977	Shirley Muldowney won National Hot Rod Association (NHRA) Top Fuel Championship
1989	First *Racial & Gender Report Card* issued by the Center for the Study of Sport in Society
1997	Dee Kanter and Violet Palmer became first females to officiate a NBA game
1999	Women's World Cup match between the United States and China drew 90,000 spectators in Rose Bowl
2002	Esera Tuaolo, former Green Bay Packers and Minnesota Vikings player, publicly announced that he is gay
2006	WNBA celebrated 10th anniversary
2008	Mean number of women's sport teams per college or university reached 8.65, up from 2.5 in 1972
2008	NCAA prohibited member use of Native American mascots
2010	Super Bowl became the most viewed television program of all time in the United States

Photo courtesy of Bowling Green State University.

18

SOCIOLOGICAL ASPECTS OF SPORT

Nicole M. LaVoi ■ Mary Jo Kane

LEARNING OBJECTIVES

1. Define sport sociology and its importance for sport managers.
2. Discuss the social and cultural significance of sport in our society.
3. Identify positive and negative social effects of sport.
4. Discuss significant research findings in sport sociology pertaining to sexism, racism, and homophobia.
5. Discuss patterns of leadership in sport and media coverage patterns based on gender and race.
6. Discuss race logic and stacking in sport.
7. Discuss how homophobia affects athletes and sport practitioners.

Key Terms

empirical
gender roles
heterosexism
homophobia
race logic
role learning
socialization
sport sociology
stacking
Title IX

GET A JOB!

☑ Continue on your journey in sport management by going to the Online Study Guide (OSG) at www.HumanKinetics.com/ContemporarySportManagement. Check out the job opportunities and consider the skills and experiences that can help you succeed in sport management.

sport sociology—The scientific investigation of relationships, social interactions, and culture that are created, maintained, changed, and contested in and through sport.

An important step in becoming a successful sport manager is gaining in-depth awareness of sport as a social, political, and economic activity that permeates our society and influences both institutions and individuals in a variety of ways. To understand the complex dynamics of how and why people participate in sport and physical activity, you must have knowledge about both individual behavior (e.g., psychological aspects such as motivation to participate) and the social context in which that behavior occurs. For nearly 40 years, the scientific investigation of the relationships and social worlds that individuals create, maintain, change, and contest in and through sport has been at the heart of an academic discipline called **sport sociology.**

The purpose of this chapter is to define sport sociology and highlight several domains of scholarly inquiry within this discipline. Particular attention is devoted to the areas where sport sociology and sport management intersect. Knowledge in this area can help you address social challenges, especially as those challenges relate to real-world concerns such as racism, sexism, and changing gender roles.

Defining Sport Sociology

Given that sport is a significant part of many societies of the world, it is not surprising that scholars would be interested in studying its dimensions, scope, and influence. According to Coakley (2009), sport sociology is the "subdiscipline of sociology that studies sports as social phenomena" (p. 11). Sport sociologists rely on sociological theories and concepts to examine institutions and organizations (e.g., the International Olympic Committee [IOC]), microsystems (e.g., women's professional basketball teams), or subcultures (e.g., sport gamblers). As part of their analyses, sport sociologists do not typically focus on the behavior of specific individuals. Instead, they examine the social patterns, structures, and organizations of groups actively engaged in sport and physical activity.

An underlying assumption of sport sociology is that sport is an important institution of the same magnitude as the family, the educational system, and our political structure. A fundamental goal of sport sociology is to describe the complex dynamics surrounding patterns of participation (e.g., the number of girls versus the number of boys involved in youth sports) and social concerns (e.g., an overemphasis on winning that may lead to the use of steroids) that make up this all-pervasive institution (Eitzen & Sage, 2009). Keep in mind that sport sociologists do far more than describe sport involvement by, for example, gathering data on how many people participate on an annual basis. They are ultimately concerned with understanding the social context in which this participation occurs, as well as the meaning of sport as an influential social, political, and economic institution.

Social Significance of Sport

Did you ever wonder why local television newscasts describe their content as "News, Weather, and Sports"? Why not "News, Weather, and Technology"? Why do they not highlight education? Or literature? Did you even wonder why so many families spend discretionary resources and time at youth sport events? Have you ever wondered why advertising rates during the National Football League's (NFL) Super Bowl are so astronomical? The entry cost for some 30-second ads for the 2010 Super Bowl eclipsed US$3.0 million, or US$100,000 per second! Perhaps it is because sport influences almost every aspect of our lives. Undeniably, billions of corporate and personal dollars are spent annually on sport-related products and services each year. In fact, in 2005 US$13.2 billion was spent on licensed sport merchandise (Sporting Goods Manufacturers Association, 2006), which demonstrates the sport industry has an enormous economic impact on US society.

Another way the significance of sport is highlighted is to see how individual acts and governance often come to symbolize broader social concerns. Some examples of this include racism (e.g., in 2008 the National Collegiate Athletic Association [NCAA] prohibited member use of Native American mascots), sexism (e.g., the public debate on whether Michelle Wie should compete on the PGA Tour), criminal behavior (e.g., NFL quarterback Michael Vick's involvement in dog fighting), and drug use and abuse (e.g., alleged steroid use among players in Major League Baseball [MLB] and the ensuing US Congressional hearings). These examples clearly indicate that sport holds a prominent place in our society and that the consumption, valuation, and participation of sports have potential for both positive and negative outcomes and consequences. Sport can be a place where sexism, racism, homophobia, and violence occur and are perpetuated. Keep in mind, however, that sport also has incredible potential to serve as a vehicle for positive youth development and social change.

Does the popularity of the Super Bowl justify the cost of TV ads aired during the game?
Photo courtesy of Paul M. Pedersen.

BENEFITS OF SPORT

Clearly, sport shapes and maintains many social values that are held in high regard, such as hard work and fair play, self-discipline, sacrifice and reliance, and commitment to oneself and others. Research documents that sport participation can lead to greater health and well-being, as well as social, emotional, moral, physical, and psychological development (LaVoi & Wiese-Bjornstal, 2007). In short, sport has the potential to contribute to the positive development and stability of both individuals and society as a whole (Coakley, 2009).

Sport as a Socializing Agent

The socialization process refers to the various ways in which a society's dominant values, attitudes, and beliefs are passed down from generation to generation. **Socialization** also pertains to the process of starting, continuing, changing, and discontinuing sports, as well as the effect of sport participation on the individual (Coakley, 2009). Children learn from coaches, parents, teachers, peers, and siblings about what is normative, important, valued, and expected in a sport context—which helps children construct meaning of their experiences. In addition, what and who are portrayed in the sport media communicate values and attitudes to consumers and spectators about what is important.

socialization—The process by which people learn and develop through social interactions and come to know the environment around them.

Sport as a Unifier

Sport can bring people together by giving them a sense of personal identity, as well as feelings of group membership and social identification (Eitzen & Sage, 2009). For example, many US citizens must have felt unified around the 2010 NFL Super Bowl, which was the most-viewed television program of all time in the United States, with 106.5 million viewers ("Game Sets Viewer," 2010). Sport accomplishes feelings of unity in a number of additional ways, from the individual level (e.g., an athlete who feels that she is part of something bigger than herself because she is a University of Minnesota Golden Gopher), to the regional level (e.g., in 2006 citizens of Louisiana rebuilt a sense of community and stability after Hurricane Katrina by rallying around the NFL's New

Orleans Saints [who played in the 2010 Super Bowl]), to the national and international levels (e.g., the entire nation rooting for athletes in the Olympic Games). Few, if any, institutions can unite people the way that sport does, largely because the popularity of sport cuts across social categories like race and class.

DARK SIDE OF SPORT

Although sport can produce unity and beneficial outcomes for both individuals and society as a whole, involvement in sport does not bring only good things; it can also be exclusionary and divisive in terms of race, class, gender, age, ability, and sexual orientation—and their complex intersections. For example, not all families can afford the rising pay-to-play fees of professionalized youth sport. Seats inside professional sport stadiums funded by public tax dollars are so expensive that only a small minority of people can afford to attend a game in the very stadium that they helped fund! Participation rates are lowest and the number of barriers to sport participation and physical activity are greatest for underserved girls—girls for whom geography, class, race, gender, and ethnicity intersect (LaVoi & Thul, 2009). Although a change in cultural beliefs pertaining to impaired athletes is occurring, improvements in access and accommodation for impaired athletes have come slowly.

As is apparent, sport participation can have a darker side. This dark side of participation includes such aspects as sexual and emotional abuse of athletes, burnout, dropout, steroid use, chronic injuries, and eating disorders. Anxiety, yet another issue in sport participation, can result from a win-at-all-cost philosophy that characterizes the pressure-cooker world of big-time athletics. Furthermore, the same inclination increasingly characterizes youth sport. Besides the concerns just listed, research findings from sport sociology highlight four areas of sport that reflect and contribute to some of the most troubling aspects of the United States as we move into the second decade of the 21st century—sexism, homophobia and heterosexism, and racism.

Sexism in Sport

In the wake of the modern feminist movement that began in the early 1970s, a number of women's roles expanded into areas traditionally occupied by men; the world of sport was no exception. As you learned in chapters 7, 8, and 17, **Title IX** of the Education Amendments Act was passed in the United States in 1972. This landmark federal legislation was designed to prohibit sex discrimination in educational settings (Suggs, 2005). Since its passage and implementation, enormous changes in the world of women's sports have taken place. For example, substantial gains have occurred in the number of sports offered, access to sport-related scholarships and facilities, and overall athletics budgets.

Title IX—Federal legislation passed in 1972 that amended the 1964 Civil Rights Act and was designed to prohibit sex discrimination in educational settings.

WEB **Go to the OSG and complete the first Web search activity, which has you analyze the outcomes of Title IX.**

Female Patterns of Sport Participation

With respect to sports offered on a nationwide basis, in 2008 the average number of teams (per college or university) that was available for women was 8.65, an all-time high. Compare that with 1972, when the average number was 2.5 sports per school (Acosta & Carpenter, 2008). The National Federation of State High School Associations (NFHS, 2010) reported that over three million girls (3,114,091) are now involved in interscholastic sports nationwide, compared with only 298,000 before Title IX. From information obtained from the National Center for Education Statistics (NCES) and the NCAA, the Women's Sports Foundation (2008) reported that 49% of high school participants are girls and 43% of all NCAA participants are women (compared with only 15% in the early 1970s). And more than just participation rates have skyrocketed in the wake of Title IX; the number of fans is exploding as well. Consider women's college basketball, one of the most popular women's sports around; 98.8% of member

NCAA institutions have a women's basketball team. In 2007–08, women's basketball fans in all three divisions broke attendance records, and the overall total topped 11 million fans for the first time in history (National Collegiate Athletic Association, 2008a). Attendance for the sport has increased for 25 consecutive years. Growth at the professional level is evidenced by the 14th season of the Women's National Basketball Association (WNBA) in 2010. These statistics make it clear that because of Title IX, millions of girls and women are participating in and consuming a variety of sports at all levels in unprecedented numbers.

Resources Allocated to Female Collegiate Athletes

Although women have made enormous progress in sport, assuming that they have attained equality would be a mistake. Consider the following examples. Over three decades after the passage of Title IX, women received 45% of athletic scholarships at the intercollegiate level, even though they represented 57% of all undergraduates nationwide (Women's Sports Foundation, 2008). Although 45% is a vast improvement from the pre–Title IX era, females received US$166 million less in scholarship money than their male counterparts did (National Collegiate Athletic Association, 2008b). Moreover, athletics budgets, salaries for coaches and athletics administrators, and access to facilities are nowhere near an equitable ratio. At the college level, women's programs in NCAA schools receive about one-third of the recruiting and operating budgets, which amounts to US$1.55 billion less than men's programs receive. These disparities not only put women's sports at a distinct disadvantage in building successful programs but also send a powerful message about which sports (and athletes) are considered the real or most important ones. These inequalities are particularly troubling given that most sports programs are housed within public institutions.

Women in Positions of Leadership in Sport

Ironically, with respect to leadership positions in women's sports, women have lost far more than they have gained since the passage of Title IX. In terms of national trends, before 1972 over 90% of all head coaches in women's athletics were female; in 2008 that figure was just 42.8% (Acosta & Carpenter, 2008). And although the overall number of head coaching positions in women's sports has increased dramatically since the mid-1980s, males have benefited from this increase far more than their female counterparts have. For example, in college sports only 20% of head coaches are female, and females continue to represent only 2 to 3% of the coaches in men's sports (Acosta & Carpenter, 2008). At the professional level, the WNBA is the only sport league to have any female head coaches, but even then, in the 2009 season only 5 of the 14 head coaches were women.

The picture for women in key administrative positions in women's sports is even more disturbing. Research indicates that before Title IX, women occupied the vast majority (over 90%) of all athletics director positions throughout women's intercollegiate sports. In 2008, however, they accounted for only 21.3% of those same administrative positions (Acosta & Carpenter, 2008). In professional sports, females in positions of power outside the WNBA are rare. Similarly, females make up less than 10% of the Associated Press sports editors, assistant sports editors, columnists, and sport reporters (Lapchick, 2009)—the people who decide what and how to write about sport.

These facts make it undeniably clear that in terms of employment opportunities, particularly in high-ranking leadership positions, men have fared far better under Title IX than women have. Even more troubling is that in spite of women's increasing experience and expertise, they remain only a token presence as leaders in men's sports and fight an uphill battle as leaders in women's sports. Some have suggested that this employment trend occurred (and persists) because men are better qualified, but **empirical** evidence does not support this belief. On the contrary, studies have indicated that

empirical—Knowledge based on experimental method and observation versus theory or supposition.

Women and Sport Leadership in New Zealand

By Sarah Leberman • NEW ZEALAND
Massey University

In 1893 New Zealand became the first country to give women the vote. As a result, a key cultural myth and official ideology concerning New Zealand is that society is, was, and should be egalitarian where everybody is entitled to a "fair go," irrespective of race, gender, or social class. As an institutionalized, privileged, cultural practice in New Zealand, sport has the potential to mirror this fair-go ideology. Deeper investigation, however, indicates that sport frequently does not represent this ideology, especially in leadership opportunities.

As an International Olympic Committee (IOC) member country, New Zealand strives to meet IOC objectives. One of the IOC's core objectives is gender equity in Olympic sports. In 1996, as a reflection of concern about the low level of women's involvement in decision-making roles within member sports organisations, the IOC set a goal to achieve a 20% participation rate of women in decision-making positions in national and international sport organisations by the end of 2005.

In 2007 research conducted under the auspices of the New Zealand Olympic Committee (NZOC) found that only 11% of paid chief executive officers (CEOs) of sport organisations were female. The sports of basketball, gymnastics, rowing, tennis, and triathlon all had less than 20% female board representation, despite the fact that 50% or more of the participants in those sports were women. By 2008 the percentage of paid female CEOs had increased to 19%. Disappointingly, however, only 44% of the executive boards met the IOC standard of 20% female representation, and 21% of the boards had no women representatives at all. In addition, although women constituted 50% or more of the athletes in badminton, rowing, swimming, tennis, and triathlon, none of those boards met the IOC goal of 20% female representation.

Photo courtesy of Hockey New Zealand.

Hilary Poole, CEO of Hockey New Zealand, is one of the few female leaders of sport organisations in New Zealand.

The New Zealand Olympic Committee (2008) study identified several barriers that were preventing women from participating in senior roles:

gender roles—A set of perceived behavioral norms associated particularly with males or females, in a given social group or system.

role learning—A social process by which children learn various roles, such as neighbor, friend, student, sibling, daughter, or son, and the characteristics associated with them.

women are often as qualified, or more qualified, than their male counterparts. Such hiring practices are rooted in "assumptions that are frequently made about employment roles and women's and men's perceived abilities to cope within those roles" (Shaw & Hoeber, 2003, p. 348). These findings suggest that sport is still a place that produces and reinforces male power (Fink, 2008) as well as perpetuates harmful gender stereotypes and traditional **gender roles** (Cunningham, 2008). The underrepresentation of females in positions of power exists even though research indicates that gender and marital and lifestyle status do not significantly affect a person's organizational commitment (Turner & Chelladurai, 2005).

Why does it matter that fewer women occupy leadership positions? In the absence of visible female role models (**role learning**), females may devalue their own abilities,

- Lack of women mentors
- Career breaks for domestic reasons
- Lack of women role models and peers
- Confidence in own ability
- Lack of childcare
- Unconscious discrimination from both males and females

The IOC's position is that the active involvement of women in sport management will lead to higher quality decision making. Additionally, unless women are in leadership positions at the national level, they are not likely to contribute at the international level. In line with the IOC philosophy and recommendations, therefore, the NZOC has developed a plan of action through its Women in Sport Committee to encourage women into leadership roles. These interventions include

- mentoring and role modelling programmes,
- strategies to build the confidence of capable women candidates, and
- social marketing that promotes the benefits of balanced decision making and leadership.

The NZOC encourages sport organisations to be mindful of the value of diversity when filling leadership positions. To quantify the results of the NZOC appeal, the Women in Sport Committee plans to continue monitoring women's representation in sport leadership positions on an annual basis.

INTERNATIONAL LEARNING ACTIVITY #1

Investigate the percentage of women serving as CEOs of sport organizations in your country. Then find the percentage of women participating on national sports teams in your country. With respect to the ratio between female CEOs and female participants, how does your country compare with New Zealand?

INTERNATIONAL LEARNING ACTIVITY #2

Read Scott Poynting's article "Bulldog Whistling: Criminalization of Young Lebanese-Australian Rugby League Fans," which is posted at www.internetjournalofcriminology.com/Poynting%20-%20Bulldogwhistling.pdf. Summarize the article and explain how the collective behavior of some fans resulted in the racial stereotyping of those labeled as deviant.

accept negative stereotypes, fail to realize their potential, and limit their own sport career aspirations. Access and exposure to female role models in positions of leadership (i.e., power) is particularly important to girls, because they have fewer such role models in their lives than their male counterparts do, especially in sport contexts (Hums, Bower, & Grappendorf, 2007; Vescio, Wilde, & Crosswhite, 2005). To create social change and challenge stereotypical beliefs pertaining to gender, power, and leadership, females must be seen in equal numbers in all positions of power within the world of sport.

Media Coverage of Female Athletes

A number of female athletes have become household names because of sport media coverage over the last several years. Annika Sorenstam, Michelle Wie, Candace Parker,

Mia Hamm, Maria Sharapova, Serena Williams, Danica Patrick, and Dara Torres immediately come to mind. In spite of such progress, sport media scholarship over the past three decades has convincingly demonstrated in two important ways how mainstream media treat sportswomen and sportsmen differently. First, although females make up approximately 40% of all sport participants, they receive significantly less coverage than their male counterparts do—on average receiving only 6 to 8% of the total sports coverage regardless of the medium. Numerous studies have documented this pattern in newspapers, in magazines such as *Sports Illustrated* and *Sports Illustrated for KIDS*, on television and sports talk radio, and through new media outlets (e.g., Duncan, Messner, & Willms, 2005; Maxwell, 2008). This finding is true regardless of the period in relationship to Title IX, the age of the athletes, race, or the type of sport in which they are involved.

WEB

Go to the OSG and complete the second Web search activity, which has you look at and analyze differences in pictures of male and female athletes.

A second way that the mainstream media treat female athletes differently involves type of coverage. Numerous investigations (e.g., Kane & Buysse, 2005; Parker & Fink, 2008) have shown that the media portray males in an array of images and stories that emphasize their athletic strength and mental toughness, but present females in ways that predominantly highlight their physical attractiveness and heterosexuality rather than their accomplishments as athletes. Similarly, sexualizing highly skilled sportswomen makes up much of the commentary of male sports reporters.

Homophobia and Heterosexism in Sport

homophobia—An irrational fear, a contempt, or an antipathy toward homosexuals and homosexuality.

Sport scholars also examine one of the most oppressive aspects of sport—homophobia. Pat Griffin (1998), a leading scholar in this area, defines **homophobia** as a universal fear or intolerance toward gay men, lesbians, and bisexuals. Although significant progress has occurred in this area, especially in women's sports, stereotypes continue to link gender roles with highly competitive athletics, particularly in team contact sports such as basketball and football. Traditional definitions of masculinity (and heterosexuality) were synonymous with "real" athletes. In contrast, traditional notions of femininity—sugar and spice and everything nice—were, by definition, the antithesis of athleticism. As a result, athletes who challenged these stereotypes were often stigmatized as not "real" women or men.

Media Portrayals of Female Athletes

As stated in the chapter text, research has shown that the media portray female athletes in ways that predominantly highlight their physical attractiveness and heterosexuality rather than their accomplishments as highly skilled and dedicated athletes. Consistently, females are significantly more likely than males to be portrayed off the court, out of uniform, and in passive and sexualized poses. Take, for example, the "historic" *ESPN The Magazine* cover in the March 23, 2009, issue of the publication. The cover shot is of former University of Tennessee basketball standout and WNBA 2008 Rookie of the Year Candace Parker. The cover is historic because in the more than five years before Parker's cover, only 6 of the 168 (3.6%) of *ESPN The Magazine* covers featured female athletes. But how she was portrayed is the issue. A very pregnant Parker was pictured in a sleeveless white sundress alongside the cover headline "How Big Can Candace Parker Get?" The lead paragraph of the story inside started with "Candace Parker is beautiful. Breathtaking, really, with flawless skin, endless legs and a C cup she is proud of but never flaunts" (Glock, 2009, p. 28). Parker's *ESPN The Magazine* cover and cover story are classic examples of how the media continue to marginalize and sexualize female athletes, and perpetuate heterosexism. To view a picture of Parker's cover shot, go to gallery.pictopia.com/espnmag/gallery/69619/photo/espnmag:7889960/?o=13.

Homophobia and Women's Sports

Although homophobia is present in both women's and men's athletics, fears or concerns about being gay have long been associated with women's sports (Krane & Barber, 2005). Such fears range from historical assertions that women's participation will harm their reproductive capacity (and make them unable to fulfill what are presumed to be appropriate heterosexual roles such as wife and mother) to modern-day claims that athletic involvement (particularly those who engage in more "masculine" sports) will turn women into lesbians (Kauer & Krane, 2006).

Jennifer Harris, a student–athlete at Penn State University (PSU), experienced first-hand how females who engage in sports such as basketball and softball are automatically assumed to be lesbian. Harris, a member of PSU's basketball team, filed a groundbreaking lawsuit against head women's basketball coach Rene Portland, PSU, and the PSU athletics director for discrimination based on race, gender, sexual orientation, and invasion of privacy after she was kicked off the basketball team in March 2005. The university's six-month internal investigation found that Portland created an offensive environment and an aura of hostility and intimidation because of Harris' perceived sexual orientation (Leiber, 2006). A settlement was reached out of court, and Portland resigned in March 2007. Harris' sexual orientation? Straight. Kauer and Krane (2006) interviewed collegiate female athletes who, regardless of sexual orientation, experienced stereotypical labeling. One athlete in their study said, "It's if you're an athlete you must be a lesbian. . . . People will just flat out say, 'Oh a bunch of dykes'" (p. 46).

As this example indicates, those associated with women's sports, from athletes to coaches to athletics administrators, have often been stigmatized with the lesbian label. Given this reality, those involved in women's sports feel a great deal of pressure to act or appear to be heterosexual: "The underlying fear is not that a female athlete or coach will appear too plain or out of style; the real fear is that she will look like a dyke or, even worse, is one" (Griffin, 1992, p. 254). To counteract such fears, female athletes have gone to great lengths to assure themselves, their parents and teammates, coaches, and corporate sponsors that sport can (and should) be consistent with traditional notions of femininity and heterosexuality.

Research has demonstrated how homophobic beliefs and heterosexist practices (**heterosexism**) affect the lives of female athletes on a daily basis. Coaches and athletics administrators often pressure sportswomen to embrace a feminine image by dressing in skirts when traveling to out-of-town games and by wearing makeup and jewelry (Krane, 2001; Theberge, 2000). Players suspected of being lesbian may be dismissed from their positions on a team—and lose their scholarships—or could be passed over in the selection of elite teams (Iannotta & Kane, 2002). We should not underestimate the harmful consequences of the homophobic beliefs and practices that surround women's sports. Although conditions for lesbian athletes (and those perceived to be lesbian) are far better than they used to be, it still remains the case that being pejoratively labeled a lesbian is to be stigmatized as abnormal or deviant, and to be threatened with the loss of employment, career, and family (Krane & Barber, 2005). Note that this labeling process affects all female athletes, homosexual and heterosexual alike.

heterosexism—An ideology and a behavior that promote privilege for dominant groups (e.g, heterosexuals are the norm and are therefore better than homosexuals).

Homophobia also puts female coaches at risk. Administrators, colleagues, and even their own athletes often monitor coaches' personal lives. For example, when a coaching position opens up, search committee members may place private, discrete phone calls to determine a female applicant's sexual orientation (Griffin, 1998). Female coaches are particularly vulnerable to being tagged (or targeted) with the lesbian label because it can affect a critical part of their job—recruiting. A dirty little secret in the world of women's sports involves a specific form of negative recruiting in which a coach suggests to a potential athlete (or her family members) that another coach or team has a lesbian reputation (Iannotta & Kane, 2002). Recent high-profile Title IX jury verdicts, settlements, and cases at Penn State, California State University at Fresno, the University of California at Berkeley, and San Diego Mesa College have raised awareness about systemic gender inequities and homophobia at major colleges and universities (National Center for Lesbian Rights, 2009). Given such an environment and the strong (and understandable) desire of many lesbians to keep their private lives private, the subject of homophobia in sport rarely surfaces, at least on any large, public scale.

Homophobia and Men's Sports

Up to this point we have focused on how homophobia affects women's sports. But as all of us know, men's sports are particularly oppressive and intolerant when it comes to dealing with gay athletes. Scholars have suggested that this intolerance is due to the historical role of sport as a training and proving ground for males to establish their masculinity and manhood (Coakley, 2009). Because traditional definitions of masculinity are synonymous with athleticism, it is not surprising that being both a male athlete and gay is seen as a contradiction in terms (Anderson, 2005). Gay male athletes know this formula all too well. Former players such as Billy Bean in MLB, Esera Tuaolo in the NFL, and John Amaechi in the NBA are a few of the male athletes in major professional sports ever to come out, but all waited until their careers were over to do so. Tuaolo stated that he knew that if his teammates discovered that he was gay, "that would be the end for me. I'd wind up cut or injured." He explained that he "was sure that if a GM didn't get rid of me for the sake of team chemistry, another player would intentionally hurt me, to keep up the image" (Tuaolo & Cyphers, 2002, ¶ 5).

Although professional female athletes, such as Rosie Jones in golf, Martina Navratilova and Amelie Mauresmo in tennis, Sheryl Swoopes in basketball, and Natasha Kai in soccer have come out during their playing careers, to date no professional male athlete has ever done so. Given the experiences of Tuaolo—who says that he spent hours lying awake, praying for his anxiety attacks and ongoing depression to end—who could blame them? When a high-profile athlete does come out, it stimulates public dialogue—both homophobic and sympathetic—around what would happen if a gay male athlete came out during his playing career. It is naive to suggest that a safe, tolerant, and open climate will soon be a reality for gay and lesbian athletes. Nevertheless, we as a society should not abandon the principles that embrace social justice in all our institutions, including sport. To achieve that end, we should remember that the "problem" of gays in sport is not the presence of gay and lesbian athletes; it is the presence of homophobia.

John Thompson (left) and Bill Russell (right) are basketball legends who encountered some of the racism so deeply entrenched in the sport industry.

Photo courtesy of Paul M. Pedersen.

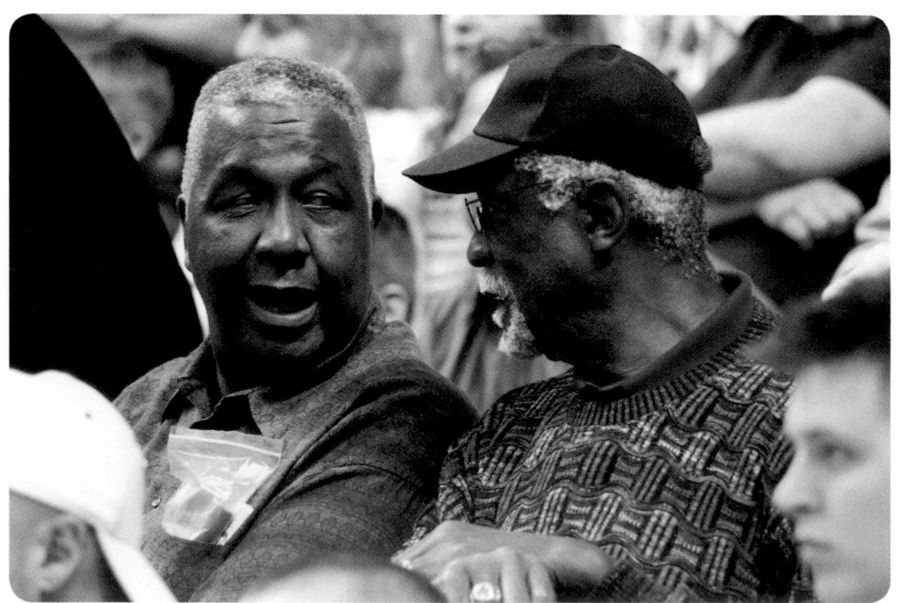

Racism in Sport

Since Jackie Robinson broke the modern color barrier in MLB in the 1940s, minorities have made important progress in all levels of sport. Even so, racism remains deeply entrenched throughout the sport world. Although sport sociologists have examined diverse ethnic minorities, the majority of research has pertained to African Americans and to the controversy related to the use of Native American mascots. Sport sociologists have identified four areas in which racial myths and prejudices about African Americans and other ethnic minorities in sport abound: assumptions about race and athletic ability, sport leadership, sport media coverage, and the role of sport in racially connected upward mobility.

Race and Athletic Ability

The popularly held belief that African American athletes owe their success to their "natural" athletic abilities suggests that they have some genetic advantage over Whites when it comes to achievement in sport (Buffington, 2005). A parallel belief is that White athletes achieve excellence because of their discipline, intelligence, and hard work. This attributional pattern is often referred to as **race logic.** Note, however, that when people of color dominate a particular sport, a strong need develops to explain this dominance, and a desire emerges to search for a "Black gene" or an "athletic gene" associated to race. Some scholars argue that the lack of visible professional success for African Americans outside sport, coupled with an overrepresentation in sport, has resulted in many scientific inquiries into the elusive athletic gene (St. Louis, 2003). Although the dialogue about the existence of the athletic gene has at times been contentious (see Hoberman, 2007; Spracklen, 2008), conclusive scientific evidence regarding the athletic gene does not exist. But when Whites dominate sports such as golf and tennis (Tiger Woods and Venus and Serena Williams being notable exceptions), the need to explain patterns of success based on the racial compositions of the players seems to vanish. A sport sociologist illustrates this in his discussion about snow skiing. "When White skiers from Austria and Switzerland . . . win World Cup championships year after year, people don't say they succeed because their white skin is a sign of genetic advantages," explained Coakley (2009). On the other hand, however, he noted that "the success of Black athletes is seen as an invasion or a takeover—a 'problem' in need of an explanation focused on dark skinned bodies" (p. 283). The implications for focusing on a genetic link to athletic success are far reaching. From a sociological standpoint, genetic-based reasoning ignores broader social and cultural explanations for ability differences such differential access, quality of coaches, community resources, and socialization.

race logic—An attributional pattern of athletic success in which Black athletes' successes are attributed to natural athletic abilities and genetic advantage and White athletes' achievements are attributed to discipline, intelligence, and hard work.

Racism and Sport Leadership

The second area and one of the most widely studied forms of racial discrimination in sport is a phenomenon called **stacking,** whereby minority groups are steered away from (or into) certain player positions that are more (or less) central to key decision-making and leadership positions on the field (Eitzen & Sage, 2009). For example, in MLB, while Whites have dominated the position of catcher, pitcher, and infielder—baseball's primary "thinking positions"—African Americans have been overrepresented in the outfield, in positions that rely on speed (Lapchick, 2009). In the NFL, African American quarterbacks such as Donovan McNabb and David Garrard are primarily drop-back passers yet are often described by the media as running quarterbacks (Buffington, 2005), a description that highlights physical characteristics. Similarly, NFL scouts rate African American quarterbacks higher on physical attributes (Bigler & Jeffries, 2008).

stacking—A disproportionate allocation of athletes to central (e.g., "thinking positions") and noncentral positions as a function of their race or ethnicity.

Although the number of African American quarterbacks starting on NFL teams has increased, the activities and attitudes surrounding stacking in sport have not been eliminated. If most African American athletes are, for example, steered away from critical decision-making positions such as catcher or quarterback during their playing careers, the practice reinforces the belief that African Americans do not have the leadership skills and judgment necessary to become coaches and managers. Stacking helps explain why, although progress has occurred, minorities remain underrepresented in proportion to the percentage of people of color in the population at nearly all levels of leadership positions in professional sports. To see the lack of racial diversity in positions of power in professional sports, look at the various tables within the links at the Web site for the *Racial and Gender Report Card* (web.bus.ucf.edu/sportbusiness/?page=1445). Racial equity is far from reality, but an example of progress is evidenced by the NFL's 2002 Rooney Rule, which mandates that each team include at least one person of color in the candidate pool for head-coaching positions. It appears that this rule has positively affected hiring practices. The number of African American head coaches in the league has increased from two in 2001 to six in 2008 (Lapchick, 2009).

As reported by Lapchick (2009), similar patterns of underrepresentation of minorities also occur in intercollegiate athletics. In fact, minority representation is even lower in intercollegiate athletics. In 2008, of the Division I athletics directors, 6.2% were African American men—nearly double the 3.4% representation in 2004. But little, if any, progress has occurred when it comes to selecting African American women to occupy leadership positions in intercollegiate sports. In 2008 few athletics directors (1%) and head coaches (4%) across Division I were African American women. The encouraging news is that all of the men's major professional leagues as well as the NCAA have undertaken diversity initiatives designed to increase the numbers of minorities and women in leadership positions. Such initiatives complement the advocacy efforts of Black Coaches and Administrators (BCA) to increase minority participation and employment, particularly in intercollegiate athletics.

Sport Media Coverage

A third area that reflects racial stereotypes of African Americans can be found in sport media coverage. For instance, scholars refer to one trend in media coverage as the hierarchy-of-naming pattern. This occurs when members of a less powerful group (minorities and women) are referred to by their first names only, whereas those in more powerful groups (White men) are referred to either by their last names or their full names. In a study by Duncan, Messner, and Cooky (2000), 90% of the cases in which male athletes were referred to only by their first names, the athlete in question was a person of color. Examples from professional sports illustrate this point. All of us know who Kobe, LeBron, and K.G. are, but we do not think of Peyton Manning, Steve Nash, or Sidney Crosby as Peyton, Steve, and Sidney. Although certainly not intentional, this type of coverage can reflect and perpetuate a lack of respect toward minority athletes.

Sportscasters in basketball and football consistently describe African American athletes as naturally athletic in comparison to their White counterparts, who are described as intelligent or hard working (Bruce, 2004; Rada & Wulfemeyer, 2005). In the 2000 Summer Olympics African American athletes were pictorially overrepresented in newspapers when they were competing in strength sports, whereas White athletes were overrepresented in aesthetic sports such as swimming (Hardin, Dodd, Chance, & Walsdorf, 2004). These subtle forms of sport media coverage perpetuate racial stereotypes and race logic, suggesting that African American athletic success is primarily attributed to physicality or athletic ability.

Sport and Upward Mobility

The fourth area dominated by racial stereotypes and myths involves the notion that African Americans and sport are linked together as part of African Americans' biological and cultural destiny, especially in certain sports (Coakley, 2009). Sport is often perceived as one of the more progressive institutions in the United States because of the prevalence, visibility, and success of minority athletes. Although African Americans constitute slightly less than 13% of the total population (United States Census Bureau, 2008), a majority of NBA (76%) and NFL (66%) athletes are African American. In short, the widely held belief is that sport—and in far too many cases only sport—offers a path to upward mobility. Americans hold this view largely because African American athletes dominate the most visible and popular sports and because athletes such as Kobe Bryant and Larry Fitzgerald earn astronomical salaries and endorsement contracts. In addition, for many years Americans have heard countless rags-to-riches stories about racial minorities making it in professional sports—from the Williams sisters to LeBron James. Probably for that reason, two-thirds of African American adolescent males believe that they can have a career in professional sports (Eitzen, 2006). How accurate are those beliefs? How often do African Americans succeed in the big-time world of sport?

Sport sociologists have addressed those questions by pointing out that although African Americans (particularly males) have been enormously successful in the most prominent professional and intercollegiate sports, the likelihood of having a professional sport career is "a dream for all but an infinitesimal number" (Eitzen, 2006, p. 178). Consider these statistics: Of all the professional sports available to men, African Americans have found the greatest success in basketball. Yet only a small percentage of high school seniors of any race continue to play football (5.7%) or basketball (3.0%) at NCAA institutions (Bracken, 2007). Additionally, Eitzen reported statistics from sociologist Wilbert M. Leonard, who calculated that for African American males, the odds of making an NBA team are 20,000 to 1 and the odds of playing for an NFL franchise are 10,000 to 1.

No one suggests that African Americans (and other racial minorities) should not strive for success in sport, despite the long odds against achieving and maintaining a professional career. But critics point out that achieving upward mobility is easier in other professions, such as medicine, law, education, science, and engineering. Equally important is the fact that people who follow such career paths have greater lifetime earnings than most professional athletes, who on average last 3 to 12 years in individual sports such as golf or tennis and 3 to 7 years in team sports such as basketball and football (Coakley, 2009). The late, great African American Arthur Ashe broke new ground in men's professional tennis. Although he used sport as a way to achieve success, Ashe understood the limitations—and warned against the dangers—of seeing sport as the only, or even the primary, path to social and economic mobility: "We have been on the same roads—sports and entertainment—too long. We need to pull over, fill up at the library and speed away to Congress, and the Supreme Court, the unions, and the business world" (Ashe, 1977, p. 2S). Unfortunately, over 30 years after those prescient remarks, the need for African Americans to fill up professions beyond the sport world remains in play—although the inauguration of Barack Obama as president of the United States may turn the tides more quickly. Besides examining African American involvement in sport, scholars in the field of sport sociology have spent a lot of time researching the controversy surrounding Native American mascots in sport. This controversy is examined later in the ethics section.

ACTION

Go to the OSG and complete the Learning in Action activity, which has you identify which sociological issue is at play in several scenarios.

SPORT AS A VEHICLE FOR SOCIAL TRANSFORMATION

Although sport certainly includes many problematic aspects, as highlighted in much of this chapter, it can also help us overcome injustice, prejudice, and oppression. Structured and reinforced with appropriate social values, the sport experience can instill people with a deep-seated commitment to make important and long-lasting contributions to society. Although we rarely think of sport in this manner, its enormous popularity, coupled with its ability to reach across social, political, and economic divides, make sport one of the few institutions that can serve as a catalyst for change. Perhaps the most celebrated example of sport as a vehicle for change occurred in 1947 when, as noted earlier, Robinson broke the modern color barrier in MLB and paved the way for countless athletes of color to participate across all levels of sport. We can only imagine what sport, and society, would be like if it were not for the contributions of athletes such as Muhammad Ali, Michael Jordan, Magic Johnson, Serena Williams, Candace Parker, Michelle Wie, and Tiger Woods.

Another area (and era) in which sport confronted society's ills and became a catalyst for significant change involved the turbulent 1960s. That period was marked by social unrest and assassinations of well-known leaders such as John F. Kennedy, Robert Kennedy, and Martin Luther King Jr. The decade was also a time of demonstrations in the streets and the killing of students on college campuses over US involvement in Vietnam. Against this backdrop, the 1968 Summer Olympic Games took place in Mexico City. During the Games, two African American athletes, Tommie Smith and John Carlos, who had won the gold (Smith) and bronze (Carlos) medals in the 200-meter dash, used the awards ceremony to protest racial injustice. During the national anthem, Smith and Carlos lowered their heads and raised their black-gloved, closed fists in a gesture that was widely seen (and criticized) as an African American power salute. Although they were stripped of their medals and vilified back in the United States, their protest brought to light many of the injustices faced by African Americans and (in some quarters) revealed the hypocrisy of America as the "land of the free." Sport sociologists argue that the protest of Smith and Carlos was not only one of the most memorable moments in Olympic history but also a milestone in the civil rights movement.

In the early 1990s, sport—and a celebrated sports figure—challenged existing stereotypes and helped to transform society. Near the peak of his career, Magic Johnson stunned not only the NBA but all of America with the revelation of his HIV-positive status. Before his shocking announcement, many Americans were aware that thousands of people had died from AIDS and that millions more were infected with the deadly disease. Although by that time the public knew that celebrities such as Hollywood icon Rock Hudson had died of complications from AIDS, education, treatment, and research about the disease remained almost invisible to the public consciousness. But that all changed with Johnson's announcement. Almost immediately, his medical condition and subsequent retirement from professional basketball became the lead story, not just in the world of sport but throughout society. The event was a dramatic illustration of the power and widespread appeal of sport. It clearly demonstrated how sport, and sport heroes like Johnson, could enable us to see AIDS as an American and world tragedy and allow us to move beyond the stereotypic and inaccurate perception that AIDS was confined to gay men and that contracting AIDS meant a death sentence.

Billie Jean King, a highly decorated tennis champion who participated in the Battle of the Sexes in 1973, founded the Women's Tennis Association and the Women's Sports Foundation and has been a pioneer in and tireless advocate of women's sports.
Photo courtesy of Paul M. Pedersen.

Another example of sport as a vehicle for change is women's increasing and widespread participation in sport and physical activity. Before the early 1970s and the passage of Title IX, many segments of society, including many kinds of sporting activities, were considered off limits to most females. But many women and their male allies began to push for greater opportunities and a more level playing field for any female who wanted to become involved in sport. Such efforts have made an enormous difference in the lives of countless girls and women, their families, and their communities. For the first time in US history, young girls, like countless young boys before them, grow up with a sense of entitlement to sport. They also experience the benefits of sport, from having a sense of identity, to being a part of something bigger than themselves, to facing (and overcoming) the physical, social, and intellectual challenges found in sport. Because of sport, girls and women feel a sense of pride and accomplishment, learn about their physical limitations and potentials, and create their own destinies, both in sport and in every part of society in which they participate. And because they do, we all benefit.

Finally, and perhaps most amazingly, sport has taken some initial steps in challenging homophobic beliefs and practices. By doing so, this all-powerful institution has created some safe space for gay and lesbian athletes, although it appears limited to individual sports like golf and tennis. Consider the case of Nike-endorsed professional basketball player Sheryl Swoopes. This four-time WNBA champion, three-time WNBA MVP, three-time Olympic Games gold medalist, and second openly gay player in the WNBA decided to come out publicly in 2005, although she had been out to her family and friends for many years. Her decision to come out to the world was one that she did not take lightly. "I'm just at a point in my life where I'm tired of having to pretend to be somebody I'm not," explained Swoopes. "I'm tired of having to hide my feelings about the person I care about" (Granderson, 2005, ¶ 2). Rosie Jones, a 20-year veteran of the LPGA, who publicly came out shortly before Swoopes did, revealed how sport and courageous athletes truly make a difference. "Many of them reminded me that times have changed," explained Jones (2004). "I wouldn't have this opportunity as an athlete and our society wouldn't be as liberated as it is if it weren't for all the professional athletes and so many others who have had the courage to come out of the closet." She added, "It certainly made my decision easier knowing that others had gone down this road before me. And all of their lives have been enriched as a result" (¶ 11).

IMPLICATIONS FOR SPORT MANAGERS

Sport sociology has a number of implications for sport managers. We have already discussed how individuals face challenges, both on and off the court, and in so doing gain feelings of self-worth and empowerment. We have also examined broader social issues like the various (and harmful) ways in which mainstream media portray female athletes, how racism is perpetuated throughout the sport world, and how homophobic stereotypes put coaches and athletes at great risk personally and professionally. At the same time, however, we have seen how the Olympic Games, professional sports, and big-time college athletics can unify cities and nations, and as a result, challenge and transcend bigotry and oppression. What all these scenarios have in common are people. And knowing about people is critical to success in sport management because the sport manager must understand the social context of sport and the meaning attached to that

Case Study

The way in which University of Minnesota sport managers used research findings to guide decision making provides a good example of how sport sociology has direct implications for sport management. Anthony Brown is the assistant director of the university's Department of Recreational Sports; his boss, James Turman, is the director. They submitted a long-range proposal for recreational sport facilities to the university planning office. To inform their decisions regarding number of participants, design issues, and other factors related to on-campus sport facilities, they examined longitudinal survey data from the National Sporting Goods Association (NSGA).

Findings from this survey provide nationwide participation rates related to age, gender, geographic location, and popularity of activity. Brown and Turman concluded that exercise for fitness and physical appearance will remain popular among college students. They also used the research data to conclude that in team sports, interest in basketball will remain strong, soccer will continue to grow, and participation in extreme sports and outdoor pursuits such as snowboarding and skateboarding will increase. Brown and Turman's use of research findings had a direct effect on their facility and program master plan—more soccer fields, facilities for roller hockey and in-line skating, a skateboard park, and inclusion of a climbing wall as well as another basketball gymnasium in the recreation center were included.

context in order to get people involved with and stay committed to a certain activity.

One example that relates to the positive and negative aspects of sport illustrates this point. As we have seen, females' mass participation in sport and physical activity is a relatively recent phenomenon. As we have also seen, many women who participated in the pre–Title IX era were stigmatized as not being real women. Yet we all know that people can gain tremendous benefits when they become involved in fitness or competitive sports programs. This is particularly true for females; adherence to sport and exercise can result in significantly lower rates of obesity and heart disease, and can serve as an important counterweight to depression or a negative self-image (Women's Sports Foundation, 2005). Clearly, getting girls and women interested in regular (and serious) physical activity and providing safe opportunities for them to do so is the right thing to do. But given historical definitions of what it means to be an athlete and a female, many older women may need a more proactive approach by sport managers to help them get, and stay, involved. Sport managers who understand and respect the concerns of older women can provide creative and sensitive sports programs that reaffirm not only the benefits of participation but also the notion that serious sport involvement can enhance, not undermine, participants' womanhood.

Critical Thinking in Sport Sociology

The following is a guest column ("Title IX Needs Change") by a male student that was published in a university newspaper:

> Title IX is not good for collegiate sports. Universities are decreasing the athletic opportunities for men in order to make room for various women's sports. There has been a net loss of more than 17,000 opportunities for men in collegiate athletics. Title IX is merely a law of proportionality. Schools need to keep the same ratio of male athletes to male students as female athletes to female students. This is not fair to men's athletics. Universities need to be concerned about the economics of athletics by focusing mainly on those sports that are the most profitable. This should be common sense.
>
> The university should be putting money toward those sports that will return the greatest profits, not using funds for state-of-the art women's athletic facilities. Earlier in the year the women's [sport withheld for privacy] team was promoting games for $1—$1 games . . . this is not a good investment. This sport does not attract fans. There are so few students that would go to a women's [sport] game for the purpose of being entertained. Most of those in attendance are family or friends that know the athletes. Now compare this to a men's [same sport] game. . . .
>
> I just don't believe it is fair for men's programs to be cut in order to have more women's sports. . . . The female teams that benefit from Title IX do very little to benefit the university on an economic level. These teams are financial burdens to the university. Title IX was never expected to last 30 years. The number of women in college has increased, so the number of females athletes needs to increase according to Title IX. This does not take into account the fact that there is a greater proportion of men interested in sports than women. Title IX is now a threat to the history of men's athletic programs across the country.

PORTFOLIO

Complete the critical thinking portfolio activity in the OSG, consulting as needed the "Eight Critical Thinking Questions" section in chapter 1.

Ethics in Sport Sociology

The debate over the use of Native American sport mascots has been contested over the last 30 years. According to Davis-Delano (2007), Native American mascots were used by five professional sport teams (i.e., the Atlanta Braves, Chicago Blackhawks, Cleveland Indians, Kansas City Chiefs, and Washington Redskins), approximately 15 to 20 colleges and universities, and more than 2,900 high schools, middle schools, and elementary schools across the United States. Among other ethnic minority groups who experienced historic marginalization and discrimination, the use of related mascots is absent.

The position of scholars and activists pertaining to Native American mascots is based on three major points—imagery reflects and reinforces stereotypes, representations harm Native Americans, and Native Americans have no control over such images (Davis-Delano, 2007). For example, the Chief Wahoo (Cleveland Indians) mascot is representative of images at the center of the debate. Stereotypical depictions and inaccurate portrayals of Native Americans assume two forms: untamed savages (Washington Redskins) or noble savages (Chief Wahoo). This unfounded dichotomy of Native American culture ignores the role that the US government played in the relocation and displacement of Native American tribes (King, 2004; Staurowsky, 2004).

In contrast, individuals and institutions who defend the use of Native American mascots claim that images are designed to honor local tribes (Hofmann, 2005) or have been supported by Native Americans (Cummings, 2008). Institutions have shown reluctance to comply or change their mascots to less offensive representations because they fear economic backlash from loyalist alumni donors (Williams, 2006). This controversy has inspired position statements from the US Commission on Civil Rights, the NCAA, and the American Sociological Association. But the NFL Washington Redskins, the team located in our nation's capitol, illustrates that the debate is far from over.

PORTFOLIO

Complete the ethical issues portfolio activity in the OSG, consulting as needed the "Guidelines for Making Ethical Decisions" section in chapter 1.

Summary

Sport sociology involves the scientific study of the social context of sport. Although sport sociologists study the various ways in which people participate in sport, they are primarily interested in the meaning of sport and its influence on our social, political, and economic institutions. Sport management is directly linked in theory and practice to sport sociology because both areas are influenced by the cultural and societal aspects of sport and physical activity.

Sport has great prominence in society, shaping and perpetuating many important social and cultural values. The social benefits of sport include teaching children positive social roles and unifying diverse groups of people as they cheer for a particular team. Sport can also engender feelings of self-worth and a sense of empowerment. But sport has negative aspects as well—sexism, racism, and violence both in and out of sport settings. Finally, sport may serve as a vehicle for social transformation. Sport figures can enhance awareness of and sensitivity to social problems such as AIDS, racial injustice, and homophobia.

Understanding and appreciating the field of sport sociology can provide an important foundation for understanding the field of sport management. To be effective, sport managers must be aware of the social aspects of sport. Considering that sport managers work with people in social settings, they must understand both individuals and their social environments because they are continuously interacting and affecting each other. Sport managers can play an essential role in developing safe, positive, and enriching sport environments. When they do so, people will participate more fully and effectively in all aspects of sport as athletes, employees, fans, clients, or consumers. As we have seen throughout this chapter, sport is a much-loved institution. The exciting challenge for sport managers is to harness that love in ways that emphasize not only sound management skills but also a sense of social responsibility that enriches us all.

QUIZ TIME

Did you grasp all the key points in this chapter? Go to the OSG for a short quiz to test your understanding of the material.

Review Questions

1. What is the definition of sport sociology, and how (and why) is it related to examining the social context of sport?
2. How and why do sports come to symbolize broader social concerns throughout society?

3. What do we mean when we say that sport is a socializing agent? How does participation in sport allow us to learn important societal roles?
4. What is Title IX, and how has it influenced participation patterns for girls and women on a nationwide basis?
5. Why has the number of women in key leadership positions in sport declined dramatically over the past three decades?
6. Do you think that stereotyping happens more often to African Americans or to Hispanics, or is the stereotyping just of a different type? Explain your answer.
7. How can homophobia negatively affect all women in sport, not just those who are gay?
8. What are some current examples of ways in which sport can serve as a catalyst for social change?
9. Why does sport sociology have significant implications for sport managers?

References

Acosta, R.V., & Carpenter, L.J. (2008). *Women in intercollegiate sport: A longitudinal, national study, 31 year update, 1977–2008*. Retrieved February 2, 2010, from http://acosta-carpenter.org/

Anderson, E. (2005). *In the game: Gay athletes and the cult of masculinity*. Albany, NY: State University of New York Press.

Ashe, A. (1977, February 6). Send your children to the libraries. *The New York Times*, p. 2S.

Bigler, M., & Jeffries, J.L. (2008). "An amazing specimen": NFL draft experts' evaluation of Black quarterbacks. *Journal of African American Studies*, *12*, 120–141.

Bracken, N. (2007). *Estimated probability of competing in athletics beyond the high school interscholastic level*. Retrieved February 2, 2010, from www.ncaa.org/wps/ncaa?key=/ncaa/ncaa/academics+and+athletes/education+and+research/probability+of+competing/methodology+-+prob+of+competing

Bruce, T. (2004). Marking the boundaries of the "normal" in televised sports: The play-by-play of race. *Media, Culture & Society*, *26*, 861–879.

Buffington, D. (2005). Contesting race on Sundays: Making meaning out of the rise in the number of Black quarterbacks. *Sociology of Sport Journal*, *22*, 19–37.

Coakley, J. (2009). *Sports in society: Issues and controversies* (10th ed.). New York: McGraw-Hill Higher Education.

Cummings, A. (2008). Progress realized? The continuing American Indian mascot quandary. *Marquette Sports Law*, *18*(2), 309–335.

Cunningham, G.B. (2008). Creating and sustaining gender diversity in sport organizations. *Sex Roles*, *58*, 1–2.

Davis-Delano, L.R. (2007). Eliminating Native American mascots: Ingredients for success. *Journal of Sport and Social Issues*, *31*, 340–373.

Duncan, M.C., Messner, M.A., & Cooky, C. (2000). *Gender in televised sports: 1989, 1993 and 1999*. Retrieved February 2, 2010, from www.aafla.org/9arr/ResearchReports/tv2000.pdf

Duncan, M.C., Messner, M.A., & Willms, N. (2005). *Gender in televised sports: News and highlights shows, 1989–2004*. Retrieved February 2, 2010, from www.la84foundation.org/9arr/ResearchReports/tv2004.pdf

Eitzen, D.S. (2006). *Fair and foul: Beyond the myths and paradoxes of sport* (3rd ed.). Lanham, MD: Rowman & Littlefield.

Eitzen, D.S., & Sage, G.H. (2009). *Sociology of North American sport* (8th ed.). Boulder, CO: Paradigm.

Fink, J.S. (2008). Sex and gender diversity in sport: Concluding comments. *Sex Roles*, *58*, 146–147.

"Game sets viewer, advertising marks." (2010, February 8). *ESPN.com*. Retrieved on February 9, 2010, from http://sports.espn.go.com/nfl/playoffs/2009/news/story?id=4897094

Glock, A. (2009). The selling of Candace Parker. *ESPN The Magazine*, *12*(6), 26–28, 30–32.

Granderson, L.Z. (2005, October 27). Three-time MVP "tired of having to hide my feelings." *ESPN The Magazine*. Retrieved February 2, 2010, from http://sports.espn.go.com/wnba/news/story?id=2203853

Griffin, P. (1992). Changing the game: Homophobia, sexism and lesbians in sport. *Quest*, *44*, 251–265.

Griffin, P. (1998). *Strong women, deep closets*. Champaign, IL: Human Kinetics.

Hardin, M., Dodd, J., Chance, J., & Walsdorf, K. (2004). Sporting images in black and white: Race in newspaper coverage of the 2000 Olympic Games. *Howard Journal of Communications*, *15*(4), 211–227.

Hoberman, J. (2007). African athletic aptitude and the social sciences. *Equine and Comparative Exercise Physiology*, *1*(4), 281–284.

Hofmann, S. (2005). The elimination of indigenous mascots, logos, and nicknames. *American Indian Quarterly*, *29*, 156–177.

Hums, M.A., Bower, G.G., & Grappendorf, H. (2007). *Women as leaders in sport: Impact and influence*. Reston, VA: NAGWS.

Iannotta, J., & Kane, M.J. (2002). Sexual stories as resistance narratives in women's sports: Reconceptualizing identity performance. *Sociology of Sport Journal*, *19*, 347–369.

Jones, R. (2004, March 21). Backtalk: First, a word about me and my sponsor. *The New York Times*, p. H9.

Kane, M.J., & Buysse, J.A. (2005). Intercollegiate media guides as contested terrain: A longitudinal analysis. *Sociology of Sport Journal*, *22*, 214–238.

Kauer, K., & Krane, V. (2006). "Scary dykes" and "feminine queens": Stereotypes and female collegiate athletes. *Women in Sport & Physical Activity Journal*, *15*, 42–55.

King, C.R. (2004). This is not an Indian: Situating claims about Indianness in sporting worlds. *Journal of Sport and Social Issues*, *28*, 3–10.

Krane, V. (2001). We can be athletic and feminine, but do we want to? Challenging hegemonic femininity in women's sport. *Quest*, *53*, 115–133.

Krane, V., & Barber, H. (2005). Identity tensions in lesbian intercollegiate coaches. *Research Quarterly for Exercise and Sport*, *76*, 67–81.

Lapchick, R. (2009). *The racial and gender report card*. Retrieved February 2, 2010, from the University of Central Florida, Institute for Diversity and Ethics in Sport Web site: http://web.bus.ucf.edu/sportbusiness/?page=1445

LaVoi, N.M., & Thul, C.M. (2009, May). *Sports-based youth development for underserved girls*. San Francisco: Team Up for Youth.

LaVoi, N.M., & Wiese-Bjornstal, D. (2007). Girls' physical activity participation: Recommendations for best practices, programs, policies and future research. In M.J. Kane & N.M. LaVoi (Eds.), *The Tucker Center research report, developing physically active girls: An evidence-based multidisciplinary approach* (pp. 1–5). Minneapolis, MN: The Tucker Center for Research on Girls & Women in Sport, University of Minnesota.

Leiber, J. (2006, May 11). *Harris stands tall in painful battle with Penn State coach*. Retrieved March 3, 2009, from www.usatoday.com/sports/college/womensbasketball/2006-0511-jennifer-harris_x.htm

Maxwell, H.D. (2008). *Women's and men's intercollegiate basketball media coverage on espn.com: A mixed methods analysis of a complete season*. Unpublished doctoral dissertation, University of Minnesota, Minneapolis.

National Center for Lesbian Rights. (2009). *Sulpizio and Bass v. San Diego Mesa College*. Retrieved February 2, 2010, from www.nclrights.org/site/PageServer?pagename=issue_caseDocket_sulpizio

National Collegiate Athletic Association. (2008a). *Women's basketball attendance*. Retrieved on April 14, 2009, from www.ncaa.org/wps/ncaa?ContentID=1522

National Collegiate Athletic Association. (2008b). *2005–2006 NCAA Gender Equity Report*. Retrieved April 19, 2009, from www.eric.ed.gov/ERICDocs/data/ericdocs2sql/content_storage_01/0000019b/80/1/c7/71.pdf

National Federation of State High School Athletic Associations. (2010). *2008–09 high school athletics participation survey*. Retrieved February 2, 2010, from www.nfhs.org/content.aspx?id=3282&linkidentifier=id&itemid=3282

New Zealand Olympic Committee. (2008). *Gender representation in New Zealand Olympic sports*. Retrieved February 2, 2010, from www.olympic.org.nz/Resource.aspx?ID=11474

Parker, H.M., & Fink, J.S. (2008). The effect of sport commentator framing on viewer attitudes. *Sex Roles, 58*, 116–126.

Rada, J.A., & Wulfemeyer, K.T. (2005). Color coded: Racial descriptors in television coverage of intercollegiate sports. *Journal of Broadcasting & Electronic Media, 49*(1), 65–86.

Shaw, S., & Hoeber, L. (2003). "A strong man is direct and a direct woman is a bitch": Gendered discourses and their influence on employment roles in sport organizations. *Journal of Sport Management, 17*, 347–375.

Sporting Goods Manufacturers Association (SGMA). (2006). *Sport licensing white paper*. Retrieved May 23, 2009, from www.sgma.com/reports/137_Sports-LicensingWhite-Paper-2006

Spracklen, K. (2008). The holy blood and the holy grail: Myths of scientific racism and the pursuit of excellence in sport. *Leisure Studies, 27*, 221–227.

Staurowsky, E.J. (2004). Privilege at play: On the legal and social fictions that sustain American Indian sport imagery. *Journal of Sport and Social Issues, 28*, 11-29.

St. Louis, B. (2003). Sport, genetics and the "natural athlete": The resurgence of racial science. *Body & Society, 9*(2), 75.

Suggs, W. (2005). *A place on the team: The triumph and tragedy of Title IX*. Princeton, NJ: Princeton University Press.

Theberge, N. (2000). *Higher goals: Women's ice hockey and the politics of gender*. Albany, NY: State University of New York Press.

Tuaolo, E., & Cyphers, L. (2002, October 30). *Free and clear*. Retrieved February 2, 2010, from http://espn.go.com/magazine/vol5no23tuaolo.html

Turner, B.A., & Chelladurai, P. (2005). Organizational and occupational commitment, intention to leave, and perceived performance of intercollegiate coaches. *Journal of Sport Management, 19*, 193–211.

United States Census Bureau. (2008). *State and county quick facts*. Retrieved February 2, 2010, from http://quickfacts.census.gov/qfd/states/00000.html

Vescio, J., Wilde, K., & Crosswhite, J J. (2005). Profiling sport role models to enhance initiatives for adolescent girls in physical education and sport. *European Physical Activity Review, 11*(2), 153–170.

Williams, D. (2006). Patriarchy and the "Fighting": A gendered look at racial college sports nicknames. *Race and Ethnicity Education, 9*, 325–340.

Women's Sports Foundation. (2005). *Her life depends on it: Sport, physical activity and the health and well-being of American girls*. Retrieved February 2, 2010, from www.womenssportsfoundation.org/binary-data/WSF_ARTICLE/pdf_file/990.pdf

Women's Sports Foundation. (2008). *2008 statistics*. Retrieved February 2, 2010, from www.womenssportsfoundation.org/Content/Articles/Issues/General/123/2008-Statistics--Gender-Equity-in-High-School-and-College-Athletics-Most-Recent-Participation--Budge.aspx

HISTORICAL MOMENTS

1896	First modern Olympic Games held in Athens, Greece
1903	First Tour de France held
1904	FIFA established
1930	First British Empire Games (now Commonwealth Games) held in Hamilton, Ontario
1950	Inaugural Formula One World Championship held in Great Britain
1960	First Paralympic Summer Games held in Rome, Italy
1972	At Munich Olympics, Israeli athletes were taken hostage and killed
1975	First International Cricket Council (ICC) Cricket World Cup held
1976	First Paralympic Winter Games held in Örnsköldsvik, Sweden
1984	At Olympic Games in Los Angeles, Joan Benoit Samuelson won first Olympic women's marathon
1987	First Rugby Union World Cup held
1989	Hillsborough Stadium disaster—96 lives claimed during soccer match between Liverpool and Nottingham Forest
1991	First Women's FIFA World Cup held
1995	Bosman case changed soccer transfer rules in European Union
2002	Japan and Korea cohosted FIFA World Cup
2006	Inaugural World Baseball Classic held
2009	IOC awarded 2016 Olympic Games to Rio De Janeiro

Photo courtesy of Paul M. Pedersen.

A NORTH AMERICAN PERSPECTIVE ON INTERNATIONAL SPORT

Ted Fay ■ Luisa Velez ■ Janet B. Parks

LEARNING OBJECTIVES

1. Explain factors to consider when defining international sport.
2. Identify five key changes that resulted in the expansion of international sport.
3. Discuss three factors that have redefined international sport.
4. Explain how advances in recruitment and marketing have affected international sport.
5. Identify emerging economies that are attractive hosts for international sport competitions.
6. Critically analyze the issue of manufacturing sport products in countries that use sweatshop labor.
7. Discuss the effect on sport governance of corporate sponsorship, drug testing, assistive devices, and the inclusion of Paralympic athletes in international competitions.
8. Identify skills, experiences, and competencies that help aspiring international sport managers prepare for the job market.
9. Discuss three factors that will affect the future of international sport.

Key Terms

ambush marketing
BALCO
blood doping
EU
FIFA
GATT
GGSP
NAFTA
position player
Title IX

GET A JOB!

☑ Continue on your journey in sport management by going to the Online Study Guide (OSG) at www.HumanKinetics.com/ContemporarySportManagement. Check out the job opportunities and consider the skills and experiences that can help you succeed in sport management.

FIFA—Fédération Internationale de Football Association (i.e., International Federation of Association Football).

During the late 20th century, a number of events, companies, teams, and personalities transcended the isolation and limitations of regional and national recognition to become international sport brands across a broad cross-section of cultures, religions, and locations around the globe. International events (e.g., Solheim Cup, Ryder Cup, **FIFA** World Cups, Tour de France, Rugby World Cup, Olympic Games [Vancouver 2010, London 2012, Sochi 2014, and so on]), professional leagues (e.g., National Basketball Association [NBA], English Premier League in soccer, International Professional League in cricket), athletic apparel and shoe companies (e.g., Nike, adidas–Reebok, Puma), and sports teams (e.g., Manchester United and Real Madrid in soccer, New York Yankees in baseball) all share a high degree of global brand recognition. Like movie stars and musicians, athletes such as Candace Parker, Sachin Tendulkar, Lorena Ochoa, Kobe Bryant, Lewis Hamilton, Serena Williams, Ronaldo, Alexander Ovechkin, Sidney Crosby, Marta Empinotti, Usain Bolt, Michael Phelps, Venus Williams, and Yao Ming enjoy near cult status. Against this contemporary backdrop, this chapter will provide snapshots of individuals, organizations, and historical events that have shaped and will continue to shape the international sport industry in the first quarter of the 21st century. As you learn about the people, organizations, and events that have been prominent or are emerging on the international sport scene, we hope that you will gain a better understanding of the ever-changing and expanding dimensions of international sport. This chapter will also emphasize the special skills, experiences, and competencies that will help you, as a new sport management professional, gain access to a career in the management of international sport.

WHAT IS INTERNATIONAL SPORT?

We consider two factors in determining whether a sport is international: (1) the context in which an individual, organization, or event operates within the international sport enterprise and (2) the degree to which, or the regularity with which, action by an organization, event, or individual focuses primarily on the international stage.

With respect to the context in which an organization operates, it is clear that the Olympic Games and Paralympic Games, world championships such as FIFA's Men's and Women's World Cups, and major annual international events such as the Tour de France, the Ryder Cup, and the tennis Grand Slam events, are among the giants of international sport. The same is true for multinational sport product and service corporations such as Nike and adidas; sport marketing and representation agencies such as Octagon and International Management Group (IMG); and sport facility design and management firms such as HOK Sport, Ellerbe Becket, AEG, and Global Spectrum.

Assessing the degree to which an organization is engaged in international sport can be more difficult, especially if it operates almost exclusively in one nation or is only occasionally involved with international athletes or clients. Examples of these types of organizations include United States, European, or Asian-based professional leagues. For example, from a North American perspective, the NBA, Women's National Basketball Association (WNBA), Major League Baseball (MLB), National Football League (NFL), National Hockey League (NHL), National Pro Fastpitch (NPF), Major League Soccer (MLS), and Women's Professional Soccer (WPS) have a wealth of talented players who originate from all continents of the world. These leagues broaden their regional or national bases through marketing, branding, and broadcasting events to international audiences. They also recruit and market international players in hopes of gaining new international fans, start developmental leagues in various countries, and allow their athletes to play for their home countries during the Olympic Games or world championships. The creation of grand tours by some of the world's most famous soccer teams (e.g., Manchester United, Chelsea, Real Madrid, Arsenal, Liverpool, AC Milan,

FC Barcelona, Juventus) to play high-profile exhibition matches in the United States and China signals the recognition of the value of creating an international brand (Foer, 2004). Clearly, we can look at international sport in several ways. To avoid confusion, this chapter addresses only the organizations, events, and governance structures that are involved internationally on a regular basis or as one of their primary functions.

EXPANSION OF INTERNATIONAL SPORT

During the last two decades, sport enjoyed unprecedented international growth, mostly in the first-world economies of North America, Europe, and parts of Asia. This growth could be seen in (1) dramatic changes in the Olympic Games; (2) increased opportunities for women in sport; (3) the redefinition of international sport; (4) extension of international recruitment and marketing efforts; and (5) the introduction of countries from emerging economies such as Brazil, Russia, India, China, South Africa, and Turkey (BRICSAT) as potential hosts for major global sporting events.

Dramatic Changes in the Olympic Games

Between 1968 and 1984, several events occurred that produced lasting effects on the Olympic Games. Change began at the 1968 Mexico City Games with the compelling and symbolic Black Power salute on the medal podium by American sprinters Tommie Smith and John Carlos. The Summer Olympics of 1972, held in Munich, Germany, marked the birth of an international sport revolution. The West German government was eager to demonstrate its rebirth as a peaceful nation free of its dark past associated with the anti-Semitism of Hitler and the Nazis at the 1936 Olympic Games and the Holocaust of the late 1930s and early 1940s (Reeve, 2000). Even as the world watched the incredible performances of athletes such as triple gold and silver medalist Olga Korbut of the USSR in women's gymnastics and Jewish American Mark Spitz, who won seven gold medals in men's swimming, the prevailing idealistic sense that the Olympic Games were above international politics was about to be shattered forever.

WEB

Go to the OSG and complete the first Web search activity, which lets you investigate the legacy of the 2008 Summer Olympic Games in Beijing, China.

The perception that the Olympic Games were immune to the evils of the world changed dramatically on September 5, 1972, with the tragic murder of 11 Israeli Olympic athletes and coaches and a German police officer by Palestinian terrorists in the Munich Olympic Village. This 20-hour saga, watched by a worldwide audience of more than 900 million viewers, sent shock waves through the international sports establishment (Reeve, 2000). This horrific catastrophe permanently altered the safety and security procedures required for all subsequent Olympic Games and other major international sporting events.

The year 1972 also witnessed conflict between the competing principles of amateurism and professionalism in the Olympic Games. At both the Winter Games and Summer Games, some sporting goods manufacturers (e.g., adidas, Puma) were accused of under-the-table payments to alpine skiers such as Karl Schranz of Austria, track and field athletes such as Michel Jazy of France, and swimmers such as Spitz of the United States. Such payments challenged the concept of amateurism that had been carefully promulgated and fiercely protected by American Avery Brundage, who reigned as International Olympic Committee (IOC) president from 1952 to 1972.

The controversy involving individual-sport athletes, however, paled in comparison to the debate over inequities in team sports (e.g., men's ice hockey, basketball), wherein the USSR was accused of fielding professional teams against the amateurs from Western countries. The fierce debate over the eligibility of professional athletes to participate in the Olympic Games reached a flashpoint in 1972 because of the controversial upset victory by the Soviet Union (51-50) over the favored US team. This game marked the

BRASIL: SETTING THE STAGE TO BE A NEW SPORT POWER

By Ricardo João Sonoda • BRASIL
Nunes Federal University of Paraná

In the world of sport, Brasil is best known for its consistent performance and international recognition in men's football (i.e., soccer) and recently in women's football as well. Brasil's first football league was founded in 1902 in the city of São Paulo. Seventeen years later, in the 1919 South American Championship of Nations (known as Copa América since 1975), Brasil enjoyed its first of many significant football victories. A passion for football continued to grow and so did Brasil's level of play, as it became the only country to win five World Cups. Information about the sport industry in Brasil follows:

- **Popular sports of interest:** soccer or futebol, volleyball, car racing, tennis, boxing, skateboarding, martial arts, swimming, sailing, surfing
- **Major international sports and Olympic Games:** volleyball, swimming, vela, gymnastics, handball, athletics, basketball, judo, taekwondo
- **Major professional sport leagues:** soccer, volleyball, indoor soccer, basketball, car racing (automobilismo)
- **Famous athletes:** Arthur Antunes Coimbra (Zico), Edson Arantes do Nascimento (Pelé), Ronaldo Luis Nazario de Lima, better known as Ronaldo (men's futebol); Gustavo Kuerten ("Guga") (tennis); Ayrton Senna da Silva, Emerson Fittipaldi, Tony Kanaan, and Helio Castroneves (car racing), Marta Vieira da Silva, better known as Marta (women's futebol)
- **Leading sport manufacturer:** Olympikus
- **Major international sporting events hosted:** FIFA World Cup 1958, Pan-American Games 2007, FIFA World Cup 2014, 2016 Summer Olympic Games
- **Popular TV and sport media:** Globo TV (Rede Globo), SBT (Sistema Brasileiro de Televisão)
- **Sport newspapers:** The newspaper of sport (*Lance*), São Paulo newspaper (*Folha de São Paulo*), *State of São Paulo* (*O Estado de São Paulo*)

Football dominance, however, is just one aspect of Brasil's aspiration to be a powerful player in international sport. In 2007 the Pan-American Games (Pan-Ams) were held in Rio de Janeiro. Also, Brasil will host the 2014 FIFA men's World Cup and the 2016 Olympic and Paralympic Games.

PA Photos.

Members of Brasil's men's football team pose wearing their 2014 World Cup bid shirts.

first loss by a US men's basketball team in Olympic history. In response to this loss, some within the US Olympic Committee and Western European national Olympic committees accused the Soviet players of being quasi-professionals who were paid by their government. Many observers believed that the idea of sending NBA all-stars instead of the best US amateur collegians gained serious momentum as a result of this

These events combined with the successful development of elite athletes in other sports, such as volleyball, and the economic growth that the country has enjoyed make a strong case for Brasil as an emerging sport power.

The 2007 Pan-Am Games marked the important stage of Brasil's emergence on the international sport scene. The Pan-Ams, the largest sport event the country had ever hosted, were both successful and controversial. They helped Brasil develop its infrastructure through the construction of sport facilities, improvements in airports, and an increase in tourism. On the other hand, the fact that some Brasilians lived in poverty while the government spent large amounts of money on sport rather than on health and education created much discontent.

Brasil approaches hosting the 2014 Men's World Cup and the 2016 Olympic Games with much anticipation. These events will also bring infrastructure, security, transportation, and sport business that Brasil needs. The Brasilian government's position is that hosting the World Cup and Olympic Games will lead to better education, health, and international relations.

In Brasil, football is the moneymaking sport because it has exclusive access to and is supported by the national lottery. Other sports do not have this luxury. Tax incentives for companies that financially support sport in Brasil have helped the funding and development of the other sports. With respect to grassroots sport development, football clubs are taking the lead in international performance, sponsorships, and infrastructure.

Volleyball, another advanced sport, is administered by the Brasilian Volleyball Confederation, which sponsors national teams for both women and men. Other sports that are beginning to emerge among Brasilians are tennis, swimming, auto racing, and sailing.

For Brasil's potential to become a reality, it will be important to develop relationships among the government, private institutions, and companies with money to invest. Toward that end, Brasilian President Luiz Inácio Lula da Silva has expressed interest in talking with US President Barack Obama, because there seems to be interest in the capitalist model.

INTERNATIONAL LEARNING ACTIVITY #1

The Brazilian government spent US$4 billion on the 2007 Pan-American Games. This amount was 18 times more than had ever before been spent on the Pan-Ams. Many people in Brazil believed that in light of the poverty in some parts of the country, the money should have been spent on health and education. Others believed that the expenditure was justified because successful Pan-Am Games were crucial to a successful bid for the 2016 Olympic Games. Using the eight critical thinking questions presented in chapter 1, critically analyze this controversy.

INTERNATIONAL LEARNING ACTIVITY #2

Choose a country other than Brazil (profiled earlier) or the United States (profiled throughout this textbook). Using the Brazilian profile examined in this sidebar as a model, create a profile of your selected country by investigating its most popular sport activities, sport facilities, and famous athletes. Describe the prime sport exports and imports of this country, including the production of goods and services, the existence of prominent sport leagues and events, the development of players and coaches in particular sports, offices of international sport federations (IFs), and so on.

loss. A month after the 1972 Summer Olympic Games, the professionalism controversy deepened when a team of Canadian NHL all-stars challenged the reigning Olympic and world ice hockey champions ("amateurs") from the Soviet Union for the first time in history. The Canadian professionals barely emerged victorious in what ice hockey historians called, "The Series of the Century."

Title IX—A US law mandating equal opportunity for women and men in programs and activities that receive federal financial assistance.

A New Dawn in Women's Sports

The year 1972 also marked the passage of **Title IX** of the Education Amendments, a law that set off a revolution in women's sports in the United States and indirectly around the world. Title IX challenged male privilege within the Olympic movement and other international sport federations. As a result, by the time of the 2004 Athens Olympic Games, the level of women's participation in both the Summer Games and Winter Games as measured by the number of athletes, number of sports, and number of events had become nearly equal to that of men (King, 2005). In the 2008 Beijing Olympic Games, a new record was set as 42% of the athletes were women (International Olympic Committee, 2008).

A critical effect of Title IX has been the slow but steady growth in the number of women who are assuming leadership roles within international sport federations, including increased numbers of women being elected as members of the IOC. In 1995 then IOC president Juan Antonio Samaranch established a Women and Sport Working Group to advise the IOC Executive Board on policies regarding women's roles in international sport. This group, chaired by former US Olympian and IOC vice president Anita DeFrantz, became a full-fledged IOC commission in March 2004.

Redefinition of International Sport

During the latter 20th century, many aspects of international sport changed profoundly. Primary among those changes were the advent of corporate sponsorship associated with the Olympic Games, a shift in the balance of power, and the emergence of soccer as a worldwide obsession.

The Olympic Games Go Corporate and Professional

Faced with possible political and financial disaster, the IOC reluctantly altered its rules governing corporate involvement for the 1984 Summer Olympic Games in Los Angeles. For the first time in Olympic history, the IOC allowed the Los Angeles Olympic Organizing Committee (LAOOC), under the leadership of its entrepreneurial CEO, Peter Ueberroth, to charge significant fees for corporate sponsorship that included the use of the Olympic rings. The financial success of these Olympic Games touched off a sport marketing and event management revolution.

In 1985, yielding to increasing pressure to allow professional athletes to participate in the Olympic Games, the IOC eliminated all references to the term *amateur* and allowed each international sport federation (IF) to determine its own eligibility rules. This landmark decision opened the door for professional athletes to compete in both Summer Games and Winter Games and helped level the playing field between the state-supported athletes of the Soviet bloc and their Western counterparts.

New Kids on the Block: A Shift in the Balance of Power and Players

Over the past several decades, the balance of power in international sport has shifted dramatically with each breakthrough victory by an individual, team, or nation. Beginning with Australia's win in the 1983 America's Cup, to the Tour de France successes of American cyclists Greg LeMond and Lance Armstrong, to China's Chen Liu becoming the first Asian to win a World Ladies Figure Skating Championship in 1995, the previously predictable world of international sport has been transformed. Although the United States claims to have the best baseball league in the world, Team USA did not make it to the semifinals in the 2006 World Baseball Classic (WBC) and lost in the semifinals in the 2009 WBC. Although Japan took the crown in the 2006 and 2009 WBCs, the Caribbean island nations of Cuba, the Dominican Republic, and Puerto Rico emerged as serious baseball contenders in both years. Europeans have taken turns dominating the professional women's and men's tennis tours, while European, African,

Asian, and Australian golfers have consistently succeeded on the LPGA Tour and PGA Tour. Clearly, single nations or regions no longer dominate specific sports.

Soccer: The World's Sport Obsession

The period from 1992 through 2009 brought a dramatic shift in both men's and women's soccer. Teams from Africa, Asia, and the United States emerged to challenge the dominance of a few select European and South American teams. In 1994 the United States successfully hosted the FIFA Men's World Cup, played before record crowds of spectators (3.58 million) and television viewers (2.1 billion worldwide). Despite scandals and fan violence, soccer has continued to expand its presence globally. New professional leagues for men have formed in Japan, Korea, and China. An elite professional league in the United States was restarted with the MLS league in 1996, and the US team surprised many by finishing second to Brazil in the FIFA Confederations Cup in 2009. The 2010 FIFA Men's World Cup was awarded to South Africa and is returning to Brazil in 2014. Clearly, FIFA has successfully expanded from its traditional roots in Europe and South America to Asia, North America, and Africa.

In 1991 the first FIFA Women's World Cup was held in China. It was followed by the 1995 Women's World Cup in Sweden and the 1999 Women's World Cup in the United States, where over 90,000 fans watched in the Los Angeles Rose Bowl as a scoreless tie between China and the United States was settled by a shootout won by the United States. This victory gave the US team its second successive World Cup title. In the 2003 Women's World Cup, Germany defeated the favored Americans and thus joined the elite group of nations (i.e., United States, Norway, and China) that had ruled women's soccer in the 1990s.

Interest in soccer in Korea exploded after the country cohosted (with Japan) the 2002 FIFA Men's World Cup. The men's professional soccer league in Korea, the K-League, consists of 15 clubs, including the two teams featured here, FC Seoul and Incheon United.

Photo courtesy of Paul M. Pedersen.

The successful US hosting of the Women's World Cup in 1999 and again in 2003 had a tremendous influence on the popularity of the game with girls and women throughout the world. Players such as Mia Hamm and Brandi Chastain (United States), Su Wen (China), Sasi (Brazil), and Birgit Prinz (Germany) became well known. Endorsements, professional league contracts, and television deals became connected with the women's game for the first time. The ascent of the United States as a world power in women's soccer is often attributed to the role that Title IX played in supporting the development of sport for girls and women at the school, college, and elite club level. Following the 2003 demise of the Women's United Soccer Association (WUSA), efforts to create another league for women were undertaken by the Women's Soccer Initiative. As a result, the Women's Professional Soccer (WPS) league was established in 2007 and held its inaugural season in 2009, culminating in a championship by Sky Blue FC (Women's Professional Soccer, 2010).

Recruitment and Marketing

Changes in recruitment and marketing that began in the late 20th century have had a profound effect on the nature and conduct of international sport. Today, athletes and teams have numerous additional options, and consumers have enhanced access to their performances, products, and services.

Chan Ho Park, the first South Korean native to play in Major League Baseball, came to the Los Angeles Dodgers in 1994. Since Park's arrival, there have been more than 10 additional South Korean natives to play in the major leagues.
Photo courtesy of Paul M. Pedersen.

Recruitment

The recruitment and development of top players from nontraditional locations has accelerated because most professional sport leagues scout the world for talent. This practice is common among the elite soccer leagues in Europe, where many of the top players on professional clubs are not from the home region, from the home nation, or even of European origin. It is common to find South American, North American, Asian, Australian, and African players starting in the first division of premier European leagues. This trend is also seen among the top North American leagues. The NBA has players from Brazil, Argentina, Canada, Australia, Germany, Croatia, Congo, Nigeria, Senegal, Spain, Turkey, and China. Korean, Japanese, Caribbean, Latin American, Canadian, and Australian players are increasing in number in MLB. Players from Russia, Sweden, Finland, Czech Republic,

Slovakia, and other European countries are prominent in the NHL; Canadians and Australians play on college teams in National Collegiate Athletic Association (NCAA) softball; and an array of international stars from Europe, Asia, Canada, Australia, and South America participate in the WNBA and WPS.

With the appearance of NBA and European league professionals in world championship and Olympic tournaments and the recruitment of foreign players in Division I college basketball, players from Europe, Asia, Africa, and South America have become a greater presence in the NBA. In 2008, 85 non-Americans played in the NBA, 46 of whom were from Europe (*Stern Lays Out*, 2008). Many of the international athletes are stars in the league, including players such as Tim Duncan (US Virgin Islands), Steve Nash (Canada), Yao Ming (China), Luol Deng (Sudan), Manu Ginobili (Argentina), Tony Parker (France), Pau Gasol (Spain), and Dirk Nowitzki (Germany).

In professional baseball the 1990s produced an unexpected star in Hideo Nomo, a pitcher for the Los Angeles Dodgers of MLB's National League (NL). Nomo was the first Japanese player to play in the major leagues since 1963, when Masanori Murakami pitched briefly for the San Francisco Giants. In 1995 Nomo was named to the 1995 NL All-Star team and was the NL Rookie of the Year. In 2001 Ichiro Suzuki, another Japanese national, became an overnight phenomenon as the first Japanese **position player** in MLB when he won the American League's MVP award, batting title, and Rookie of the Year award in the same season. The success of Nomo and Ichiro set off a groundswell of signings of other Asian players by MLB teams (e.g., Kosuke Fukudome, Diasuke Matsuzaka, Hong-Chih Kuo).

position player—Any baseball player other than a pitcher.

The increasing number of international athletes who compete in elite North American–, European-, and Asian-based professional sport leagues continues to broaden the definition of what constitutes international sport. The leagues use the influence of these players to market to new audiences at home while expanding their teams' brands through the sale of broadcast rights, team merchandise, and other product extensions overseas. An interesting result of increased access to international stars has been a corresponding drop in fan interest and attendance within regionally focused professional leagues. For example, the rise of Japanese players in MLB has resulted in an increase in interest among Japanese fans in watching Japanese players play on television for MLB teams in the United States and a drop in attendance at Japanese professional baseball league games (Maguire & Nakayama, 2005).

In light of these developments, major professional leagues in soccer, basketball, baseball, and ice hockey have formed new working agreements. Leagues and franchises have sought to create a climate of cooperation and a more orderly international transfer of players. Both of these efforts have been affected by court rulings. In the early 1990s a number of Canadian- and US-based players migrated to the national teams of their ancestry, giving rise to issues over the eligibility of dual nationals to participate in the Winter Olympic Games. Issues involving transfer fees and freedom of movement of Russian and other European players to the NHL also developed. The case that laid the foundation for future decisions occurred in 1995 when Jean-Marc Bosman, a Belgian soccer player, challenged the Belgian Football Association and the European Union (EU) of Football Associations over their system that allowed only a certain number of foreign-born players on each professional club. In this case, the European Court of Justice ruled that transfer fees for out-of-contract, foreign-born soccer players who were transferred between clubs from one EU nation to another were illegal and represented a restraint of trade.

Sport Marketing as a Global Phenomenon

The international expansion of sport has set off a flurry of activity in sport marketing. In 1989 the NBA launched a global marketing campaign to expand the brand awareness of its teams, players, and league-licensed merchandise. This campaign was perfectly positioned to capitalize on the gold medal performance of the 1992 US Olympic men's basketball team led by the NBA's best. As much by design as by happenstance, Michael Jordan and Magic Johnson became even greater international sport icons. The NBA is now one of the most recognized sport brands in the world and is poised to consider expansion of team franchises into Europe in the coming years. Evidence of the success of the NBA's global recognition and its popularity among fans is the fact that in the 2008–09 season the top-selling jersey in China was Kobe Bryant's while Yao Ming's jersey ranked 6th in sales (National Basketball Association, 2009).

Successful and popular professional sport teams such as the New York Yankees and Manchester United have experimented with forming unique business partnerships to broaden themselves as worldwide brands, particularly in China. Even the ownership of these teams is undergoing a radical international shift from national to international investment and ownership control. In 2005 American Malcolm Glazer began the invasion of American owners in English Premiership with his takeover of Manchester United. British soccer fans and sport media were outraged by this action, which was seen as anti-British and could be compared with the purchase of the Yankees by a Russian business mogul. On the sport apparel side, in 2006 adidas purchased Reebok for US$3.8 billion in an effort to boost its position in the international sport marketplace and to blunt the stronghold that Nike, an US$18.6-billion competitor, had on the sport apparel and shoe markets, including Nike's 34.6% market share of the athletic shoe market (Lefton, 2009).

Emergence of China as a Sport Superpower

The most socially and politically significant sport-related event that occurred during the latter half of the 20th century was US President Richard Nixon's decision to use sport as a diplomatic tool by sending a US table tennis team to China in 1972. This historic event, which is often referred to as Ping-Pong diplomacy, marked the beginning of the normalization of diplomatic and economic relations between the United States and China.

Since that time, China has emerged as a new Olympic power, challenging the traditional powers led by the United States, Russia (formerly the Soviet Union), and other Western countries. China has invested heavily in a government-run and government-sponsored sport model that identifies children with talent in specific sports and then trains them intensively in residential training centers for elite and promising athletes.

Similar to its Soviet and East German predecessors, China, while not forgetting to support its burgeoning men's programs, has sunk significant amounts of money and other resources into developing its women's programs in numerous sports. These efforts to develop elite Chinese athletes have produced numerous medals, as evidenced by China's finishing third overall in total medals behind the United States and Russia at both the 2000 and 2004 Olympic Games and dominating the gold medal count in the Beijing Olympic Games. China also topped the medal count at the 2004 and 2008 Summer Paralympic Games, sending shock waves through the traditional Paralympic powers.

This strategy of developing winning international teams in a variety of high-profile sports has created a strong sense of national pride. It has also assisted the government in garnering increased international respect. Many believe that the ultimate winner in the emergence of China as a world player is the sport industry itself (Power & Allison, 2000). The potential growth in real gross global sport product **(GGSP)** for all segments of the international sport industry will come from new sport media and marketing opportunities, the rise of new professional leagues, the exportation of elite athletic talent, the incredible growth of new facilities of all types, and expanded sport manufacturing and product development. With this boom in the establishment of a new sport infrastructure for China, other segments of the sport enterprise, such as finance and licensing, will continue to accelerate. We will also see the creation of joint ventures and alliances between established US and European sport firms and their Chinese partners.

GGSP—The total economic output of the sport industry worldwide.

Emerging Economies

The end of the cold war and the dissolution of the Soviet Union and East Germany in 1989 helped spawn sport market economies in the new nation states of Central and Eastern Europe. A similar emergence of sport market economies has occurred in South America, Africa, the Persian Gulf States, and Asia. A vibrant global marketplace based on new sources and pathways in both the production and distribution of goods and services has stimulated a dynamic export–import exchange among many nations and regions. Sport is often seen as a universal product that bridges cultural differences, customs, and belief systems and thus is a vital part of the growing international business exchange (Larmer, 2005).

In the first decade of the 21st century, countries new to the international sport scene have positioned themselves as attractive for global commerce and, therefore, attractive as prospective hosts of international competitions. A shift has occurred from the so-called G20 group of industrialized nations to emerging markets in Asia (e.g., China, India) and the Middle East (e.g., the Gulf States of Abu Dhabi, Bahrain, Dubai, Qatar). Host countries have ranged from South Africa with the 2010 Men's FIFA World Cup, to Turkey with the 2010 FIBA World Basketball Championship, to Brazil with the 2014 FIFA World Cup and the 2016 Olympic and Paralympic Games.

CURRENT ISSUES IN INTERNATIONAL SPORT

As a prospective sport management professional, you need to be aware of many issues in international sport. In this section, we look at several concerns associated with international sport governance. (See "Ethics in International Sport" later in this chapter for discussion of another issue, the relocation of sporting goods manufacturing companies.) A key step on your journey into international sport is developing an understanding of complicated international sport governance structures (see figure 19.1). Eligibility for each Olympic-related sport is governed and controlled by an international sport federation (IF) and its related national sport governing federation or body (NSF or NGB). Note that the IFs have relationships with the IOC, but they are not formally part of the IOC. These federations, therefore, sometimes differ with the IOC with respect to rules of control, athlete eligibility, and drug-testing procedures and consequences.

Before 1985 international sport focused on amateur sports that were included in the Olympic Games, Commonwealth Games, or hemispheric games (e.g., Asian Games, Pan-African Games, Pan-American Games). Over the past 25 years a number of new entities have become involved in international sport governance. These changes reflect the evolution of international sport from a relatively small number of organizations that emphasized amateur sport to a highly complex set of interrelated organizations with billions of US dollars at stake. The principal additions include (1) professional sport organizations, such as sport franchises, leagues, tours, and circuits; (2) professional athlete unions (PAUs), along with professional athlete representatives (PARs); (3) the Court of Arbitration for Sport (CAS), which adjudicates issues such as international athlete eligibility and breaches of fair play; (4) the World Anti-Doping Agency (WADA), an independent testing and research organization designed to eliminate the use of banned performance-enhancing substances and techniques from international sport competition; and (5) sport organization and event sponsors that provide critical support and funding to athletes, organizations, and events.

Numerous problems confront the governance of international sport. The following sections focus on four primary issues: corporate sponsorship, drug testing and arbitration, the use of assistive devices, and concerns associated with the Paralympic Games.

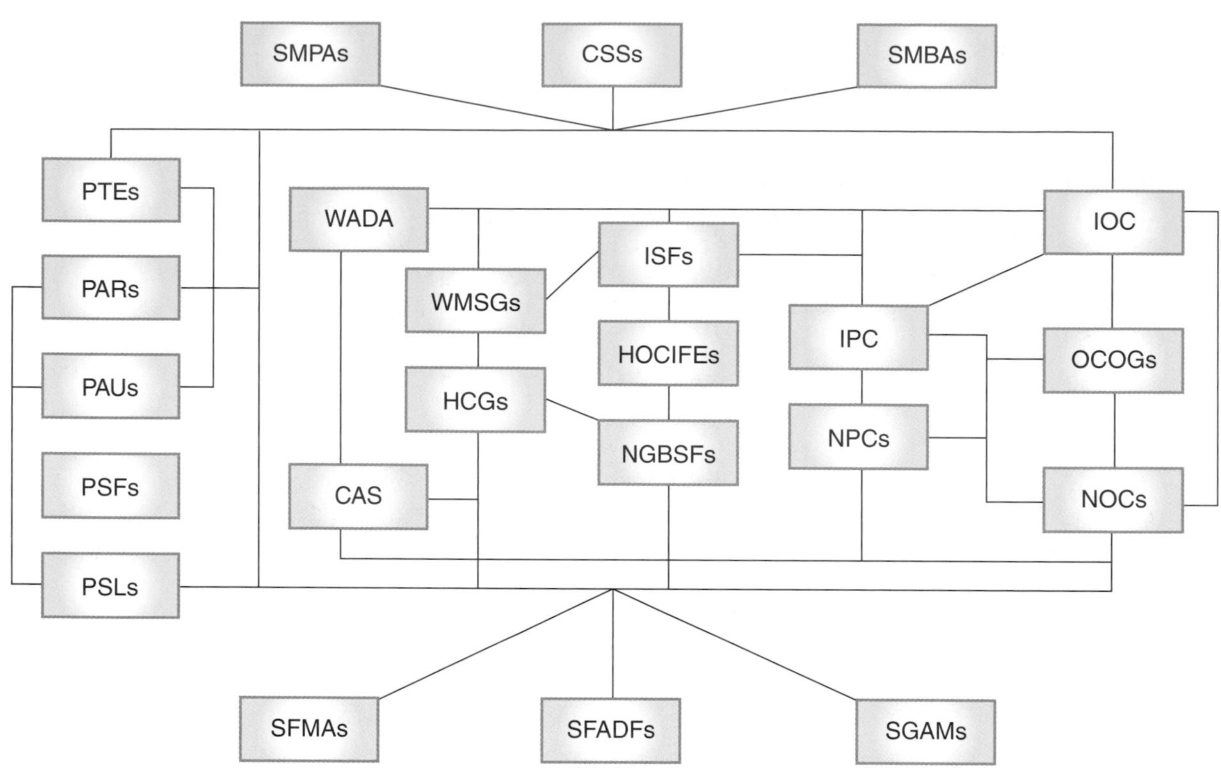

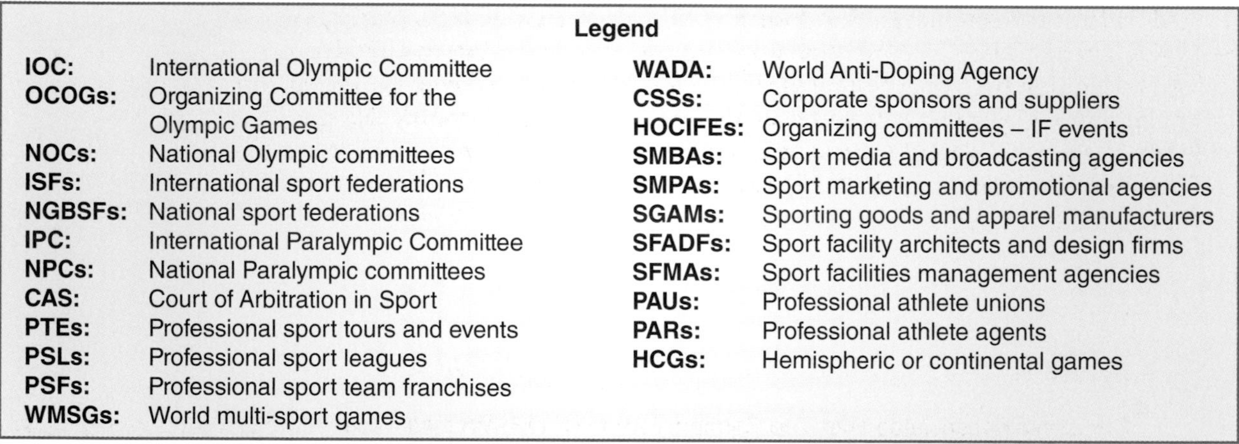

Figure 19.1 Universe of key international sport governance and industry interrelationships.
Created by Ted Fay 2006.

Corporate Sponsorship of Major International Sporting Events

A classic example of the complexities of international sport governance involved the 1992 US men's Olympic basketball team. Some members of the team were NBA players who had endorsement contracts with sponsors other than the official US Olympic team sponsors. In 1992 Reebok was the official US Olympic outerwear sponsor, providing warm-up jackets to Olympic athletes in all sports. As the gold medalist US basketball team stood on the victory podium, some of them covered the Reebok name and logo on their warm-up jackets with American flags. Michael Jordan, a Nike-sponsored athlete, initiated this action because he did not want to be seen implicitly endorsing his company's competitor. This incident thrust the United States Olympic Committee (USOC), Nike, Reebok, USA Basketball, the NBA, the NBA Players Association, and Jordan into a high-stakes public relations battle. The USOC has since amended its code of conduct to include language that requires all US Olympic athletes to wear the apparel provided by official US Olympic sponsors.

In the years following the marketing success of the 1984 Olympic Games in Los Angeles, the IOC became an international sport marketing juggernaut. It has been fueled by billions of dollars in television rights fees from NBC and others, as well as millions from corporations in the TOP (The Olympic Partner) Program. As shown in the sidebar "Rights and Opportunities for TOP Companies," TOP members have exclusive marketing rights to both the Summer Games and the Winter Games. Because of the known effectiveness of association with the Olympic Games, some non-TOP companies have engaged in **ambush marketing** by linking images of sports or athletes to the host city (e.g., "Good luck to our athletes in Vancouver"). Although these companies carefully refrain from the use of terms such as *Olympic* or *Olympic Games* in their ads, consumers psychologically infer a relationship between the product being advertised and the sporting event with which it is being linked. The IOC and its NOC members have become forceful in limiting and counteracting ambush marketing campaigns by corporations and organizations intent on circumventing the costs of sponsorship. As noted earlier, to prevent future conflicts between official Olympic team sponsors and rival companies that have endorsement deals with Team USA's players, the USOC has tightened its contracts and oversight.

ambush marketing—A tactic whereby a company attempts to undermine the sponsorship activities of a rival that owns the legal rights to sponsor an event; intended to create the sense that the ambusher is officially associated with the event.

Drug Testing and Arbitration

Another example of the complexities of international sport governance involved US track and field athlete Butch Reynolds' challenge of the 1992 Olympic drug-testing procedures. Reynolds failed an out-of-competition drug test and was disqualified from participating in the 1992 Olympic Games. He subsequently filed suit against the International Amateur Athletic Federation (IAAF), claiming that his urine specimens had been tampered with and that the analysis procedures had been flawed. The US federal court's ruling in favor of Reynolds prompted several international sport federations to join the IOC in creating the Court of Arbitration for Sport (CAS), which mediates sport-related disputes that cross national boundaries (Hums & MacLean, 2008; Thoma & Chalip, 1996).

Rights and Opportunities for TOP Companies

Companies associated with The Olympic Partner (TOP) Program receive exclusive marketing rights and opportunities within their designated product category. They may exercise these rights on a worldwide basis, and they may develop marketing programs with the various members of the Olympic Movement—the International Olympic Committee (IOC), the National Olympic Committees (NOCs), and the organizing committees (e.g., the London Organizing Committee of the Olympic and Paralympic Games [LOCOG] for the 2012 Games). Besides exclusive worldwide marketing opportunities, partners receive the following benefits (TOP Programme, 2009, ¶ 7):

- Authorization to use all Olympic imagery, as well as appropriate Olympic designations on products
- Hospitality opportunities at the Olympic Games
- Direct advertising and promotional opportunities, including preferential access to Olympic broadcast advertising
- On-site concessions and franchise, and product sale and showcase opportunities
- Protection from ambush marketing
- Acknowledgment of sponsors' support through a broad Olympic sponsorship recognition program

WEB

Go to the OSG and complete the second Web search activity, which has you investigate the influence of the World Anti-Doping Agency (WADA).

blood doping—The practice of illicitly boosting the number of red blood cells, which transport oxygen, to enhance athletic performance.

BALCO—Bay Area Laboratory Cooperative; founder Victor Conte and others have been implicated in providing designer performance enhancing drugs and steroids to Major League Baseball players and several Olympic athletes.

Reynolds' dispute and other cases that followed led to the creation of the World Anti-Doping Agency (WADA), which was established in 1999. As an independent agency, WADA has been willing to challenge sport federations and professional sport leagues by taking on the giants of sport such as Lance Armstrong and the International Cycling Union. Even so, issues related to **blood doping**, drugs, performance-enhancing supplements, steroids, and technologies that aid performance continue to challenge the foundation of international sport (Pound, 2004). Stemming from the government-sponsored cheating of the East Germans and other countries in the 1970s and 1980s and the free-market approach of companies such as US-based **BALCO**, the challenges facing sport governing bodies are staggering (Perez, 2008).

Assistive Devices

In the lead-up to the 2008 Olympic Games in Beijing, the world witnessed double-amputee Oscar Pistorius (a.k.a. the "Blade Runner") in his efforts to qualify as a South African Olympic runner in the 400 meters. First banned by the IAAF for having an alleged competitive advantage for space-age prosthetics, Pistorius subsequently won his appeal in the CAS. Classification and eligibility of athletes with disabilities to compete in open competition in many sports using radical new assistive technology is a new frontier in sport law and arbitration (Fay & Wolff, 2009; Wolbring, 2008).

Paralympic Governance Concerns

The Paralympic Games, which include elite athletes with physical or visual disabilities, are among the world's largest quadrennial sporting events. Both the Paralympic Winter Games and Paralympic Summer Games occur two weeks after the Olympic Games and since 1988 have been held at the same location and in the same facilities as the Olympic Games. An agreement between the IOC and the International Paralympic Committee (IPC) mandates that the city winning the bid to conduct the Olympic Games is obligated to conduct the Paralympic Games as well (International Paralympic Committee, 2009). The host country is expected to modify its infrastructure where necessary to meet the accessibility needs of Paralympians.

Under the leadership of the IPC and its corresponding National Paralympic Committees (NPCs), the Paralympic Games have emerged as a viable international sport movement. Following the example regarding gender equity in US sport, some people have begun to ask whether the national governing bodies of Olympic sports and the USOC should be required by law to integrate their structures, teams, management, and governance to include Paralympic athletes (Fay, Legg, & Wolff, 2005; Legg, Fay, Hums, & Wolff, 2009). In 1986 the US Ski and Snowboard Association (USSA) became the first national governing body of an Olympic sport to integrate Paralympic athletes into its operating structure. When the USSA assimilated the US Disabled Ski Team (USDST), the USDST became, at least in theory, equal to the other US ski teams (i.e., alpine and

Tool Kit for International Sport Managers

Essential equipment for a career in international sport includes an up-to-date world atlas, a current passport, appropriate visas, bilingual dictionaries, a pocket guide to currency exchange rates, several credit cards with reasonable credit lines, appropriate transportation tickets, a laptop computer with modem and WiFi capability, a personal digital assistant (PDA), a cellular phone with international calling options, and two bags packed with the items necessary to conduct business. You will be embarking on an adventure that will test your wits with respect to your personal habits, eating preferences, cultural understanding, business etiquette, patience, ability to develop a new network of friendships, and flexibility.

Sport Management Travel Tips

As a prospective sport manager preparing for a journey into international sport, what do you need to know? The first step in your journey is to develop an understanding of the primary trade treaties and agreements, such as the General Agreement on Tariffs and Trade **(GATT),** the North American Free Trade Agreement **(NAFTA),** and the rules and regulations that affect countries associated with the European Union **(EU).** This knowledge will provide a rudimentary foundation from which you can research other important trade regulations, currency exchanges, and legal issues concerning brand protection and intellectual property rights. You must also know how free or restricted the movement of goods, services, persons, and capital is from nation to nation. Knowing your rights as a foreigner when doing business in another nation is critical (Morrison, Conaway, & Douress, 2001). With an in-depth awareness of how well you, your employees, and your investments will be protected by a given legal system, you will know what recourse you have if problems occur. You also need to be highly attuned to security procedures, including visa requirements and other travel-related regulations.

GATT—An agreement negotiated in 1947 among 23 countries, including the United States, to increase international trade by reducing tariffs and other trade barriers.

NAFTA—A 1994 agreement reached by the United States, Canada, and Mexico that instituted a schedule for the phasing out of tariffs and eliminated a variety of fees and other hindrances to encourage free trade among the three countries.

EU—Known as the European Union, this is a unique economic and political partnership between 27 democratic European countries.

cross-country teams) of the USSA. This recognition allowed USDST athletes to compete in open USSA sanctioned races, including the US National Championships. In the future, governing bodies will likely continue to seek the best path to full and equitable inclusion of athletes with disabilities into international organizations and events (Fay, 1999).

ESSENTIALS FOR ASPIRING INTERNATIONAL SPORT MANAGERS

Important segments of the international sport industry include arenas, event management, stadia, sport products, ticketing, sport law, security, fitness centers, rehabilitation and sports medicine centers, sport marketing, accommodations, and travel. These segments are crucial to the conduct of international sport and are the areas in which the most growth will occur in the future, thereby providing the most opportunities for entry-level sport managers. To secure work in these venues, sports managers must master a wide knowledge and skill base.

International Sport Manager's Skill Set

Computer skills and the ability to navigate the Internet to conduct research and maintain daily business communication are basic skills for entry-level sport management positions. International sport is a personal relationship culture based on strong oral and written communication skills as well as an understanding of electronic etiquette. A sales background or experience as an athlete is not a requirement, but both can be helpful in gaining a job and succeeding in it. As an international sport manager, you must be willing and able to travel, necessitating an adequate level of fitness and health. You need to be patient, able to listen, and respectful of existing hierarchies established by various cultural and religious practices.

Being able to communicate in the language of the country where you are working is extremely important. You might be told that your colleagues from other countries understand English better than they do or that you can obtain the services of an interpreter who, as it turns out, cannot or will not convey the nuances of key oral exchanges. Consequently, in international business and sport, even a rudimentary understanding of the language of the country in which you are doing business can gain you an invaluable advantage over the competition.

International Sport Manager's Worldview

If you aspire to a career in international sport management, you should consider (1) studying abroad, preferably in a country that speaks a language different from yours, for a minimum of one semester while still in school and (2) availing yourself of a wide range of publications, including industry and trade publications, Internet resources (e.g., Web sites, blogs, message boards), professional journals, newspapers, and magazines to keep you up to date on international political, business, and sport trends. This practice will give you knowledge of general business practices in a given culture, keep you current on what is happening in the global economy, and provide up-to-date information about world events.

A basic knowledge of how a sport operates internationally, how the specific rules of the game are applied, how the sport is structured, and where the locus of power resides with the sport (politically as well as on the field of play) can enhance your marketability. An understanding of trends in licensing, marketing, promotion, event management, and contracts is also helpful. Familiarity with international geography, such as shifting borders within geopolitical regions, will prevent serious faux pas, such as forgetting that Czechoslovakia is now the separate nations of the Czech Republic and Slovakia; that Burma is now Myanmar; and that Croatia, Slovenia, Bosnia-Herzegovina, Kosovo, and Macedonia are no longer part of Yugoslavia.

International Sport Management: "It's Personal!"

Success in the international sport and business sphere is predicated on personal contact and friendship. Attending meetings of national sport federations, professional sport-related associations, and other conferences and symposia helps maintain and expand your network of professional contacts. Time availability, relevance to your professional interests, and financial resources are important factors to consider when choosing the associations or conferences and trade shows (e.g., China International Sporting Goods Show, Seoul International Sports & Leisure Industry Show) that you want to attend. Volunteering at a major international sports event, conference, or trade show is an effective way to gain access to the field and demonstrate your capabilities as a potential employee.

FORECASTING THE FUTURE: INTERNATIONAL SPORT 2010-2020

In the beginning decades of the 21st century, the international sport industry has shifted and will continue to shift from being a niche in the sport marketplace to constituting the very foundation of the sport enterprise. In the following paragraphs, we discuss several trends that are destined to affect international sport.

The Shrinking Globe

As evidenced by the worldwide recession beginning in 2008, financial and credit markets are highly interdependent. In future years, countries around the world will be drawn closer as national and international sport federations compete more directly with professional leagues and franchises for global market share of trademark licensing and merchandise. All domains of the international sport enterprise, both emerging niche sports and traditional professional sports, will profit from increased advertising revenues made possible through worldwide cable deregulation and integrated technologies that use the Internet and cell phones to deliver sport content to consumers through high-definition broadband providers. Advances in on-demand information technologies will allow the creation of strong fan affiliations and the development of new virtual fans in other nations and other continents. Cross-marketing and promotional agreements among partners on different continents and in different sports will change the way in which the sport industry organizes itself. Differences in cultures, national laws, and customs will compound the challenges of these developments (Smith & Westerbeek, 2004; Szymanski & Zimbalist, 2005).

International exchanges of athletes across a broad cross-section of sports ranging from youth to near elite levels will become commonplace. Such exchanges will continue to include showcase tournaments and camps for the benefit of US college coaches who use them to recruit athletes from Europe, Australia, and to a lesser extent Africa and South America. As the rate of export and import of international talent at all competitive levels escalates, international trade agreements will have a greater effect on the sport industry.

Social and Ethical Awareness

The United Nations (UN) proclaimed 2005 as the International Year of Sport and Physical Education. In so doing, it drew attention to its focus on a new human rights convention, which included access to sport and leisure activity for all people of the world as a basic human right. This and other trends indicate that the world will soon rediscover the importance and interrelationship of access to play and sport opportunities for all, regardless of socioeconomic status, gender, race, or ethnicity. In 2006 the United Nations passed and ratified a new UN Convention on the Rights for Persons with Disabilities that included rights to sport, play, leisure, and culture for persons with disabilities (United Nations, n.d.).

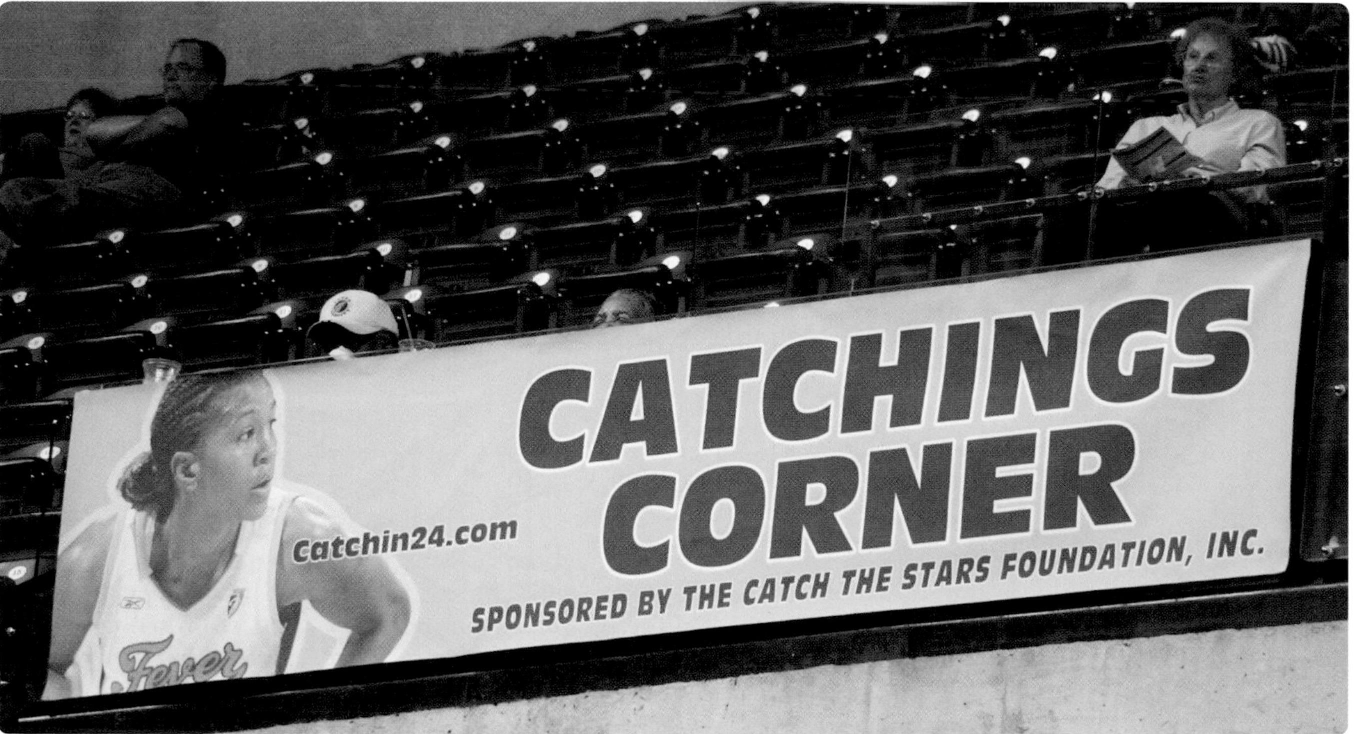

Catchings Corner is a designated section at home games for the WNBA's Indiana Fever. Tamika Catchings is a socially conscious professional athlete who gives back to her community in numerous ways, including through her Catching the Stars Foundation.
Photo courtesy of Paul M. Pedersen.

The social consciences of elite athletes will become even more pronounced. Already, we see athletes such as Dawn Staley, Drew Brees, Tamika Catchings, David Beckham, Mia Hamm, Roger Federer, Dikembe Mutumbo, Julie Foudy, Lance Armstrong, Kristi Yamaguchi, and others give back to society by establishing charities and foundations to support critical causes, from finding a cure for cancer to literacy to HIV and AIDS research. Another example of philanthropy is the generosity of Johan Olav Koss, multiple speed-skating gold medalist from Norway at the 1994 Lillehammer Winter Olympic Games. Koss used his accomplishments as an Olympic champion to call attention to a number of human rights needs by creating an organization called Olympic Aid. This organization was originally designed to support the survivors of ethnic cleansing in Bosnia in the 1990s and has since evolved into Right to Play, an international organization focused on bringing sport and physical activity to children in developing countries in Africa, Asia, and South America. American gold medalist speed skater Joey Cheek renewed Koss' pledge and commitment to worldwide human rights needs by donating all of his 2006 Olympic gold and silver medal earnings from the USOC (US$40,000) to Right to Play. Cheek leveraged the publicity surrounding this pledge to challenge more than 10 corporations to match his gift and thus created Team Darfur (Weir, 2006). Ironically, Cheek was denied a visa by the Chinese government to attend the 2008 Beijing Olympic Games based on its fear of embarrassment related to Cheek's uncompromising stand on human rights and China's role in the horrors of Darfur (Lapchick, 2008).

Within the context of human rights, an expansion and application of the principles of equity will occur throughout all cultures. Such an effort will affect not only who gets to play sports but also who gets to control the sporting enterprise. The growth and expansion of professional team sport leagues for women, particularly in North America and Europe, will give rise to expanded marketing and management initiatives (Grundy & Shackelford, 2005; King, 2005). The Paralympic Games will achieve major event status through increased television, media, and spectator appeal and perhaps be fully integrated into the Olympic Games by 2016 or 2020. These trends will provide expanded job opportunities in the international sport marketplace for women, older people, and people with disabilities. Farsighted, socially responsible, consumer-oriented companies will stand to gain the most from these developments.

A new order of elite decision makers will assume command of a global sport industry based on pragmatic alliances among leagues, international federations, television networks, and corporate sponsors. Corporations will begin to seek brand identification with particular sports, leading to the formation of corporate and national team alliances (Smith & Westerbeek, 2004). Niche and action sports such as in-line skating, triathlon, snowboarding, and mountain biking will continue to emerge and grow. Sports such as roller hockey, beach volleyball, and endurance kayaking will redefine themselves and continue to expand. All these sports will flourish because of broad, cross-generational participation and their appeal as televised events that are distributed through a new array of broadband networks.

ACTION

Go to the OSG and complete the Learning in Action activity, which has you select trends that are likely to occur in the international sport industry during the next 10 years.

CRITICAL THINKING IN INTERNATIONAL SPORT

Expanded leisure time for the elite and the growing middle classes in South America, China, India, other Asian countries, and parts of Africa will continue to fuel worldwide expansion of golf, tennis, and other recreational sports. Extended life expectancy will continue to affect the international sport and leisure travel industry, necessitating significant expansion of facilities. Serious concerns about the effect of recreational and sport facilities on the environment will accompany this expansion. Conflicts have already arisen regarding the construction of golf courses in sensitive mountain terrain and tropical rain forests. Concerns also exist about building large-scale leisure and sport resorts in the developing world and stadia and arenas in environmentally or economically sensitive areas. In response the IOC created a commission and a policy position regarding concerns about the impact of the Olympic Games on local and regional environments (Sport and Environment Commission, n.d.).

In the next decade, more career opportunities will emerge in areas dealing with jurisdiction and dispute resolution related to international athletes' rights, blood doping, drug use and abuse, relocation of franchises from nation to nation, corporate social responsibility, and other policy matters. International and national sport federations, professional leagues, sport marketing agencies, media (e.g., cable, satellite, network television and radio) and new media entities, arenas and facilities, fitness clubs, and sport product corporations will begin to give hiring preference to people with backgrounds oriented to the global marketplace.

Complete the critical thinking portfolio activity in the OSG, consulting as needed the "Eight Critical Thinking Questions" section in chapter 1.

PORTFOLIO

Ethics in International Sport

In the past, many sporting goods manufacturing companies relocated most of their production of footwear, apparel, and equipment to Asia (e.g., China, Vietnam, Pakistan, Indonesia). Currently, however, such companies are looking for other locations that have low labor costs and minimal labor rights in places such as Latin America, Africa, and the former Soviet republics. These relocations create serious financial, legal, and ethical questions. For example, does the availability of a large, cheap labor force outweigh concerns over counterfeiting made possible by weak copyright laws, currency fluctuations and devaluations, and potentially restrictive export and import laws? What are the human rights and ethical considerations when large, multinational corporations profit from the toil of children and women in sweatshop conditions in Southeast Asian or Central American countries? Is it exploitive to move footwear, equipment, and sport apparel production from one emerging economy to another (e.g., from Korea to the Philippines to China and Indonesia) in search of the cheapest labor supply? What responsibility do companies have to the workers and countries that they leave behind?

Complete the ethical issues portfolio activity in the OSG, consulting as needed the "Guidelines for Making Ethical Decisions" section in chapter 1.

PORTFOLIO

Ideally, ethical value systems and human rights principles are part of the decision-making process in the relocation of manufacturing centers. Companies should also consider the stability of political regimes and their diplomatic relations with the nations in which the corporate home offices are located. In the aftermath of the 2001 terrorist attacks in New York and terrorist bombings in Moscow (2003), Madrid (2004), London (2005), and Mumbai (2008), security issues have become paramount in decisions to locate new production facilities.

Summary

Organizations, events, and governance structures are deemed to be international if they are involved internationally on a regular basis or as one of their primary functions. Over the past few decades five key changes occurred that resulted in the expansion of international sport. These changes involved the Olympic Games; women's sporting opportunities; a redefinition of sport based on corporate sponsorship, a shift in the balance of power, and the world's obsession with soccer; advances in recruitment and marketing; and the emergence of new economies. China became a sport superpower, and Brazil became appealing as a host for international sporting events. Current issues include the relocation of manufacturing companies and governance concerns focused on corporate sponsorship, drug testing and arbitration, assistive devices, and concerns associated with the Paralympic Games. To be successful internationally, aspiring sport

QUIZ TIME

Did you grasp all the key points in this chapter? Go to the OSG for a short quiz to test your understanding of the material.

managers must have the appropriate tools, skills, worldview, and cultural understanding. The future of international sport will occur in a world that is becoming smaller because of technology, a global community that is aware of social and ethical concerns that can be addressed through sport, and a world citizenry that possesses a heightened commitment to environmental concerns related to reducing the carbon footprint. Career opportunities in international sport will expand for people who are oriented to the global marketplace and possess the ability to integrate new technologies.

Review Questions

1. What is the definition of international sport, and what factors were considered in reaching this definition?
2. What were the five key changes that occurred over the past few decades, and how have they contributed to the expansion of international sport?
3. What were the three factors that served to redefine international sport, and what was the effect of each?
4. How have advances in recruitment and marketing affected international sport?
5. What are some of the emerging economies that are now or are becoming attractive hosts for international competitions, and what makes them attractive?
6. How have corporate sponsorship, drug testing, assistive devices, and the inclusion of Paralympic athletes affected international sport governance?
7. What skills, experiences, and competencies would help aspiring international sport managers prepare for the job market?
8. What are three factors that will affect the future of international sport? Explain the effect of each.

References

Fay, T.G. (1999). Race, gender, and disability: A new paradigm towards full participation and equal opportunity in sport (Doctoral dissertation, University of Massachusetts Amherst). *Electronic doctoral dissertations for UMass Amherst.* Retrieved February 2, 2010, from http://scholarworks.umass.edu/dissertations/AAI9950151

Fay, T.G., Legg, D., & Wolff, E.A. (2005, June). *Inclusion of Paralympic events within the Olympic Games.* Paper presented at the annual meeting of the North American Society for Sport Management, Regina, Saskatchewan, Canada.

Fay, T.G., & Wolff, E.A. (2009). Disability in sport in the Twenty-First Century: Creating a new sport opportunity spectrum. *Boston University International Law Journal, 27,* 231-248.

Foer, F. (2004). *How soccer explains the world: An unlikely theory of globalization.* New York: Harper Perennial.

Grundy, P., & Shackelford, S. (2005). *Shattering the glass: The remarkable history of women's basketball.* New York: New Press.

Hums, M.A., & MacLean, J. (2008). *Governance and policy in sport organizations.* Scottsdale, AZ. Holcomb-Hathaway.

International Olympic Committee. (2008, August 18). *Record women's participation.* Retrieved July 25, 2009, from www.olympic.org/uk/games/beijing/full_story_uk.asp?id=2742

International Paralympic Committee. (2009). *IPC-IOC Cooperation.* Retrieved June 29, 2009, from www.paralympic.org/release/Main_Sections_Menu/IPC/About_the_IPC/IPC_IOC_Cooperation/index.html

King, B. (2005, April 25-May 1). What's up with women's sports? *Street & Smith's SportsBusiness Journal,* pp.18–23.

Lapchick, R. (2008, August 8). *Kept from Beijing, Team Darfur's Joey Cheek fights on.* ESPN.com. Retrieved February 2, 2010, from http://sports.espn.go.com/oly/summer08/columns/story?columnist=lapchick_richard&id=3526465

Larmer, B. (2005). *Operation Yao Ming: The Chinese sports empire, American big business, and the making of an NBA superstar.* New York: Gotham Books.

Lefton, T. (2009, April 13). What's next for Reebok? "Fun and fit." *Street & Smith's SportsBusiness Journal,* p. 1.

Legg, D., Fay, T.G., Hums, M.A. & Wolff, E.A. (2009, Fall). Examining the inclusion of wheelchair exhibition events within the Olympic Games 1984-2004. *European Sport Management Quarterly, 9,* 243-258.

Maguire, J., & Nakayama, M. (2005). *Japan, sport & society: Tradition and change in a globalizing world.* London: Routledge.

Morrison, T., Conaway, W., & Douress, J.J. (2001). *Doing business around the world.* Paramus, NJ: Prentice Hall.

National Basketball Association. (2009, October 8). Bryant's jersey remains top seller in China. Retrieved February 2, 2010, from www.nba.com/2009/news/10/08/bryant.jersey.china/

Perez, A.J. (2008, March 28). *Chemist describes work with BALCO.* Retrieved February 2, 2010, from www.usatoday.com/sports/2008-03-26-balco-chemist_N.htm

Pound, R.W. (2004). *Inside the Olympics.* Montreal: Wiley & Sons.

Power, S., & Allison, G.T. (Eds.). (2000). *Realizing human rights: Moving from inspiration to impact.* New York: St. Martin's Press.

Reeve, S. (2000). *One day in September.* New York: Arcade.

Smith, A., & Westerbeek, H. (2004). *The sport business future.* London: Palgrave Macmillan.

Sport and Environment Commission. (n.d.). *History and mission of the Commission.* Retrieved June 29, 2009, from www.olympic.org/content/The-IOC/Commissions/Sport-and-Environment

Stern lays out vision for NBA expansion in Europe. (2008, March 27). Retrieved February 2, 2010, from http://sports.espn.go.com/nba/news/story?id=3315819

Szymanski, S., & Zimbalist, A. (2005). *National pastime: How Americans play baseball and the rest of the world plays soccer.* Washington, DC: Brookings Institution Press.

Thoma, J.E., & Chalip, L. (1996). *Sport governance in the global community.* Morgantown, WV: Fitness Information Technology.

TOP Programme. (2009). *Worldwide TOP partners.* Retrieved June 14, 2010, from www.olympic.org/en/coantent/The-IOC/Sponsoring/Sponsorship/?NewsTab=1Tab=1

United Nations. (n.d.). *Convention on the rights of persons with disabilities.* Retrieved February 2, 2010, from www.un.org/disabilities/default.asp?id=150

Weir, T. (2006, February 18). Cheek's charity for a cause. *USA Today*, p. 1D.

Wolbring, G. (2008, July). Is there an end to out-able? Is there an end to the rat race for abilities? *Media/Culture Journal, 11*(3). Retrieved February 2, 2010, from http://journal.media-culture.org.au/index.php/mcjournal/article/viewArticle/57

Women's Professional Soccer. (2010). *About WPS.* Retrieved February 2, 2010, from www.womensprosoccer.com/about/about-wps

HISTORICAL MOMENTS

- **1966** *International Review for the Sociology of Sport* launched
- **1970** *Canadian Journal for the History of Physical Education and Sport* launched
- **1973** *Journal of Sport History* launched
- **1977** *Journal of Sport and Social Issues* launched
- **1984** *Sociology of Sport Journal* launched
- **1987** *Journal of Sport Management* launched
- **1992** *Sport Marketing Quarterly* launched
- **1993** *Journal of Sport & Tourism* launched
- **1994** *European Journal for Sport Management* (now known as *European Sport Management Quarterly)* launched
- **1998** *Sport Management Review* launched
- **1999** *International Journal of Sports Marketing and Sponsorship* launched
- **2000** *International Journal of Sport Management* and *Journal of Sports Economics* launched
- **2006** *International Journal of Sport Finance* launched
- **2007** *Sport Management Education Journal* launched
- **2008** *Journal of Issues in Intercollegiate Athletics* launched
- **2009** *International Journal of Sport Policy* launched

20

SPORT MANAGEMENT QUESTIONS AND RESEARCH

Jess C. Dixon ■ Wendy Frisby ■ Robert L. Boucher

LEARNING OBJECTIVES

1. Explain the value and importance of asking and addressing research questions in sport management.
2. Define research and state why it is important to sport management students, practitioners, and researchers.
3. Know what questions to ask when evaluating the quality of a research article.
4. Provide examples of the growing number of academic journals and other sources that contain relevant sport management research.
5. Describe the critical contributions of the academic community and commercial research firms in answering questions that emerge in various sport management sectors.
6. Explain the differences between scientific and pseudoscientific approaches to sport management research.
7. Differentiate between quantitative data, qualitative data, and mixed-methods approaches.

Key Terms

action research
anonymity
confidentiality
empirical
pseudoscience
reliability
research design
science
theory
validity

GET A JOB!

☑ Wrap up this journey in sport management by going to the Online Study Guide (OSG) at www.HumanKinetics.com/ContemporarySportManagement. Check out the job opportunities and consider the skills and experiences that can help you succeed in sport management.

Interest in research has paralleled the growth of the sport management industry and sport management educational programs around the world. This interest has occurred because people in business and education understand that research can inform managerial decisions, uncover solutions to managerial problems, improve organizational effectiveness and efficiency, point out inequalities in sport leadership or participation, and help sport management continue to develop a relevant body of knowledge.

Regardless of the area that you are studying, understanding research is critically important. Progressive sport organizations want to find out about the latest trends, evaluate whether their customers are satisfied, update their policies, attract new participants, provide data to sponsors and partners, and stay ahead of their competitors. Increasingly, these sport organizations are looking to sport management graduates for expertise in information searches, feasibility studies, evaluations, and marketing studies, to name a few.

Even if you do not expect research to be a major component of your future career, you need to be able to understand, evaluate, and use it when solving problems and making professional decisions. This chapter introduces key concepts and various types of research conducted in the sport management field. It also provides you with a foundation for becoming a responsible producer and consumer of research, so that you can become a more informed decision maker. To develop your skills further, you should seek out the growing list of references and courses in research methods.

RESEARCH QUESTIONS AND THEIR ORIGINS

Asking suitable research questions and getting the best possible answers are critical to every sport management sector in the current information age. Research questions are important because addressing them sets the stage for decision, action, profit, satisfaction, success, and other goals desired by sport managers. Questions in any industry, but particularly in sport, emerge because of changes in the economy, law, culture, technology, policy, politics, and other dimensions of the broader environment that affect the operations and bottom lines of organizations. Thus, sport organizations should not make bottom-line and other types of decisions without having reliable data. The starting point for obtaining information is a focused and well thought out research question. Addressing such questions through research enables sport managers to know their environment, personnel, industry, market, customers, and current trends.

Although some research questions emerge because of curiosity, most materialize as sport organizations design or revise strategies to cope with a problem or to influence change. For instance, many sport properties might be concerned about how consumers' television viewing behavior may be changing in light of new and emerging technologies. A report by Senior and Asensio (2009) indicated that the recent proliferation of digital video recorders (DVRs) and video-on-demand (VOD) programming is threatening traditional TV business models and the revenue streams that underpin them. The authors noted that "as many as 85% of consumers who own a DVR skip" (p. 6) at least 75% of the TV commercials. This type of behavior is only expected to increase in the coming years.

What are the implications of these changes in technology for sport managers? James March, senior research analyst at S.G. Cown & Co., suggested that because DVR and VOD users can skip through commercial advertisements, those messages are reaching fewer consumers, thereby forcing ad buyers to reduce their spending accordingly (Poole, 2004). Although executives of sport properties would have you believe that their television products are DVR proof, advertisers will surely need to become more creative and efficient in finding ways to integrate their messages into sport programming, or find alternative means for reaching their target markets (Poole, 2004). In fact, some advertisers and TV executives have gone so far as to project a multi-billion-dollar decrease in advertising revenue for sport properties because of this fundamental shift in how sport is being consumed on television (King, 2004). Sport managers in the second decade of the 21st century need to understand the importance of asking relevant research questions and choosing the appropriate research methods to address them.

WHY SPORT MANAGERS NEED TO UNDERSTAND RESEARCH

Students who aspire to careers in the sport industry sometimes undervalue research because they assume that it is not practical and is done primarily in universities. Current students, like others who have gone before them, appear to gain satisfaction from the practical, hands-on elements of undergraduate preparation and are sometimes unimpressed with theory and research. In truth, only those who have served in a management position can fully appreciate the importance of research in assisting with the managerial role. Now is the best time to begin developing an understanding of why research is critical to sport managers who want to stay on top of their field.

Only Research Can Keep You Current

If your family doctor graduated from a prestigious medical school in 2000, would you not expect him or her to be up-to-date with medical developments here in this second decade of the 21st century? The advances that have occurred since our doctors and countless other professionals received their initial certifications and credentials have come about largely because of research. Being able to read, understand, and apply scientific findings leads to progress. The world would be a far different place without the contributions of scientific studies.

The field of sport management is no different from other professional areas. Through the application of research findings in human resources, leadership, marketing, organizational development, and countless other areas, the practicing sport manager has a much better chance of choosing sensible alternatives to everyday managerial problems.

Emerging technology can make it more difficult for advertisers to have their messages seen by a large audience.
Photo courtesy of Hallie S. Pedersen.

Trial-and-Error Management Is Folly

Would any of us drive a car or take medicine that had not been thoroughly tested? Probably not. In similar fashion, we are well aware of the extensive research conducted on hockey sticks, baseball bats, tennis rackets, golf clubs, running shoes, and virtually every other piece of equipment related to the world of sport. We now consider it commonplace to conduct experimental studies to improve athletic performance by increments as small as a tenth of a second.

But when it comes to the management of sport, the standards

may not be as exacting. We can easily become enthralled by a new idea or by what is being done at another university or in a similar sport in another country. In real terms, the trial-and-error approach often seems to be standard practice in the everyday management of sport. Hundreds of promotions are conducted, marketing plans are formulated, and strategic plans are developed—all without research. Even with a great deal of thought, many of these ventures are doomed to failure. Having sound intuition and a wealth of experience is useful, but a trial-and-error approach can be expensive. Successful marketing strategies, comprehensive human resources policies, and many other aspects of the sport management domain are based on sound theories derived from research. Admittedly, we are all students of the trial-and-error process in that we make decisions without all possible information or may not have the time or resources to explore all the options. But why do this on purpose? Why not gather as much data as possible about your research question and make decisions based on sound information?

WHAT IS SPORT MANAGEMENT RESEARCH?

WEB

Go to the OSG and complete the Web search activity, which has you evaluate a research ethics review board at your university.

Sport management research is a systematic way of examining hunches, assumptions, and questions about a wide range of sport management phenomena. In particular, sport management researchers are interested in questions related to marketing, finance, communication, human resources, policy, and a number of other topics highlighted throughout this textbook. Sport management researchers typically use a wide range of research designs in a variety of sport settings to conduct research on people in organizations; their clients, customers, suppliers, sponsors, or partners; the media; and sport products, events, and programs. Sport management research also sometimes considers the broader economic, legal, social, cultural, ecological, technological, and political environments that shape or are shaped by sport (Slack & Parent, 2006). The findings from these research investigations can inform managerial practice, build knowledge in a subject area, or both.

Sometimes research findings support our initial hunches and assumptions, while at other times the findings contradict and challenge them. Such challenges encourage us to consider new and improved ways of managing sport. For example, we might assume that everyone in our community has equal access to the sporting opportunities available, but research might reveal considerable disparities in participation based on income, gender, race, nationality, age, sexual orientation, religion, ability, health status, and other factors. Paying close attention to this evidence will push us to consider new ways of marketing and delivering sport programs so that more people can enjoy the benefits of participation.

Regardless of whether the findings obtained from research confirm or challenge our hunches and assumptions, they will help us make better decisions. Thus, sport managers increasingly rely on research before investing financial, human, and other types of resources in new or ongoing projects. They want to avoid the costly errors that can occur when decisions are based on false or unfounded assumptions. Effective sport managers want assurances that their decisions will help them achieve desired goals based on evidence that has been carefully collected, analyzed, and interpreted.

Academic Research in Sport Management

Some authors, as noted in chapter 1, have suggested that sport management has been around since at least 11 BCE when Herod, King of Judea, staged elaborate athletic spectacles (Frank, 1984). The study and documentation of research in this area is a much more contemporary occurrence. A number of academic and professional associations formed since the mid-1980s have stimulated research and scholarly activity in sport management. The North American Society for Sport Management (NASSM), the European Association for Sport Management (EASM), and the Sport Management Association of Australia and New Zealand (SMAANZ) are examples of international associations that foster research as part of their mandates. Each association hosts an annual conference during which members and invited guests share sport management research in the form of presentations, roundtable discussions, and keynote addresses. In addition, these academic associations publish research journals to help grow the body of knowledge in sport management.

Table 20.1 provides a brief overview of academic journals that publish research related to the management of sport. Included in this table is a quality ranking for each journal based on the input of senior academics from around the world. Shilbury and Rentschler (2007) rank-ordered these journals based on their level of prestige and the contributions that they have made to theory, practice, and teaching within the field of sport management. Although these journals may differ slightly in overall quality, we can be somewhat confident in the findings published in them because they have been vetted through the peer review process that serves as the hallmark for all academic publications.

TABLE 20.1 2007 Ranking of Academic Journals Publishing Research in Sport Management

Journal	Published since	Affiliation	Ranking*
Journal of Sport Management	1987	North American Society for Sport Management	1
Sport Management Review	1998	Sport Management Association of Australia and New Zealand	2
Sociology of Sport Journal	1984	North American Society for the Sociology of Sport	3
International Review for the Sociology of Sport	1966	International Sociology of Sport Association	4
Journal of Sports Economics	2000	International Association of Sports Economists	5
Journal of Sport and Social Issues	1977	none	6
European Sport Management Quarterly	1994**	European Association for Sport Management	7
Sport Marketing Quarterly	1992	Sport Marketing Association	8
International Journal of Sports Marketing and Sponsorship	1999	none	9
International Journal of Sport Management & Marketing	2005	none	10
Journal of Sport & Tourism	1993†	none	11
Sporting Traditions	1984	Australian Society for Sports History	12
International Journal of Sport Management	2000	none	13

Notes: *Weighted journal rankings have been derived from Shilbury and Rentschler (2007); **this journal was published as the *European Journal for Sport Management* until 2000; †this journal was published as the *Journal of Sport Tourism* until 2006.

Commercial Research in Sport Management

The Council of American Survey Research Organizations ([CASRO], 2009) represents more than 300 research firms operating in the United States, each with the mission of conducting research on behalf of other organizations. An organization might need help in answering questions because in-house personnel lack expertise in newly developing areas or because the organization is unable to hire full-time research staff. When sport organizations have research questions that they are unable to answer themselves, they often hire the services of a research firm.

Several research companies specialize in providing expert research services exclusively to sport organizations. Often, the most pressing research questions of teams, manufacturers, and retailers relate to consumers and marketing. Consequently, many commercial companies address marketing and promotional issues on behalf of sport organizations. Nike, NASCAR, and other large and small sport organizations have used the services of commercial research companies in their marketing and management planning. Table 20.2 lists some of the most visible sport research companies and their services.

Although a wealth of information can be derived by contracting with commercial research firms, the uniqueness of the issues facing today's professional sports leagues has driven many of them to take responsibility for their own research undertakings. In

TABLE 20.2 List of Consultants Specializing in Sport Management Research

Consultant	Specialty
American Sports Data, Inc. Fort Mill, SC www.americansportsdata.com/dev	Specializes in consumer survey research for sport, fitness, and health industries. Provides major research for Sporting Goods Manufacturers Association and International Health & Racquet Sportsclub Association. Purveyors of the *Superstudy of Sports Participation*.
Taylor Nelson Sofres (TNS) New York, NY London, UK www.tnsglobal.com/	Leading full-service custom research company that provides advice and insight on new market segmentation, advertising and communications, new product development and brand performance, and a host of other services to national and multinational organizations. TNS Sports and Event Sponsorship division is responsible for producing the *ESPN Sports Poll,* which is quoted frequently by scholars, professional literature, and the popular press.
Joyce Julius & Associates, Inc. Ann Arbor, MI www.joycejulius.com/	Evaluates independent sports and special events programs through its *Sponsors Report* that documents in-broadcast television exposure or its National Television Impression Value Analysis (NITV) that contains full-program sponsorship analysis.
Performance Research Newport, RI London, UK www.performanceresearch.com/	Evaluates sponsorship effectiveness for sports, music, theme parks, arts, and other entertainment industries. Specializes in on-site data collection and research.
Sports Business Research Network Princeton, NJ www.sbrnet.com/	Provides continuously updated market research and industry news on sports participation, equipment sales, broadcasting, sponsorships, and marketing.
Turnkey Sports Haddonfield, NJ www.turnkeysports.com/	Specializes in providing custom market research, lead generation tools, and executive recruitment services to sport properties and sponsors. Turnkey's Team Brand Index and Sports Polls are regular features in trade publications.
Ipsos-Reid Toronto, ON www.ipsos.ca/reid	Part of the Ipsos Group, a global leader in survey-based marketing, advertising, media, customer satisfaction, and public opinion research, Ipsos-Reid is responsible for researching and publishing the *College Football Fan First Poll*.

the past decade, Major League Baseball (MLB), the National Football League (NFL), and the National Basketball Association (NBA) have all established internal research departments dedicated to collecting, analyzing, and explaining research data. Given the premium that these leagues have placed on information, sales, and marketing, executives of the future will need to be competent in conducting research (Miller, 2003). Daniel Derian, MLB's vice president of research, elaborated on this when he noted, "As decisions within our business are more reliant on measuring the opportunity and the return on investment, research and its associated functions will continue to become more prominent" (D. Derian, personal communication, June 28, 2005).

KEY CONCEPTS

Because approaches to sport management research vary, the choice of approach will depend on the purpose of the study and the nature of the question that one is attempting to address. Familiarity with the following key research concepts will be useful in understanding sport management research: (1) ways of knowing, (2) science and pseudoscience, (3) basic and applied research, (4) quantitative and qualitative data, (5) research design, and (6) validity and reliability.

Ways of Knowing

According to Peirce's classic theory (cited in Kerlinger & Lee, 2000), knowledge can be acquired in four ways: through tenacity, authority, intuition, and science. Each of these sources of knowledge has pros and cons.

1. *Tenacity.* With this form of knowledge, a person knows that a fact is true because people have always believed that it is true, even though evidence may exist to the contrary. For example, many people subscribe to the theory that sport participation builds character, although much empirical evidence shows that no relationship exists between sport and moral development, good citizenship, and other valued traits (Eitzen & Sage, 2008). In fact, some evidence demonstrates that sport might bring out the worst character traits in athletes. Yet many people still hold firmly to the belief that sport builds character.

2. *Authority.* In this case, a person knows that something is right because someone with expertise has said that it is. For instance, if the University of Tennessee's Pat Summitt explains that women play the game of basketball primarily on a horizontal plane (i.e., back and forth), whereas the men play on a vertical plane (i.e., up and down), and that both styles of play require a unique but equivalent level of proficiency, one accepts her argument because of her specific knowledge about the sport of basketball. Because Summitt is the winningest basketball coach in NCAA history (leading the Lady Vols to more than 1,000 victories and eight national championships during her tenure), when it comes to college hoops, it could be argued that no one is a greater authority on the topic. However, being an authority figure does not always guarantee that one will have accurate views. For example, few economists predicted the extent of the worldwide economic recession that began in December 2007 (Isidore, 2008).

3. *Intuition.* A person who believes that something is true because she or he thinks it is commonsense or self-evident has what is called intuitive knowledge (Thomas, Nelson, & Silverman, 2005). An example might be that Canadians are naturally gifted in the sport of ice hockey because their women's and men's teams have won more international tournaments than the teams of any other country over the years. Because this conclusion is self-evident to many around the world, it stands to reason that it must be so—at least according to the method of intuition. Research has an important role to play in

debunking commonsense beliefs that are not always accurate. For example, Canadians are not inherently better ice hockey players than athletes from other countries. Rather, ice hockey is an important part of Canadian culture and is conducive to its wintery climate, so youngsters have more coaching, facilities, equipment, and encouragement to take up and excel at the sport (Wilson, 2006).

empirical—Describes data or the results of a study that are verifiable by means of objective observation or experimentation.

4. *Science.* With this method of knowing, one assumes that information is reliable and credible because **empirical** evidence in the form of quantitative or qualitative data has been collected to address a research question of interest. Most people accept scientific information because data were collected using a systematic protocol with as few outside factors as possible swaying the results. In most cases, the scientific method is the most reliable route to information that sport managers can use to answer their research questions.

Science and Pseudoscience

science—Information based on systematic research.

When we hear the word **science,** we might associate it with experiments done in high school or with exercise physiology laboratories in which subjects' heart rates are monitored to determine fitness levels. This type of experiment-based laboratory science is known as natural science, and it has a long historical tradition in physical education and kinesiology programs in colleges and universities. Social science, another type of science, includes areas such as sport sociology, sport psychology, and sport management. In general, a social science approach to sport is concerned with individuals, groups, and organizations as they interact in a complex environment (Slack & Parent, 2006).

pseudoscience—Information that appears to be based on systematic research when it is not.

A growing body of research appears to have a scientific basis when in fact it does not. Theories promoting the latest managerial or marketing techniques that are not based on systematic research are known as **pseudoscience.** We can find numerous examples of pseudoscience in popular press books, in infomercials on TV, in newspaper or magazine articles, and on the Internet. Get-rich-quick schemes that provide unsubstantiated evidence to support the claims being made are another example of pseudoscience. Although the latest scheme or trend might be endorsed by a purported expert or authority, explained in technical language, and supported by promises of dramatic outcomes, sport managers must be skeptical of pseudoscience masquerading as science. Although several well-known management "gurus" have made personal fortunes by speaking about and selling popular how-to books on a variety of management topics, not all their theories and recommendations are supported by the systematic collection, analysis, and interpretation of data. To sort out what types of information are credible and to avoid basing decisions on information that is misleading or faulty, an understanding of sport management research is essential.

Basic and Applied Research

Social science research consists of two general types: basic and applied. Although the two types of research can be highly interrelated and may not always be easily distinguishable from one another, understanding some of the differences in their goals and approaches is helpful.

Basic research is usually done in universities or research institutes and has the goal of advancing a body of knowledge in a subject area. It focuses on developing or testing theories or explanations for why things operate in certain ways. Direct practical outcomes from basic research are not always immediately apparent, although questions often arise from practical problems and the findings can provide a foundation for developing new managerial systems and approaches.

theory—Provides an explanation for a phenomenon of interest to sport management researchers.

Simply put, a **theory** provides an explanation for a phenomenon of interest to sport management researchers. Theory is integral to basic research in three main ways: (1)

Moneyball

In essence, the book *Moneyball: The Art of Winning an Unfair Game* by Michael Lewis (2003) explained how the small-market Oakland Athletics defied all logic by finishing near the top of the MLB standings and reaching the playoffs each year from 2000 through 2003 despite operating with a payroll one-third the size of its large-market rivals. Because of its immense popularity in both the sport and business realms, the book was listed among the top 10 on *The New York Times* bestseller list every week in 2004 (Stewart, Mitchell, & Stavros, 2007). Although *Moneyball* is a book about baseball, it provides a striking lesson in the power of research and the scientific method (Dolan, 2006).

Built on more than a century of tradition, MLB clubs have long relied on the input of scouts (who travel throughout the United States and beyond to identify and evaluate playing talent) to assemble their playing rosters. Along their journey, scouts evaluate prospects based on the five tools that baseball players were supposed to exhibit: (1) hitting for average, (2) hitting for power, (3) running speed, (4) arm strength, and (5) defensive fielding ability. Despite a long history of using the five-tool approach to player selection in MLB, little empirical evidence was available to suggest that players who possessed a combination of these tools would help clubs win games. With its emphasis on the subjective observations and opinions of presumed baseball experts, player evaluation and selection in baseball had institutionalized a model of decision making based on tenacity, intuition, and authority.

According to Lewis (2003), the secret to the Athletics' success was the unique application of the scientific method to the evaluation and selection of playing talent. After taking over as the club's general manager in 1997, Billy Beane implemented a radical new system for player evaluation and selection based on the philosophy of a relatively unknown baseball writer named Bill James who argued that "the naked eye was an inadequate tool for learning what you needed to know to evaluate baseball players" (Lewis, 2003, p. 68). Through James' writings, Beane and his staff began to recognize inefficiencies that existed in the market for players when clubs made personnel decisions based on inferior or biased information. For example, players who demonstrated superior defensive abilities were expensive for clubs to acquire in comparison with those who had a knack for getting on base. Using sophisticated statistical analyses, the Athletics were able to demonstrate, in a reliable fashion, that on-base percentage (OBP) had a greater effect on a club's ability to score runs and win games than did defensive ability (or any of the other five tools promoted by baseball traditionalists). Armed with this knowledge, the A's were able to acquire a great number of effective players at low cost.

As a means of demonstrating the practical utility of incorporating the scientific method into decision making, Lewis (2003) posed the following research question: "If gross miscalculations of a person's value could occur on a baseball field, before a live audience of thirty thousand, and a television audience of millions more, what [does] that say about the measurement of performance in other lines of work?" (p. 72). This basic research question is what made *Moneyball* popular with a readership that extends well beyond the baseball diamond to include, but is certainly not limited to, general management, financial advising, academia, the film industry, and, of course, other professional sports (Gerrard & Howard, 2007).

"The race for talent and the impeding demographic challenges facing employers have been well documented for some time, yet most human resource professionals have not yet responded to this reality with new or innovative thinking. Most continue to approach talent management with the same toolbox that they have always used, relying on instinct, experience, and street smarts in much the same way that the old-school scouts of the Oakland A's did prior to the arrival of Billy Beane" (Pace, 2006, p. 140).

existing managerial theories can be used to explain sport management phenomena, (2) existing managerial theories can be built upon or extended through the study of sport, and (3) alternative theories can be proposed if existing theories do not offer adequate explanations for sport phenomena. Applying, testing, advancing, and developing new theories can further develop the body of knowledge in sport management.

Most sport managers will be interested in applied research because it is designed to help answer practical research questions, such as how to increase market share and customer satisfaction. Although applied sport management studies often have a narrowly defined purpose, do not necessarily draw on theories, and aim to produce practical results that are of immediate use, they still must use a systematic approach to research. That is, researchers must carefully define their research questions, consider how they will measure key concepts, select a sample, and collect and analyze the data before they communicate the results. Some common types of applied research in sport management include marketing research, feasibility studies, economic impact studies, and performance evaluations.

Quantitative and Qualitative Data

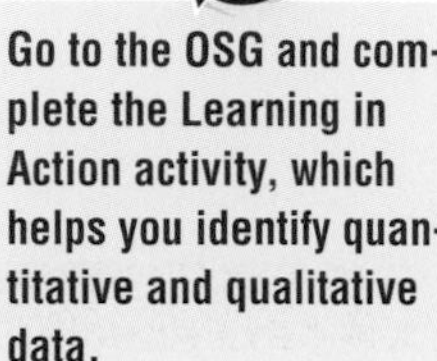

ACTION

Go to the OSG and complete the Learning in Action activity, which helps you identify quantitative and qualitative data.

One way to determine whether a study used a systematic approach is to examine the information source to ascertain whether the researchers collected empirical data. We usually associate data with numbers or statistics, but sport managers rely on many different types of data (Andrews, Mason, & Silk, 2005). Data in the form of numbers are known as quantitative data, whereas data in the form of words, pictures, or actions are known as qualitative data. The choice of data depends on the research question, and sometimes both types of data are required to address it. When investigators collect both quantitative data and qualitative data in the same study, they are using a mixed-methods approach (Creswell, 2009). For example, a program evaluation might entail counting the number of new and repeat participants as well as conducting interviews with them to determine whether any changes are desired.

Questionnaires, secondary data analyses, and content analyses are common techniques used in the sport management field to collect quantitative data for the purposes of establishing significant differences or relationships between variables of interest. In contrast, interviews, focus groups, observations, and content analyses are common techniques for collecting qualitative data to shed light on actions and the meanings that people associate with various sport-related activities. Table 20.3 summarizes some of the major advantages and disadvantages of the common methods used to collect quantitative data. Table 20.4 summarizes some of the main advantages and disadvantages of the methods that sport management researchers commonly use to collect qualitative data.

Research Design

research design—A strategy or plan of action that links the research questions to the choice of research methods and the desired outcomes.

Creswell (2009) defines a **research design** as a strategy or plan of action that links the research questions to the choice of research methods and the desired outcomes of the research. Common research designs in sport management research include experiments, surveys, ethnographies, case studies, and action research. Factors such as the purpose of the research, the research questions, the training and expertise of the researcher, available resources, and how the research will be used determine the choice of research design.

Like exercise scientists, some sport management researchers use experimental designs to test the effect of a treatment condition or an intervention on an outcome. By exposing groups to different treatments or interventions, the researcher can examine whether the treatment or intervention is causing a change in an outcome of interest (Creswell, 2009). Because experimental designs cannot answer all questions of interest, sport management researchers also use other research designs.

A survey design provides a quantitative or numeric description of trends or attitudes of a population of interest (Creswell, 2009). Researchers must carefully consider the questions that they will ask, the strategies that they will use to ensure that as many people as possible in their sample complete and return questionnaires, and the statistics that they will use to analyze the results. As more people gain access to computers, researchers are using online surveys more frequently than mail or telephone surveys.

Research questions are sometimes best answered by going out into the field and studying how sport is managed in a natural setting. Ethnography is one type of field research. The goal is often to understand the context or conditions that shape people's

TABLE 20.3 Common Methods Used to Collect Quantitative Data

Method	Main advantage	Main disadvantage
Mailed surveys	Can be used on larger samples	Low response rate
Internet or e-mail surveys	Quick response is possible	Only those with computers can participate
Telephone surveys	Immediate response	Respondents may believe that their privacy is invaded
Intercept surveys	Immediate response	Ensuring a representative sample is difficult
Secondary data analysis	Avoids costs of primary research	Not all data required may be available
Content analysis	Budgets, marketing material, planning documents, and media broadcasts are usually available	Not all data required may be available in these documents

TABLE 20.4 Common Methods Used to Collect Qualitative Data

Method	Main advantage	Main disadvantage
Interviews	In-depth responses are possible	Time intensive
Focus groups	Less time intensive than interviews	Managing group dynamics can be difficult
Observations	Can confirm or refute other types of data	Actions are often open to multiple interpretations

perspectives of their experiences as sport organizers, volunteers, consumers, or sponsors. Case studies are another popular research design in which the researcher explores a program, process, event, or organization in depth over time using a variety of data collection methods (Yin, 2008).

As a consequence of being a practically oriented area of study, the sport management field is an ideal forum for what is commonly known as **action research.** Lewin (1946) is often given credit for coining the term, which refers to generating knowledge about a social system while at the same time attempting to change it. In sport management circles, this activity involves solving problems that come directly from those who currently are or would like to be involved in sport. Although action research is not commonly used in sport management, interest in this research design is growing because it is a way of bringing study participants, practitioners, and researchers together to tackle problems of mutual concern (Frisby, Reid, Millar, & Hoeber, 2005). The overall goal of action research is to produce knowledge about how everyday experiences of people can be improved to promote social change and social justice (Reason & Bradbury, 2007). For example, we know that those living below the poverty line are much less likely to participate in sport because of the high costs of programs, apparel, and equipment. By collaborating with those living in poverty on all phases of the research process, community sport managers can identify barriers to participation and develop action strategies for overcoming them (Frisby, Crawford, & Dorer, 1997).

action research—Generating knowledge about a social system while at the same time attempting to change it.

Validity and Reliability

Before determining whether to collect quantitative data, qualitative data, or both, sport management researchers must determine how they are going to measure the various managerial concepts under investigation. Because many concepts are abstract (i.e., we cannot touch them or observe them directly), coming up with perfect measures or indicators is rarely possible. For example, managerial concepts such as organizational effectiveness and customer satisfaction are abstract and multifaceted and

APPLYING *MONEYBALL* PRINCIPLES TO EUROPEAN SOCCER

By Bill Gerrard • UNITED KINGDOM
Leeds University Business School

Michael Lewis' *Moneyball* (2003) is a case study of a successful "David" strategy in professional team sports. It explains how a resource-constrained US major league baseball (MLB) team, the Oakland Athletics, used statistical analysis as part of an evidence-based management style to challenge baseball's financial "Goliaths" such as the New York Yankees. Lewis suggested that if a team cannot spend more, then it should spend better by analysing available data to inform recruitment, team selection, tactical decisions, and remuneration decisions. General managers should approach the players' labour market like Wall Street traders, seeking to identify market inefficiencies and arbitrage opportunities if players' market valuations are out of line with their predicted performance levels.

Not surprisingly *Moneyball* struck a chord with executives and head coaches in the un-regulated "Wild West" that is European soccer. There are no salary caps, revenue sharing is limited, and the pro-motion and relegation (demotion) system in domestic leagues creates a highly incentivised merit hierarchy reinforced by the reward of qualification to the lucrative Union of European Football Associations (UEFA) Champions League tournament. In England, relegation from the FA Premier League,

The Bolton Wanderers benefited from using the *Moneyball* approach.

PA Photos.

are therefore difficult to define and capture. One way to measure abstract concepts is to create appropriate survey questions or other data collection techniques. Note, however, that our measures are never perfect indicators of the abstract concept under investigation.

validity—The degree to which measures capture the meaning of abstract concepts.

reliability—The consistency or dependability of measures of abstract concepts.

To determine how well our quantitative and qualitative data collection techniques measure abstract concepts of interest, **validity** and **reliability** are important considerations. Validity assesses how well our measures capture the meaning of abstract concepts, and reliability refers to the consistency or dependability of our measures. A sport manager can have more faith in research if the measures used capture the meaning of the abstract managerial concept and hold up over time and across different groups.

To illustrate, a manager of a fitness facility can assume that low prices, cleanliness, and qualified instructors contribute to customer satisfaction. If customers confirm that only these three factors contribute to their satisfaction, then the measures devised

the richest domestic soccer league in the world, can cost a team upwards of £50 million of lost revenue annually. For the smaller-market teams in the Premiership, the *Moneyball* approach of building a knowledge-based competitive advantage is the only prudent way to survive in the top tier.

An early proponent of the *Moneyball* approach in English soccer was the Bolton Wanderers. Under head coach Sam Allardyce, Bolton invested heavily in performance analysis as well as in fitness and conditioning and sport psychology. As a result, even with one of the smallest wage budgets, Bolton finished regularly in the top half of the Premiership.

Despite Bolton's success, the *Moneyball* approach of using statistical analyses of players' performance data remains in its infancy in European soccer. One of the principal reasons is the nature of soccer. Baseball and other striking and fielding games are atomistic in structure so that the contributions of individual players are largely independent and separable. By contrast, complex invasion team sports such as soccer and other codes of football, basketball, and hockey involve a high degree of player interdependency, creating problems in separating out and measuring individual contributions to winning and losing games. Given the fluidity of soccer, video analysis or tracking technology is necessary to collect detailed tactical data. Most elite soccer teams use a commercial tracking system such as ProZone or Amisco, but few teams analyse the data systematically, tending to retain the traditional approach of subjective assessments of critical incidents.

One of the most exciting possibilities for transferring *Moneyball* principles into soccer comes from the Oakland A's themselves. The Oakland ownership group has acquired a Major League Soccer (MLS) franchise, the San Jose Earthquakes, and have appointed the author of this essay as a technical consultant to develop a system for rating soccer players using statistical analysis of performance data. So perhaps it will be the US, not Europe, that will lead the way in applying *Moneyball* principles to soccer.

INTERNATIONAL LEARNING ACTIVITY #1

Using information and arguments posted on the Internet, discuss three evidence-based arguments for and three evidence-based arguments against using *Moneyball* principles in professional soccer.

INTERNATIONAL LEARNING ACTIVITY #2

On the European Association for Sport Management (EASM) Web site, access the list of recent articles published in the *European Sport Management Quarterly (ESMQ).* Classify the articles according to country of focus and subject area. What do you conclude about *ESMQ*'s success in offering an international outlook and covering multiple areas of sport management research?

by the manager would have high validity because they fully capture the meaning of the concept. But if customers reveal that other factors such as variety in program offerings and having the latest weight-training equipment also contribute to their satisfaction, then the survey or interview questions should incorporate those additional measures.

Using this same example, the fitness facility manager should also consider whether the measures of customer satisfaction are reliable by testing whether they are consistent over time and across different groups when all other conditions remain constant. For example, if customers were asked to fill out a customer satisfaction survey twice in a year and the results of the two surveys were similar, then the measures could be assumed to be dependable over time.

Although quantitative and qualitative researchers often use different terminology and techniques to assess validity and reliability, both groups are interested in producing results that are credible, dependable, and believable. Some of the strategies that they use to achieve these goals are carefully defining abstract concepts, examining results over time and across subgroups, and using multiple sources of data.

CURRENT CHALLENGES IN SPORT MANAGEMENT RESEARCH

Several major issues will affect sport management research as we move into the second decade of this century. A few of the most urgent are addressed in the following sections.

Judging the Quality of Research

Sport managers who lack adequate training face considerable challenges when interpreting research. Because of the information explosion that has accompanied the emergence of a knowledge-based economy, sport managers are bombarded with research from a variety of sources including the media, the Internet, trade publications, academic journals, consulting and governmental reports, workshops, and conference presentations, as well as research done for their own organizations. Because research varies considerably in quality, sport managers must be able to make accurate evaluations of the research methods used and the data analysis techniques employed to judge whether the conclusions drawn and the recommendations made are reliable and credible.

Consider the Source

The source of the research is one element to consider. Many people are suspicious of research reported over the Internet, with good reason. Although some Web sites contain research information that has been carefully monitored or reviewed, many do not. Readers often have difficulty determining whether information on the Internet is credible because the source may not report adequate details regarding the research design or the qualifications of the researcher.

Questions to Ask to Judge Research Quality

Sport managers should ask numerous questions when judging the quality of research. The following are some of the more critical questions that you should be asking:

1. Are the purposes, research questions, or hypotheses of the research clearly stated?
2. Is a strong rationale for conducting the study provided?
3. Who conducted the research, and what are their credentials?
4. Who sponsored the research, and how will they benefit from it?
5. What is the source of the research, and is a rigorous review process in place for ensuring quality?
6. Are the key concepts or variables under investigation clearly defined?
7. If applicable, was relevant literature or background information drawn upon?
8. Did the researcher consider ethical issues when conducting the research?
9. Were the methods used to collect the data appropriate?
10. What sampling techniques were used, and were they appropriate?
11. Are the measures or indicators of key concepts valid and reliable?
12. How were the data recorded and analyzed?
13. What are the limitations of the study design?
14. Were explanations for the findings provided, and are they justified?
15. Are conclusions and recommendations provided, and are they supported by the findings?

If it is not clear who conducted the research or what their credentials are, if few details are provided about the sample or research methods, and if no mention is made of the validity and reliability of the measures or indicators used, you should be highly suspicious of the claims being made. A systematic approach to research may have been used, but until you can verify that, you should critically question whether the conclusions and recommendations are justified and be hesitant about relying on the information when making decisions.

The Gap Between Theory and Practice

As discussed previously, research in the field is increasing as the study of sport management spreads to all parts of the globe. Although the field is growing and research is proliferating rapidly, an area of concern has become apparent. Parks (1992) clearly outlined the problem when she noted the struggle between those doing the research and those who must apply the knowledge. Nearly two decades later, the relationship between theory and practice in sport management remains a concern to many within the field. As Parks wrote, "Questions still remain how best to translate sport management theory into practice" (p. 221).

The key word is *translate*, and the meaning of that word leads to an important observation. Despite the proliferation of journals that have emerged in the field over the past two decades, the research that is published within them is geared toward the academic community and written in such a way that other researchers can understand it, but many practitioners cannot because they do not have adequate training in research. In fact, the readership of the theoretical journals listed in table 20.1 on page 419 is made up almost exclusively of professors and students in institutions of higher learning. Practitioners working in the field give those journals less attention, although a growing number of academic articles are discussing the practical implications of their findings for sport managers.

At the opposite end of the spectrum are a great number of trade publications that cater to a membership that is actively engaged in providing sport to the masses. These publications include numerous articles written by sport professionals for the benefit of other professionals working in the field. Written in lay terms, these articles commonly highlight best practices for managing sport teams, programs, facilities, events, and the like. These articles also provide timely statistical information regarding industry trends. Although some of these articles report on research conducted by sport managers working in the field, rarely would any of these studies stand up to scientific scrutiny. Moreover, although some trade publications, like *Street & Smith's SportsBusiness Journal*, feature articles written by academics, they are not vetted through the same peer-review process as academic journals are, so readers should be cautious when basing decisions on the findings published in these outlets.

What should become clear from this analysis is that no publications occupy a common ground, where both researchers and practitioners can contribute and reap the benefits from what is being written. Put on a continuum from theoretical to practical, the various publications show an obvious gap (see figure 20.1 on page 432). The perceived gap between theory and practice in this field can be narrowed as more sport management students learn about research. At the same time, academics cannot assume that the results of their well-conceived and eloquently written studies will reach or have an effect on the field. Consequently, some are actively striving to communicate their findings more broadly (e.g., in professional publications and conferences, in government reports, in the media). Similarly, practitioners should not assume that research is too esoteric to be of practical use and should work with academics to identify problems of mutual concern that could be addressed through research to improve policies and managerial practices. Members of both groups must make a stronger effort to answer

Using Statistics Correctly

The following two sections of this sidebar deal with research and decision making in the sport industry. The first section examines MLB salaries to illustrate how sport managers need to be aware of the consequences associated with using mean scores as the basis for any decision. While statistics such as an average can provide precise information to help in the decision-making process, such statistics only provide part of the picture and thus sport managers should be careful in drawing conclusions from the numbers alone. The second section of this sidebar uses several sport management examples to illustrate the issues surrounding surveys, sample selection and sizes, drawing inferences, and arriving at sound conclusions.

Example 1: The Well-Chosen Average

According to a report filed by the Associated Press (Bloom, 2008b), the average opening-day salary for MLB players topped the US$3 million mark for the first time in 2008. At US$3.15 million, this figure represented a 7.1% increase from the previous season and marked the fourth consecutive year that average salaries increased for MLB players. The average (arithmetic mean) is a measure of central tendency and certainly provides some information. Yet we must be aware of how this average is used and what it hides. For example, this US$3.15 million figure fails to inform us that the average player on the New York Yankees earned more than twice this amount at US$6.86 million, making the Yankees MLB's leading spender for the 10th year in a row. This spending on playing talent did not seem to help the Yankees in 2008 as they missed the postseason for the first time since 1994, when the playoffs were canceled because of a labor dispute. Nor does this average indicate that the Tampa Bay Rays leveraged the fourth lowest average salary at US$1.59 million to make their first trip to the World Series in franchise history, eventually losing to the Philadelphia Phillies, whose average salary ranked 11th in the league at US$3.39 million. Although the same study reported these figures, the US$3.15 million leaguewide average was likely the most quoted by the media and most used in salary negotiations during the off-season.

Intuitively, we also would want to question the effect that huge salaries, like those paid to the Yankees' Alex Rodriguez (US$28 million) and Derek Jeter (US$21.6 million), have on this reported average. No fewer than 85 players earned in excess of US$10 million during the 2008 season (Bloom, 2008a). Given the incredible disparity between the earnings of these players and those making the MLB minimum (US$390,000 in 2008), the average may not be the best figure for understanding MLB salaries. Of all the measures of central tendency, the arithmetic mean is the one most affected by extreme measures (either high or low). Perhaps the median (the middle salary) or the mode (the salary most commonly earned) would be a more appropriate measure to use when reporting player salaries. Some other well-chosen averages to be wary of are (1) the average income of spectators at a professional sport event, (2) the average age of joggers, (3) the average amount spent on sport equipment in a year, and (4) the average length of employment for service employees at a stadium.

To summarize, we can fairly say that statistics can provide precise information that will assist in making sport management decisions, but we must be extremely careful in drawing conclusions from the numbers alone. They provide only part of the picture. For instance, in the example of MLB salaries, by employing the critical thinking questions posed in chapter 1 (e.g., what significant information is omitted?) sport managers can expose the consequences associated with using mean scores as the basis for decision making.

Example 2: Built-In Bias

Darrell Huff wrote a book titled *How to Lie With Statistics*. "To be worth much," Huff wrote, "a report based on sampling must use a representative sample, which is one from which every source of bias has been removed" (1993, p. 18). Sometimes when we do research, we have a strong desire to produce a pleasing answer. Surveys are used to gauge customer satisfaction, fan allegiance, and a host of other factors. Because we can rarely survey the entire population, we draw samples to represent a much larger number of people. If the sample is representative of the larger population, we can draw inferences and be more assured that our conclusions are sound. In some instances, however, the sample is not representative. Analyze the following hypothetical situations to see whether you can spot the problem:

1. A Major League Soccer (MLS) franchise (e.g., DC United) surveys spectators at a game to determine fan allegiance.

2. The city council of Boise, Idaho, hesitates on plans for a multipurpose recreational facility because of an outcry of opposition in the letters to the editor section of the local newspaper.
3. The cost of playing youth lacrosse in a Canadian maritime province was increased to C$150 per season based on a survey that determined the average income of the players' parents.
4. A survey of spectators at a local harness racing track revealed that 60% would be receptive to having nutritious offerings replace junk food.

On the surface, each of the scenarios is a legitimate way to use information to improve decision making in sport management. But we must be careful what we ask, whom we ask, how we ask, and most important, what we conclude. Take, for example, the previous hypothetical situations:

1. The information derived from the DC United survey will be biased by the fact that the fan allegiance of spectators would be presumed to be quite high. A comparison between casual fans and regular fans would be more useful, but the best information might come from people who do not attend games at all.
2. People who write letters to the editor are not necessarily representative of the population of a given city. The overwhelming majority may be in favor of a new recreational facility but do not find it necessary to have their thoughts appear in print. Also, a sampling process did not preselect the letter writers—they volunteered to write, and thus they create an imbalance of opinion about which readers of the newspaper must be alert.
3. If the average income was self-reported, then the lacrosse officials should be careful in using the results because people tend to inflate their earnings when surveyed. And because we already know about the well-chosen average, we know that this income figure may not be representative of the parents of these young players.
4. When surveyed, people almost always support habits and practices that are good for them. The existence of reporting differences between attitudes and actual behavior in survey research is well established. People may say they would like to see food that is more nutritious at the concession stands, yet junk food will continue to be the biggest seller.

Refer to the critical thinking questions presented in chapter 1 to help you in your analysis of the preceding hypothetical situations. Can you think of other areas in statistics and research where you might be able to use critical thinking skills to elicit practical solutions to complex problems in the field of sport management?

questions such as these: What does this really mean? How can it be of use to me? How can we work together to promote progressive and innovative change?

FUTURE OF SPORT MANAGEMENT RESEARCH

More sport managerial issues will arise as the field grows and the century progresses. Changing technologies, environments, workforces, spectators, venues, security measures, and a plethora of other factors will influence sport and the ways in which it is managed. Sport scholars and practitioners foresee changes in media delivery, game management, and customer service to be at the forefront of concern. What issues and problems do you foresee? How will you solve them to the satisfaction of various stakeholders? What methods will you use to address your research questions?

The amount of research conducted in sport management will continue to grow to meet the demands of decision makers and to build the body of knowledge in the field. Given the importance of research as outlined in this chapter, we hope that research will eventually be included as a core content area in the undergraduate curriculum for sport management degree programs around the world. Where such classes are not

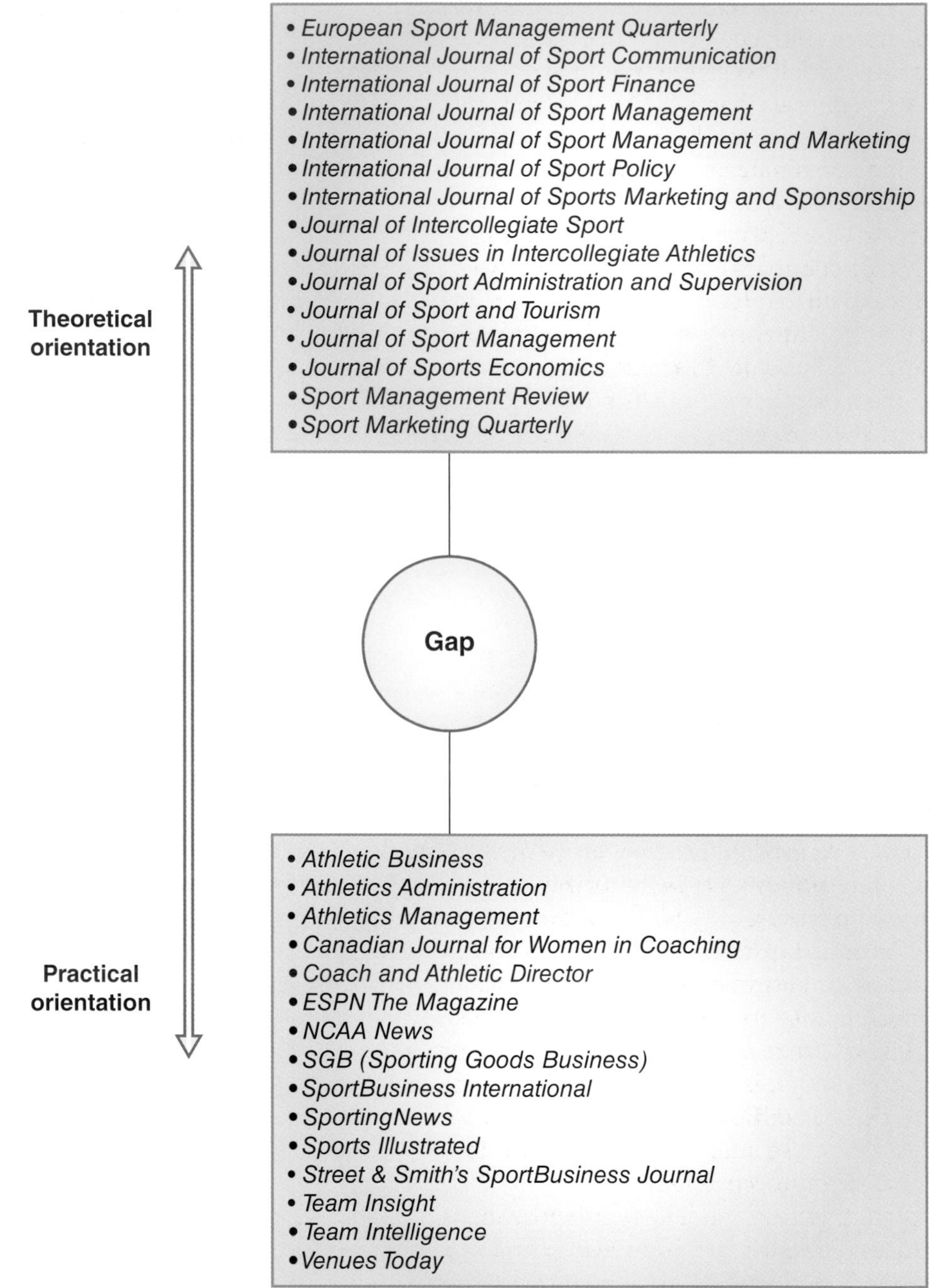

Figure 20.1 A hole in the literature!

required, sport management students should seek out courses in research methods to prepare themselves for a future based in the knowledge economy.

CRITICAL THINKING IN SPORT MANAGEMENT RESEARCH

You do not have to look far to realize that statistical information inundates our daily lives. TV commercials inform us that "four out of five dentists surveyed recommend Brand X toothpaste." News broadcasts mention that our chances of getting the flu this winter are 1 in 20 without a flu shot and 1 in 100 with the shot. Professional and amateur sport stars break records at what appears to be a record-breaking pace. Goals, home runs, coaching victory totals, and the youngest 10,000-point scorer are all examples of what we count, put in some kind of chronology, and compare or contrast.

North America has clearly demonstrated a preoccupation with sport statistics. Although statistics can be useful, those aspiring to be sport managers should be aware of the indiscriminate and in some cases intentional misuse of statistical information. As mentioned earlier, in 1954 Darrell Huff wrote a book titled *How to Lie with Statistics*. The book was reprinted in 1982 and again in 1993 and has become a bestseller in a number of countries. In a lighthearted way, Huff described how the presentation of statistical data can fool us and give us a sense of false confidence because the numbers back it up. In the earlier sidebar "Using Statistics Correctly" we adapted two of Huff's examples to illustrate how statistics influence sport managers and how they must be careful in using them. Used correctly, statistical information complements the research process. Used improperly, however, statistics can be misleading at best and incorrect at worst.

PORTFOLIO

Complete the critical thinking portfolio activity in the OSG, consulting as needed the "Eight Critical Thinking Questions" section in chapter 1.

ETHICS IN SPORT MANAGEMENT RESEARCH

A number of important ethical issues should be taken into account when conducting sport management research. Most colleges and universities have ethical guidelines that students and faculty members must follow when conducting research directly with people. These same ethical guidelines should be followed when sport management research is conducted outside the university setting to ensure that it is conducted professionally. For example, people have a right to know what the research is about and how it will be used before they agree to participate in a study, whether it is filling out a marketing survey or being interviewed on a topic of interest to sport managers. Participation in research should be voluntary, so even though researchers need to explain the importance of their studies and encourage people to take part in research, staff, volunteers, or customers should not feel as if they are being coerced into participating.

Research in sport organizations can often deal with sensitive topics, so **anonymity**, which means that names of study participants should not be included in the reporting of the results, is another ethical guideline that should be followed. Anonymity is closely tied to **confidentiality**, which means that researchers should not be specifying who said what, so study participants will feel free to speak honestly and openly about the topic without repercussions.

anonymity—Normally, the names of people who participate in research are not revealed in the reporting of the study.

confidentiality—What individual people say or report in research is not revealed in the reporting of the study.

Violating ethical guidelines in sport management research can have serious consequences. For example, if an evaluation of the leadership of a sport organization is being conducted and researchers release the names and comments made by employees who have concerns, these employees may face negative sanctions from bosses and coworkers for expressing their views. To learn more about ethical guidelines in sport management research, students are encouraged to take research methods courses and read the research ethics guidelines at their college or university.

PORTFOLIO

Complete the ethical issues portfolio activity in the OSG, consulting as needed the "Guidelines for Making Ethical Decisions" section in chapter 1.

Summary

Raising and addressing research questions are critical to sport managers in our information-based economy. Sport managers who ask relevant and focused research questions and obtain valid and reliable answers through sound research practices will enhance their planning and improve the likelihood of achieving success both on and off the playing field. The most successful sport managers in the second decade of the

21st century will be those who understand the importance of asking research questions and using research to inform their decision making.

Sport management research is available from a variety of sources. The scholarly literature and the professional literature are both excellent sources of information and often lead readers to ask additional research questions of their own. In many cases, commercial research firms are contracted to aid sport organizations in identifying suitable research questions and obtaining appropriate answers. Regardless of the source, sport managers need a solid foundation in research to be able to assess what types of information are reliable and credible. Understanding key concepts such as ways of knowing, science and pseudoscience, basic and applied research, qualitative and quantitative data, research design, and reliability and validity can help sport managers judge the quality of research so that they can make sound decisions. This understanding will also help bridge the gap between sport management theory and practice.

Engaging in the research process can be stimulating and rewarding for students. Besides incorporating research into their coursework, sport management students can attend conferences, join associations that promote sport management research (e.g., NASSM, EASM, SMAANZ), and refer to publications within the field. In addition, students can also ask professors about how they might get involved as volunteers or participants in their ongoing research studies, which often take place right on campus.

Review Questions

1. What value does a sport organization receive from research provided by the academic and professional literature?
2. Under what circumstances would a commercial research firm be able to make valuable contributions to a sport organization?
3. What are five key ways that pseudoscience differs from science, and why does the scientific approach provide sport managers with more trustworthy information on which to base decisions?
4. What are some of the differences between quantitative and qualitative data? Describe one common data collection technique for each and provide one main advantage and one main disadvantage of each data collection technique discussed.
5. What is a research design, and what are the key features of the most common research designs used in sport management research?
6. Why is it important to consider ethical issues when conducting sport management research?
7. What questions should be asked to judge the quality of sport management research?
8. Do you agree that the need for expertise in sport management research will continue to grow in the future? Justify your argument.

QUIZ TIME

Did you grasp all the key points in this chapter? Go to the OSG for a short quiz to test your understanding of the material.

References

Andrews, D.L., Mason, D.A., & Silk, M. (Eds.). (2005). *Qualitative methods in sport studies*. London: Berg.

Bloom, B.M. (2008a, April 1). *Average salary in MLB tops $3 million*. Retrieved June 12, 2010, from http://mlb.mlb.com/news/article.jsp?ymd=20080401&content_id=2479371&vkey=news_mlb&fext=.jsp&c_id=mlb

Bloom, B.M. (2008b, December 4). *MLB salary increase lowest since '04*. Retrieved February 2, 2010, from www.mlb.com/news/article.jsp?ymd=20081204&content_id=3702956&vkey=news_mlb&fext=.jsp&c_id=mlb

Council of American Survey Research Organizations. (2009). *CASRO—who we are—what we do*. Retrieved February 2, 2010, from www.casro.org/whatis.cfm

Creswell, J.W. (2009). *Research design: Qualitative, quantitative, and mixed methods approaches* (3rd ed.). Thousand Oaks, CA: Sage.

Dolan, R.J. (2006). Applying *Moneyball* ideas outside of baseball: The perspective of a business school dean. *Human Resource Management, 45*, 132–135.

Eitzen, D.S., & Sage, G.H. (2008). *Sociology of North American sport* (8th ed.). Boulder, CO: Paradigm.

Frank, R. (1984). Olympic myths and realities. *Arete: The Journal of Sport Literature, 1*(2), 155–161.

Frisby, W., Crawford, S., & Dorer, T. (1997). Reflections on participatory action research: The case of low-income women accessing local physical activity services. *Journal of Sport Management, 11*, 8–28.

Frisby, W., Reid, C., Millar, S., & Hoeber, L. (2005). Putting "participatory" into participatory forms of action research. *Journal of Sport Management, 19*, 367–386.

Gerrard, B., & Howard, D. (2007). Editorial introduction: *Moneyball* as sport finance inaction: But are the lessons from baseball more generally applicable? *International Journal of Sport Finance, 2*, 175–176.

Huff, D. (1993). *How to lie with statistics*. New York: Norton.

Isidore, C. (2008, December 1). *It's official: Recession since Dec. '07*. Retrieved February 2, 2010, from http://money.cnn.com/2008/12/01/news/economy/recession/index.htm?postversion=2008120112

Kerlinger, F.N., & Lee, H.B. (2000). *Foundations of behavioral research* (4th ed.). Orlando, FL: Harcourt.

King, B. (2004, September 13). Will rise of DVRs change sports TV? *Street & Smith's SportsBusiness Journal*, p. 1.

Lewin, K. (1946). Action research and minority problems. *Journal of Social Issues, 2*, 34–36.

Lewis, M. (2003). *Moneyball: The art of winning an unfair game*. New York: Norton.

Miller, S. (2003, August 11). Research budgets increase as leagues seek growth. *Street & Smith's SportsBusiness Journal*, p. 17.

Pace, D. (2006). *Moneyball* lessons: The transition from HR intuition to HR analytics. *Human Resource Management, 45*, 140–142.

Parks, J.B. (1992). Scholarship: The other "bottom line" in sport management. *Journal of Sport Management, 6*, 220–229.

Poole, M. (2004, February 16). Sports sponsorship will be the key to connecting with the TiVo generation. *Street & Smith's SportsBusiness Journal*, p. 11.

Reason, P., & Bradbury, H. (2007). *Handbook of action research*. Thousand Oaks, CA: Sage.

Senior, J., & Asensio, R. (2009). *TV 2013: It's all over!* Retrieved June 12, 2009, from www.oliverwyman.com/ow/8868.htm

Shilbury, D., & Rentschler, R. (2007). Assessing sport management journals: A multi-dimensional examination. *Sport Management Review, 10*, 31–44.

Slack, T., & Parent, M. (2006). *Understanding sport organizations: The application of organization theory* (2nd ed.). Champaign, IL: Human Kinetics.

Stewart, M.F., Mitchell, H., & Stavros, C. (2007). *Moneyball* applied: Econometrics and the identification and recruitment of elite Australian footballers. *International Journal of Sport Finance, 2*, 231–248.

Thomas, J.R., Nelson, J.K., & Silverman, S.J. (2005). *Research methods in physical activity* (5th ed.). Champaign, IL: Human Kinetics.

Wilson, B. (2006). Selective memory in a global culture: Reconsidering links between youth, hockey, and Canadian identity. In D. Whitson & R. Gruneau, R. (Eds.), *Artificial ice: Hockey, commerce, and Canadian culture* (pp. 53–70). Aurora, Ontario, Canada: Garamond.

Yin, R.K. (2008). *Case study research: Design and methods* (4th ed.). Thousand Oaks, CA: Sage.

INDEX

Note: The italicized *f* and *t* following page numbers refer to figures and tables, respectively.

ABOUT THE EDITORS

Paul M. Pedersen, PhD, the newest member of the editorial team, is an associate professor of sport management and the director of the sport management doctoral program at Indiana University at Bloomington. Previously, Pedersen taught sport communication and management courses at several colleges and universities, including Bowling Green State University and Palm Beach Atlantic University.

A former sportswriter and sports business columnist, Pedersen has researched, published, and presented on the activities and practices of many sport organization personnel, specifically those associated with the print media (e.g., editors, reporters) and affiliated with intercollegiate and interscholastic sports (e.g., athletic directors, student-athletes). He has lectured and presented on sport communication and management topics around the world, including China and Korea. His primary area of scholarly interest is the symbiotic relationship between sport and communication.

Pedersen has published over 60 peer-reviewed articles in journals such as the *Journal of Sport Management, Sociology of Sport Journal, International Journal of Sports Marketing and Sponsorship,* and *Journal of Sports Economics.* Pedersen has authored or coauthored *Strategic Sport Communication* (2007), *Research Methods and Design in Sport Management* (2011), and two sport history texts.

Founder and editor in chief of the *International Journal of Sport Communication*, Pedersen also serves as an editorial review board member of five national and international sport journals. He is a research fellow for the North American Society for Sport Management (NASSM), a member of the North American Society for Sport History (NASSH) and the European Association for Sport Management (EASM), and a charter member of Sport Marketing Association (SMA).

Pedersen lives in Bloomington, Indiana, with his wife, Jennifer, and their four children. He enjoys spending time with his family as well as traveling, photography, cycling, and watching sporting events. His photo is courtesy of Indiana University.

Janet B. Parks, DA, is distinguished teaching professor emerita, former graduate studies coordinator, and former sport management division chair at Bowling Green State University in Ohio. She was a founding member of the North American Society for Sport Management (NASSM), which has honored her with the Earle F. Zeigler Award for Professional Achievement (1992) and the NASSM Distinguished Service Award (2001). She is a NASSM research fellow; a fellow in the Research Consortium of the American Alliance for Health, Physical Education, Recreation and Dance (AAHPERD); and the recipient of the Outstanding Achievement Award from the Sport Management Council (SMC) of the National Association for Sport and Physical Education (NASPE) and the President's Award from the National Association for Girls and Women in Sport (NAGWS). She was twice selected as an honorary fellow in the Women's Studies Research Center at the University of Wisconsin at Madison.

Parks is a founding coeditor of the *Journal of Sport Management* and has served on NASPE's Task Force on Sport Management Curriculum Accreditation (1986-93) and Sport Management Program Review Council (1993-94). In 2005–2006, she was an SMC/NASPE representative on the Task Force on Sport Management Curriculum Standards.

During her 39 years on faculty at BGSU, Parks taught physical education and sport management and coached tennis and golf. Her published works include textbooks, book chapters, journal articles, and a computer program on sport management career guidance. Since retiring from teaching in 2004, Parks has written and produced *Title IX: Implications for Women in Sport and Education*, a three-disc DVD set designed for classroom use. Her most recent book, written in collaboration with Addie Muti and Ann Bowers, chronicles the history of women's sports at BGSU.

An avid traveler, she makes her home in Bowling Green, Ohio, where she enjoys working on projects that preserve the history of women in physical education and sport. She also volunteers for several social service agencies in her community. Her photo is courtesy of Craig J. Bell, BGSU.

Jerome Quarterman, PhD, is an associate professor in the department of health, human performance, and leisure studies at Howard University in Washington, DC. Prior to that, he was on the faculty at Florida State University and taught graduate students in research methods, organizational theory, and diversity in organizations of the sport industry. He was a tenured faculty member at Bowling Green State University of Ohio for 11 years. Prior to his position at Bowling Green, his teaching and administrative experiences were at historically black colleges and universities, including Southern, Alabama State, Kentucky State, Central State, Hampton, Florida A&M, and Lincoln universities. He is a member of the North American Society for Sport Management (NASSM) and was inducted as a NASSM Fellow in June 2010. He is also a member of the American Alliance for Health, Physical Education, Recreation and Dance (AAHPERD).

Quarterman is an active researcher who has authored or coauthored 45 scholarly publications, including peer-reviewed journal articles, book chapters, and edited books. His research has appeared in the *International Journal of Sport Management, Sport Marketing Quarterly, Journal of Sport Management, Academic Athletic Journal, Journal of Teaching Physical Education, Applied Research in Coaching and Athletics Annual, The Physical Educator, International Journal of Sport Marketing and Sponsorship, Journal of Physical Education, Recreation and Dance*, and *College Student Journal*. He has also served on the editorial boards for *International Journal of Sport Management, Athletic Academic Journal*, and *ICHPERSD Journal of Research*.

He has served on and chaired numerous master and doctoral committees at Bowling Green, Florida State, and Howard universities. He teaches students in a variety of courses at the undergraduate, master's, and doctoral levels, including organizational theory, intercollegiate athletic administration, research methods in sport management, ethics and social issues in sport, human resources management, sport marketing, and diversity in sport organizations.

Quarterman holds a doctoral degree from Ohio State University, a master's degree from Kent State University, and a bachelor's degree from Savannah State University. He is the proud parent of Terrance and Michele. His photo appears courtesy of Dr. Quarterman.

Lucie Thibault, PhD, is an associate professor at Brock University in Ontario, Canada. Before working at Brock University, Thibault taught at the University of British Columbia for 8 years and the University of Ottawa for 5 years. In more than 20 years of teaching, Thibault has instructed courses in organizational theory, organizational behavior, ethics in sport, globalization of sport, and policy and social issues in sport.

Thibault serves on the editorial board of the *International Journal of Sport Policy* as well as the *Journal of Sport Management* where she previously held the posts of associate editor and editor. She is a member of the North American Society for Sport Management (NASSM) and was named a NASSM research fellow in 2001. In 2008, Thibault was awarded the Earle F. Zeigler Award from NASSM for her scholarly and leadership contributions to the field.

Her research interests lie in the formation, management, and evaluation of cross-sectoral partnerships in sport organizations. She also investigates the role of the Canadian government in sport excellence and sport participation and government involvement in developing sport policy. Her research has appeared in the *Journal of Sport Management, International Review for the Sociology of Sport, Journal of Sport and Social Issues, Human Relations, Leisure Studies, European Sport Management Quarterly*, and *International Journal for Sport Management and Marketing*.

Thibault resides in St. Catharines, Ontario. Her photo is courtesy of Suzanne Gabriel, Brock University.

ABOUT THE CONTRIBUTORS

Robertha Abney, PhD, is an associate professor at Slippery Rock University (SRU) in the Department of Sport Management. She received her doctorate in athletics administration from the University of Iowa. Her areas of research include role models and mentoring women in sport (womentoring), and the status of minorities and women in leadership roles in sport. At SRU she teaches undergraduate and graduate courses in sport management and ethics, sport communication, and introduction to sport management. She has written several chapters in sport management textbooks. She served on six committees within the National Collegiate Athletic Association (NCAA) during her tenure as associate athletics director and senior woman administrator at SRU. She served on the NCAA Division II Management Council, Management Council Subcommittee, Committee on Infractions, Administrative Review Subcommittee, Championship Task Force Committee, and Project Team to Review Issues Related to Diversity. Also, she served on the American Alliance for Health, Physical Education, Recreation and Dance (AAHPERD) Awards Committee. She is a past president of the National Association for Girls and Women in Sport (NAGWS). Dr. Abney is a member of the North American Society for Sport Management (NASSM). She was elected to serve on the Commission on Sport Management Accreditation (COSMA) Board of Commissioners. Dr. Abney's photo appears courtesy of Herman A. Boler.

Robin Ammon, Jr., EdD, is a full professor and the chair of the Department of Sport Management at Slippery Rock University (SRU). He graduated with a doctoriate in sport administration from the University of Northern Colorado. His areas of research include legal liabilities in sport, risk management in sport and athletics, and premises liability. At SRU he teaches undergraduate and graduate courses in risk management, sport law, event and facility, management, and a senior seminar. Dr. Ammon has written more than a dozen articles in refereed journals, 11 chapters in sport management books, and three textbooks. He has presented more than 60 times at local, regional, national, and international conferences on a variety of topics including facility, legal, security, and crowd management issues. Dr. Ammon has served as an expert witness in a variety of court cases regarding several of these issues. In 2009 he was selected as a highly skilled trainer for the delivery of the Department of Homeland Security (DHS) Risk Management Training for Sports Event Security Management. This issue entails developing effective security management systems for sport events held at national intercollegiate football stadiums. Dr. Ammon's photo appears courtesy of Robin Ammon, Jr.

Ketra L. Armstrong, PhD, is a professor and the director of the graduate program in sport management at California State University at Long Beach. She is the former president of the National Association for Girls and Women in Sport. Before her arrival at California State University at Long Beach, Dr. Armstrong taught sport marketing courses at Ohio State University, where she also received her PhD in sport management (cognate area: sociology). Dr. Armstrong is a research fellow in the North American Society for Sport Management. Her research specialization is sport marketing and sport consumer behavior, and her research has been featured in numerous journals: *Journal of Sport Management*, *Sport Management Review*, *International Journal of Sport Management*, *Sport Marketing Quarterly*, *Journal of Sport Behavior*, *Journal of Sport and Social Issues*, *Women in Sport and Physical Activity Journal*, *Journal of Black Psychology*,

Quest, *Academic Athletic Journal*, *Black Coaches Association Journal*, *Physical Educator*, and *Future Focus*. She coauthored a manuscript that received the Outstanding Research Award by the Sport Marketing Association. She has conducted research for *Essence* magazine on Black women's fitness, and she received the Young Professional Award from the American Association of Active Lifestyle and Fitness. In addition to pursuing her scholarly interests, Dr. Armstrong has amassed a wealth of practical experience in the sport industry. She is a former Division I basketball player, Division I women's basketball coach, and collegiate athletics administrator. Over the years, she has performed integral roles in the research, management, marketing, and media relations for numerous community, collegiate, national, and international sport events. Dr. Armstrong is also a freelance sport broadcaster and a former board member of the National Women's Hall of Fame. Her photo appears courtesy of Ketra Armstrong.

F. Wayne Blann, EdD, earned his doctorate from Boston University and is professor and coordinator of the undergraduate sport management degree program at Ithaca College. In 1986 he developed the sport marketing course in the sport management curriculum at Ithaca College, and he continues to teach this course. He also teaches sport marketing in the Ithaca College sport management graduate program. Dr. Blann pioneered research on American collegiate and professional athletes' and coaches' career transitions. He has served as consultant to the NBA, the NFL, the NHL Players Association, and the Major League Baseball Players Association. Since 1996 the Professional Athletes Career Transition Program (PACTP) developed by Dr. Blann has served as the model for athlete career education programs. He has given numerous presentations at national and international conferences and has published articles in sport management, applied sport psychology, sport sociology, and applied research in coaching and athletics journals and newsletters. Dr. Blann was twice inducted into the Johnson State College (Vermont) Sports Hall of Fame: in 1996 as an honorary member for his leadership as athletics director and in 2003 for his basketball coaching achievements. In 2008 a group of faculty colleagues and alumni established a scholarship in Dr. Blann's name in recognition of his leadership and contributions to the Department of Sport Management and Media. Dr. Blann's photo appears courtesy of Melanie Blann, DPT, ATC, Florida Orthopedic Institute.

Robert L. Boucher, PhD, professor and dean of the Faculty of Human Kinetics at the University of Windsor, Ontario, has extensive experience as a leader in the academic and applied areas of sport management. He cofounded and has served as president of the North American Society for Sport Management (NASSM) and the Canadian Intramural Recreation Association (CIRA). He was the head of the Department of Athletics and Recreational Services at the University of Windsor from 1987 to 1996. He served as the chef de mission for the 1997 World University Games in Sicily, Italy, and as the assistant chef for the 1995 World University Games in Fukuoka, Japan. He also served as the chair of the organizing committee of the Pan-Am Junior Athletic Championships, which were held in Windsor in 2005. Dr. Boucher has published an edited book with Dr. W. James Weese and has written articles that appear in a variety of academic and professional journals. Dr. Boucher received the Dr. Earle F. Zeigler Lecture Award for contributions to sport management by NASSM in 1996 and the Distinguished Service Award in 2002. Dr. Boucher's photo appears courtesy of the University of Windsor.

Jennifer E. Bruening, PhD, earned her BA in English from the University of Notre Dame (1992), her MA in English from Morehead State University (1994), and her PhD from Ohio State University (2000). Bruening spent four years as a collegiate student–athlete playing volleyball at the University of Notre Dame. She spent eight years as an athletics administrator and volleyball coach at Kenyon College in Ohio, including two years as athletics director. She has been a part of the sport management program at the University of Connecticut since January 2002 and serves as the director of the Laboratory for Sport Management. She is also a research fellow with Northeastern University's Center for the Study of Sport in Society. Dr. Bruening's research line has focused primarily on the barriers and supports for women and minorities in sport. Dr. Bruening is also the program founder and director for Husky Sport, receiving funding from the USDA and the City of Hartford. Husky Sport has both a program and a research component. The program provides mentors (UConn students) as planners of sessions at a recreation center, an elementary school, and a neighborhood Saturday program that emphasize exposure and access to sport and physical activity and advocate good nutrition and healthy lifestyles. Research has focused specifically on the effect of such a program on preadolescent females and the effect of involvement in such a program on the college student mentors. For more information see www.huskysport.uconn.edu. Her photo appears courtesy of Jennifer E. Bruening.

Carla A. Costa, PhD, is an assistant professor in the Department of Sport, Recreation and Tourism at the University of Illinois at Urbana-Champaign. Dr. Costa earned her doctoral degree in sport management from Ohio State University. She has completed funded research projects and published findings in peer-reviewed publications on the areas of participation of youth in sport, participation and training of volunteers in sport, event and destination leveraging, and, broadly stated, the utility of sport as a community development tool. As the coauthor of *Adventure Sport Tourism in Rural Revitalization*, she explored several assumptions that are commonly present in the use of sport for community revitalization in rural areas. Some of her recent research projects focus on the challenges of aligning stakeholders' perceptions, values, beliefs, and expectations when formulating and implementing strategies and policies that incorporate sport as one of the elements in community development. She is active in the North American Society for Sport Management (NASSM) and the European Association for Sport Management (EASM) and currently serves on the editorial board of the *Journal of Sport Management*. Dr. Costa's photo appears courtesy of the University of Illinois at Urbana-Champaign.

Corinne M. Daprano, PhD, is an associate professor in sport management and the associate chair of the Department of Health and Sport Science at the University of Dayton. She graduated from Ohio State University and has more than 15 years of experience working in the sport and recreation industry. Her research interests include the study of strategic human resource management, organizational change and the factors associated with change within sport and recreation organizations, and service learning in higher education and its application to sport management programs. At the University of Dayton, she teaches undergraduate courses in sport law, human resource management, principles of management, global sport business, and women in sport. Dr. Daprano has published articles in *Sport Management Review*, *Recreational Sports Journal*, *Quest*, and *Future Focus*. She has coauthored a book chapter on the topic of service learning and has made numerous presentations at local, regional, national, and international conferences on volunteer management, organizational change, and service learning. Dr. Daprano serves on the editorial review boards of *Sport Management Review* and the *Sport Management Education Journal*. She is a member of the North American Society for Sport Management (NASSM) and the National Intramural-Recreational Sports Association (NIRSA). Dr. Daprano's photo appears courtesy of Larry Burgess, University of Dayton.

Timothy D. DeSchriver, EdD, is an associate professor of sport management in the Alfred Lerner College of Business and Economics at the University of Delaware. He earned his doctor of education degree in physical education with an emphasis in sport administration from the University of Northern Colorado. He has worked as a field economist for the US Department of Labor, served as interim associate athletics director at the University of Northern Colorado, and spent four years as an assistant professor at Western Carolina University. He currently teaches classes on sport finance and sport marketing at both the undergraduate and graduate levels. Dr.

DeSchriver's research interests are sport consumer demand, pro sport ownership incentives, and sport facility financing. He has published articles in the *Journal of Sport Management*, *Eastern Economic Journal*, *Sport Marketing Quarterly*, *International Sports Journal*, and *Street & Smith's SportsBusiness Journal*. He has been involved in research projects for the NCAA, the New York Red Bulls, the Major Indoor Soccer League, and the National Steeplechase Association. He was also coauthor of the textbook *Sport Finance* (first and second editions). Dr. DeSchriver is a member of the North American Society for Sport Management (NASSM) and the Sport Marketing Association (SMA). He has made numerous presentations at NASSM annual conferences as well as at international conferences. Before taking his position at the University of Delaware, Dr. DeSchriver was an assistant professor at the University of Massachusetts Amherst. Dr. DeSchriver's photo appears courtesy of the University of Massachusetts Amherst.

Stephen W. Dittmore, PhD, is an assistant professor in the Department of Health Science, Kinesiology, Recreation, and Dance at the University of Arkansas where he teaches undergraduate and graduate courses in the recreation and sport management program. He earned his doctorate from the University of Louisville. He also holds a visiting assistant professor position with the AACSB-accredited sport management MBA program at the Instituto de Empresa in Madrid, Spain, where he teaches a course in sport media and public relations. Dittmore's research has appeared in the *Journal of Sport Management*, the *International Journal of Sport Communication*, and the *International Journal of Sport Management*. He coauthored *Sport Public Relations: Managing Organizational Communication*. Dittmore has 10 years of practitioner experience in various sport public relations roles and served as a director of the Salt Lake City Organizing Committee for the 2002 Olympic Winter Games. His photo appears courtesy of the University of Arkansas.

Jess C. Dixon, PhD, is an assistant professor of sport management in the Department of Kinesiology at the University of Windsor. His primary research and scholarly interests are in the areas of strategic management in sport. His secondary interests include executive leadership and human resource management in sport, sport finance and economics, and sport management pedagogy. He currently teaches classes in sport management, strategic management in sport, human resource management, and sport finance. He has experience working within the golf and retail sporting goods industries, as well as with a boutique sport agency. He belongs to the North American Society for Sport Management (NASSM) and has made several presentations at its annual conference. His photo appears courtesy of the University of Windsor.

Marlene A. Dixon, PhD, is an associate professor at the University of Texas at Austin. Her research expertise is in the area of sport and life quality. In this area, she examines the ways that sport can be better designed and implemented to enhance the life quality of both sport providers and participants. Her most recent works include investigations of the work and family lives of intercollegiate coaches, sport and participation patterns of working mothers, and the role of sport in community building. Dr. Dixon completed her doctorate at Ohio State University and served for several years in the Sport Management Department at Rice University in Houston, Texas. She has over 25 publications in a variety of journals including the *Journal of Sport Management*, *Sport Management Review*, *Research Quarterly for Exercise and Sport*, *Sex Roles*, and *Quest*. She also has been named a research fellow in the North American Society for Sport Management (NASSM) and a fellow in the M.G. Seay Centennial Professorship for Education at the University of Texas at Austin. Her primary teaching areas are social and cultural aspects of sport, sport finance, and human resource management. She also enjoys mentoring graduate students and directing projects stemming from the Sport and Life Quality Laboratory. Before beginning her formal academic career, Dr. Dixon coached basketball and volleyball at the college level. She also competed as a varsity athlete in basketball and volleyball at Trinity University. She enjoys running, playing basketball, hiking, and fishing with her husband and three children. Dr. Dixon's photo appears courtesy of Stacy Warner.

Sheranne Fairley, PhD, is an assistant professor in the Department of Sport Management at the University of Massachusetts Amherst. Her primary research interests are in the consumer behavior of sport fans, sport tourists, volunteers, and umpires. Her secondary research stream focuses on the internationalization and globalization of sport practice and education. She has published in the *Journal of Sport Management*, *Sport Management Review*, *Sport in Society*, *Journal of Sport & Tourism*, and *Event Management*. She teaches classes in sport marketing, sport tourism, and international sport management. She is currently serving on the advisory board of the United States Australian Football League. Dr. Fairley's photo appears courtesy of Janis Ori.

Ted G. Fay, PhD, is a professor and chair of the Sport Management Department at the State University of New York (SUNY) at Cortland. He holds a doctorate from the University of Massachusetts Amherst, an MPA in public affairs from the University of Oregon, and a BA in government from St. Lawrence University. Dr. Fay also serves as a senior research fellow at the Center for the Study of Sport in Society at Northeastern University and as a strategic consultant related to the center's research and academic program initiatives. He has focused much of his scholarly work in the areas of social and public policy, sport governance, sport for development, and strategic management. Particular foci in his research, advocacy, and activism have been placed on diversity and social justice issues involving a sport context. Before coming to SUNY Cortland and to the Center for the Study of Sport in Society in 1999, Fay helped start the sport management program at Daniel Webster College in Nashua, New Hampshire, and taught in the graduate and undergraduate programs at the University of Massachusetts Amherst from 1992 through 1995. Fay has an extensive background in international sport including the Olympic and Paralympic movements. He has had a varied career as an educator, advocate, and activist involved in a number of human rights initiatives, environmental policy and protection campaigns, and community organizing efforts. Fay is recognized as an international expert on issues related to the integration and inclusion of athletes with a disability in mainstream sport. He was involved in the drafting of Article 30.5 of the United Nations Convention on the Human Rights for Persons with a Disability that addresses issues involving culture, leisure, and sport. Fay has been an active member of a number of professional associations including the North American Society for the Sociology of Sport (NASSS), the North American Society for Sport Management (NASSM), and the European Association of Sport Management (EASM). He has worked with or for a number of national and international sport governing bodies including the US Ski & Snowboard Association, the US Biathlon Association, USA Hockey, the US Team Handball Federation, and the International Paralympic Committee over a span of 30 years as a national team coach, program director, marketing and strategic consultant, international games and event official, and executive director of national and world championship events in skiing, biathlon, and ice hockey. Fay has been actively involved in nine Winter Paralympic Games (1980–2010) and was a member of the 1988 US Winter Olympic team in Calgary, Alberta. His photo appears courtesy of Eric Poggenpohl.

Lawrence W. Fielding, PhD, is a professor and director of the sport marketing and management program in the Department of Kinesiology at Indiana University at Bloomington. He received his doctorate from the University of Maryland in sport history in 1974. He has published more than 50 articles in sport history, sport management, and sport marketing. He has presented more than 75 papers at professional meetings. He has served on the editorial review boards for the *Journal of Sport History*, *Journal of Sport Management*, and the *Sport Marketing*

Quarterly. He is a research fellow in the North American Society for Sport Management (NASSM) and was selected for the North American Society for Sport History (NASSH) Staley Address, the highest recognition in sport history. Dr. Fielding's photo appears courtesy of Indiana University at Bloomington.

Eric Forsyth, PhD, is a professor at Bemidji State University. He received his doctorate in sport administration from The University of New Mexico, with a minor in marketing management. He teaches undergraduate and graduate courses in sport marketing, sport finance and economics, sport business management, and socio-culture and ethical issues, as well as a thesis proposal seminar. With a passion for interscholastic athletics, he has published numerous articles in both juried and trade journals, presented at various conferences on the national and international level, and written several text chapters on issues related to high school athletics. Through these endeavors he has had the privilege of working with several 'key players' within the interscholastic sport arena. He is a founding member of a panel charged with creating interscholastic athletic administration graduate curriculum standards, which are endorsed by the National Association for Sport and Physical Education and the National Interscholastic Athletic Administrators Association. Forsyth's most memorable role was having the distinct pleasure of serving as president of the Minnesota AAHPERD Association. When Dr. Forsyth is not in the classroom, you can bet he is in the woods during hunting season—he has even written stories about his bear hunting adventures, which have appeared in outdoor magazines. Despite all his successes in his field, Dr. Forsyth considers himself truly accomplished when his wife considers him a good husband and his children consider him a good father. Dr. Forsyth's photo appears courtesy of Eric Forsyth.

Nicole Fowler, MBA, MSBM, works for the National Basketball Association's Team Marketing and Business Operations department. She specializes in strategic initiatives and consults for the teams of the NBA, WNBA, and NBA Development League on ticket sales and service, sponsorship, game presentation, and customer relationship management. While a graduate student in the DeVos Sport Business Management Program at the University of Central Florida, she was Dr. Bill Sutton's graduate assistant and earned a master's of business administration and a master's in sport business management. She earned her bachelor's degree from the University of Florida's College of Journalism and Communications. During her graduate studies, she worked with the Tampa Bay Rays of MLB, the Orlando Magic and Atlanta Hawks of the NBA, the Atlanta Thrashers of the NHL, and assisted in research and business development for Bill Sutton & Associates. Fowler's photo appears courtesy of Charles Harless, DeVos Sport Business Management Program.

Wendy Frisby, PhD, is a professor in the School of Human Kinetics in the Faculty of Education and the former chair of Women's and Gender Studies (2004–2009) in the Faculty of Arts at the University of British Columbia, Canada. The overall goal of her research program is to determine how those who have the least access to sport and recreation can become more involved as decision makers and participants to promote health, policy change, and other outcomes. She conducts feminist participatory action research (FPAR) with citizens and practitioners to analyze how the social and living conditions experienced by those living in poverty, which are often exacerbated by existing policies, programs, and structures in community sport and recreation, create barriers to participation. Dr. Frisby has been awarded 25 research grants from various granting agencies and has given numerous international keynote addresses and lectures. She is a past editor of the *Journal of Sport Management* (2000–2003). She serves on the editorial boards of *European Sport Management Quarterly*, *Journal of Sport Manage-*

ment, and *Leisure/Loisir* and reviews for several other journals and research-granting agencies. Along with her colleagues, many of whom are current and former graduate students, she has over 90 publications including refereed journal articles, conference proceedings, monographs, book chapters, and professional and government reports. Her work has been published in *Action Research*, *Canadian Women's Studies*, *Canadian Journal of Public Health*, *European Sport Management Quarterly*, *International Journal of Sport Management and Marketing*, *Journal of Applied Recreation Research*, *Journal of Park and Recreation Administration*, *Journal of Sport Management*, *Journal of Travel Research*, *Leisure/Loisir*, *Leisure Studies*, *Managing Leisure: An International Journal*, and *Society and Leisure*. Besides publishing in traditional academic outlets, she makes a concerted effort to disseminate results broadly to promote knowledge uptake and policy development. Dr. Frisby is a NASSM research fellow, and she was the recipient of the Earle F. Ziegler Award in 2004. Dr. Frisby's photo appears courtesy of John MacLeod, School of Human Kinetics, University of British Columbia.

Heather Gibson, PhD, is an associate professor in the Department of Tourism, Recreation, and Sport Management at the University of Florida. She has an international reputation as a scholar in sport tourism and has presented keynote addresses at various conferences around the world. Her educational background encompasses both sport and tourism studies. She earned her doctoral degree in sport, leisure, and exercise science from the University of Connecticut. She has published both conceptual and empirical work on sport tourism and is the author of one of the most widely cited articles in sport tourism, "Sport Tourism: A Critical Analysis of Research," which was published in the *Sport Management Review* in 1998. Dr. Gibson, together with Laurence Chalip of the University of Texas at Austin, has been instrumental in bringing sport tourism to the attention of sport management professionals in the North American Society for Sport Management (NASSM). She is a member of the National Recreation and Park Association (NRPA), World Leisure, and the Leisure Studies Association (LSA). Dr. Gibson's photo appears courtesy of Kari Gunderson.

James ("Jay") M. Gladden, PhD, is dean of the School of Physical Education and Tourism Management at Indiana University Purdue University Indianapolis (IUPUI). Dr. Gladden's research expertise lies in the areas of sport brand management, sport sponsorship planning and evaluation, and college athletic fund-raising. Dr. Gladden has published numerous articles and book chapters on these topics in a wide variety of outlets including the *Journal of Sport Management*, *Sport Marketing Quarterly*, *Sport Management Review*, and the *International Journal of Sports Marketing and Sponsorship*, and trade publications such as *Athletic Management* and *Street & Smith's SportsBusiness Journal*. Dr. Gladden also brings nearly 20 years of experience working with industry, first as a project director for DelWilber + Associates (from 1991 to 1994) and then later as a faculty member at the University of Massachusetts Amherst. Dr. Gladden has worked with a variety of organizations including Compaq Computer Corporation, Iowa State University, the Los Angeles Dodgers, Major League Soccer, the National Collegiate Athletic Association, the Pittsburgh Pirates, Purdue University, and the United States Figure Skating Association. Dr. Gladden's photo appears courtesy of IUPUI.

B. Christine Green, PhD, is an active researcher who studies consumer behavior of sport event volunteers, active sport participants, and fans in a variety of sport settings. An associate professor in the Department of Kinesiology and the director of the Sport Development Lab at the University of Texas at Austin, Dr. Green earned her doctoral degree in sport management from the University of Maryland. She has published more than 50 articles that span a variety of contexts, including sport participants, fans, event volunteers, and sport tourists. Her framework of sport development, published in the *Journal of Sport Management* in 2005, provided pivotal guidance to the sport management field concerning sport and talent development at both the local and international levels. She designed and implemented the volunteer management system for the British Olympic Association's pre-Games training camp and participated in the strategic planning efforts to redesign the Australian university sport system. Dr. Green was the head of the research team that studied the motivation and commitment of the 2000 Sydney Olympics volunteers. She has also supervised a number of student-run marketing projects that significantly increased student attendance at intercollegiate sporting events. She is a research fellow in the North American Society for Sport Management (NASSM). She has also been honored with the Academic Innovation Award from the RGK Center for Philanthropy and Community Service and is a fellow in the Lee Hage Jamail Regents Chair in Education. Dr. Green's photo appears courtesy of Magdalena Zavala.

Kathryn S. Hoff, PhD, is an associate professor of human resource development in the College of Technology at Bowling Green State University, where she earned her doctorate in higher education administration and MEd in human resource development. She spent more than 20 years as a human resource development practitioner responsible for internship and cooperative education programs, college relations and recruiting, career development and management of employees, organizational change management, and training and development. Dr. Hoff recently stepped down as managing director for the Academy of Human Resource Development (AHRD), an international association of scholars and practitioners whose mission is leading human resource development through research. She is a contributor and reviewer for AHRD's journals. Her photo appears courtesy of Brandon Heiss, instructor, College of Technology, Bowling Green State University.

Mary Jo Kane, PhD, is professor and director of the School of Kinesiology at the University of Minnesota; she also serves as director of the Tucker Center for Research on Girls & Women in Sport. In 1996 Dr. Kane was awarded the first distinguished professorship related to women in sport and physical activity, the Dorothy McNeill and Elbridge Ashcraft Tucker Chair for Women in Exercise Science and Sport. Professor Kane was elected by her peers as a fellow in the American Academy of Kinesiology and Physical Education, the highest honor in her field. She is an internationally recognized scholar on sport and gender and is particularly interested in the media's treatment of female athletes. Professor Kane received the Scholar of the Year Award from the Women's Sport Foundation in 2004, and in 2007 she was named one of the 100 most influential sports educators by the Institute for International Sport. Professor Kane is a member of the North American Society for the Sociology of Sport (NASSS) and has served on the editorial review boards of the *Sociology of Sport Journal* and the *Journal of Sport & Social Issues*. Professor Kane's photo appears courtesy of the University of Minnesota.

JoAnn Kroll, MEd, has directed the Bowling Green State University Career Center since April 2, 1984. As executive director, she is responsible for several campuswide services including career planning, student employment, the university's Cooperative Education and Internship Program, and job search services. Under her leadership the BGSU Career Center has won two national Awards of Excellence for Educational Programming from the National Association for Colleges and Employers (NACE). She has taught graduate courses on career development theory and practice and administration and supervision in career and technology education. She has also designed and taught undergraduate career exploration courses. The author of numerous book chapters and journal articles on the field of career services, she has also written, edited, and published several books, including the *BGSU Job*

Search Guide; *B!G Decisions: Take Charge of Your Academic, Career, and Life Choices*; and *Co-Op and Internship Workbook*. The Ohio College Personnel Association honored her with the Gerald L. Saddlemire Mentor Award in recognition of outstanding service in the field of college student personnel. She was the recipient of the Michael R. Ferrari Award in recognition of her outstanding performance, innovation, initiative, and effective relationships at Bowling Green State University. She has also received the University Community Fellowship Award and BG Best Award for quality improvements to programs and services at the university. Kroll's photo appears courtesy of Jan Meyer, Bowling Green State University.

Nicole M. LaVoi, PhD, is the associate director of the Tucker Center for Research on Girls & Women in Sport (www.tuckercenter.org), cofounder of the Minnesota Youth Sport Research Consortium (www.MNYSRC.org), and instructor in the area of social and behavioral science in the School of Kinesiology at the University of Minnesota. Before returning to the University of Minnesota where she earned both her MA and doctorate in kinesiology, LaVoi was a research associate in the Mendelson Center for Sport, Character & Culture at the University of Notre Dame and an assistant professor at Wellesley College where she taught in the Department of Physical Education, Recreation and Athletics and served as the head women's tennis coach. LaVoi's multidisciplinary research has focused on the relational qualities of the coach–athlete relationship, the effect of adult behaviors (parents and coaches) in youth sport on children, the emotional experiences of youth sport parents, the physical activity of underserved girls, the structural and personal barriers experienced by female coaches in youth sport, and media representations of girls and women in sport. She was the coeditor and a contributing author of *The 2007 Tucker Center Research Report: Developing Physically Active Girls*. Her photo appears courtesy of the University of Minnesota.

Ming Li, EdD, is the director of the School of Recreation and Sport Sciences at Ohio University and a professor in sports administration. He received his bachelor's degree in education from Guangzhou Institute of Physical Culture, his master's degree in education from Hangzhou University, and his doctor of education degree in sport administration from the University of Kansas. Li has memberships on the editorial boards of several professional journals, including the *Journal of Sport Management* and *Sport Marketing Quarterly*. He has published more than 26 articles in refereed journals, three books (*Economics of Sport*, *Research Methods in Sport Management*, and *Badminton Everyone*), and five book chapters. Currently, he is the lead editor for a book project, *International Sport Management*. He has made numerous refereed presentations at state, national, and international conferences. Dr. Li is an honorary guest professor of five institutions in China, including Sun Yat-sen University, Central University of Finance and Economics, Beijing Sport University, Tianjin University of Sport, and Guangzhou Institute of Physical Education. He was an Olympic envoy for the Atlanta Committee for the 1996 Olympic Games and served as president of the North American Society for Sport Management (NASSM). Dr. Li's photo appears courtesy of Ohio University.

Daniel F. Mahony, PhD, is a professor of sport administration and the dean of the College of Education, Health and Human Services at Kent State University. Dr. Mahony has a BS in accounting from Virginia Tech, an MS in sport management from West Virginia University, and a doctorate in sport management from Ohio State University. He has worked for the accounting firm Peat Marwick Main & Co., the North Hunterdon High School Athletic Department, the West Virginia University Athletic Department, and the University of Cincinnati Athletic Department. He was a faculty member and administrator at the University of Louisville. Dr. Mahony is an active researcher in the areas of sport consumer behavior and intercollegiate athletics and has published over 50 articles in various journals including the *Journal of Sport Management*, *Sport Management Review*, *Sport Marketing Quarterly*, *International Journal of Sport Marketing and Sponsorship*, *International Journal of Sport Management*, and *Journal of Sport and Social Issues*. He was also coauthor of *Economics of Sport*. Dr. Mahony served as president of the North American Society for Sport Management (NASSM). He received the 2007 Earle F. Zeigler Award from NASSM and has been a NASSM research fellow since 2003. Dr. Mahony's photo appears courtesy of Kent State University.

Mark A. McDonald, PhD, is an associate professor of sport management at the University of Massachusetts Amherst, where he received a doctorate in 1996. Dr. McDonald has published in the *Journal of Sport Management*, *Sport Marketing Quarterly*, *International Journal of Sports Marketing and Sponsorship*, *Journal of Management Education*, and *Journal of Sport and Social Issues*. He served as coeditor for the special *Sport Marketing Quarterly* issue on relationship marketing in sport and is the associate editor of the *Sport Management Education Journal*. He has given more than 35 presentations in the United States and abroad, and his research interests include sport sponsorship, relationship marketing, pedagogy, and leadership in sport organizations. He has published 20 refereed journal articles and coauthored two books, *Cases in Sport Marketing* and *Sport Marketing: Managing the Exchange Process*. Dr. McDonald is a North American Society for Sport Management (NASSM) research fellow and was named the 2009 NASSM Distinguished Sport Management Educator. Dr. McDonald's photo appears courtesy of Ben Barndhart.

Anita M. Moorman, JD, is a professor in sport administration at the University of Louisville, where she teaches sport law and legal aspects of sport. She joined the faculty at the University of Louisville in 1996. Professor Moorman has a law degree from Southern Methodist University, and before beginning her academic pursuits, she practiced law in Oklahoma City, Oklahoma, in the areas of commercial and corporate litigation for ten years. Professor Moorman also holds an MS in sport management from the University of Oklahoma and a BS in political science from Oklahoma State University. Professor Moorman is the editor of a feature column in *Sport Marketing Quarterly* titled "Sport Marketing and the Law" and is coauthor of the text *Sport Law: A Managerial Approach*. Professor Moorman's research interests include disability discrimination in sport, and legal and ethical issues related to sport marketing practices, brand protection, and intellectual property issues in sport. She has published more than 30 articles in academic journals, including the *Journal of Sport Management*, *Sport Management Review*, *Sport Marketing Quarterly*, *Journal of Legal Aspects of Sport*, *JOPERD*, *Leisure Science*, *International Sport Journal*, *Journal of Sport and Social Issues*, *Journal of the Academy of Marketing Science*, and *ACSM's Health and Fitness Journal*. She has given more than 60 presentations at national and international conferences. Her photo appears courtesy of the University of Louisville.

Brenda G. Pitts, EdD, is nationally and internationally renowned in sport business management, particularly in sport marketing, and sport management program development. Dr. Pitts is a professor of sport management, director of the Dr. R. Cooter Sport Business Research Center, and program director at Georgia State University in Atlanta, Georgia. She also works as a sport marketing consultant. Dr. Pitts is distinguished as a Dr. Earle F. Zeigler Scholar and one of the first research fellows of the North American Society for Sport Management (NASSM). She is author or coauthor of six sport marketing textbooks, coauthor of the first textbook on research methods in sport management (2008), and the editor and an author in three Sport Marketing Association's *Book of Papers*. Dr. Pitts has published numerous papers in several scholarly journals such as the *Sport Management Education Journal*, *Journal of Sport Management*, *Sport Marketing Quarterly*, *Journal of Vacation Marketing*, *International Journal of Sports Marketing and Sponsorship*, *Women in Sport and Physical Activity*, *Sport Management and Related*

Topics Journal, and the *International Journal of Sport Management*. Her research, consulting, and service work have taken her around the world. Stops have included Sweden, South Africa, Hong Kong, Singapore, Malaysia, Spain, France, Australia, Germany, Hungary, England, the Netherlands, Japan, Canada, Portugal, Scotland, Cyprus, and China. On the more fun side of life, she enjoys all kinds of sports, more recently soccer, golf, boating, volleyball, jogging, tennis, and softball. Her prolific career in basketball brought her such awards as the retirement of her high school basketball uniform number, membership in the "A" Club of the University of Alabama, Huntsville (Alabama) Sports Hall of Fame Inductee, Women's Basketball Hall of Fame Inductee as a player in the first Women's Professional Basketball League (WBL), and recently (2009) as an inductee nominee for the Alabama Sports Hall of Fame. Recently, Dr. Pitts won a couple of golf tournaments but has made the wise decision to keep her day job. Her photo appears courtesy of Brenda G. Pitts.

R. Christopher Reynolds, JD, serves in the position of senior associate athletics director and adjunct professor at Indiana University at Bloomington. He has more than 12 years of experience working in athletics administration at Division I institutions in the following areas: human resource management, coaches' employment contracts, student–athlete welfare issues, legal issues, diversity matters, sponsorship contracts, and NCAA compliance. He has taught graduate level courses in sport marketing, NCAA compliance, and issues in intercollegiate athletics. Reynolds has served as chair of the NCAA Committee on Sportsmanship and Ethical Conduct, taught as an adjunct faculty member at Western Michigan University, and conducted leadership development workshops for Nike, Inc. and the NCAA. He was selected as an NCAA fellow, a rigorous leadership development program sponsored by the NCAA national office for aspiring athletics directors and conference commissioners. Besides working in a senior role as an athletics administrator, Reynolds is completing his PhD in sport management at Indiana University at Bloomington. His photo appears courtesy of Indiana University at Bloomington.

Sally Rea Ross, PhD, is an assistant professor of sport and leisure management at the University of Memphis. Before earning her doctoral degree from the University of Illinois at Urbana-Champaign, Dr. Ross gained extensive practical experience in college athletics administration as an assistant athletics director overseeing student–athlete support services at her alma mater. Before taking on that role, Dr. Ross was an academic counselor and life skills coordinator for student–athletes and was also an academic advisor for the Department of Recreation, Sport and Tourism at the University of Illinois at Urbana-Champaign. Her research interests include girls' and women's experiences and opportunities in sport, media representations of athletes, and the social responsibility of sport entities. Her work has been published in academic journals that include *Sex Roles*, *Sport Marketing Quarterly*, *International Journal of Sport Marketing and Sponsorship*, and *Sport Management Education Journal*. Dr. Ross has taught undergraduate and graduate courses in a variety of areas, including foundations of sport and leisure management, intercollegiate athletics administration, event and facility management, sport ethics, globalization, and popular culture. A former Big Ten All-Conference and Academic All-Conference student–athlete, Dr. Ross was the recipient of the Distinguished Alumnus Award from the University of Illinois volleyball program. She is a member of the North American Society for Sport Management (NASSM), Sport Marketing Association (SMA), and North American Society for the Sociology of Sport (NASSS), and is a faculty affiliate with the Collegiate Sport Research Institute. Her photo appears courtesy of Morgan E. Ross.

Ellen J. Staurowsky, EdD, is professor and graduate chair of the Department of Sport Management and Media at Ithaca College. She received her doctoral degree in sport management and psychosocial aspects of sport from Temple University. On more than 100 occasions, Dr. Staurowsky has presented to learned societies, professional associations, and conferences on gender equity and Title IX, pay equity and equal employment opportunity, the exploitation of athletes, the faculty role in reforming college sport, representation of women in sport media, and the misappropriation of American Indian imagery in sport. She has published numerous articles in scholarly and professional journals. In 1998 she coauthored the book *College Athletes for Hire: The Evolution and Legacy of the NCAA Amateur Myth*. Dr. Staurowsky is a member of the editorial board for the *Journal of Sport Management*, *Women in Sport and Physical Activity Journal*, and *Athletic Management*. She is past president of the North American Society for the Sociology of Sport (NASSS) and the Research Consortium. She is a founding member of the Drake Group, a group of faculty around the country interested in college sport reform. She is also on the executive board of the College Sport Research Institute. She is the former college field hockey and lacrosse coach at Oberlin College and was the director of athletics at Daniel Webster College and William Smith College for nine years. Dr. Staurowsky's photo appears courtesy of Ithaca College.

G. Clayton (Clay) Stoldt, EdD, is an associate professor and chair of the Department of Sport Management at Wichita State University. He teaches classes in sport public relations and sport marketing. Stoldt is the coauthor of *Sport Public Relations: Managing Organizational Communication*, and his research activities have focused on sport public relations issues such as crisis communications, the roles of sport public relations professionals, and the application of advanced public relations practices in the field. Stoldt serves on the editorial boards for the *International Journal of Sport Communication* and the *Journal of Sport Administration and Supervision*. He also serves as conference manager for the North American Society for Sport Management (NASSM). Stoldt received his doctor of education from the University of Oklahoma in 1998. His master's degree was in sport management, and his bachelor's was in journalism and mass communication. Before coming to Wichita State University, Stoldt worked in the athletics department at Oklahoma City University, where he served as sports information director, radio play-by-play broadcaster, and development officer. He also served as an adjunct instructor at both Oklahoma City University and the University of Oklahoma. His photo appears courtesy of Ryan Stoldt.

David K. Stotlar, EdD, is a professor of sport management in the areas of sport marketing and sport law at the University of Northern Colorado. He has had more than 70 articles published in professional journals and has written several book chapters in sport marketing, fitness risk management, and sport law. He is the author of several textbooks, including *Developing Successful Sport Sponsorship Plans*, which is now in its third edition. He has made numerous presentations at international and national professional conferences and has conducted international seminars in sport management and marketing for various sport councils, federations, and institutes. Dr. Stotlar served as the media subcenter supervisor for the Soldier's Hollow venue at the 2002 Winter Olympic Games in Salt Lake City. He received the Dr. Earle F. Zeigler Award from the North American Society for Sport Management (NASSM) in 1999 and was named a NASSM research fellow in 2001. Dr. Stotlar's photo appears courtesy of Sylvia Stotlar.

William A. Sutton, EdD, holds an appointment as professor and associate department head on the faculty of the DeVos Sport Business Management Program at the University of Central Florida (UCF). In this role Dr. Sutton teaches graduate courses in sport marketing and sales and promotional management in sport, and also serves as the internship coordinator for the program. Besides performing his duties at UCF, Dr. Sutton is the founder and principal of Bill Sutton & Associates, a consulting firm that specializes in strategic marketing and revenue enhancement for clients including the NBA, NHL, WNBA, Orlando Magic, New York Yankees, Phoenix Suns, Cleveland Cavaliers, and Pittsburgh Pirates. Before assuming his current positions, Sutton served as vice president, team marketing and business operations for the NBA. In this capacity, Dr. Sutton assisted NBA teams with marketing-related functions such as sales, promotional activities, market research, advertising, customer service, strategic planning, and staffing. Dr. Sutton has previously held academic appointments at Robert Morris University, Ohio State University, and the University of Massachusetts Amherst. Dr. Sutton is a coauthor of two texts: *Sport Marketing* (third edition, 2007) and *Sport Promotion and Sales Management* (second edition, 2008) published by Human Kinetics. Dr. Sutton has also written more than 125 articles (refereed and nonrefereed) and has made more than 150 national and international presentations. Dr. Sutton, a past president of NASSM, is a founding member and currently serves as president of the Sport Marketing Association (SMA). He also serves on the editorial board for the *Journal of Sport Administration and Supervision*. He is a founding member of *Sport Marketing Quarterly*, a publication for which he has also served as coeditor. He currently serves on the editorial board. Dr. Sutton is a featured author for *Street & Smith's SportsBusiness Journal (SBJ)* and for the basketball strategy and business magazines *Basketball Gigante* and *FIBA Assist*, published in Italy. Dr. Sutton's additional professional experience includes service as a special events coordinator for the City of Pittsburgh, a YMCA director, vice president of information services for an international sport marketing firm, and commissioner of the Mid-Ohio Conference. Dr. Sutton serves on the boards of the Orlando Magic Youth Fund and the Folds of Honor Foundation, which is committed to using sport to raise scholarship funds for the children of military families who have lost a family member during a military operation. A native of Pittsburgh, Pennsylvania, Dr. Sutton holds three degrees (BA 1972, MS 1980, and EdD 1983) from Oklahoma State University, where he was inducted into the College of Education Hall of Fame in 2003. Dr. Sutton is also an inaugural member of the Robert Morris University Sport Management Hall of Fame (2006). Dr. Sutton and his wife Sharon reside in Orlando, Florida. Dr. Sutton's photo appears courtesy of the University of Central Florida.

Luisa Velez, PhD, is an assistant professor at the State University of New York (SUNY) at Cortland. She teaches undergraduate and graduate courses in sport marketing, international sport enterprise, and research methods in sport management. She earned her doctoral degree in sport management from Texas Woman's University. Her research and scholarly interests include inequities in sport involving race, gender, and class. She is a board member of the Latin American Sport Management Association (Asociación Latinoamericana de Gerencia Deportiva). Dr. Velez's photo appears courtesy of Luisa Velez.

Warren A. Whisenant, PhD, is an associate professor of sport management and associate department chair in the Department of Exercise and Sport Sciences at the University of Miami (Florida). His doctorate was awarded by Florida State University. He also holds an MA in kinesiology and an MBA–management from Sam Houston State University. His research, most of which has focused on gender and organizational issues within interscholastic athletics, has been published in such journals as the *Journal of Sport Management*; *International Journal of Sport Management*; *Sport, Education, and Society*; *International Journal of Sport Management and Marketing*; and *Sex Roles*. In 2009 he became a NASSM research fellow, a designation that recognizes scholars for their achievements in sport-related scholarship. His professional background includes over 20 years of experience with three global organizations—Hewitt Associates, KFC-USA, and Frito Lay, Inc. His roles within those businesses were as an advanced project and process consultant, a director of restaurant operations (1 of 16 in North America), and region sales manager, respectively. In each of the positions noted, he was involved with coordinating promotional programs and sponsorships with various sport organizations. Dr. Whisenant's photo appears courtesy of the University of Miami.